RITUAL AND RELIGION IN THE MAKING OF HUMANITY

Roy Rappaport argues that religion is central to the continuing evolution of life, although it has been displaced from its original position of intellectual authority by the rise of modern science. His book, which could be construed as in some degree religious as well as about religion, insists that religion can and must be reconciled with science. Combining adaptive and cognitive approaches to the study of humankind, he mounts a comprehensive analysis of religion's evolutionary significance, seeing it as co-extensive with the invention of language and hence of culture as we know it. At the same time he assembles the fullest study yet of religion's main component, ritual, which constructs the conceptions which we take to be religious and has been central in the making of humanity's adaptation. The text amounts to a manual for effective ritual, illustrated by examples drawn from anthropology, history, philosophy, comparative religion and elsewhere.

ROY RAPPAPORT taught at the University of Michigan, Ann Arbor from 1965 until his death in 1997. He was President of the American Anthropological Association from 1987 to 1989. Among his many publications are *Pigs for the Ancestors* (1968; revised edition 1984) and *Ecology, Meaning, and Religion* (1979).

Cambridge Studies in Social and Cultural Anthropology

110

RITUAL AND RELIGION IN THE MAKING OF HUMANITY

Cambridge Studies in Social and Cultural Anthropology

Founding Editors
Meyer Fortes *University of Cambridge*
Jack Goody *University of Cambridge*
Edmund Leach *University of Cambridge*
Stanley J. Tambiah *Harvard University*

The monograph series Cambridge Studies in Social and Cultural Anthropology publishes analytical ethnographies, comparative works, and contributions to theory. All combine an expert and critical command of ethnography and a sophisticated engagement with current theoretical debates.

A list of books in the series will be found at the end of the volume

RITUAL AND RELIGION IN THE MAKING OF HUMANITY

ROY A. RAPPAPORT

CAMBRIDGE
UNIVERSITY PRESS

PUBLISHED BY THE PRESS SYNDICATE OF THE UNIVERSITY OF CAMBRIDGE
The Pitt Building, Trumpington Street, Cambridge, United Kingdom

CAMBRIDGE UNIVERSITY PRESS
The Edinburgh Building, Cambridge CB2 2RU, UK
40 West 20th Street, New York, NY 10011–4211, USA
477 Williamstown Road, Port Melbourne, VIC 3207, Australia
Ruiz de Alarcón 13, 28014 Madrid, Spain
Dock House, The Waterfront, Cape Town 80011, South Africa

http://www.cambridge.org

First published 1999
Eighth printing 2006

Printed in the United Kingdom at the University Press, Cambridge

Typeset in Times 10/13 pt [CE]

A catalogue record for this book is available from the British Library

ISBN 0 521 22873 5 hardback
ISBN 0 521 29690 0 paperback

Dedication

I dedicate this book to four anthropologists who have very much influenced the ideas expressed in it and who have been otherwise important in my life and career. In the order in which they entered my life, they are:

Robert Levy
Eric Wolf
Mervyn Meggitt
Keith Hart

All of them have acted like elder brothers to me, even Keith who is many years my junior.

Contents

ix

x   *Contents*

Foreword

Emile Durkheim published *Les Formes élémentaires de la vie réligieuse* in 1912, on the eve of the First World War. The war consolidated a process which had been building up for at least three decades and which we can now see laid the foundations for the kind of society familiar to our twentieth-century world. This society was organized by and for centralized states, staffed by a professional class of scientific experts. Durkheim himself, as the principal founder of the discipline of sociology, had taken the lead in establishing the new sciences of society which would underpin the activities of this class. Yet in *The Elementary Forms* he posed an immense problem for the future of humanity. Science appeared to have driven religion from the field as a serious intellectual ground for the organization of society; but it could not perform the function of religion. This left a huge hole in the spiritual existence of modern people which Durkheim knew must be filled, but he himself was powerless to imagine how.

Roy Rappaport's book, the result of more than three decades' investigation into the relationship between religion, society and ecology, is, in my view, the first systematic attempt to address the question which Durkheim left unanswered. As such, it deserves to be seen as a milestone in the anthropology of religion comparable in scope to his great predecessor's work. For Rappaport is attempting here nothing less than to lay the groundwork for the development of a new religion adequate to the circumstances humanity will encounter in the twenty-first century. His stated aims are more modest, namely to review the anthropological evidence which might allow for a more comprehensive understanding of ritual as the practical matrix of religious life. But the unity of this work derives from his implicit desire to inform future attempts to construct a religion compatible with the scientific laws ruling a world for which humanity is ultimately responsible, as that part of life on this planet which is able to think.

Religion belongs to a set of terms which also includes art and science. It is a measure of the declining intellectual credibility of established religions that science, which began as a form of knowledge opposed to religious mysticism, is now most often opposed to the arts. If science may crudely be said to be the drive to know the world objectively and art is pre-eminently an arena of subjective self-expression, religion typically addresses both sides of the subject–object relationship by connecting what is inside each of us to something outside. Religion, etymologically speaking, binds us to an external force; it stabilises our meaningful interaction with the world, provides an anchor for our volatility.

Durkheim's concept of religion was consistent with this formulation, but it contained some radically distinctive elements. He divided experience into the known and the unknown. What we know is everyday life, the mundane features of our routine existence; and we know it as individuals trapped in a sort of private busy-ness. But this life is subject to larger forces whose origin we do not know, to natural disasters, social revolutions and, above all, death. We desperately wish to influence these unknown causes of our fate which we recognize as being both individual and collective in their impact; at the very least we would like to establish a connection with them. And so, for Durkheim, religion was the organized attempt to bridge the gap between the known and the unknown, conceived of as the profane world of ordinary experience and a sacred, extraordinary world located outside that experience.

He recognized that we normally conceive of the sacred in terms of spiritual powers, summarized in the world religions as God. He proposed, however, that what is ultimately unknown to us is our collective being in society. We find it very difficult to grasp how our actions arise from belonging to others; and it is this property of collective life which is highlighted in the chief mechanism of religion, ritual. Through ritual, Durkheim argues, we worship our unrealized powers of shared existence, society, and call it God. Sometimes we objectify the spirit world as nature and worship that. This natural religion, associated at the time Durkheim wrote with the "totemism" of the Australian Aborigines, he considered to be the matrix of all systematic knowledge, including science. It was thus one of the tasks of *The Elementary Forms* to demonstrate that science springs from the same desire to connect the known and the unknown that spawned religion.

The chaos of everyday life, by this formulation, attains some stability to the degree that it is informed by ideas representing the social facts of a shared collective existence. Science, sociology for example, can help us to be more aware of this; but, in general, scientific knowledge and method undermine the coherence and stability of culture. Durkheim believed that the central task of ritual was to instill these collective representations in each of us. In a celebrated expression, he spoke of the "effervescence" of ritual experience. In a state of spiritual ecstasy we internalize the lessons which bind us to each other in social life. He did not elaborate on this rather important conception of the socialization process. Roy Rappaport's book, among other things, may be read as an extended treatment of this very point.

It is not the task of this Foreword to pre-empt the contents of what follows. Apart from anything else, Rappaport is unusually lucid in setting out his own agenda and sticking to it. Indeed I would argue that this book is as much a work in analytical philosophy as it is an essay composed within the anthropological discipline which acknowledges Durkheim as a founder. For the author is relentlessly precise in his use of words, a precision which is alleviated by the robustness of a prose which knows that it is borne along by the currents of an impressive intellectual tradition. The second chapter, for example, is as fine a review of what ritual has been taken to be as will be found anywhere. Moreover, Rappaport's own definition, starting from a parsimonious emphasis on formality, invariance and tradition, builds over no less than eleven chapters (out of fourteen) into an analysis of ritual which, for sheer comprehensiveness and consistency, has no parallel in the literature.

Roy Rappaport gives such rigorous and explicit attention to ritual because he finds in it the ground where religion is made. He is aware, as was Durkheim, that religion has not fared well in modern times, having been removed from the governance of society's leading institutions and left instead as an irrational palliative for the growing mass of the world's outsiders. He knows that, if the pattern of our own rotten century is repeated in the twenty-first, there will not be a twenty-second. This is because a pseudo-religion of money and commodity consumption is supervising the destruction of nature and society on a scale which is unsustainable in even the fairly short run. Rappaport believes that one possible answer to the world's crisis would be a religion founded on a postmodern science grounded in ecology, rather than astronomy – so that human society might be conceived of as being inside rather than outside life on this planet.

This is the meaning of the book's title. In Rappaport's usage, humanity is a personal quality, a collective noun and a historical project. The project of achieving our potential to be collectively human is, in a sense, barely begun. It is entailed, however, in our origin as a species, in the discovery of language and with it religion. The inclusive feature of religion is "holiness", a concept which embraces the sacred, the numinous, the occult and the divine. Holiness is whole (and cognate to healthy); religion, which is constantly being made and remade through ritual, is the means we have of getting in touch with the wholeness of things. Increasingly, we are becoming aware that human society has a unity defined by its occupation of a place in the life of this planet. That place has hitherto often been heedlessly destructive. The task is to assume responsibility for our stewardship of life as a whole. Religion is indispensable to that task and ritual is its active ground; hence the echoes of Durkheim's *la vie réligieuse.*

Between the two books lies almost a century of war, bureaucracy and science. Anthropology has in that time become a major academic specialization whose achievements underpin Rappaport's work. But he also looks to theologians, psychologists, ethologists and philosophers for the means of developing his arguments. In this he is true to the discipline's origins in the eighteenth-century Enlightenment. Immanuel Kant coined the term "anthropology" in its modern sense for a series of lectures (*Anthropology from a pragmatic point of view*) which was published towards the end of his life. In them he posed the question of how humanity might make a cosmopolitan society beyond the boundaries of states; and he found the answer in a comparative inquiry into cognition, aesthetics and ethics. For Kant, community and common sense were generated through social interaction; the aesthetic was primarily social, having its roots in good food, good talk and good company. This is the urbane source for Durkheim's emphasis on a more primitive conception of ritual; and Rappaport takes up once more, as Durkheim could not, the project of imagining how ritual might sustain a social life of planetary rather than merely national scope.

The universals of nineteenth-century anthropology have been discredited in our own century. And this was not difficult, since they were founded on Western imperialism's ability to unify the world as an unequal association of races governed by what was taken at the time to be the last word in rationality. Since then, another vision of world society has taken hold, a fragmented world of self-sufficient nation-states reflected in an ideology of cultural relativism which insists that people everywhere have a right to their own way of life, however barbarous. This vision has become so central to the academic anthropology of our day that Rappaport's treatise will seem to be anomalous. Of late it has come to be held that big, closely argued books on universal themes are out-of-date. Minor essays on elusive topics, ethnography for its own sake and evasion of matters of general public concern are the norm. If this book does nothing else, it makes a claim that anthropology needs to be animated by more ambitious intellectual projects which look backwards, to be sure, but also forwards to the world we hope to inhabit in the near future.

Roy Rappaport's enterprise is made possible by social conditions at the end of the twentieth century. We are living through a communications revolution sustained by the convergence of telephones, television and computers. The progressive integration of global exchange networks since the Second World War has brought about an unprecedented capacity for movement and connection on a planetary scale. At the same time we are increasingly aware of the damage being done to the environment and of the obscene inequality which marks world society. The states in which Durkheim placed implicit confidence as the sole means of organizing society are now in disarray. No government anywhere commands widespread popular support, with the possible exception of Nelson Mandela's.

We know that we are at the end of something and on the verge of something else. Rappaport does not discuss the historical context of his arguments in any way; yet this book's remarkable integrity derives from his conviction that our twentieth-century world of nation-states must soon give way to a new one premised on the need for forging a common human agenda. In other words, we need new conceptions of the universal. Religion once provided such conceptions. Anthropology filled the gap when religion was driven out by science; but it is not itself religion, merely the means towards formulating fresh approaches to religion on the basis of sound knowledge of the human condition.

It might be argued that the world is full of religion at present, as indeed it is. But the vehicles for religious experience which predominate today, especially the so-called fundamentalisms of Christianity and Islam, attract the dispossessed masses; they offer a means of connecting with world society, but they do not yet influence the institutions which rule that society. And it would be tragic if they did, since they look backwards to the certainty of religions of the Book at a time when humanity's means of communication are fast moving in a new direction.

Roy Rappaport does not engage at length with what many take to be religion's most distinctive and alarming feature, namely its capacity to fuel divisive conflicts. Instead, he focuses on the potentially constructive powers of ritual. For, as I stated at the beginning, he intends his book to be a sort of manual for those who would collaborate in the task of remaking religious life along lines compatible with the enhancement of life on this planet. It may or may not turn out to be that. What he has assembled here, however, deserves at the very least to set the anthropology of ritual and religion on a new course.

Emile Durkheim's dualistic conception of the religious life as a bridge between separate worlds, the sacred and the profane, the collective and the individual, reflected his assumption that society would continue to be defined by the impersonal institutions of the state and a market-driven division of labour. In such a world, the personal and the everyday have no meaningful connection with society and history; so that it is left to experts, sociologists and anthropologists, to discover how the abstract principles by which we live are reproduced in religious ritual. Rappaport's approach is strikingly different. His definition of ritual draws no hard line between the sacred and the everyday, between society and the individual or, for that matter, between culture and nature. And this reflects the changed circumstances of our late twentieth-century world, where faith in anonymous structures has taken something of a beating in recent years.

Rappaport's vision of the human universals appropriate to our day invites us to rethink the modernist movement which launched our century and has sustained the universities as a privileged enclave within it. In particular he insists that we find ways of reconciling science and religion, since their mutual antagonism is ruinous and their false synthesis, as in that latterday astrology, economics, is potentially even more so. The vast majority of his professional colleagues will probably be unmoved by his arguments, since they have long been committed to other ways of thinking and have too much at stake in the existing institutions. But, if there is to be a future for specialized intellectual enquiry, young anthropologists and other students of religion will be stimulated by Roy Rappaport's bold example to explore new regions of human possibility.

Keith Hart
Cambridge
April 1997

Preface

This book, as all my friends well know, has been a long time coming. Some of its ideas came to me as early as the late 1960s, and I have worked on them in fits and starts ever since. I've lectured on ritual and religion during most academic years, and published preliminary versions of some of the book's elements in such essays as the *Obvious Aspects of Ritual*, and *Sanctity and Lies in Evolution*, both 1979. An earlier version of this manuscript was accepted for publication in 1982 with requests for no more than minor revisions. Upon rereading it at that time, however, I decided it didn't say quite what I wanted to say, so I put it aside "until I had time" to revise it to my liking. But I was about to go off to do field work and when I came back I was elected to the presidency of the American Anthropological Association, an office which engaged virtually all time left over from my full-time position at the University of Michigan. And then there have always been, as for most of us, requests for articles and essays that one expects to take a week to write, but usually take me a couple of months. And so, although I made some progress on the manuscript, it was slow going. This didn't make me happy, but I was given some comfort by the feeling that my revisions were better than what I had done originally. By and large I think this is true, although the book still doesn't say quite what I would like to say, or doesn't say it as well as I would like.

In April 1996 I was diagnosed with lung cancer. To paraphrase Dr. Johnson, there really is nothing like a diagnosis of non-curable carcinoma to concentrate the mind wonderfully on what one takes to be one's priorities, what one takes to be of great significance, and, unsurprisingly, such a diagnosis encourages an ever-growing sense of the need for closure, to get it done. I walk away from the manuscript feeling that many passages could well have used more work. At any rate, they – all those passages – have come off their back burners and have, for better or worse, been front and center since the diagnosis.

I have been fortunate with my disease. So far, I've suffered no pain. My chief symptoms have been weakness and fatigue which have kept me from working more than two or three hours at a stretch. This may be a good time to thank the people most directly involved in keeping me alive and in working order over these past months: Doctors Robert Todd, James Arond-Thomas, and Michael Shea and two magnificent infusion nurses, Annkarine Dahlerus and Jennifer Welsh. Judy Federbush has not only kept me alive but reasonably sane not only during the last year but during previous periods when the manuscript and other committments were tying me in knots. I don't think I would ever have gotten done without her support.

The most crucial person in keeping me alive and functioning has been my wife, Ann. I realize that expressions of this sort are clichés in prefaces and acknowledgements, but I simply cannot imagine how anyone can get through a year or so of cancer, even with symptoms as mild as mine, without some loving support constantly there. Her support has been beyond the call of love or duty and so has, more intermittently, the help of my daughters, Amelia and Gina Rappaport.

At some point, and it might as well be here and now, I want to express my thanks to my institution, the College of Literature, Science, and the Arts of the University of Michigan, and to its Anthropology Department for providing the additional material support I've needed during this past year. I am very grateful to Dean Edie Goldenberg and Associate Dean John Cross, and to two very effective chairmen of the Anthropology department, Richard Ford and Conrad Kottak. The funds they have provided have made it possible to engage the services of Susan Else Wyman, who has overseen the production of the manuscript, and Brian Hoey, who checked the bibliography.

I am also deeply grateful for the honor bestowed upon me several years ago when I was nominated Mary and Charles Walgreen, Jr. Professor for the Study of Human Understanding. This honor provided me with additional time to work on this manuscript.

I finally can turn to acknowledgments of intellectual assistance, aid, and stimulation, a much more difficult task, given the many years I've been thinking about this material. And with all that space and time I couldn't possibly name everyone who contributed. There have been many generations of students who have heard some of this, and it seems to me that there has been at least one student in each generation who has asked a question or made a comment so penetrating that it has caused me to rethink key points.

There are many less anonymous acknowledgments to make. In the early days of this enterprise, discussions with Gregory Bateson were especially illuminating, and a leave at Cambridge in England gave me opportunities to spend time with Maurice Bloch and to talk at length with Meyer Fortes. There were also opportunities for important conversations with Eric Wolf, who was on leave in London at the time.

Robert Levy and Mervyn Meggitt gave very close readings to the early chapters of this book's early drafts, and their detailed comments were instrumental in transforming early drafts into the final work. They have both been cited in the book, but unacknowledged traces of their thought are ubiquitous in the work. Others who read portions of the manuscript and made valuable suggestions include Aletta Biersack, Ellen Messer, Sherry Ortner, and Aram Yengoyan. A Wenner-Gren Conference on Ritual and Reconciliation at Burg Wartenstein years ago, convened by Margaret Mead and Mary Catherine Bateson and attended by, among others, Roger Abrahams, Barbara Babcock, and Fehean O'Doherty was a break-through moment for me and I am deeply grateful to the Wenner-Gren Foundation's president at the time, Lita Osmundsen.

Since the onset of my illness, my most generous and helpful assistance has been offered by Keith Hart, who has visited twice from Cambridge, England, to help me give final shape to the text and, finally, to write a penetrating Foreword. That this book was concluded was as much due to Keith Hart's efforts as to mine. Finally, I am very grateful to the staff of Cambridge University Press, especially Jessica Kuper, the Anthropology editor, who in recogniton of the condition of my health, have abbreviated and accelerated their review and production procedures.

Roy A. Rappaport
Ann Arbor
July 1997

1

Introduction

The most general aim of this book is to enlarge, if only by a little, our understanding of the nature of religion and of religion in nature. Thus, it is about the nature of humanity, a species that lives, and can only live, in terms of meanings it must construct in a world devoid of intrinsic meaning but subject to physical law.

It will be centrally concerned with religion's most general and universal elements, "The Sacred," "The Numinous," "The Occult," and "The Divine" and with their fusion into "The Holy" in ritual. It will also be concerned, both at first and ultimately, with the evolution of humanity and humanity's place in the evolution of the world.

These two concerns may seem different or even antagonistic but they are not. An argument, close to explicit later in this chapter, remaining subterranean throughout most of this book, although surfacing from time to time and becoming central in the last chapters, not only suggests that religion could not have emerged in the absence of humanity's defining characteristic but the converse, that in the absence of what we, in a common sense way, call religion, humanity could not have emerged from its pre- or proto-human condition. It is, therefore, plausible to suppose, although beyond demonstration's possibilities, that religion's origins are, if not one with the origins of humanity, closely connected to them.

The absolute ubiquity of religion, however defined, supports the attribution of such profound significance to it. No society known to anthropology or history is devoid of what reasonable observers would agree is religion, even those such as the former Soviet Union (Tumarkin 1983) which have made deliberate attempts to extirpate it. Given the central place that religious considerations have occupied in the thoughts and actions of men and women in all times and places, and given the

amount of energy, blood, time and wealth that have been spent building
temples, supporting priests, sacrificing to gods and killing infidels, it is
hard to imagine that religion, as bizarre as some of its manifestations
may seem, is not in some way indispensable to the species.

These suggestions concerning religious origins and importance are
meant to provide the most general context possible for the more specific
arguments and discussions developed in the course of this work. The
validity of these less general arguments and discussions does not,
however, depend upon the acceptance of the book's more general theses.
Nevertheless, the claim that elements of religion may have been indispensable to humanity's evolution may seem to threaten to subordinate the
more abstract, rarefied and meaning-laden aspect of human life to so
coarse a utilitarian interpretation that its deep meaningfulness is rendered
invisible and inaudible. No such reduction is intended, nor will it take
place. Neither religion "as a whole" nor its elements will, in the account
offered of them, be reduced to functional or adaptive terms. An account
of religion framed, *a priori*, in terms of adaptation, function or other
utilitarian assumption or theory would, moreover, and paradoxically,
defeat any possibility of discovering whatever utilitarian significance it
might have by transforming the entire inquiry into a comprehensive
tautology. The only way to expose religion's adaptive significance (should
such there be) as well as to understand it "in its own right" is to provide
an account that is "true to its own nature." This is not to promise that the
account that follows is framed in "religion's own terms," whatever they
might be. It is not. If it is in the nature of religions to lay special claims to
truth, then "religion's own terms" would necessarily multiply into the
parochial terms of innumerable religious traditions, and we shall be
concerned with human universals, universals of the human condition,
universals of religion and the relationship between them.

This book is not a theological treatise but a work in anthropology. As
such, its ambitions are more general than those of any particular
theology. As an anthropological inquiry, its assumptions are, of course,
exclusively naturalistic, but it respects the concepts it seeks to understand, attempting not only to grasp what is true *of* all religions but what
is true *in* all religions, that is, the special character of the truths that it is
in the nature of all religions to claim. It is further concerned, particularly
in the last chapter, with how, and in what senses, the truths of sanctity
may become false. Later portions of this chapter and chapters 10, 11, 12
and 14 can almost be read as a treatise on certain forms of conventional
truth, on relations among them, and on various forms of falsehood.

It can also, and most obviously, be read, independent of any concern with religion's origins or evolutionary significance, as a treatise on ritual. One of its main theses is that religion's major conceptual and experiential constituents, the sacred, the numinous, the occult and the divine, and their integration into the Holy, are creations of ritual. To put the matter into logical rather than causal terms, these constituents are *entailments* of the *form* which constitutes ritual. Definition of all of these terms will be postponed for a little while. For the moment it is sufficient to characterize ritual as a *structure*, that is, a more or less enduring set of relations among a number of general but variable features. As a form or structure it possesses certain logical properties, but its properties are not only logical. Inasmuch as performance is one of its general features, it possesses the properties of practice as well. In ritual, logic becomes enacted and embodied – is realized – in unique ways.

Because ritual is taken to be the ground from which religious conceptions spring, the preponderance of the book – chapters 2 through 12 – will be devoted to its analysis. These chapters will, as it were, "unpack" a definition of ritual (to be offered in chapter 2), in the course of which the sacred, the numinous, the occult, the divine, and the Holy, will be derived, and it will further be argued that social contract, morality, a paradigm of creation, the conception of time and eternity, intimations of immortality, and those orderings of the world that we shall call *Logoi* (singular *Logos*) are all entailments of and are generated out of that form.

This book can, then, be taken to be a treatise on ritual: first on ritual's internal logic, next on the products (like sanctity) that its logic entails, and on the nature of their truth, and finally, on the place of ritual and its products in humanity's evolution. During the discussion of ritual that will occupy the early and middle chapters of the book, consideration of humanity's evolution, having been laid out briefly in this introduction to provide the broadest possible context for what follows, will remain in the background, present but largely tacit, emerging only for a moment from time to time, until chapters 13 and 14 when they will again move into the foreground.

We can now turn to the salient characteristics of humanity's evolution and to those of its problems that religion ameliorates.

1. The evolution of humanity
I did not say that this book would be concerned with "hominid" or "human evolution" but rather with "the evolution of humanity." "Hominid evolution," or "human evolution," would have emphasized

what our species has in common with other species, namely that we are animals living among and dependent upon other organisms, and, further, that our species emerged through processes of natural selection no different in principle from those that produced limpets or lions. These commonalties are assumed, but the phrase "evolution of humanity" is meant to emphasize the capacity that sets our species apart from all others. Our forebears became what might loosely be called "fully human" with the emergence of language. All animals communicate, and even plants receive and transmit information (Bickerton 1990), but only humans, so far as we know, are possessed of languages composed, first, of lexicons made up of symbols in Peirce's sense of the word (1960 II: 143ff.) or Buchler's (1955: 99, 102, 112f.): that is, signs related only "by law," i.e. convention, to that which they signify,[1] and second, of grammars, sets of rules for combining symbols into semantically un-bounded discourse.

It is obvious that the possession of language makes possible ways of life inconceivable to non-verbal creatures, and even "proto-language" a form of communication making use of limited vocabularies composed of symbols but possessing little or only rudimentary grammar (Bickerton 1990, chapters 6 and 7) must have conferred important advantages upon the hominids among whom they developed. With proto-language, com-munication could, perhaps (or even probably) for the first time in this world's evolution, not only escape from the confines of here and now to report upon the past and distant but also begin to order, to an increasing degree, the future by facilitating the division of labor and by making more precise planning and coordination possible. Social organization could, as a consequence, become increasingly differentiated, increasingly effective and uniquely flexible, and new dimensions of mutual support and protection could be attained.

Even more fundamentally, it is plausible to assume that increased communicational capacities both indicate and entail increased conceptual capacities. Moreover, the emergence of the symbol not only increased conceptual capacity but transformed it, and new forms of learning became possible.[2] With symbolic transmission individuals can learn from the accounts of others as well as from their own direct experience, and this learning may be transformed in its mere recounting, into public knowledge which can, by further recounting, be preserved as tradition.

The immediate advantages that such abilities confer upon those who possess them are patent, and, in light of them, it is plausible to believe that linguistic ability, once it began to develop, would have been very strongly selected for, which is to say that the anatomical structures on which it is based may have been elaborated and transformed at rates that were, in evolutionary terms, unusually rapid. Proto-language and language could well have emerged in a relatively short time.[3] Increased ability to plan, to coordinate, to report on the past and distant, to accumulate and transmit knowledge, to learn in new and more effective ways, must all have been among the early factors vigorously selecting for increasing linguistic ability.

Other rather less obvious but by no means obscure entailments of language may, however, have been as consequential in the long run. With language, discourse not only can escape from the confines of here and now to recapture the concrete past and distant or to approach the foreseeable future. It could also eventually escape from the concrete altogether. It may be suggested that the transcendence of the concrete and the emergence of grammar were mutually causal,[4] but, be this as it may, when discourse can escape from the concrete as well as the present, and when it is empowered by grammar, it finally becomes free to search for such worlds parallel to the actual as those of "the might have been," "the should be," "the could be," "the never will," "the may always be." It can, then, explore the realms of the desirable, the moral, the proper, the possible, the fortuitous, the imaginary, the general, and their negatives, the undesirable, the immoral, the impossible (Rappaport 1979b). To "explore" these worlds is not simply to *discover* what is there. It is to *create* what is there. Language does not merely facilitate the communication of what is conceived but expands, eventually by magnitudes, what can be conceived. This expansion of conceptual power as much as the ability to communicate to others the products of that expanded power – accounts, understanding, abstractions, evaluations – underlies the general human mode of adaptation and the specific adaptations of the many societies into which the species is ever redividing itself. As such, language and proto-language before it, have been absolutely central to human evolutionary success. It would not, indeed, be an exaggeration to claim that humanity is their creation.

2. Adaptation

The term "adaptation" has just been introduced. Its full discussion will be postponed until chapter 13. For now it is well to note that although the concept is central to much thought in biology as well as anthropology, it is slippery. Because not all writers mean the same thing by the term, it is always useful, if not downright necessary, for those involving it to make clear what they do mean. In this book the term designates the processes through which living systems of all sorts – organisms, populations, societies, possibly ecosystems or even the biosphere as a whole – maintain themselves in the face of perturbations continuously threatening them with disruption, death or extinction. Gregory Bateson (1972) put the matter in informational terms, stating that adaptive systems are organized in ways that tend to preserve the truth value of certain propositions about themselves in the face of perturbations continually threatening to falsify them. The preservation of "the truth" of these propositions is associated with, or even definitive of, the persistence or perpetuation of the systems of which they are elements. In organisms, these "propositions" are, as it were, genetically and physiologically encoded descriptions of their structure and proper functioning. In human social systems, however, regnant "propositions" may be propositions properly so-called: "The Lord our God the Lord is one," the invalidation of which would signify the demise of Judaism.

Adaptive responses to perturbations include both short-term reversible changes of *state* and longer-term irreversible changes in *structure*. Although the two classes can be distinguished from each other, they are not separated from each other in nature. Adaptive responses are seldom, if ever, isolated but seem, rather, to be organized into sequences possessing certain temporal and logical characteristics (Bateson 1972h, Rappaport 1971a, 1979a, Slobodkin and Rapoport 1974) commencing with quickly mobilized easily reversible changes in state (if perturbation continues), proceeding through less easily reversible state changes to, in some cases, the irreversible changes not in state but in structure that are called "evolutionary." The generalization connecting reversible "functional" to irreversible "evolutionary" changes is sometimes known as "Romer's Rule" after the zoologist, A. S. Romer (1954 [1933] I: 43ff.), who illustrated it in a discussion of the emergence of the amphibia from the lobe-finned fish during the Devonian period. These air-breathing, bottom-feeding, bony-finned denizens of shallow ponds did not first venture onto dry land in order to take advantage of a promising set of open niches. Rather, they were frequently left high and dry during that time of intermittent dessication. Under such circumstances relatively minor modifications in limb structure (heavily boned fins into legs) and other subsystems were strongly selected for because they facilitated locomotion over land back to water. Thus, the earliest terrestrial adaptation among the vertebrates made it possible to maintain an aquatic way of life. To put it a little differently, *structural transformations in some subsystems made it possible to maintain more basic aspects of the system unchanged.* This proposes that the fundamental question to ask about any evolutionary change is "*What does this change maintain unchanged?*" To translate the matter once again into informational terms, modifications or transformations in the descriptions of substructures may preserve unchanged the truth value of more fundamental propositions concerning the system as a whole in the face of changes in conditions threatening to falsify them. More detailed discussion of adaptation will be postponed until later chapters, but two brief comments are in order.

First, even this brief account of adaptation indicates that adaptive systems are generally hierarchical in structure. The parable of the transformation of lobe-finned fish into amphibia indicates that they are hierarchical in the unavoidable and irreducible sense of wholes made up of parts: changes in *subsystems* preserve the continuity of the system as a whole living entity. They are hierarchical in the secondary and derivative sense of superordination and subordination. The subsystems of a normally functioning adaptive system are subservient to the perpetuation of the system as a whole or, to put this in informational terms again, to preserve the truth value of the system's regnant proportions subordinate propositions may be modified, transformed or replaced.

Secondly, flexibility is central to adaptation so conceived, and the adaptive flexibility of humans following from the possession of language seems to be unparalleled. When social organization and rules for behavior are stipulated in conventions expressed in words rather than specified in genes inscribed on chromosomes they can be replaced within single lifetimes, even sometimes, overnight. This has made it possible for a single interbreeding species to enter, and even to dominate, the great variety of environments the world presents to it without having to spend generations transforming itself into a range of new species.

3. The symbol

Language and its entailment, culture, the general way of life consisting of understandings, institutions, customs, and material artifacts, whose existence, maintenance and use are contingent upon language,[5] must have emerged through processes of natural selection as part of the adaptive apparatus of the hominids.

But even such far-reaching claims as "Language is the foundation of the human way of life" do not do language's importance justice, for its significance transcends the species in which it appeared. Leslie White used to say that the appearance of the symbol – by which he meant language – was not simply an evolutionary novelty enhancing the survival chances of a particular species, but the most radical innovation in the evolution of evolution itself since life first appeared. Inasmuch as the symbol seems to be unique, or virtually unique, to humanity, such a claim may be uncomfortably reminiscent of theological assertions of a status for humans only one step lower than the angels but, bearing in mind the dangers of such assertions and insisting that humanity remains squarely in nature, we should recognize that White's claim was not extravagant. A quibbler could argue that the development of language was nothing more than the most radical innovation in the evolutionary process since the appearance of sex, to which it may be likened in some respects. Both, after all, are means for recombining and transmitting information, and sex laid the groundwork for a sociality that language later elaborated. The significance of language, however, is not confined to the recombination and transmission of the already existant class of genetic information. With the symbol an entirely new form of information (in the widest sense of the word) appeared in the world. This new form brought with it new content, and the world as a whole, not merely the genus *Homo*, has not been the same since.

The epochal significance of the symbol for the world beyond the species in which it appeared did not become apparent for many millennia – perhaps hundreds of millennia – after it had emerged. But earlier effects of language and even proto-language upon the lifeways of the hominids in its possession must soon have become enormous. That language permits thought and communication to escape from the solid actualities of here and now to discover other realms, for instance, those of the possible, the plausible, the desirable, and the valuable, has already been emphasized. This was not quite correct. Language does not merely *permit* such thought but both *requires* it and *makes it inevitable*. Humanity is a species that lives and can only live in terms of meanings it itself must invent. These meanings and understandings not only reflect or approximate an independently existing world but participate in its very construction. The worlds in which humans live are not fully constituted by tectonic, meteorological and organic processes. They are not only made of rocks and trees and oceans, but are also constructed out of symbolically conceived and performatively established (Austin 1962, see chapter 4 hereafter) cosmologies, institutions, rules, and values. With language the world comes to be furnished with qualities like good and evil, abstractions like democracy and communism, values like honor, valor and generosity, imaginary beings like demons, spirits and gods, imagined places like heaven and hell. All of these concepts are reified, made into *res*, real "things," by social actions contingent upon language. Human worlds are, therefore, inconceivably richer than the worlds inhabited by other creatures.

"Human worlds." Each human society develops a unique culture, which is also to say that it constructs a unique world that includes not only a special understanding of the trees and rocks and water surrounding it, but of other things, many unseen, as real as those trees and animals and rocks. It is in terms of their existence, no less than in terms of the existence of physical things, that people operate and transform not only their social systems but the ecosystems surrounding them which, in all but the cases of hunters and gatherers, they have dominated[6] since the emergence of agriculture 10,000 or so years ago. Since then, language has ever more powerfully reached out from the species in which it emerged to reorder and subordinate the natural systems in which populations of that species participate.

4. The great inversion

Although it conforms to this account to say that language is central to human adaptation, it is also clear that such a statement is so inadequate as a characterization of the relationship of language to language user as to be dangerously misleading. If, as agents, people act, and perhaps can only act, in terms of meanings they or their ancestors have conceived, they are as much in the service of those conceptions as those conceptions are parts of their adaptations. *There is, this is to say, an inversion or partial inversion, in the course of human evolution, of the relationship of the adaptive apparatus to the adapting species.* The linguistic capacity that is central to human adaptation makes it possible to give birth to concepts that come to possess those who have conceived them, concepts like god, heaven and hell. To argue that all such concepts or the actions they inform or guide enhance the survival and reproduction of the organisms who maintain them as a simple adaptive theory of language would have it, is not credible.

That language is central to the human mode of adaptation is the truth, but it is far from the whole truth. If adaptive systems can be defined as systems that operate (consciously or unconsciously) to preserve the true value of certain propositions about themselves in the face of perturbations tending to falsify them, and if the metaphor of inversion (surely an oversimplification) is at all apt, then it is appropriate to propose that the propositions favored in human social systems are about such conceptions as God, Honor, Freedom, Fatherland, and The Good. That their preservation has often required great or even ultimate sacrifice on the parts of individuals hardly needs saying. Postulates concerning the unitary or triune nature of god are among those for whom countless individuals have sacrificed their lives or killed others, as are such mundane apothegms as "Death before dishonor" or "Better dead than red."

That the implications of such an inversion for evolution may be obvious does not make them any the less profound or epochal. First, whatever the case may be for explanations of the behavior and organization of other species, and of their evolution, the extent to which concepts like "inclusive fitness" and "kin selection" can account for cultural phenomena is very limited. Secondly and related, whatever the case may be among other species, group selection (selection for the perpetuation of traits tending to contribute positively to the survival of the groups in which they occur but negatively to the survival of the particular individuals in possession of them) is not only possible among humans but of great importance in humanity's evolution. All that is needed to make group selection possible is a device that leads individuals to separate their conceptions of well-being or advantage from biological survival. Notions such as God, Heaven, Hell, heroism, honor, shame, fatherland and democracy encoded in procedures of enculturation that represent them as factual, natural, public, or sacred (and, therefore, compelling) have dominated every culture for which we possess ethnographic or historical knowledge.

Language, in sum, makes for profound changes in the nature of evolution and, even more profoundly, in the nature of evolving systems. Non-human systems are organic systems constituted largely by genetically encoded information. Human systems are cultural-organic systems constituted by symbolic (linguistic) as well as genetic information. Whereas the transformation from organic to cultural-organic must have been strongly selected for, we are coming, in this discussion, to see that the consequences of the emergence of language and its concomitant, culture, were not unambiguously advantageous to those in their possession. We may note in passing a seldom-remarked evolutionary rule: every "advance" sets new problems as it responds to and ameliorates earlier ones. Language was no exception.

We have been led from a panegyric to language to a recognition of its vices. In addition to setting up possibilities for unprecedented contradiction between the symbolic and genetic such that the propositions that humans attempt to preserve above all else may lead them to their deaths, two others seem intrinsic to language's very virtues. They may be less obvious than language's gifts but they are both profound and grave.

5. The lie

The first is this. When a sign is only conventionally related to what it signifies, as in Peirce's sense of the symbol, it can occur in the absence of its *signification* or *referent*, and, conversely, events can occur without being signaled. This conventional relationship, which permits discourse to escape from the here and now and, even more generally, to become separate and distinct from that which it merely represents or is only *about*, also facilitates lying if it does not, indeed, make it for the first time possible. The very freedom of sign from signified that enlarges by magnitudes the scope of human life also increases by magnitudes possibilities for falsehood.

The concept of lie requires some discussion. The term "Lie" will be used in this work in its most general sense to denote a family of forms of falsehood, some of whose less well-known members, those I call "Vedic Lies," "Diabolical Lies," "Gnostic Lies," "Lies of Oppression" and "Idolatrous Lies," we shall encounter later. For now we shall be concerned only with the most familiar and most fundamental form, the "Common" or "Vulgar" lie,[7] the willful transmission of information which is thought by the transmitter to be false.

The common lie (which I will simply call "lie" for now) is often associated with deceit, but deceit is more general in both occurrence and scope. The term "deceit" implies an intention to mislead to the disadvantage of those who are misled, particularly *vis-à-vis* those misleading them. "Lie" also entails intention, but the defining intention of lie is related to the signal transmitted, whereas the defining intention of deceit is concerned with the effect upon, or more specifically, the response of, the receiver. When such a distinction is made it becomes apparent that the terms "lie" and "deceit" designate overlapping but not coextensive ranges of phenomena. Deceit often employs lies, and lies are often deceitful, but it is not difficult to find instances of lying that do not seem so. Most people would not think it a deceit to say to a sick child "You are going to be well," even if the speaker really thinks the child is in danger of dying. In fact, if patients are suffering from conditions that could be exacerbated by strong emotion, like heart disease, we might think it perfidious to "tell the truth," or what we think "the truth" to be. If perfidy is a form of deceit it is clear that not all deceitful acts are lies.

Even those meant to harm dupes may not be lies in a strict sense. The horse that the Greeks left for the Trojans may not have been a lie properly so called, but it certainly was the central element in what seems a rather implausible deception.

Lying seems largely a human problem, but deceit may be more general. There are, at least, both behaviors and organic structures common among animals that do share characteristics with deceitfulness. They include such things as bluffing, broken-wing behavior, playing possum, camouflage, and mimicry. But intentionality is lacking from some of these phenomena. The fly that looks like a wasp doesn't consciously try to look that way, and playing possum may be genetically programmed. Moreover, even the intention to mislead may not be sufficient to identify deceitfulness. No reasonable person would consider a feint in boxing, a trap in chess, a finesse in bridge, a fake hand-off to the tailback[8] or even an ambush in modern warfare or possibly the ancient presentation of wooden horses to Trojans to be deceitful. The notion of deceit presupposes the existence of a relationship of trust which deceit then violates, and there is no violation in the last two cases because no relationships of trust prevailed at the time of the act. It is significant that, aside from bluffing which is often if not, in fact, usually directed toward conspecifics in contexts in which competition or antagonism is clear, the sorts of instances I have noted among animals are generally employed by members of one species to deceive members of others, usually (if not always) those preying on them or on which they prey, and with whom they certainly do not stand in relationships of trust.

In light of the absence of intentionality in some of these instances and the absence of previously existing bonds of trust in others, it seems reasonable to establish a more inclusive category, "Deception," of which deceit and lie are overlapping subclasses, lie also overlapping with a third subclass that we may, for lack of a better term, call "Innocent Deception."[9]

Deceit and deception generally are, then, more widespread among the world's creatures than common lying, but such lying does expand possibilities for deceit and deception enormously. We should also recognize that inasmuch as possibilities for lying to those with whom one does not share a language are very limited, those duped by lying humans are not only not members of other species but not usually members of other societies. Considerations of propinquity and common language both suggest that the dupes of human lies are most frequently members of the liars' own social groups, persons, that is, to whom the liars stand in relationships of trust.

The contention that lying is largely a human problem is not novel. Hobbes (1951 [1651]) said as much in the seventeenth century. Long before him, Plato's discussion of "noble" lies in *The Republic* presupposed language, as did St. Augustine's discussion in *The Enchiridion*: "Now it is evident that speech was given to man, not that men might therewith deceive one another, but that one man might make known his thoughts to another" (quoted by Bok 1978: 32). In this century Hockett and Altman (1968) added the ability to prevaricate to Hockett's earlier list of the "design features" of human language. A few years earlier, Martin Buber, not a linguist but a philosopher and theologian, opened his book *Good and Evil* by declaring the lie to be one of the two grounds of human evil.

> The lie is the specific evil which man has introduced into nature. All our deeds of violence and our misdeeds are only as it were a highly-bred development of what this and that creature of nature is able to achieve in its own way. But the lie is our very own invention, different in kind from every deceit that the animals can produce. A lie was possible only after a creature, man, was capable of conceiving the being of truth.
>
> *(1952: 7)*

W. H. Thorpe (1968, 1972: 33), an ethologist, in a discussion of Hockett and Altman, gives qualified support to Buber, observing that the ability to lie is "highly characteristic of the human species and is hardly found at all in other animals."

Sufficient research on animal deception has been conducted in the decades since Thorpe's comment to have called humanity's sole proprietorship of the lie into question. That dubious honor is probably still ours, however, although, as already noted, deception is widespread among animals, and behavior that closely resembles "true lying" has frequently been observed among apes and, possibly, canids as well (Ruppell 1986).[10] Two decades ago, for instance, Jane Van Lawick-Goodall reported the now-famous and rather spectacular case of a non-domesticated adolescent chimpanzee named "Figan" by the researchers at Gombe in Tanzania, who was observed to do something that seems on the face of it to qualify. It was the practice of the ethnologists to leave bananas in a certain clearing to attract chimpanzees for close observation. High-ranking males dominated these assemblages, of course, and appropriated most of the fruit for themselves. To enlarge his share Figan applied what it seems plausible to assume he consciously knew of his conspecifics' typical attentiveness to each other's behavior. If, after a group of chimpanzees has been at rest, one of them leaps up in an apparent state of heightened attention and agitation the others are alerted, and if he or she then moves off briskly and apparently purposefully, the others are likely to follow, probably because they take him or her to have heard something. On several occasions, Figan led the group away from the feeding area in such a manner, returning quietly and alone a little while later to gorge himself in solitude. Van Lawick-Goodall (1971: 96) states "quite obviously he was doing it deliberately." Margaritha Thurndahl, who watched Figan on other occasions, told me that his guile was even more elaborate. He not only acted as if he heard something, but dashed off into the forest after it, vocalizing and stimulating others to vocalize, returning to the clearing under the cover of the general commotion.

We can admire Figan's ingenuity, but our very admiration is a recognition of how difficult and awkward is lying that relies upon communication which is not symbolic in the Peircian sense. Figan's signals on this occasion were not symbolic but, rather, feigned indexicality, an index being, in Peirce's tripartite classification – as stated in note 1 above – a sign that is "really affected by" that which it signifies (a dark cloud does not symbolize but indicates, or is an index of, rain). Thus an agitated demeanor combined with an attitude or posture of heightened attention in one of his conspecifics might indicate to an observing chimpanzee that his associate had heard something.

With all due respect both to Figan's ingenuity and to his disingenousness we must be struck not only by how awkward and difficult is lying that is dependent upon pseudo-indices but also how limited is its scope. In the absence of the symbol, we have already noted, the significance of messages is almost entirely, if not, indeed, entirely, limited to the here and now. Lying does not escape from such limitation. Thus a female gorilla, to cite another well-attested case (Hediger 1955: 50f.), who lured her keeper into her cage by pretending that her arm had somehow gotten caught in the bars, could only transmit a false message about the *present* (here and now) state of affairs. She could not indicate or pretend to indicate that her arm had been stuck sometime last week or would be next month, much less that someone else's arm was stuck somewhere else at the present time. Furthermore, her transmissions were not only limited to the here and now but she herself had to be unceasingly engaged in the transmission of her own lie. Similarly, Figan could transmit the message "Something is out there" only by acting and *continuing* to act as if there were. (If Thurndahl's account is accurate, he was, however, able to prolong the effectiveness of his falsehood beyond the cessation of his own transmission by, deliberately or not, stimulating his dupes to continue the transmission through their own behavior.) In contrast, a symbolically transmitted lie need not be transmitted continuously. It may remain operative and continue to affect the dupe's understanding of the state of the world long after its transmission has ceased, being revived from time to time in circumstances the dupe takes to be appropriate. A lie symbolically transmitted in a sentence or even a word may, like blood libels against Jews in medieval Europe, endure for centuries. In light of these profound differences between the capacities of apes (and perhaps other animals) and humans, I think it proper to preserve the title of "World's Only True Liar" for our own species. We may admit to our society a few chimpanzees whom humans have taught to sign, but even the craftiest of unschooled apes seem incapable of more than what may appropriately be called "Proto-Lying," a form of falsehood that relies upon the use of pseudo indices.

The problem of the lie is not only embedded in language and thus in the essentials of human nature, but is a fundamental one for human society. What is at stake is not only the truthfulness or reliability of particular messages but credibility, credence and trust themselves, and thus the grounds of the trustworthiness requisite to systems of communication and community generally. The survival of any population, animal or human, depends upon social interactions characterized by some minimum degree of orderliness, but orderliness in social systems depends, in turn, upon communication which must meet some minimum standard of reliability if the recipients of messages are to be willing to accept the information they receive as sufficiently reliable to depend upon. If they are not sufficiently confident in its trustworthiness their responses are likely to become decreasingly predictable, and social life increasingly disordered. What were called "Credibility Gaps" during the Vietnam years are socially corrosive and individually demoralizing. When a system of communication accommodates falsehood, how can the recipients of messages be assured that the messages they receive are sufficiently reliable to act upon? I will argue, among other things, *that aspects of religion, particularly as generated in ritual, ameliorate problems of falsehood intrinsic to language to a degree sufficient to allow human sociability to have developed and to be maintained.* Three comments are in order.

First, I do not claim that religion arose more or less simply as an adaptive response to enhanced possibilities of falsehood, but that certain defining elements of religion, especially the concept of the sacred and the process of sanctification, are no less possibilities of language, particularly of linguistic expressions in ritual, than are lies, and that *religion emerged with language. As such, religion is as old as language, which is to say precisely as old as humanity*.

Secondly, it must be emphasized that religion provides no cure for falsehood. There is no absolute cure for the common lie, nor should there be. Most philosophers and theologians have not taken falsehood to be unambiguously evil, and we can easily recognize the social benefactions some lies provide. Most obviously, "white lies" are, by definition, lies meant to be protective of those to whom they are told. Insincerities are an important ingredient of civility and as such an indispensable lubricant of social relations. Common lies, furthermore, may also be legitimate responses to questions concerning matters which are none of the inquirer's business. They have, no doubt on innumerable occasions, helped to guard the meanings of colonized and subordinated peoples against outside threats posed by the likes of missionaries and colonial administrators. Religion, happily, is no more capable of banishing the common lie than are any other means known to humankind. It can do no more than ameliorate some of their vices.

Thirdly, not all symbolically encoded messages present the same sorts of difficulties. Those communicating necessary truths or well-known and immutable facts or empirical laws or social rules may not present problems of credence and credibility. The message $1 + 1 = 2$ does not trouble a normal receiver. Given the meanings assigned to the terms it would be self-contradictory to deny such a statement. Receivers of such messages as $1 + 1 = 3$ have available to them, at least theoretically, logical grounds for rejecting them. Similarly, the assertion that the application of sufficient heat to ice produces liquid water is not likely to excite doubt. But, such generalizations constitute only a minority of socially significant messages. A law concerning heat, water, melting points, boiling points and so on does not tell us whether a distant lake has yet thawed or whether the fish there have started to bite. That $1 + 1 = 2$ does not tell us how much treasure remains in the coffers. The laws of *Kashrut* do not tell a pious Jew whether the meat offered him by his host has been butchered according to those laws, and it is one thing for a Maring man to know that the ritual planting of *rumbim* turns war into peace, but quite another to know whether or not a particular local group has performed that ritual. It is not society's *generalizations* about the *nature* of the world in which it lives *that in the first instance* present continuing problems of credibility and credence. It is specific information concerning the *current states* of that continuously changing world, particularly its social aspects, that is problematic.

6. Alternative

The common lie is not the only vice intrinsic to the very virtue and the very genius of language, not the only worm in the apple so to speak. Language's second problem is alternative. Whereas the problem of the "Lie" follows, in the main, from the symbolic relationship between the sign and the signified, problems set by Alternatives arise, as much or more from the ordering of symbols through grammar, language's other *sine qua non*.

Grammar makes the conception of alternatives virtually ineluctable. If there is enough grammar to think and say "YHVH is God and Marduk is not," or "Socialism is preferable to capitalism" there is, obviously, enough to imagine, say and act upon the opposite.

Some ability to conceive alternatives must, of course, constitute part of the cognitive processes of most animals. It is reasonable to suppose that a squirrel pursued by a dog sees the alternative trees up which she can escape, and may even in some way assess the advantages and disadvantages of the routes available to her. But the scope of alternatives takes a quantum leap with grammar. We can infer from the squirrel's ability to undertake alternative courses of action that she can conceive of *alternative states of affairs* and even evaluate their advantages, but grammar does more than enhance the ability to conceive and evaluate alternative courses of action and states of affairs. Grammar makes it possible to conceive of alternative worlds, that is, of *alternative orders* governed by *either* the laws of Marduk *or* those of YHVH, or of worlds organized in terms of the principles of socialism or of capitalism.

The ability to imagine and establish alternative orders is not, on the face of it, problematic. Such an ability makes possible, or even itself constitutes, a quantum leap in adaptive flexibility, the capacity of a system to adjust or transform itself in response to changing conditions. This enhanced flexibility has, however, an unavoidable but dangerous concomitant: increased grounds for disorder.

No actual society is utopian. It may, therefore, be difficult for any society's members not to imagine orders in at least some respects preferable to those under which they do live and labor. If they can conceive of better orders, how are their actions to be kept in sufficient conformity to the prevailing order for that order to persist? The conception of the possible is always in some degree the enemy of the actual. As such it may be a first step toward the disruption of prevailing social and conceptual orders, whatever they may be, without necessarily being a first step toward their improvement or replacement by orders more acceptable to those subject to them. Because of its disruptive capacities, Martin Buber (1952) took alternative to constitute the second ground of human evil.[11]

Consideration of alternatives brings into view problems deeper than disorder. For there to be disorder there must be orders that can become disordered. We come to the underlying matter of the "reality" of such orders, to the matter of WHAT IS, of what is actual and what is only a figment of fear or yearning, for what, out of the range of conceived or conceivable alternatives, can "truth" be claimed? Marduk or YHVH? A Triune or Monophysite divinity? At a lower level what is honorable, what dishonorable, what moral, what immoral? In societies in which such matters are contested, such "reality," or "truth" is not, moreover, merely a matter of the civil establishment of one or the other possibility nor, necessarily, the outcome of an easy tolerance, as is made clear by the diatribes of Hebrew Prophets against both idolatry and against the habits of kings. It is not merely a question of what order *does* prevail but which one *should* prevail. For at least some of the world's symbolically contingent elements "reality" or "truth" has a moral as well as social dimension, and historical states of affairs at variance with that reality are taken to be false. We will return to this matter later especially in chapters 4 and 10. Here I will assert that the problem of WHAT IS is not, for humans other than scientists and philosophers, a problem concerning stars or rocks or digestion or the leafing out of trees, or even the photosynthesis located in those leaves, that is to say, of visible or even invisible physical components of the world, of elements constituted by cosmic, geological, meteorological, ecosystemic, genetic and physiological processes. It is primarily a problem concerning those world elements whose actuality is contingent upon symbolic-beings, like gods and demons, places like heaven and hell, virtues like honor and humility, moral qualities like good and evil, social abstractions like democracy, socialism, equality, freedom, free enterprise, fatherland; for all of these there are conceivable alternatives, and all of them may, therefore, be contested: Marduk or YHVH?

To claim that the problem of the real is a problem concerning the world's symbolic but not its physical elements is not to claim that the principles by which the physical elements of the world originated, evolved or operate, or even of what these elements consist, are fully known or understood. Obviously they are not, and there is some reason to believe that they never will be (Grim 1991). Nor is it to propose, with an equivalent absurdity, that we can ignore, even for the purposes of this book, or leave to specialists, the questions concerning the reality of the world's physical elements – creatures, objects, substances – with which humans continually interact. We shall return to such matters and to the interaction of the world's symbolic elements with them. It is simply to observe that humanity's knowledge of the reality of the symbolically contingent elements of the world and the world's "naturally constituted" element are differently grounded. If the world's physical elements and processes are to be known they must be discovered, and humanity has developed general principles and procedures for ascertaining them. The world's symbolic elements are not naturally constituted, but are, rather, human fabrications. Knowledge of their actuality – whether Marduk governs the world and YHVH is no more than a figment of heretical imagination or *vice versa* – is not primarily a matter of discovery. The actuality or reality of any symbolically contingent element of the world becomes known, in the first instance, as a consequence of its construction, establishment and maintenance by those who would take it to be actual. This is to say that knowledge of "the truths" of the symbolically contingent portion of the world is an ontological as well as, or even rather than, an epistemological matter. As Giambattista Vico put it as early as 1699:

We stand in relation to the products of the human mind as God stands to nature: "God alone is the maker of nature: the human mind may I be allowed to say, is the god of the Arts," and, as he later proposed in the first sentence of *On the Most Ancient Wisdom of the Italians* (first published in 1710) " ... *verum* [the true] and *factum* (what is made) are interchangeable ... " that is, one and the same. Having made it we can know that is the case.   *(Palmer, 1988: 9)*

The cornerstone of Vico's thought was a radical critique of certain aspects of Cartesian method and of the method of natural science, particularly those proclaiming that only objective knowledge derived through precise observation of objects by dispassionate observers radically separated from them could claim truth about the extended world, and of Descartes' claim that mathematics is the ultimate and perfect form of objective knowledge, that numerical representation provides the best guarantee of certainty, and that all other claims for truth are trivial or false.

Vico acquiesced in his early works (1709, 1710) to the superiority of truth claims for mathematics but proposed that the truth of mathematics is known to us not because we discovered it objectively but precisely because we did not. In doing mathematics we are not discovering the most immutable features of an objective world but *inventing* a logical system. We can know its truth fully because we *made* it.

He elevated this form of truth into a general principle. The only consciousness that can know a thing truly and fully is the consciousness that made it. Thus, he argued, the only consciousness that can truly know the natural world is God's, because God made it. Humans can glimpse the workings of the natural world by imitating God through experiment, but otherwise they are limited to "outside knowledge," to a knowledge of that which can be ascertained – for example, that four moons orbit Jupiter, and to inferences from that which can be directly ascertained, for instance, that the earth orbits the sun. In contrast, he argued, we can have full and true knowledge of that which we have made, of machines, for instance, or more importantly, of human images, thoughts, symbols, and institutions because we have created them, or if we ourselves did not, they were fabricated by minds which, being human, are sufficiently like our own to be, through various methods, accessible to us, as the divine mind that fashioned nature can never be. Thus, Vico stated as early as 1699, we stand in relation to the products of the human mind as God stands to nature ("God alone is the maker of nature: the human mind, may I be allowed to say, is the god of the arts").

Vico distinguished terminologically between the forms of truth available through Cartesian method applied to the physical world and those which humans can attain of "the world of civil society" (1968 [1744]: paragraph 331; Bergin and Fisch 1984: 97).

All that the former can yield is the inferior form of truth that he called *certum*, that which can be ascertained, simple fact. Humans can, in contrast, attain deeper knowledge, knowledge *per causas* (Berlin 1981: 113), inside knowledge of causes, motive, reasons, operations, as well as the knowledge provided by direct experience, knowledge of what it is to be poor or injured or a father or exultant. For such knowledge Vico reserved the term *Verum*, "the true." His general thesis was stated in the first sentence of his 1710 book *On the Most Ancient Wisdom of the Italians*: "For the Latins, *verum* (the true) and *factum* (what is made) are interchangeable [i.e., one and the same]". This is generally read as an epistemological principle and, of course, it is. But I believe it is more than that. It is at a deeper level and, in the first instance, ontological. In proposing that the human mind is to the arts as God is to nature, Vico, it seems to me, is recognizing not only the potential omniscience of the human mind with respect to the world's symbolic elements, but its omnipotence in that domain as well. It seems plausible to suggest that he had at least a glimmer of the twentieth-century development called "Speech Act Theory" (see Austin 1962; Searle 1969, and chapter 4 below).

Such truth is closely related to lie: both are fabrications, and so we are led to the question of how humanity grounds the truths it must fabricate and how it distinguishes them from falsehood.

This question is close to the one Hans Kung asks in the very first paragraph of his monumental *Does God Exist?*: "And since the emergence of modern, rational man there has been an almost desperate struggle with the problem of human certainty. Where, we wonder, is there a rocklike, unshakable certainty on which all human certainty could be built?" (Kung 1980: 1).

I would modify Kung's question only by dropping the terms "modern" and "rational." The problem is as old as humanity. Modern "rational" man may be faced with the breakdown of ancient means for establishing certainty, but that is another matter. Although the problem of certainty may have become increasingly serious, problematic and even desperate as humanity has evolved socially and culturally, I take it to be *intrinsic to the human condition*, that is, the condition of a species that lives, and can only live, by meanings and understandings it itself must construct in a world devoid of intrinsic meaning but subject to causal laws, not all of which are known. It is, further, a world in which the lie is ubiquitous, and in which the "reality" or "truth" of key elements, like gods and values and social orders, not only have to be invented but maintained in the face of increasing threats, posed by ever-burgeoning alternative possibilities, to falsify them. If the world is to have any words at all it may be necessary to establish *The Word* – the *True Word* – to stand against the dissolvant power of lying words and many words, to stand against falsehood and Babel.

It is a major thesis of this book that it is in the nature of religion to fabricate the Word, the True Word upon which the truths of symbols and the convictions that they establish stand. As I suggested at the beginning of this chapter, I take the foundry within which the Word is forged to be ritual. A definition of ritual will be offered and its general features examined. Two streams of messages carried by all religious rituals, the self-referential and the canonical, will be distinguished, and differences between them with respect to the relationship between signs and their significata will be discussed. The self-referential stream will be explored in some depth with emphasis placed upon formal features of its transmission and their implications for clarity, ambiguity, and vagueness. The relationship of self-referential to canonical messages will occupy chapter 4. I will argue there that social contract, morality, and the establishment of convention are intrinsic to ritual's form, and I address the question of why it is that virtually all rituals include acts and objects as well as words. Then I will discuss ritual's sequential, simultaneous and hierarchical dimensions from which a concept of the sacred will be derived. The relationship of sacred and sanctified truths to other forms of truth must be later explored. The relationship of sanctity to order will develop the concept of Logos. The non-discursive, affective experiential aspect of the religious and its generation in ritual will be examined, and, finally, the emergence of the concept of the divine out of ritual will also be considered there. Finally, we will return to the matter of adaptation and the place of the sacred, the numinous and the holy in adaptive structure and process and then consider the relationship between holiness and power and, further, the degradation of the sacred, the delusion of the numinous, the breaking of the holy, the contradiction between the epistemology of discovery defining science and the ontology of meaning underlying the symbolic aspect of the world, and, finally, their possible reconciliation.

2

The ritual form

It is possible, and may even be preferable, to avoid general definitions of religion any more specific than the loose characterization offered in the first chapter – that for purposes of this book the term denotes the domain of the Holy, the constituents of which include the sacred, the numinous, the occult and the divine, and also ritual, the form of action in which those constituents are generated.

Such a sketchy representation – a verbal equivalent of pointing – is sufficient to indicate the region to be explored, its very vagueness suggesting the indefiniteness of the shape and extent of the territory religion occupies and the haziness of its boundaries. The concept of religion is irreducibly vague, but vagueness is not vacuity, and we know well enough what people mean by the term to get on with things.

The situation is very different with respect to religion's elements. For one thing uses of these terms, particularly "holy" and "sacred," vary widely, and "numinous" is less familiar than the others. For another, these conceptions both participate directly in and are the specific objects of analysis, whereas "religion" is simply the domain within which these analyses are conducted. As such our understandings of them must be much more specific than our general understanding of the term "religion." Because one of the main goals of this book is to develop a fuller grasp of the nature of religion, that is a better grasp of the Holy and its constituents, they will not be defined *a priori*. We will rather work toward them. It is sufficient for now to say that in this book the term "sacred" signifies the discursive aspect of religion, that which is or can be expressed in language, whereas "numinous" denotes religion's non-discursive, affective, ineffable qualities. The term "occult" refers to religion's peculiar efficacious capacities (it will concern us least) and "divine" will signify its spiritual referents. The term "holy" (in common usage as well as in the work of many analysts often a synonym for sacred, which in turn, usually has wider and vaguer meaning than it does in this work) is distinguished here from "sacred" and will be reserved for the total religious phenomenon, the integration of its four elements which, I will argue, is achieved in ritual. This inclusiveness is apt, for the word "holy" probably shares its derivation from the Old English *halig* with the word "whole" as well as with "healthy" and "heal" (see American Heritage Dictionary, 3rd ed., 1992, Oxford Unabridged Dictionary, Partridge 1983: 292, 804).

Because the Holy and its elements are generated in and integrated by ritual, they will be approached through ritual, to whose introduction this chapter is devoted.[1]

1. Ritual defined

I take the term "ritual" to denote *the performance of more or less invariant sequences of formal acts and utterances not entirely encoded by the performers*. This definition, being extremely terse, demands elaboration and discussion. Before discussing its specific features (performance, formality, invariance, inclusion of both acts and utterances, encoding by other than the performers) several general comments are in order.

First, this definition encompasses much more than religious behavior. Psychiatrists, for instance, have used "ritual" rather similarly conceived, or the closely related if not synonymous term "ceremony", to refer both to the pathological stereotyped behaviors of some neurotics (Freud 1907), and to certain conventional, repetitive but nevertheless adaptive interactions between people (Erikson 1966: 337). In sociology and anthropology "ritual" and "ceremony" may designate a large range of social events, not all of which are religious, or may denote the formal aspects of such events (e.g. Bell 1992, Firth 1967b, 1973, Goffman 1967, E. Goody 1972, J. Goody 1961, Grimes 1990, Kertzer 1988, La Fontaine 1972, Leach 1954: 10ff., Moore and Meyerhoff (eds.) 1977), and application of the term has not been restricted to human phenomena. Ethologists have used it, virtually interchangeably with "display," to designate behavior they have observed not only among other mammals but also among reptiles, birds, fish and even members of other phyla (Bell 1992, Blest 1961, Cullen 1966, Etkin 1964, Grimes 1990, Hinde 1966, Huxley 1914, 1966, Wynne-Edwards 1962).

One may ask whether we observe, in the use of a common term by anthropologists, theologians, psychiatrists and ethologists, nothing more than a label stretched to cover phenomena of such diversity that little is gained from attending to whatever similarities may prevail among them, or whether the use of a single term for such widely differing phenomena as the courtship dance of fiddler crabs (Crane 1966) and the Roman Mass recognizes significant commonalities underlying their undoubted differences. Surely, some of the differences among instances of the general class "ritual" are both obvious and important. No one would be hard pressed to distinguish the genuflections of Catholic priests from the gyrations of impassioned crustacea, and it would be absurd to regard the former as no more than a mere complexification of the latter, or to minimize their differences in any other way. At the beginning, however, it may be more useful to attend to what is common to a class, or possible class, as vague or vacuous as these resemblances may seem, than to emphasize what may distinguish its members from each other, as striking as these differences may be. Prior attention to similarities does not preclude subsequent attention to differences, and it may help to place those differences in proper perspective. By noting first the ways in which religious and other rituals resemble each other it may be possible to distinguish them from each other more clearly later, and distinguishing religious from other ritual will be helpful in fashioning conceptions of the sacred, the numinous and the holy.

Our definition, then, encompasses not only human rituals, but also those stylized displays reported by ethologists to occur among the birds, the beasts and even the insects. Yet, as inclusive as this definition may be, not all behavior plausibly called "religious" fits comfortably within its terms. All manner of moral acts may be understood by those performing them and by the communities within which they occur to be innately religious, or at least to be informed by religious principles. There is little point, however, in attempting to force alms-giving or the avoidance of adultery, or all acts of respect for one's father and mother into the definition's mold. Not even all devotional acts are easily or properly encompassed by it. Some people experience what they take to be naked encounters, i.e., meetings unmediated by ritual, with what they understand to be the divine (James 1961[1902]: 42). We may ask, of course, whether they would have, or even could have, such "direct experiences" if they had not participated at other times in rituals which provided meaning for, or even in some way invoked, the later experience, or if they had not at least been told of them by others who had. But that is another matter, and as all ritual is not religious, not all religious acts are ritual. I will, nevertheless, argue that ritual as defined here is the ground from which religion grows.

2. The logical entailments of the ritual form

Certain features often associated with ritual are notably absent from our definition. First, the term "symbol" does not appear. Whereas ritual is often taken to be a symbolic form (see, for instance, Tambiah 1985[1979]: 128, Moore and Myerhoff 1977: 13, 14 *passim*) it is not entirely or even essentially so if "symbol" is taken in Peirce's sense, as it was in the first chapter. That ritual is not entirely symbolic is one of its most interesting and important characteristics, for through ritual some of the embarrassments of symbolic communication (notably the two vices of language, lie and the confusions of Babel) may be ameliorated.[2] We will first return to this matter at the end of this chapter and will continue to do so throughout this work.

Secondly, this definition obviously does not stipulate what ritual is "about" or what it is "for." It is neither substantive nor functional, but gives primacy to the sensible features common to rituals always and everywhere, the features that may, in fact, lead us to recognize events as rituals in the first place. As such it can claim a reasonably close correspondence both to what I believe to be a universally, or near universally recognized (if not always lexically marked) category of action, and also to popular English usage. At the same time, stipulating as it does a number of specific features, it can claim, as our loose characterization of religion cannot, considerable analytic utility. As such the definition conforms to what Kapferer (1983: 194) suggests are requisites for an adequate definition of ritual.[3]

It not only privileges ritual's obvious (i.e., perceptible) elements, none of which is in and of itself unique to ritual, but also tacitly stipulates enduring relations among these features, each of which may itself vary in some degree. It implies that the term "ritual" designates, as stated in the first chapter, a *form* or *structure*, and I will argue that, although none of the elements constituting this structure is unique to ritual, the relations among them are. To put this a little differently, ritual is a unique structure although none of its elements – performance, invariance, formality and so on – belongs to it alone. That the structure of ritual is peculiar to it is not immediately apparent in the definition and we shall better distinguish it from other formal performance forms later in this chapter.

The significance of the observation that our definition of ritual is formal, rather than substantive or functional, is not merely taxonomic. It is clear that ritual, as a form of action may have and in a trivial sense inevitably has social and material consequences (that may or may not be "functional"). To define ritual as a form or structure, however, *ipso facto* goes beyond the recognition of such effects for, as sets of enduring structural relations among specified but variable features or elements, ritual not only can claim to be socially or materially consequential, but to possess *logical entailments* as well. *I will argue that the performance of more or less invariant sequences of formal acts and utterances not entirely encoded by the performers logically entails the establishment of convention, the sealing of social contract, the construction of the integrated conventional orders we shall call* Logoi *(singular:* Logos, *see chapter 11), the investment of whatever it encodes with morality, the construction of time and eternity; the representation of a paradigm of creation, the generation of the concept of the sacred and the sanctification of conventional order, the generation of theories of the occult, the evocation of numinous experience, the awareness of the divine, the grasp of the holy, and the construction of orders of meaning transcending the semantic.* These and other secondary entailments derivative from them inhere, as it were, in the form which we have defined as ritual and will reveal themselves as we unpack that definition, particularly in chapter 4 and later chapters.

3. Ritual and formal cause

I have stated that the conception of ritual proposed here is neither substantive nor functional, but assertions like "social contract is embodied in or is intrinsic to ritual's form or structure", or that "it is in the nature of ritual to invest its content with morality" may sound very much like simple functional statements. In fact, they are not, and it is important to make the nature of the argument clear before entering it, particularly since I have been seriously misunderstood on this matter in the past. Those who are not interested in such matters may wish to move directly to section 2.4.

This is a specific point on which I believe that I have been seriously misunderstood. Maurice Bloch, for instance (1986: 4ff.), seems to think that my analysis of the Maring ritual cycle constituted a functional-ecological theory of ritual in general. It did not. At the time of writing I really was not concerned with ritual as such, but with what I took to be ritual's functions in a particular system. In fairness to him, his misunderstanding was probably at least in part my fault. In the final paragraph of *Pigs for the Ancestors* I asserted that if we are to understand what is uniquely human we must also consider those aspects of existence which man shares with other creatures. This conviction has led me to set religious rituals and the beliefs associated with them in a frame of reference that can also accommodate the behavior of animals other than man. It is this frame of reference that has exposed the crucial role of religion in the Maring's adjustment to their environment.   *(1968: 241–2)*

It did not occur to me that this, or perhaps other statements or observations about Maring ritual in particular, could possibly be construed as *specifically* ecological propositions about ritual in general. We can, after all, cite without difficulty many instances of rituals that have nothing whatsoever to do with ecological or political relations. Similarly, Catherine Bell in *Ritual Theory, Ritual Practice* (1992) indicates that she may share Bloch's misunderstanding (unless I misunderstand her) when referring to my approach to ritual as "ecological rationalism" (p. 108). I will only mention that Bruce Kapferer (1983) has denounced as "functionalist" various definitions and conceptions of ritual offered by Moore and Myerhoff (1977), Rappaport (1979d [1974]), Tambiah (1985[1979], Lévi-Strauss (1981) and Bloch (1973). His reasons for indiscriminately bagging them together and then labeling them "functional" are unclear. In describing them he asserts that in them "Ritual is characterized as action which is markedly formalized, stereotypical, repetitious, etc. Such definitions are narrow, obscurantist, often misleading and beg the nature of analysis ... They constitute in the ... definition the phenomenon to be understood ... " (p. 193). It is difficult to see how formality, stereotypy and repetitiveness even imply function, nor does he explain how their use in definition constitutes the fallacy of affirming the consequent. I think he is simply wrong.

It would be not so much wrong as utterly banal to commit the fallacy, complementary to the example just offered in which the specific is universalized, of making a formal causal statement where a final causal statement may be called for. The latter might be illustrated by an attempt to account for the division of labor in nineteenth-century France by invoking Durkheim's assertion that organic solidarity is intrinsic to the division of labor. Along the same lines, the observation that the formation of alliances (in the English as well as the French sense) is virtually entailed by exogamy is not, in the first instance, a functional (final causal) assertion, but a formal causal one.

Our argument, then, is essentially formal causal, or structural, although subsidiary discussion may take other forms.

4. Form and substance in ritual

That our definition specifies neither the contents nor the purposes of ritual requires further comment. First, concerned as it is with what is *common* to, say, the Catholic Mass, the Plains Sundance, rites of passage in the deserts of Central Australia, Papua New Guinea curing rituals and human sacrifice in Aztec Mexico, with what, this is to say, is *universal* to ritual, the unlimited content and innumerable purposes of the world's rituals could not and should not have been brought into the definition. This obviously does not mean that the invariant sequences of formal acts and utterances of which rituals are composed are without purpose or signify nothing (or even, contra Maurice Bloch (1973: 74) are devoid of "propositional force," an assertion with which I heartily disagree). In human rituals the utterances are usually predominantly verbal, that is, are expressions in words, and as such are symbolically (and often otherwise) signifying, and the acts, in being formalized, are, *ipso facto*, invested with meaning. It could be said, as Tambiah has (1985: 143) in what he took to be disagreement with me but was not, that "the ordering and the pattern of presentation of the ritual language, physical gestures, and manipulation of substances is the *form* of the ritual: form is the arrangement of contents" (emphasis his). I would put the relationship between ritual's form and substance a little differently. The formalization of acts and utterances, themselves meaningful, and the organization of those formalized acts and utterances into more or less invariant sequences, imposes ritual form on the substance of those acts and utterances, that is, on their significata. At one and the same time such formalization constitutes the specific forms of *particular* rituals and, reciprocally, *realizes* the *general* ritual form in specific and substantial instances. In the absence of specific substantiating instances there could no more be a general ritual form than there could be a general mammalian form in the absence of camels, woodchucks, sperm whales, or other species that realize or embody the set of features that together distinguish the class mammalia from, let us say, reptiles and birds. In *all* ritual performances there is a substantiation of form and an informing of substance, and I therefore fully agree that it would be an error to ignore either form or substance in the analysis of *any* ritual and have never suggested otherwise.

Form or substance. We come now to what may be a genuine disagreement between Tambiah and me, although it again may be a matter of his misunderstanding of my proposal. If he could misunderstand, anyone could misunderstand, and it may, therefore, be clarifying to go a little further into this matter than I have in earlier treatments. He continues from the last quotation as follows:

Therefore I think Rappaport (1979d) is mistaken – in the same way that McLuhan is mistaken – in thinking that the "surfaces of ritual" whose features are stereotypy, liturgical invariance and so on can be dealt with apart from the symbolism of ritual or, as he puts it, "the relations among the symbols that may appear in rituals."   *(1985: 143)*

I have already agreed that form and substance are inseparable in any performance of any ritual. But it is one thing to say that form and substance are inseparable in practice and another thing to say that they are analytically indistinguishable. They are, it seems to me, both as inseparable in practice and as conceptually distinguishable as, let us say, sentence forms – declarative, inquisitive, imperative – are from the particular statements, questions, or commands that they shape.[4]

"That they shape." It seems at the least possible – even inarguable – to propose that the ritual form is not a neutral medium that adds nothing to the contents, symbolic or otherwise, encoded in its relatively invariant sequences of formal acts and utterances. It is important to note that it is in respect to its symbolic depths that ritual is least distinctive. That Leach (1954: 13ff.) could declare that "myth implies ritual, ritual implies myth, they are one and the same," a dictum which, by only slight extension, would seem to assert that ritual signifies neither more nor less than what is signified by the references symbolically encoded in its acts and utterances, a view made more explicit by La Fontaine (1972: xvii): "In this book ritual actions are seen as exemplifying in another medium the cultural values that find expression in statements which we call beliefs and which are elaborated in narratives or myths." I disagree.

It would be well to reiterate that I am raising no objections to symbolic, structural, or any other form of analysis of ritual's contents. I am only insisting that to view ritual as no more than an alternative symbolic medium for expressing or accomplishing what might just as well – or perhaps better – be expressed or accomplished in other ways is, obviously, to ignore that which is distinctive of ritual itself. It seems apparent, and few students writing today would disagree, that ritual is not simply an alternative way to express any manner of thing, but that certain meanings and effects can best, or even *only*, be expressed or achieved in ritual. Inasmuch as the substance of rituals is infinitely various, this must mean that these meanings and effects follow from ritual's universal form. This form, moreover, cannot lie hidden in symbolic depths where all rituals differ from all others and each awaits

its particular culture-specific exegesis. It must lie at or near ritual's "surfaces", in, that is to say, relations among the *perceptible* features by which ritual is recognized as such and by which it has been defined here. Several summary comments are in order.

First, relations among perceptible features constituting the ritual form (most importantly perhaps, the relationship of performers to their own performances of invariant orders that they themselves have not encoded) are, it should now be clear, distinct (although not separated) from relations among elements (largely symbolic) constituting the particular substance of any and all rituals. *The ritual form, to say the least, adds something to the substance of ritual, something that the symbolically encoded substance by itself cannot express.*

Secondly, it follows from these observations that the contents of a ritual may be no different from the contents of, say, a myth, and that ritual form and substance are inseparable but distinct, that ritual form relates to ritual content as "frame" (Goffman 1967), or "context marker" (Bateson, M.C. 1973), or "metamessage." *If, in contrast to the infinite variety of ritual contents, the ritual form is universal, then it is plausible to assume that the metamessages intrinsic to that form are also universal.*

Thirdly, if certain meanings and effects are entailments of ritual's form and only of that form, then *ritual is without equivalents or even, for some purposes that will later become apparent, satisfactory alternatives.* This may go a long way toward accounting for the ubiquity of ritual, a ubiquity that approaches universality: no society is devoid of what a reasonable observer would recognize as ritual.

Fourthly, the gravity of ritual may also contribute to its ubiquity. Although ritual's contents may be concerned with matters as trivial and inconsequential as the doings of tooth fairies, that which can be expressed in or achieved through the ritual form, for instance the entailments enumerated in section 2 above, are neither trivial nor inconsequential but, on the contrary, are requisite to the perpetuation of human social life. *I therefore take ritual to be the social act basic to humanity.*

Although the contents of ritual will not be ignored in this book, it will mainly be concerned with the unique entailments of ritual's form, the crucial nature of which will be uncovered as we proceed. We can now turn from general comments about the ritual form to each of the several features constituting that form.

I have already noted that no single feature of ritual is peculiar to it. It is in the conjunction of its features that it is unique, but it is convenient to begin by discussing each of its elements separately. The unique ways in which they relate to each other and the implications and entailments of these relationships will unfold later in the chapter and throughout the book.

5. The first feature of ritual: encoding by other than performers

First, our definition stipulates that the performers of rituals do not specify all the acts and utterances constituting their own performances. They follow, more or less punctiliously, orders established or taken to have been established, by others.

This feature seems to run afoul of a simple and obvious problem, namely that seemingly new rituals do appear from time to time and that, unless we agree to their divine origin, human agents must be implicated in their invention. This difficulty could be escaped by simply acknowledging that although the conditions of the definition hold for an overwhelming preponderance of performers, they do not for occasional innovators. Such a qualification would do little or no damage to the argument to be developed in this book, but it would beg issues of origins.

It may first be noted that the role of deliberate and calculated invention in the establishment of rituals, particularly religious rituals with which we will be almost exclusively concerned, is problematic and probably effectively limited. Conscious attempts are sometimes made to cut new rituals from whole cloth, but they are likely to strike those witnessing them to be forced or even false. Those present may fail to become performers or participants because they may not know what is expected of them, because the expectations of the inventors may not be in accord with the impulses of the potential performers or because they may be reluctant to undertake formal, stereotyped, solemn or, possibly, grotesque public behavior unless it is sanctioned by time and custom, that is to say, by previous performances. A ritual which has never been performed before may seem to those present not so much a ritual as a charade. Rituals composed entirely of new elements are, thus, likely to fail to become established (the test of establishment being that they be performed again on categorically similar occasions). Rituals composed entirely of new elements are, however, seldom if ever attempted. "New" rituals are likely to be largely composed of elements taken from older rituals (Turner 1973: 1100). There is still room for the rearrangement of elements, and even for discarding some elements and introducing others, but invention is limited and the sanction of previous performance is maintained.[5]

A near contradiction is entailed by the human invention and introduction of new rituals when rituals are understood by performers to be ordained by the divine, or at least understood to be sanctified by association with it. Authors of change in religious ritual sometimes claim, however, that they are not inventing liturgy but merely reforming it, or they escape contradiction by claiming that they are merely divesting the ritual of the inconsequential, profane or evil accretions of time and error, returning to it the purity that prevailed in more righteous days. In other instances individuals introducing new rituals disclaim responsibility for authorship altogether. They declare, and their subjective experience may convince them, that the new ritual was revealed to them by spirits or gods in dreams or in visions (Mooney 1896: 14 and many after him, e.g., Munn 1973).[6]

6. The second feature: formality (as decorum)

Next there is formality. Formality, i.e., adherence to form, is an obvious aspect of all rituals. It is often, but not always, through the perception of their formal characteristics that we recognize events as rituals, or designate them to be such. Behavior in ritual tends to be punctilious and repetitive. Ritual sequences are composed of conventional, even stereotyped elements, for instance stylized and often decorous gestures and postures and the arrangements of these elements in time and space are usually more or less fixed. Rituals are performed in specified contexts, that is, they are regularly repeated at times established by clock, calendar, biological rhythm, ontogeny, physical condition, or defined social circumstance, and often they occur in special places as well. What is true of humans is true of other animals. As the faithful of a certain persuasion congregate at a certain church at 10: 00 am on Sunday, so do the starlings congregate on a certain tree at dusk. Some comments and qualifications are in order.

First, although the performance of many rituals demands decorum, and although the concepts of "formality" and "decorum" are overlapping, they are not synonymous, nor does formality necessarily entail decorous behavior. The greeting behavior of teenagers for example, is formal in that it is stereotyped, but it is not particularly decorous, and the formality of some rituals, as Roger Abrahams has emphasized (1973), may subsume or even specify, comic, violent, obscene or blasphemous behavior. Clowns have important roles to play in the rituals of the Tewa (Ortiz 1969) and other American Indians, in Sri Lanka (Kapferer 1983) and elsewhere; and the *Arioi* society of the Society Islands violated food taboos, performed what Captain Bligh and others took to be obscene dances, and gave themselves to what both missionaries and explorers report as heterosexual debauchery and sodomy within the sacred precincts (*marae*) in the course of certain of their ceremonies (Bligh 1937, Ellis 1853: 319–325, Van Gennep 1960: 83f.). Self-mortification was encouraged in the rituals of many American Indians (e.g., J. Brown 1971: 92ff., Jorgensen 1972: 177ff., Radin, 1923: 98, 471) and torture played a central role in the rituals of others (e.g., Wallace 1972: 30ff.).

Secondly, and more important, it would be incorrect to impose a simple dichotomy upon all behavior in an attempt to distinguish the formal, stylized or stereotypic from the "informal" or spontaneous. There is surely a continuum running from highly spontaneous interactions in which the behavior of each of the participants is continually modified by his or her interactions with the others, in which great choice of action and utterance is continuously available to them, and in which stylization is slight, to those elaborate rituals in which the sequence of words and actions, through which the participants proceed with great caution and decorum, seems to be fully, or almost fully, specified. Abrahams (1973) has suggested that for heuristic purposes we may recognize a number of levels of increasing formality and decreasing spontaneity commencing with (1) the stylized words and gestures that intersperse ordinary conversation and acts, through (2) the "everyday ceremoniousness" of greeting behavior, stylized expressions of deference and demeanor and the like, to (3) "self-consciously patterned formal interactions" of some duration. We may think here of the rather rigid or even invariant procedures of the courtroom, in accordance with which the variant substance of particular cases is presented in orderly fashion. The range of utterances considered to be in order is restricted, but sufficient opportunities are provided for the litigants to describe the particulars of the dispute. Indeed, the very rigidity of the procedure represents an attempt to insure that full and coherent accounts of more or less unique events will be presented to those who must judge them. The invariant procedural aspects of litigation are, so to speak, subservient to their variant substantive aspects. In (4), events of yet greater formality, such as inaugurations, coronations, dubbings, marriages and the like, there is an inversion of the relationship between the variant and the invariant. The invariant aspects of the event become dominant or, to put it a little differently, themselves become operative. Such stylized acts as crowning and anointing are those which transform a prince into a king; the recitation of traditional vows and the ancient act of placing a ring on another's finger transform the affianced into the wed; traditional words and the application of holy water transform a human infant into a Christian. These formal elements themselves are the main points of the events in which they occur – coronations, marriages, baptisms. This is not to say that there is no room for novelty. It is customary, for instance, for presidents and monarchs to make speeches when they are elevated to office, and many clerics insist upon preaching to those whom they have just joined in wedlock. Their remarks vary from one occasion to the next (although it is of interest that the scope of what it is appropriate to say on such occasions is rather narrowly limited to the general, the vacuous, and the inspirational), but their speeches do not in themselves effect the transitions toward which such events are directed. They are mere embroideries, elaborating events the main purposes of which are effected by more or less invariant formal acts and utterances, such as oath taking, anointing or exchanging rings.

Finally, there is (5), the category that subsumes the most formal of all events, those in which almost all aspects of performances consisting of fixed sequences of stylized and stereotyped words and acts are rigidly specified, and opportunities for performers to introduce new information into the sequence are few, themselves formalized, and narrowly defined. This most highly formalized category of behavior is, perhaps, largely occupied by religious rituals. To put it in the converse, religious rituals tend to concentrate toward this formal end of the behavioral continuum, although stereotyped allusions to supernaturals appear in the "everyday ceremoniousness" of such expressions as "godspeed," in the courtroom oath, and in the oaths and anointings of coronations.

Several points are to be made here. First, it may be useful to make a distinction between ritual, the formal, stereotyped aspect of events in general, and rituals, relatively invariant events dominated by their formal components. Be this as it may, it is not necessary to distinguish ritual radically from other events by imposing an arbitrary discontinuity upon the continuum of formality at any point. I will simply note that the phenomena with which this study is concerned lie toward the more formal, less variant end of the continuum, rituals sufficiently elaborate to include what may be called "liturgical orders": more or less invariant sequences of formal acts and utterances of some duration repeated in specified contexts. The term "liturgical order" will be extended to include not only the sequences of words and acts providing form to individual rituals but also, following Van Gennep's (1960[1909]) concerns but not his terminology, to the sequences of rituals that lead their participants around the circles of the seasons, along the straight paths that depart from birth and arrive at death, through the alternations of war and peace, or along the dream tracks crossing Australian deserts. It will also, on occasion, denote the corpora of particular traditions in their entirety (e.g., the Maring liturgical order).

7. The third feature: invariance (more or less)

Although invariance is inevitably generated by, or is a logical entailment of, formality understood as conformity to form, it is of such consequences that I have given it explicit recognition in the definition. Its profound significance will be developed later, especially in chapters 4 and 8. Here it is necessary to emphasize that the definition does not characterize ritual as invariant but as "more or less" invariant. This qualification is only in part meant to recognize the obvious: that imprecision is unavoidable in even the most punctilious performances, that, although the congregations performing them may not be fully aware of it, liturgical orders do change through time, that various elements of liturgical orders are differentially susceptible to change (a matter to be explored later in this chapter and in chapter 8) and, finally but most importantly, the details of no ritual are ever specified to such a degree that there is no room for some logically necessary or deliberate variation.

As far as logical necessity is concerned, for two or more performers to perform the "same" ritual there is obviously and unavoidably variation in performers. Performer A and performer B are two different people. That this is tautological does not make it trivial inasmuch as performance has entailments for the performers that will be explored in chapter 4.

We come here to the deliberateness of variation. There is the possibility of, or even the necessity for, some choice to be exercised by performers even within the most invariant of liturgical orders. For instance, the Mass includes the ministration of communion, but participants may or may not choose to receive it. Jewish liturgy includes a series of acts connected with bringing forth the Torah from the ark in which it resides. These acts honor those performing them, but the liturgy does not specify who is to be so honored. Among the Maring of New Guinea, certain rituals require the sacrifice of pigs, but the number to be killed is not stipulated. In addition to possibilities for variations in performance itself, there is the most fundamental of all choices, always open to the potential participant, at least as a logical, if not always viable possibility: whether or not to participate at all in a ritual which is occurring. Although this last point seems obvious to the point of being trivial, it is a matter of great importance and will be considered in a later chapter. Finally, there are, with respect to some rituals, possibilities for variation with respect to where and when to perform them, or whether to perform them at all.

In sum, there are possibilities for, and even demands for, variation within the most invariant of liturgical orders. What may vary, the significance of such variation, and the relationship of the variant to the invariant will be explored in the next two chapters.

A last point concerning formality leads to another of ritual's defining features. Whereas there is no ritual without formality, all that is formal is not ritual. Much of graphic and plastic art and music elaborates repetitive, rhythmic, stylized patterns and so does much architecture. Rituals may, and frequently do, call for the manipulation of special paraphernalia, and they are often convened in special places. These things and places may have abstract characteristics formally similar to those of ritual, and they may be indispensable to the rituals with which they are associated. We may think here of the cruciform plan of the Cathedral, the crucifix on the altar, and the act of crossing oneself. It may be that they are properly regarded as components of rituals, or even said to be "ritualized," a term sometimes applied to the apparently "useless" organs that many species of animal wave, vibrate, expand, or suffuse with color in their displays (Blest 1961). But they are not themselves rituals, for performance is as intrinsic to the notion of ritual as is formality.

8. The fourth feature: performance (ritual and other performance forms)
Unless there is a performance there is no ritual. This is obvious in the case of fleeting greeting rituals which serve to order ongoing interaction, but it is no less true of elaborate liturgical rituals. Liturgical orders may be inscribed in books, but such records are not themselves rituals. They are merely descriptions of rituals or instructions for performing them. There are, in our possession, records of liturgies performed in the temples of Sumer and Akkad (e.g., Hallo and Van Dyjk 1968, Jacobson 1976), but they are no longer enlivened by performance. Liturgical orders are realized – made into *res* – only by being performed.

It may seem unnecessary if not downright absurd to emphasize what seems not only to be an obvious aspect of ritual, but intrinsic to its very conception. It is important so to insist, however, because of a point already touched upon. Ritual is not simply one of a number of more or less equivalent ways in which the material embodied in liturgical orders may be expressed, presented, maintained or established. It may be, as

Leach (1954: 13ff.) would have it, that "myth *implies* ritual, ritual *implies*
myth," but they are not, as he proposed, "one and the same." "Myth
regarded as a statement in words" does not, contrary to Leach, "say the
same thing as ritual regarded as a statement in action" (1954: 13). Much
of what is "said" *in* ritual is, of course, "said" in myth or in lawbooks or
in theological treatises or, for that matter in novels, drama and poetry,
but, to reiterate an assertion made earlier, there are things "said" *by* all
liturgical rituals that cannot be said in other ways. They are in part
expressed by the special relationship between the liturgical order performed and the act of performing it. The act of performance is itself a
part of the order performed, or, to put it a little differently, the manner
of "saying" and "doing" is intrinsic to what is being said and done. The
medium, as McLuhan and Fiore (1967) would have it, is itself a message,
or better, a meta-message. We shall return to this matter in a later
chapter.

It is not, however, useful to consider all formal performance, even
those composed entirely of highly invariant sequences of formal acts and
utterances, to be ritual. Ordinary usage would not have it so and there is
no advantage in departing from ordinary usage here. Some scholars
would distinguish "ceremony" from "ritual" and, although ritual and
some forms of theatre resemble each other in some respects, they differ
importantly in others. Athletic contests bear some similarity to both
theatre and ritual, and both theatre and games have sometimes been
associated with ritual. There are yet other events – some political
conventions, festivals, carnivals, demonstrations – that share features
with rituals. In sum, ritual is one member of an extended family of
performance forms, to some of which it seems on the face of it to be
more closely related than to others. The matter is too complex to do
more here than note some of the distinctions that have or can be used to
distinguish major types from each other.

The forms most closely related – if, indeed, they should be distinguished at all – are "ceremony" and "ritual." Firth (1967b: 13),
Gluckman and Gluckman (1977: 231), and others do make this distinction. Gluckman and Gluckman, referring to an earlier publication by one
of them, state that the term "ritual" was stipulated "to cover actions
which had reference, in the view of the actors, to occult powers: where
such beliefs were not present, it was suggested, that the word "ceremony"
be used." Firth's distinction is slightly different.

Ceremonial I regard as a species of ritual in which, however, the emphasis is more
upon symbolic acknowledgment and demonstration of a social situation than

upon the efficacy of the procedures in modifying that situation. Whereas other ritual procedures are believed to have a validity of their own, ceremonial procedures, while formal in character, are not believed in themselves to sustain the situation or effect a change in it.   *(1967b: 13)*

There is little or no real difference between Firth and Gluckman. The sets each would distinguish as ritual and as ceremony would come close to coinciding. Of greater interest: they would probably come close to matching those placed in levels 4 or 5 in Abraham's continuum of formality. Be this as it may, it seems to me that the distinction, although it can be made and although it may in some contexts be useful, is of dubious general value because expressions "acknowledging or demonstrating social situations" may themselves constitute actions sustaining or changing those situations and, furthermore, the nature of the efficacy of such actions – whether or not they are occult – is often left unclear, perhaps deliberately.

Distinctions between theatre and ritual are more salient. The first stands on a difference in the relationships of those present to the proceedings themselves. Those present at a ritual constitute a congregation. The defining relationship of the members of a congregation to the event for which they are present is *participation*. Those present at theatrical events include, on the one hand, *performers* and, on the other hand, *audiences*. Audiences and performers are more or less radically separated from each other, always in function, almost always in space, often clearly marked off by raised stages, proscenium arches, curtains and so on. The performers perform – dance in ballets, sing or play instruments in concerts or, in the form most important to us, drama, they "act." The defining characteristic of audience in contrast to performers on the one hand and congregation on the other is that they do not participate in the performance: they *watch* and they *listen*.

To say that all those present at a ritual are participating in it is obviously not to claim that they all have the same or equivalent parts to play. Their roles may, in fact, be highly differentiated. There are obvious differences between initiators and initiates in rites of passage, and distinctions among performers can become very complex.

Gluckman has used the term "ritualization" to refer to the assignment of ritual roles to individuals in conformity to their secular relations and statuses. Thus, in the Naven rituals of the Iatmul, to cite a classic example (Bateson (1958: 6ff. [1936]), mother's brother (*Wau*) and sister's son (*Laua*) play roles defined by their kinship relationship to each other, and roles are assigned to participants in the coronation of English kings on the basis of their general social statuses. The situation is not essentially different in rituals in which secular status differences among congregants are not emphasized or are even deliberately softened. Thus, Catholic usage clearly recognizes differences in the participating roles of those present in stating that the priest presides at the Mass whereas the Congregation celebrates it.[7] Obviously, the priest has much more to do than do his parishioners, but their participation, and this seems true of all ritual, requires of them something more than, or better, other than the open passivity or receptivity of Western audiences. Congregations may be called upon to sing, dance, kneel, respond in liturgy or kill pigs in particular ways at particular moments in ritual performances. Such acts, in addition to expressing whatever particulars they represent, indicate to performers that they are indeed participating in, and not merely watching, the proceedings. The significance to them of their own participation will be taken up in chapter 4. For now it is sufficient to propose that such significance is absent from the relationship of audiences to the performances they attend. To go a little farther, the members of congregations may leave the ritual with their statuses in some way formally transformed. The social status of members of the audiences are never so transformed by dramas, although they may be deeply moved by them.

Certain qualifications or clarifications are in order before proceeding. First, the distinction between audience and congregation is not always behaviorally obvious. In a good many rituals, for instance in the Sinhalese demon exorcisms of which Kapferer (1983) writes, congregations may spend much of the time watching clowns and other performers. This spectator-like behavior obviously does not preclude acts constituting participation during other moments in the liturgy. To put this in the converse, participation is definitive of congregations, but the roles played by various members of most congregations are not all equal, and therefore certain participants are likely to become, at particular times during the ritual, objects of audience-like attention for other participants.

Second, it sometimes happens that some of those present, for instance, tourists watching a Plains Indian Sundance, are not participants but, rather, stand in an audience-like relationship to the performers. I say "audience-like" because it is questionable whether or not audiences are properly so-called when performances are not directed toward them as such. The anomolousness of their presence is often experienced by both "visitors" and their "hosts" as awkwardness, embarrassment, resentment or shame, and may even degrade the event from the status of ritual to mere mimicry of ritual.[8]

Third, there are interstitial forms, performances that, lying as they do between culturally recognized forms, derive their peculiar force from their very ambiguity. Passion and mystery plays, positioned between drama and ritual, provide instances, and in recent decades deliberate attempts have been made to draw audiences into the performances of some western dramas (see Schechner 1985). Success has been limited, perhaps because it is very difficult to transform audiences composed of strangers whose status as such is protected by rules of etiquette to such a degree that to address a person in an adjacent seat is regarded as forward, into congregations. Congregations are usually composed of people who know each other but even if they don't they can make certain assumptions about each other from the mere fact that they are participating together in a liturgical order with which, in contrast to the situation of an audience watching a drama, they are usually thoroughly familiar. They can assume that they stand on common ground and as such are members of a common community. This assumption is often reinforced formally by the requirement, or at least expectation, that congregants greet their neighbors in formulaic manner: "peace be with you," "*shabbat shalom*", etc.

Further differences between ritual and drama are, perhaps, made clearest by reference to those dramas which are, within the western tradition, most closely related to ritual, the tragedies of ancient Greece. Aristotle informs us (*Poetics*, chapter 4, McKeon 1941: 1458) that both tragedy and comedy emerged out of ritual, tragedy, more particularly, out of the *Dithyramb*, a spring celebration associated with Dionysus. Jane Harrison (1913) at the beginning of this century noted that the word "drama" is derived from *dromenon* ("thing done") an ancient Greek term for ritual. (Other authorities, e.g., Partridge (1958), derive its root *dra-* from *dran*, to do act, make). By Aeschylus' time (525–456) drama had become more or less distinct from ritual but continued to be performed in association with it. Greek tragedies, like ritual, could be said to be composed of more or less invariant sequences of formal acts and utterances encoded by other than the performers, but the two forms are invariant in rather different senses. A ritual displays or even flaunts its invariance, for in its very invariance it manifests or represents a *specific* order to which individuals *ipso facto* conform in performing them. Once performers commence their performances the only choices available to them are the narrow and formal options the performed order specifies: to take communion or not, to sacrifice one pig or two. To "choose" to act in ways other than those specified by the ritual's order is at best meaningless and as such constitutes noise, but is more likely to be disruptive and as such constitutes blasphemy.

Dramas, to be sure, are also invariant orders in the sense that the actor's utterances and movements are scripted in advance of their performance by others, i.e. playwrights. But the invariance that is intrinsic to the scripting of tragedies is not meant to represent or under-write the propriety of any specific order in any simple or straightforward way (although it may finally do so). In tragedy invented[9] characters are presented in problematic situations, situations in which, as Gluckman and Gluckman (1977: *passim*) have pointed out in a discussion of *Antigone*, it is as if the outcome (although scripted prior to any perform-ance) is represented as uncertain, and hinges on choices represented as open to them even though the world remains in the God's control. The proper order of the world, as ordained by the Gods, is established in invariant liturgical orders. The stuff of tragedies arises from the near inevitability of the destruction of fallible humans making choices, the consequences of which they cannot foresee, in worlds constituted by ritually ordained orders, elements of which may be in contradiction (in *Antigone* between obedience to the Gods and to the king and duty to and concern for kin). This is to say that that which is represented in ritual as the proper order, or the only order, or order itself is represented as problematic in drama. To put it yet differently, ritual specifies an order, tragedy reflects upon that order and, when it is successful, evokes the reflection of the individuals composing the audience. We uncover here the essential difference between the invariance of ritual and the invar-iance of drama. In ritual invariance is not only visible but emphasized for it, in *itself*, in all its punctilious repetitiveness represents the propriety of whatever is encoded. The invariance of drama in contrast, is kept hidden beneath the illusion of novelty and spontaneity that gives virtual life to the dilemmas the drama represents. Invariance here is simply part of the machinery producing an illusion, an illusion of the possibilities of varia-tion.

Another difference between ritual and drama comes to the surface here. The problems raised, illuminated and engaged by drama in general and tragedy in particular may well be the most profound facing human-ity. Nevertheless, those who act in dramas are, as we say, "only acting" which is precisely to say that they are not actually taking action but only mimicking action. The tendency of Western drama toward "realism", that is, a performance style *simulating* the "informal" behavior of everyday life, underlines this point, which is also implicit in drama's

English language synonym, "play." Ritual, in contrast, is "in earnest", that is, it is understood by performers to be taking place in the world, even when it is playful, entertaining, ludicrous, obscene or blasphemous, or even when, perhaps especially when, its actions are highly stylized, as in postures of submission or in the recitation of formulae.

That actors are "only acting" in dramas does not mean that they or the scripts they perform are not serious nor that they do not effect the world outside the play. Of course they do, but as Gluckman and Gluckman (1977: 231) put it, their enactments in themselves are not understood to affect directly the world's events. They may affect the world but the manner in which they do is essentially different from the ways in which ritual achieves its affects, a matter to be discussed later in this chapter and developed further in chapter 4.

Athletic contests resemble both ritual and drama sufficiently to warrant brief consideration. For one thing the relationship of those present to the event differs from those prevailing in either ritual or theatre. As in theatre, athletic contests separate performers from spectators, and there is often a third category of person present, namely officials, referees, umpires and the like, who represent, apply and enforce the rules of the game. Unlike theatre audiences, however, spectators are not required to attend passively to the proceedings. They are expected to be partisan and to express their preferences loudly (mainly through cheering their own teams, but also by baiting the opposition) and visibly (through wearing the colors of their teams, through gestures and movements associated with cheering, and so on). In more elaborated American performances such expressions of partisanship are in some degree formalized, being called for and coordinated by another subsidiary category of performances, cheerleaders, who are sometimes reinforced at football games by marching bands.

In the active nature of their participation "fans" at certain athletic contests resemble congregations more than they do audiences, but differ from typical congregations in frequently being raucous and always being in high degree spontaneous. No matter how frenzied their support of their team may be, however, it is clear to fans that they themselves are not participating in the game. They and their actions are already separated from what goes on on the playing field, and in this they resemble audiences more than they do congregations. Unlike theatre audiences, however, who understand that their attitudes and feelings cannot affect the outcome of the simulated events they witness, fans typically feel that their own actions can affect the outcomes of the actual event – the game – which they watch. In this respect there is some resemblance to ritual, the performances of which are taken to affect the state of the world, but the efficacious principles are understood to be different. Fans are not assisting in the proceedings as a Roman Catholic congregation used to be said to assist in the Mass, but are giving *support* to their teams, simply encouraging them or, perhaps, even inspiring them. In this the relationship of fans to the teams they support may be the reverse of that of audiences to actors in drama. Whereas the actors' performance may inspire or otherwise inform the audience, the behavior of the fans may inspire or otherwise motivate the athletes.

Another frequently remarked upon distinction between athletic contests and both ritual and drama has been implicit throughout this discussion. The actions of rituals are usually (not always) preordained, and although the outcome of dramas are represented as uncertain they are also, in fact, preordained. The outcomes of athletic contests are, in contrast, really uncertain. Whereas the invariance of ritual orders may constitute a way to impose order on a vagrant and unruly world, and the invariance hidden in drama may be in the service of posing perennial and possibly irresolvable questions about such orders, the invariance of the athletic contest is confined to its rules and does not penetrate directly to the play itself. If there are messages intrinsic to Western athletic contests they do not need to be elucidated through deep reflection, nor are they primarily concerned, as ritual typically is, to specify agreed upon orders, although they tacitly do so when "played by the rules." The messages emphasized concern the values of skill, courage, strength, determination, cooperativeness, competitiveness, loyalty and victory. There is also honor paid to "fair play" and "sportsmanship", and if there is anything like dramatic dilemma represented it is in the possibility of contradiction between victory and "playing fair"; if there is anything like tragedy involved it is in the near inevitability of defeat. The difference in this respect between *Antigone* and the Rose Bowl is not entirely in the gravity of their subject matters but in the relation of those present to them. *Antigone* represents the defeat of mortals and asks its audience to reflect upon defeat. The Rose Bowl does not represent victory or defeat. It itself, in its nature, *presents* both victory and defeat and thus itself provides the materials for such reflection, or to practice such reflection on a matter of no enduring importance to very many people. It's entertainment.

Victory and defeat lead to the contrast between games and rituals made by Lévi-Strauss in the first chapter of *The Savage Mind*.

Games ... appear to have *disjunctive* effect: they end in the establishment of a difference between individual players or teams where originally there was no indication of inequality. And at the end of the game they are distinguished into winners and losers. Ritual, on the other hand, is the exact inverse; it *conjoins* for it brings about a union (one might even say communion in this context) or in any case an organic relation between two initially separate groups, one ideally merging with the person of the officiant and the other with the collectivity of the faithful. In the case of games the symmetry is therefore preordained and it is of a structural kind since it follows from the principle that the rules are the same for both sides. Asymmetry is engendered: it follows inevitably from the contingent nature of events, themselves due to intention, chance or talent. The reverse is true of ritual. There is asymmetry which is postulated in advance between profane and sacred, faithful and officiating, dead and living, initiated and uninitiated, etc., and the "game" consists in making all the participants pass to the winning side
...
(1966: 32; emphasis his)

As Stanley Tambiah (1985[1979]: 128) has remarked, no anthropologist would take this brilliant comparison to be true of all rituals but it does shed light on such occurrences as the transformation of cricket into a ritual display by the Trobrianders, or to cite an example Lévi-Strauss himself addresses, the Gahuku-Gama of New Guinea reported by Read (1965) who, in playing football, play as many matches as necessary to even the score. "This", says Lévi-Strauss, "is treating a game as a ritual" (Lévi-Strauss 1966: 31) but it would be better to say that Trobriand Cricket and Gahuku-Gama football are instances of an intermediate form between ritual and games, one that derives its peculiar force from the achievement of the conjunctive ends of one, ritual, through the disjunctive procedure of the other, athletic contest.

There may also be forms intermediate between athletic contests and theatre, for instance gymnastics and high diving, which seem to be, essentially, displays of strength and skill integrated with an aesthetics of the body rivaling that of ballet. It may be suggested that such events differ from the frankly theatrical performances of circus acrobats and trapeze artists mainly in their contextualization. If the performance takes place in a theatre or circus the performers are entertainers or artists. If a competitive structure is imposed upon it the performers are athletes. It is unclear, however, that such intermediate forms as gymnastics/acrobatics can claim, as can mystery plays or Trobriand cricket, special forces of their own.

Finally, and a little different, ritual, theatre, athletic contests and other forms that could, possibly, be taken to be members of the same extended family, like carnival, are sometimes associated with each other in time and space. The tragedies of Ancient Greece were performed at the spring festivals honoring Dionysus, passion plays were performed at Easter, Carnival has a place in the Christian liturgical calendar, and the Olympic games were held in honor of Zeus every fourth year in the Altis at Olympia. Other Greek games held in other places also honored gods: Apollo at the Pythian games at Delphi, Poseidon at the Isthmian games at Corinth (Croon 1965: 181, 112). Their association suggests for one thing that both drama and games were sanctified by their association with ritual. Of greater interest, in the instances noted here, at least, games, drama and ritual are not, as it were, equal partners in their association. Protracted ritual cycles set the contexts within which both drama and athletic contests take, or at least took, place. Their encompassment proposes that they are in some sense subordinate to ritual, that is, that their significance derives at least in part from the ritual orders of which they are part.

9. The fifth feature: formality (vs. physical efficacy)

Because the definition of ritual offered in this chapter's beginning is very terse some of its terms are required to carry heavy, or even double, loads. "Formal" has, so far, subsumed decorousness, punctiliousness, conformity to form, repetitiveness, regularity, and stylization. The term "formal" is also meant to contrast with the "functional" or, to be more precise, with the physically efficacious. That ritual is "in earnest" does not mean that the formal action of ritual is instrumental in any ordinary sense. It is not. Many scholars would agree with Homans' observation of long ago, "ritual actions do not produce a practical result on the external world – that is one of the reasons we call them ritual" (1941: 172), and would take lack of material efficacy to be one of ritual's defining features.[10] It is worth plowing some old fields here.

Two main lines of thought, at first sight competing but ultimately converging, have elaborated the theme of ritual's lack of material efficacy. The first was clearly enunciated by Leach years ago. He would distinguish, in activity generally, two interwoven strands one of which is materially instrumental and one of which is not. Writing of the people among whom he worked in Highland Burma he says:

In Kachin customary procedure the routines of clearing the ground, planting the seed, fencing the plot and weeding the growing crop are all patterned according to formal convention and interspersed with all kinds of technologically superfluous frills and decorations which make the performance a Kachin performance and not just a simple functional act. And so it is with every kind of technical action; there is always the element which is functionally essential, and another element which is simply the local custom, an aesthetic frill.   *(1954: 12)*

Leach would include within the category ritual, then, the locally specific, formal, technologically superfluous "frills and decorations" informing procedures that may also include a component or aspect which he labels "technique." "Technique has economic material consequences which are measurable and predictable; ritual on the other hand is a symbolic statement which 'says' something about the individuals involved in the action" (p. 13). This view accords with the continuum of formal behavior proposed by Abrahams, and also with the distinction made earlier between ritual and rituals, for it does not insist on the separation of ritual behavior from everyday technological activity and it recognizes that even highly formalized liturgical rituals may have technical components.

> From certain points of view a Kachin religious sacrifice may be regarded as a purely technical and economic act. It is a procedure for killing livestock and distributing the meat, and I think there can be little doubt that for most Kachins this seems the most important aspect of the matter ... But ... there is a great deal that goes on at a sacrifice that is irrelevant as far as butchery, cooking and meat distribution is concerned ... and it is these other aspects that I describe as ritual.
>
> *(1954: 13)*

The other general view, which initially appears to differ from the first more than it actually does, takes seriously the understanding, made explicit by some people at least, that when they perform a ritual they are not simply "saying something" about themselves but "doing something" about the state of their world. That such an understanding is frequently entertained by performers is implicit in the terms some people use to designate some of their rituals, or even rituals in general. For instance, the ritual cycle in accordance with which Tikopian society is organized is called "The Work of the Gods" (Firth 1967a), the fundamental rituals comprising the annual cycle of the Tewa Indians are referred to as "works" (Ortiz 1969: 98ff.), the Maring of New Guinea frequently refer to rituals as *raua kongung*, literally spirit work (the word *kongung* also being used for garden work, etc.), *dromenon*, a Greek term for ritual, meant "a thing done," according to Jane Harrison (1913), the term "liturgy" is derived by way of *leitourgia*, public service from the Greek *leos* or *laos*, the people or the public, and *ergon*, work or service, and the English term "service" connotes more than talk. But only a portion of what is done *in* rituals and little or none of what is done *by* ritual is accomplished through material techniques directly affecting physical causal processes, and Goody (1961) once characterized ritual as "a category of standardized behavior (custom) in which the relationship between means and ends is not intrinsic." If ritual (in contrast to technique) does anything at all it doesn't do it by operating with matter and energy on matter and energy in accordance with physical laws of cause and effect, but by focusing agencies or forces of another sort upon whatever is to be affected.

This difference is likely to be understood by the actors who, although they may not make a clear distinction between what is natural and what is not, know the efficacy of spells to be different from that of spears. Terms like "supernatural" and "preternatural" have been used to refer to the non-physical agencies posited by people and invoked by them in their rituals. But Fortes, for one, (1966) objected that the term "supernatural" is an artifact of literate cultures, and claimed that the actor, in tribal societies at least, sees the world as composed of the patent and the hidden – or occult – which present themselves in mixed sequences and which are interwoven into a unified reality. He took this distinction to be wide-spread, or even universal. The patent can be known in the last resort by sensory experiences and it conforms to the regularities of material cause. The occult presumably, cannot be so known nor does it so conform. Ritual, in his view, is distinguished from non-ritual, not only by the analyst but by the actor as well, in that it derives its efficacy from the occult, and not the patent.

While Fortes claimed that the distinction between the occult and the patent reflects a general folk distinction, he as an analyst derived the occult from "the unconscious (in the psychoanalytic sense) forces of individuals' actions and the existence of their social equivalents, the irreducible factors in social relations ..." (1966: 413). Questions concerning folk notions of the bases of occult efficacy and the suggestions of anthropologists concerning the occult's foundation in what they take to be reality will arise from time to time later and need not be considered in detail here. In some – probably very few – instances effects for which the occult is credited are, in fact, achieved through obscure physical causal processes, which may even be hidden from the performers themselves (see note 10), but such processes do not provide a plausible basis for a general analytic theory of occult efficacy, nor do they seem to be sufficiently common to have lead to world-wide or even widespread acceptance of the idea of the occult. One large and rather heterogeneous body of analytic theories would derive the occult from the affective force and persuasiveness of ritual performance[11] and we may note in passing that some students would take some sort of systematic relationship to the emotions to be an aspect of all ritual.[12] Whether or not this is the case it is indubitable that emotions are regularly stimulated in many rituals, that these emotions may be strong and they may seem persuasive. It is not unreasonable, therefore, to take them to be a source of ritual's "power" or of the participants' ability to bring about the states of affairs for which they strive, also a source of ritual's actual, as well as putative, efficacy.

But perhaps not the only source, for it might well be asked how inchoate emotions could possibly lead to well-defined acts and ends. Other analytic theories would found the occult upon features of language, particularly as it is used in ritual, and we may note that all human rituals include words or acts informed by, and equivalent to, words. Inasmuch as the acts and ends of ritual are not related to each other through the operation of physical principles their relationship cannot be physically self-evident. If it cannot be perceived it must be specified, if it is to be conceived at all, and the specification of the imperceptible is contingent upon symbols in Peirce's sense, that is, on words. This contingency pertains even when an effect is achieved through such physical metaphors, or icons, as sticking pins into images. That the act is, in fact, a representation, and not simply a way to park pins, and that a particular person is the target of the attack must be stipulated, at least implicitly, by words. This is to say that the verbal specification of the relationship of act to effect is an important component of the act itself. This view accords nicely with the near universal attribution of magical or creative power to words and to certain acts informed by words. Finnegan (1969), for instance, invokes J. L. Austin's (1962) theory of performativeness, something to which we shall return in chapter 4. Tambiah (1973) and Fernandez (1974) speak of metaphorical predication. Tambiah has argued in a more general vein that it is the perception of certain characteristics of language that has brought about the elevation of the word as supremely endowed with mystical power.

There is a sense in which it is true to say that language is outside us and given to us as part of our cultural and historical heritage; at the same time language is within us, it moves us and we generate it as active agents. Since words exist and are in a sense agents themselves which establish connection and relations between both man and man, and man and the world, and are capable of "acting" upon them, they are one of the most realistic representations we have of the concept of force which is either not directly observable or is a metaphysical notion which we find necessary to use.   *(1968: 184)*

There is also style. Ritual utterances are not "mere words," but frequently possess special characteristics – stereotypy (Bloch 1973), weirdness (Malinowski 1965[1935] II: 218ff.) and repetitiveness – that may enhance their seeming force, and so may the often noted emphasis upon propriety and precision in uttering them. We shall return to these matters later.

The views of occult efficacy as founded upon word or upon emotion are neither exhaustive nor, for that matter, mutually exclusive. The point of importance here is that if the occult efficacy of ritual rests in whole or in part upon words (both in folk and analytic theory) then the distinction between ritual as communication and ritual as efficacious action breaks down. This is not to claim that all rituals, even those for which efficacy is claimed, are deemed by those performing them to possess occult efficacy, but simply to take efficacious ritual to be a sub-class of a larger class, ritual, itself one of many modes of communication. Leach (1966) stated, or perhaps overstated, this or a similar point when he asserted that the distinction between communication behavior and behavior potent in terms of cultural conventions (rather than instrumental or physical terms) is trivial.

10. Ritual as communication

In taking ritual to be a mode of communication some of its strangest features – the separation in time and space of some rituals from daily life, the grotesque quality of some ritual postures and gestures, the weirdness of some ritual utterances, the exuberant elaboration of some objects and structures used in rituals – become clear. The effectiveness of signals is enhanced if they are easy to distinguish from ordinary technical acts. The more extraordinary a ritual movement or posture the more easily it may be recognized as a signal and not a physically efficacious act. Among animals ritual gestures seem to be based largely upon instrumental movements like those of walking or nesting or feeding, but ritual imposes what has been called a "typical form" on those movements. Their scale may be exaggerated, their tempo changed, or they may be elaborated in other ways (Cullen 1966: 365). Instances of ritualized elaborations of functional movements and objects are also to be found among humans (e.g., processional paces, the wielding of swords of state), although many of the artifacts and gestures of human ritual probably have nothing to do with forms of technical activity.

Special time and places may, like extraordinary postures and gestures, distinguish ritual words and acts from ordinary words and acts. In ritual's time or place, words and acts that may be indistinguishable from those of everyday sometimes take on special meaning. (Think here of "I do.") The designation of special times and places for the performance of ritual also, of course, congregates senders and receivers of messages and may also specify what it is they are to communicate about. In sum, the formality and non-instrumentality characteristic of ritual enhances its communicational functioning.

It may be objected that a view of ritual as communication comes up against the fact that many rituals are conducted in solitude, and that to refer to solitary actions as communications events is to dilute the meaning of "communication" to the point of meaningless. The subjective experience of private devotions is however one for which the term "communication" is appropriate, for in such rituals the performers presumably do feel themselves to be communicating with spiritual beings.

Moreover, given the extent to which in solitary rituals various parts of the psyche ordinarily inaccessible to each other may be brought into touch, and given the extent to which the emotions of participants may respond to the stimuli of their own ritual acts, it is reasonable to take ritual to be auto-communicative as well as allo-communicative (Wallace 1966: 237ff.). Auto-communication is, I will argue, of utmost importance even in public rituals. In fact, *the transmitters of ritual's messages are always among their most important receivers*, a matter to be elaborated in chapter 4.

To understand ritual to be a mode of communication does not restrict its scope. On the contrary, it entails an expanded notion of communication. It is possible to distinguish, although not to separate, two large classes of natural processes. First, there are those in which actions achieve effects in simple accordance with the laws of physics, chemistry and biology, through the direct application of matter and energy to whatever is to be effected. Secondly, there are those in which transmitters achieve effects by informing – representing form to, transmitting form to, injecting form into, more simply transmitting messages to, receivers. In this view, which is in accord with certain developments in linguistic philosophy (Austin 1962, O'Doherty 1973, Searle 1969, Skorupski 1976) over the past few decades and anthropology (Finnegan 1969, Bateson 1972b, Rappaport 1979, Silverstein 1976, Tambiah 1985) as well as information and communication theory and cybernetics (Bateson 1972, Wilden 1972), communication includes not only simple "saying," but also the sorts of "doing," in which the efficacious principle is informative rather than powerful.[13]

Although we may recognize that even efficacious ritual is a mode of communication it may be well to recall, if only to dispense with it, Fortes' (1966) warning, in response to Leach's (1966) mistaken suggestion that speech be construed as "a form of ritual" with "non-verbal ritual [being] simply a signal system of a different less specialized kind," that "it is but a short step from the notion of ritual as communication to the non-existence of ritual *per se*." To say that ritual is a mode of communication is hardly to suggest that it is interchangeable with other modes of communication. It is a special medium peculiarly, perhaps even uniquely, suited to the transmission of certain messages and certain sorts of information.[14]

11. Self-referential and canonical messages

There seem to be two broad classes of messages transmitted in human ritual. First, whatever else may happen in some human rituals, in all rituals, both animal and human, the participants transmit information concerning their own current physical, psychic or social states to themselves and to other participants. As Leach put it, ritual serves to express "the individual's status in the structural system in which he finds himself for the time being" (1954: 11), but the status of groups as wholes, as well as individuals, may also be communicated (Rappaport 1968: 23 *passim*). I shall refer to this class of messages as "self-referential."

In some human rituals, and perhaps in all animal rituals, there is no more. When one male baboon presents his rump to another he is signaling submission, when the other mounts he signals dominance. The message content of the ritual is exhausted by information transmitted by the participants concerning their current states and relations among their current states. The ritual is self-referential and self-referential only. The same can probably be said of such stylized human gestures as bowing, saluting and tipping one's hat to what used to be called "ladies."

We come here to a radical distinction between some human rituals and all animal rituals. In some human rituals the sum of the self-referential information transmitted among the participants does not exhaust the message content of the ritual. Additional messages, although *transmitted* by the participants, are not *encoded* by them. They are found by the participants already encoded in the liturgy. Since these messages are not encoded by the performers, and since they tend toward invariance, it is obvious that these messages *cannot in themselves* represent the performers' contemporary states. For instance, the words and acts comprising the Roman Mass (some of which have remained unchanged for more than a millennium) do not *in themselves* represent or express the current states of those uttering and performing them. In recognition of the propriety with which they are invested and surrounded and of their apparent durability and invariance I shall refer to this class of messages as "canonical."

In distinguishing between the canonical and the self-referential we are, among other things, recognizing a distinction between the significance of what is encoded in the invariant orders of liturgy on the one hand and the significance of the acts of transmitting those invariant messages on the other. That the *Shema*, the Ultimate Sacred Postulate of the Jews, may not have changed in 3000 years (Idelsohn 1932) is one thing, that a particular person recites it on a particular occasion is another. The *Shema* remains unchanged, but those who utter it, and thus place themselves in a certain relationship to it, continue to change as circumstances change and as generation succeeds generation.[15] We will discuss this relation later, especially in chapter 4.

Whereas the referents of self-referential messages, i.e., the current physical, psychic or social states of individual participants, or of the body of participants as a whole, are confined to the here and now, the significata of the canonical are *never* so confined. They always include, in words and acts that have been spoken or performed before, orders, processes or entities, material, social, abstract, ideal or spiritual, the existence or putative existence of which transcends the present. The self-referential represents the immediate, the particular and the vital aspects of *events;* the canonical, in contrast, represents the general, enduring, or even eternal aspects of *universal orders*. Indeed, its quality of perdurance is perhaps signified iconically – its sense is surely conveyed – by the apparent invariance of its mode of transmission.

We may recall that even the most invariant of liturgical orders make room for some variation. The Canon of the Eucharist, for example, has remained more or less unchanged for over a millennium, but who receives communion varies from one Mass to the next, the rituals commencing the *kaiko* festivals of the Maring people of Papua New Guinea proceed in conformity to well-established orders that include pig sacrifices, but the number of pigs to be offered is not specified, nor is the time when the ritual is to be performed or who among other groups will be invited to attend. Furthermore, individuals always have (at least logically) a choice as to whether to participate in rituals that are being performed. We see here that self-referential and canonical messages are not transmitted in separate rituals but that their strands are interwoven throughout all liturgical orders. We further see that *the canonical stream is carried by the invariant aspects or components of these orders, self-referential information is conveyed by whatever variation the liturgical order allows or demands.*

12. Symbols, indices and the two streams of messages

In considering differences in the ways in which canonical and self-referential messages are transmitted we are led back to fundamental semiotic matters broached in the first chapter. Most important: the relationship of signs to that which they signify differs between the two message streams. Canonical messages, which are concerned with things not confined to the present in time or space, which may even be conceived to stand outside the time-space continuum altogether, and whose significata may be, indeed, usually are spiritual, conceptual or abstract in nature, are and *can only be* founded upon symbols (i.e., signs associated by law or convention with that which they signify) although they can employ, secondarily, icons[16] and even make limited use of indices.[17] In contrast, the transmission of information concerning the *current* state of transmitters, being confined to the here and now, may transcend mere symbolic signification and be represented indexically. This is of considerable importance given the vices, discussed at length in the Introduction, to which symbolic transmission is prone: those of lie and of Babel. The use of indices in ritual to convey self-referential information may circumvent some of their disruptive possibilities.

An index, to recall Peirce's phrase, is "a sign which refers to the Object it denotes by being really affected by that Object" (Buchler 1955: 102). This seems clear enough, but differences between indices and the other Peircean signs – icons and symbols – and differences among various forms or instances of indices may not be as straightforward as this most simple of Peirce's several characterizations of the index would suggest. Some commentators, notably Arthur Burks (1949) has argued, with justice, that Peirce became confused in discussing the index, but to make matters yet more complicated, in my view, Burks, in attempting to clarify and correct Peirce, in his turn made matters yet more confused.

Because a close reading of Peirce and such later writers as Burks, Jakobson (1957) and Silverstein (1976) would indicate that my understanding of indices differs more or less subtly from any and all of theirs, as well as from aspects of Peirce's conception, a discussion of this class of sign and its relationship to the others is warranted, if not requisite if my usage is to be justified. The matter is, however, too intricate to dispose of briefly and has, therefore been exiled to an Appendix to this chapter.

Here it is only necessary to make my own usage clear. I am following, as literally as possible, the simple conception Peirce formulated in the sentence just cited. Thus, a rash indicates (is an index of) measles, the rustling of the peacock's spread tail fan indicates his sexual arousal, the weathervane indicates the wind's direction, the Rolls Royce or sable coat indicates the wealth of its owner, May Day parades indicated the strength of Soviet armaments, or aspects of that strength, the March on Washington of November 15, 1970 indicated the size and social composition of opposition to the war in Viet Nam.

There is, obviously, considerable variety among these examples. For instance, the rash indicating measles is what might be called a "natural index," or "symptom," for it is simply a natural effect of a cause which, although it can be read to denote a disease, probably did not emerge or evolve as such and certainly was not deliberately "transmitted" as a sign at all. The peacock's fan and its display is also, presumably, a natural effect of his sexual arousal, as intrinsic to it as his tumescence, but it may not have evolved as a sign. The March on Washington was what is called a "demonstration", an event in which the strength of a political position is not simply asserted, reported, or recounted, but *displayed* and thus *demonstrated*. Although important differences distinguish these instances from each other all of them are comfortably subsumed under a conception of the index as a sign which is caused by, or is part of, or, possibly, in the extreme case, is identical with, that which it signifies. To put it differently, they are perceptible aspects of events or conditions signifying the presence or existence of imperceptible aspects of the same events or conditions.

"Events" or "conditions." Given the relationship of indices to that which they denote they are, as it were, tied to such events and conditions, and cannot *genuinely* occur in their absence. This implies, and we have been so instructed by Figan and other apes, that indexical communication does offer some limited possibilities for deceit.

Opportunities for falsehood are, however, multiplied by magnitudes and the consequences of falsehood made more comprehensive and grave by the symbol, which allows the lie to be elevated from the "proto," to the "true" level. But the hospitality of the symbol to lie is in some degree overcome, or at least ameliorated, in ritual by eschewing its use in favor of indices in the transmission of self-referential information, information concerning the current states or conditions of the transmitters. We may note here that, although some indices can be falsified – accomplished actors can weep when they do not grieve, apes can feign indices of alarm and thus alarm others, Rolls Royces can be rented, borrowed or stolen –

and although some indices can be misconstrued – the driver of the Rolls Royce may be the chauffeur and not the owner, slurred speech may be the effect of drunkenness rather than stroke – ritual relies heavily on indices that are virtually impervious to falsification and resistant to misinterpretation. It is of wry interest that when humans wish to make themselves more than ordinarily credible they may leave behind the subtleties of language and communicate in a manner more closely resembling that of the speechless beasts.

I do not claim that all self-referential messages transmitted in ritual are indexical, but that some of them are patent. When, for instance, a Goodenough Islander (Young 1971) or a Siuai of Guadalcanal (Oliver 1955) gives away large numbers of pigs, seashells or yams in a competitive ritual feast he is not simply *claiming* to be a man of influence, importance, prestige or renown – a "Big Man" – he is *demonstrating* that he is. The amount that he gives away, furthermore, may be a more or less precise index of just how big he is, inasmuch as that amount is "really affected by" that which it signifies – his influence, prestige, authority, industry, renown, all of which, alone or in combination, are attributes of "bigness." Thus, when Soni of Turonom village, a Siuai *muminai*, or Big Man, gave away thirty-two pigs valued at 1,920 spans of cowrie shells one day in 1937 he indicated to 1,100 witnesses (Oliver 1955) just how big he was, at least in relative terms – slightly bigger than a man who could give away thirty pigs, considerably bigger than one who might have managed twenty-five.

It may be well to call attention here, although the matter will be more fully discussed in chapters 3 and 5, to an inversion, in the illustration just offered, of the qualities verbal humans usually expect in signs and their significata. As language users we are accustomed to the sign being relatively insubstantial and the signified substantial, as, for instance, in the relationship of the word "dog" to an animal that it denotes or designates. It may be suggested that in instances in which claims are made concerning valued states or qualities themselves devoid of essential physical properties (e.g. prestige, worth, valor, "bigness") the sign *must* be substantial (e.g. thirty-two pigs given away) if it is to be credited. If the sign for such qualities were not substantial it might be discounted as mere words: vaporous, boastful, "hot air."

Be this as it may, the indices of ritual are usually if not always at least in part substantial. As such they are very resistant or even impervious to falsity. That Soni was able to dispose of thirty-two pigs was, in the Siuai case, all that finally mattered. That some of the pigs were his own, but others borrowed may have been of interest to some of his witnesses but was beside the point. If he were not wealthy enough to have thirty-two pigs of his own to give away he was influential enough and creditworthy enough to borrow what he needed or powerful enough to coerce others into providing them.

The indexicality of other cases is less patent, but more interesting. Among the Maring, a people occupying a domain in the Jimi and Simbai Valleys of Papua New Guinea, men would signify, by dancing at the *kaiko* festival of another group, that they would give their hosts military support the next time they went to war. There is surely no intrinsic or causal relationship between dancing and fighting, particularly dancing *now* and fighting *later*, but the dance is nevertheless indexical. What it indicates is not fighting in the future, but, rather, a *pledge undertaken in the present* to fight in the future. Such conventional acts as pledging and swearing oaths are, of course, symbolic at least in the sense that they would be impossible to conceive or denote in the absence of language. That dancing signifies pledging is also conventional. Some other act, like raising one's right-hand or even, possibly, some verbal formula like "I swear" or "I pledge" could, conceivably, do as well (in chapter 5 I will, however, argue that acts do better than words in such matters). Nevertheless, dancing does not simply symbolize the Maring man's pledge. It indicates it because the conventional act of pledging is understood by the Maring to be *intrinsic* to, an aspect of, the conventional act of dancing. To dance is to pledge. In terms that will be more fully discussed in chapter 4, dancing at a *kaiko* is a "performative" (Austin 1962), a conventional act bringing into being a conventional state of affairs. Inasmuch as dancing brings a pledge into being it cannot help but indicate it.[18]

We note in this instance an indexical relationship between two conventions, dancing and promising. We also note that in this case it would be impossible for deceit to hide within a cloud of vagueness or ambiguity because there is no ambiguity or vagueness. To dance is to pledge and that is that.

But that is not the end of the matter. The case of the Maring dancer not only illustrates indexicality, but its limitations as well. Dancing may indicate a pledge of support, but a pledge of support obviously does not in and of itself honor that pledge. To put this a little differently, to pledge is to undertake an obligation, but it is one thing to undertake an obligation now and another to fulfill it in the future. Fulfillment of the pledge is not an ineluctable effect of the pledge as the pledge is of dancing.

The indexical transmission of self-referential information is, thus, only a partial antidote to the problems generated by falsehood and its corollaries, those of establishing credibility and establishing credence. What may make Maring hosts confident that their guests will honor in the future the pledges that they are undertaking in the present is another matter relating to other aspects of the ritual. We shall return to this question later, only noting now that *this confidence, such as it is, is contingent upon the association of the indexically transmitted pledge with messages borne by the liturgy's invariant canon.*

In sum, two classes of information, then, are transmitted by ritual. All rituals, both animal and human, carry self-referential information, information concerning the current states of the participants, often if not always transmitted indexically rather than symbolically.[19] The second class, the canonical, is concerned with enduring aspects of nature, society or cosmos, and is encoded in apparently invariant aspects of liturgical orders. The invariance of a liturgy may be an icon of the seeming changelessness of the canonical information that it incorporates, or even an index of its actual changelessness, but canonical messages rest ultimately upon symbols.

There is a self-referential component in all rituals, but it might seem that in some rituals its significance is so far outweighed by the grandeur of the canonical that it appears trivial, as, for instance, in the case of the Mass. Consideration of this matter must be delayed until chapter 4, but it may be well to assert – or reassert – now that in all liturgical rituals, and most clearly *in all religious rituals, there is transmitted an indexical message that cannot be transmitted in any other way and, far from being trivial, it is one without which canonical messages are without force, or may even seem nonsensical.*

If it is the case, as I have claimed, that some self-referential messages are dependent for their acceptability on their association with the canonical, and if canonical messages are without force, or even sense, unless accompanied by certain self-referential messages ritual is not merely a mode of communication in which two sorts of information maybe transmitted. *It is, rather, a very complex form in which the two classes of messages are dependent upon each other.*

Appendix
Peirce, as well as others following him, characterized the index in a number of slightly, but nevertheless significantly, different ways. His simplest formulation, relied upon in the main text, defines the index as "a

sign which refers to the Object it denotes by being really affected by the Object" (Buchler 1955: 102).

He also defined it as

a sign, or representation, which refers to its object not so much because of any similarity or analogy with it, nor because it is associated with general characters which that object happens to possess, as because it is in dynamical (including spatial) connection both with the individual object, on the one hand, and with the sense or memory of the person for whom it serves as a sign on the other hand ...

(Buchler 1955 107)

We will only note here that there are some differences between these characterization of indices (particularly the first) and those of Burks for whom an index is a sign "in existential relation with its object (as in the case of the act of pointing)" or "a sign which determines its object on the basis of an existential connection."

Subsequently (p. 108) Peirce elaborates by telling us that

Indices may be distinguished from other signs ... by three characteristic marks; first, that they have no significant resemblance to their objects; second that they refer to individuals, single units, single collections of units, or single continua; third, that they direct attention to their objects by blind compulsion.

Here are some of Peirce's examples.

I see a man with a rolling gait. This is a probable indication that he is a sailor. I see a bowlegged man in corduroys, gaiters and a jacket. These are probable indications that he is a jockey or something of the sort. A sundial or a clock *indicates* the time of day ... A rap on the door is an index. Anything which focuses the attention is an index. Anything which startles us is an index in so far as it marks the junction between two portions of experience. Thus a tremendous thunderbolt indicates that *something* considerable has happened, though we may not know precisely what the event was. But it may be expected to connect itself with some other experience.

... A low barometer with a moist air is an index of rain; that is we suppose that the [forces] of nature establish a probable connection between the low barometer with moist air and coming rain. A weathercock is an index of the direction of the wind; because in the first place it really takes the self-same direction as the wind, so that there is a real connection between them, and in the second place we are so constituted that when we see a weathercock pointing in a certain direction it draws our attention to that direction, and when we see the weathercock veering with the wind, we are forced by the law of mind to think that direction is connected with the wind. The pole star is an index, or pointing finger, to show us which way is north. A spirit-level, or plumb bob is an index of the vertical direction. *(Buchler 1955: 108–109)*

Two comments are in order before proceeding. First, I believe that the statement of his first "characteristic mark" would be improved by modifying it to say that indices *need* have no significant resemblance to their object. As it stands it is not entirely consistent with all of his examples. "A ... plumb bob is an index of the vertical direction" in part because its line, by virtue of the law of gravity must itself be vertical. As such it resembles, to say the least, its object, the vertical direction. Much the same can be said about the weathervane's direction.

It is striking how different some of these signs are from others. The North Star, for instance, and the finger pointing north, both seemingly understood by Peirce to be indexical equivalents of synonyms, not only for each other but, no doubt, for compass needles as well, are radically different in their relationship to their Objects. The act of pointing a finger in a particular direction in response to the question "which way is north?", a deliberate act on the part of the signer, is not really affected by its object, the direction north, but, at best, by the direction the signer believes to be north, a very different matter. I said "at best." It is possible for a signer to point, quite deliberately, to what be believes is south when asked for the north.

In contrast, the Pole Star happens to be at or near the zenith at the North Pole. As such it stands in a static spatial (not what most of us mean by "dynamical") relationship to the North Pole and therefore cannot help but indicate north to whoever has knowledge of the relationship and can find the star.

There are yet other differences. Some of Peirce's examples make clear that the objects of at least some indices can be very vague (as in his account of the thunderbolt), and that others can easily and plausibly be misunderstood or mistaken. I may construe the rolling gait of the man I see to indicate that he is a sailor but in reality he may be a drunken attorney or a stockbroker suffering from a central nervous disorder. Others, in contrast, like the plumb-line attaching the plumb-bob to the tripod are close to perfectly clear and difficult or impossible for a normal person to misunderstand.

Further problems vex this list. It may be, for instance, that both sundials and clocks indicate the time of day but they do so very differently. The sundial's shadow is a product of the intervention of its style between its face and the sun. The sun's position is what is meant by "time of day", at least during the daylight hours, and thus the position of the shadow on the face is, inarguably, "really affected by" it object, the time of day. It is, in contrast, difficult to see how the positions of the clock's hands are "really affected by" or are in "dynamical connection" to the time of day. That they are not is to be inferred from the fact that there is often disagreement between clocks in the same place at the same moment. Peirce, then, left many important distinctions among indices (and between them and other sign types) unremarked. As Arthur Burks put it many years ago "A study of Peirce's theory of signs is difficult not only because of the unusually fragmentary character of his writing on this subject but also because of the presence of certain inconsistencies and confusions" (1949: 675)." Burks cleared up some of these inconsistencies and confusions but, I believe, introduced others. These need brief discussion.

First, he misconstrued what Peirce meant by the term "interpretant" or at least uses it in a very different sense from Peirce. For Peirce an interpretant is an aspect of the sign itself:

A sign, or *representamen* is something which stands to somebody for something in some respect or capacity. It addresses somebody, that is creates in the mind of that person an equivalent sign, or perhaps a more developed sign. *That sign which it creates I call the interpretant of the first sign ...* (*Buchler 1955: 99, emphasis mine*)

Burks, in contrast, uses the term "interpretant" to denote the "somebody who is addressed, and not the sign created in his or her mind." This is clearly indicated in the following:

A sign represents its object to its interpretant symbolically, indexically, or iconically ... Consider ... the word "red." The word "red" is a symbol because it stands for the quality red to an interpretant who interprets it in virtue of the conventional linguistic rule of English establishing the meaning of this word.

(*1949: 674*)

Two problems are raised. First, in the disappearance of interpretant as an aspect of the sign, or more precisely, the refraction of the object through the "something" which stands for that object, an important question concerning the nature of indices is dissolved without being resolved. It is the question of disparity between the object and the interpretant. The object of the rolling gait in Peirce's first example is "sailor" but, as I have suggested, the interpretant (in Peirce's sense) could have been "drunk" or "cerebral palsy" instead. Peirce does not seem to me to have expressed himself very clearly on this matter and Burks' apparent misinterpretation doesn't help.

Secondly, and perhaps more importantly, it may be that Burks' use of the term "interpretant" to designate the "somebody" who does the interpreting is a response to the near absence from Peirce's formulation of any discussion of senders and receivers as such, that is, the encoders and decoders of signs, and of distinction between these agents (although he does mention the "intelligence using [signs]" [Buchler 1955: 98] and of the "somebodies" who are "addressed" by signs, that is receivers or decoders). His is a theory of signs and not of communication. Although it is reasonable to take the position that no theory can, or even should, aspire to account for everything, neglect of senders and receivers in the case to hand makes problems for the theory of signs, even narrowly defined, particularly with respect to the nature of the relationship of signs to objects. Pointing a finger, as we have seen, does not relate to the direction north in the same way that the Pole Star does. Pointing a finger toward the north requires a conscious agent to do the pointing (transmitting of the message) in every instance. The relationship of Polaris to the North Pole, in contrast, once it was *discovered* could stand forever as an indication of the direction north. That is, a conscious transmitter is not required every time someone looks to Polaris to locate north, nor is a conscious transmitter required every time a compass is consulted. Once it was *invented*, the compass, like Polaris, could forever indicate the north (when corrected for deviation and deflection). There are differences, however. That Polaris indicates the direction north is a convenient spatial happenstance. That a compass indicates north is the result of a "dynamical connection" between magnetic needles and the magnetic North Pole. It is, this is to say, a function of the operation of universally operating "forces of nature." In sum, if indices are by definition "really affected by" their objects or significata, neglect of the agencies engaged in encoding and transmitting them (not necessarily the same) and the agencies receiving and interpreting them will necessarily neglect important differences among them.

This leads to what I take to be Burks' most serious confusion, which is based upon his attribution of a "basic confusion" to Peirce.

Peirce confuses the cause–effect relation with the semiotic relation. Thus he says that ... a weathercock is an index of the direction of the wind ... but a weathercock is not a sign in the sense of Peirce's definition – the interpretant does not use the weathercock to represent or denote the direction of the wind. What the interpretant does is to infer the direction of the wind from the weathercock's position, on the basis of his knowledge that this position is the effect of the wind.

(1949: 679)

First, I do not think that Peirce's inclusion of weathercocks, barometers, spirit-levels and the like among indices is the result of any confusion of the causal and the semiotic, or of anything else, for that matter. Although he did not develop an adequate taxonomy of indexical forms, the conflation of the causal and semiotic seems *in its essence* to characterize one of the index's basic classes, the class that seems to me to be the "purest" or most fundamental of all indices. Let us call them "True Indices." A "True Index" is one in which there is a perfect correspondence between the sign–object relationship and either an effect–cause or part–whole relationship. That is, a True Index is a sign that is either an effect of, or an aspect of, or a part of its object.

It may be useful to distinguish two subclasses of True Indices. First there are what might be called "natural indices" or "symptoms." They include the dark cloud that indicates rain, the rash that indicates measles, the star Polaris that indicates north, the rolling gait that indicates "sailor."

Secondly, there are what may be called "Constructed Indices." They include the weathercock that indicates the wind's direction, the barometer that indicates air pressure, the plumb line that indicates the vertical, and the rap on the door indicating the presence of someone or something (a raven, maybe) seeking the attention of an occupant, a presentation of thirty-two pigs indicating bigness, dancing indicating pledging and so on. They differ from natural indices most fundamentally, of course, in that they are deliberately constructed and employed by humans to indicate whatever they do indicate.

As deliberate constructions Constructed Indices are *in their very nature* semiotic, and as such they differ from natural indices which are, simply, perceptible aspects of phenomena the presence of which may indicate to observers aspects of phenomena that are "really affected by," "in existential relation with," or in "dynamical" relation with other less perceptible aspects of those same phenomena. (A dark cloud is not in its nature a sign of rain or of anything else, although it can *serve* as a sign.) Constructed Indices nevertheless qualify as True Indices in that the relationship of sign to object among them is, no less than among Natural Indices, that of effect to cause or as part or aspect to whole. That is, signs constituted as Constructed Indices are caused by or are parts or aspects of their objects. This may hold, as we have seen in the main text, even when the object is a convention, like pledging or bigness, and when the sign is a convention, like a presentation of pigs or participation in a dance.

That the constructed index is in its nature semiotic whereas the natural index is not proposes another difference between them which may sometimes be of considerable importance. To put it in ordinary language natural indices are usually more diffuse, less focused than constructed indices. What the thunderbolt indicates is, according to Peirce, vague, what the rolling gait indicates is ambiguous, what the rash indicates may be very general as well as highly ambiguous, and what the dark cloud indicates – the likelihood of rain – is uncertain. In contrast, what is indicated by the weathervane and the plumb-line and the thirty-two pigs is not in the least vague, ambiguous, general or uncertain. They are as specific as it is possible to be: the weathervane indicates wind direction and wind direction only. The plumb line indicates no more and no less than verticality. The gift of thirty-two pigs specifies how "big" the donor is.

It is useful to put this in Peirce's terms. His conception of the sign is not limited to the three elements so far discussed, namely the sign (or sign vehicle) the object and the interpretant. It also includes a fourth: "The sign 'stands for ... [the] object, not in all respects, but in reference to a sort of idea, which I have sometimes called the *ground* of the representamen'" (Buchler 1955: 99). Thus, the plumb-line suspended from a beam next to a post does not indicate whether the post is made of oak, but only that it is vertical. Similarly, the weathervane does not indicate the wind, but only the direction of the wind. Verticality and direction are the grounds of these indices, and it may be suggested that constructed indices *always* have a ground whereas natural indices may not, or at least not definite ones.

We can now return to what I take to be Burks' confusion. Burks as we have seen disqualifies weathervanes, plumb-lines and the like as indices or, for that matter, signs of any kind, on the grounds that they do not represent or denote the direction of the wind, etc., but are used by their interpreters to *infer* such things. I am neither a philosopher nor a psychologist, but would suggest, first, that the logical distinction between inference and interpretation may be clearer than the behavioral distinction in particular cases; secondly, that in instances in which the conclusions to be drawn from the state of a device are limited to one (e.g., that the plumb-line is vertical, that the direction of the wind is the direction in which the weathercock points) there is a simple and straightforward indexical relationship between the sign and the object; thirdly, and related, if those who use the weathervane take its direction to indicate the wind's direction then it is an index, regardless of what their mental operations might be, unbeknownst to themselves; fourthly and related, even if it could somehow be demonstrated that every time a farmer observes his weathervane he commences an inferential process, it would be so short, informal and unconscious that it would hardly deserve to be called "inference" and would be experienced as indication. Indeed, if inference is, by definition, the drawing of conclusions from premises then in the case at hand the conclusion "The wind is north-westerly" is virtually identical with the premises (1) The weathercock points in the wind's direction, (2) The weathercock points northwest; fifthly, one of the main points of such devices is to reduce or eliminate the need for inference which is in its nature more open to error than are True Indices. It could also be argued, sixthly, that even if one wished to consider the conclusion "The wind is northwesterly" an inference from premises constituted by the weathercock and its position, indication and inference are not mutually exclusive. An index, it could be said, consti-tutes a premise. Furthermore, indexicality is an aspect of the relationship between the sign vehicle and the object whereas inference is an activity of the interpreter of the sign.

Although I believe Burks to have been mistaken with respect to such devices as weathervanes it may well be that inference plays a much more important role in the interpretation of natural indices. To interpret the rolling gait of the man I see as indicative of intoxication, nervous disorder or a maritime way of life requires the interpreter to take other indications (dress, location, speech, etc.) into consideration and to infer from them all, in light of each other, what the sign does, in fact, indicate. Inference may also be important, of course, in "secondary interpreta-tions" of whatever is indicated by a constructed index. A barometer, for example, indicates atmospheric pressure, no more, no less. It does not indicate what tomorrow's weather will be although we may infer from such an indication (with a degree of reliability that is unclear or uncertain) that it will rain or that the sun will shine. That tomorrow's weather is not fully predictable from either the dark cloud or the barometer reading does not, however, disqualify either from membership in the general class of signs that Peirce called "indices," and I respectfully suggest that it was Arthur Burks and not Charles Sanders Peirce who was confused in this regard.

In sum, two types of indices, the natural and the constructed have been distinguished, and I have further proposed that they are subclasses of a more inclusive class, here called "True Indices." The label "True Index" seems appropriate for two reasons: first it distinguishes its members as a class from certain mixed forms alluded to by Peirce (Buchler 1955: 108) and discussed further by Burks (1949), Silverstein (1976) and others. Secondly, the label recognizes that when a sign is the effect of a cause it cannot help but indicate that cause and as such cannot help but be true, although its object can be misconstrued or misunderstood by a receiver. Inasmuch as a degree of ambiguity inheres in silence I will make explicit that the omission of the finger pointing north from the class of True Indices was deliberate. We will return shortly to the matter of index and truth. First, a brief discussion of mixed forms is necessary.

Peirce (Buchler 1955: 108) noted that "it would be difficult, if not impossible, to instance an absolutely pure index, or to find any sign absolutely devoid of the indexical quality." I believe that this is an overstatement, but it nevertheless proposes, reasonably enough, that the terms "index", "icon" and "symbol" should be taken to be possible *aspects* of signs rather than labels for necessarily *separate* and *distinct* signs. Whether it would be difficult or impossible to instance "absolutely pure" types need not be discussed here. It does seem to me that most of the examples of True Indices already adduced would come reasonably close to indexical purity, but even if they don't there is reason to believe that pure indices do exist, if it is the case as I, following others, have argued (in the last chapter for the most part) that animal communication is largely indexical and, with the *possible* exception of minor use in a handful of intrahuman species, totally devoid of symbols.

The situation is different with respect to icons, we may note in passing. As noted above, iconic actions, like sticking pins into an image of a victim, rests upon the use of symbols – ultimately words – to specify that the image is a representation of a victim, the pins a representation of occult attack and who, precisely, the victim may be. Burks took Peirce to task on this point.

Peirce ... failed to recognize that since any sign embodies or exhibits a number of qualities and relations, some symbolic means is required to communicate both the fact that a sign is an icon and the respect in which it is iconic, and so also failed to see that there can be no pure icons.   *(1949: 676)*

The assertion that there "can be no pure icons" seems plausible with respect to humans, but if animal communication is also taken into consideration it may not hold. The primary questions are, first, whether such phenomena as genetic mimicry (e.g. the edible moth that looks like an inedible one to knowledgeable birds) and such activities as honeybee dancing (which seems to indicate, iconically, the distance and direction of pollen sources) are to be regarded as iconic and secondly, if they are is their iconicity contingent upon indexicality? These questions need not be addressed here, but it is worth noting that we may be observing in such cases a stage in the evolutionary emergence of icons, whether out of indices or not is another matter.

Although we can, I believe, find instances of both pure indices and pure symbols, signs possessing both symbolic and indexical properties play an important, or even indispensable part in human communication. Such signs were recognized by Peirce and have been further and more elaborately discussed by Burks (1949) Jakobson (1957) and Silverstein (1976) among others. I need not attempt to summarize these complex discussions here. Suffice it to say that words can be, and often are, used indexically. The word "this" for instance, can indicate something in the immediate environment in precisely the same way that pointing a finger can. As such it is an index, but inasmuch as "this" is a word it, like all words, is a symbol. "A symbol is a Representation whose Representative character consists precisely in its being a rule that will determine its Interpretation" (Buchler 1955: 112). This is simply to say that referential meaning of a symbol is conventional.

The range of word types that commonly serve as indices, according to Peirce and following him, Burks and Silverstein, include time and place references and various forms of pronoun. The possibility of indexical relations between symbols or symbolically constituted phenomena becomes more or less clear in these discussions. Thus, for instance, Silverstein tells us that

a distinct nonreferential bifurcation of lexical items into complementary indexical sets was widespread in Australian Aboriginal speech communities. As described by Dixon (1971) for Dyirbal ... there is an "everyday" set of lexical items, and a "mother-in-law set" which had to be used by a speaker only in the presence of his classificatory mother-in-law or equivalent affine. In other words, the mother-in-law vocabulary, totally distinct from the everyday one, indexes the specified affinal relation between speaker (X) and some "audience" – not the socially defined addressee (Y) – in the speech situation. As such the switch in vocabulary serves as an *affinal taboo index* ... maintaining and creating sociological distance.

(*1976: 314–15*)

We see here an indexical relationship between two forms, *both of which are essentially symbolic*, a special vocabulary and an affinal taboo.

This instance can be distinguished in a fundamental way from the instances of indexical relations between conventional signs and objects earlier discussed – dancing and pledging, pigs and social bigness. In the latter instances the signs and their objects are absolutely inseparable – to dance is to pledge, to give away thirty-two pigs is to be big. The signs in these instances are really affected by the Objects because they, in fact, effect the Objects. Inasmuch as this is the case it is impossible for them to be false. I therefore place them in the category of True Indices.

The Dyirbal case is different. The connection between the Object – the presence of the mother-in-law – and the sign – use of the special vocabulary – is much weaker. It is possible for a boorish Australian to fail to use the special vocabulary when his mother-in-law is visiting or, conversely, he could use it when she is nowhere to be seen. It may be that an Australian can infer the presence of a man's mother-in-law from his vocabulary, and we may even be willing to say that his speech *indicates* his mother-in-law's presence but truth is not intrinsic to this form of sign, and inasmuch as the Sign in the Sign–Object relationship is relatively weak I would not place this instance in the class of True Indices. I have similar reservations about such putative indices as pointing fingers.

3

Self-referential messages

We shall be concerned in this chapter with self-referential messages and their transmission. A consideration of the self-referential aspects of ritual will lead us naturally to a consideration of the canonical, but the self-referential and its mode of transmission are of great interest in their own right.

We noted in the last chapter that, even in the most invariant of liturgical orders, there is some room for variation and that, in fact, variations of one sort or another may be intrinsic to particular elements of ritual performance. For instance, pig sacrifices may be demanded in a particular ritual, but the number of pigs to be slaughtered left unspecified. We also noted, although only in passing, that canonical messages are conveyed by the invariant aspects or components of liturgical performance; self-referential messages, by whatever variation performance of the liturgical order allows, entails or demands. We shall be concerned in this chapter with variation in liturgical performance, considering first variation and indexicality. We shall proceed to numerical variation in the contents of ritual and to the substantial representations of abstractions and to the digital representation of what are called analogic processes. Consideration of the effects of these aspects of ritual communication on the clarity and informativeness of its transmissions will lead to a discussion of the occurrence of rituals as binary signals, and to the role of ritual in transmitting information across the boundaries of unlike systems. We shall conclude with discussions of the self-informativeness of ritual, and the relationship of the self-referential to the canonical stream of ritual's messages.

If there could be no variation in liturgical performance there could hardly be self-referential transmission. How, after all, could an age-old canon punctiliously performed in the day of the year upon which it had always been performed communicate information about the particularities of the performers' contemporary states? How, indeed, could it communicate anything about them at all? Information in the technical sense (Shannon and Weaver 1949) is that which reduces uncertainty. The minimal unit is a "bit," the amount of information reducing the uncertainty between two equally likely alternatives, the answer to a "yes/no question" when yes and no are equally likely. If there are no alternatives, no information *in this strict sense* can be transmitted (see chapter 10). This raises important questions, to which we shall return in a later chapter, concerning the canonical as well as the self-referential aspects of liturgy. Here we may reiterate that even in the performance of the most invariant liturgies there is opportunity for variation of a fundamental sort. Potential performers have available to them, at least as a logical possibility, the alternatives of participating or not in a ritual that is being or could be held. This minimal and seemingly trivial possibility for variation not only may carry socially significant information of a rather specific and often precise nature, but also infuses participation itself with a profound and general significance to be discussed in the next chapter.

1. On levels of meaning

Before going on, it may be well to allay a possible concern that some readers may soon begin to feel: that I am reducing ritual's meaning to information narrowly defined. I am not. I understand information to constitute a *type* of meaning that does have a place in ritual, but I do not take it to be coextensive with ritual's meaning, much less meaning in general. I have neither the time nor the credentials to broach the matter of the meaning of meaning. Suffice it to say that although the kinds of meaning to be found in ritual might be indefinitely manifold, for the purposes of this book we can, in a rough and ready way, distinguish three types or, better, three levels of meaning.

First, there is what I have elsewhere (1979a, 1992) called *low order meaning*, meaning, that is, in its simple, everyday semantic sense. The meaning of the word "dog" is *dog, dog* being distinct from *cat*, which is signified by the contrasting word "cat." Low order meaning is grounded in *distinction* and, as such, is closely related to, if not coextensive with, what is meant by information in Information Theory. Taxonomies are the typical, but, of course, not the only, structures organizing low order meaning.

When, however, we wish to go beyond simple semantic meaning to *meaningfulness* (whatever we mean by the term) we become concerned not only with rationally drawn distinctions but with emotionally charged values as well, and we employ means other than distinction to convey or evoke such meaning. The sense of meaning to which the question "What does it all mean?" points – when asked by one confronted by a complex mass of information – is surely not that of further distinction. In responding to such a question we do not attempt to multiply distinctions but, on the contrary, to *decrease* their number and import by discovering similarities among apparently disparate phenomena. In what I have elsewhere (1979a, 1992) called "higher-order meaning" but might better be called "*middle-order meaning*," such similarities, hidden beneath the surfaces of apparently distinctive phenomena, become more significant than the distinctions themselves. They may, indeed, when illuminated or discovered, strike us with the force of revelation.

Whereas the paradigmatic household of low order meaning is the taxonomy, the vehicle of higher order meaning is metaphor. Metaphor, we may note, enriches the world's meaningfulness, for the significance of every term that participates in a metaphor is transformed into more than itself, into an icon of other things as well. It is significant that art and poetry rely heavily upon metaphor, a mode of representation that, perhaps because of its connotative resonance, is affectively more powerful than straightforward didactic discourse, and it may well be more convincing.

I have not yet exhausted meaning's levels. Whereas low-order meaning is shaped by distinction and middle-order meaning is carried by the discovery or revelation of similarities (often hidden) among apparently disparate things, what I shall call *high-order meaning* (in previous publications "highest-order meaning") is grounded in identity or unity, the radical identification or unification of self with other. It is not so much, or even at all, intellectual but is, rather, experiential. It may be experienced through art, or in the acts of love, but is, perhaps, most often felt in ritual and other religious devotions. High-order meaning seems to be experienced in intensities ranging from the mere intimation of being emotionally moved in, for instance, the course of ritual to those deep numinous experiences called "mystical." Those who have known it in its more intense forms may refer to it by such obscure phrases as "The Experience of Being" or Being-Itself. They report that, although it is beyond the reach of language, it seems enormously or even ultimately meaningful even though, or perhaps because, its meaning is ineffable.

If distinctions are radically reduced in middle order meaning they are annihilated by high order meaning in its ultimate manifestations, as the last distinction, the one between that which is meaningful and she for whom it is meaningful, is obliterated in *unio mystica*, the experience of unification with another, or others, or the cosmos, or the divine. Whereas low-order meaning's home is taxonomy and middle-order meaning's vehicle is metaphor, *participation* is the way to high-order meaning. We have already noted that participation is a *sine qua non* of ritual.

In sum, we have distinguished three bases of meaningfulness – distinction, similarity, and unification or identity – all of which are important in ritual. It is interesting that each level of meaning seems to be roughly associated with a different class in Peirce's tripartite classification of signs. Low-order meaning, based on the semantic distinctions of language, relies upon symbols in Peirce's sense, that is signs "associated by law," as he put it, with their significata. Middle-order meaning, which is derived from the recognition of formal (or perhaps other) similarities among disparate phenomena, is conveyed iconically. High-order meaning, founded upon unification, may be experienced as indexical, that is, as effects of or as *parts* of, that which they signify.

It is worth noting that it is low-order meaning elaborated by language, that is the *sine qua non* of humanity. The ultimately meaningful is largely, if not entirely, non-discursive. It could be objected, however, that the terms "low," "middle," and "high" are not neutral and that they, or the way that I have assigned them to the three levels is arbitrary, prejudiced, and prejudicial. A Cartesian might invert my ordering; a logical positivist might banish the middle and the high from meaning's realm entirely.

My ranking is, I believe, justified because it is not simply an ordering of three types of signification but a hierarchy of *meaningfulness*. Distinction, similarity, and unification not only imply or even entail different relations – symbolic, iconic, and indexical – between signs and their significata, but different relations between signs and those for whom they are meaningful. The semantic distinctions constituting low order meaning are intrinsic to messages or texts. As such they are separate from, and are perceived to be at some distance from, those for whom they are meaningful. They distinguish physical, social, or conceptual objects from each other and we treat them as "objective," a term which not only refers to objects, but contrasts with "subjective." Subjectivity becomes important if not dominant in middle order meaning. Dependent on pattern recognition, it engages cognitive operations that seem to be more affect-laden than the objective operations of low-order meaning (see Fenischel 1945: *passim*; on primary process, Langer 1953: *passim*, and chapter 12 below), and such recognition is not always contained by the particular similarities to which attention is called in the poem, narrative, or ritual. It reverberates through the mind and body, bringing to consciousness or subconsciousness other parts of experience. Persons, signs, and significata are drawn closer together than they are by the distinctions of low-order meaning; meaning becomes strongly subjective and as such more immediate.

In high-order meaning the distance between signs, significata, and those for whom they are meaningful may be greatly reduced, if not annihilated, as he for whom it is meaningful feels himself uniting with or participating in that which is meaningful to him. Meaning stops being referential, becomes a state of being, and as such seems totally subjective. Our hierarchy of meaningfulness is, among other things, a hierarchy of subjectivity.

To distinguish three levels of meaning is not, of course, to separate them. It is unfortunate that students of each level tend to be different people, for surely these levels must be related to each other in systematic ways. One may suggest that association with, or subsumption by middle-order meanings invests low-order meanings with value, that is, makes mere information more meaningful. Conversely, low-order meanings provide the distinctions upon which meanings of higher order operate. It is not possible to illuminate similarities among disparate phenomena unless distinctions among those phenomena have been recognized. It would not be possible to dissolve all distinctions and similarities into a transcending unity if there were no distinctions and similarities to dissolve.

Our hierarchy is not only one of subjectivity but also of integration. The distinctions of low-order meaning, lodged in language, divide the world into discrete objects; the recognition of similarity constituting middle-order meaning makes connections among those objects; high-order meaning unifies the world into wholeness. Middle-order and high-order meaning may thus prevail, at least from time to time, over the experiences of fragmentation and alienation that are, possibly, concomitants of language's objectifying powers, but it is important to note that the three levels of meaning do not always live easily together. Naive scientism and naive rationalism tend to deny the validity of middle- and high-order meaning, and it is ironically interesting that information may become the enemy of meaningfulness. Conversely, untempered commitment to middle- and high-order meaning may ignore crucial distinctions in the natural and social world.

Although this account of meaning's hierarchical structure will not be continually made explicit and will, rather, largely remain implicit in the background, it outlines, in a rough way, the general trajectory of this book's argument. Thus, it may be helpful to some readers to make this trajectory explicit. Having laid its foundations in the first two chapters, now the exploration begins of what may be thought of as ritual's surfaces, with meanings, in their most obvious aspects. In subsequent chapters, we plumb ever deeper into ritual's depths (or, if you prefer to maintain consistency with our ordering of meaning into low, middle, and high, to scale its heights). This chapter, concerned with self-referential messages, emphasizes, although this will remain implicit, low-order meaning. This is not to imply that self-referential messages possess only low-order meaning or that meanings of higher-order are confined to canon. That this is not the case is implicit in this brief discussion of objectivity and subjectivity in meaning, and should become more apparent as we approach, without calling continual attention to the matter, higher- order meanings in later chapters.

2. Variation and indexicality in the Maring ritual cycle

There are possibilities for variation in both the contents of ritual and in their time and place of occurrence. All of these possibilities are nicely illustrated by certain rituals performed by the Maring, a group of slash-and-burn horticulturalists living in the Simbai and Jimi Valleys of New Guinea's Central Highlands (Rappaport 1968).

The Maring had little contact with Europeans before I first sojourned among them in 1962 and 1963. There were at that time about 7,000 Maring speakers organized into twenty or more autonomous local groups or populations ranging in size from 100 to 900 members, each composed of one or more putatively patrilineal clans, and each occupying a territory of several square miles, in most instances running from river bottom to ridge top on one side or the other of either the Jimi or Simbai valleys. Political relations are such that each local group has a Maring enemy across at least one of its borders on the same valley wall, and intermittent warfare characterized relations between such enemies until the mid 1950s. The rituals of interest here are among the many that together comprise an elaborate and protracted liturgical order, cyclical in form, taking a dozen or more years to complete. This ritual cycle and the individual rituals of which it is made have been described in detail elsewhere (see Rappaport 1984); we can therefore confine our discussion here to certain of its features. Ritual cycles are conducted separately by each local population. In fact, that they join in conducting a ritual cycle is what defines aggregates of clans occupying contiguous territories as local populations (see chapter 8). The ritual cycle can be said to start during the course of warfare. If it becomes clear that hostilities – always engaging adjacent groups – are not going to be swiftly composed, the antagonists hang certain ritual objects called *mbamp ku* (fighting stones) from the center poles of their *ringi yin* (ringi houses). These small round structures are associated with the spirits of men killed in warfare (*rawa mugi* red spirits). When the fighting stones are hung, a charcoal, called *ringi*, laden with occult virtue, is prepared inside the *ringi* houses. The rituals occurring at this time are elaborate and costly. Both red spirits and other ancestors are invoked, and pigs sacrificed to them. They are also momentous. Hanging the fighting stones transforms opponents into formal enemies (*cenang yu* "ax men": those to whom one relates through the sharp edge of an ax). Rigid and enduring taboos separate *cenang yu* in peacetime as well as during war, and it takes four generations to remove all impediments to social relations between groups who have declared each other to be such. With the hanging of the fighting stones combat is escalated from *ngui mbamp* (brother fight) or *ura awere* (nothing fight), in which only bows and arrows are used, to a much more lethal form, in which spears and axes also figure. Moreover, a great many taboos – most noticeably on all sexual relations and on a great many foodstuffs – come into effect with the hanging of the stones. All of them last for the duration of the warfare, but some for many years longer. Some, indeed, are permanent for those subject to them.

While local populations are presumably or ideally composed of groups of agnatically related men and their in-married wives, a substantial portion of the male population of any local population is, in fact, made up of non-agnates living uxorilocally, sororilocally or matrilocally.[1] When the local population among whom such a man lives hangs its fighting stones he may choose to fight at the side of his hosts not as a mere ally but as one of them. The choice may be almost academic because, if he is a long-term resident, he would probably be ashamed to do other than to declare himself not to be one with his hosts, and might not be allowed to remain in residence if in fact he did. Be this as it may, if he does choose to be numbered among those with whom he lives, he joins them in having *ringi* applied to his face and his body.[2]

Allies do not have *ringi* applied to them. By wearing it a man therefore signifies that he comes to battle not as an ally, but as a principal antagonist. The role of a principal antagonist may well be more dangerous than that of an ally because enemies are more motivated to kill principal antagonists than they are their antagonists' allies. Indeed, they even may attempt to avoid killing or injuring their antagonists' allies.[3]

Should a local population remain in possession of its territory at the conclusion of a round of warfare (in most cases neither side is dislodged) it conducts further rituals that, among other things, provide its erstwhile resident aliens with further opportunities to identify with it. First, if such a man is in possession of any mature or even adolescent pigs he will join the other locals in sacrificing them to various categories of spirits, and in presenting the bulk of the pork to men from elsewhere who have fought as allies. That is, he acts towards others as do the men among whom he has been living and at whose sides he has fought. The role he takes in these rituals – sacrificer of pigs and donor of pork – cannot help but *indicate* that he shares with his erstwhile hosts the burden of debts to allies and spirits that warfare entails for the principals.

The final and most important act in the rituals terminating hostilities is the planting of small trees or shrubs called *yu min rumbim* (*yu* [men]; *min* ["soul," life principle, shadow]; *rumbim* [*Cordyline fruticosa*, pidgin English: *tanket*]) by each of a local population's sub-territorial groups (usually patriclans or clusters of them). All men participate in this ritual by grasping the *rumbim* as earth is tamped around its base. Some informants say that they are actually injecting their *min* into the plants. Be this as it may, they are signifying their connection to the land in which it is planted and to each other. The former alien, having defended the land upon which he lives in the same fashion as its native sons and having sacrificed his pigs as have they, joins them in clasping the *rumbim*, possibly mingling his *min* with theirs, but at any rate joining them and, in effect, rooting himself in the land.

We note, then, three ritual contexts associated with warfare in which, as Leach would have it, the individual expresses his "status as a social person in the structural system in which he finds himself for the time being." Participation in them by native sons, although important, is hardly noteworthy, for it doesn't indicate anything not already established and well-known. Much more noteworthy would be their failure to participate. On the other hand, the participation of resident aliens, anomalous figures whose positions are ambiguous, is much more noteworthy, for it indicates clearly what has not previously been entirely clear: the groups with which they align themselves.

Their participation *indicates* membership. It does not simply symbolize it, despite the fact that the association of *ringi*, presentations of pigs and the planting of *rumbim* seem to be, or in fact are, only conventionally related to membership. To apply *ringi* to oneself before going into battle is not merely to report or assert that one will accept the dangers of group membership, or to symbolize one's acceptance of those perils. It is in itself to accept them. There is no possibility for dissembling. Similarly, when one who was previously a resident alien joins native sons in sacrificing pigs and presenting pork to allies he is not symbolizing his willingness to discharge the responsibilities of membership in the local group. He *is* discharging them. His actions indicate his position because: (1) they are highly visible; they constitute a display and (2) they are intrinsic to, an aspect of, that which they signify. To attach oneself to a territory by planting a tree into which one has poured one's life principle, and to join a group by mingling one's life principle with those of others surely has an iconic aspect, for the acts bear formal resemblance to that which is being signified. Yet planting the *rumbim* is also an index of membership because the planting brings the membership into being if it did not previously exist.

This account may suggest, among other things, that the information transmitted in ritual may be highly redundant. Three successive rituals speak of membership. Leach (1966) and others (Bloch 1973) have stressed the ways in which ritual reiterates messages. It should be noted, however, that for the erstwhile alien these three rituals are not entirely redundant. In the first he accepts the dangers of membership, in the second its economic and ritual responsibilities. It is only later that he participates in the ritual which gives him rights of membership.

We note finally that what is being indicated, the membership of a previous alien, is on the face of it simple – a man is either a member or an alien. This clear and simple indication, however, emerges out of a rather complex process. Not only is the willingness of the former alien to accept duties and responsibilities prerequisite to his membership, so is his acceptance by the body of members. That his act of clasping the *rumbim* is, so to speak, a summary of complex private and public decision-making processes is a matter to which we shall return.

3. Index, icon, and number in the Maring ritual cycle

The planting of the *yu min rumbim* terminates hostilities and a truce ensues. Some years later – it may be more than a decade – when the group has what it considers to be sufficient pigs to discharge to ancestors and allies the debts incurred in the last round of warfare, the *rumbim* is uprooted and a year-long festival, or *kaiko*, is staged. During the *kaiko* debts to allies and ancestors are repaid in pork, and when it is finished the group may again initiate warfare.[4]

A local population entertains members of other friendly local groups from time to time during its *kaiko*, and it is useful to examine these festivals in some detail, for they are full of self-referential messages of great significance to the participants. They commence with the arrival, generally late in the afternoon, of the visitors. The most prominent feature of such occasions is the dancing of the local and visiting men to the accompaniment of their own drumming and singing. Dancing continues from the time the visitors arrive until early next morning, interrupted only at dusk for a formal presentation of food by the hosts to their guests. At dawn the dance ground becomes a trading ground; people from as much as a day's walk away, most of whom are members of neither the host nor visiting groups, convene to exchange, traditionally, bird plumes, shell ornaments, axes, native salt, and baby pigs.

We may recall that by dancing at the *kaiko* of another group a man signifies that he will come to his hosts' aid in future rounds of warfare. Given the structure of Maring society, ritual provides an especially effective medium for the transmission of this information.

The Maring are highly egalitarian. There are no political authorities capable of commanding men into the wars of others. Whether or not to assist another group in warfare is a decision resting with each individual male, and is made on the basis of his own considerations. Allies cannot, therefore, be recruited by appealing to other local groups as such. Rather, each member of the groups primarily engaged in hostilities appeals to affines, cognates and sometimes trading partners in other groups for help. These men, in turn, urge their co-residents and even kinsmen from yet other local populations to "help them fight."

The channels through which invitations to dance at a *kaiko* are extended are precisely those through which appeals for military aid are issued. Invitations to dance are not extended from one group to another but from individual men to kinsmen and trading partners, and these men, in turn, ask their co-residents and, possibly, kinsmen from elsewhere to "help them dance." The equivalence of dancing and fighting is, perhaps, further signified by the similarity of the pre-dance rituals performed by contingents of visitors to pre-fight rituals. A certain clay (*gir*) is ritually applied to the ankles and feet to strengthen them for both fighting and dancing, and certain pouches called *mbamp yuk* (fighting packages) in which are secreted occultly powerful materials including the exuviae of enemies, are applied to weapons, drums, shoulders, heads and feather headdresses to make them sharp, strong, ardent, and, in the case of the plumes, vibrant, fascinating, and attractive. The martial character of the dancing is also reflected in the stylized way in which visiting contingents enter onto the dance grounds of their hosts. They charge over the fence, voicing the long, low Maring war cry, led by a small vanguard of men brandishing axes or *mbamp yuk*, running back and forth in the peculiar stylized fighting prance of the Maring and other Papua New Guinea Highlanders. Their women come in quietly behind them, to be greeted by local women on the edges of the dance ground.

At first the visitors alone occupy the dance ground, but when they finish singing their entrance song the formation of local men joins them. The two groups dance separately for a while but gradually they merge and dance together until dusk when speeches are made by hosts, and food is given the visitors. The food consists, for the most part, of cooked vegetables – with taro being especially important – but also includes quantities of sugar cane for quenching thirst. It is presented to those visitors specifically invited to the *kaiko* by the men who invited them. The recipients immediately and publicly redistribute the food to those who have come to "help them dance." The hosts have displayed to them, in the course of this distribution, the number of followers each of those whom they have invited has been able to mobilize. In like manner, the food distribution provides some grounds for the visitors to assess the local status of the men inviting them. Donors assemble the foods to be presented to visitors by calling upon the men helping them to bring forth their contributions. How many men have assisted each donor, as well as the gross amount of food each donor has been able to assemble, is a matter for all to see. In sum, both hosts and guests are provided information concerning the social status of the men who connect them.

With darkness, dancing begins again and continues around low fires until dawn; women are the most numerous and significant spectators. The dancing is tacitly competitive. Men boast of dancing and singing without respite through the night, although most of them do take frequent breaks, and, by dawn, when trading replaces dancing on the *t'p kaiko*, (dance ground), only a few die-hard young men, weary, footsore, and hoarse, are still at it.

That the networks through which dancers are assembled and fed are icons of those through which military assistance is mobilized seems apparent, for the two are formally similar. But the term "icon" hardly does justice to their relationship. The dancing network is not simply "like" the mobilization network. The men invited to dance are men who are likely to be importuned for help in wartime, and those who "help them dance" are likely to be among those who help them fight. Given the near identity of dancing and alliance networks, and given the understanding that to dance entails a pledge to fight, the mobilization of visiting dancing contingents for *kaiko* has indexical as well as iconic value. Such events, in which alliance networks are, as it were, displayed in dance, are perhaps best regarded as iconic indices.

4. Natural indices in the Maring cycle

The self-referential messages indexically transmitted at *kaiko* entertainments have not been exhausted. There are yet others of a much simpler and more straightforward sort. We may turn here to the way in which men present themselves on these occasions. Their personal adornment is sometimes breathtaking.[5] The visitors come crowned in feathers of eagle and parrot and bird-of-paradise plumes, their heads encircled by bands of marsupial fur or iridescent beetles set in orchid fiber. They are adorned with fine nose pieces, ear plugs and pendants of pearl, conus and green sea-snail shell; about their necks hang strings of cowrie shells, trade beads, and Jobs' Tears, their arms are encircled by bracelets, and their waists by girdles of finely woven orchid fiber, through which are draped elegant striped loin cloths embellished with marsupial fur and into which are set elaborate bustles made from a variety of ornamental plants. Their faces glow with designs executed in red, blue, yellow, green, black, and white pigments, and their bodies glisten with pandanus oil. When they charge onto the dance ground shouting, their brilliant plumes bravely vibrating, their drums beating, their dancing bustles rustling, they are greeted by the cheers of the spectators, mostly women, standing on the periphery. The local men, who have taken equal pains to bedeck themselves in similar fashion, are also very attentive to the arrival of the visitors, but are usually much less vocal in their appreciation. There is considerable competitiveness among men concerning their finery, and they express both the hope that their own will awaken desire in the breasts of the women of the other group, and the fear that their own women will be attracted by the splendor of the others. A prominent aspect of the ritual that precedes such an occasion is to make one's own appearance and performance irresistible to women, to protect one's own women from being dazzled by men of the other group, and to prevent them from running off with those men. Such ritual includes not only spells made upon ornaments or upon objects that are then applied to parts of the body or to paraphernalia such as drums, but also, for host groups at least, public entreaties to certain spirits.

It is not necessary to dance all night to indicate future military support; that pledge is signaled simply by dancing in the formation as it enters the dance ground. Most older men drop out at, or soon after, the food distribution, but the younger men continue, only in part for the sheer pleasure of dancing. By continuing, they signify their interest in the unmarried female spectators, who they hope will find them attractive and make overtures to them.[6] The dancing of men at *kaiko* may be regarded as instances of what ethologists call "epigamic display," amatory displays forming all or part of courtship procedure and noted in species as different from our own as the Great Crested Grebe and the Fiddler Crab.

At Maring festivals, then, samples of eligible males are presented to sets of eligible females who may not be familiar with them. Moreover, the mode of presentation permits young women to compare the men along lines that have bearing upon other matters. A man's wealth and connections are signified in some degree by the quality and amount of his ornamentation, his general endurance, as well as his comeliness, by the vigor, grace and endurance of his dancing. To put the matter in the converse, since the richness of his finery is really affected by his wealth and connections, and since it is plausible to assume that his dancing prowess is really affected by the physical, mental and emotional characteristics collectively making for grace, vigor, and endurance, information concerning both the economic status and psycho-physical characteristics of men is indexically signaled to women (and others as well) at *kaiko* entertainments. The men are not merely *symbolizing* these personal characteristics by adorning themselves and dancing. They are *displaying* them. It may be noted that the indexicality of these displays seems to be, in a sense, more simple and direct than some of the other instances of indices we have adduced. For instance, the indexical relationship between dancing and pledging to fight is an indexical relationship between two conventions. As such, it is what might be called a "second order index." In the case of dance networks displaying mobilization networks the signal is iconic as well as indexical. The relationship between a man's dancing prowess and his endurance, in contrast, seems almost as simple and direct as the relationship between a dark cloud and rain. It is "naturally" indexical.

At the last events of the festival, a little more than a year after its commencement, the hosts finish discharging their debts to their ancestors (for help in the last round of warfare) by sacrificing most of their pigs to them, and they discharge their obligations to allies and affines with the flesh of the selfsame pigs. Their accounts with the living and the dead squared, they may once again attack their enemies, secure in the knowledge that they will receive the help of both the living and the dead, and warfare was likely to break out soon after *kaiko* was completed. Be this as it may, the completion of a *kaiko* was an index of – i.e., indicated – the martial, ecological and economic competence of the group sponsoring it, for to stage a *kaiko* required, first, that it successfully defend its territory, and, subsequently, that it successfully raise sufficient pigs to discharge its debts.

5. Ordinal and cardinal messages

One other aspect of the events culminating the *kaiko* is of interest here. The day after the pigs are sacrificed the hosts invite all those whom they have entertained on separate occasions during the year. A thousand or more people from a dozen or more local populations may be present at once on the dance ground. One by one the names of the men of the other groups to whom appeals for help were made in the last round of warfare are called out by a herald standing astride the *pave*, a high (fifteen to twenty foot) ceremonial fence built of poles and saplings specially for the occasion at one end of the dance ground. When his name is announced an honored man, followed by his retinue, battle-chanting and drumming, charges toward a window in the *pave* through which a hero's portion of salted pig belly is thrust into his mouth. He dances away, the fat dangling from his clenched teeth, brandishing his ax; the spectators cheer. There is a rough gradation of honor indicated in the order in which names are called out, the first being most honored, and the next few highly honored. One whose name is called last is inclined to feel insulted when he discovers that no name follows his. In some cases, it is clear who should be accorded highest honor. Kinsmen of allied men slain in aid of the local group are most honored, and are called first. Next in honor are those men who killed enemies, followed by men who have sustained or inflicted wounds on the local behalf. Others who helped follow. Since there is likely to be more than one man in each category, decisions concerning precedence usually must be made. Self-referential messages may be transmitted by groups as well as by individuals, for the order in which men are honored is an outcome of group processes. In the course of some rituals, performers not only transmit messages concerning their status as social persons in the structural systems in which they participate, but they may also be informed of their statuses in those systems.

Allied men thus have indicated to them their places in a structured system by giving them positions in its roster of honor. In another ritual mentioned earlier, the acquiescence of the other men is surely required before an erstwhile alien can join them in planting *rumbim*, and thus join their group. Their acceptance of him, no less than his acceptance of membership, is indicated by the performance of the ritual. Acceptance is signified indexically in this instance, since to allow him to participate in the ritual itself constitutes acceptance.

To summarize, a range of self-referential messages are transmitted through participation in Maring rituals. They are, moreover, transmitted indexically. Although the bases of their indexicality may vary, as in the Maring case, it is doubtful if ritually transmitted self-referential messages are ever totally devoid of indexical components. This is of considerable importance in light of the problems of falsehood, credibility and credence raised in the first chapter.

A concern with variation in the participation of individuals (whether or not they participate) has led us to consider variations in contents. The two are hardly distinct. The "shapes" of the networks displayed in dancing, for instance, are organized outcomes of many individuals' decisions concerning participation.

There are usually possibilities even in the most invariant of liturgical orders for variations of a numerical sort, with possibilities for both their cardinal and ordinal characteristics to be significant. The capacity of the ordinal to convey information is nicely illustrated by the events at the *pave*. A number of men are placed in an order differentiating among them in honor. In other rituals the cardinal aspects of variation are more important. *Kaiko* entertainments not only provide opportunities for individuals to transmit information concerning their own individual states, but this information must be summarized, and such summarizations may be what is most significant to the receivers. The hosts of *kaiko* seemed to me more keenly interested in the size of visiting dancing formations than they were in their finery or fettle, because the quantitative information concerning future military support produced by the series of summations that *kaiko* made possible was significant in their deliberations concerning the actions they might take in the future.

The summative aspect of some public rituals, while straightforward and simple, does merit some further discussion. First, following Wynne-Edwards (1962)[7] and others, *kaiko* entertainments may be termed "epideictic." Epideictic displays are those which communicate to the participants information concerning the size, strength or density of the group of which they are members through the simple expedient of displaying the membership to itself. Widespread among animals, examples of epideictic displays include the "dancing of gnats and midges, the milling of whirligig beetles, the maneuvers of birds and bats at roosting time, the choruses of birds, bats, insects and shrimps" (p. 16). Epideictic displays, Wynne-Edwards further observes, usually occur at conventional times and in "traditional places" (p. 17). Wynne-Edwards' further specification, however, that such displays precede actions that restore or shift the relationship of the population to its resources, may not be as generally applicable to events displaying populations to themselves. It is reasonable to take the Sunday service at the local Methodist church to have an epideictic aspect, for it does display to the congregation its own size, but the display of this information is not usually a prelude to actions restoring or shifting the relationship of the congregation to its resources. *Kaiko* entertainments, however, seem epideictic even in Wynne-Edwards' narrow sense. One of the ways of restoring or shifting population balance is by redispersing organisms over land. The *kaiko* takes place near the end of a ritually established truce, and, after its termination, the existing pattern of population dispersion may again be tested, and possibly modified, through warfare. The *kaiko* permits a group to assess the strength of the military force it may be able to field while the truce is still in effect. Other Maring rituals have an epideictic aspect; these include the planting of rumbim which indicates to those participating not only who is or is not in fact a member of their group but how large the group is. The epideictic aspect of such rituals follows as a consequence of the simultaneous public transmission of indexical messages by individual participants.

6. Quantification and the substantial representation of the incorporeal

In the case of the epideictic rituals, populations are directly represented by their own metrical characteristics, samples (of either the whole or a part) of themselves. As such they are simply and directly indexical. But the indexical transmission of quantitative information in ritual is not limited to variations in numbers of performers, and may concern matters other than group size and strength. Moreover, quantitative representations do not always seem to be intrinsic to that which they represent. In the potlatches of the northwest coast Indians (Codere 1950, Drucker 1965: 131ff.), in the *abutu* of Goodenough Island (Young 1971), and in the *muminai* feasts of the Siuai of Guadalcanal (Oliver 1955), to cite some well-known examples, information concerning status, worthiness and political influence is indicated by variations in the amount of food and valuables distributed, destroyed or consumed.

These rituals do more than count and total. They translate such important but incorporeal, complex and non-metrical aspects of social life as prestige, worthiness, honor, shame and influence into terms that are not only simple and metrical but also concrete. We note here an inversion of the more familiar qualities of the sign and the signified. We are more accustomed to the sign being insubstantial and the signified substantial as, for instance, in the relationship of the word "dog" to the animal it designates. The representation of the incorporeal by the substantial is of considerable interest and, perhaps, even of fundamental significance, but its consideration must, in the main, be postponed. Here we need only suggest that in cases in which representations are made of states, conditions or qualities such as prestige or valor which are themselves without physical properties the sign may have to be substantial if it is to be taken seriously. If the sign were insubstantial it would be nothing more than a claim, mere words, "hot air." Be this as it may, ritual signs are frequently substantial, a matter to which we shall return. Other aspects of rituals in which self-referential messages are carried by variations in number of objects employed do bear discussion here.

First, it may be objected that in rituals such as potlatches and *muminai* feasts prestige or worthiness are not so much signified as achieved. Moreover, more is being accomplished than the acquisition of prestige or influence. Large quantities of foodstuffs are being distributed and so on. The economic and ecological functions of such rituals seem to me to be reasonably well-founded but, in light of the distinction between ritual and rituals made in chapter 2, do not need to be discussed here.[8]

It is no doubt the case that men achieve status as well as communicate information about it in the course of such rituals. The distinction, however, is not a sharp one, for the achievement of status entails its recognition. Status, by definition, is public, but to be recognized, information concerning it must be transmitted, and such information clearly and effectively transmitted in the displays central to these rituals. Prestige and worthiness are not simply being described, claimed or reported in them; they are being substantiated. To foreshadow some of the concerns of chapter 4, doing and saying are not only inseparable, but are virtually indistinguishable in these events.

One implication of this argument is that the concrete representations of incorporeal qualities in these rituals are *necessarily* accurate. If a society accords prestige on the basis of competitive public distributions, then he who distributes more has more prestige. If this were all, these displays might not amount to much more than a wasteful pastime (which *might* have been the case in the instance of the late post-contact potlatch). It is obvious, however, that the worthiness, influence or renown being represented are related to states of affairs external to their display. The amount a man distributes can hardly be other than a function of his own and his wives' hard work, his skill in mobilizing supporters and his ability to cajole or coerce them into contributing to his efforts. The display, therefore, stands in a direct indexical relationship to that which it represents.

It is worth noting that although the signal – the display – in these cases stands in an indexical relationship to that which it represents, it is simpler. To simply recognize as more influential he who has distributed more does not in itself attend to the nature of the networks through which he or his rivals have assembled that which they later distributed, what their strategies of accumulation were, or what they had to promise to whom. Some of these nuances may be communicated in details of the events, (as when a sponsor's supporters bring forward their contributions separately – see, in addition to the Maring example already offered, Young (1971: 199) concerning tardy helpers at Goodenough *abatu*), but in general the display communicates less than is there. Such simplification may sometimes be misleading – for instance, the man who has put on a big display may have overextended himself to do it, and his position may be much shakier than it appears to be – but it also reduces complexity to manageable dimensions, facilitating comparisons between men.[9]

7. The digital representation of analogic processes
We have been concerned in the last pages with the assessment of such aspects of social life as prestige, influence, shame and worthiness by counting numbers of pigs, pearl shells, blankets, coppers, plaques, and other valuables, and it is now obvious that some rituals operate as public counting and ordering devices. But it is important to note that their operation includes more than simple counting or ordering. Fundamental to the operation of counting are things that may be counted, that is, discrete entities of some sort. In these rituals, incorporeal qualities, in their nature only vaguely metrical and certainly not numerable, are given a form that is not only material but clearly metrical, like numbers of pigs, coppers, and copper plaques. In this regard, ritual display illustrates a more widespread phenomenon, the digital representation of analogic properties or processes.

Communications engineers distinguish between two types of computation, analogic and digital, and between the entities and the processes employing them. Speaking roughly, the distinction is that between measuring and counting. The term "analogic" refers to entities and processes in which values can change through continuous imperceptible gradations in, for instance, temperature, distance, velocity, influence, maturation, mood, prestige and worthiness. Signals, like other phenomena, may be analogic. Cries of pain, for instance, can proceed through continua of imperceptibly increasing intensity that may indicate the intensity of the suffering they signify. The term "digital," in contrast, refers to entities or processes whose values change not through continuous infinitesimal gradations but by discontinuous leaps.

Examples of discontinuous phenomena that lend themselves "naturally" to digital representation are the beating of the heart and changes in the size of animal populations. Some objects include both digital and analogic elements. Thus, a thermostat contains both an analogic element, a column of mercury or a bimetallic bar, either capable of and subject to continuous change, and a digital element, a switch which fluctuates back and forth between two discontinuous positions, "on" and "off." As there are analogic signals so may there be digital, employing discontinuous terms or scales like numbers of pigs or blankets. Analogic processes can be, and often are, represented digitally. Although time is continuous, and may even be conceived as such, it can be represented digitally, and is on many watches; so can distance. We can measure time and distance, but we can also count days, minutes, light-years, and miles. Prestige and influence, like time, distance, and angular displacement may be continuously variable, but they can be represented precisely through, say, the distribution of numerable objects, for example, blankets at a potlatch or pigs at a Melanesian feast.

The rituals we have been considering are instances in which continuous phenomena are represented digitally. There seem to be some clear advantages in digital representation in these instances. Indexical information concerning prestige, influence and the like transmitted through such indices as pigs, coppers and blankets is more precise than that to which it refers, and the imposition of the metrics of discrete units upon phenomena which are not themselves composed of discrete units, that is, the imposition of digital computation and signaling upon continuous processes or undifferentiated phenomena, helps to define – make definite – important but vague aspects of the world. Comparing the status of contending men becomes relatively easy when status can be assessed by the numbers of coppers, yams or pigs given away, consumed or destroyed. Thus, a Siuai man who wished to contend with Soni of Turunom village for prestige and influence in 1937 needed to match or better him at the *muminai* feast in which, before 1100 people, he distributed exactly thirty-two pigs worth precisely 1920 spans of shells (Oliver 1955: 439).[10] Precision is not accuracy, and sometimes there may be loss of accuracy in the representation of analogic processes or entities digitally. The advantage of digitalization is that it increases clarity. The representation of influence, prestige or worth in numbers of discrete units, such as pigs, reduces the vagueness of social and political situations by facilitating comparison. To the extent that digitalization depends upon material representation this reduction of vagueness is a function of substantiation as well. Be this as it may, thirty-two pigs thrown into a feasting competition are, simply and obviously, more than twenty-five.

Two qualifications are in order here. First, the extent to which ritual displays decrease vagueness may vary. Maring *kaiko* hosts here witnessed the entrances of their guests, but they were not, until the arrival of Europeans, accustomed to count past twenty, and their estimation of how many warriors attend their festivals remain imprecise. Even in high order precision ambiguity may remain. Thirty-two pigs may be clearly more than twenty-five, but in the course of events rather than in the procedures of arithmetic it may not be so clearly more than thirty-one. The outcomes of some Goodenough *abutu* are, in fact, unclear despite their precision, because of the incommensurability of the different commodities distributed. Concerning the aftermath of such a competition Young writes:

The principal *Inuba* counts his *liva* measures and finds, perhaps, that he has a platform of taro ten feet long and a dozen yams of various types and sizes still to pay back. His enemy, he notes, owes him eighteen bunches of bananas, a couple of wooden platters of *tait* and six yams of an impossible size. Their pigs were equal. He may conclude that he has won because of the bananas, while his opposite number, making similar calculations in his own house, may conclude that victory is his because of the taro. A few months later they will tend to agree with everyone else that it was "fair," a drawn contest. Only unmatched pigs and a wide discrepancy in the amount of vegetable food (particularly yams) can add up to victory or loss.   *(1971: 203)*

The second qualification, related to the first and implied in the passage just cited, is that vagueness and ambiguity also have a positive place in human affairs. Young continues: "Moreover, one *Inuba* might win in yams and his opponent in pigs – an ultimately satisfactory state of affairs because it enables the descendants of each to claim partial victory and obliges neither to admit total defeat" (p. 203).

To say that the digital representation of continuous phenomena intrinsic to some ritual displays decreases vagueness by increasing precision is not to claim that clarity always becomes crystalline, nor that clarity is in all instances to be preferred to vagueness and ambiguity. Orderly social life requires that some distinctions be made as sharply as possible and that others be fudged.[11] We have been concerned in this chapter, and will continue to be until its conclusion, with digital aspects of ritual communication. This does not imply that ritual communication is only digital. It is not, but attention to its analogic characteristics must wait until a later chapter.

8. The binary aspect of ritual occurrence

The representation of continuous phenomena by digital metrics and signals leads us from the contents of ritual to its occurrence. Whereas vagueness is reduced by the digitalization of aspects of ritual's contents, ambiguity concerning the current state of the performers may be reduced, or even eliminated by ritual's occurrence. The occurrence of ritual – like an individual's participation in a ritual – carries the digital to the extreme or, rather, to one step away from the extreme. That is, it brings it to the binary, to the reduction of discrete units or states to two only. Any ritual included in the repertoire of a society can at any given time only be occurring or not occurring. The occurrence of a ritual transmits a binary (yes/no, 0/1, on/off., either/or, boy/man, war/peace, etc.) signal. Indeed, binary signals are intrinsic to ritual occurrence, and they are, in their very nature, free of ambiguity.

It may be objected first, that this assertion is too true to be good: the binary characteristic of an occurrence for which significance is being claimed is intrinsic not only to the occurrence of ritual but to events generally. Information is intrinsic to observable difference,[12] and occurrences other than those of rituals are surely observable. We may ask, however, "what is an event?" When and how does it start or conclude? What constitutes its occurrence? The formality and non-instrumentality of ritual makes its occurrence clearer than that of many other "events," whose demarcation in time and space is arbitrary. The same characteristics also indicate that a message is being transmitted and what the message is. Further, "the meanings" of other sorts of events, events in which spontaneous novel or idiosyncratic features (rather than stereotyped, formal, repeated, traditional features) are most prominent cannot be immediately apparent. They are, rather, products of interpretation and, of course, interpretations may vary. Finally, while information can surely be gleaned from all events that can be recognized as such, not all events can properly be regarded as communication events.

It may also be objected that the significance of ritual occurrence is often trivial. The parishioners of the local Methodist church are, after all, not told much by the occurrence of a service at their church at 10:00 am on Sunday. At best the occurrence of a calendrical ritual is a "match signal" indicating that the system of which the ritual is a part continues to function. The *failure* of a calendrical ritual to occur, on the other hand, indicates that something extraordinary, probably bad, has happened. In contrast, occurrences of *non-calendrical* (and non-circadian) rituals often constitute signals of great significance, and it is with them that we shall be concerned. The question of first importance concerning the occurrence of such a ritual is "What caused it to be performed?" In some instances the answer is obvious. A curing ritual is performed, let us say, in response to the appearance of whooping cough symptoms in a child. But triggering factors are not always so clear or simple.

Although the occurrence of a ritual *transmits* a yes/no, or either/or signal, it may have been *triggered* by the achievement or violation of a *particular* state or range of states in a continuous, or at any rate, more-less process (such as physical maturation or changes in the size of a herd of livestock), or even of a *complex* state or range of states defined by relationships among a number of such processes. As such, the occurrence of a ritual may be a simple qualitative representation of complex quantitative information. Since the latter may be analogic, or if not itself analogic, comprised of digital representations of continuous processes, the occurrence of a ritual may summarize information concerning complex continuous processes and translate them into the simplest possible digital signal. To put it differently, the occurrence of a ritual may impose a "yes/no," "either/or" summary or decision upon a "more-less" process. The inauguration as President of *either* one *or* the other of a pair of contenders is a simple example of such an imposition. One candidate is inaugurated and the other is not, whether they were separated by one vote or millions. In the reduction of the electoral results to the either/or summary of the inauguration there is, of course, a great loss of information concerning both the results and their causes. The ritual makes, so to speak, a sharper distinction than is "in" that which it summarizes.

The social importance of this simplifying operation is perhaps most

generally illustrated by "puberty rites." Physical and intellectual development is generally continuous and gradual (although marked by certain
periods when growth is especially rapid or slow). Considerable vagueness
and ambiguity surrounds individual maturation, particularly during
adolescence; it alone would hardly be sufficient to order behavior. If
guided by nothing more than their own development, individuals might
well be uncertain as to whether to act as children or adults, and others
would be equally uncertain of what to expect from or to demand of
them. Behavior, however, is ordered more in terms of categories of
persons than in terms of the continuities of individual maturation, and
the categories are at least as social as they are physical and intellectual
(child/adult, boy/man, girl/woman, etc.). Van Gennep (1960[1909]: 65ff.)
long ago observed that "social puberty" and "physiological puberty" are
"essentially different" and "rarely converge." He was surely correct, but
this is not to say that they are unrelated. Categories signifying degrees or
stages of social maturation may impose upon the continuities of physical
and intellectual development distinctions otherwise not there. Rituals
concerned to apply such categories to persons or to transfer them from
one such category to another – rites of passage – bring clarity and
certainty to an ontogeny which would otherwise remain obscure and
uncertain.

   In a few societies young people themselves dispel uncertainty concerning their status by initiating their own rites of passage. In the Society
Islands, for instance, boys between the ages of eleven and fourteen decide
to have themselves supercised,[13] thus passing from the status child to
that of *taure'are'a* (Levy 1973: 117ff., 368ff.). The latter status contrasts
with the former in several ways. It is characterized by greater autonomy,
and by an attenuation of the boy's connection to his parent's household,
and there is also, according to Levy, a concomitant shift in his "desires
and activities." Moreover, although the custom is sometimes breached,
supercision is supposed to precede first intercourse. It is said that sex
might split an unsupercised foreskin, and that girls dislike the unsupercised penis. Lads are thus motivated to undergo the operation, and they
are further goaded by the teasing of older boys. Usually small groups of
close friends decide to go through the operation together, arranging with
a knowledgeable man to operate on them. They do not consult or even
inform their parents of their intentions (they say it would worry their
mothers),[14] and the operation is performed secretly in a secluded place.
But the boys advertise their new status over the next few days by their
exaggerated manner of walking, and perhaps, by indicating – or feigning

indications of – tenderness in the genital region in other ways. That a boy has undergone the operation signals unambiguously to the community that certain complicated biological, social and psychological developmental processes have not only reached a point at which he is prepared to leave the status of child and assume that of *taure'are'a*, or a point at which they could or might do so, but that he has done so. Much complex, unobservable and unclear "more-less" information concerning continuous processes is reduced by supercision to a single highly visible "either/or" signal.

It may also have been the youth who declared his changed status among the Thomson River Indians of Western Canada, for among them, according to Teit (1906: 317ff.), a boy would undertake a vision quest sometime between his 12th and 16th year after having dreamed of an arrow, a canoe or a woman. But the matter is perhaps not so clear among the Thomson River Indians as among the Tahitians, and it is even less clear among other American Indians. Winnebago girls and boys, for instance, may have finally decided for themselves whether to begin "fasting," but they were cajoled and browbeaten by their elders if they did not (Radin 1923: 87ff., 243ff.), and so Pettitt observes (1946: 90ff.) were Crow, Sioux, Hidatsa, Ojibwa, Delaware, Nez Perce and Salish children.[15] In light of such pressure and of the fact that children were brought up with the expectation of seeking visions, Pettitt questions the generally accepted belief that the beginning of vision quests should be ascribed to the initiative of the youthful questors. Be this as it may, the commencement of fasting, whether the child was chased and kicked into the forest, as seems sometimes to have been the case, or whether he ran off willingly to seek his vision or to find his guardian spirit, indicated a social transformation, or at least the first step in one.

More often than not, initiative for changing the status of children or youths comes from their elders (although the youngsters may be eager to be transformed). For instance among the Ndembu of Zambia (Turner 1967: 152ff.) boys between approximately six and sixteen years of age are circumcised, undergo other ordeals and receive instruction while secluded during an elaborate and protracted set of rituals called *Mukanda*. *Mukanda* is held in any "vicinage" (Turner 1967: 156) only once every decade or so, its occurrence seemingly being induced by changes in the distribution of the population among the categories of which the society is composed.

The occurrence of the *Mukanda*, even more than the occurrence of supercision in Tahiti, summarizes in a single highly visible yes/no signal a

great deal of vague information concerning complicated and not altogether observable processes,[16] including increasing shortage of boys to
do chores, increasing attachment of boys to their mothers, and the men's
anxieties about this, men's anxieties about pollution and the increasing
inconvenience of avoiding it, the increasing obstreperousness of undisciplined boys, the increasing antagonism between younger and older boys,
and probably, agitation by the boys themselves to be circumcised, as well
as by the desire of some men to compete for positions of honor in the
Mukanda.

Occurrence may be of importance in all rites of passage, but its importance is not limited to such rituals. We may return here to the planting of
rumbim by the Maring, and we may also allude to its subsequent
uprooting, for both rituals are induced by, and therefore their occurrence
indicates, the achievement, in continuous processes, of complex states
which are difficult or impossible for crucially interested parties to observe
directly or even, for that matter, to define. In the last section it was
pointed out that the planting provided an opportunity for men to
demonstrate their membership in a local group. It was, however, performed for another reason, namely to terminate warfare. *Rumbim* planting indicated that a local group had broken off hostilities.

Planting *rumbim* is induced by the formation of a consensus among the
men of one or both of the principal antagonistic groups to terminate
hostilities. The various and complicated factors affecting this consensus
include honor, anger, the number of casualties suffered and inflicted, the
willingness or reluctance of allies to continue their assistance, the call of
garden work. The enemy is not witness to these deliberations, and even
for those participating they must seem vague, ambiguous and confusing,
for the Maring do not make decisions through such devices as votes.
Eventually, they say, "The talk becomes one;" that is, sufficient agreement prevails to allow action to be taken, in this instance *rumbim*
planted, without anyone being adamantly opposed to doing so. Planting
rumbim signals unambiguously that the group has, in response to
complicated, continuous or at least more-less, processes, switched from
one to the other of its two possible states; that is, from a condition of
belligerency to one of non-belligerency. In most instances a group
responded to the news that its enemies had planted *rumbim* by planting
its own, if it had not done so already. The planting of *rumbim* by
antagonists, although conducted separately, seems generally to have been
roughly coordinated, possibly by word of each side's condition and

explicit intentions passing to the other through neutral populations (see Rappaport 1984).

The planting of *rumbim* initiates a truce which prevails until there are sufficient pigs to repay the ancestors and allies for their help in the fighting just finished. When consensus has it that there are sufficient pigs – often ten to twenty years later – the *rumbim* is uprooted, and the debts are discharged, largely in pork in the course of a *kaiko*. The uprooting of the *rumbim* and the several other sacrificial rites following it during the festival signal a transition from non-belligerency to potential belligerency. The occurrence of these rituals is induced by, and thus *indicates*, the achievement of a particular state ("sufficient animals to reward ancestors)" in a continuous process, the growth of the pig population. Since I have discussed this process elsewhere (Rappaport 1984), it is sufficient to note here that demographic change among Maring pigs is no simple matter. Among the important factors affecting it is the frequency of human misfortune, for serious illness, injury and death call for pig sacrifices. The alternation between nucleation and dispersion characterizing Maring settlement patterns may also affect the rate of the herd's growth. Since all domestic male pigs are castrated, pregnancies among domestic sows result from unions with feral boars, who seem to be loath to approach areas in which human habitations are dense. Sows are allowed to range freely, but there may be greater likelihood of their finding a boar when settlement is dispersed.

The number of pigs sufficient to reward ancestors is not given numerical specificity, but empirical investigations indicating "sufficiency" approximates the number of animals which the local group can support and tolerate: pigs must be fed, and, because of their propensity to invade gardens, they can become nuisances. But many factors affect the number that can be tolerated: the number, health and age of a group's women (women care for the pigs and do most of the work in gardens from which pigs are fed), the ratio of taro and yams to sweet potatoes in the gardens (pigs are fed mainly on sweet potatoes, people prefer taro), and the frequency of trouble and violence caused by pigs (the invasion of gardens by pigs frequently leads to strife between the pig owner and the garden owner). Moreover, people might not find a smaller number of pigs sufficient to reward ancestors should their enemies be preparing to pay off their ancestors. This choice is agonizing. If the number of pigs with which they reward their ancestors is small, their erstwhile allies, who receive most of the resulting pork, might conclude that they are people of little account and not worth supporting again. If they delay until they have more animals, they leave themselves open to attack by their more successful enemies. The rate of growth and maximum size of a pig population is an index of the general well-being or success of its owners. Given the number of factors affecting pig demography, the "general success" or "well-being" signaled by up-rooting *rumbim* is a highly complex state involving not only a large number of continuous and fluctuating variables, but also relations among those variables. Now this complex and fluctuating quantitative information, summarized or reduced by the uprooting of the *rumbim* into a single "yes/no" or "either/or" statement, is not available in entirety to anyone, not even to the group performing the ritual. But even if it were, its relationship to the belligerency status of the local group would be a matter for interpretation which, given its complexity, vagueness, and lability would, in its nature, be highly vulnerable to error. *But this difficulty is overcome if a mechanism, like the occurrence of a ritual, is available to summarize this unstable, uncertain, and complex quantitative information and translate it into a qualitative or yes/no signal.* Uprooting the *rumbim* is such a mechanism. Although the fluctuating processes inducing its occurrence are known only vaguely, ambiguously and incompletely, *its occurrence signals unambiguously* that the general condition of a local group is such that it may now undertake actions previously forbidden to it. Its occurrence is an unambiguous signal, not merely of a "more-less" change in the continuous processes of its ecological relations, but of a transformation from one to the other of two possible states with respect to warfare: from that of truce to non-truce.

In sum, the clarity of the messages of supercision and circumcision, of *rumbim* planting and uprooting derives from the opposition of ritual occurrence to non-occurrence. This opposition reduces great masses of complex "more-less" information to the answer to a single "yes/no," "on/off" or "either/or" question. In the terms of information theory the occurrence of a ritual contains one bit of information, a "bit" being that which eliminates the uncertainty between two equally likely alternatives. Single bit answers are both the simplest possible and, in the ordinary course of things, free of ambiguity. Since this is the case, ritual occur-rence may impose sharp, *unambiguous qualitative distinctions* upon *continuous ambiguous quantitative differences*, and so it does in the instances noted above (see Wilden 1972: 177).[17]

This chapter is generally concerned with the self-referential content of ritual, but the effectiveness of ritual's ability to impose clear distinctions, such as boyhood/manhood and belligerent/non-belligerent, upon continuous and otherwise ambiguous processes, and to signal those distinctions clearly is not confined to the self-referential. Ritual occurrence, which separates the before from the after with absolute clarity, is admirably suited to impose upon the continua of nature, generally, distinctions much sharper than nature's own. Annual rounds of festivals, for instance, distinguish the seasons from each other more sharply than do changes in the weather. The existence of such festivals makes clear that, although predictable, the occurrence of calendrical (and perhaps circadian) rituals is not always without significance. The certainty of their occurrence stands as if in defiance of the vagaries of weather as it careens from the hottest time of year to the coldest.

The binary characteristic of ritual occurrence does not limit it to single distinctions, for rituals are often arranged in series: rites of passage stationed along the straight paths leading each human from his birth to his end, festivals joining the seasons into circles, alternating rituals turning men from war to peace and from peace to war again, sabbaths punctuating sequences of days into weeks, the rituals set at the ends and beginnings of years. The durations between such rituals become, in part because they are set apart by rituals, not simple times when there has been more growth or the weather has grown warmer, but significant periods: childhood, youth, manhood; spring, summer, fall, winter; war and peace. Bound together by the very rituals distinguishing them, they form significant wholes: lives and histories, and the weeks and years that set lives into histories and societies and, in turn, societies and histories into the order of the cosmos. We will discuss ritual's role in the construction of time in chapter 6.

Ritual occurrence resembles digital computing machinery in its manner of operation as well as in its effects upon continuous processes. In an introductory textbook concerned with the logical design of digital circuits, C. M. Reeves wrote some years ago, "The successful operation of a real machine depends upon being able to separate the time intervals at which variables have their desired values from those in which they are changing. Logically, therefore, the passage of time is discrete where physically it is continuous" (1972: 7). Modern machines usually confine the time intervals in which the values of variables are changing in a continuous manner to micro- or nano-seconds, which, taken to be instantaneous, are ignored in its computations, which are based on values as they stood either before or after the change. In some rituals, similarly, the values of some variables are changed during the course of a ritual or series of rituals (Van Gennep 1986, Turner 1969). Between an act of separation from daily life and an act of reaggregation into it there is a liminal period during which some aspect of the condition or state of some or all of the actors is transformed. As in the case of the digital machine, the time during which the values of variables are changing in ritual is out of ordinary time, as Eliade (1959, etc.) and others have observed. In contrast to the machine, however, in which the "time between times" is virtually infinitesimal, liminal or marginal periods demarcated ritually may last for hours, days or even months or years. Moreover, we know that which occurs during rituals and that which is instrumental in transforming some aspect of the actors' states, is not always entirely discursive or digital. In the interstices of time, in the times out of time that lie between the befores and afters that rituals distinguish so clearly, there may be a time of continuous, highly affective performance in which boundaries and distinctions are obliterated rather than clarified. To emphasize, as I have in this section, ritual's digital aspects is not to deny its analogic aspects. In a later chapter we shall return to the analogic heart held both safe and harmless within the brackets of ritual's occurrence.

9. Ritual occurrence and the articulation of unlike systems

The occurrence of ritual not only articulates what it itself distinguishes, as the seasons by festival or sacrifice, or that it itself separates, as war from peace by formal declaration. We may note in the cases we have cited that it also facilitates – or even makes possible – the transmission of information across the boundaries of "unlike" systems. There are difficulties in defining whatever it is that distinguishes the systems that seem to be unlike, but, for now, such distinctions may be illustrated by the contrasting terms "private" vs. "public," processes or systems in our illustrations concerning rites of passage, and, in the Maring case, by the opposition "local system vs. regional system." In Tahitian supercision, information concerning the psychic and physical processes unfolding within a youth's privacy is summarized and transmitted into a public (social) system. In the Ndembu *Mukanda*, performed when the adult men decide to perform it, the flow from the public into the private system seems to be more significant. It is the men who transmit social information – information concerning their new status and its duties and prerogatives – to the boys who not only must, as public actors, incorporate this new information into their public persona, but must also somehow accommodate it into their private psychic processes.

In the Native American instances there seem to be important flows in both directions. In a formally similar way, uprooting *rumbim* transmits information concerning a local ecological system (a system of interactions between a local human group and the members of other species with which it shares its territory) into a regional system (a system of transactions including warfare, marriage and trade among a number of local human groups occupying a broader region).

Transduction (the technical term for the transmission of information or energy from one form or system to another) is not always a matter of mere transmission. It is often necessary to translate information into terms which are meaningful to the receiving system or subsystem. Sometimes translation, if it should even be called so, is a simple matter of changing modality, for instance from the grooves of a phonograph record to the sounds emanating from a speaker. The "languages" or metrics of the two subsystems, the record's grooves and the vibrations of the speaker, are supposed to correspond to each other perfectly. For every groove of a particular dimension there is a vibration of proportional frequency and volume, and continuous, analogic translation of information from groove to vibration of the needle to electrical impulse to vibration of the speaker to sound is both possible and desirable. But such nice correspondence between the organization and activities of interacting systems or subsystems is not common in nature, and certainly does not pertain in our examples. Public systems are not icons of private systems, nor does the Maring regional system correspond in structure or function to the local ecosystems in which its constituent populations also participate. Moreover, relations between public and private systems and between regional and ecological systems are not fully coherent. That is, the frequency, intensity and nature of social interactions among Tahitians, or any other people for that matter, do not vary in direct proportion to changes in the affective and physical states of the participants, nor do the exchanges of pork, pearl shells, and women among Maring local groups wax and wane in direct and proportional response to changes in garden yields or fluctuations in the sizes of the pig herds of the exchanging groups. Although they are related, and although the same entities – individual humans – are continuously participating in both, public and private processes are quasi-autonomous with respect to each other, and the same can be said for the relationship between ecological transactions of Maring populations and their regional social, economic and political relations. Neither member of either pair is a direct function or outcome of the system to which it is joined. Since this is the case, the processes inhering in, or even defining, the contrasting members of these pairs are not only distinctive but incommensurable. Public systems and private systems are not, to put it loosely, "about the same things," nor are they even in equivalent metrics or "languages."

The subjective metrics or languages of private systems are concerned with the organic and psychic; the phenomena to which they refer are many, varied and often unknown to or hidden from those experiencing them. They may include levels of blood sugar and caloric and protein intake; rate of growth and size; levels and types of physical and psychic stress; feelings of well-being, depression, anxiety, confidence, fear, frustration, anger, hate, love and reverence; wishes, drives and goals; the amounts and types of knowledge learned, and countless other things. The system is "about" the growth and health of the organism, the gratification of its needs and desires, and, finally, its own survival. "Primary process thinking" which is characterized by imagery, allusion, analogy, metaphor, metonymy and symbolism, rather than verbal formulation, from which there is an absence of negative conditional, or qualifying conjunctions and which is highly charged emotionally (Bateson 1972e, Brenner 1957: 534, Fenichel 1945: 47) has a prominent, perhaps even dominant place in private systems, or at least in some of the subsystems of private systems.

The metrics or languages of public systems, in contrast, refer to social, economic, demographic and political events, entities or processes: statuses and roles; marriage, trade and vengeance; birth rates and death rates; fission and fusion; social and cultural differentiation and homogeneity. Such systems "are about" the maintenance and transformation of social orders or perhaps about the persistence of associations of organizms whose interactions are governed in accordance with the conventions of social orders. "Secondary process thought," conscious, rational, largely verbal and obeying the laws of syntax and logic (Brenner 1957: 52, Fenichel 1945: 49) dominates in the ordering of public systems.

The terms of Maring local systems, although in large measure summarized in the dynamics of pig populations, are ecological. They refer to acreage in production and acreage in fallow, the organic content and structure of the soil, the proportions of crops in gardens, energy expenditure in various activities, energy and nutrient returns per unit area, and to energy expenditure, species diversity, the size and dynamics of the human population and their pig herd and many other things. The system is "about" trophic exchanges and the populations of different species participating in them. The metrics of the Maring regional system are concerned with the numbers of women given and received, valuables owed and exchanged, the numbers of men killed by enemies. The system is explicitly about alliance, trade and warfare, and implicitly about the continuity of a regional population, or a society, or even, possibly, a culture.

These distinctions fall short of providing unambiguous criteria by which to distinguish systems of different types, but it should be clear that to distinguish unlike systems is not necessarily to distinguish or separate *discrete* entities. Any human embodies a private psychophysical system (within which subsystems may, of course, be distinguished) at the same time that he or she participates in, or is a component of, a public system, and public systems may themselves be composed of more or less incommensurable subsystems. Local Maring groups participate in both local ecosystems, systems of trophic exchanges among sympatric populations of unlike species, and a regional system, a system of exchanges of personnel, goods and (through warfare) land, among allopatric populations of the same species. The term "system" refers here to more or less coherent sets of processes, and *not* to distinct entities. Unlike systems may share components, but they are composed of incommensurable transactions, have different goals, and are "in" different "languages" or metrics.

Since the processes of each of the systems we have taken as examples are distinct from those defining the system with which it is in interaction, and since their metrics are incommensurable, continuously fluctuating quantitative information from the one cannot be directly meaningful in the other. I use the term "meaningful" here to refer to the effect that information has upon the operations, particularly the regulatory operations, of the receiving system. To say that information is "not directly meaningful" is to say that it is expressed in terms that cannot, without translation, enter into the information processes of the receiver. But to say that information concerning the processes occurring in one system is not directly meaningful in another system is *not* to say that it is irrelevant. It is beyond argument that changes in the physical and psychic condition of the organisms composing a social unit may finally affect its operation, albeit probably not immediately or proportionately, and the same can be said of the relationship of the local ecological system to the Maring regional system. The problem, then, is to translate information *relevant* to the receiving systems into terms that are *meaningful* to it.

Ritual offers a solution to this problem. As we have observed, the on/ off of ritual occurrence may simplify the quantitative information that induced it into a simple yes/no or either/or signal. Such a signal is not only unambiguous, but, may also be meaningful to a receiving system of a type different from that of the transmitting system. For instance, supercision may be taken to be an either/or response to the question "boy or man?" Boy/man is a public or social distinction that may be imposed upon the continuous process of male maturation out of which, however, it seems to observers to arise. This is to say that the terms "boy" and "man" have meaning in both a public and a private system. Similarly, uprooting *rumbim* may be taken to be an answer of "yes" to the question: "Do the Tsembaga have sufficient pigs to repay their ancestors?" Sufficient pigs to repay the ancestors is, at one and the same time, a meaningful statement concerning both local environmental relations and regional political relations. To put it differently, it signifies an intersection of two sets of continuous and related but incommensurable processes, local ecological processes on the one hand and regional socio-political processes on the other.

We are noting here a cultural manifestation of a widespread or even universal phenomenon. Control transduction between unlike components of organic systems also seems to rely heavily upon binary mechanisms because of the difficulty of translating quantitative information directly between incommensurable phenomena (Goldman 1960), and Wilden (1972: 159) has written "[A] feature which emerges from the study of the nervous system seems to be that digitalization is always necessary when certain boundaries are to be crossed, boundaries between systems of different 'types' or 'states,' although how these types or boundaries might be operationally defined is unclear." This proposition, he argues, is supported by the application of the analog/digital distinction to phonology, psychoanalysis, play, exchange theory and anthropology.

10. Ritual occurrence and buffering against disruption

Ritual occurrence thus is suited, because of its binary nature, not only to make distinctions in continuous phenomena, but also to articulate processes that are unlike or incommensurable. Distinguishing and articulating are contrasting functions, but they are not contradictory. Times of war and times of peace are not only distinguished and signaled by Maring rituals, but they are articulated by the self-same rituals that distinguish them into a regulated alternation. The distinction between the private system of psychic and physical processes and the public system of status and roles is not an artifact of distinctions made by the occurrence of (and participation in) ritual, but ritual occurrence does sharpen the boundary between them, insulating them from each other at the same time and in the same way that it articulates them. As such, it protects the quasi-autonomy of each of the systems it articulates. This has adaptive significance.

We have already noted that the frequency, intensity and nature of social interactions do not vary in direct proportion to changes in the psychic states of those party to them. It may now be added that it would be disastrous if they did. The same may be said for the relations between other articulated systems, those both alike and unlike. It is a truism that no living system could survive without interacting with others, but it is no less true that nothing could survive if there were not partial discontinuities in chains of cause and effect. If there were not, disorders originating anywhere could quickly spread everywhere, and everything in nature would be continuously subject to intense and contradictory stresses. Causal discontinuities and the quasi-autonomy of the systems of which the world is composed are not only obvious aspects of nature; they are crucial. But to say that they are both obvious and crucial is not to say that they are to be taken for granted. Years ago Geoffrey Vickers (1968) observed that the problem of contemporary civilization is not that we are not one world, but that we are. Elsewhere (1969, 1977, 1994) I have argued that "hypercoherence," too great a degree of systemic coherence,[18] can be as lethal as too little.

Widespread disruption becomes increasingly likely with increasing coherence. It may be sown by word as well as by forceful deed, and it may arise in response to messages which are themselves innocent. But transduction through ritual occurrence reduces the likelihood of such disruption by reducing, simplifying and making the information transmitted both unambiguous and meaningful. This is to say that by establishing or protecting distinct and quasi-autonomous systems, ritual helps to limit the world's coherence to tolerable levels. Put a little differently, ritual occurrence not only may first distinguish and then articulate quasi-autonomous and distinctive systems, it may also reduce the likelihood that they will disrupt each other.

The matter is complex and even obscure, and therefore requires discussion and exemplification. We have already seen that the occurrence of a ritual may eliminate the ambiguity enshrouding the conditions invoking its performance. Continuous more-less processes, we have observed, may trigger the performance of a ritual, but it is in the binary nature of such occurrence to signal the transition from one to the other of two possible discrete states. Such a reduction of ambiguity, I have argued (and it is tantamount to tautology) enhances the clarity of messages so transmitted. I would now add that it "purifies" them, so to speak, as well. That is, although it may not eliminate all of the ambivalence that may attend their transmission, it does tend to neutralize the possibly polluting social effects of that psychic condition. For example, the planting of *rumbim* does not wait for each man, having fully reconciled all his anger, hostility, grief, doubt and other conflicting emotions, to come to a conviction, in agreement with all of his fellows, that now is the proper time to perform that ritual and thus break off warfare. The *rumbim* may be planted while many men remain ambivalent. Similarly, the young Tahitian male may arrange to be supercised while he continues to entertain doubts about leaving boyhood to become a *taure'are'a*. The planting of the *rumbim* signals to those planting it, as well as to others; the slash of the supercisor's knife signals to the boys having themselves cut even more than to others, that *regardless* of their continuing ambivalence they have taken *definitive* action, action, that is, redefining their social status. and that, in social terms, is that. For better or worse, the Maring man has, for the time being, left off being a warrior to become a gardener; the young Tahitian has irrevocably left boyhood to become a youth. The new social status is not nullified or even modified by ambivalence with respect to its assumption, or even by emotions and attitudes incompatible with it. Such attitudes are, as it were, "filtered out" in the process of ritual transduction: they are "private" psychic phenomena which have no place in the public social system. To put it differently, ritual occurrence protects social processes from infection by inimical psychic processes. This account underlines a point made in chapter 2, that performers themselves are likely to be the most important of ritual's addressees.

The protection of social processes from psychic "noise" (to employ another, common, communicational metaphor) is not limited to defensive "filtering." Decision is formally intrinsic to the occurrence of non-calendrical rituals, and thus is signaled by their occurrence. But the signal of decision does not simply reflect one of the many, countless, or even infinite number of states possible in continuous processes. The yes/no act of decision, implicit in the occurrence of the ritual, terminates the process of deciding. Thus, the occurrence of rituals (which may be indistinguishable from the decisions to perform them) are not merely induced by more-less processes. They are reflexively, imposed upon them, and set their limits. It may thus be suggested that the occurrence of, for instance, supercision or circumcision rituals cuts boys away from childhood, and may be important in elimination of childish attitudes which, if allowed to persist uninhibited, could impede their development toward manhood. Such rituals deprive juvenile attitudes and dependencies of institutional support, and since they are no longer appropriate and no longer supported they may be expected soon to wither. The single bit of information implicit in the occurrence of the ritual not only terminates boyhood, but (since the ritual's occurrence is the answer to an either/or question), by terminating boyhood, it commences another life stage. By participating in the ritual a boy effects one of the transformations in the process of his social ontogeny, a process only grossly correlated and insufficiently guided by physical maturation, by irrevocably informing himself of it. Similarly, the pursuits of war and the pursuits of peace, which would interfere with each other if they were not separated in time and space, are clearly separated by the *rumbim* rituals which, terminating the time for one and commencing the time for the other, impose upon political relations an order of sharp and unambiguous alternation, an order that is not intrinsic to the complex, continuous fluctuations in men's warlike ambitions, peaceable plans, economic well-being, feelings of honor and shame, or ecological and demographic fortunes. In planting or uprooting *rumbim* a group is informing itself, as well as others, of its change of state. It is probable that in *most* rituals participants transmit information concerning their own current states *to others, but in all rituals they transmit such information to themselves. Participation in ritual*, as observed in the last chapter, *is not only informative but self-informative.*

The content as well as the occurrence of rituals may be self-informative; for instance, a group is informed of its own size and strength in an epideictic display, although here we are more concerned with ritual occurrence. For ritual occurrence to inform the transmitter of his own state is more than simply reflecting, in the manner of a mirror, all of the complexity, ambiguity, vagueness and lability of his condition. It must *define* this state for him in terms that are almost the simplest conceivable, that is, as one of a pair of alternatives. He is either a warrior or a farmer, a "boy" or a "man," a member of this local group or of that one, regardless of whatever ambivalence continues to vex him privately. And, as the occurrence of one ritual alleviates the uncertainty of the moment by informing the transmitters of their immediate states, so may the successive occurrence of a series of rituals introduce enduring order into their days, their years, their lifetimes.

For participation in a ritual to indicate her state to a participant is for it to impose form upon her amorphous condition. Yet some question may be raised concerning the assertion of the self-informativeness of ritual participation, and it is well to make clear that this claim does not deny that in some rituals different participants have different functions, and that some seem to, and do, inform others. In rites of passage, for instance, there are novices and initiators, the bride and groom do not recite the entire liturgy transforming them into husband and wife, the communicant takes the Eucharist from the hand of the priest. There are in many rituals celebrants who present to other participants the definitions suitable to their states. But participation is nonetheless self-informative; it is only through participation that participants open themselves to such definitions of their states. An individual's participation is a result of, or an aspect of, his or her own action, which is frequently his or her own choice; even in instances in which he or she has, as a practical matter, little choice but to participate, he or she could at least conceivably do otherwise.

In some rituals, local ecological systems may be articulated to regional political systems, and in many others social units of different magnitude or type may be brought together. Our argument proposes, however, that in *all* rituals private psychophysical processes and public orders are at once articulated to each other and buffered against each other. This was clear in the case of the Tahitian youth, and it is no less so in the case of planting or uprooting *rumbim* among the Maring. By participating in these rituals each Maring man imposes upon his own private self a transformation of his public state. By uprooting *rumbim* he transforms himself from husbandman into potential warrior, by planting *rumbim* from warrior into husbandman.

The term or form by which the performer defines his state – man, warrior, knight, king, subject, penitent, citizen, sick man – does not arise fresh for the occasion out of his own understandings or out of those of his initiators, should there be initiators. Such are encoded in both the ordered sequences of events occurring within rituals and in the ordered series of ritual occurrences that bind together lives, societies, and the cosmos. They are, that is to say, carried by canon, and it is in canon that the participants both find and enliven them. They have meaning, first, within the canonical orders in which they are found, which is to say that their relationships to other terms found there are established and in some sense known, usually explicitly. They also have social and cosmological referents beyond the ritual's performance in space and time. By participating in a ritual the performer reaches out of his *private* self, so to speak, into a *public* canonical order to grasp the category that he then imposes upon his private processes. Canon, which is more or less invariant, provides very limited sets of categories in whose terms the participants' states may vary, either through irreversible transformations such as rites of passage, or through shorter term fluctuations, such as purity and pollution, trespass and atonement, the declaration and abrogation of taboos, alternations between war and peace. It is in the canon that the selves engaged in ritual find meanings which they refer to themselves. Without canon, ritual's self-referential messages would be meaningless or even non-existent as such. To dance at a *kaiko* would be no more than to dance. The canonical guides, limits and, indeed, defines, the self-referential. But this does not mean that the self-referential is unambiguously subordinated to the canonical. There is, as we noted at the beginning of this chapter, in all rituals of sufficient length to constitute liturgical orders, a self-referential message without which the canon would be without force, or even nonsensical. Discussion of ritual's self-referential messages thus leads naturally to ritual's canonical content. The next chapter will be concerned with their relationship.

4

Enactments of meaning

The complex relationship between the self-referential and the canonical streams of ritual's messages is best approached through further exploration of the relationship between saying and doing. After a preliminary discussion of general principles of efficacy we will consider a crucial indexical message, intrinsic to ritual's very form, alluded to at the end of the second chapter, in the absence of which the canon would be inconsequential. We approach here what I understand to be ritual's fundamental office and will discuss in this light the establishment of convention in ritual and the social contract and morality that inheres in it. These observations provide grounds for taking ritual to be humanity's basic social act.

At the end of the last chapter I argued that participation in rituals might not only indicate aspects of performers' contemporary states but impose transforming decisions on those states. A clumsy bit of sleight-of-hand may seem to be poorly hidden in that argument. To claim on the one hand that supercision, for example, indicates the achievement of a certain stage in a boy's maturation and, on the other, that it imposes a dichotomous decision on that process, may seem either ingenuously confused or disingenuously confusing. To indicate a condition would be one thing, to transform it another. The two, however, are not being confused. They are being conflated. Some, if not most, of the self-referential messages occurring in ritual do not merely "say something" about the state of the performer. They "do something" about it. That a Tahitian boy indicates something about his ontogenetic stage by having himself supercised is indubitable. It is no less indubitable that he has done something about it. Similarly, by dancing at a *kaiko*, a Maring man signals his pledge to help his hosts in warfare.[1] Dancing cannot help but

107

signal that pledge because, among the Maring, dancing brings that pledge into effect. This is further to say that that signal is indexical (and not merely symbolic) because the acts of dancing and pledging are one and the same. Such a pledge can, of course, be violated but, on grounds discussed in chapter 2, it may be asserted that there is no way to lie about having made the pledge.

It was earlier argued that many, if not all, of ritual's self-referential messages are indexical in character. I would now emphasize a point noted in passing in chapter 1: that the indexical nature of acts signalling conventional states (such as pledging) is a consequence of their accomplishment of whatever it is that they indicate. We earlier noted that the relationship between sign and signified in indexical self-referential transmissions is the inverse of what it is in more familiar symbolic transmissions. In the casual usage of everyday, we usually, and rather carelessly, take signs, indexical or otherwise, to report, describe, represent, denote, designate, reflect or otherwise signify states of affairs existing independent of, and usually previous to, our references to them. In the case of the ritual acts and utterances with which we are concerned, the sign brings the state of affairs into being and – here is the sleight-of-ritual – having brought it into being cannot help but indicate it. We shall return, a little later in this chapter, to ritual's one indispensable indexical message. We are further concerned in this chapter with the ways in which conventional states are transformed and, at a deeper level, how conventions themselves are established in ritual. Because, however, the significance of what I have been proclaiming to be ritual's most profound indexical message is best elucidated in such a context, we will first consider principles of efficacy.

1. The physical and the meaningful

Both the occurrence of ritual and ritual's contents form and transform that upon which they are imposed, but, as we noted in chapter 2, not primarily by force of energy or expenditure of matter. What is often called their "power"[2] rests upon other means or principles. We may discern in nature two general classes of efficacy – the physical and the meaningful. The efficacy of what Leach calls "technique," achieving as it does its results through the deployment of matter and energy in accordance with the laws of physics and chemistry is, largely if not entirely, physical, but prayer is not, nor is ritual, nor are words. Their efficacy is grounded in principles of communication.

Bateson has noted some general differences between the two classes:

when you enter the world of communication, of organization, etc., you leave behind the whole world in which effects are brought about by forces and impacts and energy exchange. You enter a world in which "effects" – and I am not sure one should still use the same word – are brought about by differences [bits of information] ...

The whole energy relation is different. In the world of mind nothing – that which is not – can be a cause. In the hard sciences, we ask for causes and we expect them to exist and be "real." But remember that zero is different from one, and because zero is different from one, zero can be a cause in ... the world of communication. The letter which you do not write can get an angry reply; the income tax form that you do not fill in can trigger the Internal Revenue boys into energetic action, because they, too, have had their breakfast, lunch, tea and dinner and can react with energy which they derive from their metabolism. The letter which never existed is no source of energy ... what we mean by information, the elementary unit of information, is a difference which makes a difference, and it is able to make a difference because the neural pathways along which it travels and is continually transformed are themselves provided with energy ...

The pathways are ready to be triggered. We may even say that the question is already implicit in them.

There is, however, an important contrast between most of the pathways of information inside the body and most ... outside ... The [external] differences ... are first transformed into differences ... of light or sound and travel in this form to my sensory ... organs. The first part of their journey is energized in the ordinary hard science way, from "behind." But when the differences enter my body by triggering an end organ, this type of travel is replaced by travel which is energized at every step by the metabolic energy latent in the protoplasm which *receives* the difference, recreates or transforms it and passes it on.

(1972d: 452–453; emphasis in original)

Because, in possible disagreement with Bateson, I take information to be no more than one form of meaning and because I do not think that all forms of meaning can be reduced to information in the strict sense, I designate the class into which ritual falls as that of "meaningful (rather than informational) acts."

To distinguish the meaningful and the physical as two distinct classes of efficacy, is not to propose that they are separate or separable in nature. That ritual achieves its effects through the communication of meanings does not imply that it does not both consume and mobilize energy and material, nor that technique proceeds in some mindless way without the guidance of meaning. Matter-energy devoid of information is necessarily devoid of life: information and other forms of meaning separated from matter-energy could be conceived as mathematical or formal abstraction, pure spirit or Platonic ideal, but the act of conceiving it as such, being a biological process like all other acts of conception, could not occur in the absence of matter and energy. Although there seems to be no direct relationship between the meaningfulness of messages and the amount of energy required to transmit them, the communication of meaning, both informational and of higher order, always requires energy and sometimes matter as well. Even speech is propelled by energy, and information is inscribed on paper, engraved on stone, combined in DNA and encoded on magnetized tape. Conversely, any change detected by an organism in the energy flux to which it is subjected, or any change it detects in its material environment conveys information to it, for information is, in one of its aspects, detected, or at least detectable, difference. Moreover, as Bateson observes, matter-energy and informational processes frequently cannot be separated from each other because the receipt of information leads organisms to expend their own energy to bring about effects that may include both material and informational elements. Matter-energy processes and informational processes, although they can be distinguished, are inseparable in nature, and it is of interest that the myths of many peoples, including both Australian aborigines and ancient Hebrews, describe creation, either in whole or in part, as an act or set of acts, imposing form upon an already existent but inchoate primordial matter (Bateson 1972b: xxiii ff.). Creation, this is to say, is conceived as the informing of substance and the substantiation of form. Higher-order meaning comes later.

Information and matter-energy processes may be inseparable in nature, but they, the objects they affect, and the ways in which they achieve their effects may be distinguished. Matter and energy, it seems clear, operate most effectively, that is with most predictable results, upon inert materials. The efficacy of information and other forms of meaning, on the other hand, rests not only upon the ability of senders to encode and transmit information, but upon the ability of others to receive those messages, that is to recognize, comprehend and take account of them.

Not all entities are equally capable of being informed. Mythic acts of creation aside, insensible and inert objects cannot receive messages at all. They can be formed and transformed and arranged so that they can convey information to others but they can't be informed. Organisms, social systems, and perhaps some machines constructed by humans can be informed, that is, receive messages and modify their behavior or understandings in light of such receptions. Obviously there are great differences among systems in their receptive capacities. Dogs probably have greater absolute capacity for being informed than do snails, and humans greater capacities than dogs.[3] While there are not known to be differences in the average capacities of the memberships of different human populations for receiving and processing information, there surely are differences between individuals *per se*. Moreover, common sense, if not empirical studies, suggest that there are differences among human groups as groups in their capacities to receive information and to be transformed by the information they receive, owing to differences in their size, literacy, technology, and special institutions for receiving, storing, interpreting and disseminating information.[4]

That there are differences in what members of different human groups take to be meaningful is, of course, the *raison d'être* of comparative anthropology. Be this as it may, it is obvious that few Americans would be informed of much by a speech in Mongolian, and the same may be said of some of the non-verbal as well as verbal messages transmitted in rituals. Most American youths might be deeply impressed by being subincised, but none, it is probably safe to say, would be hastened on the road to sociological manhood by such an operation, as would young Walbiri or Arunta. The ritual form may be universal, but all human rituals include signs specific to the society, church, or congregation in which they are performed, and the arrangement of sign elements into liturgical orders is also in some degree socially and culturally specific. If the reception of the messages encoded in liturgical orders requires that they be in some sense "understood" (which is not to say that they may not at the same time be mysterious), then it is necessary that they be in some way learned, because the understanding of signs only conventionally related to their referents could not possibly be specified genetically. This is to say that participants must be trained, indoctrinated or otherwise prepared to receive the messages rituals transmit. The work of Campbell (1959), Erikson (1966), Turner (1969) Wallace (1966) and Goodenough (1990) suggests that the ability to be informed by ritual is itself established in the individual, in part in the course of a series of rituals starting in early infancy and proceeding to maturity. Erikson (1966) has referred to this process of preparation as "ritualization," and we shall return to it in a later chapter. Here it is necessary to note only that the informative capacity of ritual, its ability to form and transform, rests not only upon its special mode of transmission but also upon its reception by specially prepared receivers.

The effects that can be achieved by the deployment of motion and energy on the one hand and meaning on the other are also obviously different. Physical effects – weights lifted, ditches dug, billiard balls knocked into pockets, acids neutralized, metals smelted, plants cultivated

– must rely upon physical processes for their achievement. Conventional effects, on the other hand – princes transformed into kings and words into promises, the profane made sacred and truces declared – can *only* be achieved by meaningful acts. Whatever energy may have been required by a young man to fulfill the responsibilities of knighthood, or even required to complete his transformation to knighthood, did not flow into his shoulder from the sword with which he was dubbed, nor from the voice of whomever it was who dubbed him. It came, to recall Bateson, from his breakfast and dinner. Dubbing transformed him into a knight not by the force of its blow but by informing him of his knighthood, or better, informing him *with* knighthood. (In fact, according to the Oxford Unabridged Dictionary, a man is dubbed *to* knighthood, the transformative aspect of being informed being emphasized.) Although certain physical acts were performed with certain objects in dubbing, whatever transformation took place in the passage to knighthood was neither a physical alteration of the young man, nor was it effected by a process that can be comprehended as physical, chemical or biological. The transformation was, and could only be, effected by communicating meaning to whomever was the locus of the transformation, and to other concerned persons, in accordance with the conventions of the society in which it was occurring. The same may be said of the transformations in group membership and belligerency status effected by the planting of *rumbim* among the Maring, and even of those rituals in which the initiate is subjected to severe pain and by which he or she may be left physically marked for life: scarified, subincised, circumcized, canines removed, septum pierced, fingers lopped off. The significant transformations produced by such operations are obviously not physical, nor are they outcomes of the physical changes *per se* wrought by such operations but of the meanings those changes carry.

Ritual acts, such as body mutilation, planting *rumbim* and dubbing are, to use Van Neumann's term, "markers," that is "observable bundles, units or changes of matter-energy whose patterning bears or conveys the informational symbols from the ensemble" (James Miller 1965: 164). It is, of course, a matter of great interest that humans, who have a range of codes and markers to choose from, employ precise, subtle, energetically and materially inexpensive speech for the transmission of some messages and comparatively crude, expensive and sometimes painful physical acts for the transmission of others. We touched upon this question peripherally in the last chapter, and will discuss it in greater detail in the next.

To distinguish between the domains in which the physical and meaningful prevail is not to declare that the boundary between them is sharp
or clear. It is unlikely that any sea has ever been parted by prayer or
turned back by command, and we may be equally confident that no
prince has ever been transformed into a king, no man and woman into
husband and wife, by matter and energy alone. But prayer as well as
drugs may have an effect upon the physical well-being of those praying
and even upon the health of those for whose sakes prayers are offered.
So may sorcery. Accounts of "voodoo death" are well-documented (for
recent discussions of such matters see Lex 1979, d'Aquili and Laughlin
1979) and provide us with reason to believe that the efficacy of some
rituals rests upon the ability of human organic processes to translate
information conventionally encoded in such utterances and acts as
cursing, bone pointing and shamanic projectile removal into chemical
and neural signals. These, in turn, may have further physical consequences, either beneficial or harmful, for the organism receiving the
message. It is significant that the ritual acts initiating attempts to achieve
organic effects are often simple and easy to observe, but the subsequent
neural and hormonal processes directly producing the effects are not.
They are extremely complex and they are hidden from direct view. The
precise nature of the causal principles relating the act to its ultimate
effect is, thus, obscure and even mysterious. The location, within human
organic processes, of the boundary between the domains of the physical
and the meaningful is not well known but cannot be a sharp one. It is
plausible to believe that the very obscurity of this region is one basis of
notions concerning the occult efficacy of ritual words and acts.

2. Speech acts

There are important differences among the occurrences that have been
rather casually included here in the class of meaningful acts. Events, such
as dubbings, *rumbim* plantings and supercision must be distinguished
from messages which simply inform receivers of conditions in their social
or physical environments.

First, such rituals are more likely to inform the participants of changes
in themselves or perhaps it would be better to say *with* changes in
themselves, than they are of changes in their surroundings.

Secondly, whereas simple messages concerning environmental conditions leave the responses of receivers to their own devices, rituals specify
their responses, often very precisely. When, in medieval Europe, a youth

was dubbed he was not stripped of his status to become anything desire or imagination suggested to him. He became a knight and nothing but a knight. When an alien grasps the *rumbim* of a Maring local group he becomes a *de jure* member of that local group, and nothing else. When they uproot *rumbim*, Maring husbandmen become potential warriors. When they are supercised it is *t'aure'are'a*, and nothing else, that Tahitian boys become.[5]

Thirdly, while a message concerning the state of the social or physical environment may lead us to undertake an action which will transform ourselves or the conditions surrounding us, at least some rituals themselves complete the transformations with which they are concerned. Dubbing, we have observed, does not tell a youth to be a knight, nor does it tell him how to be a knight. It makes him a knight.

Ritual is full of conventional utterances and acts which achieve conventional effects. "I dub thee to knighthood," "I name this ship the Queen Elizabeth," "I swear to tell the truth," "I promise to support you in warfare," "We find the defendant guilty." The importance of such utterances in the conduct of human affairs is so patent as to obviate the need to argue it, but philosophers, in the last few decades especially, have given considerable attention to their peculiar characteristics. J. F. Austin (1962) has called them "performative utterances" and "illocutionary acts," J. R. Searle (1969) includes them among what he calls "speech acts," F. O'Doherty (1973) refers to an important sub-class as "factitive" acts or utterances, J. Skorupski (1976) uses the term "operative acts" for a class resembling them closely.

It is important to make clear that the force of what I shall call "performatives," following Austin's earlier and simpler terminology, does not depend in any simple and direct way upon the effect of these acts and utterances upon the minds and hearts of those exposed to them. Whether or not he has reservations, planting *rumbim* joins a man to the group with whom he plants it. Regardless of what they may think or feel about it those who are excommunicated, outlawed, found guilty or demoted in rituals properly conducted by authorized persons are thereby excommunicated, outlawed, made felonious or degraded. If authorized persons declare peace in a proper manner, peace is declared whether or not the antagonists are persuaded to act accordingly. This is not to say that acts and utterances which are performative may not be persuasive, threatening, inspiring or otherwise affect the receiver in ways inducing him to act in particular ways. In the language of speech act theory they may have "perlocutionary" as well as "illocutionary" force.[6] It is to say that an action having a conventional effect is completed in the gesture or utterance itself.

Performatives differ in the scope of the action they complete. If an authorized person, following a proper procedure, names a ship the Queen Elizabeth, the ship is so named. Others may, if they like, call it "Hortense," but its name happens to be Queen Elizabeth, and that's really all there is to it. On the other hand, if a man has danced at another group's *kaiko*, thereby promising to help his hosts in warfare, that is *not* all there is to it, for it remains for him to fulfill his pledge and he may fail to do so. The naming, which not only constitutes an action but actually brings into being the state of affairs with which it is concerned, is of the class of performatives that we may call "factive."[7] Whereas many actions completed in ritual – dubbings, declarations of peace, marriages, purification – are factive, it is obvious that all are not. Some – among which are those that Austin called "commissives" (1962: 150ff.) – do not bring into being the states of affairs with which they are concerned, but merely bring into being the commitment of those performing them to do so sometime in the future.[8]

3. The special relationship between rituals and performativeness

While many liturgies are performative, where some sort of performative act is the main point of the performance, transforming war into peace, restoring purity to that which has been polluted, joining men and women in wedlock, performativeness is not confined to ritual. There is no advantage to be gained, for instance, in taking the publican's utterance "The bar is closed" to be ritual, but when he says "the bar is closed" it is thereby closed, and you are not likely to get another drink. Performatives are not confined to ritual, but there is a special relationship between ritual and performativeness.

First, the formal characteristics of ritual enhance the chances of success of the performatives they include. Like any other acts performatives can fail. If, for instance, I were to dub one of my junior colleagues Knight of the Garter he would not thereby become a Knight of the Garter, even if the conduct of the ritual were letter perfect. Conversely, if Queen Elizabeth dubbed Princess Anne's horse to knighthood it probably wouldn't make him a knight, even granted the well-known English tolerance of eccentricity. And if a befuddled cleric recited the funeral liturgy rather than the marriage service I doubt if the couple standing before him would thereby become objects of mourning (Austin 1962: *passim*). All of these instances of faulty performatives are of ritual performatives and ritual performatives can misfire. The ludicrous nature of these instances suggests, however, that they are less likely to do so than are other non-ritualized performatives because the formality of liturgical orders helps to insure that whatever performatives they incorporate are performed by authorized people with respect to eligible persons or entities under proper circumstances in accordance with proper procedures. Moreover, the formality of ritual makes very clear and explicit what it is that is being done. For instance, if one Maring casually said to another whom he happened to be visiting, "I'll help you when next you go to war" it would not be clear whether this was to be taken as a vague statement of intent, as a prediction of what he would be likely to do, or as a promise, nor would it necessarily be clear what might be meant by "help." To dance this message in a ritual, however, makes it clear to all concerned that a pledge to help is undertaken, and it is conventionally understood that that help entails fighting. Ritual, this is to say, not only ensures the correctness of the performative enactment, but also makes the performatives it carries explicit. It generally makes them weighty as well. If a message concerning the current states of participants is communicated by participation in ritual it will not be vague, and the formality, solemnity and decorum of ritual infuses whatever performatives the ritual incorporates with a gravity that they otherwise might not possess. In sum, simply by making their performatives explicit rituals make clear to their participants just what it is that they are doing and thus they specify, at least tacitly, what would constitute an abuse or violation of whatever obligations those performatives entail. Clear definition itself may reduce the likelihood of abuses and violations simply by leading people to "think twice" before acting. To put this a little differently, clear definition, which is intrinsic to the formality of ritual, itself possesses perlocutionary force, and so do the gravity, solemnity and decorum characteristic of many rituals. Reflexively, the perlocutionary force inhering in the formality of a ritual supports whatever performatives are enacted in that ritual.

There are two other closely related reasons for considering the performativeness of ritual. First, the association of the sacred and occult with performatives in magical and religious rituals may mystify their conventional nature, and this may enhance their chances of success. To take the state of affairs established by a king's enthronement to derive from the sacramental virtue of crown and chrism may be more effective with respect to the maintenance of the social order over which the king reigns than would be the recognition of enthronement as a naked performative, a mere conventional act, the effects of which could, for instance, in response to the short-run displeasure of his subjects, easily be reversed.

Second, as Ruth Finnegan (1969: 50) has suggested, albeit rather unspecifically, the "truth lying behind" assumptions concerning what is often called "the magical power of words" may be related to their illocutionary force or performativeness. It may be proposed, rather more specifically, that the magical power of some of the words and acts forming parts of liturgies derives from the relationships between them and the conventional states of affairs with which they are concerned. As we have already observed, the relationship of performatives to the states of affairs with which they are concerned is the inverse of that of statements. The facts, events or situations to which a statement refers presumably exist independent of and previous to the statement referring to them, and a statement is assessed true if it accords in some sufficient degree to those previously existing and independent states of affairs. Since performatives bring about the facts, events, situations, etc., with which they are concerned, these facts are subsequent to and contingent upon them. Performatives, and most unambiguous factives, are self-fulfilling: they make themselves true in the sense of standing in a relationship of conformity to the states of affairs with which they are concerned. In light of this it may be suggested that the performativeness, and more especially the factiveness of ritual acts and utterances provide a basis for occult efficacy in general, including the magical power of words in particular. Ritual's words do, after all, bring conventional states of affairs, or "institutional facts" into being, and having been brought into being they are as real as "brute facts" (Searle 1969: chapter 2, *passim*). It may also be that magical power is attributed to other words by extension of the principle of factiveness beyond the domain of the meaningful, in which it is clearly effective, into the physical, in which it is not, but we must be very careful about stipulating the limits of the effects ritual can accomplish. We have already argued in somewhat different terms that their illocutionary force may be augmented by perlocutionary force. The effectiveness of persuasion, threat, cajolery, inspiration and ecstasy may well thrust beyond the purely conventional, and beyond discursive consciousness into the organic, as in the cures of healing rituals and in the injuries of ensorcellment.

4. Ritual's first fundamental office
Performatives are not confined to ritual, and there seems to be more to some or even all liturgies than the performatives that they incorporate.

Indeed, some liturgies may not seem to include performatives in any simple sense at all. Many religious rituals do not seem to be directed toward achieving simple conventional effects through conventional procedures. If, however, simple performativeness is not criterial of ritual, something like it, but of higher order, may be. Although not all rituals are obviously and simply performative, performativeness itself may be made possible by ritual. We approach here the conjunction of formality and performance noted but not discussed in chapter 2. We come, this is to say, to what is intrinsic to the act of *performing* a liturgical order, and thus to the heart of the relationship between the self-referential and canonical.

The characteristic of liturgical orders salient here is the simple fact of their performance; that they must be performed. Without performance, there is no ritual, no liturgical order. Records or descriptions of liturgies performed in Ur and Thebes survive but they are merely *about* liturgies not themselves liturgies. They are remains of the dead, for the liturgical orders they recall are no longer given life and voice by the bodies and breath of men. Performance is not merely one way to present or express liturgical orders but is itself a crucial aspect or component of the messages those orders carry. The following may seem involuted. The involution is intrinsic to the phenomenon, and not to my account of it. A liturgical order is a sequence of formal acts and utterances, and as such it is realized – made real, made into a *res* – only when those acts are performed and those utterances voiced. This relationship of the act of performance to that which is being performed – that it brings it into being – cannot help but specify as well the relationship of the performer to that which he is performing. He is not merely transmitting messages he finds encoded in the liturgy. He is participating in – that is, *becoming part of* – the order to which his own body and breath give life.

To *perform* a liturgical order, which is by definition a more or less *invariant* sequence of formal acts and utterances *encoded by someone other than the performer* himself, is *necessarily to conform to it*. Authority or directives, therefore, seem intrinsic to liturgical order (see Maurice Bloch 1973). The account just offered suggests, however, something more intimate and perhaps more binding than whatever is connoted by terms like "authority" and "conformity." The general notion of communication minimally implies transmitters, receivers, messages, and channels through which messages are carried from transmitters to receivers. Sometimes, furthermore, as in the case of canonical messages, which ritual's performers find already inscribed in prayer books or prescribed by tradition, transmitters should be distinguished from encoders, whose identities may be lost in time and whose dicta are, in part for that very reason, timeless. We earlier noted a peculiarity of ritual communication, namely that in ritual the transmitter and receiver are often one and the same. At least the transmitter is always among the most important receivers. Now we note another of ritual's peculiarities. *To say that performers participate in or become parts of the orders they are realizing is to say that transmitter-receivers become fused with the messages they are transmitting and receiving. In conforming to the orders that their perfor- mances bring into being, and that come alive in their performance, performers become indistinguishable from those orders, parts of them, for the time being. Since this is the case, for performers to reject liturgical orders being realized by their own participation in them as they are participating in them is self-contradictory, and thus impossible. Therefore, by performing a liturgical order the participants accept, and indicate to themselves and to others that they accept whatever is encoded in the canon of that order.*

This act of acceptance is the first of ritual's fundamental offices. The self-referential and the canonical are united in the acceptance of the canon. Acceptance is the self-referential message intrinsic to all liturgical performances, the indexical message without which liturgical orders and the canonical messages they encode would be without consequence, non- existent, or vacuous. It is not a trivial message because humans are not bound to acceptance of particular conventional orders by their geno- types. They are often free not to participate in rituals if they do not care to, and refusal to participate is always a possibility, at least logically conceivable, by potential actors. Participation, and thus acceptance, always rests in logic and in some degree in fact, upon choice. Such choices may sometimes be extremely costly, but are always possible.

5. Acceptance, belief, and conformity

The assertion that acceptance is intrinsic to liturgical performance may still seem to be either dubious or indubitable. It therefore requires some elaboration and clarification in this section and the next.

First, *acceptance is not belief.* The concept of belief is difficult to define and the occurrence of belief difficult to establish (see R. Needham 1972). Let us say that the term "belief" at least suggests a mental state concerning, or arising out of, the relationship between the cognitive processes of individuals and representations presented to them as pos- sible candidates for the status of true. As such, "belief" is a second-order process, that is, one concerned with the relationship between a first order process and external reality. By this account, belief is an inward state, knowable subjectively if at all, and it would be entirely unwarranted either for us or for participants or witnesses to assume that participation in a ritual would necessarily indicate such a state.

Acceptance, in contrast, is not a private state, but a public act, visible both to witnesses and to performers themselves. People may accept because they believe, but acceptance not only is not itself belief; it doesn't even imply belief. Ritual performance often possesses perlocutionary force, and the private processes of individuals may often be persuaded by their ritual participation to come into conformity with their public acts, but this is not always the case. Belief is a cogent reason, but far from the only reason, for acceptance. Conversely, belief can provide grounds for refusals to accept. Reformers and heretics, for the very reason that they believe deeply in certain postulates concerning the divine, may refuse to participate in the rituals of religious institutions they take to have fallen into error or corruption.

This account suggests that although participation in liturgical performance may be highly visible it is not very profound, for it neither indicates nor does it necessarily produce an inward state conforming to it. Such a view is widely held by critics of religion who are inclined to take ritual participation to be nothing more than empty or even hypocritical formalism, a view reflected in one of the term's common modern meanings, formal behaviour devoid of substance or consequence. But, paradoxically, it may be, and it surely has been implied by religion's defenders, that the acceptance indicated by liturgical performance, being independent of belief can be more profound than conviction or sense of certainty, for it makes it possible for the performer to transcend his or her own doubt by accepting in defiance of it. Even the most devout, indeed especially the most devout, sometimes harbour doubts or even voice scepticism concerning propositions expressed in liturgies to which they scrupulously conform, and acceptance in this deep sense has much in common with certain Christian notions of faith. Fehean O'Doherty, a Catholic priest, writes "faith is neither subjective conviction nor experienced certitude, but may be at its best where doubt exists" (1973: 9), and Paul Tillich has said that faith *necessarily* includes an element of uncertainty or doubt (1957: 16 ff.). It is also of interest in this regard that Judaism does not require the devout to believe, for belief is not subject to command. It does, however, demand of them that they *accept* the law, and this acceptance is signalled by, and is intrinsic to, conformity to the ritual observances that pervade all of life.

Be this as it may, there may well be, and often are, disparities between the act of acceptance and the inward state associated with it. One can accept publicly not only that which one doubts but that which one privately despises or secretly denies. But if acceptance is intrinsic to performance it is not vitiated by secret denial. To recognize that secret denial may hide beneath the acceptance inhering in the act of perform-ance is to recognize that the grounds of acceptance may vary widely, that acceptance is not necessarily founded upon belief, and that it does not even necessarily imply the subjective state termed "approval."

Acceptance, then, can be unconvinced and "insincere," *but insincerity does not nullify acceptance.* In what appears to be a flaw of sufficient seriousness to vitiate its meaningfulness lies the very virtue of acceptance through liturgical performance. Its social efficacy lies in its very lack of profundity, in the possibility of disparity between the outward act and the inward state. The distinction between belief and acceptance corre-sponds to the distinction made in the third chapter between the public and private. Participation in ritual demarcates a boundary, so to speak, between private and public processes. Liturgical orders, even those performed in solitude, are *public* orders and participation in them constitutes an acceptance of a public order *regardless* of the private state of belief of the performer. We may cite here Austin's views on a great range of performatives – promising, swearing, repudiating, commending, assessing – among which accepting is to be included:

we must not suppose ... that what is needed in addition to the saying of the words in such cases is the performance of some internal spiritual act, of which the words are then the report. It's very easy to slip into this view at least in difficult portentous cases ... In the case of promising – for example, "I promise to be there tomorrow" – it's very easy to think that the utterance is simply the outward and visible ... sign of the performance of some inward spiritual act of promising, and this view has been expressed in many classic places. There is the case of Euripedes' Hippolytus who said "My tongue swore to, but my heart did not" – perhaps it should be "mind" or "spirit" rather than "heart," but at any rate some kind of backstage artiste.   *(1970: 236)*

It is gratifying to observe in this very example [that of Hippolytus] how excess of profundity, or rather solemnity, at once paves the way for immorality. For one who says "promising is not merely a matter of uttering words! It is an inward and spiritual act!" is apt to appear as a solid moralist standing out against a generation of theorizers: we see him as he sees himself, surveying the invisible depths of ethical space, with all the distinction of a specialist in the sui generis. Yet he provides Hippolytus with a let-out, the bigamist with an excuse for his "I do" and the welsher with a defence for his "I bet." Accuracy and morality alike are on the side of the plain saying that our word is our bond (Austin 1962: 10).

Acceptance in, or through, liturgical performance may reflect an inward state of conviction; it may also encourage "the mind," "the heart" and "the spirit" into agreement with itself. It does not necessarily do either, however, and therefore it does not eliminate all of the shenanigans of which the mind, the heart, the spirit, and other "back-stage artistes" may be capable, but my argument, based on Austin's, proposes that although liturgical performance does not eliminate insincerity, it renders it publicly impotent. It is the visible, explicit, public act of acceptance, and not the invisible, ambiguous, private sentiment, which is socially and morally binding.

Because public and private processes are (and must be) related, but only loosely related, a range of what Austin (1962: 95ff., *passim*) called "infelicities" – insincerities and the like – are possible. But if, somehow, public orders could be required to depend upon the continuing belief, sincerity, goodwill, conviction or enthusiasm of those subject to them, the possibility of insincerity or deceit would surely be replaced by the high probability of non-order or disorder because of the near impossibility of meeting such a standard. This is not to say that the private processes may not be important in the dynamics of ritual. In a later chapter we shall take up belief and religious experience. It is simply to recognize that the private states of others are in their nature unknowable and even one's own attitudes may not always be easy to ascertain, for we are inclined to be ambivalent about matters of importance, like the conventions to which we are subordinate, and private states are likely to be volatile. "Common belief" cannot in itself provide a sufficiently firm ground upon which to establish public orders, even in very simple societies. We cannot know if a belief is common, for one thing, and whereas belief is vexed by ambivalence and clouded by ambiguity acceptance is not. Liturgical orders are public, and participation in them constitutes a public acceptance of a public order, regardless of the private state of belief. Acceptance is not only public but clear. One either participates in a liturgy or one does not; the choice is binary and as such it is formally free of ambiguity.[9] While ritual participation may not transform the private state of the performer from one of "disbelief" to "belief," our argument is that in it the ambiguity, ambivalence and volatility of the private processes are subordinated to a simple and unambiguous public act, sensible both to the performers themselves and to witnesses as well. Liturgical performance is, thus, a fundamental social act, for the acceptance intrinsic to it forms a basis for public orders which unknowable and volatile belief or conviction cannot.

That a liturgical order is accepted in its performance does not, further-more, guarantee that the performer will abide by whatever rules or norms that order encodes. We all know that a man may participate in a liturgy in which commandments against adultery and thievery are pro-nounced, then pilfer from the poor box on his way out of church, or depart from communion to tryst with his neighbor's wife. To recognize such sordid realities is not to agree that liturgical acceptance is hypocri-tical, trivial or meaningless (Douglas 1973: 30), nor is it to dismiss claims for the social efficacy of acceptance through liturgical performance. It is, in fact, to affirm them, for such violations do not nullify acceptance, nor render it trivial. It is in such instances that the importance of ritual acceptance is most dramatically demonstrated. The primary function or metafunction of liturgical performances is not to control behavior directly, but rather to establish conventional understandings, rules and norms in accordance with which everyday behaviour is *supposed* to proceed. Participation in a ritual in which a prohibition against adultery is enunciated by, among others, himself may not prevent a man from committing adultery, but it does establish for him the prohibition of adultery as a rule that he himself has both enlivened and accepted. *Whether or not he abides by that rule, he has obligated himself to do so.* If he does not, he has violated an obligation that he himself has avowed. The assertion here is similar to those of Austin (see above) and of the philosopher John Searle, who has argued that

when one enters an institutional activity by invoking the rules of that institution one necessarily commits oneself in such and such ways, regardless of whether one approves or disapproves of the institution. In the case of linguistic institutions like promising [and accepting] the serious utterance of words commits one in ways which are determined by the meaning of the words. In certain first person utterances the utterance is the undertaking of an obligation.   *(1969: 189)*

Searle later notes that the notion of obligation is closely related to those of accepting, recognizing, acknowledging. This suggests that there is no obligation without acceptance, and perhaps that morality begins with acceptance.[10] We may also note that while the acceptance of conventional undertakings, rules and procedures is possible outside of ritual, the formal and public nature of liturgical performance makes it very clear that an act of acceptance is taking place, that the acceptance is serious, and what it is that is being accepted. In Austin's terms (1962: *passim*) it is "explicitly performative." *In sum, it is not ritual's office to ensure compliance but to establish obligation.*

6. Performativeness, metaperformativeness, and the establishment of convention

We may now return to the assertion that although all ritual may not include simple performatives – conventional procedures for achieving conventional effects – something formally similar to simple performativeness, but of higher order, is intrinsic to ritual's form, and that this characteristic of ritual makes performatives possible.

Austin (1962: 26ff.) listed six conditions that must be fulfilled if performatives are to be successful (see also Searle 1969: *passim*). These include a number of obvious stipulations already noted at least tacitly – that they be performed by properly authorized persons under proper circumstances, and that they be executed correctly and completely. We have observed that the formality of ritual goes a long way to assure that those conditions are met, but ritual's contribution to performativeness is not limited to its service as a protocol, conformity to which assures full and correct performance. Its significance is much more fundamental.

Austin states the first and most basic condition for performative success, that which he labels A.1, as follows: "There must *exist* an *accepted* conventional procedure having a certain conventional effect, the procedure to include the uttering of certain words [or the performance of certain symbolic acts] by certain persons in certain circumstances" (1962: 14) (emphasis mine). Conventional effects cannot be achieved without conventions for achieving them. If young men are to be transformed into knights there must be a procedure for doing so, and this procedure must be acceptable to the relevant public. We may also note, although Austin does not, that the acceptance of a procedure for dubbing knights tacitly but obviously entails an acceptance of the convention of knighthood itself. Yet further, if the young man is "armed as a knight for the service of Christ" by priests or bishops, an acceptance of Christ's divinity is also entailed (Marc Bloch 1961: ch. 33).

Austin's basic condition seems obvious, but it is not trivial because its violation is possible. A performative attempt could misfire because, for instance, no one but the performer recognized the procedure which it employed or the state of affairs it sought to achieve. An attempt by an American citizen living in the United States to win a divorce by repeating to his wife "I divorce you" three times would not rid him of matrimony's burdens, nor would any divorce procedure whatsoever succeed in a society not recognizing divorce at all (Austin 1962: 27). Conventional procedures and conventional states, or even entire conventional codes, may be accepted by some and not by others and there are surely changes in the conventions of any society through time, with the scope of their applicability expanding or contracting, some disappearing altogether while others appear. Conventions can cease to exist because they are no longer accepted (Austin 1962: 30), as, for instance, in the case of the code of honor of which duelling was a part. It is unlikely, to say the least, that in contemporary United States or Great Britain a slap of a glove across a cheek would lead to a duel. The conventions of which this ritual act was an element are no longer accepted. They are, as we say, "history."

Austin stipulated as requisite to the effectiveness of performatives that relevant conventions exist and be accepted, but he gave only scant attention to the ways in which this prerequisite might be fulfilled. The argument being presented here is that ritual may fulfill it. To establish a convention – a general public understanding, a regular procedure, an institution – is *both* to ascribe existence to it *and* to accept it. The two are hardly distinct, as Austin (1962: 26) understood, for the existence of a convention, given the meaning of the word, is a function of its acceptance (see Bateson 1951: 212ff.).[11] To perform a liturgy is at one and the same time to conform to its order and to realize it or make it substantial. *Liturgical performance not only recognizes the authority of the conventions it represents, it gives them their very existence.* In the absence of performance liturgical orders are dead letters inscribed in curious volumes, or insubstantial forms evaporating into the forgotten. A ritual performance is an instance of the conventional order to which it conforms. Conversely, a ritual performance realizes the order of which it is an instance. Participants enliven the order that they are performing with the energy of their own bodies, and their own voices make it articulate. They thereby establish the existence of that order in this world of matter and energy; they *substantiate* the order as it *informs* them.

If performatives are to be understood as conventional procedures for achieving conventional effects, rituals are, by this account, more than simple performatives. We have already noted that a dubbing did more than transform a particular young man into a knight; it also repeatedly established (accepted the existance of) a conventional procedure for transforming young men into knights. It further established and re-established the conventions of knighthood itself, and of the divinity of the god in whose name and service knights were dubbed. The mass, in contrast, establishes a more general conventional understanding of the relationship of humans to the divine. The act of acceptance intrinsic to ritual performance is not simply performative, as are specific conventional acts occurring within rituals – crowning, marrying, dubbing, purifying – but *meta-performative*. Rituals do more than achieve conventional effects through conventional procedures. They establish the conventions in terms of which those effects are achieved.

The establishment of convention is the second of ritual's fundamental offices. It is fundamental because all of ritual's simple performative functions are founded upon, or presume it, and so may conventional procedures outside of ritual itself. It is fundamental, this is to say, because the establishment of convention is what might be called a "*meta*function" making possible the fulfillment of particular functions by the particular conventions established.

It is fundamental in a second, formal sense, because the establishment as convention of whatever is encoded in canon is intrinsic to the form of ritual, that is, to the performance of more or less invariant sequences of formal acts and utterances not encoded by the performer. We observe here the profound importance of invariance and formality. These are the features that maintain constant that which is accepted. In the absence of such constancy that which is accepted would not be conventional. Indeed, acceptance would be inconsequential, meaningless, or even logically impossible if the canon were made up afresh by each participant for each performance.

We note in passing that as one of "the realities" lying behind notions of the *magical* power of words may be simple performativeness or factiveness mystified, so may widespread notions concerning the *creative* power of *The Word* rest upon meta-performativeness or meta-factiveness mystified, upon the realization of conventions through participation in invariant liturgical orders.

7. Ritual and daily practice in the establishment of convention

That the obligations clearly and explicitly accepted in liturgical performance are nullified by neither disbelief nor violation has a significance transcending the problems of insincerity and deceitfulness. We approach here a matter of profound importance, the relationship of convention to behavior and, more particularly, difficulties in establishing convention through ordinary usage. I have argued that one of ritual's fundamental offices is the establishment of convention, but no claim was made that convention is established only in ritual. It therefore may seem in this regard that ritual is no different from usage or practice in general. Convention, be it noted, may also be established by decree. There are important differences, however, between liturgical performance and other means for establishing convention.

First, we may contrast liturgical performance with quotidian practice. As Bateson (1951: 214) long ago remarked, "every statement in a given codification is an affirmation of that codification and is therefore in some degree metacommunicative (when I say 'I see the cat' I am implicitly affirming the proposition that the word 'cat' stands for what I see)". The core meaning of the term "code" is linguistic, in some usages it denotes vocabularies and the rules for combining their elements into larger mean-ingful units *without reference to or restriction upon what can or may be said.* While linguistic conventions may be taken to be paradigmatic of those established in ordinary practice, it should be kept in mind that the concept of code has been extended beyond language by some cognitive anthropologists, who tend to see cultures generally as complex codes made up of "shared finite cognitive set[s] of rules for the socially appropriate construction and interpretation of messages and behaviour" (Kernan 1972: 333, cf. Frake 1964). But a liturgy is not a code in this wide and semantically unspecifying sense. It is a more or less fixed sequence of stereotyped actions and utterances and as such what can be expressed in it is narrowly circumscribed. Permissible variations in some aspects of performance do allow or require the participants to encode indexical messages, but the content of the canon, the invariant aspect of the liturgy in respect to which the indexical messages may vary, is fixed, and therefore the range of indexical messages that may be transmitted in any liturgy is restricted. Moreover, as we have noted, the participants do not encode but only transmit the invariant messages the canon embodies. Since this is the case, the term "liturgical *order*" seems more appropriate than "liturgical *code*." It follows that the acceptance of an order, because it is in its nature highly restrictive, is therefore more socially consequen-tial and significant than the affirmation of a more or less unrestrictive code. High valuation of the qualities of the consequential and the restrictive, as previous discussion suggests, invites the application of liturgical order, for liturgy tends to make explicit precisely what is being stipulated, it is in its very form constricting, and further, liturgical form and decorum tends to make its substance seem grave.

It would, of course, be mistaken to impose the simple dichotomous distinction of "codes" versus "orders" upon the conventions organizing social life. Linguistic codes and the conventional dogmatic understandings embodied in some liturgies stand at opposite ends of a continuum of constraint. Between them are stretched the conventions which organize not merely what people say to or about each other or the world, but what they do to and with each other and the world around them. Little is known about the order of this continuum, whether certain domains of culture are more likely to be subject to narrower or more rigorous constraints than others, or whether variation from one society to the next is wide. We shall return to this general question in a later chapter when we discuss sanctification. For now it may be noted that comparatively high degrees of constraint seem entailed by the invariant nature of liturgy, and it may further be suggested that the more highly motivated people are to violate a convention or the more consequential its violation is deemed to be, the more likely it is to be established in liturgy than in daily practice, or the more closely and strongly will it be associated with conventional understandings that are so represented (see the discussion of sanctification in chapter 10 below). Be this as it may, certain conventions, for instance, those of speech, emerge out of ordinary usage and are maintained by ordinary usage in sufficient stability to allow meaningful and orderly social interaction. In such cases, "the norm is identical with the statistical average" (Leach 1972: 320). It may be suggested that variation with respect to such conventions can be comfortably tolerated and day-to-day usage may be allowed to establish, maintain or change them. But ordinary practice or usage is not in itself sufficient to establish all conventions, nor are statistical averages arising out of behavior always coextensive with conventions.

First, it is impossible for ordinary usage to establish conventions to which no ordinary usage corresponds. Such conventions include most importantly, and perhaps exclusively, the understandings upon which religions are founded, dogmas and mysteries concerning gods and the like which, being typically without material referents and always being taken to be extraordinary, cannot grow out of ordinary usage. The fundamental importance of these conventions will be discussed in later chapters.

Secondly, statistical averages arising out of usage represent no more than common practice, summations of behavior, and the utility of summations of behavior for guiding or assessing the behavior of which they are summations is limited, at best. They are particularly inadequate, first, in the case of conventions with moral import, for they tend to reduce the notion of immorality to deviation from a statistically average behavioral range – to that which "is not done," and the moral to that which "is done." Such a notion of morality and immorality is, on the one hand, descriptively erroneous – no society operates with such a conception of morality – and, on the other hand, operatively inadequate. No society could so operate, at least for long, because it would be without any means for assessing common practice itself, and a common practice may, even in terms of the moral code of the society in which it occurs, be vicious, anti-social or self-destructive. Common practice, statistical average, ordinary usage will have difficulty establishing conventions concerning aspects of social life that are obviously restrictive, obviously arbitrary, highly charged emotionally, especially dangerous, or require obedience conventions, this is to say, that demand of individuals that they subordinate their self-interests to the common good. Behavioral variation may be less tolerable with respect to these matters than with respect to linguistic usage, and uncertainty as to the precise nature of the conventions themselves, a different matter, may be even less tolerable than variations in the practices which they presumably direct. Ordinary usage always varies, and in ordinary usage rules and conventions are frequently violated. Leach was generally pointing in the right direction but did not go far enough when he suggested that "if anarchy is to be avoided, the individuals who make up a society must from time to time be reminded of the underlying order that is supposed to guide their social activities. Ritual performances have this function for the group as a whole. They momentarily make explicit what is otherwise fiction" (1954: 16). Although usage may not be faithful to it, that which is represented in a liturgical order is not a fiction, (except in the sense of being "made up," rather than given by non-human nature, see Geertz 1973: 15), and the performance does more than remind individuals of an underlying order.

It is well to make explicit an assumption tacit in our general argument. The orders of societies, like the order of the universe in general, tend to degenerate into disorder. Their material elements disintegrate or decay into non-functioning fragments if they are not maintained, and their meaningful elements, including conventional understandings and rules, dissolve into error, nonsense, ambiguity, vagueness, hypocrisy and meaninglessness unless continually clarified, corrected and re-established. Far from clarifying and reasserting conventions, the vagaries of practice may tend to erode them. It is therefore necessary to establish at least some conventions in a manner which protects them from dissolution in the variations of day-to-day behavior and the violations in which history abounds. Liturgy does not simply remind people of the orders which usage – behavior and history – violates and dissolves. It establishes and ever again reestablishes those orders. *Liturgy preserves the conventions it encodes inviolate in defiance of the vagaries of ordinary practice, thereby providing them with existence independent of, and insulated against, the statistical averages which characterize behavior.* That "everyone does it" exonerates no one. For people of the Book adultery would remain a sin even if every married person indulged in it.

It should be noted, however, that the violation of convention is not always simply a matter of entropy, chaos or anarchy asserting itself against an ideal but not fully realized order. The constitution of some societies is such that the violation of some conventions is not only frequent but systematic, and yet the convention has a vital part to play in the life of the society. Gluckman long ago (1954) considered certain African rituals in this light, and we may note that among the Maring and other Highland New Guinea peoples, a strong patrilocal patrilineal ideology prevails. It is putatively patrilineal clans that hold territories and putatively patrilineal sub-clans that claim smaller tracts (Rappaport 1968: ch. 2). Rituals, addressed largely to patrilineal ancestors, are conducted by these groups at special places on the land which they and their deceased ancestors are said to occupy together. But the exigencies of life and death are such that the demographic fortunes of these small groups (sub-clans among the Tsembaga ran, in 1963, from almost none to about thirty-five persons, clans from sixteen to seventy persons), fluctuate widely, and fluctuations may lead to the violation of the patrilineal patrilocal ideal. Groups must maintain their strength *vis-à-vis* their neighbors, and when their numbers are low the members of a group will attempt to attract outsiders to settle among them. Their kinship terminology, which is Iroquois on ego's generation, but generational on all descending generations, as well as on the second ascending generation and above, seems well suited to the assimilation of strangers, obliterating as it does distinctions between agnates, other cognates and affines in two generations, and *rumbim* planting can be seen as the beginning of a process by which cognates are transformed into agnates. This ritual transformation of non-agnates into agnates is able to preserve the *conventions* of patrilocality and patrilineality, if not patrifiliation, inviolate in the face of continual violation in usage (see LiPuma 1990). This is of considerable adaptive importance. Densities sometimes become high in the New Guinea highlands and therefore it sometimes becomes necessary or desirable to exclude people who would like to immigrate (Meggitt 1965b). Agnatic rules, necessarily violated by practice but preserved by ritual, provide a basis for such exclusion when there is need.

The formality definitive of ritual and distinguishing it from ordinary behavior is clearly of importance in preserving the conventions it encodes from the errors and trespasses of daily practice. Because preservation is virtually entailed by ritual's formality, and because the acceptance as well as the precise stipulation of convention is intrinsic to ritual's form, ritual may well be without functional, or metafunctional, equivalents.

Ritual, to be sure, is not altogether unique in establishing conventions at the same time that it insulates them from the variations and violations of behavior. Conventions may also be promulgated by decree and maintained by force. But the acceptance of those subject to a decree is not intrinsic to the promulgation of that decree. In contrast, it is one and the same ritual act that both realizes and accepts a liturgical order. Furthermore, the act of acceptance establishes an obligation with respect to the convention accepted, an obligation that is not specifically under-taken and may not be felt by those subject to decrees.

It is of interest in this regard that even in those instances in which conventions are self-consciously promulgated by kings or parliaments the act of promulgation and those participating in it are surrounded by ritual. Kings are crowned, public officers sworn into office, meetings of parliaments are ceremonially opened and closed, and their deliberations set within a more or less invariant procedure. Moreover, their decrees may be accepted, albeit indirectly and non-specifically, by those subject to them in such ritual acts as pledges of allegiance to the entities, or symbols thereof, from which the promulgators derive their authority. To accept an order is to ascribe legitimacy to its terms. To ascribe legitimacy to its terms is to oblige oneself to abide by them, or to put it a little differently, to agree to their application as a set of standards against which the acceptor's own actions are properly judged. Insofar as partici-pation in a liturgical order is an acceptance of that order, it legitimizes that order.

It may also be suggested, although there is no way of knowing, that ritual, in the very structure of which both authority and acquiescence are implicit, may well be the primordial means by which humans have established conventions. The conditions that make it possible for some men to promulgate conventions by directives to which other men must conform seem to have developed relatively recently, probably not ante-dating by much, if at all, the appearance of plant and animal cultivation 10,000 years or so ago.[12] Ritual, on the other hand, does not require superordinate human authorities to establish conventions and must have antedated procedures that do.

8. The morality intrinsic to ritual's structure

The performance of a liturgy not only brings conventions into being but invests them with morality. Moral dicta are not explicit in all liturgies, but morality, like social contract, is implicit in ritual's structure.

We have, following Searle, noted that obligation is entailed by the acceptance intrinsic to participation in ritual. Breach of obligation, it could be argued, is one of the few acts, if not, indeed, the only act that is always and everywhere held to be immoral. Homicide, for instance, is not. There are conditions, so common as to require no illustration, under which killing humans is laudable or even mandatory. What is immoral is, of course, killing someone whom there is an obligation, at least tacit, not to kill. A similar point can be made about most or possibly even all other specific acts generally taken to be immoral. Breach of obligation is of a higher order of generality than any such specific breach as murder, rape or robbery and it may be suggested that it is breach of obligation that transforms otherwise morally positive, neutral or empty acts into crimes such as murder or robbery. Breach of obligation may, then, be *the* fundamental immoral act, the element in the absence of which an act cannot be construed to be immoral, in the presence of which it is ipso facto immoral. The topic is a difficult one, and surely cannot be settled here. I will only emphasize that failure to abide by the terms of an obligation is universally stigmatized as immoral. To the extent, then, that obligation is entailed by the acceptance intrinsic to the performance of a liturgical order, ritual establishes morality as it establishes convention. The establishment of a convention and the establishment of its morality are inextricable, if they are not, in fact, one and the same.

We may refer again in this regard to the relationship of performatives to the states of affairs with which they are concerned. Austin initially tried to say that performatives differ from statements in that performatives are neither true nor false (1970: 233ff.) whereas statements are either true or false. Later he found this view to be questionable because certain performatives, notably verdictives, are supposed to stand in a relationship to states of affairs similar to that of true statements to states or affairs. Later he found this not always to be the case. Performatives do, however, differ from statements in a related way which he did not note but which does have to do with truth, and with the foundations of morality.

In discussing their indexical nature, we have observed that the relationship of performatives to the states of affairs with which they are concerned is the inverse of that of statements or descriptions. Statements

report autonomously existing states of affairs. Performative acts re
states of affairs. The inverse nature of these relationships has ob.
implications for assessment. The adequacy of a descriptive statement is
assessed by the degree to which it conforms to the state of affairs that it
purports to describe. If it is in sufficient conformity we say that it is true,
accurate or correct. If it is not we say that it is false, erroneous,
inaccurate or lying. *The state of affairs is the criterion by which the truth,
accuracy or adequacy of a statement is assessed.* In the case of performatives there is an inversion. If, for instance, a man is properly dubbed to
knighthood and then proceeds to violate all of the canons of chivalry, or
if peace is declared in a properly conducted ritual but soon after one of
the parties to the declaration attacks the other, we do not say that the
dubbing or the peace declaration were faulty, but that the subsequent
states of affairs are faulty. *We judge the state of affairs by the degree to
which it conforms to the stipulations of the performative act.* Liturgical
orders provide criteria in terms of which events – behavior and history –
may be judged. As such, liturgical orders are intrinsically correct or
moral. Morality is inherent in the structure of liturgical performance
prior to whatever its canons explicitly assert about morality in general or
whatever in particular may be taken to be moral. Morality derives
ultimately not from statements about what may be right and wrong but
from what liturgy establishes as right or wrong. To put it a little
differently, to establish a convention independent of usage is to establish
an "ought" against which the "is" of behavior may be judged.[13]

The establishment of morality is clearest in the case of simple factiveness and the commissive implications thereof. It is patently immoral to
act incompatibly with the terms of a conventional state of affairs that
one has ritually participated in bringing into being. My argument
implies, however, that morality is also intrinsic to the meta-factiveness of
ritual, that is, to the establishment of particular conventions and conventional orders. One who violates not merely the terms of a conventional
state of affairs, but of the conventional order defining such states of
affairs is not guilty of a simple immoral act, but of apostasy. It is of
interest here that in Zoroastrian Persia and Vedic India states of affairs
that departed from the proper liturgically established order were designated by terms that also seem to have meant "lie," *druj* in Persia and
anrta in India (Duchesne-Guillemin 1966: 26ff., N. Brown 1972: 252ff.,
Orlin 1976). What may be called "Vedic lies" or "Zoroastrian lies"
(Rappaport 1979b), states of affairs that their perpetrators are aware do
not conform to prevailing liturgically established orders, are the inverse

of "vulgar lies," statements that their transmitters believe misrepresent the states of affairs which they purport to report.

9. Ritual and myth, and drama

Acceptance entails neither belief nor obedience. To say that in performing a canon the participant accepts whatever conventional understandings, principles, rules or procedures it encodes is simply to say that he has obligated himself to abide by its terms regardless of his private opinions and feelings about them. In slightly different terms, an act of acceptance invests the objects accepted with the qualities of correctness, propriety, legitimacy and morality, and thus establishes them as criteria in terms of which common practice, behavior, events, history and especially the acceptor's own conduct, may be judged.

It is obvious but nevertheless worth making explicit, if only to take issue with a loose anthropological truism, that the ritual relationship of performers to what they are performing distinguishes ritual from myth on substantive as well as formal grounds. Ritual actions cannot be seen as simply "exemplifying in another medium the cultural values that find verbal expression in statements about the world, society, man – statements which we call beliefs and which are elaborated in narratives or myths" (La Fontaine 1972: xvii). And while it may be, as in Leach's phrase of four decades ago (1954: 12), that "myth is the counterpart of ritual, myth implies ritual, ritual implies myth," they are not, to complete the famous dictum, "one and the same." They are *never* one and the same, even when they are about the same things, or even when the ritual is simply an enactment of the myth. Myth as such carries no self-referential information, nor does its telling either presuppose or establish any particular relationship between the myth and he or she who recounts it. The narrator may tell it as priest to novice, entertainer to audience, sorcerer to apprentice, father to child, French structuralist to students, literary critic to ladies' club, folklore collector to those who read his anthology. This is to say that the telling of a myth, even in the case of the priest, does not necessarily imply that the teller accepts the myth as part of an order in which she herself participates, or to which she subordinates herself. The relationship of narrators to the myths they narrate is often unknown to auditors or readers, and is, at any rate, irrelevant to them. What may be relevant to them is the substance of the myths themselves, something which can as well be read as seen, heard, voiced or acted. As narrators do not necessarily accept the myths which they narrate as anything more than stories, neither do their audiences, and such acceptance as they might accord to such stories is responsive to their perlocutionary force, the ability of the stories to move them, and not through conformity to their form. Myths, like rituals, can "die" (Eliade 1963), but they do not, as do rituals, become dead letters if they are preserved only in writing.

In contrast to myths, rituals even when they seem to be no more than detailed reenactments of myths always stipulate a relationship between performers and that which they perform. Such rituals communicate more than their myths. They communicate the indexical message of the participants' acceptance of those myths as well.

It may be suggested that myth and drama are closer to being "one and the same" than are myth and ritual. A drama based upon a myth is no more nor less than an enactment of a version of that myth. As such, its performance, unlike ritual performance, does not indicate acceptance of the narrative being played. But ritual and drama have sometimes been taken to be closely related in one way or another and Jane Harrison long ago (1913), observed that the origins of Western drama lay in ritual. She observed that the term "drama" comes from the Greek *dromenon*, literally, "thing done," but early denoting religious ritual. It may be well, in view of their putative relationship or similarity, to note in more detail than was appropriate in chapter 2 some further differences between ritual and drama.

Perhaps most important is that which distinguishes an audience from a congregation. The congregation participates in the ritual, with all that participation entails. The audience at a performance of a Western drama merely watches and listens. It is present for the performance, but is not part of it. A congregation is generally required to do things in the course of a ritual: sing, dance, read responsively, kneel, eat, drink. In contrast, the members of a Western audience are not required to do anything and may even be required to do nothing. Whereas a congregation joins the celebrant in performing the acts that comprise the ritual, an audience does not join the actors in the performance of a drama. The actors act on one side of the proscenium arch, the audience refrains from action on the other.

Secondly, the acts of those who celebrate rituals express or enliven the orders to which the congregation acquiesces. But in theatre, actors play parts which, when they come together in the totality of the drama, comprise fictions which none of those present need or is expected to accept as anything other than fiction. Even when audiences accept dramas as great fiction, true as some of Shakespeare's plays are true, they do not accept them as literal reality, in some degree concrete, of which they are parts, but as representations of some sort. As in the case of myth audience, acceptance rests upon the ability of drama to persuade or move, and not upon its demand to act in conformity to its form. In Austin's terms, drama, like myth without ritual, has *at best* perlocutionary *but not* illocutionary force.

It is interesting in this regard to compare the "acts" of those who participate in rituals and those who "act" in drama. For one who performs a ritual "to act" is to take an action that affirms or even brings into being a significant order and also states his acceptance of it. It may even transform that order or himself. The ritual act, this is to say, "does something," it is an action that is meant to affect the world and it is likely to do so. To act in a drama, in contrast, is not to take an action affecting the world, but only to imitate doing so. That acting in a drama is not acting in the non-dramatic sense is, moreover, clearly signalled to those present by a whole set of context markers setting the dramatic action apart from "real life": the seats, the curtain, the program providing the worldly names of those who, for an hour or two, will act out a temporary identity in the playwright's words and the director's gestures. To act in the dramatic sense is precisely not to act in the non-dramatic sense. This contrast is strongly suggested by the alternative term for drama in English. It is "play," a term which, of course, also denotes lack of earnestness. Whereas a worshipper takes part in a ritual, thus participating in the enduring order that his own performance helps bring into being, an actor plays a part in a play, a part which evaporates when the curtain falls and when his own identity is supposed to return to guide his actions once again.

We note here what distinguishes ritual from drama, but of course, particular events are not always purely one or the other. Some performances include elements of both, or better, stand somewhere on a continuum lying between the polar forms. We may think here of miracle and passion plays and concert performances of religious music in churches. The effectiveness of some performances may arise out of the ambiguities of this continuum, and so may the failures of others. "Living theatre," for instance, is likely to be unsuccessful because an audience is asked to take upon itself congregation-like duties while, lacking the well-rehearsed certainties of liturgy, not knowing in what they are being asked to participate or with whom they are participating. But surely, through time, the character of some performances changes, the relationship of those present being transformed from that of congregation to audience or audience to congregation (see Kapferer 1983: esp. ch. 8). Harrison argues (1913: 35–38) that the transformation from *dromenon* to *drama* in ancient Greece may be traced archaeologically through changes in the use of space occurring during the fifth and sixth centuries BC. At the beginning of the period there was only the orchestra, a round area in which everyone present joined together in the dances of the dithyramb, the spring festival. Later, however, a theatre, that is to say rows of seats, came to tier the hillside above the orchestra, and spectators came to be separated from dancers and actors. According to Harrison this separation from the action in space was concurrent with and inseparable from a trend toward the detachment of those present from the action taking place, and she distinguished ritual from drama on the grounds of the distinction between participation and contemplation, that is to say, congregation and audience. Conversely, in our own day there seems to be a transformation of audiences into, or at least in the direction of, congregations in certain performances, notably rock concerts. In the absence of canon in these events it is not surprising that their stars are virtually apotheosized.

10. Ritual as the basic social act

To summarize, the existence of a conventional order is contingent upon its acceptance; in fact a rule or understanding cannot be said to be a convention unless it is accepted. In ritual, however, acceptance and existence entail each other, for a liturgical order is perforce accepted in its realization, in, that is to say, the performance which gives it substance. Since obligation is entailed by acceptance, and the breaking of obligation is *per se* immoral, the existence, acceptance and morality of conventions are joined together indissolubly in rituals; they are, in fact, virtually one and the same. The same cannot be said of principles, rules, procedures or understandings established by proclamation, or legislation on the one hand or by daily practice on the other. This is to say that there is a logically necessary relationship between the form which is ritual, the performance of more or less invariant sequences of formal acts and utterances not encoded by the performers, and the messages rituals contain concerning both what is performed and the relationship of the performer to what he performs. Ritual is not merely another way to "say things" or "do things" that can be said or done as well or better in other ways. The form which is ritual is surely without communicational equivalents and thus, possibly, without functional or metafunctional equivalents. That ritual's abilities are intrinsic to its form and in indissoluble association *only* with its form, goes far to account for its ubiquity.

In attending to ritual's form we must not lose sight of the fundamental nature of what it is that ritual does as a logically necessary outcome of its form. In enunciating, accepting and making conventions moral, ritual contains within itself not simply a symbolic representation of social contract, but tacit social contract itself. As such, ritual, which also establishes, guards, and bridges boundaries between public systems and private processes, is *the* basic social act.

Competing ritual sets for binding convention >
new method for comparing relative worth of
conventionalized morals — >.
Ethics

5

Word and act, form and substance

Humans possess the ability to speak, yet their rituals include acts as well as utterances, and in many of them special objects and substances are used or manipulated. Even rituals conducted in solitude often require the assumption of special postures, the performance of stereotyped movements or the manipulation of special paraphernalia and, like public rituals, they are often performed in special places at special times. We have a vision, all the more true for being idealized, of children reciting their daily prayers not anywhere at any time, but kneeling, eyes closed and hands clasped, by their beds at the very end of their day, and orthodox Jews bind phylacterie to their arms and foreheads before morning prayer even when they are alone. Physical display is a widespread, if not universal, aspect of solitary as well as public ritual, and it is plausible to take it to be an aspect, and an important one, of ritual's self-informing operation.

To note that physical acts and material objects and substances are components of virtually all human rituals is hardly to account for such a fact. Physical display in ritual may, of course, be archaic. In their use of posture and movement the rituals of humans come closest to those of the speechless beasts, and it may be that the material aspect of human ritual survives from a time when our forebears were without language. But to suggest that something is a survival is not to account for why it should have survived. Even if the antiquity of ritual postures and gestures were to be demonstrated we would not thereby know why this peculiar mode of non-verbal communication should have persisted many thousands or even hundreds of thousands of years into the time of language. If it is objected, as well it should be, that ritual display is not to be construed *a priori* to be a manifestation of continuity with the pre-linguistic past of the species a related, but more fruitful question may be asked. Why is it that humans, who can communicate with ease, efficiency and subtlety through language should also employ such an awkward, limited and expensive mode of communication as physical display? An obvious answer, of course, is that physical display indicates more, more clearly or other than, what words are able to communicate. This chapter is concerned with whatever that might be. Yet more generally it is concerned with the particular communicative capacities of various classes of acts, objects and substances employed in ritual, and also those of gesture, posture, wounds, and words.

Two comments are in order before proceeding. First, the topic is obviously one which overlaps with the concerns of paralinguistics and kinesics. Ritual display may, however, be distinguished from much of their subject matter, albeit in a rough and ready way. Paralinguistics and kinesics are concerned to elucidate non-linguistic signals either accompanying speech or emitted as autonomous messages through perceptible changes in the state of the body. Many of these signals – blushing, stammering, posture in sitting, body movement in walking, distance maintained between interlocutors – are unconscious. They are indexical, indicating physical and psychic conditions – the states of the private processes and changes in those states. They are symptoms of nervousness, illness, pain, anger, embarrassment, sexual arousal, resentment, elation or other affective or physical circumstance. They generally accommodate gradation in expression and they may change continuously. They are, this is to say, analogic signals. In contrast, ritual's physical display is under conscious control. It stands in an indexical relationship not to private processes, physiological or psychological, but to conventions and conventional states. That is, it is concerned with the public order and the individual's participation in it. Finally, ritual acts as such communicate primarily in the digital rather than the analogic mode. They may of course carry messages analogically as well, but this is not fundamental to them. In fact, it may be strongly suggested that the digital messages of ritual display override, and possibly suppress, the analogic messages continuously and inevitably transmitted kinesically and paralinguistically, thus rendering them irrelevant.

Secondly, the general topic of ritual display also overlaps with the question of the use of icons or metaphors in ritual, a subject broached by Van Gennep (1960). He observed that particular kinds of rituals tend to include physical acts that seem to be formally similar to whatever it is that they seek to accomplish. Rites of separation, for instance, often include such acts as cutting something, perhaps the hair. More recently such scholars as Tambiah (1973) and Fernandez (1974) have been concerned with metaphor, particularly material metaphor, and metaphor making use of the body of the performer. We shall return to the matter of metaphor *per se* later. At the beginning, however, we shall be more concerned with what might be called the metaphor of matter. That is, we shall not be concerned with what may be represented in physical display but with *what may be represented by the sheer material nature of that display.*

1. Substantiating the non-material

That material display communicates more, or other than, what may be communicated by words is clear in some cases. In earlier chapters we were concerned with displays, such as the *Muminai* of the Siaui, the *Abutu* of of Goodenough Island, and the potlatch of the Northwest coast in which such incorporeal qualities as worthiness, prestige, political influence, or rights to titles are represented by objects – pigs, yams and copper plaques – and actions taken with respect to them – distributing them, destroying them, eating them.

In such representations, we noted, an aspect of the relationship between signs and significata to which we are accustomed is inverted. It is more usual for the subject matter of messages to have weight and dimension, and for the signs representing them to be insubstantial: words, spoken or written. But, it was suggested, when that which is signified is incorporeal, like worthiness or influence, its representation may have to be material if it is to be taken seriously. Claims to rank and honor are empty unless made substantial. To use the phrase of the Limba people of Sierra Leone (Finnegan 1969), such words "must be made heavy" if they are to be convincing. Corporeal representation gives weight to the incorporeal and gives visible substance to aspects of existence which are themselves impalpable, but of great importance in the ordering of social life. It may be recalled in this regard that displays such as those of Goodenough Island and Guadalcanal big men stand in an indexical relationship to that which they represent, and that, therefore, they do not simply symbolize influence or prestige. They *demonstrate* it in a way that leaves little room for empty boasting.

The indexical messages made heavy by material representation in ritual are not, of course, confined to those concerning prestige and influence. Among the Limba ritual announcements of binding intentions, for instance by a man to his affines when he takes a bride, or when he announces to a chief that he wishes to take up residence in his territory, require a gift to "make his words heavy" (Finnegan 1969). And we may be reminded here of the proposal advanced long ago by Mauss (1954) concerning the moral obligation to return gifts, an obligation intrinsic to their very acceptance. Conventional bonds cannot be specified without words, but cannot always be established by words alone. The passage of something of value may be necessary to realize or establish them – that is, to stipulate them, accept them and give them weight. Thus, in Western law contracts are usually not binding unless there is a consideration. It is significant that even in instances in which valuables do not change hands words may not be enough to establish bonds or obligations. The deal may be "closed" or "sealed" with a hand clasp, or a toast or something of the sort.

Bonds among the living are not alone in requiring substantiation. The substantiation of the conventional by the material is also an aspect of sacrifice, whether the sacrificial act is understood to be an offering or a communion. If an offering, devotion is made substantial; if a communion, that which might otherwise remain an abstraction is first made substantial and then informs the performer as it is assimilated into his substance.

The advantages of communication through physical display over verbal communication are not as obvious in other instances as they are in the potlatch, the *abatu* or Limba declarations. Not all of the messages transmitted in the physical acts of ritual, or through the use of objects and substances would resist what would seem to be adequate translation into words.

Postures and movements seem to be more problematic in this regard than do prestations of yams, blankets or pigs. In many parts of the world, for instance, postures of subordination – kneeling, prostration and the like – are assumed by the lowly before those of high rank. It would seem that the messages transmitted by such displays could be adequately rendered verbally as "I submit to you" or something of the sort. But since such messages are often transmitted by physical display rather than speech it is plausible to assume that the display indicates more, or other, than what the corresponding words would say, or indicates it more clearly. By kneeling or prostrating himself a man seems to be doing more than *stating* his subordination to an order. He is *actually subordinating himself* to that order. In fact, he is so subordinating himself, at least for the time being, because, in line with previous discussions, the signal is performative. It may be factive, and it is likely to have commissive implications.

It may be objected that the connection of the formal physical acts of ritual to the states with which they are concerned is no less conventional than words would be and that, as Austin and others have argued at length, and as the last chapter attempted to make clear, words too have performative or illocutionary force. Words should, therefore, be as effectively subordinating, to continue with the present example, as postures. Indeed, without language which is the foundation upon which all the conventional signals of humans stand and without which the conventions by which humans live could not be stipulated, there would be no performative or factive acts. To claim illocutionary force for postures or movements is not to distinguish them from utterances. It may be suggested, however, that more ambiguity veils the informative force of speech than it does such physical acts as bowing or saluting. If a man only voices subordination he may seem to be doing no more than stating, reporting or asserting it (since stating, describing and asserting are always or almost always done verbally). But if he kneels he is more clearly displaying his subordination (since stating, describing, reporting and asserting are almost never done through posture or gesture) by performing an act taken to be in itself subordinating. This is to say that the performative nature of physical acts is likely to be clearer than the equivalent utterance, which could possibly be taken for a mere report or statement.

There is a related, but perhaps more important point. For lack of better terminology, it may be suggested that physical display is "performatively stronger" or "performatively more complete" than utterances. Whereas a performative utterance achieves a purely conventional or institutional effect through a conventional informative procedure, posture and movement, in adding physical dimension to the procedure, may seem to add physical dimension to the effect as well. That is, the effect achieved is not only conventional but material. The act brings into being not only an institutional fact but a correlated "brute" or physical fact, as "palpable" – while it lasts – as water or wind or rock. Through kneeling, bowing, saluting, tugging the forelock, uncovering the head or covering it, subordination, piety, devotion (or whatever the gestures represent), are "realized," that is, made into *res*, and as such achieve an apparent naturalness equal to that of flowers or wind, if not rock. Taboos are of interest in this context. Requiring the individual to refrain from physical acts of which he or she is capable, or to avoid certain persons, objects or substances, may not only substantiate obedience and, possibly, like sacrificial offerings, devotion, but may also give substance to conventional distinctions. Moreover, taboos, while often or usually liturgically assumed, are generally realized outside of ritual. The orders from which they spring are thus extended by them into the secular world where they become not only material but apparently natural as well. We shall return to the "naturalizing" of convention at the end of the chapter. For now we may simply note that as "saying" may be a form of "doing," so may "doing" be a substantial way of "saying."

2. Special and mundane objects

To say that both ritual acts and the use in ritual of material objects and substances may substantiate – make substantial – that which would otherwise remain weightless is not to say that all acts, objects and substances are equivalents. It seems obvious that there are differences among what various materials and objects can effectively substantiate, and more general differences between postures and movements on the one hand and the use of materials and substances on the other surely prevail. Some brief suggestions are in order. They are not meant to be comprehensive.

The special objects manipulated in ritual, and the special places set aside for ritual performance may substantiate aspects of liturgical orders that cannot be substantiated by physical acts. The simple fact of the continued existence of the 1,000-year-old cathedral, for instance, does more than speak of the endurance of a liturgical order and its relationship to a place and a group. It demonstrates it. Even a new cathedral built to a traditional plan demonstrates the endurance of the plan, and thus the order specifying it, and so does the manipulation of sacra which are either themselves ancient or which conform to ancient patterns. In being fashioned to conform to an ancient form, moreover, the newly made object or building substantiates the continuing vitality, propriety or correctness of that form. In this it is no different from liturgical performance. (Indeed, in some instances, the manufacture of sacra is itself a liturgical performance.)

Obviously, there are, on the other hand, aspects of liturgical order than cannot be substantiated by buildings, new or old. The concept of the sacred will not be defined until a later chapter, but we may for the present rely upon a common sense understanding of it to observe that although an enduring sacred precinct can sanctify the performers or their current states, or their representations of their current states, it cannot substantially represent those states nor fluctuations in them, as can the yams and pigs given away in a Melanesian feast. The use of everyday objects or valuables in rituals may substantiate self-referential messages, making certain of them indexical. Buildings in which rituals are conducted, monuments and some smaller sacra on the other hand, seem to substantiate canon. We have noted too an indexical relationship between some common aspects of such objects – their age, their conformity to specification – and some aspects of liturgical orders – their endurance and their propriety.

Some manipulable sacra, such as the crowns of kings and the chrism with which they are annointed seem to be intermediate. On the one hand they represent enduring orders, but it is one man and not another who is crowned, and crowning is a simple performative affecting both the current state of whomever is crowned and the current state of social relations generally, The sacred pipe of the Oglala Sioux and some other American Indians is an icon of both the cosmos and the human being, and in smoking it the smoker became one with the cosmos (J. Brown 1971: 21, *passim*). Manipulable sacra, this is to say, in the mere fact of their material existence, may substantiate, or make material, aspects of enduring canonical orders, and at the same time, in their manipulation relate the enduring order to the particulars of the contemporary situation. To put it a little differently, such objects are themselves parts of canonical orders, but their manipulation is in part self-referential.

3. Acts and agents

Ancient sacra can substantiate the enduring nature of the canonical order, something which probably could not be substantiated by the use of the body alone. Nor could the body alone represent what can be represented by valuables. Pearl shells, blankets, yams, pigs, since they can be appropriated, collected, distributed and consumed, may substantiate certain aspects of the accumulator's relations with others – in taking his influence or authority, in giving his largesse and nurturance. Authority and generosity could not be substantiated by movement or posture. Indeed, a movement or posture unaccompanied by objects or substances of value would be mere posturing – vainglorious and boastful.

Acts, however, have virtues of their own, virtues possessed by neither the words of ritual nor the objects and substances that rituals may employ. Earlier it was proposed that in ritual, transmitter, receiver and canonical messages become one – are fused – in the participant, and it was argued that in ritual the performer accepts the liturgical order in which he participates. But since acceptance is not belief, and since belief can be withheld even when acceptance is given, a crucial question becomes: who or what is the performer, who or what is the accepting self or agent, of what is the accepting self constituted?

It now may be proposed that the use of the body defines the self of the performer for himself and others. We have seen, following Austin, that for this crucial self to be defined as the secret "heart" or "soul" of the actor, or as some other "backstage artiste" will not do. The accepting self must be palpable to others as well as to itself since acceptance is neither more nor less, necessarily, than a public act on the self's part. The words of acceptance alone, although audible, might well seem to be ephemeral, or to be separate or separable from the speaker – something distinct from himself. In contrast, a movement or posture is directly and immediately sensible to the performer as something inseparable from his being. The knees he bends, the head he bows are not ephemeral and they are not dispensable. The use of the body in ritual posture or gesture defines for the performer especially (but for witnesses as well) the nature of the accepting self. The self defined by the body drawn into a ritual posture is not composed of ephemeral words fluttering away from the speaker's mouth to dissolve into silence, nor is it yet his elusive "heart" or "mind" or "soul." When he kneels it is his inseparable, indispensable and enduring body that he identifies with his subordination. The subordinated self is neither a creature of insubstantial words from which he may separate himself without loss of blood, nor some insubstantial essence that cannot be located in space or confined in time. To put all of this a little differently, the use of the body to transmit the message of acquiescence or subordination constitutes a non-discursive meta-message about the discursive message being transmitted. It communicates both to the self and to others not only what could be conveyed by an apparently corresponding set of words (e.g., "I accept Allah"), but also a commitment of the living self to that message. Such physical acts seem to be more than "mere talk." It is the visible, present, living substance – bone, blood, gut and muscle – that is being "put on the line," that is "standing up [or kneeling down] to be counted," that is "putting its money where its mouth is," that constitutes the accepting agent.

Some brief elaboration is in order. First, it is not being claimed that all uses to which the body may be put are equivalent. There is a considerable difference between, let us say, kneeling or dancing on the one hand and undergoing circumcision, tattoo or scarification on the other. The worshipper gets off his knees sooner or later, but the scars of such wounds as circumcision are with their bearers always. They are irreversible, indelible and ever-present, distinguishing those who have suffered them from those who have not in contexts outside of ritual as well as in. This does not endow the irreversible and enduring stigmata of single rituals like circumcision with a moral, cosmic or semiotic superiority over more ephemeral postures or gestures. Such ineradicable marks are well-suited to indicating irreversible changes in whoever bears them, but they cannot, as can such gestures or postures as kneeling, genuflecting or baring the head, indicate reversible changes of state or renewal of commitment. Postures and scars have different liturgical import.

The distinction between ritual acts and objects is not always as clear as might be suggested by our discussion. A subincised Australian is himself a sacral object, at least his penis is. Conversely, he was subincised in a ritual. Similarly, the sun dance lodge of the Sioux was both a sacral object and the product of a series of ritual actions (Dorsey 1894, J. Brown 1971: 160). It is not always clear whether it is the object itself or the act producing the object which is of significance. For instance, the blessing of holy water could probably be regarded as nothing more than the consecration of water to ritual use, which is to say that the sanctified substance itself is of greater significance than the act of producing it. In contrast, the location of many paleolithic paintings in the dark and inaccessible depths of caves, and the fact that such paintings were some- times executed one on top of the other in palimpsest, strongly suggests that the act of painting them was of greater significance than the paintings themselves. In yet other instances both the act producing the object and the object itself are significant. The mark of subincision may be regarded as that which makes a man a sacral object, or as itself a sacral object, and as such is of continuing significance. But the ritual act of subincision, part of an elaborate liturgical order, is in itself of great significance, a significance surely related in considerable degree to the pain suffered in its course. Such pain must have great perlocutionary force. He who experiences it will never be the same again, and he who experiences it is clearly separated from those who have not, by the ordeal as well as by the mark the ordeal leaves.

4. Predication and metaphor

We are concerned here with, among other things, the matter of predication. Predication, the attribution of qualities to objects, is one of the fundamental processes of language and is impossible or even inconceivable in the absence of language. In the presence of language, however, acts given meaning by words as well as words themselves can be predicating, and our argument proposes that the perlocutionary force of physical predication is far greater in some circumstances than that of words alone. To say "John is a changed man" is one thing. For John to emerge from the ordeal of subincision is quite another.

I have not suggested with what John is predicated when he is subincised. Such is the order of Australian society that it can at least be said that he is predicated with manhood. After his subincision an Australian male may assume all the functions, ritual and social, of a mature man. But such an understanding, while it is correct is incomplete, for it does not propose why it is that young men are subincised, and do not suffer instead, let us say, the lopping off of a finger.

I do not believe that such a question can be answered definitively, but we may be helped by considering the matter of metaphor. Fernandez (1974) has suggested that the first mission of metaphor is to predicate "sign-images" upon inchoate subjects. In his view humans achieve their identities through a series of predications, some of which are imposed upon them by others, some of which are of their own choice, some of which are literal, others metaphoric.

"Metaphor is generally defined as 'a means of expressing one thing in terms of another,' or as Robert Frost said in his informal way, 'just putting this and that together'" (Thomas 1969: 3). A metaphor stipulates a formal similarity between two (or more) relationships, and may be expressed formally as A:B::C:D. To cite as an example one notion concerning the metaphor underlying Australian circumcision: as the foreskin is cut away from the boy's body so is he separated socially from his mother, and other women (Roheim 1945: 73ff.; Campbell, 1959: 93ff.). The foreskin, which, when it is removed, forms a ring of flesh, is being likened to the vulva. The youth's final separation from his mother's vulva seems prerequisite to his entrance into the vulvas of other women, and, as he is predicated with independence from his mother he is also predicated with a new degree or level of socio-sexual maturity.

There is surely more to circumcision among the Aranda and other Australians than this, and other interpretive suggestions have been made. We need not discuss them here. The point necessary to make is that the people themselves may not be altogether clear about precisely what it is that circumcision represents. As Fernandez (1974), Firth (1973: 75) and others have noted, the significata of such representations are often difficult or even impossible to put into words. Subincision is perhaps even more obscure than circumcision. It may be, as Bettelheim (1962: 45, 100, *passim*) and others have suggested on the basis of considerable evidence, that the subincision is a representation of the vagina and that, in being carved into the penis, the genitalia of both sexes are brought together on men in a way which gives to them a kind of reproductive completeness, or a mastery over procreative processes.

Their bodies, or at least their genitalia, may become more generally representations of the unification of opposites. But it is not clear to what in the natural, social or mythic world this completeness and unity point, to what other relations subincision and the subincised penis stand as a metaphor. They are left unspecified. The metaphor is incomplete, but in remaining incomplete it remains open and its scope of application can be expanded or changed. We may note too that the notions – they are hardly clear concepts – of completeness and unity are extremely abstract, so abstract that it is difficult to put them into words.

The matter of metaphor leads us back to the metaphor of matter. In subincision and similar events notions so abstract that words can barely grasp them are represented by material signs. The most abstract products of human thought and feeling are thus made substantial and in being made substantial, are being made comprehensible. When that sign is carved on the body the abstract is not only made substantial but immediate: nothing can be experienced more immediately than the sensations of one's own body – and if the mark is indelible, as in the cases of the subincision, the excised canine, the lopped finger, the scarified face, chest or back, it is ever-present. As the abstract is made alive and concrete by the living substance of men and women, so are men and women predicated by the abstractions which they themselves realize.

Possible grounds for notions of occult efficacy are implicit in this argument, particularly when it is taken together with previous discussions concerning the performativeness of ritual acts and their perlocutionary force.

That metaphoric thought is a component of notions of magic is, of course, a very old understanding in anthropology: it is implicit in both Frazerian categories of magical act, the sympathetic and the contagious. Tambiah (1973) has suggested that the logic of magical action is not merely metaphoric, but that it involves metaphoric manipulation, more specifically the correction of imperfect metaphors. Among the Zande, for instance, Evans-Pritchard (1937: 485) reports that chicken manure is used as a poultice to cure ringworm. Ringworm resembles chicken manure; in fact, the disease is called *Imanduraukondo*, literally fowl house sickness. Tambiah notes, however, that ringworm and the excrement of chickens stand in radically different relationships to the organisms with which they are associated. The chicken naturally voids itself of its feces. In contrast, it is the nature of ringworm to cling to the skins of those whom it afflicts. The point of the ritual application of chicken feces to ringworm is to change the relationship of the disease to patient to one which is similar to that of chicken manure to chicken.

The logic of this action can be represented verbally, and words do enter into it. But the fact is that real chicken manure is actually applied to the affliction. The efficacious principle, this is to say, is carried by a substance, or better, is intrinsic to the relationship between a substance and that which it aims to affect. It may be suggested that the substantial nature of the representation is as important to its success as are its metaphoric characteristics. The logic is metaphoric, but logic is not in itself action, and a plan or conception is not in itself an effect. The conception must be associated with the result. When the effect sought is material, substantiating the association, that is, representing it in a material fashion, associates the conception with the effect sought. It may be suggested that the distinction between powerful and occult efficacy would appear to the performers to be blurred in such an operation. Be this as it may, there may be a lesson of moral value in observing that under certain circumstances the feces of barnfowl are more convincing than the words of men.

The incompleteness characteristic of some metaphors may also make a contribution to notions of occult efficacy, particularly when combined with performativeness. We have noted that in some of the metaphors in which ritual abounds one "side" is left unspecified. In the example we cited it was not clear what entities or concepts may be related in a manner similar to the relationship of subincision to penis. We noted, however, that the relationship of subincision to penis is really very abstract. It can perhaps be pointed to by such terms as "inversion," "completeness," and "unification" and there are surely others. The abstractness of the relationship and the vagueness of its domain of application may well provide it with mystery, the aura of which may veil from the participants the simple performative nature of a ritual which transforms youths into men, that is, which predicates them with manhood. To put this a little differently, the abstract nature of the relationships represented in incomplete metaphors may be one more basis for notions of occult efficacy.

5. Ritual words

Having noted the special virtues of ritualized postures and gestures, we should not overdraw the distinction between them and words. We have been contrasting display with ordinary language, but not all language is ordinary. Words themselves may become ritualized, and ritualized words may also be clear and carry conviction. It is of great interest that ritualized utterances eschew one of ordinary language's special talents: its ability to split and split again the world into ever finer categories and conditions and conditionals. It is virtually definitive of ritual speech that it is stereotyped and stylized, composed of specified sequences of words that are often archaic, is repeated under particular, usually well-established circumstances, and great stress is often laid upon its precise enunciation. As Maurice Bloch (1973) has emphasized, in contrast to ordinary discourse in which considerable choice is open to speakers at a number of points in any utterance, in ritual formulae the "features of juncture," those components of speech indicating relations among the referents, are immutable. In M. C. Bateson's (1973) terms, ritual utterances are "fused." This is to say that meaning is derived from them as unsegmented wholes, or as wholes only segmented into minimal meaningful units of considerable length, usually much greater length than is the case in ordinary speech. We shall return to further implications of the rigidity of ritual speech in the next chapter. Here we need note only that because of its fixity ritual cannot exercise language's ability to express gradation, qualification and the uniqueness of the here and now. But if flexibility and subtlety is eschewed, clarity is gained. A man swears an oath or he does not, he pledges fealty, or he does not. The distinction between recitation and non-recitation is unambiguous and so are differences in at least some of the formal aspects of the conventional states of affairs contingent upon these alternatives. If peculiarities unique to the present state of affairs are not obliterated by the standardization intrinsic to the formula, which assimilates the present states of affairs to an enduring category of states of affairs, they are at least subordinated to it.

As far as form is concerned, ritual formulae are to ordinary language as ritual postures and gestures are to ordinary instrumental activity. Leach (1966) was undoubtedly correct in stating that ritual cannot be distinguished from myth on the grounds that myth is in words while ritual is "in action." Words themselves, when they are no longer "just talk" or "mere words" but ritualized formulae as stylized as curtseys or genuflections, may, and often are themselves, constituents of display. If it is clear that the words spoken are ritual words and not simply ordinary

speech, they may transmit indexical meanings as clearly as ritual postures. It may be suggested, however, that they are not as convincing, for
ritual words by themselves lack the ability to substantiate the messages
they transmit. Yet, such messages may be affirmed by further words, a
matter to which we shall return in discussing sanctity and sanctification.

It should not be imagined, however, that ritual words are simply a
poor substitute for ritual acts and objects. The relationship between the
physical and the spoken in ritual is, rather, complementary, each class
claiming virtues the other lacks.

As ritual acts and objects have special communicational qualities so, of
course, do words have others, as Tambiah (1968) has argued. Whereas
acts and substances represent substantially that which is present, the
words of liturgy can connect that which is present to the past, or even to
the beginning of time, and to the future, or even to time's end. In their
invariance itself the words of liturgy implicitly assimilate the current
event into an ancient or ageless category of events, something that
speechless gesture or mortal substance of expendable objects alone
cannot. Because of their symbolic quality, this is to say, invariant words
easily escape from the here and now and thus can represent felicitously
the canonical, which is never confined to the here and now. Objects like
the cross can have symbolic value, it is true, and thus signify that which
is present in neither time nor space, but such objects must be assigned
symbolic value by words, and words are ultimately necessary to representations of the canonical.

Ritual words, then, are not altogether ineffective for the transmission of
self-referential messages, but it is in other aspects of ritual communication
that words are indispensable. While acceptance of, or participation in,
canon is easily – and best – signaled by physical display, canons themselves must be specified in words or in material symbols assigned meaning
by words. Gods, dead ancestors and the like, not existing materially in the
here and now, cannot be referred to by acts whose designata are limited to
the present. Reference to them is impossible without words. The same
may even be said for conventions having existence in the contemporary
social order – knighthood, kingship, pollution – and the conventional acts
relating to them – dubbing, crowning, the violation of taboo, for, as we
have observed, behavior is not convention.

6. The reunion of form and substance

The relationship of ritual's reliance upon language to its reliance upon
material representation is, roughly, that of the canonical to the self-

referential. This is obviously not to say that self-referential messages are never transmitted by ritual formulae, nor that canon may not be translated into and made substantial by physical display. It is simply to recognize that, on the one hand, canon is contingent upon words and, on the other, that the material components of ritual are especially appropriate for the indexical transmission of messages concerning the current state of the transmitters. Indeed, given the problematic nature of the accepting self, movement or posture may be crucial to the indexical transmission of the message of acceptance. The message of acceptance is itself a meta-message concerning the canon. The use of the body is of yet higher order. It is a meta-message concerning the nature of the acceptance – that it is the act of an identifiable living person.

The informational virtues of the physical and verbal aspects of liturgy seem to complement each other, although it may be that a term like "complement" does not express their intimacy. It might be better to say that they complete each other. As the material aspects of ritual provide the liturgical order with substance, so its words provide it with form. Form and substance, norm, convention or ideal on the one hand and behavior on the other, are united in ritual. Indeed, ritual can perhaps be regarded as the reunion of forms and substances forever coming apart in the stresses of daily usage. By drawing himself into a posture to which canonical words give meaning the performer incarnates or embodies a canonical form. As he participates in the form or order he incorporates it into himself. His body gives substance to the canon as the canon provides his body with form.

It seems that the cosmic, social, psychic and physical become, as it were, fused in such a representation. That is, in the successful conjunction of word and act there may be, or seem to be, a unification of first, the physical, affective and cognitive processes constituting the self; of second, the unified self with its visible representation; and, finally, of the self and its representation with the canon in which it participates. A ritual posture or gesture, moreover, is the specified one of the enormous number of positions or movements the body *could* assume that it *does* assume. Its assumption or enactment thus not only indicates, *ipso facto*, conformity to an order, it also poses the restricted nature of that order. The performer lives both the order and his acceptance of it in the formal posture or gesture. A living metaphor of the union of form and substance is generated as the self-referential and canonical come together in the ritual act.

That ritual is a union of form and substance is explicitly recognized and emphasized in eastern and western Christian thought concerning the sacraments and their performance. In the Orthodox Church a sacrament is a "mystery," that is, "a rite which under some visible form is the cause of and conveys to the soul of the faithful man, the invisible grace of God; instituted by our Lord, through whom each of the faithful receives divine grace." Mysteries were instituted to be "badges" of the "true sons of God," "sure signs of faith" and "indubitable remedies against sins" (Peter Moglia, cited in R. Parsons 1918: 902). In addition to celebration by an ordained priest, (a requirement that may be dispensed with in some instances) mysteries have two requirements: proper matter as, for instance, water in baptism and the joining of hands in marriage, and the invocation of the Holy Spirit with forms of words "whereby the Priest consecrates the mystery by the power of the Holy Spirit." The proper matter makes visible and substantial that which because it is only spirit would otherwise remain impalpable. Spirit cannot manifest itself separately from substance in this world of substance, and thus the "badges" of the "true sons of God," the "sure signs of their faith" are *necessarily* material.

In the western church too, a sacrament is a *signum rei sacrae*, the *signum* being palpable, the *res* impalpable. Since a sacrament is a sensible sign it is obvious that something visible or tangible is requisite, and, as in the eastern church, each of the sacraments has its proper matter: water in baptism, the laying on of hands in ordination, oil in unction, bread and wine in communion, and so on. Speaking of baptism in particular, Augustine spoke of "adding word to matter to make sacrament" (Lacey 1918: 907). It is perhaps significant in this regard that until well after Augustine's time the term "sacrament" referred to much more than the seven rites which have, since the Council of Trent, comprised the "sacraments properly so-called." His usage seems to have had much in common with that of Tertullian and Cyprian for whom it tended to encompass all Christian ritual or even the whole Christian religion.[1]

In the thirteenth century substance *per se*, rather than substance as visible or material sign of the invisible, became of interest to Catholic thinkers when William of Auxerre applied to sacraments the distinction derived from the Peripatetic metaphysic, between matter and form: "The sensible act or thing used in the administration of a sacrament was likened to formless matter, being indeterminate in use and adaptable to many purposes; it was determined to a spiritual significance by the use of words, which then played the part of the metaphysical *forma essentialis*" (Lacey 1918: 907). As matter is by itself formless, so is form lacking in matter without efficacy, indeed, without worldly existence. Although this doctrine was becoming explicit at a time when the narrow definition of sacrament as rite conveying grace was emerging, it seems to have been implicit in earlier thought and usage; and, moreover, the term "sacrament" was still being used by some writers in a rather more general way. Be this as it may, the seven sacraments "properly so-called," are not unique in including word and act, thereby bringing together form and substance, nor even are these seven augmented by the so-called "sacramentals," such as the anointing of kings and the consecration of nuns. Indeed, the burden of our argument is that the inclusion of both word and matter is characteristic of ritual in general, and it may be suggested that the union of form and substance is latent in the structure of ritual generally, whether or not it becomes manifest in the doctrines of performers.

7. The union of form and substance as creation
In including within itself both word and substance ritual may contain within itself a paradigm of creation. It is at least possible to say that in its unification of form and substance ritual bears formal resemblance to a large array of accounts of creation far-flung in time and space. Many myths of the world's origin, as Bateson has (1972b: xxiiiff.) reminded us, do not take creation to be, simply, or even at all, the production of matter *ex nihilo*. Indeed, the origin of matter is often ignored, or it seems to be taken for granted that a primordial matter always existed. That aspect of beginnings to which attention is explicitly paid is not the creation of matter *per se* but giving form or order to a previously existing but inchoate primordial substance. Creation, this is to say, is represented as the informing of substance and substantiation of form, a union of form and substance.

Creation as described in Genesis provides a familiar example. The translation by Speiser (1964: 3) from oldest sources would render the opening phrases (less majestically but perhaps more faithful to the original than more familiar English texts) as follows: "When God set about to create heaven and earth – the world being then a formless waste, with darkness over the seas and only an awesome wind sweeping over the water – God said 'Let there be light' and there was light." We may note first that the matter existing in the beginning seems to have been water, which is perhaps as close as it is possible to come in ordinary experience to formless substance. Some ambiguity must, of course, be recognized. The Hebrew phrase *Tohu wa-bohu* rendered by Speiser as "formless waste" is a hendiadys meaning, literally, "unformed and void" and the term "void" does suggest the creation of formless matter out of nothing previous to its shaping into cosmos, the ordered world of form and difference. But be this as it may, the creation of matter is no more than implied in this passage, and as Gregory Bateson has observed (1972b: xxiii), if it is noticed at all it is summarily dismissed. No procedure by which matter was first created is described, whereas that which transforms already existent but inchoate matter into formed matter – a sequence of utterances – is, in sharp contrast, set out in detail. It is clear that the origin of substance is of little interest to the author, or authors, of the first chapter of Genesis, and seems not to be given much attention by myth-makers generally, perhaps because it is something about which not much need be said, for the appearance of primordial matter does not bear on the problematic aspects of human experience to the degree to which the outlines of primordial ordering do. That substance exists is obvious and its creation is likely to be taken for granted or assumed, as it is in some of the formulations of modern cosmology.[2] Moreover, it is hard to imagine substances radically different from those which one has experienced, and to do so is hardly more than idle and harmless entertainment. Why the existing order rather than others that could easily be imagined prevails is a very different matter.

If the first chapter of Genesis provides us with a familiar instance of creation represented as the informing of substance, it is far from unique. It is, rather, a late and well-wrought example of what may have been rather general in ancient near-eastern thought. According to the Babylonian Enuma Elish, upon which the Genesis account may well have drawn, there was first "a watery chaos composed of the mingled waters of Apsu, the abyss of sweet waters, Tiamat, the salt water ocean, and Mummu who may ... represent cloud banks and mist (Hooke 1963: 60ff., Heidel 1951: 18ff.). There was not yet dry land, nor had even the Gods come into being. Apsu belonged to the orderly framework of nature, and it was out of Apsu that land, and all other things in the orderly universe were eventually formed. Tiamat who is personified as a she-dragon, and who is perhaps echoed in the Old Testament in the figures of Tehom, Leviathan and Rahab, was, in contrast a yet older principle whose archaic waters still exist beyond the limits of the orderly universe, and remain ever ready to burst into the world if the laws excluding or confining them are removed. The ordered world is created or formed when Marduk, himself a descendant of Tiamat, slays her in single combat by driving the winds, which are his followers, into her open mouth distending her belly. He then administers the *coup de grâce* by piercing her with an arrow. Splitting her in two "like a shellfish," he fixes half of her carcass on high to hold back the waters of heaven, the other half remaining underfoot to serve as ground. Apportioning functions to others of the new gods of light he establishes order in the universe occupying the space between the two halves of Tiamat's corpse.

Ancient Egyptian representations of creation, although much more varied and complex, (see Frankfort 1948: 148ff.) and free of the conflicts that wrack creation in Mesopotamia, share with the latter the idea of the pre-existence of a primordial chaos and its personification by monsters. The Hermopolis cosmology speaks of

eight weird creatures fit to inhabit the primeval slime. Four were snakes and four frogs or toads ... They were not part of the created universe, but of chaos itself, as their names show. Nun was the formless primeval ocean, and his female counterpart, Naunet, was the sky over it. Or perhaps it would be better to say that Nun was chaotic primeval matter, Naunet primeval space ... The next pair of the ogdoad were Kuk and Kauket, the illimitable and the boundless. Then came Huh and Hauhet, darkness and obscurity; and finally Amon and Amaunet, the hidden and concealed ones. If we allow that some of these gods, such as Nun and Naunet represent primordial elements, the uncreated material out of which cosmos came forth, then Amon and Amaunet represent air and wind ... [which are] ... chaotic elements. They [the eight] were male and female, and they brought forth the sun ... the eight mysteriously made the sun-god come forth from the waters and therewith their function was fulfilled.   *(Frankfort 1948: 154f.)*

Subsequent creative or formative functions were attributed to many gods; "in fact, most temples claimed it for their deities" (Frankfort 1948: 150). Khnum shapes all living things on his potter's wheel; Ptah-The-Risen-Land, the primeval mound, the first dry ground to emerge above the waters, shapes the sun and moon on his potter's wheel, and creates all living things by *Maat*, that is, by truth, order and exactness; Osiris forms the earth, water, plants, fowls, animals with his hand; Thoth creates Seb and Nut, earth and sky, by his word while he is still submerged in the chaos of Nun; and creative functions were also attributed to Aten, Atum and others (Frankfort 1948: 148ff.; Petrie 1911: 184f.). In sum, in ancient Egypt creation was not viewed as "the bringing forth of something out of nothing ... to the eastern mind it contains the idea of regulation, of cosmos. To a large extent the material is there already and the act of creation consists of forming the chaotic material into a living organism" (Wensinck 1923, cited by Frankfort 1945: 150).

Some, but not all, of the deities to whom Egyptian cosmologies attributed the shaping of the cosmos are aspects of the sun (Ptah, for instance is not, nor is Thoth). As Wensinck suggested, the sun seems a particularly appropriate creator in systems emphasizing the formative aspects of creation for it is not only an obvious source of energy, it also "rules the changes of day and night, of the seasons, and of the years."

A number of Greek cosmogonies also seem to proceed from primordial unorganized matter, rather than from the void, although this may not be as clear as in the instances already cited. The Iliad makes Oceanus, the ocean, the father of all the Gods, and it may be that Oceanus, like the primeval waters of the Babylonians, Egyptians and Hebrews, can be taken to be primordial matter, although behind him and Tethys, earth and first mother, stands the goddess Night who may represent the void (Burns 1911: 145). The theogony of Hesiod commences with Chaos, out of which came Gaia and Eros on the one hand and Erebus and Night on the other, and from them proceeded the ordered cosmos. It is unclear whether Chaos was – as we generally take the term to suggest – formless unordered matter, or whether it was void. Etymology suggests the latter (Burns 1911: 146), but whether or not Chaos, and possibly Night are representations of nothingness, attention is focused upon the ordering of matter already in existence rather than upon bringing matter into existence. Later cosmogonies continued this emphasis. That of Phere-cydes derived the cosmos from three principles that were alike eternal, these being Zeus, spirit; Chronos, time; and Chthonia, primary matter. One of its variations is reminiscent of and was no doubt affected by cosmogonies of the near East. Before Cosmos is formed by Zeus (who, since he is pure spirit and thus stands outside of the world, has transformed himself into Eros to undertake this activity) a conflict between Cronos (a descendant of Chronos) and the dragon Ophioneus for the lordship of nature develops. Only after the victorious Cronos casts the dragon into the sea can Zeus set about his task. The details of this myth are not entirely compatible with other aspects of the Cos-mogony, but as Burns (1911: 147) observed, "the meaning is entirely clear: before the ordered world, the Cosmos, can be established, a victory must be won over disorder." Zeus can then embroider "earth and ocean and ocean's dwellings" upon the world mantle.

The notion of creation as the informing, rather than the production, of substance is not confined to the Eastern Mediterranean, nor is it characteristic only of high civilizations, such as those appearing early in that region. A similar emphasis is found in the myths of some tribal peoples, even in those of hunters and gatherers. The myths associated with the Gadjari and other rituals of the Walbiri people of Central

Australia, and those concerning the Wawilak sisters of
people of Arnhem Land, may be cited here, as could those
their neighbors. The Gadjari rituals of the Walbiri are ¹
exploits of the two Mamandabari brothers who emerge f
the Mulungu hill in the dreamtime, the mythical time ⸣
still in some sense persists. "Their first action is to sing about tnen ...
in order to establish or validate their identity and efficacy" (Meggitt
1966: 5). They then begin to travel southeast across Walbiri territory, at
first continuing to sing their names. As they proceed, however, they see
and sing of places and species, their seeing and singing bringing them
into being, and, as they fashion bullroarers, they sing that the patterns
with which they inspire the sacred objects will represent the path they
intend to travel.

The singing and the incisions, be it noted, do not represent a path that
already exists, but a plan for a path and the features it connects, which
are yet to be brought into existence. It is, as it were, a blueprint rather
than a map. Contemplating the patterns on the bullroarers – lines of
points, each of which are composed of concentric circles, the several
points being connected by both straight lines and arcs – they set off
singing, each brother venturing out in arcs from the straight line of
advance from one represented point to the next. "In this way they can see
and by doing so 'create' more of the country they traverse. At the same
time each carries a bullroarer in each hand and swings his arms out to
form the same pattern of arcs as their walking takes, and so to mark the
country ... as they walk in wide sweeps they swing their arms so
vigorously that the bullroarers cut the ground deeply to form the creek
now known as Gadara" (Meggitt 1966: 8). Thus they progress, singing
and swinging, across the country, "creating" species and places by seeing
and singing them, that is, by comprehending them, bringing them into
the world by subsuming them under the pre-existing order of bullroarer
and songs, if not into actual material existence. In the course of their
travels they not only establish places and species but also rituals, and in
crossing many dreaming sites and tracks established by other creatures,
they assimilate knowledge of the rituals associated with them, and the
crossing of tracks itself weaves a larger and more comprehensive order
than is established by the creation of one track alone.

The creative activities of the Wawilak sisters of Murngin myth are not
dissimilar from those of the Mamandabari men (Warner 1937). Coming
out of the far inland, they walk toward the sea naming places, and
when they kill animals for food they give them the names they bear to

his day, telling each thing killed that it will soon be sacred. This elaborate myth, which also provides charter for circumcision, treats of the transcendence of linguistic differences by totemic affiliations, considers the origins of female pollution and establishes the grounds for several complex sets of rituals, culminates in the swallowing and regurgitation of the Wawilak women and their offspring by the great python Julunggul, but these aspects of it do not concern us now. What is of interest is that creation is represented in this myth, as in that of the Mamandabari brothers of the Walbiri, as the informing – the forming, shaping, or ordering – of previously existing but inchoate substance and the substantiation of previously existing but incorporeal form.

The cosmogony and cosmology of the Navajo bear a family resemblance to those we have been discussing. Witherspoon (1977: 47) states explicitly that the Navajo take cosmic order to have been produced by the informing of substance and the substantiation of form, and form is associated in a complex way with language. For the Navajo "in the beginning were the word and the element, the symbol and the symbolized." The first lines of the "emergence myth" reads:

The One that is called "Water Everywhere"
The One that is called "Black Earth"
The One that is called "First Words"   *(1977: 45–46)*

Words as well as formless substances are among the world's primordial constituents. "To the Navajo, man can only think with symbols, so some symbols must have existed before thought" (Witherspoon 1977: 43). Words – symbols – are, as it were, elements of order or form, but do not themselves constitute order or form. Order or form, it is true, is imposed upon the world and its processes through speech but speech is not itself word, nor is it language. It is, rather, uttered words. Speech is the outer form of thought, thought, in turn, is the outer form of knowledge. Knowledge, finally, is for the Navajo an awareness of the primordial constituents of the universe, among which are First Words. "Unlike Adam, First Man did not go about naming things (creating symbols), he went about learning the names of things (interpreting reality through already established symbols)" (Witherspoon 1977: 43).

"Although First Man and First Woman were not the originators or inventors of the symbol, they were the originators of form. The capacity to organize, arrange and pattern symbols is found in the intellect. Symbols are the building blocks of mental images, and just as man cannot build a house without materials, so he cannot construct mental images of the universe without symbolic elements" (Witherspoon 1977:

43). Having gained knowledge of, that is to say having become aware of, primordial symbols, First Man and First Woman thought them into an order in accordance with language, which is not only a congeries of words but a set of rules – a form or pattern – for representing knowledge in words. Knowledge, represented in language and ordered by thought, is then imposed upon the world through acts of uttering words, that is, performatively through speech.

We cannot fail to note a progression in this account. Form and then order emerge as one proceeds from what the Navajo take to be inner forms to ever more outward forms, as primordial constituents are embraced by the awareness of knowledge represented in language, then organized by thought patterned in language and finally projected upon the world through speech.[3]

As Witherspoon points out, the accomplishment of Navajo First Man – the learning of previously existing names of things – does seem to be different from that of Adam, who named things himself. In fact, however, medieval Jewish mystical thought, including exegeses of the scriptural account of man's creation, comes close to the Navajo view:

Kabbalistic speculation and doctrine is concerned with the realm of the divine emanations, or *Sefiroth*, in which God's creative power unfolds ... Insofar as God reveals himself, he does so through the creative power of the *Sefiroth* ... God ... is always conceived under one or more [there are ten emanations] of these aspects of His Being ... The [creative] process described as the emanation of divine energy and divine light [the Sefiroth] was also characterized as the unfolding of the divine language ... [The Kabbalists] speak ... of spheres of light; but in the same context they speak also of divine names and the letters of which they are composed ... The secret world of the godhead is a world of language, a world of divine names that unfold in accordance with a law of their own.

(Scholem 1969: 35f.)

A remarkable book from pre-Kabbalistic times, the anonymous *Sefir Yetsirah* (Book of Creation, or Book of Formation) of the third to sixth century AD, should also be mentioned here. This work, according to Scholem, played a crucial part in the development of the *golem* concept.

The term "golem," in its one occurrence in the Bible [Psalm 139: 16] and in some later sources, seems to have meant "unformed" or "amorphous," and was used as an equivalent for the Greek *hyle*. It came, however, to designate in legend, folklore and mystical literature creatures resembling Frankenstein's monster, creatures fashioned from earth to whom life had been imparted by the magicians or mystics who were their makers.   *(Scholem 1969: 161, passim)*

The parallel to the creation of Adam (the Hebrew for earth being Adamah, for man being Adam) is obvious, and ritual procedures for producing golems may have taken place as mystical exercises or initiations.   *(Scholem 1969: 184, passim)*

Significant for the creation of the golem were the names of God and the letters, which are the signatures of all creation. These letters are the structural elements, the stones from which the edifice of creation was built. The Hebrew term employed by the author in speaking of the consonants as "elementary letters" undoubtedly reflects the ambivalence of the Greek word *stoicheia*, which means both letters and elements.

we read in the second chapter [of the *Sefir Yetsirah*]: "Twenty-two letter elements: He outlined them, hewed them out, weighed them, combined them, and exchanged them [transformed them ...] and through them created the soul of all creation and everything else that was ever to be created" ... How did he combine, weigh and exchange them? A [... in Hebrew ... a consonant] with all [other consonants] and all with A, B with all and all with B, G with all and all with G, and they all return in a circle to the beginning through two-hundred-thirty-one gates – the number of the pairs that can be formed from the twenty-two elements – and thus it results that everything created and everything spoken issue from one name.

Both the context and linguistic usage make it clear that ... this name ... is the name of God [That is, His Name, or rather one of them, is the utterance produced by following the formula A with all and all with A, B with all ... etc.] .... Thus, at every "gate" in the circle formed by the letters of the alphabet there stands a combination of two consonants, which ... correspond to the two letter roots of the Hebrew language, and through these gates the creative power goes out into the universe ... every thing or being in it [the universe] exists through one of these combinations.   *(Scholem 1969: 168)*

In accounts taking creation to be the informing of substance and the substantiation of form, we note that form is not always, but often, associated with word. The heroes and heroines of the Australian Dreamtime, as we have seen, provide form to things by naming them in speech or song; in Genesis Chaos is ordered into light and darkness, dry land and ocean by the utterances of God; and Thoth also created by word. We could also have cited here the Dogon theologian Ogotemmeli's account of creation (Griaule 1965: *passim*), and the views of the Nuer, who identify God's will and God's creative activity with his word (Evans-Pritchard 1956: 6, 12). The association of "form" and word was patent in ancient Greece where Logos was not only word, but an order that was possible for men to discover through use of the reason they possess by virtue of their possession of language, and Christ, the Second Adam who brought a new order to humans, was Logos become flesh. "As the word is the utterance of the thought and at the same time its representative and equivalent and as it were its image projected beyond the speaker, it was an apt term for the Son of a purely spiritual Being" (Attwater 1961: 528), "who we may add is himself, unlike his father, not entirely spiritual. As Christ was *Logos* incarnate, so in the *Targums*, the Aramaic version of the Old Testament, God was sometimes referred to as *Memra*, meaning utterance."

Christ is not, in this conception, simply the Word, but the *living* word, and *Memra* is not merely word, but *utterance* – breathed word. It is of interest to note here that the Nuer word for God, *Kwoth*, derives from the word for breath, as do the Latinate spirit (from *spirate*, to breathe) and the Greek form *pneuma*. The Hebrew *Ruah Elohim*, the primordial wind that sweeps the formless waste in the first lines of Genesis, may be rendered as the breath as well as the wind of God, and *Ruah* carries the meaning of spirit as well as breath and wind. It was, moreover, *Ruah* that God breathed into the earth (*Adamah*) that was to become Man (*Adam*) and finally the first particular man, Adam.

Breath is obviously associated with living processes themselves, but the mouth, through which the breath flows and into which in some creation myths spirit is breathed, is also the organ of speech. While the association of God's Ruah with speech is not made explicit in Genesis, it is assumed in the Book of Creation and commentaries on that work. The rite of the 231 gates, an epitome of Hebrew phonemics, morphemics and canonical form, initiated the inspiration of insensible earth by language into living and intelligent man.

Language and life are thus joined in utterance, and in the notion of breath-spirit. We may recall here that for the Navajo it is not word or language or thought that finally orders the world. It is utterance or speech. Now speech in the Navajo view itself partakes of substance as well as form, for the Navajo take air to be a substance. It is, however, a substance with peculiar properties. "Air is the only substance or entity in the Navajo world with an inherent capacity to move and to bear knowledge" (Witherspoon 1977: 53). Speech is the substance air modulated – formed, that is to say, by thought, itself composed of words organized in accordance with the rules of language. Speech is air in patterned motion, and motion for the Navajo is one with animation. Without air there is no motion, without motion there is no life. "Without air ... the digestive and respiratory systems cannot function, the mind cannot think, and the body cannot produce sound or movement. The body has no inherent capacity for thought, speech or movement; it acquires these capacities from air" (Witherspoon 1977: 70). Speech – breathed word, enlivened language, thoughtful air – is intermediate between insubstantial form and formless substance, for it partakes of both form and substance and its motion carries form to substances that without it would remain inert.

8. Ritual, creation, and the naturalization of convention

Representations of creation, then, like the performance of liturgies, often, if not always include both word and matter. In both myths of creation and in the enactments of ritual two seemingly primitive categories, form and substance, are united, and it may be suggested that in ritual there is a representation, or even reunion of this primordial union.

It could be argued, however, that any deliberate act unites form and substance and so are they united in any artifact. So does anything made or done in accordance with a pattern, whether or not it was fashioned by man, and we may ask, then, what is special about ritual with respect to the representation of such a union?

We may recall here an argument advanced in the last chapter. Usage always varies, and therefore usage tends to dissolve the form with respect to which it is undertaken and by which it is informed or guided. In ritual, however, there is not only reiteration but a re-establishment of the form itself. What better way to represent form than through the invariant words of a liturgical order, or to provide substance to that form than by drawing the body into a ritual posture? In the ritual act, itself specified by words and undertaken with respect to that which can ultimately be designated only in words, the self-referential and the canonical unite and become indistinguishable. Form is substantiated and substance informed as they were at the time of creation. They are one, as they were before behavior and history departed from the ordered ideal. There is in ritual not only a representation of creation, but a re-creation of the primordial order, the primordial union of form and substance which forever comes apart as the usages of life depart from the Order that should be.

To argue that both myths of creation and ritual establish order by uniting form and substance is not to account for why it is that humans should take the distinction between these categories, and their union, to be problematic, and more remains to be said about why it should be that form is so often associated with words. Nature, after all, is as full of form as it is of substance, and, as Bateson (1972b: xxv) points out, the distinction between form and substance does not arise naturally and spontaneously out of direct experience. No one has ever observed chaos. Some humans may, in their meditations, have contemplated pure form but none have witnessed it. Form and substance are inseparable in physical nature. They are obviously not inseparable in the language that distinguishes them, however, and it may well be that it is to linguistic phenomena that we should look for the grounds of the problem.

Bateson suggests that the distinction could have arisen as "an unconscious deduction from the subject-predicate relationship in the structure of primitive language" (1972b: xxv). Let us enlarge a little upon this profound insight. A predicate invests its subject with qualities or characteristics, and subjects are in some sense inchoate until they are predicated (see Fernandez 1974). Predicates, as it were, give form to subjects and thus stand to subjects as form does to substance. This is to suggest that the form–substance dichotomy applied to the world at large is a metaphor of the predicate–subject relationship fundamental to language and thought framed in language. However, there are few subjects that can be predicated only in a single way, and there are few predicates that can be applied to one subject only. All languages are constituted of lexicons that include many items which can serve as subjects and predicates and, of course, objects, conjunctions and modifiers as well. Syntax makes it possible to substitute many of the items in any class for each other, which is to say that in its very nature language makes alternatives conceivable. Indeed, it makes the conception of alternatives inevitable. The conception of alternative, moreover, is not limited to the conception of mere *circumstances* differing from those occurring, but includes as well the conception of *orders* different from those prevailing. If it is possible to say "This king is evil," it is possible to say "Kings are evil." The conception of alternative orders entails the conception of disorder, for alternative orders can hardly avoid being in disagreement or conflict, and it further entails the realization of disorder. Even if the prevailing order is not challenged by actions based upon alternative possibilities, the psyches of those who perceive alternatives may become arenas of internal conflict.[4] If humans have never witnessed chaos or formlessness they surely do have living experience of disorder, and some of them, at least, can sense the fragility as well as the arbitrariness of the orders under which they do happen to live.

We face here something which approaches paradox or contradiction, a problem which, like the facilitation of lying inherent in the symbolic relationship, is intrinsic to the very virtues of language. Language has made it possible for the members of a single species to specify conventionally an innumerable range of orders appropriate to differing environmental and historical circumstances. It thus frees the species from the limits of the genetic determination of the specifics of any socio-cultural order, and it has made it possible for the species to invade and dominate the great variety of environments of which the world is made. Conventional orders can be specified in language, but almost anything can be said in any language, and if there are any words there will be many words. The very flexibility of language which is fundamental to the adaptive flexibility of the species therefore threatens with confusion, with babel and with discord, the unique and particular orders specified by all particular groups within the species.

If there are going to be any words at all it is necessary to establish *The Word*. The Word is implicit in ritual, for the very invariance of canon is a meta-message concerning the words it includes: these words and not others. The Word is also established in cosmogonic myths by the assertion that it has established the natural world. We approach here the "naturalizing" so to speak, of convention.

In the primordial union of form and substance expressed in myth, of which ritual may be a representation, natural orders are apparently formed by and subordinated to orders over which words or utterances or primoridal languages preside. Language and its constituents are the essence of convention, and it would seem that in such conceptions nature is absorbed by convention or, to put it a little differently, subsumed by culture. But it should be kept in mind that the Mamandabari brothers and Wawilak sisters named and sang into being not only species and places but also rituals and principles of social life, and the God of Genesis not only brought into being man, woman and the animals, he specified proper relations among them. No distinction is made between the conventional and the natural in their manner of formation or in the agencies forming them. If the existence of both the natural order and the conventional order are accounted for by similar operations of the same creative agencies, the conventional and the natural remain indistinct from each other: the conventional remains as apparently natural as earth or trees or light.

It is entertaining to note that convention becomes part of nature by being accounted for supernaturally. Whereas many creation myths suggest, on the face of it, the assimilation of the natural by previously existing and more encompassing orders founded upon cultural constituents – a "culturizing" of nature, so to speak – the deeper message may be the converse. In assimilating natural orders to themselves cultural orders assimilate themselves to nature. Cultural or conventional orders, by themselves arbitrary and fragile, thus come to partake of the necessity and durability of natural law and brute fact.

Liturgy as well as myth transforms the conventional into the natural. Some of the ways in which this may be accomplished have been touched upon in this and previous chapters, but it may be well to bring them together here.

First, as we noted above, the conventional understandings expressed in liturgical orders may stipulate that the same creative agencies are responsible for the existence of both the facts of convention and those of the physical world, and the manner in which both are thought to have been brought into being may not differ.

Secondly, as we observed early in the chapter, the use of substances, objects, postures and gestures in what are essentially performative or meta-performative acts seems to bring into being not only institutional facts but correlated physical or brute facts, as material as scarred or gesturing flesh, as real as water, oil or ashes, pigs, scepters or masks.

Thirdly, and also implicit in some earlier discussions, time and circumstance transform the factive into the descriptive, thus masking the conventional nature of effects. That is, utterances or acts equivalent to utterances which, when first performed or uttered are factive, become, subsequently, descriptive. For instance, supercision for a Tahitian boy is equivalent to the sentence "I am now a *taure 'are' a*," and is factive. But for him to utter this sentence a month or even a day after the operation would not be factive. It would be a simple description of a state of affairs. Factives and meta-factives make facts. These facts seemingly become facts of nature and can be described or reported, like any other facts of nature, in sentences that differ little from the factives that in fact created them. We may only note in passing that the transformation of factives into statements may be another ground upon which notions of ritual's occult efficacy – particularly the magical or creative power of words – are founded.

Fourthly, liturgical orders, to the extent that they are invariant, present the conventions they express to be without alternative. That which is without alternative is likely to be taken to be inevitable, and thereby natural. We shall be specifically concerned with invariance in a later chapter.

In the last chapter we noted the morality intrinsic to liturgical form, now we are attending to the quality of the natural inhering in that form. That we have discussed these qualities separately is not meant to deny that the concepts of the natural and the moral are closely related. They may, indeed, become conflated in some rituals. The abstract notion of order is common to both concepts of created nature and to all conceptions of the moral, and the same liturgical orders at one and the same time order nature and morality, moralizing nature and rendering morals natural. But, as liturgical orders make natural and moral the conventions they encode they tacitly suggest, if they do not stipulate, that conventions in conflict with those they encode, the conventions, that is, of other groups are unnatural and immoral, which is to say abominations.

The naturalization of culture in myth and ritual emphasized in these last pages seems to stand opposed to a conception of myth more widely accepted in anthropology, namely that in myth humanity is distinguished from nature. I do not wish to argue the matter here and will only suggest that the disagreement is more apparent than real and stems from different emphasis being given to different stages, levels or aspects of the process of creation. In the first chapter of Genesis, for instance, Man and Woman are surely distinguished from the rest of nature, but only after they are brought into being by the same agent who brought into being the rest of creation by a procedure similar to that which produced light, darkness, water, birds, land and trees. It is these latter aspects of creation – which seem to me to be fundamental – that I have emphasized.

There is, in the union of form and substance in myths of creation, and in their reunion in the re-creations of ritual, a reunion of culture with the nature from which language, with its intrinsic capacity to objectify, to distinguish, to separate and to conceive the imaginary and the alternative, has alienated it. And, of course, the apparent reunion is, despite its curious legerdemain, proper, for culture is, after all, as natural as the seas out of which all life emerged, and it must, ultimately, conform to the laws of nature no less than, although in a manner different from, the ways in which protoplasm must so conform.

6

Time and liturgical order

I have used the term "liturgical order" to refer not only to individual rituals, but to the more or less invariant sequences of rituals that make up cycles and other series as well. My terminology differs from Van Gennep's (1960 [1909]), but my usage is similar to his, for he too was as much concerned with such sequences as he was with single rituals.

I refer to rituals and sequences of rituals as "liturgical orders" because I take them to be orders in virtually every sense of the word. First, they constitute orders in the sense of such phrases as "the moral order" or "the economic order" or "the natural order" – more or less coherent domains within which generally commensurable processes are governed by common principles and rules. As such they represent and maintain enduring relations among the elements they include, keeping them "in order," and thus establishing or constituting order as opposed to disorder or chaos. In so doing they may also distinguish orders of persons, for instance, those "in orders," such as Benedictine monks, from others. These orders may be ranked, and rank or hierarchy is implicit in some usages. Architects, for instance, speak of elaborate arches composed of four or five orders, one above the other. Further, inasmuch as liturgical orders are more or less invariant sequences encoded by persons other than the performers their performance entails conformity. This is to say that, although their words are not usually cast in the imperative mood, they constitute orders in the sense of directives. Finally and most obviously, they are orders in that they are more or less fixed sequences of acts and utterances, following each other "in order."

1. The dimensions of liturgical orders

Liturgical orders are realized in three "dimensions." First, there is what may be called the *simultaneous* or *synchronic* dimension. This dimension, which may be likened to the width of a room, and which has been well-studied by Turner and others, is the dimension emphasized in symbolic analyses of the multivocal significata of liturgical representations. At any moment an array of "meanings" may be represented simultaneously by the same object or act. Turner's (1967) *mudyi* tree is a famous example. We will discuss the simultaneous dimension in chapter 7.

The second dimension, which could be likened to the height of the liturgical chamber or volume, may be called *hierarchical*. It is the least well-understood of the three, having, with notable exceptions (Dumont 1980; J. Smith 1987), been largely ignored or overlooked by most anthropologists and other students of such matters. The multiple understandings encoded in and organized by any liturgical order are not in all ways equivalent. They differ in logical typing, concreteness, specificity, mutability, reversibility, contingency, authority and the ways in which they are meaningful (see Rappaport 1979b: 117 ff.). Moreover, they are not represented in haphazard fashion, but are organized into coherent structures. Discussion of this dimension will also be postponed until chapter 8.

In this chapter we shall be concerned with the third dimension, the sequential, which can be likened to the length of the liturgical chamber. This is the dimension with which Van Gennep (1960 [1909]) was most obviously concerned. Although nothing could be more banal than the observation that one thing follows another, the implications of one thing following another are not at all obvious or banal, as he showed us long ago. We shall, however, be concerned here with aspects of sequence different from those engaging Van Gennep. He was primarily interested in the transformations in the social condition of performers effected in rituals, but the concern here is only secondarily with them. The sequential is the dimension with the most obvious and immediate temporal entailments, and it is upon the organization, or even the construction of time (and in chapter 7 eternity as well), that we shall focus. The spatial aspects of sequence will also receive brief attention.

2. St. Augustine, St. Emile, time and the categories

Time is surrounded by the deep mystery peculiar to the absolutely familiar. St. Augustine captured this singular aspect of its enigmatic nature so well that after sixteen centuries he continues to be cited with great frequency: "What, then, is time? If no one ask of me, I know; if I wish to explain to him who asks, I know not" (*Confessions*, Book XI, Ch. XIV). After eleven more chapters of attempting to undo time's knots he pauses for a moment to

confess unto Thee, O Lord, that I am as yet ignorant of what time is ... I know I speak of these things in time, and that I have already long spoken of time, and that very "long" is not long save by the story of time. How, then, know I this when I know not what time is? *(Confessions, Book XI, Ch. XXV: 270)*

Emile Durkheim, fifteen centuries later, in the introduction to *The Elementary Forms of Religious Life*, in the course of locating the concept of time in the general structure of human understanding, may have elucidated the special ground of its paradoxical mysteries:

At the roots of all our judgments there are a certain number of essential ideas which dominate all our intellectual life; they are what philosophers since Aristotle have called the categories of understanding: ideas of time, space, class, number, cause, substance, personality, etc. They correspond to the most universal properties of things. They are like the solid frame which encloses all thought ... [they] appear to be nearly inseparable from the normal working of the intellect. They are like the framework of the intelligence. *(1961[1915]: 21–22; emphasis mine)*

The "solid frame enclosing all thought." "Inseparable from the working of the intellect." "The framework of intelligence." Such expressions suggest why it is that time should be enigmatic. The categories, as Durkheim (and others) saw them, were not so much objects of thought as means of thought. Bateson argued a half century later (1972e [1967]: 136) that "the conscious organism does not require (for pragmatic purposes) to know *how* it perceives – only to know *what* it perceives." It can even be argued that organisms are better off if they remain innocent of "the how" of it. To have perceptions of objects and actions in the external world cluttered up with a continuing awareness of the electro-chemical or cognitive processes constituting them would certainly ambiguate and possible destroy them. The matter is, of course, hypothetical. No organism in this world, it is safe to say, not even any experimental psychologist, is conscious of how she is perceiving what she is perceiving while she is perceiving it. We are concerned here with conceptions rather than perceptions, of course, but questions may be more appropriately raised concerning conception than perception, particularly with respect to fundamental concepts like "the categories," those comprising the "solid frame," the "normal working," the "framework" of conscious thought itself.

As is the case with perception, it can be argued that the organism does not need to know how it is that it can, say, conceive of quantities, but merely be able to do so, and it could also be argued, although perhaps not as forcefully as in the case of perception, that it is better off (at least for "pragmatic purposes") if the grounds of thought remain, by and large, unexamined. Gains in knowledge, after all, generally entail corresponding losses of innocence, and such losses tend to render previously simple and straightforward aspects of the world increasingly complex and problematic. Be this as it may, never do the basic assumptions of any society simply stand naked to the view of its members. Such assumptions, those upon which its consciously recognized understandings are founded, Bateson long ago (1951) argued, are not only outside the ordinary awareness of the society's members, but may be virtually inaccessible to them. We will take up the matter of such inaccessibility in chapter 10. The point here is that if the basic assumptions of *particular* cultures are relatively inaccessible to their members, how much more inaccessible must be the grounds of *general* categories of human understanding?

In approaching "the categories," we may be approaching the top of the ladder, as it were, of the logical types (Bateson 1972a, Whitehead and Russell 1910–13) of conscious human thought. The mechanism constituting or governing any level of knowledge or consciousness is of "higher logical type" than that level. Thus, we say, the grammar of a language constitutes a "meta-level" in relation to that language and its use. The production of utterances – speech – is, by and large, a conscious activity: speakers usually know more or less what they want to say, and their choice of words is at least in large part a matter of conscious decision. But, although their utterances generally conform to rules constituted at the level of grammar, they may never have brought that grammar into consciousness, and most, if not all, non-literate societies lack the analytic tools to do so. The grammatical meta-level, this is to say, may not be conscious. If the most fundamental level of consciousness is considered, then Durkheim and others propose that the concept of time and other categories are located at such a level, the meta-level constituting it cannot be other than unconscious. As such it is inaccessible to direct conscious awareness, and its accessibility to objective Cartesian investigations is full of difficulty. It would be anachronistic to claim that Durkheim, who was writing in the first and second decades of this century, was concerned with a problem not yet clearly formulated. His argument, nevertheless, does conform to the expectation that if a consciously recognized concept does constitute a category *fundamental* to conscious thought, its own ground must be, in some sense, unconscious.

Unconscious *in some sense.* The ground in which the categories are rooted, according to Durkheim, does not lie within Freud's unconscious, nor within the more capacious unconscious outlined by Bateson (1972e), nor in that of the neurophysiologists. It lies not only outside the organism's consciousness but outside the organism altogether. He argued that the categories are, and must be, held in common by collectivities: "They are the most general concepts which exist because they are applicable to all that is real, and since they are not attached to any particular object, they are independent of any particular subject; they constitute the common field where all minds meet" (1961: 26). As collective representations the categories are *necessarily social,* and they are constituted, *outside the participants' awareness,* in social processes. The social processes of a society, this is to say, relate to the conscious thought of members of the society as (among other things) an aspect, or type of, or component of their unconscious.

In attributing a dominant role to social processes in the establishment of the categories Durkheim obviously set himself squarely against those who accounted for them as either *a priori* structures of the mind or products of individual experience. Whether or not it was correct to do so, to privilege social over mental processes in the establishment of what appear to be intellectual constructs was a move of stunning boldness, great profundity and exceptional power.

Further aspects of Durkheim's argument were less compelling, however. It is one thing to claim that the categories, as collective representations, are (and must be) socially constituted and it is quite another to claim (as he did) that social life itself provides the categories that are then applied to other domains. This assertion was criticized effectively by Rodney Needham (1963) in an introduction to a modern edition of *Primitive Classification* (which Durkheim wrote with Mauss and published in 1903), but applied just as well to Durkheim's later work. Needham's critique also extends to Durkheim's assertion that it is out of religion in particular, and not simply part of social life generally, that the categories emerge. No matter how insightful, the assertion that the categories "are born in religion and of religion; they are products of religious thought" (1961: 21) is not logically well-founded when it stands on the observation that "when primitive religious beliefs are systematically analyzed, the principal categories are naturally found" (p. 21). If, after all, the categories ground all thought, we would expect them to pervade all thought, and therefore their presence in any particular domain cannot be counted as evidence of that domain's precedence.

Difficulties at least as serious are generated by Durkheim's treatment of all of the categories as if they were logically, ontologically, epistemologically and ontogenetically equivalent; it presumably follows that they are all established in the same way. However, they may differ in important ways. The concepts of number, space and substance, for example, may be sufficiently distinctive to allow or require different means for their establishment. There is certainly no apparent reason to believe that they all need to arise out of religion, and there may be important inter-societal differences in this respect (see below, chapter 9, The truths of sanctity and deutero-truth). It is not even clear that they all need arise out of social life. The separate experiences of individuals are likely to be so similar with respect to certain categories, like substance, that, it could well be argued, individual experience could be relied upon for their establishment. More generally, given the universal structure of the human brain and, indeed, the human organism as a physiological system, there is a point below which the roles of neither *a priori* structures nor individual experience can properly be reduced. Memory and anticipation, which most thinkers agree enter into the experience of time, may be shaped by social processes and cultural particulars, but they must, after all, have roots in brain physiology and individual experience.

This leads us to an even more serious problem with the category of time as such. Durkheim seems to have assumed that it and the other categories are conceptual monads. Yet thinkers since the ancients, while treating time as somehow unified, have made it clear, either tacitly or explicitly, that the concepts of time and temporal experience are composed of a number of distinct although interrelated elements, including duration, change, motion, frequency, rhythm, velocity, passage, simultaneity, conception of a present, extension, succession and perhaps others as well. There is no compelling reason to believe that all of these elements are grounded in the same aspects of human experience and considerable reason to believe that they are not (J. T. Frazer 1966, 1975, Jacques 1982, E. Parsons 1964, Ornstein 1969, etc.).

In sum, Durkheim, in arguing for a place for social processes in the establishment of categories, made an important contribution to the understanding of human understanding, filling lacunae with which neither *a priori* structuralism nor the empiricism of individual experience could plausibly deal, notably those associated with observable inter-societal variation and problems arising from the possibilities of difference between individuals. But Durkheim overstated his case at the same time that he underdemonstrated it. In both the introduction and conclusion of

The Elementary Forms, Durkheim argued brilliantly for the social construction of the categories. Between the introduction and conclusion lay what is arguably one of the most important accounts of religion ever written by a social scientist. It does not, however, make explicit, much less detail, how the concept of time, or any of the other categories, are actually formed in religious thought or practice.

The most defensible position to take is that individual experience and *a priori* structures, as well as social processes, participate, to a greater or lesser extent, in the establishment of grounds of thought, even when it is recognized that those grounds are and must be held in common by collectivities. To go a step or two beyond this simple and unarguably sensible position, it is plausible, or perhaps even commonsensical, to suppose that, in the complex of determinants, social processes will manifest themselves most assertively in the formation of those categories and aspects of categories in which significant variation, both between societies and between individuals within the same society, is most possible and most likely. The relative importance of the several foundations is also likely to be correlated with, it is almost tautological but nevertheless important to say, the degree to which the category has immediate social entailments, as time or its elements (being central to coordination) do and as substance does not. I will not pursue these questions systematically here, for the claim being made is much less grandiose than Durkheim's. It is simple, that liturgical orders can and do organize, or even construct socially, the temporal orders of at least some societies, and that "temporal" orders, when organized by ritual, make a place for eternity as well as for mundane time.

3. Temporal experience and public order

It would be exaggerating to claim, then, that the sense of time is fully constructed *ex nihilo* by each society; for all normal human beings past infancy must distinguish *now* from past and future and, *pace* Edmund Leach (1961), past and future from each other as well. They recognize that some events are periodic and recurrent,[1] while others are not, and perceive some events to be further in the past or future than others. Although memory, hope, and expectation have no place in the time of the physicist or astronomer they do, to say the least, enter into the temporal experience of the living.

We obviously cannot discuss anything like the range of temporal constructions that anthropologists or others might encounter. We can, however, note that some temporal conceptions, including modern ones (see Milne 1948: para. 2, 7, E. Parsons 1964: ch. 3, Whitrow 1972), seem more closely related to individual experience than do others. St. Augustine, for instance, was especially concerned with the sense (perhaps universal to everyday human consciousness) of a future flowing continuously into a present and on into a past. Like virtually all others who have recorded their thoughts on time, motion, change and their perception were essential to his concept:

> Thou mightest make all these things of which this *changeable* world consists, and yet consisteth not; whose very *changeableness appears* in this, that times can be *observed* and *numbered* in it ... *times are made by the changes of things.*
>
> *(Confessions, Book XII, Ch. VIII, 19072–283; emphasis mine)*

In chapter 11 of the same book he reiterates, "Without the change of motions times are not."

Whether change or motion is in and of itself time, or whether time is the duration in which motion or change takes place was answered by Augustine in favor of the latter: "Let no man tell me that the motions of the heavenly bodies are times," because at the Battle of Jericho, in answer to Joshua's prayer, the sun stood still "but time went on" (Book XI, Ch. 23). Still mystified by the nature of time, he confessed three chapters later that "time is nothing else than extension, but of what I know not." Finally, he takes the human mind to be the critical locus of temporal process: "But how is the future diminished or consumed which as yet is not? Or how does the past, which is no longer, increase, *unless in the mind which enacts this* there are three things done? ... it ... expects, and considers and remembers" (Book XI, Ch. 28). This world of change, of expectation, of memory, of constantly shifting foci of attention, is contrasted with a divine world, unchanging, after which Augustine yearns:

> forgetting the things that are past; and not distracted but drawn on, not to those things which shall be and shall pass away, but to those things which were before ... where I can contemplate their delights, *neither coming nor passing away* ... I have been divided amid times, the order of which I know not, and my thoughts ... are mangled by tumultuous varieties.   *(Book XI, Ch. 24; emphasis mine)*

We shall return later to the relationship of the unchanging to the changing. Of concern here is that not only that what humans experience in time may be tumultuously varying, but temporal experience itself may not be constant or uniform.

Although various biological clocks exist, and although certain very short cycles may be related to the sense of the present and the perception of simultaneity (E. Hall 1984, Ornstein 1969, etc.), they do not account for the sense of longer durations. There seems to be no universal temporal sense guiding all humans through their lives at apparently uniform rates. Nor is there even subjective constancy of rate, for the chronicles of memory and anticipation are private and idiosyncratic, and they may be bent or reordered by regret, nostalgia, pain, delight, foreboding and hope, or disarranged by disease, age, and simple forgetfulness. The sense of passage that all normal humans possess, being idiosyncratic and unreliable, or at least subject to distortion, not only cannot itself serve as the ground for temporal ordering but may itself generate a need for the public ordering of time, not simply to coordinate social life, but to provide a well-marked road along which each individual's temporal experience can travel. Be this as it may, it seems safe to say that all societies recognize public temporal orders.

4. Succession, division, period and interval

Societies differ widely in what they use to make time. Nature is, of course, a general source of temporal raw material, and societies may and do found time upon its periodicities. But this does not propose that times are simply given by nature, although they may so appear to those whose lives they frame. While time may be *founded upon* natural processes – the circle of the seasons, the waxing and waning of the moon, the alternation of day and night, it is not *established* by those processes themselves. The only natural cycle that seems universally significant is that of day and night. Although cultures may make use of a range of natural cyclicities in their construction of time, time needs always to be constructed. The materials out of which it is constructed, moreover, are not limited to natural recurrences. There are olympiads, five day "weeks," seven day weeks, nine day "weeks" and ritual cycles of variable duration, such as that of the Maring, which takes anywhere from eight to twenty or so years to come full circle. In ancient China, a world-cycle of 23,639 years was recognized (J. T. Frazer 1975: 40, Needham 1966) and the Vedic doctrine of the *yugas* provided ancient India with cosmic cycles varying from 360 years to lengths unimaginable (Eliade 1957a: 177ff.).

Aristotle (*Physics*, Book IV ch. 10, McKeon 1941), and many since Aristotle, have suggested that the experience of time and, indeed, time itself is, in essence, a matter of succession, recurrent or non-recurrent. Whitehead (1927: 158) took it to be the "sheer succession of epochal durations"; a little earlier in the century J. S. MacKenzie (1912), in a discussion of eternity, went further, defining time as "simply the form of succession in a developing process."[2]

This may *sound* clear, but succession of what? When we speak of successions we must be speaking of more or less distinct events or states of affairs. But, as we asked in chapter 3, "what is 'a state of affairs' or an 'event'?" Each of us interprets the occurrences we separately experience in more or less idiosyncratic ways, and each of us punctuates continuous experience differently. Furthermore, even such regular, repetitive, natural transitions as spring turning into summer are vague, for nature does not mark such transitions sharply. Most natural processes are continuous rather than discontinuous, and continuity generates both vagueness and ambiguity.

The formal characteristics of ritual contrast sharply with the indistinct character of "natural" or "ongoing" events. Rituals are more or less invariant from one performance to the next, and great emphasis is often placed upon punctiliousness of performance. This is to say that they are among the most perfectly recurrent of cultural events. As such the fact of a ritual's occurrence – that a ritual is, in fact, recurring – is among the clearest of all humanly constructed social events. Furthermore, and in consequence, the task of interpreting the significance of a ritual is less difficult than that of interpreting other events because both the contents and occurrence of rituals, being elements in liturgical orders, have previously established public meanings.

Clarity of occurrence suits ritual admirably for the task of imposing on natural processes discontinuities much sharper than those intrinsic to the natural processes themselves. It may even be claimed that the occurrence of ritual imposes discontinuities upon processes that are themselves seamlessly continuous. As such ritual can be relied upon to distinguish succeeding from preceding unambiguously, thus distinguishing in continuous processes what may be called *"phases,"* that is *stages*, in what can now appear as *series* of distinct states of affairs. These phases – whether parts of "developmental" or recurrent processes – may then serve as characterizations of the *durations* during which they unfold and, in effect, transform those durations into *periods*.[3] Periods, to put it conversely, are temporal durations within which phases are encompassed, phases like spring/summer/autumn/winter, childhood/youth/manhood/death, night/day. Thus, through the series of rituals comprising them, liturgical orders can sever seamless durations into distinct periods and can also invest those periods with significance. Moreover, as liturgical orders may distinguish periods from one another, so may they unite those distinguished into larger meaningful entities. Childhood, youth, manhood and old age are joined into coherent and orderly lifetimes;

spring, summer, autumn, winter into years. If, as MacKenzie said, in general agreement with many others, time is "simply the form of succession in a ... process" (developing or otherwise), then liturgical orders impose form on processes to make succession. There can be no succession without things – periods – to succeed each other. It is of interest that the English word "time" derives from the Indo-European root *di*, or *dai*, "to divide" (American Heritage Dictionary 1992). Liturgy, in dividing continuous duration into distinct periods, provides the wherewithal of succession, and further provides for those successions to be joined into larger wholes. This is the beginning of temporal construction.

But only the beginning. The temporal significance of ritual is not limited to punctuating indefinite durations into significant periods, for ritual times themselves are significant, often, indeed, of greater cultural significance than the durations lying between them. Geertz has gone so far as to claim that in Bali in particular and, by implication, more generally in Indonesia, the durations distinguished by the ten concurrent cycles (that possibly make time-reckoning there the world's most complex) are devoid of cultural significance.

> The cycles and supercycles [formed by the juncture of two or more primary cycles; e.g., the 35-day cycles made by the simultaneous completion of five seven-day cycles and seven five-day cycles] are endless, unanchored, uncountable, and, as their internal order has no significance, without climax. They do not accumulate, they do not build and they are not consumed. They don't tell you what time it is. They tell you what kind of time it is.
>
> *(1973: 393)*

The sort of time-reckoning that Indonesian permutational calendars facilitate is, he says, "punctual" rather than "durational":

> It is not used ... to measure the rate at which time passes, the amount which has passed since the occurrence of some event, or the amount which remains ... it is adapted to and used for distinguishing and classifying discrete self-subsistent particles of time – "days."
>
> *(p. 393)*

Geertz later notes that the days of juncture are often referred to as "times" or "junctures" and other days as "holes" (p. 394). The "holes" are comprised of days on which nothing, or at least nothing much, goes on, whereas "times" are days on which something important, perhaps a religious celebration, occurs, but the permutational calendar also marks days auspicious or inauspicious for secular activities as well.

It is difficult to disagree with the contention that ten primary cycles operating concurrently do not demarcate significant periods, for it is difficult to see how they possibly could. This is not to say, however, that one or another of them, or one or more of the "super-cycles," do not.

Ignoring Geertz's objection (p. 394n) to the use of the term "week" to refer to what we may call the "temporal extensions" formally (although perhaps not culturally) marked off by the various cycles, because the term "week" at the least connotes significant durations, Becker (1979: 198ff.), writing about Java, tells us that "the five-day week cycle [based on the frequency of markets] and the seven-day cycle [both cycles being named and composed of named days] are the two calendrical systems most used ... for daily affairs." Soebardi (1965) also uses the term "week," and it is not clear in either his discussion or Becker's (or for that matter in Geertz's own) that all of the durations (particularly the five-day "market week") are devoid of significance as such.

If Geertz means to advance a yet stronger implication of his argument, namely that with a punctual rather than durational mode of time reckoning dominant the Balinese (and, by extrapolation, other Indonesians) are without well-defined senses of duration or temporal passage he is on ground that is yet less solid. For one thing, as he himself notes, there exist alongside the permutational calendar a lunar-solar calendar, access to "absolute dates through the so-called Caka system" and "Hinduistic notions of successive epochs" (p. 391n). Perhaps even more significant, Soebardi notes that there were "still in use among certain ethnic groups, for instance, among the Javanese, Niasese, the Dyaks, the Toradja, the Achehnese and several others," various "traditional systems of time indications," and, by his account, the durational aspects of these systems were emphasized. Thus, among the Niasese:

The word for a year is *dofi*, meaning star; however when the Niasese wish to indicate a period of time more than one year, they use the word *faghe*, meaning rice, for instance, or *mendruwa faghe*, two years. Thus these people count years by the number of times they have had their harvest. The word "year" here is in fact only of six months duration.   *(1965: 49ff.)*

Similarly, among the Toradja "the period when plants grow and ripen is called *ta'u. San ta'u* means a year and this expression has the meaning of 'one rice-year,'" which lasts only six months.

The general point that we can take away from Becker, Geertz and Soebardi's discussions of time-reckoning in Indonesia is, as we have already noted, that the temporal significance of ritual goes beyond the punctuation of meaningless durations into significant periods. The occurrence of the rituals themselves are usually, if not always, moments of heightened significance and, further, there are intersocietal differences in the ways and extent to which periods and the rituals distinguishing them respectively figure into daily life. We will touch upon some of these matters in later sections of this chapter.

Although societies differ in the extent to which they focus upon periods or the rituals punctuating them, it is probably a mistake to characterize any society's mode of temporal construction as either "durational" or "punctual." Too much shouldn't be made of it, but the term "punctual," furthermore, is an unfortunate one because it connotes, at the very least, the concept of the point. A point in space is a location without extension and, by analogy, a point in time is an instant. But no ritual is instantaneous. The ritual of, say, Midsummer Night's Eve lasts from dusk until dawn *thereby comprising a duration of sensible length.* This duration, part of neither the preceding springtime nor the succeeding summer, itself constitutes a significant *interval* between those periods. *In distinguishing periods from each other liturgy cannot help but distinguish periods as a class from the intervals separating them as a class.* These intervals may be confined within boundaries of single rituals or they may be more protracted, beginning and ending with distinct rituals, and complex patterns of nesting also occur: ritually marked durations may be encompassed by ritually demarcated durations of greater length.

The distinction between intervals and the periods they separate corresponds to a frequently remarked distinction between two "kinds of time" or, to be a little more formal and correct, two "temporal conditions." On the one hand, what is called "ordinary" or "mundane" or "profane" time prevails in periods, but intervalic "time" is said to be different. Mysterious phrases, such as "extraordinary" or "sacred" time, or even "time out of time" are used. Van Gennep (1960), Turner (1967, 1969), Leach (1961), Wallace (1966) and others have been concerned with the peculiar characteristics of actions and events occurring in these intervals, emphasizing that transitions are effected in them and that neither quotidian logic nor ordinary social relations always prevail during them. We shall return later to these matters and also to something with which they were not importantly concerned, namely the peculiar characteristics of extraordinary time itself. I will argue that "time out of time" really is out of time.

5. Temporal principles

It would obviously be incorrect to claim that time is constituted by liturgy always and everywhere, or even that time's passage is always experienced in terms established liturgically. It should not be forgotten, however, that the liturgical calendar remains significant in the experience of the year's turning even in contemporary secular societies that number their days and years, and although writing and the numbering of years tends to replace liturgy by history and geology in the conceptualization of long duration, we still reckon duration from the birth of Christ.

Societies obviously differ in what their liturgies seize upon to distinguish periods and thus to make time. Evans-Pritchard (1940) was pointing to two general classes of processes in widespread use when, in a discussion of Nuer time-reckoning, he distinguished "oecological time," constituted "mainly [of] reflections of ... relations to environment," from "structural time," which reflects social process and social relations. He argued that "time reckoning based upon changes in nature and man's response to them is limited to an annual cycle and therefore cannot be used to differentiate longer periods than seasons" and, further, that "the larger periods of time are almost entirely structural because the events they relate are changes in the relations of social groups."

The distinction between the oecological and structural seems useful although it is not always to be as clearly distinguished as Evans-Pritchard or the Nuer would have it. Among the Maring, for instance, changes in the size of the pig populations, an aspect of the relations of human groups to their environments, are ordered by liturgy into significant periods in total comprising sequences six to twenty years in length. These periods, much longer than seasons or years, have their ground in environmental relations, but also affect and are affected by relations among local territorial groups and by changes in them.

Evans-Pritchard made no general claims for the principles he identified in his study of the Nuer. Although their application is widespread, they alone would hardly be sufficient to account for time construction generally. Our own society, for instance, makes some use of the oecological principle in the ordering of the year but, with its numbered years stretching backward into the past and forward into the indefinite future, it seems to make little or no use of the structural principle. 1776 would have been 1776 even if the United States had not declared itself independent of Great Britain. The principle of indefinitely continuous annual numeration, limited in its distribution until recently to very few complex societies, separates the conception of time from structural processes and reduces the natural processes upon which time is dependent to those occurring in the heavens.

It might be well to distinguish the celestial from the oecological not only in this regard, but also because the apparent relationship of humans to events observably occurring in the heavens differs in simple and seemingly significant ways from their relationship with elements of their more immediate environments. First, as already implied, the distinction between time itself and significant changes in the world is unclear when a structural, oecological or ontogenetic (see below) periodicity is used. The distinction is much clearer when time is constituted in the heavens. Significant events in the world, be they structural, ecological, ontogenetic, cyclical, rectilinear, entropic or progressive take place *in* time. Time as such becomes more distinct from whatever occurs in time. Secondly, whereas humans interact with the other species among which they live and can even manipulate and modify nonliving features of their immediate habitats, the movements of the sun, the moon, the stars are absolutely beyond manipulation. To use their movements in the construction of time is to make time absolute, inelastic, inexorable and certain, when otherwise it might not be.[4]

Principles other than the oecological, celestial, structural and numerical are, of course, sometimes used by liturgy in the construction of time. For instance, rites of passage order the lives of individuals into distinct periods, and, for societies in which age-grades are prominent, it may be possible to distinguish an ontogenetic principle of temporal construction from Evans-Pritchard's structural principle. Such a distinction may have significance in matters more important than those of classification. We may return here briefly to Evans-Pritchard's simple distinction between oecological and structural time, for in making it he proposed that the former "appears to be, and is, cyclical," whereas the latter "appears to an individual passing through the social system to be entirely progressive." He adds, however, that "in a sense this is an illusion" (1940: 95), because

> the structure remains fairly constant, and the perception of time is no more than the movement of persons, often as groups, through the structure. Thus, age-sets succeed one another forever, but there are never more than six in existence and the relative positions occupied by these sets at any time are fixed structural points through which actual sets of persons pass in endless succession. Similarly ... the Nuer system of lineages may be considered a fixed system, there being a constant number of steps between living persons and the founder of their clan, and the lineages have a constant position relative to one another. However many generations succeed one another the depth and range of lineages does not increase ...
>
> *(1940: 107)*

In sum, Evans-Pritchard makes a distinction between two experiences of succession, the "cyclical" and the "progressive," but immediately declares the "progressive" to be "in a sense, illusory."

It seems to me that he became confused in this matter. That structural processes are, in fact, repetitive or cyclical is one thing. That particular persons passing through them experience a "progress" is quite another. If the experience is one of progress, and if the experience of time is not to be distinguished radically from time itself, then it is not illusory to suppose that "progress" is an aspect of the experience of certain successions even while agreeing that aspects of the selfsame successions are, in an abstract or formal sense, recurrent. To say, for instance, that age grades, their number and their relationship to each other are enduring aspects of a social structure does not constitute a claim that the movements of particular age-sets through them one after another is in any sense illusory. The class of 1996 is not the class of 1949, although the members of both were seniors when they graduated from the same university. This confusion is elementary yet easy to fall into. To decrease its likelihood it is well to distinguish structural time from ontogenetic time, the former standing to the latter as age-grades stand to age-sets, as enduring institutions stand to more-or-less transient actors, indeed, as changeless rites stand to the successive persons or states of affairs they transform. Although the recurrent and non-recurrent aspects of events cannot be separated, they can be distinguished from each other.

Leach has also addressed the matter of recurrence and non-recurrence in temporal experience:

all other aspects of time, duration for example, or historical sequence, are fairly simple derivatives from ... two basic experiences:
    a) that certain phenomena of nature repeat themselves,
    b) that life change is irreversible.   *(1961: 125)*

Leach then takes issue, albeit tacitly, with Evans-Pritchard's association of repetition with cyclicity. Although he stops short of denying the propriety of the association altogether, he does propose that it derives from the formulations of astronomers and mathematicians, and that

in a primitive, unsophisticated community the metaphors of repetition are likely to be ... much more homely ... vomiting, for example, or the oscillations of a weaver's shuttle, or the sequence of agricultural activities, or even the ritual exchanges of a series of interlinked marriages ... Indeed, in some primitive societies it would seem that the time process is not experienced as a "succession of epochal durations" [Whitehead's definition or characterization (1927) earlier cited by Leach] at all; there is no sense of going on and on in the same direction, or round and round the same wheel. On the contrary, time is experienced as something discontinuous, a repetition of repeated reversal, a sequence of oscillations between polar opposites: night and day, winter and summer, drought and flood, age and youth, life and death ... the past has no depth to it, all past is equally past; it is simply the opposite of now.

(1961: 126)

It may well be that the use of a cyclical metaphor for time is more obvious in societies that possess wheels and astronomers (although there are temporal cycles in societies possessing neither). We can also agree that recurrence may sometimes take the form of alteration rather than cyclicity. Such an agreement, however, does not constitute a denial of the aptness of the cyclical metaphor. It seems reasonable to recognize that recurrence can take the simple or minimal form of alternation or the complex or elaborated form of cyclicity, in which three or more phases succeed each other in regular order repeatedly. It is necessary to specify three or more phases because in formal terms an alternation between two states may be a form of cyclicity, albeit the limiting case,[5] in which the cycle includes only two phases. This, however, may be as experientially false as it is formally true, and it seems as wrong to dissolve the experience of alternation into that of cyclicity as it is to deny the reality of the experience of cyclicity itself.

A more important point needs to be made here. Complex recurrent processes may, at one and the same time, be both cyclical and alternating. Maring liturgical orders, for instance, distinguish a number of periods, succeeding each other cyclically and distinguished from each other by rituals. Each of these periods is characterized by dominant activities of different sorts – warfare, pig husbandry, garden cultivation, marsupial hunting, entertainment, eel-trapping, fulfillment of obligation and warfare again. At the same time that liturgical order imposes a *cyclical* repetitiveness upon all major activities, it imposes a sharp and discontinuous *alternation* between war and peace.

More fundamentally, whereas the succession of recurrent periods may be experienced as *either* cycle or alternation, the experience of the succession of period by interval and interval by period is *in its nature* that of alternation. Leach (pp. 129ff.) argues that in ancient Greece, the dynamic of time is that of alternation between "contraries" (e.g., active/inactive, good/bad), and the states prevailing in periods on the one hand and intervals on the other may be radically different. Indeed, an inversion of the order prevailing during periods is commonly reported to occur during the intervals which rituals mark off. This alternation may lie beneath notions of immortality and eternity, a matter to which we shall return. Leach further observes that the ancient "Greeks conceived the oscillations of time by analogy to the oscillations of the soul," and argues that in doing so they were using a concrete metaphor. Basically it is the metaphor of sexual coitus, of the ebb and flow of the sexual essence between sky and earth (with the rain as semen), between this world and the underworld (with marrow-fat and vegetable seeds as semen), between man and woman. In short, it is the sexual act itself which provides the primary image of time. In the act of copulation the male imparts a bit of his life-soul to the female; in giving birth she yields it forth again. Coitus is here seen as a kind of dying for the male; giving birth as a kind of dying for the female. *(1961: 127)*

Leach suggests that such a view of time's foundation, although it seems strange, throws light upon the mythic accounts of the relations between Uranus, Cronos and Zeus. While it does seem to me that it would be strained, and perhaps arbitrary, to take the sexual metaphor to underlie the dynamics of time generally, the concept of fertilization or birth that it implies may well be illuminating with respect to the relationship between periods and intervals. We shall touch upon a related view of that relationship later.

Leach associates the experience of irreversibility with life change, but life change is certainly not all that is experienced as irreversible. Structural processes, in Evans-Pritchard's sense, no matter how recurrent they may be, not only seem to be, but are unique for those living through them: it is *this* clan that flourishes and *that* clan that is driven from its land. It is *my* grandfather who dies as *my* son is born, my father's estate that I share with *my* brothers, *my* extended family that fissions. Events and states of affairs shaped by recurrent processes are experienced as unique; that which is unique does not recur, successions of the unique are irreversible, or virtually so. It is out of infrequent novel events – the coming of traders and missionaries with steel axes, money, measles, and new Gods, the introduction of the stirrup, the invention of the wheel – and continuously generated unique aspects of recurrent processes that history emerges. But even in societies which have been relatively well-insulated from outside events and in which novelty is of great rarity, the uniquenesses of history are never limited to the particulars of biographies, as one chief replaces another, or even to the particulars of general social process, as one clan declines and another becomes ascendant. Secular trends are inherent in many, if not all, recurrent processes. Through the annually repeated activities of cultivation land is deforested, irrigation systems extended, deserts enlarged. Through recurrent episodes of warfare, a structural process among the Maring, larger polities are amalgamated out of smaller ones. The recurrent and the irreversible may be conceptually contrary, but they are not separate in nature.

Histories, like lives, being made in some degree of successions of particulars, are in their nature irreversible, and as such they are likely to be oriented. As Lévi-Strauss observed in a comparison of what he calls "statistical time" to "mechanical time,"[6] "an evolution which would take contemporary Italian society back to that of the Roman Republic is as impossible to conceive of as is the reversibility of the processes belonging to the second law of thermodynamics."

Tacit in this observation are two directions, as apparently opposed as north and south, toward which time's arrow may point. On the one hand, there is progress, on the other, entropy. Evans-Pritchard's equation of irreversibility with progress was inadequate, for decline, death and decay are at least as salient and powerful associations of irreversibility as progress, growth and advance. Histories are continuous processes producing pasts made not only of recollections of stirring achievements and challenges triumphantly met, but also of lands and causes forever lost, men and women irrevocably dead. Indeed, loss rather than gain may be the dominating experience of irreversibility as people, at least those beyond a certain age, become increasingly aware that they are losing their lives day by ever briefer day.

Earlier we noted that whatever the recurrent structure of mundane time may be, *overall* temporal structure when constituted by a liturgical order is an *alternation* between "periodic," or "mundane" time and intervalic "time out of time." It is important to note again, now with respect to this alternation between the temporal conditions, that rituals, which encompass times out of time and distinguish them from mundane periods, are, as invariant sequences of formal acts and utterances in which emphasis is typically placed on punctilious performance, among the most clearly recurrent of social events. There is, in ritual participation, reenactment of that which *in its very essence* is invariant.

Recurrence is not confined to ritual, of course. Much of what occurs in mundane time is also recurrent. Spring comes every year. But mundane time is also the time to which the continuous, oriented and nonrecurrent processes of nature are largely confined – the irreversible changes of growth and progress, to be sure, but also those of decline and death. The ceaseless and ineluctable changes of life and history are of mundane time.

In contrast, that which occurs in liturgical time out of time, the invariant canon and the myths some canons enact, is characterized by punctilious repetition, *and is thus represented as never-changing*. The relationship, then, of that which occurs in liturgical intervals to that which occurs in mundane periods is *the relationship of the neverchanging to the ever-changing.* We shall return to this. First, there are some things to say about the organization of mundane time.

6. The grounds of recurrence

To speak of the construction of time by ritual is, in part, to speak of its shaping in conformity to differing "shapes" or "forms" of liturgical orders. Possible varieties were implied in the last section. There are, first, what Van Gennep called "rectilinear" orders (1960) a class exemplified but not exhausted by the sequences of rites leading from those surrounding birth to those following death. Although the preponderance of the rituals composing such sequences may, for any individual, be non-recurrent, they are oft-repeated in any society, for many of its members will proceed through all of them.

There are also "closed" or recurrent orders – those that lead back, so to speak, whence they came. Cycles are familiar, and many liturgical orders, most obviously calendrical orders, take a "circular" form. As we have seen, however, recurrence can assume at least one other form, namely alternation or oscillation.

Liturgical orders may, furthermore, differ in ways other than "shape." There are also, obviously, differences among them in length. Some rectilinear orders, notably those guiding individuals from their births to their deaths, are as variable in length as are the lengths of the lifetimes they mark at beginning and end. Others, of cyclical form, take one solar year or one lunar year, or seven days or five days or one day to complete, while the "temporal circumferences" of other cycles, such as that of the Maring, are as elastic as the amount of time it takes to accumulate the pigs necessary to conclude them.

Even such a brief list indicates clearly enough that there are differences among orders in the particular grounds upon which the recurrence of the rituals composing them are based. In some a ritual is repeated every month when the new moon appears, in others on every seventh day, in yet others when there are "sufficient pigs," or when the taro is ripe or when someone dies or has her first menses. All of this is obvious to the point of banality but less obvious differences lie beneath the surfaces of these commonplaces.

The recurrences marked by some liturgical orders are external to themselves. They are properties of processes unfolding in society or nature independent of liturgy. Day and night will alternate, the moon will wax and wane, the seasons change, solar years turn, children mature, whether or not ritual marks the transitions. The recurrence of a ritual may make it clear that, at a particular moment, night has replaced day, spring has replaced summer, the boy has become a man, but the liturgical order itself does not engender the differences in light or temperature, rainfall, plant growth, animal sexuality or celestial movement upon which its distinctions are based. The cyclicities of such liturgical orders do more than reflect the cyclicities of nature and society, of course, for they sharpen transitions in nature's or society's cycles, but they themselves do not provide the rationale for the distinctions they mark. Their performance sometimes coordinates the activities of communities in ways that conform to nature's recurrences, but such performances do not cause, nor are they usually taken to cause, those recurrences. (Although construing a ritual that marks a natural transition to be one that causes it may be one ground of the conception of ritual's occult efficacy.)

There are other instances in which the liturgical order does not simply mark transitions external to itself but itself provides grounds for recurrence. In contrast to rituals that, let us say, greet the arrival of the new moon, and thus distinguish one month from another, sabbath rituals distinguishing one seven-day week from the next do not simply reflect a rhythm intrinsic to nature onto social life. They fabricate an arbitrary periodicity in accordance with which society can organize its activities; in the case at hand, six days of labor and one of rest.

Of yet greater interest are non-calendrical liturgical cycles. The occurrences of the rituals constituting the Maring ritual cycle are a function of certain environmental and demographic processes. But this cycle does not simply reflect these processes, nor does it merely provide an arbitrary periodicity in terms of which humans may organize their management. *It itself imposes recurrence upon those processes.* In the Maring case, when the number of pigs is "sufficient," that is to say, when the pig population has grown so large as to have become a burden or nuisance, a *kaiko* is commenced. The *kaiko* entails sacrifices of large numbers of pigs, which reduces the population drastically, after which it can again grow to sufficiency, and again be sacrificed.

This is a matter of considerable importance. To impose recurrence upon a process is, in a strict, formal sense to regulate it. To regulate, in its very cybernetic essence, is to maintain the reversibility, and thus the recurrence, of processes that, if left to themselves, might well move rectilinearly in the direction toward which the second law of thermodynamics points: toward environmental degradation, social disruption, political anarchy and even biological annihilation. Processes that would otherwise proceed in "statistical" or "historical" time are brought into the domain of "mechanical" or "structural" time (see Lévi-Strauss, 1953: 530).

7. Schedules and societies

Discussion of the imposition of the cyclicity inherent in liturgical orders upon the social and natural world external to them leads from the ordering of time *per se* to the closely related matter of scheduling, that is, to the temporal organization of activities.

First we may observe that those whose activities are organized by common liturgical orders thereby constitute social entities of some sort. Indeed, coordination of ritual performances may actually define discrete social groups. Among the Maring, autonomous local populations are fused out of adjacent clusters of agnatic clans through the coordination of their ritual cycles (Rappaport 1984 [1968]: 19). The local group called Tsembaga, for example, was the product of the coordination of the ritual cycles of two adjacent but initially autonomous clusters, the Kungagai-Merkai and the Kamungagai-Tsembaga, following wars each fought against its own distinct enemies within days of each other. These wars were separate, but the two clusters supported each other, by and large during both of them, as allies.[7] Both the Kungagai-Merkai and the Kamungagai-Tsembaga were successful and, following their near-simul-taneous victories, proceeded through truces subsequent to the planting of *rumbim* more or less simultaneously. Years later they seem to have coordinated the uprooting of their separately planted *rumbim* and went through their *kaikos* together, or at least at the same time. Informants say that at that *kaiko* there were three dance grounds, the Kamungagai and Tsembaga clans each had one while the eastern cluster, Kungagai-Merkai, cleared only one. At two subsequent *kaiko*, the western as well as the eastern cluster shared one ground. At the 1962–1963 *kaiko* all five clans then comprising Tsembaga shared a single *tup kaiko*, or dance ground.[8]

Conversely, significant social distinctions may be established and maintained by adoption of and conformity to distinct liturgical calendars. Familiar examples are provided by differences in the holy days of Jews, Christians and Muslims. First, there is the sabbath. For Jews, the day has been regarded since biblical times as more than a day of rest and worship. It is a recurrence of the day on which God rested from his labors and as such is part of the very fabric of the universe. The observance of the sabbath "constitutes a sign at once of Israel's and God's fidelity to the covenant" (Abrahams 1918: 891), and is, thus, a matter of great significance for Jewish identity, particularly in the diaspora. The observance of the sabbath distinguishes those who participate in the covenant from those who do not. In this light, it is of equally great significance that Christians observe Sunday rather than Saturday as a devotional day. Indeed, this difference in observance may well have been part of a more or less deliberate attempt to distinguish Christianity from Judaism. "Though not quite conclusive, the evidence makes it probable that the observance of Sunday began among St. Paul's churches, which were predominantly gentile," and Paul urged his followers "to protest against having the sabbath imposed upon them" (Glazebrook 1921: 103). Churches in whose congregations persons of Jewish origin predominated were slower to abandon the sabbath for Sunday observance. Sunday was regarded not as the sabbath but as the Lord's Day, and *The Apostolic Constitutions* (fourth century) recognized parallel observance of the sabbath and Sunday. Whereas sabbath observance disappeared from Christianity earlier, the conception of a Sabbath (Saturday) distinct from the Lord's Day (Sunday) persisted until the ninth century (Glazebrook 1921: 104f.; see also John Miller 1959: 631ff.).

That there is a distinction between the conception of the Sabbath and the conception of the Lord's Day is of interest here, for it permitted Christians to distinguish themselves liturgically from the practice of the Jews without renouncing the account of creation offered in the first chapter of Genesis, and with it the Old Testament in its entirety. On the one hand, there is no explicit renunciation of the traditional sabbath, on the other hand, the elevation of Sunday is also rationalized in terms of the Genesis account of creation.

The Jews called Sunday the first day of the week since it was on this day, according to Genesis, that God began the work of creation; the Christians, though accepting this, went a step further and regarded Sunday as the first day of the second creation. Thus, in Eusebius of Alexandria we read: "It was on this day that the Lord began the first-fruits of the creation of the world, and on the same day He gave the world the first-fruits of the resurrection." *(John Miller 1959: 362)*

The young church was thus able to maintain its grasp upon the ancient source of sanctification while it was separating itself from the liturgical order that had been identified with that source from earliest times. We will return to related matters in chapter 9.

Similar considerations seem implicit in the Muslim selection of Friday as a "day of assembly" distinct from both the Lord's Day of the Christians and the Sabbath of the Jews. Margoliouth observes that it is conceivable, and may even be regarded as probable, that, if the Prophet had succeeded in attaching a great number of Jews to his cause, he might have made the Sabbath the sacred weekly day for his followers. But ... events having made this impossible, and the Christian Sunday being *per se* excluded ... he naturally settled instead on the old day of assembly ...   *(1918: 894)*

Although Friday "was a day of assembly of some kind long before the Prophet's time," it is of interest that the reasons provided for its selection by him were also consonant with the creation according to Genesis: it is the day upon which Adam was created, upon which he was taken into paradise and upon which he was expelled from it. Furthermore, resurrection will occur on a Friday. For these reasons Friday is "the best day upon which the sun appears." It is stated in Qur'an (iv, 50) that the "people of the Sabbath" must adhere strictly to the Sabbath order, "but for the followers of the Prophet of Allah the truly excellent day, namely Friday, has been ordained as the great day of the week" (Margoliouth 1918: 894).

That significant social identities and distinctions may be established by conformity to or departures from particular liturgical schedules is also exemplified by the Quartodeciman heresy, one of the earliest in Christianity. The Quartodecimans were those who celebrated Easter on the fourteenth day of the Hebrew month of Nisan, which is to say on Passover. Those who would "celebrate Easter with the Jews" (Jones 1943) were finally anathematized at the Council of Nicea (AD 325), but several councils called by Victor, Bishop of Rome, long before – at the end of the second and beginning of the third centuries – declared against the Quartodecimans. Indeed, Victor excommunicated them, and attempted to induce other Christian churches to do the same (Carleton 1910: 88, Jones 1943). Subsequent to the Council of Nicea it became impossible for Easter and Passover to coincide, but with the adoption of solar reckoning, new problems came to vex the computation of Easter, and its proper dating remained a matter of bitter controversy for centuries. A difference in the basis of this calculation was the most important of the distinctions separating the Irish and Roman churches, a difference that was not reconciled until the year 747 (Carleton 1910: 89); between the Roman and Orthodox churches these differences never have been resolved.[9]

In a process that seems the inverse but nevertheless illustrates the same general point, Christian missionaries to Great Britain at the end of the sixth and beginning of the seventh centuries, in apparent compliance with the spirit of Gregory the Great's instructions for attracting Anglo-

Saxons into the fold (see note 12, chapter 10), adapted their liturgical calendar to the previously existing cycle of the north by emphasizing saint's days coinciding with pagan festivals and times of sacrifice. That the feast of the Merovingian St. Martin fell on the same day, November 11, as the Winter's Day sacrifice to the Germanic gods largely accounted for its elevation to special importance in early Christian England, and other Christian holy days also stood in close temporal relation to pagan predecessors (Chaney 1970: 57ff., 240ff.). Although such adaptations of the Christian liturgical calendar might not have been absolutely crucial to the conversion of the Anglo-Saxons to Christianity, they were importantly facilitating.

8. The temporal organization of activities

We may turn now from the matter of the identities produced by the coordination of activities to those activities themselves. Calendrical liturgical orders, leading their congregations around the year's circle, may not only distinguish seasons one from another and then join them into years, but may also organize their mundane activities. Some activities, of course, may seem to be demanded by the qualities of the seasons themselves, but others, particularly those not immediately or narrowly entrained by environmental exigencies, may be set in time by the liturgical order itself. These activities are more likely to be concerned with distribution and with the maintenance and reproduction of society and cosmos than with food production. Among the Tewa of the San Juan pueblo, for instance, rituals are more densely concentrated during the period between the autumnal and vernal equinoxes than during the warmer months when subsistence activities are more pressing (Ortiz 1969: 104). A good many of these "works" – rituals called "Of the middle of the structure," "Days of the Sun," "Of moderation," "Bringing the birds to life," and "Bringing the leaves to life" – are concerned with cosmic order, but these (and other rituals contingent upon them) activate the mutual dependencies of the community's constituent associations and groups – the moieties, the ceremonial societies, the "three statuses." Moreover, the canons of many of these winter rituals stipulate the distribution of significant amounts of food, a matter of considerable significance in a society in which differences in the agricultural success of separate households is likely (Ford 1972).

The ordering of activities as well as of time is more obvious, and perhaps more significant, in liturgical orders the cyclicities of which are independent of seasonality. Once again, we may turn to the Maring whose ritual cycle distinguishes a number of periods of varying length in each of which the dominant activities are distinct from those of the preceding and succeeding periods. Planting *rumbim* terminates warfare and commences a protracted period of peace during which gardening and pig husbandry dominate activities. When, as described in chapter 3 (and at greater length in Rappaport 1984) the "pigs are sufficient," usually ten or fifteen years after *rumbim* planting, stakes are planted ritually marking the borders of the local group's territory. Preparations for the *kaiko*, or pig festival, dominate the following months. The work includes such chores as planting large gardens (already cut in secondary forest), constructing dance grounds and houses for visitors, making ovens, and gathering firewood, but of greatest significance is the trapping and smoking of *ma*, a category of animals that includes marsupials and large rodents, all said to be the "pigs of the Red Spirits."

When the fruit of the marita pandanus variety called "*pengup*" matures about five months after the stakes are planted, the *rumbim* is uprooted and the *kaiko* commences. The *kaiko*, which is devoted to entertainment, ritual, sacrifice and the fulfillment of obligations to both ancestors and allies, lasts for a little more than a year. It itself is divided into two phases, the second being set apart from the first by a ritual called "*kaiko nde*," after which different songs are sung, taro is added to the foods offered to *kaiko* visitors and, finally, men go into seclusion to trap eels, said to be the pigs of the spirit Koipa Mangiang. Preparations for the pig sacrifices, taboo abrogations, debt settlements, entertainment and public distributions culminating the *kaiko* ensue. The *kaiko* having been completed with the ritual recognition of key allies at the ceremonial fence called the *pabe* (see chapter 3 above), warfare could again be initiated, and usually did soon break out. If it were not settled quickly (and if the enmity were of long standing it almost never was), a ritual called "hanging the fighting stones" was performed, after which the level of violence escalated. Warfare terminated, for those remaining in possession of their territories, with the planting of *rumbim*.

In sum, in the Maring ritual cycle, which takes eight to twenty years to complete, a sequence of rituals distinguishes a number of major periods in each of which the dominant activity is different from the activities dominating the preceding and succeeding periods.

1. Planting *rumbim* terminates warfare and commences a period of six to twenty years during which gardening and pig husbandry are the focus of activities.

2. Planting stakes commences a period of several months during which trapping and smoking marsupials and planting large *kaiko* gardens are the main activities.

3 Uprooting the *rumbin* commences the *kaiko* festival, a little more than a year in length, during which pigs are sacrificed to ancestors, friendly groups are entertained, payments are made to affines and alliances are strengthened. The *kaiko* itself was divided into two periods, first *kaiko wobar* and then *kaiko nde*, distinguished by different songs, different foods included in prestations and different activities (see Rappaport 1984).

4. The *pabe* ritual terminates the *kaiko* and permits the local group to initiate warfare again. Wars sometimes, probably usually, developed through two phases or periods, marked off from each other by rituals, which were characterized by different levels of violence (see Rappaport 1984).

The Maring ritual cycle, it is clear, not only separates periods dominated by different activities from each other, but it provides an overarching structure within which those activities are organized.[10] Given the requirements of slash-and-burn horticulture and pig husbandry it is only occasionally that the efforts of an entire Maring local population need be concerted, but the cycle coordinates the subsistence, exchange and affinally directed activities of more or less autonomous household production units, thereby consolidating them into a general communitarian effort. Because every man pays his debts to affines, allies and ancestors at the same time, because all persons abrogate the taboos separating them from other members of the local group on the same day, and because these simultaneous transformations of social relations entail simultaneous ritual performances, the group, at particular moments in its history, is unified within itself, and it stands once more as a unified whole, in relationships of parity with ancestors, allies, affines and the other species with whom it shares its territory.

We have, through consideration of the temporal organization of activities, returned to the role of joint participation in, or coordination of, ritual performances in the definition and maintenance of autonomous social groups, for Maring ritual cycles also organize relations among the many autonomous local groups of which Maring society is composed. The separate ritual cycles of its independent local groups constitute, along with affinal relations, virtually all the infrastructure upon which Maring areal integration stands (see Rappaport 1984: ch. 4).

Coordination, as important as it is, does not exhaust the significance of the ritual cycle for the mundane activities of the Maring. It also provides all of these activities – production, reproduction, exchange, warfare – or rather, these activities taken together, with a general rationale transcending their immediate material effects. Ancestors and allies are repaid and the slain are avenged in conformity to and in reaffirmation of principles of reciprocity that are constituent of the world's natural order, and the wounds of a world repeatedly sundered by inevitable human strife are ever again healed in accordance with that order, *Nomane*, a cosmic conception bearing a family resemblance to the Heraclitan Logos (see chapter 11 below).

9. Regularity, length, and frequency

Liturgical sequences differ not only in shape, length, mode of regulation and bases for the occurrence of the rituals composing them, but also in the frequency of the rituals composing them, in the regularity with which those rituals occur, and in the length of individual rituals. Little thought has been given by anthropologists to such differences, and I can do no more here than speculate upon some of their possible correlates and concomitants.

Regularity and regulation

Turning first to the general nature of the periodicity predominating in different liturgical orders: a major distinction – perhaps the major distinction – among orders in this regard contrasts those in which the periods lying between one ritual and the next are of equal duration, as in the cases of Sabbath and Lord's Day services among Christians and Jews, with those in which the length of periods demarcated by rituals vary.

Few, if any, liturgical orders are organized along only one of these lines. Contemporary Christianity is liturgically calendrical, and thus largely regular in its periodicities, but performances of certain of its rituals, for example funerals, are responses to events in the world rather than regular reactions to date or time of day. On the other hand, the Maring were traditionally without a calendar, and were without even a clear conception of the year. The periods that were demarcated by the rituals constituting their cycle were of variable length, as was the cycle as a whole. Nevertheless, the *kaiko* year itself included among its rituals several inaugurated in response to such natural indicators as the ripening of pandanus varieties, which are themselves annually recurrent.

Regular versus irregular periodicity, it may be cautiously suggested, seems to be associated with two distinctive modes of regulation found not only in social life but throughout phenomena of all sorts. They can be observed in organic processes and in such mechanical and electronic devices as traffic lights, thermostats and gun-sights. A comparison of elements of the Tewa cycle (Ortiz 1969) which is calendrical, and the Maring, which is not, may be illuminating.

The Tewa calendrical cycle is predominantly *time-dependent* in its regulatory operation. That is, its regulatory actions take place at points fixed in time regardless of the state of the phenomena regulated. For instance, as we have noted, disparities among households in the amounts of corn they have stored tend to be reduced by the food distributions concomitant to festivals, and it is therefore fair to say the size of these disparities is subject to the generalized regulatory operation of the ritual cycle. These festivals take place at calendrically fixed times whether disparities between households are large or insignificant, just as Christian church services are held at, let us say, 10:00 am on Sunday morning regardless of the spiritual condition of the congregation, and regardless of the states of whatever other variables may be affected by that particular performance. Both of these instances bear formal resemblance to the operation of traffic lights, which turn from red to green when they do whether or not any cars are waiting.

The Maring cycle, in contrast, is predominantly *variable-dependent* or *cybernetic*. *Kaikos* are initiated and pigs are sacrificed not at fixed times but when a particular variable, the ratio of pigs to pig keepers, exceeds a tolerable range. As such, the operation of the ritual cycle bears a formal resemblance to that of the thermostat, and the durations between rituals were *necessarily* variable in length.

Invariant versus variant recurrence and thus periodicity, then, may be related to contrasting forms of regulation. When temporal construction itself is a function of variable dependent regulation (as it seems to be in the Maring case) the conception of time distinct from occurrences *in* time is much less clear than in systems in which time-dependent regulation is embedded in a periodicity seemingly independent of the regulated variables. A clear conception of an autonomous time is intrinsic to time-dependent but not to variable-dependent regulation.

Regular liturgical periodicity is, of course, highly correlated with the presence of calendars and the numeration of time, and these, in turn, are correlated with social complexity (although some rather simple societies do possess calendars). Our discussion nevertheless suggests that inquiries into the grounds for the periodicities prevailing in societies should include questions concerning modes of regulation and the nature of the variables to be regulated.

It may be that when the environment is characterized by regular and predictable changes, such as those in which seasonality is marked, or in which fluctuations in the states of other important variables are more or less regular, we should expect to find time-dependent regulation and calendrical rituals dominant. Non-calendrical rituals and variable-dependent regulation, in contrast, may predominate in situations in which seasonality is not strongly marked or in which changes in the states of other important variables are a function of so many factors as to be highly unpredictable.

Other things being equal, time-dependent regulation, and hence calendrical ritual cycles, may be favored over variable-dependent regulation for reasons of simplicity. It is, for example, simpler to make sacrifice on, say, November 11, or to redistribute food at an annual calendrical ritual, than it is to reach consensus that there are now sufficient pigs to uproot the *rumbim*. Variable-dependent regulation requires the monitoring of the states of variables, such as the numbers of pigs, or at least means for detecting deviations in the values of those variables from ideal or tolerable states and, in some instances, further requires means for developing and consolidating consensus and moving from consensus to action. In contrast, no judgment or decision that this is the proper time to perform a calendrical ritual need be made. It is the fourteenth day of the month of Nisan, or the 11th day of November or the summer solstice. But this isn't quite the end of the matter. The peculiar length of the solar year, for instance, made sufficient difficulties in determining the precise date of Easter to have provided some of the best minds in early medieval Europe with a major intellectual industry – developing methods for reckoning Easter's recurrence. These difficulties were so intractable as to resist definitive resolution and thus remained to provide grounds for major divisions within Christendom.

Frequency and length

The frequency and length of rituals also vary. Orthodox Jews join in public prayer three times every day, performing, in addition, briefer rituals in private and with their families, and there are additional observances on the sabbath and on holidays. Catholic monks, priests and some other clerics are obliged to recite the Divine Office, a daily order of seven rituals ancillary to the Mass. The divine office takes about one and a half hours to recite privately, much longer if sung in choir during the canonical hours distributed through the day. In contrast, months or even years may separate performances of community-wide rituals among the Maring, and any Maring's participation in the rituals of less inclusive congregations is also likely to be less regular and less frequent than among Jews or lay Christians, to say nothing of Christian monastics or Orthodox Jews. When Maring rituals do occur, on the other hand, they tend to be lengthy in comparison to those performed in Western societies.

If liturgical orders do in fact distinguish two temporal conditions, mundane time and time out of time, the frequency and length of rituals will affect the proportions of their lives that individuals spend in each. Rituals may be so frequent in some monasteries, and the duration of these rituals so long, that periods spent in mundane time may seem encapsulated in what is experienced as a virtually continuous liturgy. Not only may the proportion of time spent in liturgy be high, but the mundane periods between them may be so brief as never to be fully out of their "shadow" or "afterglow." Discussion of the nature of experience in ritual must be deferred for a little while. Suffice it to note here that it may be very different from that normally prevailing in mundane time. The degree to which that experience departs from quotidian experience may well be related to the proportion of life spent in ritual and out of it.

There seems to be a range of social conditions in which high proportions of time are spent in ritual. In complex societies it is largely, if not entirely, religious specialists, particularly those in cloistered communities, who are thus engaged. Among Australian aborigines (Meggitt n.d., Stanner n.d.) and Southern Africa Bushmen (Katz 1982), in contrast, all individuals spend a high proportion of their time in ritual on occasions when large numbers of people can come together, although such assemblages may themselves not be very frequent.

I would suggest that the high proportion of time spent in ritual by desert hunters and gatherers provides a way to overcome some of the difficulties their environments make for social life, whereas, for cloistered Christians, it provides a way to escape them altogether. It is plausible to argue, generally following Durkheim (1961), that the extraordinarily intense sociability generated in frequent, lengthy and effervescent rituals Australian aborigines and Bushmen (Katz 1982) perform during limited and infrequent periods establishes social bonds of a strength sufficient to countervail the centrifugal tendencies inherent in a way of life in which families are not only economically autonomous but live in isolation for months on end. As for cloistered communities of Catholic contemplatives, it is important to note that

> the original [Catholic] religious foundations existed for the spiritual good of the members rather than for any service to the church or to one's fellow man. The life of the evangelical counsels [i.e., the poverty, chastity and obedience freely vowed by those entering such communities] is supposed to imitate more closely than secular life the manner of living which Jesus himself followed.
>
> *(MacKenzie 1969: 97)*

This life is, in the contemplative orders, "built round the daily praise of God in the Divine Office or *opus Dei* ... where the whole concern is the Lord's service" (Bullough 1963: 247). Physical and mental work as well as prayer is also understood to be done in the Lord's service. Those entering such communities do so, as far as the Church is concerned, voluntarily, and if they remain they do so, presumably, because they have a "vocation" for living in such a way. St. Benedict, the father of Western monasticism, deliberately formulated the Rule governing this mode of life in Western Christianity to teach men to "run in the era of God's commandments," and to provide a few persons of extraordinary spiritual concern with a solution to the problem of "living in the world" in a manner which is not "of the world" (John 17.11.14; see Bullough 1963: 244ff.). Men and women following Benedict's Rule do, in significant degree, at least in theory, escape from the mundane world of expectation, reason, memory and shifting foci of attention, for they are separated from it in space and spend much of every day's waking hours outside its time as well, contemplating, through the never-changing Divine Office, God's "delights, neither coming nor passing away." They have, this is to say, leaped out of this world's troubles and gotten a head start on the way to Heaven.

But cloistered monastics are not the only Catholics obligated to recite the offices. Priests, who are fully immersed in the world, are also charged to do so, although they may recite them privately and quickly rather than chant them at length in choir. And Orthodox Jews, obviously not cloistered, and not a body of religious specialists set off from the rest of their community, also participate in several rituals each day.

In moving from cloistered clergy through priests to Orthodox Jews, we have shifted ground. Both the priests and the Jews participate in frequent rituals, but their devotions are briefer than those of cloistered communities and therefore the proportion of their time actually spent in them may not be high. Although frequency and length together produce a "product" in the mathematical sense – the amount of time spent in ritual and out of mundane time – and although this product constitutes one term in the ratio of mundane time to extraordinary time, it is also useful to approach frequency and length separately. In doing so, we may recall, from chapter 4, that the performance of a ritual entails formal acceptance of the order encoded in that ritual. Such an act of acceptance establishes an obligation to comply with that order, but does not guarantee compliance. Without acceptance there is no obligation, it was argued in chapter 4, and without obligation there can be no violation of obligation, but once obligation is established it *can* be violated. Ritual acceptance therefore establishes conventional rules and understandings in a way that insulates them from the vagaries and violations of ordinary usage and that then permits them to be used as standards against which the propriety and morality of daily behavior can be judged. Actual compliance with the order accepted, it was further argued, is a matter distinct from the act of acceptance. I now suggest that both the length and frequency of rituals bear upon compliance and upon the motivational, cognitive and affective grounds underlying it. High frequency and lengthiness together may, as we have already noted, augment each other in the production of powerful and pervasive effects, but when length is great and frequency is low or frequency high but length brief they may be put to ends and have effects that are the inverse of each other.

Length

Length can be discussed only briefly here, its implications being further developed in later sections of this chapter and yet more fully in chapter 11. At this point it seems reasonable to suppose that the longer a ritual continues the fuller can be the development of the peculiar characteristics of time out of time (alluded to earlier in this chapter but remaining to be discussed) with, possibly, more profound alterations of consciousness and deeper and more enduring effects upon the psyches of participants (d'Aquili, Laughlin, and McManus 1979, Lex 1979). This further suggests that the length of rituals could be related to the profundity of the transformations, social, cognitive or affective, to be effected in them. Other things being equal, we would expect, for example, rites of passage in societies in which ontogenetic statuses are radically distinct to be long. Among the Maring the *ngimbai*, a ritual to send the ghosts of deceased persons to the world of spirits, performed after all of the flesh has rotted off the bones of the exposed corpse, begins at dusk and lasts until shortly after dawn. Rituals lasting all night are common among the Maring, and in 1963 older men told of a ritual, no longer performed, often lasting three days or more, in which a shamanistic spirit known as the *Kom-Wok Ambra* (Kom-tree bark woman) selected her novices. The eligible young men were confined to an elevated platform in a darkened house and, deprived of drink and food (except for a certain species of web-spinning spider) were kept awake the whole time while the older men chanted. Those whom the *Kom-Wok Ambra* "struck," as the Maring put it, would gibber, twitch, fall into trance, and upon recovering, report flying to the spirit's house on top of Mt. Oipor in the Jimi Valley, where they became something like her bridegrooms.

The *Kom-Wok Ambra* had been succeeded by another female spirit, *the Kun Kase Ambra* (the Smoking Woman) long before I arrived in the field in 1962. There remained only one elderly man who had been struck by the *Kom-Wok Ambra* in his youth. He stated that he remained celibate for several years after being struck by her because she was jealous of other women and, had he made love to his wife, the *Kom-Wok Ambra* might have killed him.

There may, of course, be alternatives to length for reaching psychic depths. The intensity of the ritual state is not a function of length alone but of such elements as tempo, unison, density of symbolic, iconic and indexical representation, sensory loading, strangeness, drug ingestion, or pain, every one of which may, by itself, be affectively powerful and cognitively dis- or re-orienting, and may be even more so in concert. Among Australian aborigines, for whom the distinction between initiated and uninitiated men is sharp and wide, rites of passage, through which males pass only once, are both long and intense.

Frequency

Whereas the length of rituals may be related to an intention to work deep psychic transformations or to maintain those previously effected, the frequency of rituals could be related to the extent to which liturgical orders are, as it were, called upon both to guide or govern daily behavior and to penetrate to, and thus to shape and maintain "proper" cognitive and affective bases for that behavior. The need to shape or constrain the grounds of behavior, and not simply the behavior itself may, in turn, be related to (1) the degree to which the understandings encoded in the liturgical order are exposed to dissolution by the corrosive power of frequently encountered experience or alternative understandings; (2) the extent to which the rules and moral dicta the order represents are vulnerable to violation by actions motivated by the pressures, temptations, and usages of daily life, and by the unruly emotions they may generate; and (3) the weakness or absence of other means to guard against such threats. For instance, the ritual recitation with sabbatarian frequency of an order that not only stipulates the name and nature of the divinity, but emphasizes the golden rule of charity, and which admonishes its faithful to love neighbors or even enemies, may be related to the impersonal nature of much of daily life in complex Judeo-Christian societies, to the ease with which persons in such societies can avoid community responsibility or even prey anonymously on strangers and to the strength of temptations to do so. It may also be related to the lack of other mechanisms for insuring that ethical prescriptions in these and similar matters are fulfilled. The even greater frequency of ritual performance demanded of Roman Catholic priests is at least correlated with austere restrictions upon their sexual behavior, and may be systematically related to them. The argument developed here subsumes one which is both more specific and more familiar: frequent rituals may be important in the sublimation or denial of more or less continuous psychological and physiological processes and in coping with hostile social conditions. (We may recall here Freud's (1907) proposal that ritual provides some fulfillment of that which it prohibits or denies.)

The high frequency of the rituals constituting the Orthodox Jewish liturgy is understandable, first, in terms of *Halakha*, the rules constituting comprehensive observance not confined to practices in their nature obviously or explicitly devotional. The proximate aim of *Halakha* is to guide the faithful in their efforts to lead their entire lives in accordance with the will of the ever-present God (Adler 1963: ch. 3). Its ultimate aim is, explicitly, to bring the divine order into this world (Soleveitchik 1983). It is plausible to suggest that so comprehensive an order and so difficult a goal could not rely for its realization upon mere formal acceptance of rules, but must seek the willing or even enthusiastic acquiescence of those realizing it. Thus, *Halakha* "is concerned with motive as well as action, with ... attitude as well as behavior" (Adler 1963: 66). A "[righteous] act is not a substitute for an inner feeling but an expression of it" (Adler 1963: 63).

Halakhic observance, Soleveitchik (1983) argues, is, in a sense, the inverse of mystical practice. The mystic attempts to escape from the mundane world into the world of the divine. The "Halakhic Man" attempts to bring divine order into the world of everyday, and to maintain it in the everyday world in the face of daily vicissitudes. Such strenuous spiritual and moral exertion may well call for the psychic reinforcement of frequent ritual. More fundamentally, however, performance of the rituals realizes, *ipso facto*, the divine order with a frequency that cannot help but pervade the mundane world. The divine is continually realized in the mundane. Whereas mystical states may be encouraged by, and therefore their cultivation may call for, lengthy ritual the frequency of which may be irrelevant, liturgical orders which attempt to bring the divine into everyday life may favor brief but frequent rituals.

It may also be significant that Halakhic practice seems generally to be rabbinic in origin (Adler 1963: 60ff.), and thus is associated with the diaspora, during which Jews have everywhere been a minority (and not infrequently a persecuted one). The high frequency of the ritual performance of Orthodox Jews not only gives frequent expression to their cultural distinctiveness, but may well cause participants to internalize that distinctiveness. This internalization has been of central importance in preserving the identity of the Jews in alien environments through the eighty or so generations that have lived and died since Titus took Jerusalem.

Frequency, ethics, and social complexity

Examples so far offered may seem to suggest that ethical dicta encoded in the liturgical orders of complex societies require frequent reiteration in ritual because other means for assuring behavior conforming to them are inadequate, and because prevailing social forces tend to violate or even dissolve them, whereas, in contrast, the social forces at work in simpler societies do not. There are, I think, some grounds for such a view. In tribal societies, ethics are an immediate and perceptible aspect of relations among people who are, for the most part, not only known to each other but stand in well-defined relationships to each other. Reciprocal (although not necessarily symmetrical) obligation is the cement if not, in fact, the ground of all such relationships, and the obligations they entail are usually quite clearly specified. Violations of obligation inevitably become evident, often quickly, and sanctions against breach of obligation are essential elements of reciprocity's fundamental structure. Whereas the response to a specific offense may be specific and proportional (an eye for an eye, a pig for a pig, a death for a death or a wife for a wife) it often entails the termination or suspension of the *general* relationship within which the *specific* offense is located. Furthermore, the logic of reciprocity, in which meeting or failing to meet *specific* obligations strengthens or weakens *generalized* personal relationships, encourages performance which is not merely adequate but exemplary. That prestige as much as or even more than wealth is among the chief rewards of life properly lived in societies in which reciprocity prevails also encourages vigorous, valorous and generous fulfillment of obligation.

It would be wrong to claim that the sanctions of reciprocity are not in force in societies in which specialized transactions between parties otherwise unrelated or even unknown to each other are the rule. Dissatisfied customers can always take their business elsewhere. But such sanctions are not as compelling or coercive as they are in societies in which the preponderance of everyone's transactions engage a limited number of well-known others. Legal sanctions are more highly developed in complex societies, of course, but legal actions constitute realistic remedies in no more than a small minority of cases. Moreover, they are more effective in providing punishment for prohibited acts than they are in encouraging virtuous behavior. It may, indeed, be logically impossible, at least with respect to some virtues, to establish laws requiring them. Generosity, for example, by definition must exceed whatever is ordained. Legal sanctions, it can be argued, support, and even represent as exemplary, the logic of minimal rather than maximal performance, of the least that you can possibly get away with rather than the most you can possibly afford.

In sum, in simple societies ethics are firmly grounded in face-to-face social relations. In complex societies they are not. Where there is obligation in simple societies there are, in complex societies, conceptions like charity, the golden rule, the virtuousness of loving neighbors and even enemies, the blessedness of giving. Not founded upon or growing out of the impersonal and commoditized nature of prevailing social relations, such conceptions can hardly stand unsupported.

This argument builds on one advanced in chapter 4. It was proposed there that ritual provides a means for establishing (i.e., specifying and accepting) conventions, including rules, understandings, values, procedures, in a manner which insulates them from the violations and vagaries of everyday usage. Thus, behavior departing from the convention merely violates it. It does not dissolve it. Here it is further proposed that if, in the absence of behavior consistently and reliably conforming to them, the ethical conceptions established in the rituals of complex societies are to be more than honored in their breach, but are, rather, to be effective in shaping actual behavior, they may have to be reiterated with sabbatarian or even daily frequency. In contrast, such conceptions as "charity" may not even be formulated in simple face-to-face societies.

Frequency and restraint
Such societies have other problems which frequent ritual performances may ameliorate, however, and reciprocity itself may be a source of some

of them. It may, for instance, ordain that injuries be revenged, and ritual restraints on violence may be more highly emphasized, more frequently invoked, and more heavily relied upon in smaller, simpler societies than in larger ones in which, in elaborated divisions of labor, special agencies are charged to maintain public order. The taboos on interdining, food sharing and certain aspects of sociability ritually assumed by Maring between whom serious grievances lay are of special interest in this regard.

Homicide was the grievance most frequently leading to proscriptions on the consumption of food grown by the antagonists, or their kin, or of any food cooked over a fire on which food eaten by the antagonists' party has been cooked, or entering houses which have been entered by them. The most frequent cause of homicide was warfare. These taboos (and a good many others) dominate relations between principal antagonists, that is, local groups that had fought against each other, but they were not confined to them. Principal antagonists, as noted in note 8 above and in chapter 3, recruited allies, but not by enlisting the aid of friendly local groups as corporate wholes. Rather, their members appealed to their affines and cognates in other local groups to "help them fight," and it was a shameful breach of obligation for those called upon to withhold their support without compelling reason.

Patterns of marriage were such that it was not unusual for both sides to recruit allies from the same local groups, and it was therefore not unusual for men of the same group, or even the same clan, to find themselves facing each other across raised shields as allies of antagonistic groups whose quarrels were not their own. Principal antagonists seemed to have suffered more casualties than allies, but allies sometimes got killed. Thus, Tsembaga men fought on both sides of the Monamban-Kauwassi war of 1955 and two (both Monamban supporters) were killed in the rout that ended the day. The Tsembaga were fragmented and in exile at the time, having taken refuge with seven different local groups following their defeat at the hands of the Kundagai some months earlier. When, in the following year, they were returned to their own territory by pacifying agents of the Australian government, those between whom blood grievances lay – the kinsmen of the two slain men and those who fought on the side of the killers and *their* kinsmen (not mutually exclusive categories, by the way) – had once again to become members of a single co-residential and (intermittently) cooperating group.

Death can be avenged by death, but Maring usage ordains that principal antagonists should compensate their allies for injuries and deaths suffered in their service. Such compensation is postponed, however, until the principal antagonists stage their *kaiko*, at least six or eight years after the termination of warfare. (If a group had been driven from its land and, therefore, had not planted *rumbim* it was never in a position to host a *kaiko*.). Until its *kaiko* was completed, erstwhile principal antagonists were not only forbidden to attack their enemies, but from even entering enemy territory. Such a prohibition obviously could not prevail within the local groups from which they had drawn their allies, however, and if such a group had suffered casualties, relations within it remained delicate until compensation was received. The Monamban *kaiko* had not yet taken place during my 1962–63 sojourn among the Tsembaga, and blood grievances among them not only remained formally unresolved but were very much alive in their minds and hearts (or, as they would say, "bellies").

The frequent expression of interdining and other interpersonal taboos played an important part, I believe, in preventing these grievances from exploding into violence. They defined specific forms of behavior in which the anger generated by death and injury could be expressed while permitting cooperation in most important tasks. In Freudian (1907) terms, the taboos represented a compromise between the needs both to express and repress dangerous feelings, for they allowed or required grievances to be stated frequently and formally in highly specified ways: by men cooking their food side by side over separate fires, by the refusal of one man to enter another's house, by the refusal to eat food grown by another. The frequent but relatively harmless statement of antagonism in areas of behavior narrowly defined by taboos inhibited, I believe, their more generalized, less predictable and therefore more dangerous expression. Further, such narrow expression could not help but call attention to the wider context of amity encompassing them: not only would two men cook food each had separately grown over separate fires, but would chat amiably while doing so as they rested from the heavy work of, for example, building a fence together. The sanctified and categorical nature of the taboos, moreover, may have further relieved tension between those separated by them by elevating the issue from one of personal animus to impersonal spiritual duty. Be this as it may, frequent observation of these taboos, I think, prevented ill feeling from contaminating all aspects of the relationships of parties between whom grievances lay, and thus facilitated their continuing cooperation and amity. Men who disdainfully refused to eat each others' crops or eat at each others' fires helped each other to clear forest and to build fences, granted land to each other, and assisted each other with affinal payments.

That it is taboo – sanctified proscription of physically feasible activity – rather than positive ritual to which the expression and suppression of antagonism is assigned is of significance. Taboo, it is plausible to argue, is better suited to the purpose than ritual, for the very act of observing interpersonal taboos turns the principals *away* from each other, thus permitting the expression of grievances in ways that tend to avoid dangerous confrontations.

Regularity, length and frequency: a summary

The form of periodicity dominating a liturgical ordering may be related to the mode of regulation in which the order is predominantly engaged. Variable dependent regulation, if it is implicated in temporal construction at all, produces periods that vary in length or circumference from one instance to the next. Thus, Maring ritual cycles, from *kaiko* through warfare and raising pigs until the next *kaiko*, took anywhere from six to over twenty years to complete. Time-dependent regulation produces or is produced by periods of invariant length. Variable-dependent ritual regulation is likely to be found in societies in which a few key variables whose values may fluctuate more or less unpredictably, are the foci of regulation. Unpredictable seasonality (e.g., unpredictable variability in the onsets and intensities of wet and dry seasons) may also favor variable-dependent regulation, or at least inhibit the development of time-dependent regulation in simple societies, and an unelaborated division of labor may be requisite for a society to live by a predominantly variable-dependent regulatory mode or variant periodicity. Time-dependent ritual regulation is more likely to occur in simple societies in which fluctuations of regulated variables are predictable and where seasonality is clearly marked. In societies with complex divisions of labor, regular periodicity – weeks, months, years – may well be distinguished by ritual but the rituals themselves may not be regulatory, that is, their performances do not, in and of themselves, correct conditions deviating from ideal. They merely mark or establish periodicities in accordance with which non-ritual agencies may conduct and regulate a range of activities within a common temporal regime. When a temporal regime is contingent upon variable-dependent regulation there is no clear distinction between time and processes occurring in time. With time-dependent regulation the distinction is clear.

The length of rituals may be related to the profundity of the transformations to be effected in them. The longer a ritual the more deeply it may alter the consciousness and affective condition of the participants and, possibly, the nature of their social condition as well.

The frequency of ritual performances may also be related to the extent to which the liturgical order not only guides continuing daily behavior but constitutes an attempt to penetrate to the grounds of that behavior, which in turn may be related to the vulnerability of the order being realized to violation or even dissolution by the pressures and temptations of everyday life. Frequent performance of brief rituals, like the round of daily prayers of Orthodox Jews and their continued observance of *mitzvot* (commandments) in the details of daily life may penetrate to the cognitive and affective bases of that behavior, and thus strengthen the ground upon which the order realized stands. The length and frequency of rituals have some similar cognitive, affective and social consequences, but they also may be eschatological inversions of each other. The lengthy but infrequent ritual, in profoundly altering the consciousnesses of the participants, lifts them out of mundane time and the mundane world to assimilate them, for the time being, into what may be represented as a never-changing divine order, returning them transformed to the mundane world at the ritual's end. Brief but frequent rituals, in contrast, do not transport participants to a divine world but attempt an opposite movement; they attempt to realize a divine order in mundane time. This is explicit in the Orthodox Jewish conception of *Halakha*.

Finally, when a liturgical order is composed of rituals that are both lengthy and frequent, participants are maintained more or less continuously outside of mundane experience, permanently in the case of religious specialists spending their lives in cloistered communities, and for limited seasons in the case of groups which, like Australian aboriginal hunters and gatherers, assemble from time to time for such events as initiation.

10. Sequence and space

As consideration of the sequential dimension of liturgical order leads to time and its ordering, and consideration of time to schedule and to the organization of activity, so are we led by sequence to organization both of and in space. Liturgical orders unfold in, or proceed through, space as well as time, and so, of course, do the activities they may regulate.

Eliade has argued that the sacred is experienced most fundamentally in spatial terms. Ritual or revelation establishes centers – earth navels, axis mundi – through which the divine enters the material world and from which that world is oriented.

If the world is to be lived in it must be *founded* – and no world can come to birth in the chaos of the homogeneity and relativity of profane space. The discovery of a fixed point – the center – is equivalent to the creation of the world.

(1957b: 22; emphasis his)

There is, then, a sacred space and hence a strong significant space; there are other spaces that are not sacred and so are without structure or consistency, amorphous.

(1957b: 20)

In my view Eliade seriously overstated the case for the priority of space in "the religious experience," and he also overemphasized the significance of centers (see J. Smith 1987: ch. 1). But we need not accept his thesis that always and everywhere "the religious experience of the non-homogeneity of space is a primordial experience homologizable to a founding of the world" (p. 20–21) to recognize that ritual may transform mere extent into ordered cosmos and that, as liturgical sequences distinguish mundane periods from the extraordinary intervals between them, so do they distinguish the extraordinary space at or inside loci of orientation – shrines, temples, mountain tops, caves, be they "centers" or not – from the ordinary, or profane spaces surrounding or extending from them.

Time and space, of course, are not altogether distinct conceptually. The term "sequence" itself, in applying to both of them seems to pull them toward each other, and common terms for temporal and spatial relations – the English "before" which can signify both "prior to" and "in front of," and "present" which can be a synonym for either "here" or "now," are examples – are found in many languages. Ordinal numbers generally have both spatial and temporal significance, and we may recall that Van Gennep used a spatial metaphor – that of crossing thresholds – to discuss transitions seemingly temporal in nature.

Perhaps nowhere else are time and space more closely bound together conceptually than they are by liturgy among certain Indians of the American Southwest and Mexico. Among the Hopi the ritual calendar rests upon the sun's rising at particular points upon the horizon in its progress from solstice to solstice. Two chiefs are designated Sunwatcher: the Horn Chief follows the sun's journey from summer solstice to winter from his observatory at the buffalo shrine, the Gray Flute Chief monitors its journey north, following the winter solstice, from his observatory on the roof of the Sun Clan house. The rise of the sun at named points of the horizon constitutes the occasion for major rituals; solstitial rituals have great importance, and the points of sunrise and the solstice are marked on the horizon by shrines (Titiev 1944). Among the Chamula, who live in the Central Chiapas Highlands of southern Mexico, the sun, conflated since the Spanish Conquest with Christ, is the central deity and "was responsible for delimiting the major temporal and spatial cycles by means of his death and subsequent ascent into the sky, thus defeating the forces of chaos, cold, and evil" (Gossen 1972: 136). Both time and direction are established by the sun's movement, two of the cardinal directions being given labels that seem as temporal as spatial: the term for "east" may be translated into English, according to Gossen (1972: 138), as "emergent heat (or day)," and west as "waning heat." North and south, respectively "the edge of heaven on the right hand" and "the edge of heaven on the left hand" are oriented in accordance with the sun's daily path from the point of its rising, a path which also lays out the "principle divisions of the day." The temporal divisions of the year "are expressed most frequently in terms of the fiesta cycle" (p. 138), but the fiesta calendar is based upon the annual journey of the sun between the solstices (140, 142, 147 *passim*), a phenomenon that has directional as well as temporal aspects. In this regard we may note that the processional circuits taking place in rituals begin in the real or conceptual east or southeast (the intercardinal direction of sunrise at the winter solstice) and proceed in a counterclockwise direction. Similar orientations of ritual circuits are found among the pueblo Indians of the southwest (White 1962: 110; Ortiz 1969: 18). Among the Chamula, at least, "This direction is the horizontal equivalent of the sun's daily vertical path across the heavens from east to west" (p. 138). In this horizontal representation of the vertical, north becomes the equivalent of the zenith, the height of the day, and it is also associated with warmth and growth because such are the conditions prevailing at the summer solstice, that is, when the sun has reached the northern destination of its annual journey. The south, in contrast, and all that is on the sun's left hand as it crosses the heavens, is, by a counter rotation of the land to the vertical orientation of the sun's movement, associated with night, darkness and the underworld and, of course, when the sun is in the region of the winter solstice far to the south, the nights are long, the days are cold, and growth is in abeyance.

   In sum, among the Chamula the movements of the sun, both diurnal and annual, are the ground of both temporal and spatial order and of liturgical order as well. Yet, time and direction are not simply established by the sun's movements. They are constructed by the Chamula, the Tewa, the Hopi and others out of the sun's movements. The shifts between the northerly and southerly stages of the sun's passage do, of course, provide the basis for a division of the year into two natural periods, but to provide a basis for a distinction is not to make the distinction. Even in the case of the major division between the period of the sun's northward and southward journey, the distinction is made by ritual, and shorter periods are obviously the products of the imposition of sequences of rituals upon the continuous and repetitive process of the sun's annual migration. Moreover, in seizing upon the sun's movements to order time and space, liturgy binds the spatial and temporal order to the source of warmth and growth and life to which it has also attributed goodness. Being fixed, furthermore, to a spatial-temporal framework constructed out of solar movement, the liturgical order is assimilated into nature or the cosmos and thus partakes of the certainty of nature's most inexorable and regular change and repetition.

Time and space are not bound as closely together among the Maring, who were traditionally without a calendar, as they are among the Chamula or the Hopi, but the organization of ordinary space is ordered by the ritual cycle in a manner which lashes the waxing and waning of the territories of local groups to the periodicities of Maring life. We may consider especially the planting of stakes at territorial borders. This ritual, it has been noted, precedes the commencement of the *kaiko* by some months and follows, usually by a decade or more, the planting of *rumbim*. *Rumbim* planting itself has an important spatial aspect, for it signifies the attachment of a group composed of specified individuals (those grasping it as it is planted) to a demarcated territory. *Rumbim* planting is, thus, central to the social organization of space,[11] and certain ritually planted *rumbim* are the conceptual centers of the land to which their planting constitutes a claim of title or sovereignty. This is not only true of the relationship of *yu min rumbim* ("men's souls *rumbim*") to the territories of the clans or clusters of clans on which it is planted but also that planted as *nduk mndai* ("garden heart") in the "centers" of major gardens.

Certain rules govern the planting of stakes many years later. If, after a round of warfare, both antagonists remain in occupation of their territories, the stakes are planted on their common border as it had been demarcated previous to the fighting. If one of the parties has been driven off its territory, its fragmented remnants taking refuge with friendly groups, it was not in a position to plant *rumbim* at the end of the fighting. Therefore, it could neither reconstitute its membership ritually nor reestablish through ritual its connection to the land which it had, perhaps for generations, been occupying. If a group does not plant *rumbim*, it cannot demarcate its border with stakes when it comes time to do so because the time to do so, being determined by a ritual cycle which in this instance was never commenced, never arrives. The victors, however, do not immediately annex the land from which they have driven their enemies. Indeed, it is their understanding that it would be dangerous for them to do so because, although that land has seemingly been abandoned to them by their living antagonists, the spirits of those antagonists' ancestors remain to guard it. If, however, the routed do not return to plant *rumbim* by the time the victorious group has assembled sufficient pigs to commence a *kaiko* it is assumed that even the ancestors have departed, to take up residence near their living descendants who, as they are being assimilated into the groups with whom they have taken refuge, offer them sacrificial pork from time to time at their new residences. Under such circumstances, when the time comes for them to do so, the victors plant stakes at a new border encompassing at least part of the land from which their enemy has fled.

Among the Maring, then, the social dynamics of space are ordered by the interplay of ritual cycles. A different relationship of liturgy to space prevails among Central Australian groups such as the Walbiri (Meggitt 1965a). We have already noted that their Gadjari cycle, which is concerned with the creation of a portion of the world – particular places and species – reenacts the dreamtime journey of the Mamandabari men who, emerging from Mulungu Hill where they bring themselves into full and distinct being by singing their own names, set out across previously featureless space singing places into being, thus transforming what had been an undifferentiated extent into an ordered and populated landscape. As their track crosses the tracks of other dreamtime heroes, it weaves with them the fabric of the world.

It should be noted, if only in passing, that the heroes, the world they create and, indeed, those participating in the Gadjari, are not altogether distinct. Early in their journey the Mamandabari begin to fashion bullroarers, upon each of which they incise designs representing the segment of the track that they will next traverse. These engravings also represent the ceremonial grounds and paraphernalia the heroes make at certain campsites, the bodies of the heroes themselves, and the novices participating in the contemporary ritual (Meggitt 1965a: 8, 34 *passim*). And as they make their way singing the world, their creative song is augmented by the roar of the incised bullroarers, which they swing continuously. The track, the participants, the heroes, the bullroarers, if not one and the same, are icons of each other.

The track is of enormous length – 1,000 miles or more – and the myth is elaborate. No one Walbiri knows either it or the entire corpus of 200 songs it includes. But the heroes' journey takes them through the territories of all four major Walbiri "countries," and certain men in each of them act as custodians of the songs and the portion of the myth concerning the passage of the heroes through their lands. In light of the dependence of the reproduction of the Mamandabari myth and the Gadjari rituals upon the combined and sequentially ordered participation of many men, the etymology of "Mamandabari" is of some interest. It seems, according to Meggitt (n.d.), to be "the mutually dependent (*Mamanda*) initiated men (*-bari*)."

As consideration of the liturgical ordering of mundane time leads to the liturgical ordering of activities in time, so does consideration of the liturgical ordering of mundane space lead to consideration of the liturgical ordering of the social dynamics of that space. Whereas the ritual cycle of the horticultural Maring accommodates and regulates the formation and dissolution of Maring groups densely settled in a lush forest, and the waxing and waning of the territories they contentiously occupy, the Gadjari cycle protects the continuity of small and labile groups of hunters and gatherers thinly scattered over an immense desert. Along with other of their rituals and other aspects of their organization, the Gadjari cycle itself seems to devise an interdependence that does not grow naturally out of the environment nor out of the ways in which the Walbiri gain a living from it. Indeed, the sociability of those people may well be in danger of dissolving into the desert's great distances or of fragmenting into the tiny bands sufficient to gain a living by hunting and gathering from it (Yengoyan 1972, 1976). But to participate in the liturgical ordering of physical space among the Walbiri is, at the same time, to participate in the liturgical ordering of a conceptual space, and that space is more capacious than any one person's mind. Whereas the bullroarers tell us that the body of the myth and of its heroes is both the track and those who perform the Gadjari upon it, so the great mind of the myth is assembled by the Gadjari out of the mutually dependent thought of all of those joined together by their participation in it.

The imposition of the Gadjari upon the desert turns an aggregate of physiographic and biotic features into a meaningful landscape composed not only of landmarks but also of conventions originated by the Mamandabari men at various places in the journey. In the myth of Gadjari the natural world is brought into being and ordered by the *sine qua non* of culture, the creative word (uttered by the heroes) at the same time that, conversely, the conventions specified by that word are assimilated to the landscape, and thus come to participate in the same naturalness that is the property of rock and birds. Gadjari, like Halakha, reduces the distance between the mundane and the extraordinary.

The Gadjari is imposed upon mundane space and the objects of the daily world, but the myth in which men participate in performing the Gadjari does not occur in ordinary time. It occurs in the dreaming, a time of origins that in some sense continues to recur or be recovered in ritual. It is noteworthy that myths are properly recounted among the Pitjandjara not in a past perfect but in a continuous tense (Yengoyan 1979: 327), and that men enter the dreamtime when they perform rituals. It is time to turn from mundane time to the extraordinary times out of time that ritual sequesters in its intervals.

7

Intervals, eternity, and communitas

We have been led out of mundane time and into the extraordinary time of ritual intervals. I have referred to the durations encompassed by rituals themselves as "times out of time," "sacred time," and extraordinary time," and other writers have used similarly mysterious language. We will now consider how times out of time really are out of mundane time. This will lead to a consideration of eternity and to a discussion of the relationship of tempo to the state of mind and society that Turner (1969) called "communitas" and to the simultaneous grasp and synthesis of the multiple significata of ritual representations (like Turner's *mudyi* tree (1967; *passim*), into more comprehensive meanings.

1. Time out of time

In making sense out of such obscure phrases as "Time out of time" we may heed an observation made but not developed in chapter 3. In distinguishing two temporal conditions from each other, ordinary periodic time and extraordinary intervalic time, liturgical orders operate in a manner which bears formal resemblance to the operation of digital computers. To quote from the introduction to an old textbook on circuit design:

The successful operation of a real machine depends upon being able to separate the time intervals at which variables have their desired values from those in which they are changing. *Logically*, therefore, the passage of time is discrete where physically it is continuous. *(Reeves 1972)*

Before and after the moment of change the variables have their "desired values," that is to say, the values that enter into the machine's computations. The intervals during which the values of variables are actually changing are *outside* the times during which the computer's operant logic

216

prevails and are ignored in its computations. But, although the processes of change themselves are ignored in the machine's computations, the values of the variables that *do* enter into the computations are *contingent* upon those changes.

The logic of the machine, in sum, is digital. Computations take the values of components to be either 0 or 1. The transition from 0 to 1 taking place *in the ignored interval* is not a digital but an *analogic* process. The processes occurring in the intervals are *literally* governed by a logic *other* than that in terms of which computation proceeds.

The resemblance to ritual seems patent. Like the intervals produced by the operation of digital computers, the intervals produced by the distinctions of liturgical orders are outside of "ordinary" or "periodic" time – the time of mundane activity, discursive logic, digital computation and the ever unique successions of events that are the stuff of histories. Moreover, as the values of variables in computers are contingent upon transformations occurring in preceding intervals, so are social states in mundane periods in some degree outcomes of transformations occurring in previous rituals, and while the states of affairs before and after ritual transformations can be distinguished by the digital logic of either/or (e.g., single/married, youth/man, war/peace), the logic of the interval, when transformation is actually effected, is not that of either/or, but of neither/nor, more-less and continuity (Turner 1969).

There are, of course, obvious differences between computers and liturgical orders. Duration is the most marked. Intervals in computers were first measured in milliseconds, then microseconds and then nanoseconds – billionths of seconds – and the analogic processes occurring in them are of the temporal order of picoseconds – thousandths of billionths of seconds. The intervals marked by liturgical orders are, in contrast, hours, or even days, and occasionally weeks or months in length. They are always long enough to experience being in them.

Long enough to experience *being in* them. I emphasize both "in" and "being." To say that these intervals are long enough to experience being *in* them is to say that they are long enough to experience *being* in them. The states of both individual consciousness and the social order may be very different during ritual from those prevailing in mundane time.

During mundane or periodic time society conducts itself in accordance with the canons of what Victor Turner (1969, *passim*), in general accord with traditional British usage, terms "structure," the more or less highly differentiated organization of statuses and roles through which fundamental biological, economic and social needs are fulfilled and even, in some degree, defined. The activities of mundane time, as we have noted, are guided by rational discursive thought, or so it is assumed by the actors. When people are engaged in farming, trading, cooking, arranging marriages, hunting, fighting, prosecuting court cases and composing quarrels it is "normal" for them to "act rationally," or at least to believe that they are acting rationally. Their motives and values – the bases of their decisions – are not always put into words, but presumably they could be, and actors are likely to assume that discursive logic, to which number, distinctions and sanctity are intrinsic, plays a predominant role in the calculations informing their conduct. If someone's everyday behavior seems to be guided by other than discursive reason, he may be taken to be quixotic, eccentric or even insane.

The states of society and the quality of experience dominating many rituals stand in profound contrast to those of ordinary time. Turner (1964, 1969), building upon Van Gennep, has argued (as did A. F. C. Wallace (1966) in somewhat different terms) that the states of society and experience during these intervals are at once "destructured" and "pre-structured." Relations are no longer what they were and not yet what they will be. Inversion and disorder sometimes preside briefly during such moments. Some of the liturgical orders of Christianity, for instance, include carnivals during which the proprieties of structure are lampooned and even violated, blasphemy is encouraged and "Kings of Misrule" are crowned. But the order is almost always restored, and "interstructural" times do not lack structures of their own. Relations among the participants do, after all, proceed in regular ways in accordance with generally acknowledged rules and expectations. Indeed, a heightening of order is characteristic of ritual. The organizations within which order is heightened differ, however, from those of everyday. They are generally simpler, for one thing. Most of the distinctions among persons prevailing during mundane time are likely to be obliterated, according to Turner, and for another thing, those remaining are more marked than usual. Among the Ndembu (Turner 1967), for example, the generalized and, possibly, lax authority that mature men, as a class, exercise over youths may be replaced by the absolute authority of instructors over neophytes, but commonalities are also emphasized. As neophytes the sons of chiefs and of commoners are at least said to be equals. At the shrine of St. Patrick's Purgatory in Donegal, distinctions among pilgrims are dissolved by the rigorous terms of the penitential rites they all must perform and by the common form of their humbling: they all must put aside their shoes and do penance barefoot (Turner and Turner 1978: ch. 3).

As the condition of society prevailing in ritual contrasts with that of everyday, so does the quality of experience. As social organization may be destructured in ritual so may the identities of the participants themselves. This is particularly obvious in the case of novices in the rites of passage. Like the changing variable in the computer, the novice in transit is, as Turner notes, in a curious state of "no-longer and not-yet" with respect to the social categories of which mundane structures are made. It is a state which cannot be classified in accordance with the status distinctions of mundane structure or the "either-ors" of the digital logic informing such structures. He is, rather, "neither-nor." His condition is ambiguous, and as Mary Douglas has pointed out (1966), may be dangerous or polluting. In the condition of "neither-nor" one in passage may be "symbolically" destructured to the undifferentiated state of generalized matter. Identified with the dead or unborn, perhaps naked and filthy, possibly deprived of his name and forbidden to speak, he is, as much as it is possible to be, reduced to unformed substance. Sometimes that substance, now deprived of its old form, is subjected to ordeal, perhaps increasing its malleability and thus facilitating its reformation into that which it is to become. The destructuring of identity in certain rites of passage is especially profound, but destructuring is not confined to novices nor, for that matter, to rites of passage.

It is a matter of observation that as distinctions of mundane structure are reduced in the condition of society that prevails during rituals – the condition that Turner (1969) calls "communitas" – so may the distinctions of discursive logic be overridden. Participation in ritual encourages alteration of consciousness from the rationality which presumably prevails during daily life and which presumably guides ordinary affairs, toward states which, to use Rudolph Otto's (1923) term, may be called "numinous" (see chapter 11 below). In such states discursive reason may not disappear entirely but metaphoric representation, primary process thought, and strong emotion become increasingly important as the domination of syntactic or syllogistic logic, or simple everyday rationality, recedes. It becomes normal for people to behave in ways that would in other contexts seem bizarre. Trance and less profound alterations of consciousness are frequent concomitants of ritual participation. Communitas is a state of mind as well as of society. The relationship between alterations of the social condition and alterations of consciousness is not a simple one, but it is safe to say that they augment and abet each other.

Whereas psychiatrists might view the numinous state as *dis*sociated, the experience is often reported to be what might better be characterized as *re*associated, for parts of the psyche ordinarily out of touch with each other may be united, or better, in light of ritual's recurrent nature, *re*united. Reunion, furthermore, may reach out from the reunited individual to embrace other members of the congregation, or even the cosmos as a whole. Indeed, the boundary between individuals and their surroundings, especially others participating in ritual with them, may seem to dissolve. Further discussion of religious experience must await chapter 12. We will only note here that such a sense of union is encouraged by the coordination of utterance and movement demanded of congregations in many rituals. To sing with others, to move as they move in the performance of a ritual, is not merely to symbolize union. It is *in and of itself* to reunite in the reproduction of a larger order. Unison does not merely symbolize that order but *indicates* it and its acceptance. The participants do not simply *communicate* to each other *about* that order but *commune with* each other *within* it. In sum, the state of communitas experienced in ritual is at once social and experiential. Indeed, the distinction between the social and experiential is surrendered, or even erased, in a general feeling of oneness with oneself, with the congregation, or with the cosmos.

2. Tempo and consciousness

The achievement of such special states of mind and society in ritual is, I would suggest, largely an outcome of ritual's peculiar temporal characteristics. It is of interest in this regard that the reunion of "mind," "heart," "body" and "society" may well be most fully realized in ritual dancing, as Radcliffe-Brown proposed long ago in *The Andaman Islanders* (1964 [1922]: chs. 2 and 5, *passim*). He argued that the dance produces a condition in which the unity, harmony and concord of the community are at a maximum, and one in which they are intensely felt by every member, and he takes the production of this condition to be "the primary social function of the dance" (p. 252). I have observed, in somewhat more general terms (and, further, putting the matter in a formal causal, rather than the final causal formulation of Radcliffe-Brown) that unification is intrinsic to unison. One may sing or simply recite in unison as well as dance in unison, but dancing, for reasons that have been discussed in chapter 5, and will be taken up again in chapter 12, may well have been more compelling than verbal forms. Radcliffe-Brown would have agreed:

The Andaman dance, then, is a complete activity of the whole community in which every able-bodied adult takes part, and is also an activity to which, so far as the dancer himself is concerned, the whole personality is involved, by the intervention of all the muscles of the body, by the concentration of attention required, and by its action on the personal sentiments. In the dance the individual submits to the action upon him of the community; he is constrained, by the immediate effect of rhythm, as well as by custom, to join in, and he is required to conform in his own actions and movements to the needs of the common activity. The surrender of the individual to this constraint or obligation is not felt as painful, but on the contrary as highly pleasurable. As the dancer loses himself in the dance, as he becomes absorbed in the unified community, he reaches a state of elation in which he feels himself filled with an energy beyond his ordinary state … at the same time, finding himself in complete and ecstatic harmony with all the fellow-members of his community …   *(1964[1922]: 251–252)*

In dancing the whole body enters into the computations of the prevailing consciousness, this at the same time that the individual's sense of his or her separation from others is submerged or overwhelmed as a function of continuous, tight coordination with them. The communitas engendered by dancing is, this is to say, an outcome of heightened coordination, and heightened coordination, in turn, an outcome of imposing upon social interaction special tempos – tempos that may be difficult to achieve under mundane circumstances or that are inappropriate to all but a very few ordinary activities.

The tempos typical of such coordination, and perhaps requisite to it, are quicker than those characteristic of ordinary social interaction and the coordination is itself tighter. The rhythm of the drum may approximate the rapidity of heartbeats and, as it synchronizes the movements of the dancers' limbs and unifies their voices into the unisons of chant or song, it may entrain their breaths and pulses, or at least be experienced as if it does. We note here that the tempos and the degrees of coordination in conformity to which congregations proceed through some rituals are more characteristic of organic processes than they are of ordinary social processes.

Some of the activities of mundane time are also rapid and rhythmical and tightly coordinated, of course, and it is of interest that such activities seem to generate an *esprit de corps* among participants similar to ritual communitas. But tightened coordination and quickened tempo are not all that is distinctive of the rhythm of liturgical orders. In emphasizing the organic frequencies of ritual's rhythms we must not lose sight of their much slower frequencies. Rituals are among the most precisely recurrent of social events. Not only may there be repetition at organic frequencies *within* the ritual itself but there is recurrence of the ritual *as a whole* from week to week or month to month, year to year, death to death. That which is performed now will be performed again, a week or year from now, or when someone is again troubled by similar symptoms or when the pigs are sufficient to repay the spirits once more. Not only is there likely to be continuous and rapid recurrence in the tempo of any performance but there is recurrence, often very precise, of canons as wholes. At the same time that the tempos of particular ritual performances proceed at frequencies in the range of those of breath, heartbeat, or brainwave, the tempos of liturgical orders, marked by the recurrence of rituals as wholes, are of an entirely different magnitude. The rhythms dominating a certain ritual may be of the order of heartbeats, but that ritual may recur only once a week, or a year, or even less frequently. It is worth noting yet again the emphasis on punctilious performance characteristic of ritual, to underline further that that which is performed at rapid tempo and in tight coordination, and which through that tempo and coordination unites participants more tightly than they are under ordinary circumstances, is, *in being punctiliously repeated from one performance to the next, experienced as never-changing.* We observe in liturgical orders that which is at once both quick and changeless.

3. Tempo, temporal regions, and time out of time

We are led by these considerations to a clearer understanding of what may be meant by some of the mysterious phrases used to characterize ritual time, phrases like "times out of time," and through that understanding to conceptions of eternity. Herbert Simon's discussions (1969, 1973) of temporal aspects of complex physical organization are illuminating in this regard. He argues that we can approach the problem of distinguishing "levels of organization" in complex physical reality in temporal terms:

if we ... observe the behavior of a system over a *total time span*, T, and our observational techniques do not allow us to detect rhythmical or fluctuating changes during *[brief] time intervals* shorter than [what we may call] it, we can break the sequence of characteristic frequencies into three parts: (1) *low frequencies* much less than 1 [per] T, (2) *middle range frequencies* [T<->t], and (3) *high frequencies* ... [greater than] 1 [per] t. Motions ... determined by the low frequency modes will be so slow that we will not observe them; they will ... [appear to be] constants.

Motions of the system determined by the high frequency modes will control ... the internal interactions of the components of the lower level subsystems ... but will not be involved in the interactions among those subsystems. Moreover, these motions will appear always to be in equilibrium ... In their relations with each other the several subsystems will behave like rigid bodies, so to speak.

(1973: 9–10)

Simon was concerned, in this discussion, with physical systems in general, including those describable in terms of macromolecules, molecules, atoms, and subatomic particles. To apply this hierarchical model to the matter at hand and, incidentally, to clarify the model itself, let us take the following steps:

1. First, we shall assign to "T" (the total time span over which we "observe the system") a value corresponding to a society's historical memory. Among the Nuer, for instance, Evans-Pritchard (1940) tells us that six generations lie between the living and the first man. Among Polynesians, who carefully kept (and manipulated) genealogies, T was much longer, and of course, literacy lengthens T by magnitudes. For Western civilization it approaches 5,000 years.

2. Secondly, let us assign a value to "t" slightly slower than the rhythms or fluctuations characteristic of basic organic processes, such as pulse, breath and brainwave. (Such a value would probably be in the neighborhood of a second or less). More rapid fluctuations, particularly if rhythmical, are likely to go unnoticed (Ornstein 1969).

3. Assignments of such values to T and t distinguish three "temporal regions."

   a. First, there is the low frequency region, slower than one fluctuation per T, in which change *proceeds so slowly that is unlikely to have been observed during the historical memory of the society, and if it has, it is remembered as epochal.* This is the temporal region of the cosmic.

   b. Secondly, there is the high frequency region, that characterized by frequencies more rapid than t (t being as brief as a second or less). This is the temporal region characteristic of "rhythmical or fluctuating changes" internal to the organisms comprising the society. It is, this is to say, the temporal region characteristic of such physiological processes as breathing, the circulation of blood, the secretion of hormones, the reactions of nerves, and of some related psychic processes, such as fluctuations of emotion, mood and attitude. Let us call this high frequency region "the region of organic time."

c. Thirdly, there is the temporal region lying between T and t, the region within which mundane social life proceeds through minutes, days, months, years and lifetimes. This temporal region, the region within which mundane social interactions seem largely to be played out, may be called "the region of social time."

We have, in sum, distinguished three temporal regions, the organic, the social and the cosmic. Ritual performance involves all three, I suggest, in the following way.

First, individuals, whose obscure internal states are characterized by high and more or less idiosyncratic frequencies, enter into the ritual, thereby indicating that, despite whatever internal fluctuations of mood, attitude or emotion they may be experiencing they are, in Simons' terms, "rigid bodies," that is to say stable components of the next more inclusive system, in this instance the social system. In terms proposed in chapter 4, their participation in the ritual indicates public and binding acceptance of the order it encodes, whatever internal doubts or ambivalences may be felt. To recall a discussion developed in chapter 3, fluctuations in variables internal to private systems – individuals – are either unobserved or ignored in the public system except insofar as they are expressed in a binary summarization indicated by *either* participation *or* non-participation.

As the ritual proceeds, however, the entire congregation, as its actions become more highly coordinated, moves, *as a unified whole*, across the temporal border, so to speak, from the social into the organic temporal region. This is to say that *interactions among members of the social unit assume temporal frequencies more characteristic of the internal dynamics of single organisms than of social groups.*

But the pattern of the actions specified by the liturgy's canon is invariant, and thus may be understood to be never-changing. Canon – the punctiliously recurring and therefore apparently unchanging spine of liturgical order – is of the temporal region characterized by temporal frequencies slower than one per T, the cosmic region. Thus, *the order to which the congregation is at high frequency conforming is of the low frequency region*, the region of the apparently immutable. At one and the same moment the congregation moves out of social time toward both the organic and the cosmic, toward both the quick and the changeless.

The tempos characteristic of daily social intercourse are abandoned as the activity of the congregation is coordinated by the more rapid and more rhythmic pulsations characteristic of breath, pulse and perhaps other organic processes as well. At the same time, the realization of changelessness is implicit in the punctilious recurrence characteristic of rituals as wholes. In sum, the tempos of everyday social life are replaced in liturgical intervals by an extraordinary union of the quick and the changeless, and that union implies eternity and, perhaps, immortality as well. We shall return to eternity shortly. For now, we may conclude that "liturgical time," "sacred time," "extraordinary time," is literally time out of ordinary social time, for the temporal region characteristic of mundane social interaction is vacated.

4. Frequency and bonding strength

A further observation of Simon's concerning the relationship of frequency of interaction to bonding strength also bears upon social and experiential conditions prevailing during "time out of time." He notes that in non-living matter higher energy, higher frequency vibrations or interactions are associated with less inclusive subsystems, vibrations or interactions of lower frequency with the larger systems into which the subsystems are assembled.

Thus protons and neutrons of the atomic nucleus interact strongly through the pion fields, which dispose of energies of some 140 million electron volts each. The covalent bonds that hold molecules together on the other hand, involve energies only on the order of 5 electron volts. And the bonds that account for the tertiary structure of large macromolecules, hence for their biological activity, involve energies another order of magnitude smaller – around one half of an electron volt ... Planck's Law prescribes a strict proportionality between bond energies and the associated frequencies.
(*1973: 9f.*)

I would not wish to argue that social processes, which belong to the general class of informational processes, conform to Planck's Law, which is concerned not with information but with energy in physical systems. It may be, however, that, as a social group moves as a coordinated whole into the temporal region of the organic, members may sense that they are, for the nonce, bound together as tightly as the parts of a single animal. Under such conditions the existence of a larger being of which the participants are parts may become palpable to each of them as each of them gives up his or her separate identity for the time being. When a group conducts itself in conformity to a rhythmic tempo of organic frequency, for instance that of drumming, it may seem to be an organism to the organisms composing it and they each may seem to themselves to be its cells. Neurological research gives some support to this view (see d'Aquili, Laughlin and McManus 1979).

I am not sure what to make of this similarity between social systems on the one hand and physical systems on the other (just as I am unsure what the significance of the similarity between the operation of digital computers and liturgical orders may be). It is conceivable that the relationship between frequency and bonding strength in social systems, and in elementary matter-energy systems as specified by Planck's Law, could both be subsumed by a formulation of such generality that it applies both to informational and energetic phenomena. If so we may be approaching here a principle in conformity to which all hierarchically structured complex systems, regardless of their content, must be organized. If, as Simon seems to suggest (1969: ch. 4), all complex systems not only may be, but may have to be, hierarchical in organization, it would be a fundamental ordering principle. If this isn't the case at least we have a nice analogy.

5. Coordination, communitas, and neurophysiology

I have argued that conformity to invariant orders not only makes it possible for members of congregations to indicate acceptance of those orders but to become unified through the coordination of their individual acts of acceptance. This coordination often has cognitive and affective as well as social consequences, producing a state of mind, as well as society, pointed to by Radcliffe-Brown in his discussion of Andaman Island dancing, the occasion of which is ritual.

As the dancer loses himself in the dance, as he becomes absorbed in the unified community, he reaches a state of elation in which he feels himself filled with an energy beyond his ordinary state ... at the same time finding himself in complete and ecstatic harmony with all the fellow members of his community ...

(1922: 252)

This is more than reminiscent of Durkheim's "effervescence" and to the state of mind and society that we, following Turner (1969) have called "communitas," a ritually-generated state of mind and society very different from the rationally-dominated organization and mode of thought prevailing in mundane time, through which individuals and groups do their daily business. According to Laughlin, McManus and d'Aquili,

The principal neurophysiological effect of ritual behavior individually, and ritualized sensory input contextually, may be to block the activity of the dominant cerebral hemisphere and reduce the normal adaptive surface of ego to non-linear, image- and affect-ridden thought processes ... a decrement in dominant lobe functioning invites a shift in predominance toward the atemporal image-based functioning of the non-dominant hemisphere.

In essence ritual techniques neutralize ... the functioning of the analytic conceptual mode, bringing to the fore developmentally earlier functioning ... This mode associates aspects of experience transductively; that is, it makes lateral associations ... based upon similarity, overlapping class membership, or emotional affinity.

This mode is more participatory and less decentered than is conceptual thought and consists of images embedded in fields of affect rather than concepts embedded in fields of logical relationships.   *(1969: 277)*

I have already argued that the ritual generation of *communitas* often rests in considerable degree on ritually imposed tempos, on their repetitiveness and, more fundamentally, on their rhythmicity.[1] To recall that discussion, the tempos responsible for coordinating ritual singing, chanting and dancing are typically more rapid than those characteristic of ordinary social interaction, thus producing a synchronization much tighter than is usual in mundane social activity. Indeed, the tempos of some elements of ritual performances may be more characteristic of organic than social processes: the drumbeat's tempo may approximate that of the heartbeat and, as it synchronizes the movements of dancers and unifies their voices into the unison of hymns, it may seem to entrain their breaths and heart rhythms, and thus seem to unify the congregation's separate members into a single larger, living being.

This account leads to consideration of the neurophysiological consequences of ritual participation. Although it may seem bizarre to the members of a society that puts exceptionally high value on what it understands to be unmodified rational thought, and is unusually suspicious of other states of mind and their insights, ritually altered consciousness is widespread if not, indeed, culturally universal. Bourguignon (1972: 418) years ago found institutionalized forms of dissociation in 89 percent of a sample of 488 societies for which ethnographic data sufficient to make a judgment were available.

Substantial research, much of it experimental, has been done on the specific neurophysiological nature of the ritual consciousness, and how it may be induced by particular features of ritual performance. Eugene d'Aquili, Charles Laughlin, and John McManus in an earlier work (1979) and Barbara Lex (1979) have summarized the results of much of this research in the course of discussions of their own. This important work has largely been ignored by cultural anthropologists.

It is of importance, first, that the biological effects of participation in ritual are not limited to brain functions. The nervous system as a whole is affected, and so may be the viscera and the striated muscles. As Lex (p. 119) points out, the nervous system operates as a unit, and the organs of the body are homeostatically interconnected by the nervous system. The effects may not even originate in the nervous system. Sustained movement, as in dance, may stimulate proprioceptors in the muscles, tendons and joints, and excitement may thus seem to rise from the organism's least conscious depths into its fully conscious awareness.

The repetitive and rhythmical nature of many rituals seems to be of basic importance, for the rhythms of the order entrain the biological rhythms of the performers. That is, "The external rhythm becomes the synchronizer to set the internal clocks of these fast rhythms" (Chapple 1970: 38, cited by Lex 1979: 122). At the same time, according to d'Aquili and Laughlin (1979: 158) "there is increasing evidence that rhythmic or repetitive behavior coordinates the limbic discharges (that is, affective states) of a group ... It can generate a level of arousal that is both pleasurable and reasonably uniform among the individuals ... " *Thus the rhythms of the order reach in two directions at once – into each participant's physiology on the one hand and outward to encompass all of the participants on the other.* As we have noted, the sense of "being" constituted by synchrony bears closer temporal resemblance to that of organisms than to that of societies.

At the same time that sustained rhythmic motion of dance stimulates proprioceptors in the muscles, the auditory stimulation, or whatever establishes the rhythm of the dance, may entrain brain wave rhythms, and hyperventilation may act as an "adjunctive aid" to alterations of body chemistry (Lex 1979: 122 ff.). "All of these physiological manipulations, complexly combined in the context of a ritual, ... generate stimulus bombardment of the human nervous system" (Lex 1979: 124).

The non-dominant (usually the right) cerebral hemisphere seems to become predominant in the ritual condition. Indeed, the mechanisms of ritual – rhythmicity, repetition, drug ingestion, overbreathing, pain, and so on – seem naturally to engage the right hemisphere, or to "carry" or "drive" the state of mind toward it, and for that general reason Felicitas Goodman calls them "driving behaviors" (1972: 74, cited by Lex 1979: 121). In contrast to the left hemisphere, in which speech, linear analytic thought, and the sense of duration are mainly located, the specializations of the right hemisphere include spatial and tonal perception, pattern recognition "including those constituting emotion and other states in the internal milieu," and holistic and synthetic comprehension. The linguistic ability of the right hemisphere is limited and it is devoid of a temporal sense. In the general terms of this work, the left cerebral hemisphere is associated with discursive thought, with mundane time and with the sacred, the right hemisphere with non-discursive experience, with "time out of time" or eternity, and with the numinous.

That the non-dominant hemisphere is the locus of holistic comprehension would suggest that the grasp of an encompassing holy is also grounded in its function. It may be, however, that the integration of the holy arises from a union of the functioning of both hemispheres. In fact, d'Aquili and Laughlin (1979: 175) propose that in the ultimate state of ritually altered consciousness both hemispheres function simultaneously rather than alternately. This may parallel, or be causally related to, the situation in the two subsystems of autonomic nervous systems, of which the hemispheres are the "cerebral representations" (d'Aquili and Laughlin 1979: 175). According to Lex (1979: 137), in the first phase of arousal the reactivity of either the sympathetic or parasympathetic (sub)system increases while that of the other decreases. If stimulation continues the second stage commences when the non-sensitized system is completely inhibited. Stimuli usually eliciting a response in the inhibited system then evoke responses in the sensitized system. These are termed "reversal phenomena". In the final phase reciprocity between the two subsystems fails or is overridden, and both discharge at once. This third stage is reached in orgasm, REM (Rapid Eye Movement) sleep, Zen and Yogic meditation and ecstasy states, but also under prolonged stress and in certain psychopathic conditions.

At a yet deeper level the two subsystems of the autonomic nervous systems articulate with non-neural somatic structures. Lex (1979: 135), following Hess, speaks of the autonomic-somatic integration in terms of the ergotropic and trophotropic systems. The first "consists of augmented sympathetic discharges, increased muscle tonus and excitation in the cerebral cortex manifested as "desynchronized" [cortical] resting rhythms; the *trophotropic* pattern includes heightened parasympathetic discharges, relaxed skeletal muscles, and synchronized cortical rhythms." Ecstatic states are marked by simultaneous relaxation characteristic of trophotropic response and the cortical alertness of ergotrophic response.

The cognitive effect of the simultaneous functioning of the ergotropic and trophotropic, the sympathetic and the parasympathetic, the left hemisphere and the right is, according to d'Aquili and Laughlin (1979: 175ff.), a sense of the unification of opposites, of harmony with the universe, of Oneness with the other members of the congregation, and even of Oneness of the self with God. The numinous and the holy are thus rooted in the organic depths of human being.

6. Eternity

Let us return to the apparent paradox of a movement out of social time in two opposite directions simultaneously. In chapter 4, we may recall, I argued that in ritual, performers fuse with the order they are performing. What considerations of clarity have led me to call a two-way movement out of the temporal region of social action is really not, for the quick and eternal become one in the performers. The eternal is made vital as the living – the quick – participate in, become part of, the never-changing order. And as the eternal is made vital, so the vital may seem to be made eternal. Intimations of immortality may be entailed in performances consonant with liturgy's multi-temporal rhythms and we may be un-covering here possible experiential ground for belief in immortality, or even for the idea of immortality itself.

I have, as it were, smuggled the term "eternity" into the discussion without definition. There is more than one concept of eternity, of course, but at least two seem intrinsic to ritual's form.

The first is recurrence without end – ceaseless repetition. This notion is, of course, implicit in the recurrence of rituals, and we have observed in an earlier section of this chapter that periodic recurrence imposes a rejuvenating cyclicity upon mundane processes that would otherwise follow a rectilinear path leading in the direction toward which the second law of thermodynamics points – the direction of environmental degrada-tion, social disruption, anarchy and death (see Eliade 1959). Liturgical orders may, in fact, seem to do the impossible or miraculous, that is, to transfer not only that which is forever lost to history, but lost to death itself, from the domain of the irreversible to the domain of the recurrent. As Leach points out, it is common to assert in ritual, tacitly if not explicitly, "that death and birth are the same thing – that birth follows death just as death follows birth. This seems to amount to denying the second aspect of time [irreversibility] by equating it with the first [repeti-tiveness]" (Leach 1961: 125). It is significant in this regard that representa-tions of birth are common in rites of passage and that, of necessity, they generally follow representations of death. If icons and symbols of birth were not preceded by those of death they could not represent rebirth. Rites of passage thus provide models for successions in which biological death and the rites associated with it are as much beginning as end. Even in the absence of explicit reversals of the sequence of birth followed by death that inevitably prevails in mundane time, the very performance of rituals, among the most perfectly recurrent of all social events, implies that all is not lost to time, and that which is not lost may include life itself. A precisely recurrent order is made vital in ritual performance at the same time that the requisites of the performance make the vitalizing activity more or less precisely recurrent, and in this too may lie intimations of immortality.

The irreversible or "rectilinear" journey through life is, through such sleights-of-ritual, not only made to seem recurrent – an endless repetition of cycles or an increasing alternation between life and death – but also natural or even cosmic. Van Gennep concludes his book by observing

Finally, the series of human transitions has, among some peoples, been linked to the celestial passages, the revolutions of the planets, and the phases of the moon. It is indeed a cosmic conception that relates the stages of human existence to those of plant and animal life and, by a sort of pre-scientific divination, joins them to the great rhythms of the universe.   *(1960: 194)*

The recurrence of lives is a conception that may be played out in the realm of mundane time. Those who are born again may be born here and, if not now, in a period similar in essentials to that of the present. So ceaseless repetition returns us ever again to mundane time. It may, thus, stand as an alternative to the conception of a comprehensively irreversible flow, but it does not escape history or its karmic miseries.

If, however, recurrence without end is one conception of eternity it is hardly the only one, nor is it even self-sufficient, for recurrence is inconceivable without an assumption of changelessness. That is, for anything to recur it must be assumed to be changeless, for if it were not the succeeding event could not be a recurrence of the preceding. And so there is a yet more profound sense of the eternal, not as endless repetition, but as the sheer successionless duration of the absolute changelessness of that which recurs, the successionless duration of that which is neither preceded nor succeeded, which is "neither coming nor passing away," but always was and always will be. In ritual one returns ever again to that which never changes, to that which is punctiliously repeated in every performance. As the rejuvenation of what Eliade (1959: *passim*), following Nietzsche, calls the "Eternal Return" is entailed by the precise repetition of rituals and entire liturgical orders, so is immutability necessarily a quality of that which is precisely repeated. In the punctilious recurrence of ritual that which never changes is at least brought into view and perhaps glimpsed, if not grasped, by those making it available to their own senses.

It may be suggested that the notion of the changeless points away from the physical world, away from that which can be dissolved or transformed in time, for the changeable nature of physical objects may be an ineluctable extrapolation from sensory experience. This is to suggest that the notion of absolute changelessness entails the notion of absolute truth, for if all that is physical changes all that can possibly be forever changeless is that which is forever true. Mathematical statements were taken by St. Augustine to be "eternal verities," and so may be the apparently unchanging conceptions encoded in precisely performed canons. We shall return to the relation between ritual representation and truth in chapter 11. Here I would only propose first that whereas ceaseless recurrence fends off, as it were, time's directional flow, the changelessness of that which recurs transcends that flow. As Buber (1952: 14) put it, "the truth, the divine truth, is from eternity and in eternity, and ... devotion to the truth, which we call human truth, partakes of eternity." This leads to a second observation. In the fusion of the quick and the eternal taking place in the intervals that liturgy sequesters outside of mundane time there are to be found intimations of an immortality more profound than the rebirths and rejuvenations implicit in ceaseless recurrence. There is union with eternity itself in the mystical state called "Nirvana" by Buddhists and Hindus but known by others as well. Truth, immortality and eternity may merge and be grasped in liturgy's moment.

To summarize, two rather different notions of eternity have been remarked: endless repetition, and absolute changelessness. Both are intrinsic to the punctilious repetition of rituals; eternal return to repetition itself, changelessness to the canon which is punctiliously repeated. Eternity in either or both senses is, thus, an attribute of whatever order is encoded in the canon.

Discussions throughout this work should have made clear that the eternal is not all that is represented in liturgical intervals, of course. Changes in states prevailing in mundane time are also effected during them, just as in the almost-instantaneous operation of computers, the significant values of variables are consequence of transformations completed during the intervals preceding them. An emphasis on the changelessness of canon does not deny the variations in performance allowed or even demanded by the canon, those variations discussed in earlier chapters carrying self-referential messages, nor does it discount the performative consequences of the conjunction of the canonical and self-referential. That changelessness is represented at the same time that transformations are effected in ritual is not paradoxical. An image that comes easily to mind, perhaps vulgarly mechanical but enjoying the virtue of familiarity, is that of the revolving drum of a printing press. As the press imprints an apparently invariant message upon the paper passing through it, so a liturgical order imprints apparently invariant messages upon individual lives and upon society as a whole at intervals that it itself imposes upon continuous duration.

7. Myth and history

We have considered mundane time on the one hand, liturgical intervals on the other and have now been brought to a consideration of the interplay between them. Typical forms of narrative for recounting events in mundane time are, to use the terms broadly, chronicle and biography, while the occurrence of eternity and eternity's connection to time are represented in myths, accounts of unique occurrences in which the stuff of life and history came into being, and of how and why they have taken the forms subsequently experienced. The uniqueness of all mythic occurrence is radically different from the particularities of events in the sequences that make up lives and histories, for they are unconstrained by whatever culturally constructed "natural laws" are taken to prevail thereafter. Occurring once and once only they may be informational equivalents of the class of events that modern cosmologists, in thinking about the origins of the universe, call "singularities" (see Hawking 1988). In contrast, although no biography replicates any other, biographies in all their variety are composed of ontologically similar events and experiences. Furthermore, the irreversibility of history is "statistical" in its basis (the improbability of a historical sequence that would lead us back to, let us say, the reconstruction of the Roman Empire is incalculably high), but the irreversibility of mythic occurrence is "mechanical" or "structural." As such it is absolute. The terms of creation may, of course, propose that the world will become undone if men do not perform certain rites, but for the terms of creation themselves to be undone is impossible, and not merely improbable.

The structures in accordance with which mundane activities are conducted comprise the orders prevailing in particular places during particular periods. In contrast, as Turner has suggested (1967: 98), the destructured intervals between periods represent "what is, in fact, often regarded as the unbounded, the infinite, the limitless." That which is represented in liturgy's "times out of time" is likely to be regarded as free of particular times and places or, at least, not bound to or limited by them. If the essence of history is the passage of the particular, the essence of liturgical order is the recurrence of the changeless. Mundane activities are intrinsically ambiguous, and the events which they form or to which they respond are continuously lost to an irretrievable past. In contrast, liturgical acts repeatedly recover the eternal which, being nothing if not immutable, is intrinsically true, and thus moral and even proper. The enactments of time out of time may account for or explain the origins and states of historical events and processes, and thus provide grounds for understandings of them, but they are not themselves of history. Indeed, they stand against history and may even propose standards in whose terms the events of history are to be judged. As with histories, so with lives.

That which occurs in ritual's intervals is not historical but, happening once, is timeless, and to participate in a canon is to escape from time's flow into "what is, in fact, often regarded as the unbounded, the infinite, the limitless," the everlasting, the unambiguously moral, the absolutely true and the immortally vital. In a later chapter we shall consider how these and other notions may join in the experience of divinity. For now I shall only reiterate that the imposition of liturgical sequences upon duration establishes a temporal order composed of two temporal states, the characteristics of each being the virtual inverse of the other. But liturgy does more than create two "states" of time. It relates them to each other.

8. The innumerable versus the eternal

We can recognize that the recording of history, particularly in writing, may be eternity's enemy. Written history expands the scope of T, taken to be a society's historical memory, from a few generations to thousands of years in some cases, thus letting the literate know that more and more of that which the non-literate take to be neverchanging is, in fact, changing, albeit at rates or frequencies imperceptible in single lifetimes or even in the course of a few generations. Numeracy abets literacy in dissolving changelessness. Perhaps as a consequence, the conception of eternity (if it can properly be so-called) dominant in our own society is neither ceaseless repetition nor absolute undivided duration. It is endless and unabating irreversibility. The imposition of a continuing series of numbers upon duration may even entail such a notion. When years are numbered in indefinitely continuing sequence, earth's first orbit around the sun is within time's reach, and so, by extension, is the even more remote singular event that some say brought the universe into being. And the selfsame time can also reach forward to the world's end.[2] But nothing remains changeless in all of the years that numbers distinguish except the years' numbers: they go by one by one. When years are numbered, irreversibility without cessation continues until judgment, or until heat-death finally freezes the cosmos' last motion. Whatever cyclicity or alternation inheres in liturgical orders performed in numbered years may seem subordinate to time's inexorable rectilinear flow. Under such circumstances even the most punctiliously recurrent ritual may seem no more than similar to performances that have taken place in the past. Their force as enactments may be diminished as they become mere reenactments.

Irreversibility without end is, at best, an impoverished conception of eternity, and it is comfortless as well. Indeed, inasmuch as it lies entirely within ordinary time it may be improper to think of such a conception as a form of eternity at all. It may be more accurate to say that numeration, when imposed upon time, replaces the eternal with the innumerable. Be this as it may, whereas other conceptions of eternity enlarge lives by offering relief from time's undoing through respites in intervals during which a sense of immortality may be fleetingly grasped, the numbering of years, stretching backward and forward relentlessly and forever emphasizes the transience and insignificance of humans' ephemeral spans. It is against a comprehensively metrical sense of duration that ritually generated conceptions of eternity must contend not only because what transpires in mundane time is fleeting but because mundane time itself may become immense. But the eternal is at an increasing disadvantage in its struggle with the innumerable as the dominion of number becomes ever stronger.

It follows that the numbering of days and hours and, finally, minutes and seconds, joins the numbering of years in undoing eternity. If durations great and small are all numbered, we can no longer escape time's undoing by entering ritual's eternity even for a little while, for when we return we can hardly avoid knowing that our sojourn in ritual lasted, let us say, from 3:00 until 5:00 pm on a certain day of a certain month in a certain year. Endless time not only is not eternity but overwhelms eternity, reducing it to insignificance or to superstition. When moments of eternity are fully encompassed by a time which moves inexorably toward entropy the intimations of immortality experienced in them are likely to seem no more than illusions, and eternity's only plausible resting place becomes an increasingly dubious hereafter. Number gives eternity, which once informed life and was infused by it, into the hands of death. As the eternal is banished from life by the merely innumerable, we are left to what Eliade (1957a) called "the terrors of history," hopelessness and dread in the face of inevitable and meaningless annihilation.

8

Simultaneity and hierarchy

At the beginning of chapter 6 I suggested that liturgies, in an analogy to chambers, are realized in what may be taken to be three dimensions. Chapter 6 was itself devoted to the sequential dimension, the most obviously temporal of the three, the one that can be likened to the length of the chamber or, more dynamically, to striding the length of that chamber and, in the course of that procession, organizing time or, more properly, temporality. Consideration of the division of unmarked duration into the periods constituting mundane time led, in chapter 7, to a discussion of the intervals separating mundane periods and to the temporal condition and states of consciousness and society prevailing in those intervals, and thus to the generation within them of eternity.

We have, at the same time, been led to what I shall call the simultaneous dimension of synchronic liturgical orders. I deliberately avoid the term "synchronic," reserving it for a general mode of analysis whereas here I am concerned not with a mode of *analysis* from which temporality has been eliminated but *perception*.

I have argued that the significance or meaning of any liturgical order in some degree unfolds as one thing follows another in fixed order, but only in some degree. At any, if not every, moment during the sequence's unfolding, participants may face a multiplicity of significata embedded in one or more representations perceived simultaneously. We are primarily concerned now to illuminate the range of significata concurrently represented and meant to be simultaneously grasped.

Such ritual representations are said to be "multivocalic." By far the most celebrated example in the anthropological literature is the Ndembu people's Mudyi Tree, which Victor Turner has discussed brilliantly in a

236

number of publications in which he enumerated nineteen different significata simultaneously present (e.g., 1967: *passim*).

1. The *yu min rumbim*

The *yu min rumbim* of the Maring, like the *Mudyi* a small tree, is at least as complex. A brief account of the Maring "pantheon" and some aspects of the Maring ritual cycle is a necessary preliminary to our understanding of this "ritual representation," which can be used to exemplify all three liturgical dimensions.

In chapter 3 we were concerned with indexical qualities of the planting of *rumbim*, in chapter 6 with its place in the construction of time and the scheduling of activities. The discussion that follows will emphasize the understandings that it represents in what is usually called "symbolic" fashion. Portions of this discussion have been presented in more or less detail in a number of other publications (Buchbinder and Rappaport 1976, Rappaport, 1968, 1979), but convenience and continuity suggest integrating them here.

The planting of *rumbim*, it was noted in earlier discussion, terminates warfare and commences sanctified truces. But its significance is exhausted by neither its political consequences nor its indexical content. It also represents, or even constitutes, the fundamental terms of Maring cosmology, the spiritual and structural terms by which the world is understood and relations within it governed.

Before proceeding to the ritual cycle and ritual itself a brief account of the spirits toward whom it is directed, the qualities they embody, and relations among them is necessary.

Maring spirits fall into two contrasting sets, one of which inhabits high places, the other the low. Those dwelling on high include Red Spirits (*Raua Mugi*) and Smoke Woman (*Kun Kase Ambra*). The Red Spirits of each patrilineal clan inhabit that clan's high altitude forest. Smoke Woman is said to have a residence at the highest point in the clan's territory, but her home is understood to be on the summit of Mount Oipor, the highest peak in the Simbai-Jimi River area.

Smoke Woman was never human. She acts as an intermediary between the living and all other categories of spirits. Shamans (*kun kase yu*) communicate with her in seances, conducted in darkened men's houses and often lasting all night, by inhaling deeply the smoke of strong native cigars and sending their *nomane* (a term which in some contexts means "thought" and in others "tradition" or "culture" but here the conscious aspect of the self that survives death) out of their noses to fly to the houses of the Smoke Woman in the high places and escort her back to the seance. She enters the shaman's head through his nostrils and, speaking through his mouth, informs the living of the wishes of the dead. Shamans commune with the Smoke Woman before all important rituals and upon many other occasions as well.

Although this spirit is female, she has no association with women. Female shamans are virtually non-existent: the one of whom I know was regarded as preposterous by most men. Smoke Woman has no connection whatsoever with fertility either, and while not antagonistic to women generally, is perhaps antagonistic to the sexuality of living women. When a man is "struck" by her for the first time, he should abstain from intercourse for an indefinite period because, it is said, he has become a husband to Smoke Woman who might, out of jealousy, do mischief to any woman with whom he consorted.

The Red Spirits are spirits of those who have killed or been killed in warfare. Species included in the category *ma* – mostly high altitude arboreal marsupials but including some large rodents – are said to be the pigs of the Red Spirits, but aside from some concern with the hunting and trapping of these animals, they have no more interest in subsistence activities than does Smoke Woman. As they are associated with the upper portion of the territory, so are they associated with the upper part of the body. They may cause illness of the head and chest, and their help is solicited when such afflictions have other causes. Their most important concern, however, is with the relations of their group to other local groups, particularly in warfare. Warfare rituals are largely addressed to them, and they enforce the taboos associated with warfare.

Their general qualities are reflected in the terms by which they are addressed in ritual. Often they are called *Norum-Kombri* and *Runge-Yinye*. *Kombri* are cassowaries, large dangerous birds living mainly in the high forest whose oily flesh is more highly prized than pork. Cassowary plumes adorn the heads of men when they go to war. *Norum* are epiphytic orchids with strong stalks growing high on high-altitude trees. *Runge* is the sun; *yinye* is fire. The Red Spirits are said to be *rombanda*, which in other contexts may mean simply "hot," but in relation to them it also implies dryness, hardness, strength, bellicosity, and ferocity.

The two classes of spirits that dwell in the lower portions of the territory are sometimes called collectively *Raua Mai*. *Mai* seems to mean antecedent in a biological sense: a taro (*ndong*) corm from which rhysomes have grown is a *ndong mai*; a woman who has borne children is an *ambra mai*; old men are *yu mai*.

Included among the *Raua Mai* is, first, *Koipa Mangiang* who, like Smoke Woman, was never human. He is said to dwell in pools in the streams dissecting the mountainside and, as marsupials are the pigs of the Red Spirits, eels are said to be his pigs.

Living nearby, in the trunks of the largest trees in climax forest remnants are the *Raua Tukump*, the spirits of those who have died of illness or accident. The term *tukump* refers both to a supernatural corruption that may pollute places and harm people, and to the mold, sometimes said to be faintly luminescent, that develops on rotting objects or substances.

As the Red Spirits are associated with the upper part of the body, so the "Spirits of Rot" are associated with the lower – with the belly, the reproductive organs, and the legs – and they may both afflict those parts and cure afflictions of them. They and *Koipa Mangiang* have minor parts to play in warfare rituals, but their major concern is with the fruitfulness of women, pigs, and gardens, and rituals concerned with fertility are mainly addressed to them. *Koipa Mangiang* has authority in these matters, the Spirits of Rot acting as his intermediaries, but his dominion is not limited to fertility. He alone among the major spirits kills (although other spirits may request him to do so). *Koipa Mangiang* has, therefore, a fearful as well as a benign aspect.

As the spirits of the high ground are said to be "hot," so those of the low ground are said to be *kinim*, which sometimes means, simply, cold. Here *kinim* carries an implication of wetness as well: the juice of sugar cane is *kinim*. So is water and all of the creatures that live in water. Women are also said to be so because of their vaginal secretions.

Maring observe that cold and wet conditions induce decay, the dissolution of organic matter and its reabsorption into earth from which it sprang. The decay of vegetation is seen by them to favor the fertility of gardens. New life grows from the rot of things once living; that which is living will in its turn dissolve, supporting life yet to come. But whether or not it is beneficial to growth, that which is decaying is, after all, itself dead or dying. Fertility is, thus, closely related to death in Maring cosmology. This closeness is indicated by their union in the figure of *Koipa Mangiang*.

Both hotness and coldness, both strength and fertility are, in the Maring view, qualities necessary for survival – to the successful defense of the land and to the successful cultivation of the land defended. But the two sets of qualities are contradictory and thus dangerous to each other. Some activities must, therefore, be segregated from others in time and space, and some objects and persons must be insulated from contact with other objects and persons during certain periods or even permanently. Thus, men at war who have taken into themselves the heat of the Red Spirits should avoid contact with women, because the coldness and wetness of the women would extinguish the spiritual fires flaming inside them and thus soften their strength. Like many other New Guinea Highlanders, the Maring have well-developed notions, expressed in a welter of taboos, concerning the polluting qualities of women, and too much contact with women at any time is said to be debilitating (see Buchbinder and Rappaport 1976).

In sum, the virtues of the two sets of spirits stand in clear contrast to each other. It may be that the Spirits of Rot and the Red Spirits, who were kinsmen in life, stand between Smoke Woman and *Koipa Mangiang* in some logical sense, and thus mediate their opposition. But of greater importance than logical mediation is the dynamic mediation of the Maring ritual cycle. We may illustrate this by reference to the cosmological consequences of Maring warfare, and to the ameliorative effects of planting *rumbim*, and other rituals, in its aftermath.

We have noted that the qualities of the Red Spirits, who are primarily associated with warfare, stand in opposition to those of the spirits of the low ground. Indeed, the virtues of the latter are thought to be inimical to those of the Red Spirits, and could nullify the military assistance that they might provide. It is therefore necessary, when war is "declared," to segregate the two sets of spirits and everything associated with them as much as possible, and to identify the community, especially the men, more closely with the Red Spirits. This is accomplished in an elaborate ritual during which certain objects called fighting stones (*bamp ku*) are hung from the center post of a certain ritual house (*ringi ying*). This ritual transforms the relationship of the antagonists from one of brotherhood (*ngui-ngui*: "brother-brother") into one of formal and sanctified enmity (*cenang yu*: "ax men"), if that relationship had not already been so transformed in earlier rounds of warfare. The territories of *cenang yu* may not be entered except to despoil them, and enemies may not be touched or addressed except in anger.

I have noted in passing that in the course of this ritual, in which only men participate, the Red Spirits are taken by the warriors into their heads, where they are said to burn like fire. Sexual intercourse is henceforth tabooed, of course, because contact with the cold, wet, soft, women would put out the fires burning in the hot, hard, dry men's heads. Conversely, some Maring men say that women would be burned by contact with the men. For similar reasons food cooked by women, moist foods, soft foods, and foods identified with the lower altitudes become tabooed to the warriors, who also suffer a taboo on drinking any fluids while actually on the battleground. The segregation of that associated with the high from that associated with the low, a segregation which is at its most extreme when warfare is initiated, is indicated by these and other taboos. It is perhaps most clearly represented by the prohibition against consuming marsupials, the pigs of the Red Spirits together with the fruit of the Marita pandanus, which is associated with the Spirits of Rot (parts of whose mortal remains are buried in pandanus groves). Marsupials and pandanus may each be cooked and consumed, but not in mixture or even at the same meal.

Not only are the two sets of supernaturals segregated from each other, but the living are separated from both by heavy obligations. These are owed even to the spirits of the low ground who are asked, when the stones are hung, to strengthen the warrior's legs. Because of these debts a taboo on the trapping of marsupials goes into effect, although they may be eaten if shot, a very rare occurrence. Eels may neither be trapped nor eaten. Men cannot eat them because eels, being cold and wet, would be injurious to their hotness, of course, but they cannot even be trapped for consumption by women because they are the pigs of *Koipa Mangiang*, and while a debt to him remains his pigs may not be taken.) Warfare (in sum) tears the universe asunder, requiring the radical separation of the hot from the cold, the high from the low, the strong from the fertile, male from female. When war is "declared" (by hanging objects called "fighting stones" from the center post of a small ritual house) a great range of taboos prohibiting certain objects, substances, foods, classes of persons and activities from coming into contact with each other[1] are therefore activated, and heavy debts in favor of the dead are assumed by the living, for the dead must be repaid for their assistance in the fighting.

With the termination of warfare reintegration of the universe commences. Indeed, to reintroduce the concerns of chapter 6, from the Maring point of view the sequence of rituals that, in invariant order, constitute the ritual cycle is an elaborate and protracted procedure for mending the world that warfare has broken. Each of its steps absolves those participating from certain taboos, and thus allows objects, persons and activities that hostilities have segregated to come together once again. Planting *rumbim* signifies that men and women can once again become intimate, and taboos on certain foodstuffs are also abrogated at this time. Planting *rumbim* separately buys each agnatic group both its autonomy and its connection to the particular piece of land.

When it is agreed by the antagonists[2] that warfare is to be discontinued, everyone in the local group – women, children, warriors, and their allies as well – assembles to prepare for the *rumbim* planting. All possible varieties of edible wild animals are taken: marsupials, snakes, lizards, frogs, rats, insects, grubs, birds; and wild greens are gathered. These wild foods, along with a little fat from the belly of a female pig, are cooked in a special oven (*pubit*) said to be about three feet square, made of bark, and set directly upon the ground. While the food is steaming in the oven, the warriors ritually remove the "hot" charcoal called *ringi* that they had applied to themselves when the objects called "fighting stones" were hung when hostilities were confirmed. When the oven is opened, they, as well as their womenfolk and children, partake of its contents, although mixed throughout it are meats at all other times forbidden to them, some because they are "cold," some for other reasons.

What seems to be represented by the oven and the consumption of its contents are both the fruitfulness of nature, and a natural precultural state in which men, like animals, knew no taboos and ate anything that nature offered them. The very position of the oven may be significant with respect to the lack of discriminations that seems to characterize the Maring conceptualization of the state of nature. It rests directly upon the ground. In contrast, ovens in which pigs dedicated to the Red Spirits (sometimes called "head pigs") are cooked are raised above the ground, while those in which pigs are offered to the spirits of the low ground ("leg pigs"), as well as those in which non-ritual meals are prepared, are proper "earth ovens": they are dug into the ground. It may further be suggested that the fruitfulness of nature represented in the feast of wild foods and by the oven itself are associated with procreation. We shall return to this matter shortly.

The feasting finished, the women are sent away and a young *tondoko*, a red leafed variety of *rumbim* (*Cordyline fruticosa*), is planted in the middle of the emptied oven. This is the *yu min rumbim* (*yu*/man, *min*/ shadow, life stuff). Each man clasps it as it is planted, and some men say that by laying hold of it their *min* flows into the plant where it remains for safekeeping. Be this as it may, although the *rumbim* seems to be planted primarily for the well-being of those planting it (women may not even touch it), they are not the only beneficiaries. It is said that children begotten by the participants will quickly become "hard" (*anc*); that is to say they will grow quickly, become strong and remain well. While the men are planting the *rumbim*, a *mbamp kunda yu*, a man knowledgeable in war ritual, addresses the ancestors thanking them for their help in the hostilities just terminated, especially in defending successfully their occupation of their territory. Every act of support or help requires, in the Maring view of the world, reciprocation. Nothing is for nothing and the ancestors are told that they will now be given a presentation of pork in reciprocation for their support. No matter how many pigs are slaughtered, the ancestors are told that they are but few, and that the living will devote themselves primarily to raising pigs until they have accumulated a sufficient number to discharge the debt to ancestors (and allies) properly. This can take years, a decade or more is usual (see Rappaport 1984: chs 4 and 5). Until such debts are discharged, the local group cannot initiate hostilities because the ancestors would be unwilling to help descendants who had not paid previously assumed debts, and a truce therefore prevails. When, years later, there are sufficient pigs to repay the ancestors, all adult and adolescent pigs are sacrificed. Only juveniles survive. The ancestors consume the *min* of the pigs, the allies receive most of the flesh.

In chapter 3 it was noted that by joining in the planting of *rumbim* men who were previously aliens are attached to territories and assimilated to the groups occupying them. *Rumbim*, thus, seems not only to be associated with individual men, and with the quality of hardness or strength, but also with territoriality. Claims to territory reside in corporations of men who are, ideally, agnatically related, but by grasping the *rumbim* an erstwhile outsider mingles his *min* with theirs, taking the first step toward the assimilation of his descendants into the agnatic clan upon whose territory he is living. Although the several patrilineal clans that form a local population coordinate the planting of *rumbim* (as we noted in chapter 6 such coordination defines them as a corporation), they usually plant their *rumbim* separately, each clan on its own ground. *Rumbim* is, thus, associated with patrilineality as well as with territoriality and men's strength and well-being. By grasping the *yu min rumbim*, not only does an outsider seemingly mingle his *min* with those of the clansmen, thereby taking the first step toward assimilation, but he incidentally resettles his ancestors at his new home, for he accompanies his participation in this ritual with the sacrifice of pigs, and he calls out to his dead kinsmen to come to the new place to partake of the pork. Given structural pressures, short genealogical memory and the prevailing kinship terminology (which obliterates the distinctions between agnates and other cognates in two generations), for a man to resettle his ancestors is for him to take the first step in assimilating them into the general class of ancestors (*ana-koka*) of the group into which he is assimilating.

Although it is with their *min* (their "shadows," or life stuff) that men invest the *rumbim* that they plant, it may be that the association of *min* with agnatic corporations imbues the comingled *min* which infuses the *rumbim* with, if not immortality, a perdurance beyond that of individual lives. By clasping *rumbim*, a man participates in, as it were, a corporate life whose span is greater than his own. Such a view of clan *min* is suggested by a standard phrase in the speech of heroes in accounts of how brave men face death. "It does not matter if I die. There are more Merkai (or Kamungagai, or Kwibigai, etc.) to hold the land and father the children." The clan is not immortal, but it is subject to extinction rather than death, and thus its mortal span is prolonged beyond that of the individual and territorial corporations. The spiritual qualities of *rumbim* act so that the men will remain well and the children begotten by them healthy. Spirituality, strength, health, agnation, territoriality, continuity and something like immortality are represented in the planting of *rumbim*.

When the men unclasp the *rumbim*, they plant *amame* (Coleus) around the oven. Some belly fat of pig cooked with the wild foods has been reserved and is buried among the *amame*, which is called, in fact, the *konc kump amame* (pig belly *amame*). While it is being planted, the spirits of the low ground are entreated to care well for it, that the pigs will be fertile and grow fat, that the gardens flourish, and that the women be healthy and bear children. As the oven rots, the *amame* overruns it and the space that it occupied. Cuttings are then taken from it to plant at the women's houses for the sake of the human and porcine residents.

The sexual symbolism of the *rumbim*, which is a long, slim little tree being planted in the center of the oven seems obvious, but it probably does not represent the procreative act in any simple sense. It employs a relationship between objects similar to that of male and female organs in intercourse to represent metaphorically a union of a more abstract nature. For now it is sufficient to observe that the spatial relationship of *rumbim* to *amame* does suggest that the oven is in some sense a vaginal representation. This identification receives some support from the oven's bounty: as human children emerge from vulvas, so do the fruits of the earth from the oven. Although neither Buchbinder nor I got corroborating exegeses from Maring informants, and would not have expected them, this interpretation does not rest entirely on exogenous theories of symbolism. There is a theme in Maring stories of an apparently pregnant woman from whom bursts forth not a child, but a great flood of wild vegetables and animals. The story of such a miracle reached me in the field as the report of a current event in Ambrakwi, a distant Maring community.

If the oven represents a vulva through which the fruits of the earth come forth, the earth is thereby assimilated into a class with other entities possessing vulvas, notably women. We have already seen that the earth and women share certain qualities or attributes, of course. Both are fruitful and, moreover, their fruitfulness is related to their "coldness," a coldness which is dangerous as well as fertile. In light of this, it is significant that the spatial relationship of *amame* and *rumbim* to each other produced by their planting and subsequent growth over the area occupied by the oven recalls the spatial relationship of these two plants on burial sites. As *rumbim* and *amame* are spatially related to the oven, so are they related to graves. If the oven is a vaginal representation this suggests that vaginas and graves are conflated. As the earth possesses a vagina in the oven, so women possess, in their vaginas, graves. In the symbolism of ritual, then, we find corroboration of the identification of fertility and death implicit in avoidance behavior almost explicit in cosmology, and we gain some insight into the nature of men's pollution fears. As that which emerges from the earth is eventually reabsorbed by the earth, so re-entry by men into that from which men emerge, although necessary for procreation and pleasurable as well, is dangerous. As the earth dissolves the creatures sprung from it, so those sprung from vaginas can be dissolved be re-entry into them. It is of interest that pollution by women is said to cause putrescence, a condition of deterioration similar to that of corpses. (A process with which the Maring are familiar because until the 1970s they exposed cadavers on raised platforms, where they were attended by widows or close female agnates until reduced to skeletons.) In light of this it may be suggested that Maring men's fear of pollution by women's sexuality on the one hand and by the association of women with corpses on the other, are one and the same.

We may reflect here upon some of the implications of symbolic representations of the human body, in particular of their sexual features, for those who use them. Now it may be that the distinction between male and female, being universally and immediately experienced is naturally significant, and thus an obvious cognitive tool for marking opposing classes. Among the Maring it serves as a living summary and representation of all the abstract conventional distinctions they impose upon the world. It is what Ortner calls a "root metaphor."

High/hot/hard/dry/strong/spiritual/immortal:
low/cold/soft/wet/fecund/mundane/mortal::male:female (1973)

It is important to recognize, however, that the relationship male: female is not merely a convenient metaphoric formulation. It is also material, thus providing substance to the abstractions for which it is providing an epitome.

An innumerable class of objects and substances can serve as material metaphors but the male/female distinction is to be distinguished from all or almost all of them on a further ground of great significance: it is *not* distinct from those who use it to make distinctions and to understand the distinctions they have made. As inseparable aspects of thinkers themselves it may be that the male/female distinction provides them with an intuitive understanding of the world which seems to have especially great power, generality and concreteness. But the price may be high. As the concrete and familiar, proximal terms of a metaphor may *illuminate* the abstract, strange and distal terms, so the distal relationship may *predicate* the proximal (Fernandez 1974). Thus, in making the physical differences between men and women stand for all the conceptual oppositions they have imposed upon the world, the Maring have opened their bodies to all of those conceptual oppositions. As Buchbinder and I have argued (1976) the conventional world's terrors and dangers storm back across the metaphoric bridge, so to speak, to seize the bodies of men as well as women. Their living substance is possessed by the abstract furies which the ancestors imagined into being. Such reflexive action may be intrinsic to the use of body metaphors and certainly underlies notions of female pollution among the Maring. Women are not primarily polluting for their natural qualities. They are, rather, polluted by the qualities for which they stand because those qualities are dangerous to the qualities associated with men. That they have suffered some oppression because of the meaning vested in their sexual characteristics goes without saying, but men also are victimized by metaphoric use of the male/female distinction. They are fearful of sex.

The process of the natural world is the cycle of fertility, growth, and death, and the planting of *rumbim* and *amame* seems to represent an attempt by men to impose their own cultural order upon the bounties and dangers of the nature by which they are both sustained and threatened. If the oven is a representation of a vulva, it may signify not only that the bountifulness of the wild is an aspect of the wild's fecundity, but that fecundity itself is an aspect of the wild. The planting of *amame*, itself a cultigen, around the oven which it eventually overruns is an attempt to capture for the cultivated the fecundity of the wild. *Amame* is explicitly planted for the benefit of women, domestic pigs, and gardens, and to plant it is to lash sociocultural ends onto natural processes, or to assimilate the processes of nature into those of society.

It is important to note here that the opposition of wild to cultivated is intrinsic to Maring thought. The distinction between *t'p wombi* and *t'p ndemi*, approximating that between things domestic and things wild, is an important one. It is in accordance with our general discussion, however, that *ndemi* carry the meaning of dangerous as well as wild, and that some creatures or entities not in a meaningful sense either cultivated or uncultivated, such as enemies and the ghosts of those who have not been given proper mortuary rites, are said to be *ndemi*.

Whereas the planting of *amame* may be interpreted as the imposition of cultural purposes upon the fruitful but dangerous and purposeless process of nature, the planting of *rumbim*, a plant which men clasp and invest but which women may not even touch, makes clear that insofar as the cultural order is in the hands of mortals, it is literally in the hands of men. Moreover, since Red Spirits are associated with the *rumbim* as well as with the living men who plant it, since the *amame* is associated with the spirits of the low ground, and since seances with the Smoke Woman always precede the planting of *rumbim*, the cultural order that men dominate is a spiritual order as well.

The planting of *rumbim* in the oven does not, then, represent a procreative act in any simple sense, but, rather, the union of nature, associated with death and fertility, with spirituality, associated by the Maring with the cultural order. It is of interest in this respect that the word "*nomane*," which in some contexts denotes "thought" or" soul," can in other contexts be glossed as "custom" or "culture" (chapter 11). This union implies, we may note, an ordering of living and non-living beings. Smoke Woman, associated with words, thought, and breath, as insubstantial and ethereal as the hot vapors through which men commune with her, flies high above the world. *Koipa Mangiang*, who is concerned with fertility, decay, and death, swims in its depths. If Smoke Woman, who is above the world and who provides to the world the words by which it is ordered, is supernatural, *Koipa Mangiang* who swims beneath the world is infranatural, for the world rests upon the processes over which he presides. Between them and the living, dwelling in trees in the low ground and, burning on the high ground, are the spirits of those who once lived, the Spirits of Rot, and the Red Spirits.

The houses of the living are, for the most part, built in the middle altitudes, and it is there that most of the gardens are planted.

"Primitive society," says Douglas (1966: 4), "is an energized structure at the center of its universe." At the center of the Maring universe, in the world of life, these two sets come together in the relationship between men and women. Society is possible only in their union, a union represented in the planting of *rumbim* and *amame* in and around the oven. Avoidance and taboo facilitate their union, for they are not only mutually dependent, but also in some degree inimical. At least the spiritual and cultural order, embodied in men particularly, is in danger of being engulfed by the natural processes necessary to its perpetuation. In this view, Maring beliefs concerning female pollution are not simply an outcome or an aspect of an opposition between nature and culture, an opposition which is virtually explicit in the dichotomy Maring make between *t'p wombi* and *t'p ndemi*. It is an aspect of their union as well.

Absolution from the taboos assumed when the fighting stones were hung, and, thus, the mending of the world that warfare tore asunder, requires reductions in the debt owed by the living to the dead. These obligations are fulfilled through the sacrifice of pigs, and all adult and adolescent animals owned by members of a living group are offered to the spirits of their ancestors when they plant *rumbim*. Only juveniles escape the slaughter. The dead are said to devour the spirits of the pigs, while the flesh of the animals is consumed by the living. Although the Red Spirits are more important in warfare, the sacrificed pigs are offered to the Spirits of the Low Ground because the flesh of pigs dedicated to them can be presented to allies, and allies as well as spirits must be repaid for their assistance. Only agnates may consume the flesh of pigs offered to the Red Spirits.

The pork presented to ancestors and allies with the planting of rumbim constitutes no more than a first payment to them. A large debt remains outstanding, and therefore many taboos, including those on marsupials, eels, and those dealing with the enemy and forbidding trespass on enemy territory remain. Because Maring doctrine holds that warfare can be successful only with the assistance of spirits, and because the aid of spirits will not be forthcoming if debts to them remain outstanding, a group cannot initiate a new round of warfare until it has fully repaid its debts from the last. A sanctified truce thus comes into effect with the planting of *rumbim*. This prevails until there are sufficient pigs to repay the spirits.

The question of how many pigs are sufficient and how long it takes to acquire them has been dealt with elsewhere (Rappaport 1968). Here I need only note that there are sufficient pigs to repay the ancestors when the size of the pig population approaches the limits of the ability of their owners to feed them and to control their destructiveness, and that it takes from ten to twenty years for such a number to build up. When it does, the reintegration continues through a *kaiko*, a year-long festival consisting of a series of rituals and entertainments requiring the sacrifice of pigs during which hospitality is offered to friendly groups.

In preparation for the *kaiko*, stakes marking the boundaries of the local group's territory are ritually planted. If the enemy remains on his territory, they are planted at the old border. A few pigs are sacrificed at this time and, if the enemy was driven off his land in the last round of warfare, the taboo on entering the land that he had previously occupied is now abrogated, and the boundary stakes may be planted at new locations incorporating some or all of his land. It is assumed that by this time even the spirits of the enemy's ancestors have departed to take up residence with their living descendants, who, after they were routed, sought refuge with kinsmen elsewhere. Erstwhile enemy land is thus considered unoccupied, and as such may be annexed.

Also abrogated at this time is the taboo on trapping marsupials, and a ritual trapping period, lasting for one to two months (until a certain variety of pandanus fruit ripens), commences. This culminates in an important ritual where there is further debt reduction and further reintegration of the cosmos. The beneficiaries of the slaughter of pigs when the *rumbim* is uprooted are mainly the Red Spirits. The pigs offered them are, in part, payment for their past assistance and, in part, in exchange for the marsupials (their pigs) that have recently been trapped and smoked and are now consumed. A relationship of equality with the Red Spirits, replacing the former indebtedness, is now being approached by the living. Correlated with this, the communion entered into years before by men who took the Red Spirits into their heads when they hung the fighting stones is now concluded. The Red Spirits are asked to take the pig being offered them and leave.

The cassowary, we have noted, is associated with the spirits of the high ground. From the point of view of reintegration, perhaps the most interesting act in the elaborate ritual is the piercing of a pandanus fruit with a cassowary bone dagger by a man dancing barefoot on heated oven stones. The pandanus is then cooked with marsupials, and the mixture consumed ceremoniously. Thus spirits of the high and the low, long separated, are being drawn closer together, and the congregation, gradually absolving its debts, is drawing closer to both.

With the uprooting of the *rumbim* the taboo on beating drums is abrogated, and the *kaiko* commences. During this festival other local populations are entertained from time to time at elaborate dances, and about six months after the uprooting of the *rumbim*, when the taro has begun to ripen in the gardens, a few pigs are sacrificed at the fighting stones, eel trapping becomes permissible, and one to three months later traps for them are placed in special places in various streams. In the meantime, friendly groups continue to be entertained, but taro is now the focus of the food presentations to the visitors. Taro is to the Maring the most important of foods; even sacrificial pig is called "taro" in addresses to spirits, and ritual presentations of taro to guests symbolize the ability of the hosts to maintain gardens on the one hand and social relationships on the other. Among the Maring food sharing is synonymous with friendship; people will not eat food grown by enemies. To eat a man's taro is to say that he is your friend.

The festival concludes in a series of rituals occurring on successive days. First, a few pigs are offered to the Red Spirits in rituals abrogating some residual taboos on relations with other groups arising out of warfare in earlier generations. At this time, too, inter-dining taboos among members of the local population assumed with respect to each other in moments of anger are lifted. The renunciation of these taboos permits the locals to perform the community-wide rituals which bring the entire cycle to its climax. Performed at sacred places in the middle altitudes, and accompanied by the slaughter of great numbers of pigs, the rituals call sexual generation to mind.

The trapped eels, kept alive in cages in nearby streams, are carried by young men to the sacrificial places (*raku*) up newly cut pathways, through frond-bedecked arches, where they are joined by the women and young girls. The young men, women and girls proceed together to the center of the *raku* where the eels are removed from their cages and, grasped by their tails, flailed to death on the flank of a newly-killed female pig. The eel and the pig are then cooked together in the *tmbi ying*, a small circular house with a pole projecting through its roof. On the previous night both *Koipa Mangiang* and Smoke Woman had been called into the *tmbi ying* at the same time. The universe has finally been reintegrated.

The next day there is a massive distribution of pork. All locals sacrifice their adult and adolescent pigs to their ancestors to whom their obligations for their help in the last round of warfare are now discharged, and they present the pork to kinsmen from other groups who "helped them fight." Payments in pork are made by individuals but the coordination of such payments give them a corporate character.

On the same day, hero's portions of salted pig belly are publicly presented to leading allies through a window in a ceremonial fence erected on the dance ground for the occasion. When the pork has been distributed, the hosts, who have assembled behind the fence, crash through to join the throng now dancing on the dance ground. Yesterday they reunited the high with the low and themselves with both in what appears to have been a great procreative act. Today, in what seems to be a rebirth, they have broken through the restrictions separating them from their neighbors. Their debts to both the living and the dead have been repaid and, if the central government had not recently pacified the area, they would have been again free to initiate warfare. The sanctified truce had ended.

2. Language and liturgy

Some writers, among them Charles Frake (1964) and Edmund Leach (1954: 14b, 1966) have likened ritual to language. Both are modes of communication, both use words and, as languages have syntactic structures, so do rituals have regular structures that may at least be likened to grammars. The foregoing account of the *yu min rumbim* and its planting, however, makes us skeptical of any easy assimilation of ritual into a more general category, language.

To note similarities between or among apparently disparate phenomena is to cast light upon them, but we should not be so taken by similarities that we overlook differences. Indeed, those who have discerned the similarities between ritual and language have issued such warnings themselves, and it does not derogate the significance of the similarities between ritual and language as modes of communication to propose that the differences between them are profound.

First, it was observed in chapter 4 that language is a *code*, but liturgies are *orders*. Codes consist of lexicons and rules for combining them into meaningful messages and for interpreting such messages. Linguistic codes – natural languages – do not themselves restrict the messages that may be constructed by the application of their rules to their lexicons, but the range of messages that can properly be transmitted through any ritual is highly restricted. Indeed, the range that may be transmitted in the canon is often reduced to unity as the proper words and acts follow each other in more or less invariant order. As Maurice Bloch (1973) has put it, the "features of juncture" are open in language but fixed in ritual.

It follows that ordinary verbal discourse can easily accommodate nuance, gradation, modification, and disputation but that the rhetoric of ritual cannot. This does not mean, as Bloch has (mistakenly, in my view) proposed, that canon is not rational. It means, simply, that liturgies do not argue. They assert and, given their performative qualities, often bring into being or establish whatever it is that they assert.

The flexibility of ordinary discourse is such that it can be responsive to the ever-changing present, and continuous modifications or shifts in the utterances of speakers are expected. Indeed when a speaker's remarks do not take account of what is said to him we take it to be a sign of deficiency or even pathology. He is, we say, obtuse, boring, rude, snobbish, fanatical, insane or perhaps deaf. Conversely, inflexibility is what we take to be proper in liturgical discourse. If someone does make changes in ritual we may consider him to be committing an error, or to be unknowledgeable, unorthodox, blasphemous or even heretical, his words inefficaceous, unhallowed.

A second point of difference also discussed earlier is that although language plays an important part in human ritual, few, if any, human rituals are entirely verbal. They use objects and substances, as well as the bodies of the performers, to transmit messages and meta-messages difficult or even impossible for language alone to convey. Notable among these meta-messages are those *indicating* the substantiality or existence of whatever is signified *symbolically*, by the canon's words. I suggested in chapter 5 that the use of the body in ritual indicates the living materiality of the accepting agent.

This second contrast implies a third. A purely linguistic transmission is a single channel transmission. It is spoken and then heard, or written and then read. Ritual, on the other hand, may use all of the sensory modalities – sight, hearing, touch, smell, kinesthetics – at once. This more comprehensive and thus more engrossing mode of communication must, in itself, invest messages with meanings beyond those that can be conveyed by any single modality. Moreover, these complex transmissions may, and often do, point to multiple significata simultaneously. Ritual's simultaneous or chord-like aspect has been nicely illustrated through the account of Maring ritual seen in the previous section and elsewhere.

3. Analysis vs. performance

The account I have given of the Maring ritual cycle presents it *in its integrated entirety*, a representation of the world's order as the Maring have conceived it. The analysis woven into the description of the cycle has, however, broken it into some of its constituent events and meanings. Disassembly is inevitable in analysis (in fact, the Random House Collegiate Dictionary defines analysis as "the separating of any material or abstract entity into its constituent elements"), and is not in error, for the parts may be of great significance in and of themselves. There are, however, dangers attending analytic operations and, to put it mildly, not all interpretations of rituals have escaped them.

First, in attending to the significance of the separate elements that an analysis isolates, sight of the significance of the *relations* among those elements might be lost, and thus meanings intuitive to liturgical orders *as wholes* may be missed. The breaking of the world and its subsequent reintegration animating the Maring ritual cycle from beginning to end is an instance of such a meaning.

The second danger is perhaps subtler. Any analysis of canonical signs or "symbols" must, to find their significata, take apart what are presented *as unities*. It may then seem that these significata comprise the meanings of the representation or sign. *But to perform a ritual is not to analyze it.* Indeed, the import of performance is exactly the converse of that of an analytic operation. *Whereas an analysis distinguishes the multiple significata of a canonical sign or representation, in performance those many significata come swooping into that sign from all over experience simultaneously and they are not merely summarized but integrated by that sign.*

Let us return here to the *rumbim* and its planting. We have seen that at one and the same time *rumbim* signifies peace, Red Spirits, spirituality and the spiritual order in general, patrilineality, particular patriclans, membership in particular patriclans, patrilocality, territoriality, boundaries, immortality, maleness, fire, hotness, blood and perhaps the male organ. Victor Turner similarly tells us that the *Mudyi* Tree represents womanhood, motherhood, the mother-child bond, a novice undergoing initiation into womanhood, a specific matrilineage, the principle of matriliny, the process of learning women's wisdom, the unity and perdurance of *Ndembu* society, breast milk, mother's breasts, and the body slenderness and mental pliancy of the novice.

Further significata could surely be found in the *rumbim* itself even before we attend to the other objects with which the planting associates it, the *pubit* and the *amame*. The *pubit*, it was proposed, signifies nature's bounty as an aspect of fecundity, and fecundity itself as a quality of nature. The *pubit*, it was further proposed, is also a vaginal representation. *Amame*, a cultigen, represents a mediation between nature's fertility and the designs and ends of men. It is explicitly a plant of *Koipa Mangiang* and is planted especially for the benefit of women, children, and gardens.

The spatial relationship of the *rumbim* and the *amame* to the *pubit* resembles plantings on graves. This suggests the conflation, at some level of Maring thought, of vaginas and graves, and thus of fertility and death. More explicitly, in the planting of *rumbim* in the *pubit* and of the *amame* around it, the subordination of fertility-death to spirituality, and thus of nature to culture and women to men are all represented.

The *mudyi* and the *rumbim-pubit-amame* complex are "multivocalic," to use Turner's term (1967: 50, *passim*; 1973). Although certain of these significata may be emphasized in particular rituals, all of them are, in fact, *signified simultaneously* whenever the canonical sign is represented.

It may be of interest that, as Victor Turner (1973) has pointed out, "dominant symbols" (Schneider 1968) – representations central to liturgical orders, for instance the Cross, the subincision of the Australians, Zoroastrian fires, the lotus – are likely to be very simple. The *rumbim* in the *pubit* surrounded by the *amame* is, perhaps, a degree more complex, but be this as it may, the simpler the sign the more general it is and the more it can encompass. The more complex the representation the more specific it becomes and the more it rules out. A simple representation is not only more encompassing than a more complex one, but also remains open, and can assimilate new significata and divest itself of old ones as circumstances change (see chapter 5). To put this a little differently, and to emphasize a slightly different aspect of its significance, what are called "dominant," or "key" symbols are of high taxonomic order. The Cross, for example, is related to the more specific signs constituting the various sacraments as the taxonomic category primate, an order, stands to the category *Macaca fuscata*, a species. A similar case could be made for the relationship of *rumbim, amame,* and *pubit* to the consumption of marsupials and Marita pandanus together at the *rumbim*'s uprooting.

The many significata of "key" or "dominant" representations are not randomly distributed, as it were, throughout the domains of culture. Joseph Campbell (1959, particularly the concluding chapter), as well as Victor Turner (1967: 28, 1973) has noted their bipolar distribution. At the pole that Turner calls "normative" or "ideological," components of the cosmological, social and moral orders are clustered. In the case of the *rumbim* these would include Red Spirits, spirituality, the spiritual order, patriliny, a particular patriclan, membership in the patriclan, patrilo-cality, territoriality, boundaries and immortality. At the other pole, which Turner calls the sensory or "orectic," the significations of phy-siology, sensation and emotion congregate. Those of the *rumbim* include maleness, fire, hotness, blood and the male organ. Such significata are closely associated with powerful emotions and can be expected to stimulate them.

Ortner (personal communication) has observed, in my view correctly, that the image of two poles is too simple to represent adequately the complexity of signification of important canonical signs. It may be better to conceive of a number of domains – the cosmological, the moral, the social, the psychic and the physiological, to make only gross distinctions – lying between the two poles. Be this as it may, both Turner and Campbell have argued that abstractions lying toward the ideological end of the continuum are infused with immediacy and power by their union in the canonical sign with the psychic and physiological significata. Campbell (1959), who has given this point great emphasis, refers to the two directions in which meanings may proceed from canonical signs by the Indian terms *marga* and *desi*. He says *marga*, "path" or "way," designates the direction of universally human aspects of life. *Desi*, "of the region" or locality, is that of the culturally particular. The universal human significata are, of course, those that lie toward Turner's sensory pole: *marga* points toward performers and their pan-human psychic and physiological constitutions; *desi* leads in the direction of ideology, of culturally particular meanings. In the canonical sign the universally human is lashed to the culturally specific, giving the power of the immediately experienced to the culturally specific even as the culturally specific guides it. *Desi* sublimates *marga* – makes *marga* sublime – at the same time that it is empowered or energized by *marga*. In the union of *marga* and *desi* in liturgical representations cultural forms are substan-tiated – given substance – by universal aspects of human experience.

Earlier in this chapter a number of differences between canonical signs and the words of ordinary language were noted. We may now elaborate upon them. Ordinary discourse is sequential. One meaning follows another. Liturgical orders have a sequential dimension, to the examin-ation of which chapter 6 was devoted, and which was explicit in our account of the Maring ritual cycle, but the representations following each other in fixed sequences also possess a chord-like structure with multiple significata being represented simultaneously. Words often have more than one meaning also, but in everyday declarative usage contexts usually eliminate all but one of them. If the context fails to do so we say that the verbal expression is ambiguous, and we usually take that ambiguity to be a fault. The simultaneous representation of multiple significata in canonical signs is, in contrast, the very essence of their meaningfulness. *A ritual sign does not derive its meanings from each of its significata separately so much as it derives its meaning from their union. This is to say that what is noise in ordinary language is meaning in liturgy.*

That the meaning of a canonical sign emerges from the union of its significata, and not from their mere summation, was, of course, explicit in the discussion of the relationship among *rumbim, amame,* their planting, and the *pubit,* but the apparent clarity of the interpretation offered should not be construed to be an indication of its exhaustiveness, nor to represent the degree of clarity and explicitness of canonical signs generally. The meaning that may finally be derived from the concatenation of the significata of a ritual may be so abstract, complex and emotionally charged as to be "ineffable." As we observed in a discussion of subincision in chapter 5, that the meanings of canonical signs may be beyond words is a further reason for representing them substantially.

I shall only recall in passing that the simultaneous dimension of liturgical orders is not exhausted by the multivocalic significance of the separate signs following each other in fixed order. Liturgical orders may communicate over a number of channels simultaneously: through words and non-verbal uses of the voice, through instrumental music, through graphic and plastic art, pageantry, dramatic display and physical movement, and even through the senses of smell and taste and variations on touch, including pain. It may be suggested that all of the senses are occupied, none is free to dwell upon other things or even to reflect upon the immediate experience. It may be suggested that when experience is deprived of reflective capacity its immediacy becomes in and of itself deeply meaningful. We shall return to this in a later chapter.

Not only, then, may a number of significata be represented simultaneously in a canonical sign, but all sensory channels may participate in representation. Further enriching communication, a number of canonical signs may be presented, and apprehended, simultaneously. Although they may sometimes have significata more or less distinct from the others with which they are concurrent (perhaps yielding a unified meaning more highly abstract than any of them), Babcock (1973) has argued that often they all may be signifying the same or similar things. During the High

Mass in a Gothic cathedral, for example, sunlight through stained glass, the music of choir and organ, the vestments and intonation of the celebrant, the Cross on the altar, the cruciform shape of the encompassing space, the vaulting which covers it, the odor of incense, the taste of wine and wafer, the movements of one's own body may all join as an immediate sign of God's glory. In contrast, the plethora of simultaneous representations that are characteristic of carnival's excess signifies a disorder approaching chaos (Babcock 1973). Such a "surplus of signifiers," employing a range of modalities and possibly evoking a range of associations, magnifies the shared significance into one of encompassing generality and overwhelming meaning.[3]

4. Ritual representations and hyperreality
We have noted, in the last chapter, that the tempos characteristic of ritual performance may affect the conciousness of performers, leading them into the social and cognitive condition that we, following Turner, designate *communitas*. In this chapter we have further implied that the multiplicity of the significata of such ritual representations as *rumbim* brought together in ritual may construct meanings so abstruse and so charged as to be ineffable and thus force consciousness out of the mundane. We may add here that the physical characteristics of the representations themselves – objects, acts, or combinations of the two – are often themselves of a nature to encourage profound alterations of consciousness quite separately from what they signify. The primary purpose of some ritual constituents, like the use of drugs, sensory overload, sensory deprivation and alternation between overload and deprivation, seems to be to disrupt mundane canons of reality. Some of these features have been touched upon earlier and need not be considered further, while others merit review or further discussion.

In chapter 5 we considered the characteristics of ritual places and, in retrospect, can readily understand that the characteristics of many of them would deeply affect the consciousness of those inside them. They are often unusual, or even remarkable, in several respects. They may be difficult of access, located in high places, for instance, or in the depths of caves. As such they are separated from the daily world, but even when the separation from the daily world is not great there is likely to be a boundary between them, the crossing of which is a marked act, not always open to all and often requiring some sort of formal gesture or posture.

Some ritual places are themselves overwhelming. They are often large, beautiful and full of objects both rich and strange. The architecture itself may represent a *Logos*, as in a Gothic cathedral, with its cruciform design, representations of supernatural beings ordered on the upper reaches of the walls and ceilings, its arrangement of Biblical episodes rendered in stained glass on its east, west, north and south walls, its general proportions based upon the intervals in Gregorian chant (von Simpson 1964), and, more profoundly, upon discussions of Pythagorean numbers and relations among them (St. Augustine). The individual is thus physically encompassed by an extraordinarily compelling representation of the Christian cosmos.

And such places soon become ancient. In non-literate societies, as we have seen, five or so generations – not much more than a century – is sufficient to exceed the limits of living memory. It thus may not have taken many generations for the frequenters of Lascaux or Altamira to take the works on their walls and ceilings to have been eternal. Among the literate, it takes longer for places to become ancient, and it is difficult or even impossible for them to attain the status of the eternal, but the literate are nevertheless moved by the fact that the 1,000-year-old temple is, indeed, 1,000 years old. As such its perdurance is an index of the perdurance of the order it represents and it becomes venerable in both senses of the word, tending to lead those it encloses out of ordinary consciousness into the state of mind or attitude called veneration or reverence.

We have also noted that the multivocal nature of ritual's representations has a cognitive effect. Turner's *mudyi* tree, the Maring *rumbim*, each bring together multiple significata which, if not grouped around two poles, do range in nature from the physiological and sexual through the organizational to the ideological and cosmic. The contemplation of such representations, in which the ideological significata are emotionally saturated by their association with the physiological, constitutes an attempt to grasp whatever may be similar in or common to the significata somehow unified by their integrated, or at least singular representation. Given the disparate nature of the significata such similarities or commonalities may be so abstract as to be inarticulable in ordinary discourse. Their grasp may push consciousness in the direction of metaphor and gestalt thinking and away from the rationality implicit in linear discourse. To anticipate a later section, it moves away from what William James meant by the term "thought" toward what he meant by "experience".

Intensification of emotion is an aspect of consciousness alteration, and

it almost goes without saying that the significata of ritual representations
– the general points of the ritual – are generally capable of arousing
strong emotions, thus altering consciousness. Also obvious, but less
frequently remarked upon and therefore meriting rather more discussion,
is that the physical nature of some signs themselves, distinct from their
significata, can carry consciousness away from rational thought toward
an awareness characterized more by feeling than by logic. We can think
here first of ritual acts themselves. Consider the Maring pig sacrifice. The
killer, having worked himself into a sobbing state in an address to the
ancestor to whom the pig is offered, runs back and forth, screaming,
before the tethered animal, who becomes alarmed a second or two before
it is dispatched, usually by a single blow delivered on the run with a
heavy club. The animal's eyes roll up into its head, blood drips from its
nose and ears. Death has been witnessed and death, even of livestock, is
strong stuff. But a Maring pig is not mere livestock. Pigs are named and
live in individual stalls separated from the front rooms of their mistress's
houses by nothing more than railings between which they can project
their snouts, to be petted, scratched, or hand-fed tid-bits, and when they
were piglets they were led by women to their gardens on leashes where
they could be looked out for. If the garden were distant the piglet might
even be carried there and back in a string bag. Maring pigs, all in all, live
more like pets than livestock until they are killed by those who have
named and nurtured them. Both their deaths and the act of killing them
seem deeply moving to their killers and to witnesses, and it is hardly
surprising that women keen as if for deceased kinfolk when their pigs are
sacrificed.

Other foods and their ingestion figure, albeit rather less dramatically,
in many Maring rituals. When the Maring uproot *rumbim* they cook
marsupials and the fruit of the *marita pandanus* (from which a rich sauce
is made) together for the first time since the *rumbim* had been planted a
decade or more earlier. After pigs are sacrificed to Red Spirits, the
pandanus fruit is presented to the Smoke Woman by chanting men
proceeding in a circle around the fire upon which stones for the ovens
have been heating. When the chant is finished one of the men seizes the
fruit – which is about three feet long – leaps onto the hot stones barefoot
and there, bounding up and down, he pierces it with a cassowary bone
dagger, which also serves as a spoon to feed each person his or her first
mouthful of *marita* and marsupial after they are cooked together. (For a
fuller account of this ritual see Rappaport 1984: 174ff., picture following
page 140.) This ritual seemed very moving to the participants in Tsem-

baga in 1962, many of whom broke into sobs during the presentation of the *marita* fruit to the Smoke Woman. The significata of the marsupials and the pandanus, their being brought together, and the achievement of the social and ecological conditions allowing them to be brought together must have accounted for much of the effect. Marsupials are said to be the "pigs of the Red Spirits," who, like Smoke Woman, dwell in high places. Pandanus fruit is, for the most part, grown in the lower altitudes and is associated with spirits of the low ground. Cooking and eating them together is an important step toward mending a world broken by the last round of warfare.

But, granting to all of these significata their emotional due, we may ask why the reintegration of the world is represented by food, its cooking and its consumption. It would seem, from a consideration of the significata alone, that they could have been as well represented by bringing together anything from the high and low regions, but it may be that steaming in an oven integrates, mixes, blends, dissolves distinctions to a degree not easily duplicated by other semiotic means available to the Maring, and the dissolution of a distinction is one of the main points of the ritual. I would, nevertheless, suggest that food in and of itself is powerfully evocative, especially for people who, in the absence of cash economies, produce what they themselves need both to sustain themselves and to fulfill their social obligations. Food for such people is stuff of the deepest concern, equivalent in seriousness to money in Western society. Whereas their significata may invest the pandanus fruit and the marsupials with some of their affective potency, so may the fruit and marsupials, reciprocally, invest the significata with some of theirs, and ingestion establishes an extraordinarily intimate relationship of participants to representations.

Death, killing and eating may form the subject matter of much discourse, ritual and non-ritual. We are not, however, concerned here with death and killing as significata but as *signs*, and ask what, as signs, they can possibly represent, and what such powerful signs can bring to ritual. Similar questions can be asked about certain bodily substances, blood and semen, both commonly and prominently used in rituals in aboriginal Australia (blood, see Meggitt 1965, 1966, Stanner n.d.) and Papua New Guinea (blood and semen, see Van Baal 1966, Kelly 1974, Herdt 1984 *passim*, Herdt (ed.) 1982: *passim*, etc.)

Blood and semen, as profoundly associated as they are with pain, pleasure, procreation and life itself must have extraordinarily profound signifying capacities. Clearly, it is one thing to say wine represents blood, another to use blood itself as a sign. The same can be said of phallic representations. It is one thing to represent the male organ by a long object and to take its further signification or object to be the god Shiva, or perhaps fertility, procreation, sex, fruitfulness or whatever, quite another to use sexual substance itself as a sign.

And whereas wine may be used to represent blood, what can blood itself be representing? Or semen? It may often be that they participate in such culturally organized processes as gender construction (see Herdt 1982, 1984, G. Lewis 1980), but sometimes they may seem to signify no more than themselves. Yet they do so with a "force" so far exceeding that of wine or long objects as to be "something else". Whereas wine merely symbolizes blood, blood *indicates* blood. The use of such a substance as a sign differs, however, from the use of wine, for example, not only in being indexical rather than symbolic but in pointing to further meanings so profound as not to be articulable in words but unplumbable by any of the ordinary forces of human signification, and representable only by the stuff of life itself.

The use of such substances as blood and semen as signs thus points to the limitations of signification, and may constitute attempts to push past representation in all its forms to naked, immediate existence, to the *Ding an Sich*, or, more clearly, to what C. S. Peirce called "Firstness," "the utter Thisness, or existence of things" (Hoopes 1991: 10); "the consciousness which can be included within an instant of time, consciousness of quality, without recognition or analysis" (Peirce 1885, reprinted in Hoopes 1991: 185); "that whose being is simply in itself, not referring to anything or lying beyond anything" (Peirce, in Hoopes 1991: 189, see also Carrington 1993: ch. 3).[4]

This account proposes that using "The Real Thing" as a sign establishes for the entire ritual proceeding and for its ineffably profound significata a condition that might be called "Hyperreality" beside which mundane reality pales and is, for the duration of the ritual at least, dismissed.

A sense of Hyperreality constitutes a movement of consciousness away from mundane rationality and this movement may well be aided and abetted by the intimate relationship of ritual's performers to such signs. That performers participate in the representations they enact has, of course, been emphasized since chapter 4 but here we note a further degree of intimacy in the relationship between performance and representation. If blood and semen are to be used in ritual they must first be obtained. The stuff, therefore, is not simply blood or semen but *my* blood or *our* semen. That this is the case, it is plausible to assume, magnifies its signifying power substantially, and must help to move consciousness away from domination by quotidian thought.

The intimacy of the relationship between ritual participant, sign and signification in the ritual projection, as it were, of one's own life-stuff out of one's body and into the world recalls the widespread class of practices, touched upon in chapter 5, of modifying the human body in conformity to culturally-ordained patterns. Familiar examples of such incarnation or embodiment include circumcision, subincision, scarification, and septum-piercing,[5] all of which not only transform the body permanently in manners which tacitly proclaim the enduring predominance of the conceptions being embodied, but achieve such transformation through the infliction of considerable, often great, pain. E. Valentine Daniel has argued (1984: ch. 7) that ritually inflicted pain leads consciousness to Peirce's Firstness which is, in its purity, far from the rational consciousness that is supposed to prevail in everyday life.

5. Mending the world

We have approached here profound differences in the nature of the meaningfulness of liturgical representation on the one hand and ordinary prosaic discourse on the other. It may finally be observed that the distinctions of language cut the world into bits – categories, classes, oppositions, and contrasts. It is in the nature of language to make distinctions that not only serve as grounds for meaning, but for boundaries and barriers as well. It is, on the other hand, intrinsic to the chord-like or simultaneous dimension of liturgical representations, at once indexical, iconic and symbolic, to unite or reunite, the psychic, social, natural or cosmic processes which language distinguishes and which the exigencies of life pull apart.

Another point follows from the complexity of liturgical representations. Although liturgical orders are important in the regulation of social, political, and ecological relations in many societies, they cannot be said to "reflect" or "represent" those relations in any simple way. Liturgical orders are not simply social or psychic orders played out and mystified in public representations. Some liturgies make no reference to existing social arrangements or, if they do, they may at the same time signify entities transcending the existing social order and values from which the social order has, in fact, fallen away, as well as processes internal to individuals. Liturgical orders in their wholeness do not simply or ultimately represent the social, economic, political or psychic orders prevailing. They represent – which is to say they re-present – themselves (see

Babcock 1973). Liturgical orders bind together disparate entities, processes, and phenomenal domains, and it is this bringing together, rather than what is bound together, that is peculiar to them. They are meta-orders, or orders of orders. If we were to characterize in a phrase their relationship to whatever lies outside of them, we might say that they mend ever again worlds forever breaking apart under the blows of daily usage and the slashing distinctions of language.

Having proceeded through accounts of the sequential dimension in which significance is derived from one thing following another, and of the simultaneous dimension in which meaning is fabricated from the concurrence of significata, we are in a position to approach liturgy's third dimension, the hierarchical.

6. The hierarchical dimension of liturgical orders

When they are taken to be a unified whole, the corpus of understandings represented by the more or less invariant sequence of complex multi-vocalic representations that constitute the Maring liturgical order seem to be hierarchically organized, and this hierarchy has certain formal properties.[6]

At what may be considered the apex of the Maring conceptual structure are certain understandings, formal expression of which is largely confined to ritual, concerning the existence of spirits. These understandings, which I shall call "Ultimate Sacred Postulates," have certain interesting properties which, along with their basis in ritual's form and performance, will be discussed in the next chapter. Here I would simply note that the class of Ultimate Sacred Postulates includes such familiar examples as the Jewish declaration of faith called the *Shema* (Hear, O Israel, the Lord our God, the Lord is One) and the Creeds of Christians. No such creed or declaration is made explicit by the Maring, but postulates concerning the existence and power of spirits are implicit in the highly stylized addresses to those spirits occurring in all major rituals.

A second class or level of understandings, a level composed of what may be called "cosmological axioms," is closely associated with Ultimate Sacred Postulates. I include in this category Maring notions of the world as constituted by a set of oppositions between certain qualities which are, on the one hand, associated with the two general classes of spirits and, on the other hand, manifested in the social and physical world. Thus the hot, hard, dry, strong, cultural, spiritual and immortal are associated with the Red Spirits and substantiated in men, patrilineages, territori-

ality, warfare, high land and the upper portion of the body. In opposition, the low, soft, cold, moist, fecund, natural and mortal are associated with the Spirits of the Low Ground and substantiated in women,
gardening, pig husbandry and the lower portion of the body. I further
include among Maring cosmological axioms their conceptions concerning the mediation of these oppositions through ritual. Whereas the
oppositions *per se* are irreducible, the relationship of the opposed terms
is transformed, through the course of the cycle, from inimical to complementary.

Whereas some cosmological axioms are explicit in Maring exegeses of
their liturgical cycle and its elements, others are implicit in that cycle's
formal actions, in the transformations achieved by those actions and in
their order and progress. First among these implicit principles is that of
reciprocity. All assistance must be reciprocated, all trespasses compensated or avenged. A second concerns the relationship of humans to
spirits. All important human undertakings require at least the acquiescence of spirits, and for many activities, particularly warfare, their active
assistance is crucial. Like the principle of reciprocity, this undertaking is
seldom, if ever, explicitly articulated, but it is implicit in virtually all
invocations of spirits. A corollary of both of these axioms taken together
is that spirits must be repaid for their help in past warfare if they are to
provide the help needed for success in the future.

It should be clear that I have been using the term "cosmological
axioms" to refer to assumptions concerning the fundamental structure of
the universe or, to put it differently, to refer to the paradigmatic relationships in accordance with which the cosmos is constructed. I do not
identify this class with what are generally called "values," but values may
be implicit in them, entailed by them, or even be derived as theorems for
them. For instance, the high value that the Maring place upon unity or
integrity is at least implicit in the progress of the ritual cycle from a
condition of maximum segregation of parts of the universe from each
other to one in which segregation is radically reduced. The negative value
placed upon the failure to fulfill reciprocal obligations follows from the
assumption that reciprocity is fundamental to cosmic structure. Given
this assumption, lapses in reciprocity are violations of the order constituting the world.

I have distinguished cosmological axioms as a class from Ultimate
Sacred Postulates as a class on several grounds. First, and most obviously, Ultimate Sacred Postulates are typically devoid of material significata, whereas cosmological axioms are concerned with relationships

among qualities that may themselves be sensible (e.g. hot and cold), and which are manifested in physical and social phenomena (e.g. relationships between men and women). It follows that if cosmological axioms are manifested in social and physical phenomena, the occasions for their expression and the manner of their expression are more general and varied than those in which it is appropriate to express Ultimate Sacred Postulates. The proprietous expression of the latter is largely confined to ritual, whereas the expression of the former is implicit in much of daily life. Thirdly, and related, whereas Ultimate Sacred Postulates, by themselves, are either devoid of explicit social content or very vague in this regard, cosmological axioms are more specific and often do have direct explicit and substantial political, social and ecological import. Fourthly, cosmological axioms serve as the *logical* basis from which both specific rules of conduct and the proprieties of social life can be derived. Ultimate Sacred Postulates are more remote from social life. They do not themselves provide a logical foundation for it, nor even for cosmological structure (which, I have asserted, is axiomatic). But they are not otiose. They *sanctify*, which is to say *certify*, the entire system of understandings in accordance with which people conduct their lives. Without sanctification the axioms of cosmology would remain arbitrary, constituting nothing more than attempts at explanation. When a cosmology is sanctified it is no longer merely conceptual nor simply explanatory nor even speculative. It becomes something like an assertion, statement, description or report of the way the world in fact *is*. Cosmological axioms are performative, or rather, metaperformative. To invert the hierarchical metaphor, whereas Ultimate Sacred Postulates do not themselves provide the logical ground upon which the usages and rules of social life are established, they provide the ground, deeper than logic and beyond logic's reach, upon which cosmological structure can be founded. It follows that cosmological structures can change – expand, contract, or even be radically altered structurally – in response to changes in environmental or historical conditions without changes in, or even challenge to, Ultimate Sacred Postulates. Being devoid of material terms, Ultimate Sacred Postulates are not fully of this world and can be regarded as eternal verities. Being devoid of explicit social content they not only can sanctify any and all conventions, but changes in them as well, for they remain irrevocably committed to nothing specific.

A third and yet "lower" level in hierarchies of understanding is composed of the yet more specific rules (to which I have already alluded) governing the conduct of relations among the persons, qualities, conditions and states of affairs whose oppositions are decreed by cosmological axioms (e.g., between men and women, men and "cold" foods, etc.). These rules are, of course, expressed in the performance of rituals, but they also govern the behavior of everyday life. Among the Maring, taboos of all sorts are prominent among such rules.

The oppositions of the cosmological level, including as they do terms that may be materially manifested, are more concrete and have more direct social import than do the Ultimate Sacred Postulates sanctifying them. So, in turn, are rules of conduct more concrete than the cosmological oppositions which they substantiate. They are, therefore, able both to "realize" those oppositions and to provide them with the specific social import that they by themselves do not clearly and unambiguously possess. It is one thing to establish men and women cosmologically as members of opposing sets. It is quite another to exclude women from participating in ritual on such grounds.

The rules of the third level, then, transform cosmology into conduct. It is important to note that, as the cosmological structure of the second level can be modified without challenge to Ultimate Sacred Postulates, so can these rules accommodate change without affecting the oppositions they make material. I shall return to this matter shortly.

Although I have observed in passing that cosmological axioms and the rules which make them concrete may change in response to historical or environmental change, our account so far may seem to suggest that liturgical orders somehow manufacture understandings which are then imposed upon the world external to them. So they do, but this is not the whole of the matter. Liturgies also import understandings of the external world in the form of formal indices of prevailing conditions. These importations form a fourth level in hierarchies of understandings.

Liturgical orders obviously differ in what conditions prevailing in the external world their performance may indicate, but intrinsic to all rituals is indication of some aspect of the contemporary social, psychic or physical state of the performers or their environments. States of affairs indicated by Maring rituals were discussed in detail in earlier chapters. Here it is sufficient to recall that indications of the states of environmental relations are prominent among the understandings imported into the Maring cycle. The uprooting of *rumbim*, for instance, indicates that relations among such phenomena external to ritual as the size and rate of increase of the pig population, the amount of land in cultivation, the intensity of women's labor, the patience and health of women, the frequency of garden invasions by pigs, and other factors as well, have reached a certain complex composite state which, in material terms, can be described as "all the pigs the groups can maintain or tolerate." When imported into the liturgical order, however, this description of a material condition is invested with cosmological meaning and transferred into "sufficient pigs to repay the ancestors."

It is important to emphasize the highly flexible nature of the relationship of rules to indicators of environmental conditions. For instance, the rules concerning what and when to repay spirits specify neither precise numbers of pigs nor particular dates. What constitutes a sufficient number of pigs to repay ancestors, being a function of relations among a number of variables whose states may be constantly changing, varies from instance to instance, and the length of time required for their accumulation is elastic. But the rules are not only flexible. They are also readily changed. Late pre-contact Maring history provides an example. In 1955 envoys from the Kauwassi, the largest of the Maring groups, invited the Tukmenga to join them in a concerted attack upon the Monamban whose territory lay between theirs. The Tukmenga at first refused, protesting that their *rumbim* remained in the ground, for they had not yet fully repaid the spirits for their help in the last war. After prolonged discussion they were persuaded by the Kauwassi that the spirits could be satisfied by a different procedure requiring killing fewer pigs and no delay. A few pigs were, accordingly, immediately killed and laid on the roofs of *ringi ying*, no doubt as offerings to Red Spirits, and the Tukmenga stormed off to join the Kauwassi in routing the Monamban. Informants told Vayda that this procedure had always been acceptable, but could not, or at least did not, cite any precedents, although asked to do so (Rappaport 1968: 152). We note in this example that axioms concerning reciprocity, reintegration and the necessity to enlist the aid of spirits in important enterprises remained unchallenged while the rules for realizing those axioms in human affairs were changed.

It should be noted here, if only in passing, that in our accounts of the hierarchical and sequential dimensions of liturgical orders, we have touched upon their adaptive characteristics. The sequential dimension of the Maring liturgical order is able to expand and contract, in response to fluctuations in indications of material conditions. Such *adaptive elasticity* may be a property widespread among non-calendrical ritual cycles especially. Flexibility is inherent not only in relations among the levels of understanding hierarchically ordered by the Maring ritual cycle, but in the low specificity of the terms for conforming to rules and the openness of rules themselves – and, possibly even cosmological axioms – to change if historical and environmental pressures are strong enough. It is of interest that when the Kauwassi were persuading the Tukmenga to change their rules concerning the repayment of the spirits they were the largest of the Maring local groups in their own right; their numbers were further swollen by refugees, and their land was the most degraded in Maringdom.

In this brief discussion of adaptive aspects of the relationship between the understandings generated by liturgical orders themselves and understandings imported into them, I have touched once again upon ritual's sequential dimension. I have approached the three dimensions of liturgical order separately, but it is well to keep in mind that the place of any component of ritual may be defined in terms of all of ritual's dimensions concurrently. The Maring ritual cycle is a *sanctified rule-governed sequence* of formal acts and utterances during which *cosmological oppositions* substantiated in *multivocalic representations* are transformed from a state of antagonism and fragmentation into one of complementarity and wholeness. Concomitant to these transformations are transformations in relationships among persons, social groups and ecological systems. This characterization of Maring liturgical order recognizes the concurrence not only of its sequential and simultaneous dimensions, but also of its hierarchically organized understandings.

At the apogee of this hierarchy stand a limited number of postulates concerning spirits. The significata of such Ultimate Sacred Postulates are not material in any ordinary sense, and whatever it is that they postulate is taken to be immutable. Cosmological structure is elaborated in a second class, a class of axioms by or through which the spirits postulated are associated with elements and relations of the material and social world in a set of abstract structural oppositions that apply to both: as the Red Spirits are hot, hard, dry and strong, so are men; as the Spirits of the Low Ground are cold, soft, wet and fertile, so are women. These relations are given greater concreteness and further specificity in yet a third level of understandings constituted of rules and taboos concerning action appropriate or inappropriate in terms of the understandings of the cosmological structure which inform them. Indications of material and social conditions immediately prevailing in the everyday world are imported into ritual, where they constitute a fourth level of understandings, and are translated there into cosmological terms.

It is clear from this account that the hierarchical organization of the understandings encoded in the Maring liturgical order, and liturgical orders generally, has several aspects or, to put it differently, is expressed along several continua. The significata of Ultimate Sacred Postulates are conceptual, the significata of informative sentences indicating environmental conditions are social and physical. Rules concerned with *classes* of conditions and actions, and principles stipulating structure lie between the concreteness of the significata of environmental indicators and the immateriality of whatever is represented by Ultimate Sacred Postulates. Related to materiality and explicit in the account just offered is a continuum of social specificity. Indications of environmental conditions are high in specificity (whether they are *precise* is another question), whereas Ultimate Sacred Postulates in themselves are low in material or social specificity, or even devoid of such specificity altogether. ("The Lord Our God the Lord is One" in itself specifies nothing in this world of matter and energy.)

It has also become clear that the temporal entailments of liturgical orders are not limited to their sequential dimension, but are intrinsic to its hierarchical dimension as well. We may consider here the differences in the longevity of the understandings assigned to the several levels of these orders. Ultimate Sacred Postulates are taken to be ageless and do seem, in fact, to persist for long durations. The *Shema* of the Jews may have endured for 3,000 years; the Nicene Creed has remained unchanged since AD 325. Cosmological axioms may be taken by those accepting them to be as enduring as Ultimate Sacred Postulates, but are probably less so, and the specific rules which, in realizing those axioms, govern social behavior are likely to be yet shorter-lived. Because their significata are relatively ephemeral, so must be indications of contemporary conditions. Differences in the longevity of understandings may or may not be recognized by those entertaining them, but whether or not they are, in ascending from understandings of contemporary conditions to Ultimate Sacred Postulates there is a progression from the quick to the eternal.

It has also been evident that the relationship of the ephemeral to the eternal is a relationship between the ever-changing and the never-changing. The most labile of the values (in a broad sense) represented in liturgical orders are both the most specific and the most concrete. The number of pigs sufficient to repay spirits varies from one *kaiko* to the next in response to changes in demographic, social, political and environmental circumstances. Such variation in the number of pigs deemed sufficient is in conformity to highly flexible rules which may themselves be maintained unchanged through changes in the magnitudes of the reference values they set. But as we have seen, such rules can themselves be changed while higher order cosmological axioms or principles remain unchanged. In like manner, the latter can be elaborated, modified or changed without Ultimate Sacred Postulates being affected. These, taken to be immutable, can remain unchanged as all understandings of "lower order" change. Indeed, they are likely to be changed only in response to, or as an effect of, fundamental social or political change, but they may persist even in the face of profound upheaval. We may contemplate all of the change that has occurred in Catholic countries since the Creeds were first enunciated. The hierarchy is one of mutability as well as longevity, specificity and concreteness.

Other aspects of hierarchy, although they may be present in the Maring ritual cycle, seem more apparent in the liturgical orders of other societies. Rituals vary, of course, in their gravity and in the nature of their significance. The consequences of some seem limited to the performative achievement of particular social effects, while the impact of others appears broader and more varied. The planting of *rumbim* not only transforms war into peace, warriors into farmers and aliens into brothers, all performative actions; it establishes as institutional or social fact Ultimate Sacred Postulates and elements of both cosmic structure and the social conventions through which cosmic structure is realized. In contrast, the Mass hardly refers to the existing social order at all. It simply establishes the existence and identity of the Trinitarian God and the terms of His relationship with the faithful and, in the communion, it provides an opportunity for the ritually pure (those in a state of Grace) to indicate their participation in this relationship. The Mass thus seems to be more limited in its scope than the planting of *rumbim*. This is not to say that Catholicism ignores social affairs in the societies in which it prevails. It surely does not. Its liturgical order simply relegates the establishment of the particulars of social orders and the performative achievement of social effects to other rituals.

We approach here relations of contingency among the rituals constituting liturgical orders. If, for instance, a king is to be crowned in the name of God in a coronation ritual, or if a person is to swear in the name of God in the ritual of a courtroom, it is necessary for the existence of that God to have already been established. This is done in Catholic countries in a distinct (but not always separate) ritual, the Mass. This is to say the coronation ritual and the Courtroom oath are contingent upon the Mass.

Relations of contingency may become several layers deep. For instance, the efficacy of the ritual in which a Christian king laid hands on an afflicted person to cure him of scrofula, the disease called "The King's

Evil," was contingent upon the king in fact being the properly anointed king. The ritual for curing the King's Evil was, thus, contingent upon the Coronation which, in turn, was contingent upon the Mass.

There may be certain advantages in establishing fundamental and contingent understandings in distinct rituals. It can at least be argued that the segregation of the ultimate insulates it from the vicissitudes and exigencies of social life. Ultimate Sacred Postulates are more easily preserved immaculate if they are kept at some distance from the instrumental acts that they endorse.

Liturgical orders surely differ in the extent to which they segregate the fundamental from the contingent. It may be suggested that such segregation is to be expected in religions possessed of universalizing aspirations, for their Ultimate Sacred Postulates must gain the acceptance of individuals living in a range of societies differing in their institutions, and supra-cultural acceptance may be facilitated by the separation of universal postulates from social particularities. For similar reasons we would expect such a separation even within particular societies if the division of labor is complex and subcultural distinctions are elaborated. Subcultural distinctions may, of course, be grounded in ethnic, regional, occupational or class differences. It may be suggested that participation in that for which ultimacy is claimed establishes unity, whereas contingent rituals and contingent understandings establish distinctions. Complex societies face problems of maintaining unity, and the separation of the unifying ultimate from contingent distinctions may abet unity.

But even in "simple" societies, societies in which the division of labor is undeveloped, regional differences slight, and "stratification" limited to relations between persons of different age and sex, there is likely to be some segregation of fundamental and contingent elements into separate rituals. The planting of *konc kump amame* around women's houses not only follows but is contingent upon the *rumbim* planting ritual. The dedication of all marsupials hunted and trapped to the Red Spirits who provided them is also contingent upon the establishment of the existence of the Red Spirits as a social fact in *rumbim* planting and other rituals.

The segregation of the fundamental from the contingent may be most developed in "complex" societies, perhaps for the reasons already addressed. That there is some segregation in "simple" societies may propose, however, that there are further and more general grounds for it. I would suggest, in light of our brief discussion of adaptiveness, that the separation of the fundamental from the contingent enhances flexibility and continuity. It may be easier to modify, transform, replace or simply dispose of contingent elements if they are less tightly bound to the fundamental.

It is well to emphasize at this point, however, that to distinguish the fundamental from the contingent is not necessarily to separate them in time and space. Fundamental and contingent elements can often, if not always, be distinguished within the same ritual. In a modern Jewish sabbath service the *Shema* is fundamental, the sermon is contingent. The pig sacrifices associated with *rumbim* are contingent; the *rumbim* planting itself may be taken to be fundamental. The pervasiveness of the fundamental/contingent distinction suggests that it is to be accounted for in terms at least as general, or even more general, than those of adaptive logic. These considerations may include the structural requisites of complex systems that include understandings, institutions, and physical phenomena and also, possibly, the structure of human comprehension. Be this as it may, the hierarchy of understandings ordered by liturgy is, among other things, a hierarchy of contingency.

The distinction between the fundamental and the contingent is closely related to the distinction between the fundamental and the instrumental. The coronation, for instance, is not only contingent upon the Mass. It is also socially instrumental, transforming princes into kings. Its instrumentality is not limited to the merely social, however. It is also presumed to serve the divinity whose existence is constituted in the Mass, the ritual upon which it is contingent, for it furthers the establishment of his order on earth.

It may be suggested that Ultimate Sacred Postulates are often, if not always, taken to set the ultimate goals which instrumentality serves, but to be themselves devoid of instrumentality or purposefulness. They are also, of course, low in social and material specificity. These ultimate goals – the wills of the Gods which humanity serves, or to which, at least, it must conform – are given increased specificity in cosmological axioms and the values that can be derived, perhaps as theorems, from them. To maintain the world order stipulated in cosmological axioms and sanctified by Ultimate Sacred Postulates is to serve the divinities established by those postulates. In the Maring case, the world order is maintained through obedience to rules for conducting a ritual cycle, which is to say that the rules are instrumental with respect to the maintenance of cosmological structure at the same time that they transform social and environmental relations in conformity to that structure. Indications of contemporary conditions – the fourth of the levels of sentences ordered by liturgy – are not in an explicit or obvious way instrumental. The conditions which they represent do, however, stimulate, at least as far as non-calendrical rituals are concerned, the liturgical performances that serve divinity by maintaining the cosmic structure it has ordained. When a Maring group has as many pigs as it can support, there are sufficient pigs to repay the ancestors. A *kaiko* is held which maintains a sanctified cosmic structure by reintegrating the broken world through reduction in taboos upon fulfillment of debts to spirits. If ultimate goals are implicit in Ultimate Sacred Postulates, and if the specification of those goals inheres in cosmological axioms, then indications of environmental conditions are representations of the efficient causes of the purposeful instrumental actions stipulated by the rules for conducting ritual cycles. The hierarchy, this is to say, proceeds down from ultimate goal, through specific goals to instrumental and purposeful formal action to, finally, stimuli to action.

A related way to approach the hierarchical dimension of purposefulness and instrumentality is to note that the four types of sentences involved in liturgy constitute directives of different order. Cosmological axioms can be taken to be *principles* stipulating enduring features of the cosmos' general structure and values (e.g., reciprocity and wholeness) with which there must be compliance and which may need to be maintained through human action. They themselves do not stipulate the ways in which compliance is to be achieved. The stipulation of procedures lies in the domain of the *rules* prohibiting, requiring or permitting particular actions under particular categories of circumstances. In contrast to rules, sentences informative of prevailing states of affairs are situation- rather than category-specific. As such they may, in effect, constitute *commands*, although if they are cast in language at all they are unlikely to be put in the imperative mood. That there is "a sufficient number of pigs to repay the ancestors" is a command to a local group of Maring to stage a *kaiko*.

It is less obvious that Ultimate Sacred Postulates constitute directives than it is that the other types of sentences do. They are, it is true, even lower in behavioral or social specificity than are principles, but this neither disqualifies them nor vitiates their importance. They themselves do not stipulate the actions to be undertaken in particular circumstances, nor under particular categories of circumstances, nor do they even enunciate the general principles in the service of which these actions should be undertaken. They do, however, provide the ground for those principles. If cosmological axioms or principles reveal the divine will and its effects, then Ultimate Sacred Postulates point to the divinity that possesses that will and who is to be served by conformity to it. Moreover, such postulates may seem to provide ultimate criteria with respect to which principles, or even entire systems of principles, may be assessed and found wanting, and criteria are, of course, tacit directives. We are all too familiar with orthodoxy's and establishment's defense of their interests by declaring principles, or cosmological axioms, other than those they espouse to be heretical or "Godless," but it should be kept in mind that orthodox cosmological and social principles can be threatened as well as confirmed by reference to Ultimate Sacred Postulates. The motto of the English peasants' rebellion of 1381, "When Adam delved and Eve span who was then the gentleman?" challenged the principles in accordance with which medieval society was governed. It is true that no Ultimate Sacred Postulate was explicit in the dictum guiding Wat Tyler, John Ball and their followers, but such a postulate is surely implicit in its invocation of the first chapters of holy writ with their accounts of history's beginning, and it is tacitly to such a postulate that appeal was made for the endorsement of principles of social relations radically different from those prevailing. In this instance the alternative principle for which the endorsement of the ultimate was invoked was social equality, but it is important to distinguish this principle, at once cosmological, social and moral, from the postulate endorsing it, which can be assumed to correspond in substance to the creeds of Catholicism.

To note, as we did a few paragraphs ago, that the efficient cause of a ritual's performance may lie outside of the liturgical order of which it is a part is not to propose that the efficacy of that performance also has its source in the everyday world outside of the liturgical order. It does not. Our account suggests, indeed, that the hierarchical dimension of liturgical orders has an efficacious aspect. The healing efficacy of the king's laying on of hands follows from his being crowned and anointed king by the grace of God, who is the ultimate font of all efficacy. Efficacy, this is to say, flows from the fundamental and ultimate to the instrumental and contingent, through which it is focused upon the social or physical processes that originally stimulated its invocation.

Authority is closely related to efficacy, of course, and that the fundamental and ultimate is more authoritative than that which is contingent upon it seems too obvious to require comment. It also seems obvious, although the formal definition of sanctity awaits the next chapter, that the hierarchy is one of sanctity as well. Commonsense notions of sanctity are sufficient for us to have noted that the ordering of sentences encoded in liturgical orders proceeds from postulates which are ultimately sacred through cosmological axioms which are not sacred but are highly sanctified to rules, which may also be rather highly sanctified to, finally, sanctified indications of prevailing conditions.

In sum, relations among the understandings represented in liturgical orders are organized into concurrent hierarchies of specificity, concreteness, longevity, mutability, contingency, instrumentality, efficacy, authority and sanctity. The Ultimate Sacred Postulates crowning these hierarchies of understanding are devoid of concreteness, low in social specificity, and taken to be eternal, immutable, ultimately efficacious, absolutely authoritative, fundamental rather than contingent or instrumental and, of course, intrinsically sacred. Indications of current states of affairs, in contrast, are high in specificity and concreteness, ephemeral, labile, contingent, subject to authority rather than authoritative, acted upon rather than instrumental or efficacious, and merely sanctified rather than inherently sacred. The ordering virtues of the hierarchical principle are not limited, in liturgy, to the understandings represented. They are also expressed in rhetorical, logical and formal aspects of the representations themselves. Understandings of different order constitute directives of different order. That they may also be of different "logical type" has been implied by the terms referring to them – axioms, theorems, procedural rules and statements of fact. Ultimate Sacred Postulates comprise a further type, standing beyond fact or logic but serving as a ground for them.

One further aspect of the hierarchical dimension of liturgical orders, although implicit in the foregoing discussion, should be made explicit at the end. After consideration of the formal characteristics of the concepts ordered hierarchically in liturgy, and of differences in the nature of their meaningfulness, the matter of the invariance of ritual representations may be obvious and even seem trivial. It will be argued in the next chapter, however, that liturgical invariance is the ground of the sacred.

It is important to note that the most durable elements of liturgical orders, and those performed with greatest punctilio are usually those whose significata are spiritual, or primarily spiritual, rather than those whose significata are social or material or mainly so. Ultimate Sacred Postulates are likely to be least variant of all of ritual's elements. Our hierarchy is not only a hierarchy of understandings and meanings, authority and efficacy, logical type and imperative form, but of invariance of expression as well. That invariance is associated with sanctity was, perhaps, suggested by the discussion of eternity in the last chapter, but will be explored more explicitly in chapter 9.

At the end of these chapters on ritual's dimensions it is worth observing that a single liturgical order may encompass understandings that include Ultimate Sacred Postulates; cosmological axioms concerning the structure of relations among spirits, qualities, persons, things, and processes; rules for transforming these relations; and indications of prevailing states of society and nature. This is to establish a unity or integrity of understanding that may seem highly meaningful to those grasping it and that may be tenuous or lacking in societies poor in ritual. It may further be suggested, in light of discussions in chapter 5, that the understandings embodied by liturgical orders may seem particularly meaningful not only because of their relatively high degree of coherence, consistency and integrity, but also because rituals are constituted of acts as well as words and concepts. When an actor performs a liturgical order he participates in it, which is to say that he becomes a part of it, thus investing it with meaning of a profundity far beyond the ordinary. We shall return to this meaning in chapter 11.

9

The idea of the sacred

The terms "sacred" and "sanctity" have so far been left to whatever understandings readers have brought to them. It is time to develop a more explicit concept, and to explore its relationship to liturgy.

1. Sanctity defined

The sacred may be approached through consideration of a class of expressions in the last chapter called Ultimate Sacred Postulates. Examples include such familiar utterances as the *Shema* of the Jews, in abbreviated form, "Hear O Israel, the Lord Our God the Lord is One," and in the *Kalimat al Shahada* of Islam, "I testify that there is no god but One God, and I testify that Mohammed is his prophet" (Lane-Poole 1911). Catholic equivalents are summarized in the Creeds, but are expressed at greater length in the canon of the Eucharist, particularly in the preface, the closing doxology and the words of institution (see John Miller 1959: 183ff., 272ff.). The rituals of the Maring, and those of many other societies, probably including a great majority of non-literate peoples, are lacking in such formal credos, but the postulation of the persistence of deceased ancestors as sentient beings is implicit in the formal, stereotyped addresses to them that precede all sacrifices. Sioux doxologies accompanying the smoking of sacred pipes may also fall short of being formal credos, but are more explicit in expressing Ultimate Sacred Postulates than are Maring addresses to ancestors, establishing as they do the pervasiveness of Wakan-Tanka, the "Great Spirit," or "Great Holiness" (J. Brown 1954: 314, *passim*) and the existence of the spiritual beings associated with the six directions. Moreover, the act of smoking itself establishes the relationship of the smoker and those for whom he smokes to the spiritual beings postulated in a way which seems to resemble the way in which the

Eucharist serves the Catholic (J. Brown 1971: *passim*). Among the Navajo, according to Witherspoon, "Nearly every song and prayer in the elaborate ceremonial system uses [the expression] *sa'ah naaghaii bik'eh hozho* in its benediction. In fact, the entire ceremonial system is primarily designed to produce or restore the conditions symbolized by the phrase" (1977: 19). It is not easy to translate. The word *hozho*, which Kluckhohn took to be "the central idea in Navajo religious thinking" (1949: 368), "refers to the positive or ideal environment. It is beauty, harmony, good, happiness, and everything that is positive" (Witherspoon 1977: 24). *Sa'ah* "denotes something mature, ripe, experienced or aged" (Witherspoon 1977: 19). The verb form *naaghaii* means "to repeat" or "recur," *bik'eh* "according to," (Witherspoon 1977: 23). The phrase, then, which expresses the ideal of recurrence of the processes of growth, maturation and life in accordance with the principle of *hozho*, can be taken to be the Ultimate Sacred Postulate of the Navajo. Equivalent expressions are implicit if not explicit in the rituals of all religions, even those claiming to postulate no spiritual beings, or to espouse no creed. It is, in fact, by the presence of such sacred postulates, implicit or explicit, that we finally take liturgical orders to be religious.

Such understandings have peculiar qualities. The first is implicit in the word "postulate" itself. *To* postulate is to claim without demonstration; *a* postulate is that which is so claimed. Self-evidence or obviousness may be the basis, merely "for the sake of discussion," as we say, for demonstration to confirm or reject later.

All postulates are in a strict and almost trivial sense the products of performative acts (Austin 1962; see also chapter 4 above) because to postulate is to take an action of a sort. Ultimate Sacred Postulates are the products of illocutionary force in a deeper sense, however. Their substance is not merely claimed, postulated or advanced, but is constituted by the performativeness intrinsic to liturgical orders themselves. The performative establishment of convention, including conventional understandings, was discussed at some length in chapter 4. We may recall that if performatives are understood to be conventional acts achieving conventional effects then ritual is not simply performative, but meta-performative as well, for it not only may bring conventional states of affairs into being, but may also establish the very conventions in terms of which those conventional effects are realized. These conventions may include not only the procedures for achieving states of affairs, but the conventional understandings defining both those states of affairs, and the character of the cosmos in which those states of affairs, procedures, and understandings have their places. For instance, the Mass establishes as a social fact the existence of the God in whose name men are elevated to such conventional offices as kingship[1], through such conventional procedures as crowning, anointing and oathtaking.

Ultimate Sacred Postulates are, then, established by ritual's metaperformativeness. It is important to keep in mind, however, that the distinction between performative sentences and those that Austin called "constatives" (1962: 3, *passim*), statements, reports, descriptions and the like, is not always clear and straightforward. We touched upon this ambiguity at the end of chapter 5 in a discussion of the naturalization of the conventional, and it is highly relevant here. When that which is performatively established is a concept or understanding, the performative is immediately transformed into a constative. That is, a performative expression which in its liturgical utterance establishes some cosmic entity, quality or power as a social or cultural fact makes it subsequently possible to construe that self-same expression as a statement. To establish God's existence as a social fact through the ritual recitation of, say, the *Shema*, makes it immediately possible to interpret the sentence "The Lord Our God the Lord is One" as a report or description of a state of affairs existing independently of the sentence or, at least, any instance of its utterance. Such a construction is, of course, validated by the enduring public nature of Ultimate Sacred Postulates. None of those who has recited the *Shema* in the last 3,000 years or so has enunciated it *de novo*. They have been reiterating a formula which had established the One God long before they were born. Ultimate Sacred Postulates thus appear as statements to those who give voice to them. Their ultimately performative grounding nevertheless becomes clear when the effects of the cessation of their liturgical expression is considered. If no one any longer recited the *Shema*, "The Lord Our God the Lord Is One" would cease to be a social fact, whatever the supernatural case might be. As far as present day society is concerned, Jupiter, Woden, En-Lil and Marduk are no longer anything more than figments of ancient imaginings, for no one continues to establish or re-establish their being by calling their names in ritual. Recognition of the place of ritual in maintaining the ground of cosmic order seems explicit in some religions. We shall return to this later.

Neither the rhetorical ambiguity of Ultimate Sacred Postulates nor the metamorphoses which ambiguity may engender distinguishes the utterance of Ultimate Sacred Postulates from other performative acts. If, for instance, peace is established between warring parties by the ritual recitation of the words "Peace prevails," subsequent utterances of those same words can properly be construed as reports or descriptions. There are important differences, however, between Ultimate Sacred Postulates and the conventional states of affairs resulting from ordinary performative acts. First, as just noted, the Ultimate Sacred Postulate never wholly escapes from its performative grounding because the persistence of its validity as a social fact is contingent upon its continual enunciation. The sentence "Peace prevails," in contrast, may become fully constative because the persistence of the state of peace is not contingent upon the liturgical repetition of the words "Peace prevails" but on social behavior distinct from the ritual declaration.

This leads to another difference. The accuracy or truth of sentences such as "Peace prevails" *as statements* can be tested by reference to the world of events, and the same can be said for many postulates initially asserted without demonstration. This is not so of Ultimate Sacred Postulates because of their second major characteristic: they are generally devoid, or close to devoid, of material significata. They are, therefore, invulnerable to falsification by reference to evidence naturally available in this world. Even when some of their key terms are material others are not and so these postulates remain beyond the reach of evidence. Although the pharaohs were clearly alive and accessible to the sight and hearing of their subjects there was no way to falsify the postulate that they incarnated Horus. The divinity of Roman emperors, in similar fashion, could not be falsified. In a later chapter I shall consider problems intrinsic to the apotheosis of the living, and shall adduce material, social and logical reasons for taking such representations to be inappropriate, although not impossible, as subjects of ultimate sacred postulation. The point of importance here is simply that material evidence can never falsify Ultimate Sacred Postulates if all, or even some, of their key terms are non-material, as they seem always to be. We may note in passing a general point of contrast between Ultimate Sacred Postulates and constatives. Whereas Ultimate Sacred Postulates can be invalidated simply by being ignored or rejected, they cannot be falsified. On the other hand, constatives are open to falsification, but are not invalidated by being ignored or rejected.

It is less clear that Ultimate Sacred Postulates are beyond empirical verification. We may be confident, of course, that they cannot be verified by procedures acceptable to science. Even the apparently miraculous can always (at least in principle) be otherwise accounted for, and men of science are by principle committed to, and have been remarkably successful in, reducing the marvelous to the mundane. But canons of verification are culturally various, and evidence inadequate for scientists may be regarded by others as compelling. To say that a postulate is not verifiable scientifically is not to say that it cannot be verified by procedures that adduce what is asserted to be direct physical evidence. If a relativistic view of epistemology is adopted it becomes clear that what may be counted as knowledge can be secured by means that do not conform to the requirements of scientific validation. In a later chapter we shall return to subjective experience and examine its material nature. The point here is that the sense in which Ultimate Sacred Postulates are unverifiable is weaker than the sense in which they are unfalsifiable. Although they are absolutely unfalsifiable they are merely "scientifically" or "objectively" unverifiable.

The qualities of Ultimate Sacred Postulates that place them beyond empirical falsification or objective verification are matched by others that also render them invulnerable to falsification or verification by logic. Such sentences as "The Lord Our God the Lord Is One," and "There Is no god but God," and '*sa'ah naaghaii bik'eh hozho*' are not logically necessary (as is 2 + 2 = 4), nor does apparent violation of logical necessity (as in the notion of the unity of the trinity) seem to invalidate them for the congregations giving them voice. On the contrary, violation of logic makes their acceptance *ipso facto* consequential, their "non-rational," counter-intuitive, or even self-contradictory qualities invest them with mystery.[2]

In sum, the expressions I have called "Ultimate Sacred Postulates," those crowning bodies of religious discourse, typically possess certain peculiar features. On the one hand they can be falsified neither logically nor empirically. On the other hand they can be verified neither objectively nor logically. *And yet they are taken to be unquestionable.* I take this characteristic to be of the essence, defining sanctity *as the quality of unquestionableness imputed by congregations to postulates in their nature objectively unverifiable and absolutely unfalsifiable.*[3]

2. Sanctity as a property of discourse

Sanctity by this account is a property of religious discourse and *not* of the objects signified in or by that discourse. In this usage it is not Christ, for example, who is sacred, but the liturgical works and acts proclaiming his divinity that are sacred. Christ's divinity, distinct from its stipulation and acceptance, is another matter. Whereas sanctity in my usage is a quality *of discourse itself*, divinity, when it is stipulated, is a putative property of the subject matter asserted *in* that discourse.

As a quality of discourse, sanctity is to be distinguished not only from the divinity that may be attributed to the objects of that discourse, but also from *all* of the putative properties of such objects that they are dangerous or powerful or set apart or forbidden or awesome or "wholly other" or One, or whatever. It may well be that such objects, be they gods, spirits or cosmic processes, are often taken to be dangerous or merciful or creative or absolutely good. But the qualities attributed to divine objects are everywhere various and nowhere clear. Although some of their putative characteristics are widespread none (beyond, perhaps, a vague essential non-materiality) seems universal. In contrast, it is indisputable that divine objects are always identified as such in discourse and discourse is requisite to the predication of these objects with whatever more particular properties they are understood to possess. That a divine object is understood to be absolutely good, or dangerous, or set apart, or all-knowing, or all-encompassing, or an eternal being once incarnated through a virgin birth, is stipulated as unquestionable truth in liturgical discourse. It is the unquestionable quality of this discourse, and not the objects of this discourse or their putative qualities, that I take to constitute sanctity. To put this in another way, the characteristics of discourse are of higher logical type than are the characteristics of the objects of that discourse. Sanctity is a quality of meta-language, whereas divinity is a concept in object language. Sacred discourse is about, *among other things*, the divine.

Having distinguished the sacred from the divine, I must immediately warn that this distinction is sometimes systematically blurred in practice. Later we shall examine the tendency for unquestionableness itself to become apotheosized as a divine object, only noting here that the objects with which sacred discourse is concerned may themselves be conceived as elements of discourse. Language itself was apotheosized as a goddess in Vedic religion (Deshpande 1990) and there are other well-known instances of divinity conceived as Word. The conflation of the names of spirits and gods with the spirits of gods themselves also occurs. Such a view seems to be represented in Jewish mystical thought by the conception of the Torah as "not only made up of the names of God but as a whole the one great Name of God" (Scholem 1969: 30), or even God himself. As Gikatila put it: "His Torah is in Him, and that is what the Kabbalists say, namely that the Holy One, blessed be He, is in His Name and His Name is in Him, and that His Name is His Torah" (Scholem 1969: 44). Similarly, it seems clear that when Durkheim (1961) defined "sacred things" as those which are protected and isolated from the profane by interdiction he was referring to objects of discourse, but it does seem that sacred discourse and its material representations are often if not always protected by interdictions, that is, set apart from the quotidian by prescription, proscription and punctilio of expression. Such insulation of course contributes to unquestionableness, a matter to which we shall return.

3. The ground of sanctity

The definition of sanctity as the quality of unquestionableness imputed by congregations to certain postulates and to expressions associated with those postulates raises many questions. First, and most fundamental: if the unquestionable status of Ultimate Sacred Postulates rests upon neither logic nor mundane experience, upon what does it stand? I propose three grounds, all of which are located in ritual. Discussion of one of them must be postponed until a later chapter, but the other two, which are more closely related to each other, may be approached here.

The first has in fact already been discussed at some length. I argued in chapter 4 that by participating in a liturgical order a performer accepts, and indicates to himself and to others that he accepts, whatever is encoded in the canons of the order. To accept the canon is, after all, to agree not to question it, which is tantamount to declaring it to be unquestionable. One of the grounds of the unquestionableness of Ultimate Sacred Postulates is, then, the acceptance intrinsic to the performance of the canons in which they are represented.

As I further argued in chapter 4, acceptance does not in and of itself indicate belief or dissolve doubt, but that the acceptance indicated by participation in a liturgical order, being independent of belief, can be more profound and consequential than belief, for it makes it possible for the performer to transcend his own doubt, experience and reason by accepting in defiance of them. I also noted that some prominent theologians have suggested that faith necessarily includes an element of doubt. Indeed, faith may be at its most intense when the faithful suppress the questions that strong doubt raises.

It might be objected that faith is one thing and sanctity is another, and that I am confusing an attitude entertained by subjects' willingness to accept and a quality of the accepted object, namely its sanctity. But if postulates are invested with sanctity by those for whom they are sacred, such a conflation of the subject's attitude and the object's quality must be part of the process of sacralization. Tillich implied a similar conflation of subject and object in the conception of the divine as "ultimate concern":

"God is that which concerns man ultimately ... It means that whatever concerns a man ultimately becomes God for him, and conversely, it means that a man can be concerned ultimately only about that which is God for him" (Tillich 1951 I: 211). Earlier (1951 I: 1) he proposes that "Faith is the state of being ultimately concerned" and "Ultimate concern is the abstract translation of the great commandment, The Lord Our God the Lord is One, and you shall love the Lord your God with all your heart and with all your soul and with all your mind, and with all your strength." These passages apparently indicate an attempt to break down the distinction between ultimate concern as an attitude and as an object toward which such an attitude is directed. If the subject–object distinction is dissolved it becomes possible for humans to participate in the divine, a matter to which we shall return.

If their acceptance by individuals and congregations is one ground of the unquestionableness of Ultimate Sacred Postulates it is not the only one. The attitude of subjects who accord unquestionable status to certain expressions, namely Ultimate Sacred Postulates, is reinforced by an apparent quality of these postulates themselves. It is of interest that this quality is entailed by the self-same feature of liturgical performance that entails acceptance. Let us, therefore, review briefly the liturgical basis of acceptance.

It was argued in chapter 4 that acceptance is intrinsic to ritual because to perform a liturgical order (which is by definition a more or less invariant sequence of formal acts and utterances encoded by other than the performer) is perforce to conform to that order. As such, authority is intrinsic to liturgy. It was further argued, however, that participation in a liturgical order expresses a more intimate and binding relationship between the performer and the order which he is performing than may be connoted by such terms as "authority" and "conformity." We had earlier noted that in ritual the performer himself is always among the most important receivers of the messages he is transmitting. A further fusion could then be noted, a fusion of the sender-transmitter with the message being sent and transmitted. In conforming to the order to which his performance gives life the performer becomes indistinguishable from that order for the time being. He *realizes*, makes real, makes into a *res*, that order, providing it with the substance of his own breath and body as it, reciprocally, invests him with its own form. The distinction between the participant (as subject) and the object in which he is participating dissolves. In such a union of performer and performance there can be no rejection of that which is being performed. The performer, in performing a liturgical order, cannot be doing other than accepting whatever it encodes. *If conformity to an order encoded by other than the self is required for such identification to be achieved and I have argued that it is then the invariance of the liturgical order is indispensable to acceptance.*

The second ground of unquestionableness, one intrinsic to Ultimate Sacred Postulates themselves rather than to the relationship of the performers to them, also rests upon invariance. An insight of Anthony F. C. Wallace is of fundamental importance here. He observed that in terms of formal information theory ritual (by which he meant what has been called "canon" in this work) is a very peculiar form of communication because it is devoid of information:

each ritual is a particular sequence of signals which, once announced, allows no uncertainty, no choice,[4] and hence, in the statistical sense of information theory, conveys no information from sender to receiver. It is, ideally, a system of perfect order and any deviation from this order is a mistake.   *(1966: 233)*

Wallace therefore proposed that "Ritual may, perhaps, most succinctly be classified as communication without information" (1966: 233). But, he further argues (1966: 236ff.), meaning and information are not one and the same:

Not all meaningful messages are informational; not all informational messages are meaningful. In other words, *a sequence of meaningful signals whose order is fixed,* so that the receiver always knows what signal will follow the preceding one, *will have no information value because there is no uncertainty to be reduced* by the outcome of each successive event. Conversely, *a message may be meaningless either because its information value is too high* or because the component signals are arbitrary.   *(1966: 236; emphasis mine)*

Meaningfulness, Wallace asserts, does not depend upon whether or not a message contains information but, rather, "has to do with the receiver's ability to respond to a message: that is, to respond to a small stimulus with a relatively large response" (1966: 236). This notion of meaning is similar to the aspect of meaningfulness emphasized in the discussion of transduction in chapter 3. In discussing levels of meaning in a later chapter we shall turn to other aspects of the relationship between messages and receivers. Of fundamental importance here, and virtually explicit in Wallace's discussion: *the meaning of ritual's informationlessness is certainty.*[5] Later he writes that even though the particular meanings of specific rites may be as numerous and varied as the rites themselves there is

always one other message, which is implicit rather than explicit. This is the message of organization. The stereotyping of ritual is orderliness raised to an extraordinary degree; rituals are predictable, the contingent probabilities in chains of ritual events are near unity; the myth upon which ritual is based described a world in which chaos is being, or is to be, replaced by order.

(1966: 238)

To put this in terms of this work, that which is represented in an invariant canon is thereby *indicated* to be changeless and without alternative and, thus, certain. The relationship of certainty to unquestionableness is so close that in a looser usage they would be regarded as synonymous.

There are, then, two bases for the unquestionableness of Ultimate Sacred Postulates. On the one hand, there is their acceptance *by* subjects, on the other, the certainty of their expression. Both emerge from the same general characteristic of liturgy: canonical invariance. *Insofar as the quality of unquestionableness is the essence of the sacred, the sacred itself is a product of the very form which is ritual*, or rather, of the incorporation of language into the ritual form which, we noted in chapter 1, is widespread if not, indeed, universal among animals (e.g. the courtship rituals of great crested grebes and fiddler crabs, the agonistic rituals of Sticklebacks and gulls, and possibly the "rain dances" of chimpanzees).

Although there is no way to demonstrate it, the argument unfolding here suggests that the idea of the sacred emerged in the course of evolution, perhaps inevitably, as expressions from developing language were assimilated into and subordinated to the orders of non-verbal rituals in which, it is plausible to assume, our infra-human forebears participated. *The concept of the sacred thus may be as old as language, which is a way of saying as old as humanity itself.*

We may be reminded here that, in chapter 7, it was argued that notions of eternity are also entailed by the invariant recurrence of liturgical orders. The qualities of unquestionableness and eternity not only spring from the same liturgical order but from the self-same features of those orders. If sanctity and eternity are not one and the same they are sisters. The organic relationship within which the notions of sanctity, unquestionableness and eternity are bound becomes manifest in liturgical orders.

We may also be reminded here of a certain inversion or sleight-of-ritual first touched upon in a discussion of acceptance in chapter 4. Ultimate Sacred Postulates are given perduring unquestionable status they become "eternal verities," through continuing social action, that is, through their recurrent representation in performances of liturgical orders. As eternal verities, however, they are taken to be the grounds upon which are founded the cosmic orders of which those liturgical orders are parts, and by which the performers are supposed to live. The ultimately sacred, which is generally understood to be the ground of existence, must be continuously or recurrently represented to themselves by those subordinate to it. The importance of the unbroken continuity of their own ritual performances to the maintenance of eternal cosmic order, often masked, is recognized in the religious thought of some peoples. Australian aborigines, for instance, may understand rituals not to be mere reenactments of events that brought the world into its order during the dreamtime, but to be reentries into the dreamtime to participate once again in the unique acts that once, once only, and once forever constitute the world's order. That order can only continue if men ever again enter into the one eternal performance of those unique events (Stanner 1956: *passim*; Meggitt n.d.: *passim*).

That the ultimately sacred itself rests upon the acts of those subordinate to it suggests cybernetic processes at the very heart of religion's relationship to society and its evolution. I have written about these processes in previous essays (1971b, 1971c, 1979b) and will elaborate those earlier discussions in the final chapters, where we shall also consider the place of sanctity in the adaptive structure of social formations and the related problem of pathologies of sanctification. Now we must return to the matter of unquestionableness.

4. Axioms and Ultimate Sacred Postulates

It may be objected that the conception of the sacred advocated here does not distinguish adequately Ultimate Sacred Postulates from the axioms of mathematics and logic. Both Ultimate Sacred Postulates and axioms are taken to be true without proof, and neither stands isolated. Both serve as foundations of discursive structures which include more than themselves. They do, however, differ in several respects.

First, there are important differences in the place of axioms and Ultimate Sacred Postulates in the discursive structures of which they are parts. As Whitehead and Russell showed long ago (1913), it is not possible to construct a logical system without resort to axioms. Although undemonstrable in the logic of the systems which they ground, axioms may, at least in theory, be derived as theorems in theories of higher logical type. The logics of higher type also rest upon axioms, of course, which would be theorems in yet higher logics. Infinite regress is intrinsic to the structure of logic.

Ultimate Sacred Postulates are not subject to this entailment. Unlike axioms, they cannot be derived from systems of higher logical type, for they themselves claim, as it were, to stand at the apex of the structures of discourse in which they appear. Indeed, that which they postulate is often understood to be an uncreated creator, the origin or the ground of all things. As such, Ultimate Sacred Postulates call a halt to the infinite regress that logic by itself cannot terminate. They sometimes even establish, as unquestionable, postulates that appear to human intelligence to be self-contradictory, like the plural nature of the One God, in effect posting notice that ordinary logic cannot grasp them, much less push beyond them. They tacitly assert that mundane understanding must be left behind if they are to be comprehended. *Credo ut intelligam.*

As Ultimate Sacred Postulates cannot be derived as theorems from systems of higher logical type, neither do they play the part of axioms in the discursive structures in which they do appear. This point was made in the last chapter. Here we may note that Ultimate Sacred Postulates usually[6] do not specify particular relations changelessly manifested in phenomena, as do axioms and laws of nature. That divinity is One, Two, Three or Multitudinous does not stipulate the social, moral, or physical particulars of this world, the strenuous efforts of some theologians notwithstanding. Both the multiplicity and the unity of the divine have been read from the same nature, and great ranges of institutions, many of them antithetical to each other, have been sanctified by reference to the same gods established by the same Ultimate Sacred Postulates, enunciated in the same liturgical orders. To put this a little differently, such sentences as the creeds of the Christians, the *Shema*, or the *Shahada*, *in and of themselves* do not entail particular physical, social or logical relations as do the laws of nature or states or the axioms of logic.

Axioms and Ultimate Sacred Postulates also differ in generality. Whereas axioms are valid only within particular logical systems or within physical systems of a particular class (for example, the axiom that the shortest distance between two points is a straight line holds true only on planes), the domains of Ultimate Sacred Postulates are not so narrowly limited. They may, indeed, be boundless, held to be good always and everywhere. "There is no god but One God and Mohammed is his prophet" is understood by the faithful to be as true on spheres as it is on planes. In short, the scope of Ultimate Sacred Postulates, unlike those of axioms or laws, is not typically limited to particular physical, topical, political or logical regions.[7]

A distinction of a very different sort passed over quickly in the first section deserves elaboration here. It is not equivalently consequential to accord unquestionable status to axioms on the one hand and to Ultimate Sacred Postulates on the other. For one thing, some axioms appear to be immediately and intuitively self-evident. To deny seriously that the shortest distance between two points on a plane is a straight line, or to deny straightforward derivations from axioms, such as $2 + 2 = 4$, would be to deny what is ordinarily taken to be obvious and rational and would, for many observers, constitute *prima facie* evidence of mental impairment. The same might be said about many empirical generalizations, for instance that things fall down, not up, in the general region of the earth. Conversely, the acceptance of such propositions as true by anyone beyond childhood indicates nothing more than minimal intellectual competence. As such their acceptance is close to inconsequential. In contrast, the significata of Ultimate Sacred Postulates are neither apparent nor necessarily manifested in material relations nor logically necessary. Indeed, not only are they not immediately apparent, they are often if not usually or even always counter-intuitive. As we have already observed, because they may even contradict ordinary reason or everyday experience, they cannot claim their support. To accept the trinitarian nature of the one God may not be to deny ordinary logic and worldly experience, but it certainly is to ignore or even to defy them. To grant unquestionable status to such sentences as the Nicene Creed is, therefore, highly consequential ontologically, epistemologically and socially.[8] To accept "There is no god but One God and Mohammed is His prophet" is obviously to declare oneself to be a member of a particular community and not of others, and to obligate oneself to be a member of a particular community and not of others, and to obligate oneself in ways discussed in chapter 4.

It may be objected that many axioms, for instance those of non-Euclidean geometries, are far from self-evident and that, therefore, their acceptance is not trivial. It can nevertheless be asserted that their acceptance is in one respect less, or at least differently, consequential than the acceptance of Ultimate Sacred Postulates: no social obligation is entailed.

A further, more fundamental, objection might be raised to the general account of sanctity being developed here. Despite the attempt to distinguish Ultimate Sacred Postulates from axioms the conception may seem excessively rational, for it in itself takes no notice of ineffable, subjective religious experience. It did not, however, mean to deny the importance or force of such experience. As I indicated briefly in the first chapter, the sacred, as I am defining it, is *only one* of the *two* fundamental elements of the more inclusive category that I shall call "The Holy." The sacred in this more limited and special usage is the Holy's discursive component: that part of it which can be expressed in language. Chapter 11 will treat the other major aspect of the Holy, the non-discursive, experiential aspect that I, following Rudolph Otto, call the "numinous," and which we already mentioned briefly in chapter 7. It will be concerned with the further unification of the sacred and the numinous to form the Holy, and with the conception of the divine as an offspring of that union.

5. Sanctity, heuristic rules, and the basic dogma

The association of the sacred with unquestionableness, and the distinction between the ultimately sacred and the contingently sanctified, conform generally to the conception of religious discourse developed by the Dominican philosopher-theologian Joseph Bochenski in *The Logic of Religion* (1965), although his analysis does not involve liturgy at all. It is based upon the discourse of five religious traditions, Buddhism, Christianity, Hinduism, Islam and Judaism, all of which he had found to be constructed according to a common logic out of similar classes of sentences. He designates four such classes.

First, there are "Rho sentences," the class of sentences that express "what the believers believe," as he puts it. These are the sorts of sentences that Bochenski tells us are likely to be found in creeds and catechisms: "Christ is the son of God," "Mohammed is the prophet of Allah." I have been calling such expressions "Ultimate Sacred Postulates."

Secondly, there are what he calls "heuristic rules." These are rules indicating which sentences are to be given the status of Rho sentences, or Ultimate Sacred Postulates. Heuristic rules, he emphasizes, do not stipulate the sentences to be included in the Rho category by reference to their substance but by reference to their form or context (e.g., "All statements in the book of Genesis are to be regarded as Rho sentences"). In the religious traditions which engage Bochenski, scriptures form the texts to which heuristic rules are applied to derive Ultimate Sacred Postulates. The role of the theologian in such literary traditions is to refine, or perhaps even to devise, heuristic rules and to interpret whatever postulates are yielded by their expression, for they are often obscure or cryptic. More important for us: ritual itself embodies heuristic rules or, better, *liturgical orders constitute heuristic rules.* That is, I am claiming that the recurrent, punctilious and perduring expression of a particular sentence or set of sentences in ritual selects it out of the infinite possibilities of discourse and represents it as an Ultimate Sacred Postulate. This is one of the most fundamental and crucial entailments of canonical invariance.

The third type of sentence included or implicit in ritual discourse is what Bochenski calls "the Basic Dogma." The basic dogma stipulates that every sentence designated by a heuristic rule to be a Rho sentence (or Ultimate Sacred Postulate in my terms)

has to be *accepted* as true. Thus a Mohammedan would admit that whatever has been revealed to Mohammed has to be considered as true; and a Catholic catechism says that whatever God revealed and the Church proposed to be believed is true and so on.   *(1965: 61; emphasis mine)*

Bochenski, whose interest is limited to discourse *per se*, does not tell us what constitutes this acceptance. It would seem to be an attitude toward Rho sentences possibly held by communicants, an attitude that he does not clearly distinguish from belief. Nor does he tell us how acceptance may be indicated to the acceptor and to others. Few ritual traditions encapsulate their Ultimate Sacred Postulates in formal catechisms, nor are they enunciated in churches over which preside priests whose pronouncements express "what the church proposes to be believed." Even in societies that do possess institutionalized churches distinct from society as a whole, "what God revealed" is not usually related mainly through such documents as catechisms or scriptures but through punctiliously recurring rituals. I have argued in chapter 4 and in this chapter that the performance of the selfsame rituals in which Ultimate Sacred Postulates (or Rho sentences) are expressed constitutes an acceptance of them. An apparent difference between Bochenski's formulation and that being developed here is that for him acceptance seems to be an attitude, or subjective state not clearly distinguished from conviction or belief. I have argued, in contrast, that acceptance is a *public act* visible both to the performer and to others. As such, ritual performance not only constitutes acceptance of that which it represents as sacred, but *indicates* that acceptance as well. I have further argued that acceptance as public performative act does not entail "belief in" that which is accepted although it probably encourages it.

Acceptance, however, is only one basis of the unquestionableness of Rho sentences or Ultimate Sacred Postulates. The other, I have argued, is the *apparent certainty* of the expressions themselves. Bochenski has, in a similar vein, observed:

At the same time the BD [basic dogma] also states something which is rarely explicit in it, but is known to be understood by all believers, namely, that all sentences designated by the heuristic rule have to be considered as possessing the probability 1.   *(1965: 61)*

I have argued that, at the same time the performance of an invariant order indicates an acceptance of whatever the order represents, the invariance of the order itself invests its substance with certainty. In sum, what Bochenski calls *the Basic Dogma as well as the heuristic rule is embodied in the liturgical form itself.*

A fourth category of sentences are included in Bochenski's analysis, those he designates "tau' rho." Tau' rho sentences, which are derived from combinations of Rho sentences and profane discourse, approximate those that I have been calling "sanctified sentences." He recognizes that some tau' rho sentences, particularly ethical directives, may be derived in more than one way, and that some of these ways may be exclusively "profane." For example, that it is good to honor one's father and mother could be taken to be a dictate of God, a purely moral imperative, a derivation from sociological postulates alone or, for that matter, from some biological assumptions concerning kin selection. He argues, however, that a sentence is not to be excluded from the general religious discourse of that society because it may also be profanely derived any more than sentences concerning the age of the earth grounded in plate tectonics are to be excluded from the discourse of geology because the age of the earth may possibly also be deduced from astronomical evidence.

The conception of the sacred and the sanctified being developed in this work is generally compatible with Bochenski's analysis of religious discourse; it augments his discussion with an account of ritual's role in the constitution of what he calls "heuristic rules" and "basic dogma." It also elucidates another matter upon which Bochenski touches. Having noted that the basic dogma stipulates that sentences designated Rho sentences possess the probability 1 he continues:

In most theologies it is even asserted that the certainty of the Rho sentences is by far greater, indeed belongs to a quite different order, than the certainty of any other sentence. This, however, is a psychological matter, logically there is no probability higher than 1.   *(1965: 61)*

It may not be logically possible for anything to possess a probability higher than 1. Nevertheless, our discussion proposes that the certainty attributed to Ultimate Sacred Postulates is conceptually distinct from that which may be attributed to other expressions, for they may not be falsified either logically or empirically but, as we shall see in later chapters, are amenable to validation which subjectively seems undeniable. Even the unquestionableness of highly sanctified sentences may seem to be of a different – and somehow more certain – order than statements based upon law or logic, for they do not seem to be invalidated by states of affairs running counter to time. In fact, in such circumstances, the states of affairs are invalidated. Further questions are raised here about the nature of unquestionableness.

6. Sanctity, unquestionableness, and the truth of things

Like relative or comparative invariance, the notion of unquestionableness is less clear than it may seem to be at first sight. We are concerned here with elements of discourse, in particular of liturgical discourse, a class of postulates being fundamental to them. With respect to such expressions, and to most others to which it may be applied, the term "unquestionable" in general parlance is closely related to, subsumes, or is subsumed by, the term "truthful," if, indeed, it is not synonymous with it.[9] In ordinary usage "truth" is a quality which it is possible for reports, descriptions, statements, hypotheses, propositions, postulates and theories to possess. Such locutions are said to be true if they "agree with reality" or if they conform to "knowledge, fact, actuality, or logic," to invoke two common dictionary definitions (Oxford English and American Heritage Dictionaries) that seem to correspond most closely to what is generally known as the "correspondence theory of truth." This theory, because it seems to be the most naive and straightforward of those current,[10] may be closest to what people other than philosophers have in mind when they speak of the truth of expressions. Thus, it is privileged as a widespread folk theory.

Aristotle laid a formal foundation for the correspondence theory in *Metaphysics* (Book IV 1011b, chapter 7) simply and straightforwardly enough "to say of what is that it is, and of what is not that it is not, is true." Later he proceeded as follows:

This being so, when is what is called truth or falsity present, and when is it not? We must consider what we mean by these terms. It is not because we think truly that you are *pale* that you *are* pale, but because you are pale we who say this have the truth. *(Book X 1051b, chapter 7)*

A modern theologian-logician, commenting on this passage, states:

The truth ... exists in two situations: first in the situation of being a state of affairs, whether one knows that state of affairs or not, e.g., the truth lies in your being pale; secondly, the truth lies in the situation of our knowing a state of affairs, e.g., in our knowing you are pale. *(G. Smith 1956: 3)*

Other philosophers (e.g., White 1971: 104) have raised objections to characterizing that to which an expression corresponds as a "situation" or "state-of-affairs" or "object," in part because of some embarrassment in the case of the negative statements, or in part because of the restrictiveness of such terms. White prefers the vaguer but more inclusive term "fact":

> To say what is said is true is to say that what is said corresponds to a fact; to discover whether what is said is true is to discover whether there is such a corresponding fact.   *(1971: 109)*

> Whatever is truly said has its corresponding fact ... Conversely, for every fact something corresponding could be, though it need not actually be, truly said.
> *(1971: 108)*

A variety of tests differing in formality, rigor and nature may be applied to come to judgments concerning correspondences. Some are empirical, others logical, some statistical, some unconditional, some depend directly upon sensory evidence, others relate to evidence indirectly, yet others rely upon their coherence with other expressions that are empirically grounded.[11] By one means or another, particular expressions can be judged true or false by reference to facts independent of themselves. The term "contingent truth" is sometimes used to refer to the veracity of expressions which happen to be true although they could have been false and may well be false at other times or in other places.

Our discussion of Ultimate Sacred Postulates should have made it clear that, although they are expressions, they are not true in the merely contingent sense. They are not taken to be true because they have survived tests that, assessing them against facts, could have found them false. They are not amenable to such tests. Although Ultimate Sacred Postulates are elements of discourse, the truth ascribed to them resembles more closely what Smith, following Aristotle, could designate the "Truth of Things" the absolute truth of that which simply *is*, than it does the "truth of thought" or of expressions.

The Oxford Unabridged Dictionary provides a number of definitions of truth expressing the notion of the truth of things rather than the truth of expressions: "7. Genuineness, reality, actual existence ... 10. That which is true, real or actual (in a general sense, reality ...) ... 11. The fact or facts, the actual state of the case ... the real thing ... the actual property or nature (of something)." Such truth is not simply *veracity*, a *possible* property of expressions, but *verity*,[12] a necessary property of what *is*.

In an earlier section we discussed the way in which a truth status otherwise reserved for fact is bestowed upon expressions that to all appearances seem not to be facts but, at best, sentences corresponding to facts. We need not reiterate the argument here, but should simply recall that these expressions are taken to be unquestionable, or true, because they are *represented* as *certain* and *accepted* as *beyond question*. Both the acceptance and the certainty are entailments of liturgical form; thus their truth is *not discovered*, proven or confirmed through explorations of their conformity to fact but *is established in the mode or manner of their expression*. That this is the case does not, however, invalidate the correspondence theory of truth with respect to them. To establish the truth of a representation, even if that truth is simply an entailment of that representation's expression as it is in liturgy, seems to establish the factuality, actuality, or truth of that which the representation represents. The relationship between fact and utterance that is the essence of the correspondence theory, I would suggest the most commonsensical, popular and intuitive of the several theories of truth is simply inverted. In the instances at hand a fact comes into correspondence with an expression that has, for reasons independent of the fact, been granted an unquestionable status. This operation is, of course, readily, easily, and perhaps naturally and inevitably, mystified. The ease of its mystification immediately strikes us when we dwell upon the ambiguity of White's statement cited above: "Whatever is truly said has its corresponding fact ..." *The fact, inferred as an entailment of an expression "truly said," comes instantly to be, apparently, that to which the expression, now taken for a statement, corresponds.*

I am obviously addressing here a dimension of illocutionary force inherent particularly in the class of performatives earlier (chapter 4) labeled "factives." As in the case of performatives generally those inverting the correspondence theory of truth are subject to restrictions, among which is the stipulation that they can be effective, or "felicitous," only with respect to appropriate objects. The appropriate objects in the class of cases at hand does not include what Searle and others have called "brute facts," nor physical entities of any sort, nor even the facts of logic. It would not bring a second sun into the heavens to represent such an object in liturgy, nor would such an attempt make the sum of two plus two equal three. Appropriate objects are neither physical nor logical, nor do they include all of the social. They are metaphysical. The most obvious of the metaphysical objects established by being truly said in ritual are divine beings, but they also include divine orders, the subject of chapter 11.

We must recall Giambattista Vico here. The sacred is the primordial foundation upon which fabricated *verum* has stood. The subject matter of Ultimate Sacred Postulates is generally, if not always, the divine, and Vico claimed that the gods were the first great invention of the gentiles (1988 [1744]: para 9, 10, *passim*) more particularly of their early theological poets (1988: paras. 199, 200), and thus *verum* originates in poetic truth. Whereas it originates in the fabrication of gods it is not confined to this primordial function. Vico further claimed that all human institutions, conventions, symbols, and arts are built upon foundations laid down by those gods. *Verum* is thus very different from empirical truth, the *certum* of Descartes, and is founded in historical mythology. Thus:

> These fables are ideal truths ... and such falseness to fact as they contain consists simply in failure to give their subject their due. So that, if we consider the matter well, poetic truth is metaphysical truth, and physical truth which is not in conformity with it should be considered false. Thence springs this important consideration in poetic theory; the true war chief, for example, is that Godfrey of Torquato [that] Tasso imagines; and all chiefs who do not conform to Godfrey are not true chiefs of war.   *(1988: para. 205)*

We may summarize here certain crucial differences between the truths of nature and the fabricated truths peculiar to humanity. The truths of nature, that is, of nature's regularities, must be discovered if they are to be known, but are the case whether they are known or not. Our grasp of them can claim no status more certain than *certum*, and as such may be off the mark or even dead wrong. In contrast, the fabricated truths particular to humanity, *verum*, are true *only* if they are known, for they must be known to be accepted and are true only so long as they are accepted. We may recognize them to be truths of sanctity and that they are, in essence, moral. They declare the truths of "should" against which actions and actual states of affairs are judged and often found to be wanting, immoral, or wrong. They also include expressions declaring the ultimate metaphysical ground upon which the moral stands; that, for instance, Yahweh is god and Marduk is not, or vice versa. They are the truths upon which social systems have always been built and in the absence of adequate alternatives continue to be built.

Because *certum* is no more than that which can be ascertained and thus can be radically wrong, Vico implied that it is inferior to *verum*, which is, in its nature, absolutely true. In this he went seriously and, ultimately, dangerously wrong. The domain of *verum* is that of human symbols, conventions, arts and institutions. The domain of *certum* is the physical world. The assessment of essentially human elements of the world in terms of the epistemologies producing *certum*, or of the physical world in accordance with the understandings of *verum*, constitutes the most profound and destructive fallacy threatening humanity and the world it increasingly dominates. We will return to this matter in the last chapter.

Bochenski, we may recall, has noted that "most theologies" grant to the expressions with which we are dealing here – Rho sentences, or Ultimate Sacred Postulates – probabilities greater than 1. Although he may be correct in stating that proposals of probabilities exceeding one certainly violate logic these expressions are taken by those accepting them to provide the ground of certainty itself. We have noted that they themselves are, in their nature, invulnerable to falsification in logic or by fact, and that even the sentences they sanctify are not invalidated by states of affairs at variance with them. It is of interest in this regard that in Vedic India and Zoroastrian Persia states of affairs, such as revolts, violating liturgically specified (and thus sanctified) orders of the world were characterized by terms that also denoted what we call "lies": *druj* in Persia, *anrta* in India (Duchesne-Guillemin 1966, N. Brown 1972: 252ff.). What I have elsewhere called "Zoroastrian lies" or "Vedic lies" (Rappaport 1979b) are the inverse of "common lies." Common lies are a subclass of the class of incorrect statements, statements that do not correspond to the states of affairs they purport to describe or report. Vedic lies are incorrect states of affairs, states of affairs that do not conform to the stipulations of expressions "truly said" in liturgy. In sum, the truths of sanctity do not violate the correspondence theory of truth. They merely stand it on its head.

7. Divinity, truth, and order

Early in this chapter I distinguished the sacred from the divine, proposing that sanctity is a quality of discourse, and that divinity is a property of objects of that discourse. I was quick to qualify this distinction, however, proposing that it may be systematically blurred in many if not all ritual traditions. The discussion of liturgy as a mode of "true expression," inverting the correspondence theory of truth and granting to its expressions the "truth of things," suggests how such blurring takes place. If metaphysical objects corresponding to true expressions are established in ritual performance, then the distinction between properties of sacred and sanctified discourse on the one hand and of the objects of that discourse on the other breaks down. Truth, an aspect of unquestionableness which, I have argued, is a property of sacred and sanctified discourse becomes an explicit property of the divine objects with which that discourse is concerned.

Attributions of truth to divinities are common. The instance likely to be most familiar to Christians is found at the beginning of the Gospel according to St. John: "the Word became flesh and dwelt among us, full of grace and truth; we have beheld His glory as the only son of the father ..."

The association of truth with divinity is also explicit in Judaism. In early rabbinic thought, according to Kittel, "the very essence of God is truth, so that it may be said conversely that truth has its essence in God" and according to the Talmud "the god of truth is the 'Judge of Truth'." I take this to mean that God as the "truth of things" is that against which the truth of words are to be assessed. "As thou art truth, so is thy Word truth," and the "Torah as the expression of the divine Word and essence is truth" (Kittel 1965 I: 237).

The Hebrew word for truth, *emet*, "is used absolutely to denote a reality which is to be regarded as ... 'firm' ... 'solid,' 'valid' or binding. It thus signifies *what* is 'true'" (Kittel 1965 I: 232f., emphasis mine), that is, "the truth of things." In the exegetical word play of the rabbis, the word "emet" came to be the seal of God. Composed of the first, the last and one of the middle letters of the alphabet (aleph, mem, tov), it encompasses all things, and it was observed to be formed from the initials of the words "*Elohim*," "*malak*" or "*melek*", and "*tamid*" (Kittel 1965 I: 237). As a sentence, this could be read "God is king forever" or "God rules eternally" (David N. Freedman, personal communication). In a legend anciently attributed to Saadia, the last Gaon of Babylon but probably not of his authorship, *emet* was represented as prerequisite to life. Before God breathed life and voice into the earth that was to become man, he engraved its three letters on the creature's forehead. When Adam committed a vedic lie, that is, violated the one commandment prevailing in Eden thus producing a state of affairs at variance with God's word, God erased the letter most closely associated with Himself, the first, Aleph, leaving engraved on Adam's brow the word *met*: death (Scholem 1969: 179ff.).

Later we shall touch upon similar conceptions of divine truth developed in other archaic civilizations, but the association of truth with divine objects is not limited to the self-conscious theological thought of literate societies possessed of scriptures. Among the Dakota and other Sioux, as we have seen, ultimate sacred postulation of the sovereignty of *Wakan-Tanka*, the Great Holiness that encompasses all things, is represented by calumets and the ritual act of smoking them (J. Brown 1971: *passim*). In Sioux thought, and in the thought of other North American

Indians, sacred pipes are "dominant" or "key" symbols (Ortner 1973), having in that respect the significance of the Cross for Christians. There are important differences, of course. The pipe's physical complexity contrasts with the simplicity of the cross, and the way in which the two are used ritually also distinguishes them. The intimacy of pipe, smoker and tobacco is unparalleled in the relationship of Christians to the Cross, but may be approximated in the relationship of Christians to the Eucharist.

According to the Sioux holy man Black Elk, the pipe represents nothing less than the universe (J. Brown 1971: *passim*, esp. 5–26). The bowl represents the earth, and the buffalo carved on the bowl all of the "four-legged peoples," that is, all terrestrial animals. The wooden stem represents the "standing people," the world's vegetation, and the eagle feathers adorning the pipe signify the "winged peoples," who are, of course, the birds. At the same time that the pipe represents the macrocosmos it also represents the microcosmos of the human anatomy. This identification, if not made explicit by the Sioux, is by the Osage who, in a text collected by LaFleshe, liken each part of the pipe to a part of the body (J. Brown 1971: 21).

In filling a pipe, according to Brown,

all space (which has been engaged through offerings to the powers of the six directions) and all things (signified by the mixture of tobacco, herbs and bark stuffed in the bowl) "are contracted ... within the bowl or heart of the pipe ... so that the pipe contains, or really *is*, the universe. But ... it is also man, and the one who fills a pipe should identify himself with it ... he so expands that the six directions of space are actually brought within himself. It is by this 'expansion' that a man ceases to be a part, a fragment, and becomes a whole or holy; he shatters the illusion of separateness."

(1971: 21)

From this account, it would seem that the smoker smokes for the benefit of all of the "peoples" of the universe; to smoke must be to give breath to, or share breath with, the universe. To smoke a sacred pipe is to perform an act of high solemnity, and it constitutes a ritual of considerable complexity in its own right. Elaborate formal addresses to Wakan-Tanka are elements of this ritual, and part of such an address, as recounted by Black Elk and translated by Brown, identifies Wakan-Tanka with both the universe and truth:

Our Grandfather, Wakan-Tanka, you are everything, and yet above everything! You are first. You have always been ...
O Wakan-Tanka, You are the truth. The two-legged people who put their mouths to this pipe will become the truth itself; there will be in them nothing impure ...

(1971: 13)

Smoking the calumet certifies the truth of the smoker's testimony. Black Elk reports the following admonition to one who is about to smoke after returning from crying for a vision:

Ho! You have now sent a voice with your pipe to Wakan-Tanka. That pipe is now very sacred, for the whole universe has seen it. You have offered this pipe to all the sacred Powers; they have seen it! ... And since you are about to put this pipe to your mouth, you should tell us nothing but the truth. The pipe is *Wakan* and knows all things, you cannot fool it. If you lie, *Wakinyau-Tanka*, who guards the pipe, will punish you! *Hechetu welo.*   (*Brown 1971: 60f.*)

The canon of the calumet seems best known as part of the rituals through which truces and treaties were established, probably because it was in the course of establishing peaceful relations with the native people of North America that early observers of European extraction actually saw the pipe used ritually. Catlin (1844 I: 228) tells us of a feast tendered to the Indian agent Major Sanford by the Sioux chief Ha-wan-je-tah in a semi-circular area at the center of which "was erected a flag staff on which was waving a white flag and to which also was tied the calumet, both expressions of friendly feelings toward us." After feasting on dogs sacrificed to mark the importance of the occasion, and after exchanges of gifts and speeches expressing amity,

a handsome pipe [was lit] and brought ... to Ha-wan-je-tah to smoke. He took it, and after presenting the step to the North, to the South, to the East, and to the West and then to the Sun that was over his head, and pronounced the words "How-how-how!" drew a whiff or two of smoke through it, and holding the bowl of it in one hand, and its stem in the other, he then held it to each of our mouths, as we successively smoked it; after which it was passed around through the whole group, who all smoked through it ... This smoking was conducted with the strictest adherence to exact and polished form, and the feast the whole way, to the most positive silence. After the pipe was charged, and is being lit, until the time the Chief has drawn the smoke through it, it is considered an evil omen for anyone to speak ...   (*Catlin 1844 I: 229*)

Later Catlin tells us that this "mode of solemnizing [treaties constitutes] ... the most inviolable pledge that they can possibly give, for the keeping of the peace" (I: 235). This statement corroborates the much earlier account of Marquette who, in the late seventeenth century, reported of the inhabitants of the Mississippi Valley:

There remains no more, except to speak of the Calumet. There is nothing more mysterious or more respected among them. Less honor is paid to the Crowns and scepters of Kings than the savages bestow upon this. It seems to be the god of peace and of war, the Arbiter of life and death. It has but to be carried upon one's person, or displayed, to enable one to walk safely through the midst of Enemies who in the hottest of the fight lay down their arms when it is shown. For that reason, the Illinois gave me one, to serve as a safeguard among all the Nations through whom I had to pass during my voyage.

(*Marquette quoted in R. Hall (1977: 504)*)

The place of the calumet in the solemnizing of truces and treaties is so well known that they have come to be popularly called "peace pipes." Such a characterization does not do justice to their significance, for smoking the calumet is not merely an indispensable element in all seven major rituals constituting the liturgical order of the Sioux. It is the element fundamental to them all. In Sioux myth the gift of the sacred pipe from the divine White Buffalo Woman preceded all other rites, and all of them are founded upon sanctification by the canon of the calumet. It is, in Ortner's term, a key symbol, at least equivalent in its sanctity to the Christian cross. I say "at least" because the act of smoking it as respiration for the entire universe may seem to assimilate the smoker into *Wakan-Tanka* in a fashion similar to the way in which Australian Aboriginal performance assimilates the performers into the very persons of the creative heroes of the dreamtime. Although Christian worship may be deeply moving it does not assimilate the worshipper into the Beings venerated.

We can also cite here a concept which seems to have been fundamental in Nahuatl thought, the concept of Nelli. Leon-Portilla (1963: ch. 3) renders it not only as "true" in the ordinary sense, but also as "firm" and "well-founded." Molina (1571: 57) glosses it "certain," "certainly" and "truth," and its stem *nel*, "to be diligent or careful." This stem also appears in other words which Molina translates as "thing that has a root," "basis, foundation, beginning, source," "to get rooted." Of the Nahuatl notion of "truth," Leon-Portilla (1963: 73) states that nothing could be so regarded unless it was both rooted and enduring. All of this suggests that *Nelli* signified the absolute and eternal truth of things, and not merely the ephemeral and contingent truth of words. That it was an aspect or quality of the divine is explicit. In a poem recorded by Sahagun, the "true God," *Nelli Teotl*, dwells above the heavens where "he is king, he is Lord" (Leon-Portilla 1963: 82). *Moyocoyani*, "He who invents or gives existence to Himself" was among his many names (p. 91); and thus *Nelli Teotl*, the "true, well-founded God" seemed to have been an uncreated creator "who is mother and father of the gods or, in abstract terms ... origin of the cosmic forces" (p. 90). Another of the True God's names was *Ometeotl*, "God of Duality," at once male and female, and as such "an ambivalent being, an active generating principle which was at the same time a passive receptor capable of conceiving. The powers of generation and conception, requisites for the appearance of life in our world, were thus combined into a single being who created the universe" (p. 82ff.). The True God was also called *Xuitecuhtli*, the "Lord of Fire and Time" (p. 96), and thus identified with the sun, an identification that may also be implicit in "Giver of Life," a phrase by which this deity was sometimes addressed. In the heads of priests and philosophers, at least, the pantheon of the Nahuatl seems to have drawn together into a deified unity of many aspects and many names, one of which was *Tloque Nahuage*, the "Lord of Everywhere," "The All-Encompassing" source from which the universe came:

In Omeyocan "in the thirteenth heaven, of the beginning of which nothing was ever known," dwelled the true god ... founded with and upon himself. Through his generating and conceptive powers, his divine activity came to be. In the first act of his dual being, he begot four sons, and from that moment he was "mother and father of the gods." ... The powers of Ometeotl found further outlet through his four sons; "he spread out" ... over what was to be the navel of the universe in order to "endow it with truth," to support it, thus allowing his sons to begin the various ages of the world .... It was Ometeotl who endowed with truth, with a foundation, that which his offspring had accomplished ...

During the present age, the age of the Sun of Motion, Ometeotl established harmony among the four elements. He endowed with truth a world in which time became oriented and spatialized in terms of the four directions of the universe (p. 97).

Whether Nelli Teotl was an esoteric name for the supreme deity is not altogether clear. This account does indicate, however, that Nelli was in any case a virtue originating in, but not confined to the deity. It was a principle with which the true God, or Truth as God, endowed the universe, and to which all in the universe, including the subsidiary gods, whose creative tasks are more specific than those of Nelli Teotl, should conform.

In more general terms, this account of Nelli implies that when a version of the truth of things is extended to embrace the cosmos in its entirety it becomes more than that which simply *is*. It becomes the eternal and unifying order in accordance with which the universe was created and by which it persists. It is sometimes a part of such understandings that the truth with which the universe is endowed, its eternal and unifying order, although it commands the gods themselves, is violable, and its violation may be construed to be the ground of wrong or immorality. It may further be conceived not only to be subject to violation by human acts or failures to act, but vulnerable, through such violation, to disruption or even to reconquest by primordial chaos. We shall return to such eternal orders in chapter 11.

It is of interest with respect to the responsibility of humans to conform to such orders that one of *Nelli Teotl*'s names or titles was *Tezcatlanextia* "The Mirror that Illumines Things." In his brief comment on this epithet, Leon-Portilla (1983: 86) observes only that mirrors are likely to be luminous. The defining characteristic of mirrors, however, is not that they are luminous, but that they reflect the faces of those who peer into them. As such, they may not only be icons of reflexivity, but are themselves reflexive, rendering the distinction between subject and object indistinct. One may suggest that the polarity joined into unity by Ometeotl, God of Duality, was that of subject and object. In any case, the conflation of subject and object was conceived by the Nahuatl to be an aspect of Ometeotl. Conformity to the true order with which the universe is endowed by the true God reflects that true order to those conforming to it, and also illuminates it for them. To put it differently, the universe is "endowed with truth" through conformity to the truth with which it is presumed to be endowed. Nelli, the truth of things, was completed, if not indeed constructed, by those who conformed to it in ritual's true expression.

The general argument presented in the previous section and in this one implies that notions of the divine as well as the idea of the sacred spring from the "true expression" of invariant liturgies. Maurice Bloch (1973) has argued in such a vein, observing that the words spoken by those participating in rituals are not their own words, are often extraordinary, are obviously in some sense authoritative, and are often immemorial. They imply extraordinary speakers who first uttered them in antiquity, or even at the beginning of time. The notion of divinity might not be quite *entailed* by the inference of extraordinary first speakers from extra- ordinary and immemorial sacred words, but it is an obvious possibility. The implication is that if the first speakers were not themselves divine they had direct knowledge or experience of the divine or were somehow close to it.

The suggestion advanced here is similar. If those participating in a liturgical order take its canonical words to be those of God, the recitation of those words established God's existence as a social and, more particularly, a metaphysical fact. In this light, it is hardly surprising that gods are frequently associated explicitly with the creative Word, for such an association is ultimately true in a literal sense. Whereas it is often stipulated in myth that Divine Word created the world and, possibly first established the liturgy (see chapter 5 above), the social fact seems to be the inverse. The God of Word is established as a social fact in the liturgies that establish the truth of the Words of God. It is of interest that the English word "God" seems itself to manifest this reflexivity. The preferred etymology derives it from the Indo-European form *gheu(e)*. According to the Oxford Unabridged Dictionary, "There are two Aryan roots of ... this form ... one meaning 'to invoke' ... the other 'to pour, to offer sacrifice.' Hence **g,huto-m* the pre-Teutonic form, descended from *gheu*, from which was derived the Teutonic *gud^m*, the direct antecedent of the English 'god' has been variously interpreted as 'what is invoked' and as 'what is worshipped by sacrifice' ... " If truly expressed canonical words, perhaps given substance by the materials of sacrifice or other sacrament, can bring gods into being *ex nihilo* they are truly creative. The God of Word may have first been created in the ritual that first established the truth of the Word of God. This is to suggest that the notion of the divine, like the idea of the sacred, is as old as language.

8. The truths of sanctity and deutero-truth

The truths of sanctity, it should now be patent, are not in the same class as the necessary truths of logic, nor are they to be counted among the empirical truths of experiment or discovery. They belong to a third general class. Whereas the truth of logic lies in internal consistency, and that of empirical truth in correspondence to states of affairs existing independently, the validity of truths of the third class is a consequence of their acceptance. Such conventional truths are as important in human affairs as are logical and empirical truths, but they are much more problematic. The class as a whole therefore merits some discussion.

As Gregory Bateson pointed out many years ago (1951: ch. 8), there are, in addition to those of sanctity, at least two categories of truths falling within the class of truths whose validity is a function of their acceptance.[13] First, there are the truths of codification. Any word provides a fundamental example. That the word "cat," for instance, stands for individuals of the species *Felis domesticus* depends upon a tacit agreement among English speakers that it is true, and it remains so as long as people act as if it were true. Semantic meanings are truths of codification. More important to our discussion are propositions that come out of what Bateson in his earlier work (1951) called "deutero-learning,"[14] a form of learning very much like, if not identical with, what Harlow called "set-learning" (1949), and rather similar to what much later (1977) Bourdieu called "habitus." Deutero-learning is "second-order" learning: generalizing extrapolation from "first-order" learning, which is the learning of particular facts or tasks. In learning a set of nonsense syllables, for instance, a subject not only learns that set of nonsense syllables but also learns how to learn sets of nonsense syllables. This sort of learning is not confined to our species; it has been experimentally demonstrated in dogs, cats, primates (Bateson 1951, 1972a: 279f.) and porpoises (Bateson, personal communication). It must be widespread among higher animals generally, and is so crucial to the organization of human understanding that we could not imagine thought devoid of it.

Deutero-learning is a matter of generalizing from particular learning situations, of developing informal theories about what may be expected under particular categories of circumstances, and how best to cope with them. Some of these theories may be amenable to experimental validation, and thus may achieve the status of experimental or empirical truths, but most such generalizations, particularly those concerning human motives and the behavior of complex systems, are not rigorously demonstrable. In taking them to be true we tend to act in accordance with them, however, and our actions may well be self-validating. As our assumptions guide our actions so do the results of our actions tend to reinforce our assumptions; therefore, it becomes extremely difficult to dissuade us from them. Such propositions form the second category of truths whose validity is a function of their acceptance. Because they are deutero-learned in everyday experience we may call them "deutero-truths."

A great deal of personality and character structure, Bateson argued (1951), is based upon deutero-learning which begins in earliest childhood (see, for example, Levy 1973; esp. 430ff.). To the extent that the experiences of the members of any society are similar they will learn similar deutero-truths. Deutero-learning is, therefore, implicated in the construction of what have been called "Basic Personality" and "National Character," and Bateson's discussion also suggests that what anthropologists sometimes mean by such terms as the "ethos" of a society is a more or less integrated set of generally held deutero-truths. This notion of ethos does not refer to the cultural specifics of cosmologies so much as it does to those abstract assumptions concerning the nature of the world and of human destiny developed through living and implicit in such terms as "fatalism," "instrumentalism," "competitiveness," "cooperativeness," "passivity," or "individualism." The assumptions about the world that such terms imply, that it can be manipulated, that it is predictable, that it is unpredictable, that it is impervious to manipulation, that all things in it are pitted against each other or, conversely, support each other, are neither logically nor empirically true. Their validity depends upon the degree to which the members of a community accept them and, acting accordingly, increase the likelihood that the conditions they assume will, in fact, prevail. The orderliness of a community's social life should be enhanced if its members share assumptions about the nature of the world.

In sum, the culture and personality school argued that much of the general aspects and attitudes of any culture are assimilated and reinforced through deutero-learning commencing in early childhood and continuing through life. Deutero-learning is a self-validating process which, largely unself-conscious and hardly conscious at all, sequesters its truths beyond easy reach of criticism. Deutero-truths are assumptions about the *nature* of things and, as such, seem as unarguable as the green of oak leaves, the hardness of rocks, or any other obvious aspects of what is taken to be indubitably natural. The arguments of more recent practice theorists (e.g., Bourdieu 1977) reach rather similar conclusions.

Although it is plausible to assume that deutero-learning is important in the establishment and maintenance of all cultures, the line of argument summarized here does suggest (albeit implicitly) that the capacities of deutero-learning to maintain public understandings and agreements, conventions, sufficient to ground orderly social life, are limited. Certain characteristics of deutero-truths with which Bateson did not deal must be made explicit.

First, as high-level generalizations, deutero-truths are low in specificity, or are even downright vague. They are, consequently, relatively invulnerable to review or criticism. Some, and these are the ones with which Bateson seemed most concerned, are beyond consciousness and as such are inaccessible, or almost so, to those who possess, or are possessed by them. But another aspect of their vagueness and generality is salient here. It is one thing to hold as deutero-truths propositions or assumptions like "Crime does not (or does) pay," or that "You can't (or can) fight City Hall" or that "Reciprocity makes the world go round," but quite another to specify *what* is criminal, *what* the legitimate prerogatives of governments and private citizens may be, *what* may be the specific equivalencies constituting reciprocity. At least some such specifics may have to learned directly, explicitly or even didactically, although their *propriety, morality* or *naturalness* may become deutero-truths.

This account may seem to suggest that deutero-learning with its products, deutero-truths, may serve as the ground upon which convention stands and as such may constitute a "functional equivalent" of sanctification. I do not believe this to be fully the case. We broach here the second characteristic limiting the culture-grounding capacities of deutero-truth. It is simply this: in no society does everyone have the same life experiences. Each person, therefore, is likely to extrapolate somewhat unique sets of generalizations from his or her unique experiences. Each person's deutero-truths may be expected to differ in some degree from those of others, even of the same society or, for that matter, even of the same family. It would therefore be extremely difficult or impossible for any society to found convention and to insure orderly social life on the ground of deutero-learning alone and, in fact, no society does.

Robert Levy has suggested (personal communication) that societies probably differ in the degree to which they can depend upon deutero-learning to establish the public understandings that underlie social life. The tacit assumptions of isolated societies (such as those of Pacific islands lacking in culturally distinct near neighbors), are not subject to the implicit questioning entailed by continuing exposure to alien practice and ideas. In such societies deutero-learning might be able to play a larger part than it does under less isolated conditions. Levy also suggests that the degree to which societies are internally differentiated may also be significant with respect to deutero-learning's role in the establishment and maintenance of public understandings and attitudes. It is obvious that one consequence of the elaboration of the division of labor is increasing divergence of individuals' life experiences resulting in, it is plausible to suppose, increasing disparity in the deutero-truths different individuals learn.

It is not merely that the deutero-truths of different individuals, or of different segments of populations, may be so different as to make understanding difficult and interaction awkward. In some instances, as we know too well, the deutero-truths held by different persons or different groups within complex pluralistic societies include assumptions that bring them into direct conflict with others. Racial and ethnic stereotypes are unpleasantly familiar examples. Those of us who were at universities in the United States in the late 1960s and early 1970s will not easily forget the deutero-truths that students and police held with respect to each other. In their confrontations, each side, acting upon its assumptions, elicited responses from its opponents tending to reinforce those assumptions, forging with ever-increasing violence what Bateson called in an earlier work (1958[1936]) "schismogenic systems." In the jargon of the times, "things got polarized."

There seem to be formidable impedances standing in the way of the modification or change of one's deutero-truths. They may not be as firmly grounded as propositions necessarily true in logic or demonstrated by experiment or discovery, but they are, nevertheless, often taken to be self-evident because they are understood to be objective products of experience. They are products of experience, of course, but are highly subjective and usually strongly charged emotionally. In differentiated societies they are often forged in opposition to the deutero-truths of others and are likely to stand in a relation of reciprocal support with political or social position, or economic interest. We may think here of the contrasting assumptions of liberals and conservatives, or, until very recently at least, of southern blacks and southern whites. Deutero-truths seldom stand alone. They form parts of systems which, although inexplicit and vague, are in some degree coherent. The abandonment of a deutero-truth may jeopardize a general systemic understanding of the world and for that reason is likely to be strongly resisted. Finally, if the acceptance of a deutero-truth is widespread individuals may endanger themselves by acting as if it is not the case. To cite an example that, for all its crassness, can claim the virtue of clarity, if enough people accept Leo Durocher's dictum "Nice guys finish last" it becomes perilous to act in a spirit at variance with that pronouncement, which not only expresses a world view but coerces compliance with it.

Despite such impedances some people do, as the saying goes, "learn from experience," which is a way of saying that they modify their deutero-truths, or replace them with others, in response to events. It is, for example, probably safe to suppose that the assumptions of most police and most of those who were students in the late 1960s concerning each other have changed over the course of the intervening years as a consequence of changed experience flowing from changed circumstances, and it may be that more accessible, more specific and perhaps more partisan deutero-truths require intermittent reinforcement if they are to be maintained. But even if some of the deutero-truths held by members of a society do change through time, there is no reason to believe that their unanimity will always or even usually increase. Indeed, increase in variation among the members of complex societies, if not, indeed, in all societies as they mature, is to be expected simply because the experiences of adults are probably more divergent than are the experiences of infants. Movement toward greater variety is also to be expected from long historical sequences if those sequences are marked by increasing social and economic differentiation.

Evolution thrives upon variety, but it is still necessary to recognize that individual variation, as inevitable and as desirable as it may be, sets problems for the societies it enriches. All societies must maintain some

degree of orderliness among the variety that is requisite to †
bility. Because no society can operate by coercion alone, or e
by coercion, and because coercion tends to destroy variety,
tant, and it may even be necessary, that there be widespread a͜.
of what are taken to be the unquestionable assumptions within the limits
of which variation can be tolerated or even encouraged. Deutero-learned
truths, I have been arguing, are not able *by themselves* to provide such a
ground and, for reasons which we shall touch upon shortly, would
probably be inappropriate if they could. That the truths of sanctity can
serve as that foundation has been implicit in this work since chapter 4. It
is, nevertheless, important to make some of the differences between
deutero-truths and the truths of sanctity explicit here.

Fundamental to these differences is that Ultimate Sacred Postulates
cannot be derived from ordinary experience. The notion of the triune
nature of God, for example, or of God's Oneness are not ideas that
would emerge out of anyone's daily life, nor even from extrapolations
from it. Indeed, if sacred postulates are without material significata and
are in contradiction of ordinary logic, they stand in opposition to
ordinary experience. In contrast, deutero-truths, which are generalized
from ordinary experience, require reinforcement by ordinary experience,
and can, therefore, be modified or replaced in response to more or less
radically new experience, albeit with pain and difficulty. Ultimate Sacred
Postulates not only stand beyond the reach of falsification by the
rigorous procedures of logic or science, but are also impervious to
disproof by the less formal but more compelling rigors of daily life.
Their independence from ordinary experience, moreover, makes it possible for people of widely divergent experience to accept them. This is
important in all societies, but is especially so in those which are highly
differentiated.

If they are not learned from the contexts of ordinary experience they
must be learned in experience that is out of the ordinary. The extraordinary context fundamental to their learning is that of ritual.[15] In
chapters 6 and 7, the durations encompassed by ritual were described as
"times out of time," and were identified with eternity. That which is
represented in such times is represented by the punctilious performance of
invariant sequences of acts and utterances understood to be never-changing. It may be added here that the self-same liturgical invariance from
which the concept of eternity emerges ensures that whatever is represented
in the liturgy is at least represented in identical terms to all participants.
Liturgical representations, such as Ultimate Sacred Postulates, are often

if not always mysterious, and may be understood rather differently by each person accepting them, *but ritual does insure that the representation possibly being interpreted idiosyncratically by each participant is one and the same for all of them.* Each person's understanding of the oneness of the godhead, for example, may be different, but all agree that it is the oneness of the godhead that they are attempting to understand.

As unquestionable and eternal, sacred truths are set above deutero-truths, and people do hold them with remarkable tenacity not only in the absence of supporting experience but even, if needs be, in defiance of ordinary experience, as in the case of Job or in the case of the psalmist who guards his own virtue, not only in defiance of his own suffering but also in the face of the unfailing prosperity of the ungodly (Psalm 73. See Buber 1952 for a discussion of this and certain other psalms).

The precedence of the truths of sanctity over those of experience is not limited to Ultimate Sacred Postulates but extends to other sentences concerning human action and human relations associated with them. If ordinary experience teaches deutero-truths that are at odds with the truths of sanctity it is ordinary experience that is, in the first instance, wrong. Variant and questionable experience must yield to the invariant and unquestionable sacred and to what it certifies to be correct, legitimate, moral and truthful.

The truths of sanctity can seldom refute directly the experiential truths entertained by individuals, but they may counteract them in at least two ways. First, they set limits on the deutero-truths upon which it is permissible or acceptable to act. Even if experience has taught the deutero-truth that crime does in fact pay, sanctified truth may forbid such activity. Secondly, and more important, the truths of sanctity set limits, albeit not always effectively, on the deutero-truths that are learned. Existing before the birth of the individual, the truths of sanctity guide his or her socialization and experience generally, and guide his or her interpretation of it in ways which tend to inhibit the development of anti-social deutero-truths.

We have come here to another profound problem that all societies must face, a problem which may lie in the nature of the species or even in the nature of animals. Deutero-learning, and perhaps learning in ordinary experience generally, inasmuch as it has its locus in the consciousness of individual organisms, must in some degree be concerned with the self-interest of those organisms. Self-interest may be generously conceived to the point of "selflessness," but it obviously need not be. It is often narrowly defined or even anti-social, and it may be that with the elaboration and differentiation of society and with the increase in production for gain rather than for use, individual self-interest has become ever more naked and narrowly conceived. The pursuit of self-interest, furthermore, has concurrently been legitimized by formal economics, the discipline in possession of the social paradigm dominating contemporary society's attempts to contemplate itself. Be this as it may, the philosopher Henri Bergson argued that intelligence, by which he meant ordinary consciousness and everyday rationality, itself poses threats to social life. "Intelligence is a faculty used naturally by the individual to meet the difficulties of life." It will not, if left alone, follow a course which is in the interest of the group or species. Rather, "It will make straight for selfish decisions" (Bergson 1935: 83). It has not been left unfettered, however. What Bergson termed "static religion" is society's defense against "the dissolvent power of intelligence" (Bergson 1935: 112). Its "truths of sanctity," set limits upon what an intelligence developed in ordinary experience can know and act upon. In the realm of conventional truths, truths the validity of which is a function of their acceptance, the truths of sanctity *ordinarily* hold sway.

The qualifying term "ordinarily" italicized in the last sentence needs to be emphasized. Although deutero-truth is ordinarily subordinated to the truths of sanctity, the sovereignty of the latter is not absolute. The relationship of the truths of sanctity to deutero-truths is ultimately one of reciprocal limitation. This matter will be discussed more fully in the final two chapters. Here we may recall that the truths of sanctity *take precedence* over the truths of experience. That is, on occasions of conflict, sacred and sanctified truths *in the first instance* prevail. Although the truths of sanctity may be beyond the reach of ordinary experience they are not beyond the review of extraordinary experience, such as prolonged oppression. In the next chapter we shall see that sanctity must be ascribed to postulates and to other expressions associated with them, through participation in ritual. Inasmuch as this is the case sanctity may be withdrawn from such expressions by discontinuing their enunciation in ritual or by withdrawing from rituals in which they continue to be represented. If a sanctified authority becomes oppressive, as has often happened in the course of history, that authority may be deprived of its sanctity by those subordinate to it. The threat of desecration may stimulate reform, but, if reform fails, prophets may arise, and may sanctify new political movements that may challenge the traditional sanctity of existing institutions, even if they do not challenge Ultimate Sacred Postulates themselves. Such challenges are extraordinary, are likely to be long-postponed, and their occurrence indicates crisis. Nevertheless, as the truths of sanctity set limits upon what in ordinary experience can claim validity, so does experience grounded in the psychic, organic and social processes of daily life set limits upon what may be taken to be sacred or sanctified. We shall return to these matters in the final chapters.

10

Sanctification

I have been speaking in loose and general terms of the "truths of sanctity." Although sanctity's apparent source is in Ultimate Sacred Postulates (which, being expressions concerning gods and the like are typically devoid of material significata) it is not confined to them. We noted in the course of discussing the hierarchical dimension of liturgical orders in chapter 8 that sanctity seems to flow from sacred postulates to other expressions which do include references to the here, the now and the material.

In literate societies, theological discourse may sometimes serve as a channel through which sanctity courses from Ultimate Sacred Postulates to other expressions but for reasons developed throughout this work the liturgical conveyance of sanctity is more compelling even among the literate. It is one thing for an exegete to derive a rule of conduct from an interpretation of a sacred text. It is another for the people to accept such derivations as binding upon them. Agreement, acquiescence or even belief *may* follow new theological argument, but acceptance is not its ineluctable entailment as it is in formal ritual performance.

The reach of liturgical sanctification is also more comprehensive. For instance, in light of the argument developed in chapter 4, it is difficult to see how commissives and testimony could be sanctified without being enunciated ritually inasmuch as it is not always or even often clear that an utterance is meant to be taken as a commissive or testament (and not merely a vague prediction or expression of intent or opinion) unless ritually marked as such.

Be this as it may, sanctity's domain, it is implicit in this account, includes two subclasses or categories of expressions. There is, first, the *sacred*, a category composed entirely of Ultimate Sacred Postulates.

Secondly, there is the *sanctified*, a category of expressions *associated* with Ultimate Sacred Postulates but not themselves ultimately sacred. Sanctified sentences are not in and of themselves unquestionable, but are contingent upon Ultimate Sacred Postulates from which they derive whatever degree of sanctity they possess, and, unlike Ultimate Sacred Postulates, *sets* of sanctified expressions are internally differentiated.

First, some are more highly sanctified than others. This was noted in the discussion of hierarchy in chapter 8, when it was proposed that the ordering of the corpus of expressions represented in a liturgy proceeds from postulates which are themselves ultimately sacred and thus, in and of themselves unquestionable, through cosmological axioms which are very highly sanctified, to rules which are likely to be less highly sanctified than cosmological axioms, and finally to other sentences perhaps even less highly sanctified. I suggested that the degree of sanctity accorded to liturgically ordered expressions should be *directly correlated* with the longevity, generality, efficacy, authority and immutability of that which they represent, and *inversely correlated* with their social and material specificity, concreteness and the instrumentality of their significata. The Ultimate Sacred Postulates standing at the apogee of such discursive structures are typically low in social and material specificity, devoid of concreteness, long-lived and taken to be eternal, fundamental, immutable, intrinsically efficacious, and self-sufficient rather than contingent or instrumental. They are also *intrinsically* sacred rather than *derivatively* sanctified. Cosmological axioms are more general, less specific, longer lived and more highly sanctified than the rules which specify the ways in which the principles expressed in the axioms are to be realized in conduct. Indications or reports of states of affairs (which are self-referential messages) are, in contrast, highly concrete, very specific, ephemeral, fluctuating, contingent, acted upon rather than efficacious, sanctified at best, possibly profane, and certainly not sacred.

This rather abstract and complicated description of the hierarchical organization of bodies of sacred and sanctified discourse is perhaps made more readily comprehensible by an example. A brief illustration offered in chapter 8 may be considered further here.

From the eleventh until the eighteenth century in England, and perhaps from an even earlier time in France, the king's touch was taken to cure scrofula, the disease known as "The King's Evil," and rituals in which the king laid his hands upon large numbers of sufferers occurred with some frequency. The successful cure required that the person laying on hands be in fact the king, which is to say that it derived from, and was contingent upon, the coronation ritual in which the king had been anointed in the name of God whose divinity had been continually established since earliest Christian times in the Mass.[1] We see here a flow of sanctity from Ultimate Sacred Postulates concerning God, expressed in the Mass, to the king, through the coronation ritual, and from the anointing of his hands in that ritual to, finally, the cure of scrofula in the ritual of laying on hands (Axon 1914: 736ff.).

The significatum of the Ultimate Sacred Postulate expressed in the Mass is not material, and it is taken to be eternal and immutable. The postulate is virtually devoid of social specificity, for it decrees neither particular institutions nor particular forms of social behavior as correct, moral, or legitimate. It is, nevertheless, ultimately and universally authoritative, for all of creation is subject to it, and it is that from which particular social conventions and institutions derive whatever legitimacy, morality, propriety and authority they may possess. As the ground of the universe it is understood to be contingent upon nothing, but is fundamental to all things. Although it is the source of all authority and legitimacy it is not conceived to be an instrument in the service of anything else. Ultimate Sacred Postulates are understood to represent the fonts from which sanctity flows and so participate in the maintenance of the orders whose elements they sanctify. These sources of sanctity are, however, represented as the principles or beings which the specific directives, expressed or implied in sanctified sentences, are understood to serve: *Hozho*, *Wakan-Tanka*, or in the case at hand, the Trinitarian God. As such, Ultimate Sacred Postulates constitute the form of directive implicit in such notions as ultimate concerns, goals and ends, although they may be extremely low in or devoid of social or behavioral specificity, and are not cast in the imperative mood. Ultimate concerns, goals and ends, moreover, may imply criteria against which more specific "lower order" goals and ends may be assessed. In chapters 13 and 14 we shall return to the place of such high order directives in the adaptive structure of human societies. Here I will only assert in adumbration that they stand in relation to the social elements of the world as do the energy conservation laws to the world's physical processes.

In contrast to Ultimate Sacred Postulates, the sentences and acts transforming persons into Christian kings by the act of coronation, and those by which such kings subsequently reign, contain indications that they and their significata are not fundamental but are, rather, contingent upon Ultimate Sacred Postulates, whatever they may signify. Henry is king by "Grace of God," Charles is "The Most Pious Augustus ... Great

and Peace-keeping Emperor" because he has been "crowned by God."
Christian kingship is not sacred but merely sanctified, albeit highly so.
Sanctification certifies not only the expressions transforming persons into
kings, but also those through which kings reign.

We approach the sanctification of instrumentality. The performative
ritual of curing the King's Evil is specifically instrumental and so,
obviously, are those that transform private persons or princes into kings.
Less obvious, the institution of Christian kingship itself was conceived as
an instrument in the service of God. Thus, in Visigothic Spain where
theories of kingship long influential in Christendom were being worked
out in the seventh century, the king came to be a *ministerium* in the
hierarchy of the Catholic Church, and *laesa maiestas* came to be
interpreted as Christian *infidelitas* (Wallace-Hadrill 1971: 55).[2]

Kingship, standing between God and man, became, as it were,
axiomatic in the constitution of medieval Christian society. That the
doctrines of kingship occupied such a position suggests that the authority of kings was understood to be general. But even the authority of
emperors was not conceived to be as comprehensive as that of the God
whom they served. Nature as well as society was subservient to God, as
were all Christian kings. Moreover, that which was owed by their
subjects to Christian kings was not unbounded. They were required to
render to Caesar's successors only what it was proper for Caesar to
demand. Moreover, a distinction between the sanctity of kingship as an
institution and that of particular kings seems to have been recognized in
the Christian World. The Germanic peoples seem never to have been
fully persuaded by the doctrine, promulgated in Visigothic Spain by
Isidore of Seville (Wallace-Hadrill 1971), of the necessity for a people to
suffer for their sins the rule of an incompetent, oppressive or unsuccessful king. Such a view, in fact, contradicted general pre-Christian
Germanic doctrine and practice. Pre-Christian kings among the German
peoples were generally taken to rule not merely by "grace of God," but
by right of divine descent. If, however, a king "lost his luck," as it was
said, a condition indicated by defeat, poor harvests, plague or disorder,
it was not merely the right but the duty of his people to depose him and
to elevate another member of the divinely-descended lineage to the
throne.

Kingship was, clearly, more highly sanctified than were kings but, as
kings could be deposed without challenge to the more highly sanctified
institution of kingship, so does the political condition of contemporary
western Europe testify that kingship, although in an earlier era "axio-

matic," could itself be disestablished without challenge to the Ultimate Sacred Postulates of Christianity.

In sum, relations of sanctification should have a certain logical structure: the degree of sanctity accorded expressions *should be* correlated directly with certain of their qualities, inversely with others. This claim is ambiguous, for it is possible to construe the conditional "should" as a qualification weakening the assertion to one of mere expectation or probability. Such a qualification is implicit but only because it follows from another, stronger sense of "should" that I mean to be primary here, namely its normative sense. I am asserting that the correlations I propose are "in order" or correct, but it is possible for understandings comprising discursive structures to become "out of order" or disordered. Some expressions may, for instance, become more highly sanctified than their specificity warrants or their communities can bear. Such disorders present serious problems to the societies in which they occur. We will return to these matters later.

1. Sanctified expressions
The discourse through which sanctity flows may include expressions widely variant in both content and rhetorical form. Myths – narratives in which humans are made of earth by words, or the world is sung into its shape by heroes, or first ancestors emerged from the tribal ground – are often intimately related to canon. They are, if not themselves ultimately sacred or the locus of Ultimate Sacred Postulates, highly sanctified, as may be other sanctified expressions which, in their enunciation, select as true particular understandings of the world from the great range of understandings and words the world makes possible. But sanctification is obviously not limited to discourse guiding thought or representing values. It also invests sentences stipulating specific actions or classes of actions to be undertaken or avoided. Prescriptions for ritual performances comprise an important class of such directives. In light of our discussion in chapter 4, they stipulate where, when and how Ultimate Sacred Postulates and other sanctified directives are to be unambiguously accepted. The proscriptions called "taboos" comprise another important class, especially significant because they reach out into everyday life. Dietary and interdining taboos, for instance, impose a sanctified order, in some instances (among the Maring) liturgically established, upon a fundamental biological activity. To put it conversely, taboo appropriates for liturgy important aspects of daily life. When such taboos become comprehensive, as among Orthodox Jews and the

Maring[3] the distinction between ordinary life and liturgy becomes indistinct.

Sanctified expressions may, in fact, be implicated in all aspects of social life. An important class is composed of acts and utterances certifying testimony and commissives: "I swear to tell the truth, the whole truth and nothing but the truth, so help me God," with one hand raised and the other on the Bible, "I pledge allegiance ... " with one hand on heart and, "I pledge to help you in future rounds of warfare," expressed in dance at a Maring *Kaiko*. There are also commandments such as "Thou shalt not kill," and homilies like "It is more blessed to give than receive." Performatives by which single people are transformed into married couples, war into peace, and princes into kings are regularly sanctified. Expressions like "Charles the Most Pious Augustus crowned by God Great and Peace-keeping Emperor" legitimize the authorities established by sanctified performatives. And if it is liturgically stipulated that Charles is crowned emperor by God, both the empire and the office of emperor, as well as Charles' occupation of that office, are at least implicitly sanctified. So, at one remove, are Charles' laws and commands and so, at a further remove, are the laws and commands of his duly appointed officers. Similarly, the sanctification of such healing procedures as monarchs' attempts to cure the King's Evil with their touch followed from the anointment of their hands during the rituals in which they were crowned by God or in his name.

Although sanctity has its apparent source in ritual and is in fact a product of ritual's form, it escapes from ritual's confines not only to enter everyday life but, in many societies, to pervade it. To suggest, following this account of sanctity's flow, that the sanctification of authority is universal in human societies is to approach tautology, for the sanctification of expressions is one way to make them authoritative. It is nevertheless worth noting that ethnography and history present to us a panorama ranging from small hunting and gathering societies, such as those of Australia, and tribal horticulturalists, such as the Maring, among whom sanctified directives emanate directly from liturgical orders, through societies in which authority is vested in sanctified chiefs, kings or emperors, to the enormous states of the twentieth century which, although claiming to be secular, also claim sanctity: the United States portrays itself to itself as "One Nation under God," its motto is "in God we Trust," and it swears officials into office with their hands upon the Bible. Its founding document grounds the rights of man whose security, it states, constitutes government's reason for being, not only in nature and in reason, but in God. To go further, it is a commonplace that, even in societies claiming to be atheistic, certain writings – the works of Marx, of Lenin and of Mao, for instance – are invested with a degree of sanctity comparable to that accorded scripture by god-fearing Americans; association with these writings through arguments that seem theological, and through such ritualized events as May Day parades, sanctifies the acts of their rulers.

In its flow from Ultimate Sacred Postulates to other expressions we also may note that the generalized quality of unquestionableness that I have said is definitive of the sacred is transformed into the more specific qualities appropriate to a range of markedly differing contexts: trust-worthiness in the case of oaths, truthfulness in the case of reports and testimony, legitimacy in the case of directives, propriety and morality in the case of conventions, and effectiveness in the case of performatives.

That occult efficacy may be included among the transformations of unquestionableness is implicit here, for it may, at least in part, be an effect of the sanctification of performatives, such sanctification enhancing their perlocutionary as well as illocutionary force. Sanctity's investiture and mystification of performative acts and utterances was taken up in the course of discussing the illocutionary force of rituals in chapter 4. It is possible, of course, to regard a coronation ritual as no more than a performative act, whose illocutionary force is simply legitimized by sanctity. Faithful subjects, on the other hand, can as easily understand it as a mystical transformation effected by God's Grace which, among other things, invests the king with a thaumaturgic capacity to cure "The Evil" with his touch. It can be argued that in such cases the understanding of the faithful is not only richer than that of an objective analysis but also in a sense "truer," for belief in the efficacy of an act of ritual healing may augment whatever effects illocutionary force may achieve with those achieved by the perlocutionary force of belief. That conviction may sometimes have powerful physiological effects seems well established.

2. Falsehood, alienation, sanctity and adaptation

I asserted in the second chapter that liturgy ameliorates two of the vices intrinsic to symbolic communication. The first, soon made explicit, is the facilitation of falsehood. I have argued that ritual ameliorates the problems of falsehood by moving, so to speak, in two directions. On the one hand, as proposed in chapter 2 and explored in chapter 3, ritual avoids the use of symbols (in Peirce's sense of the term) and favors the use of indices in at least some of its self-referential messages, its representations of the current states of performers, their societies, and their relations with their environments. We have seen in this chapter, on the other hand, that it also sanctifies representations of that which is *not* confined to the here and now. Thus, to return to a question raised but not answered in the second chapter, Maring hosts' confidence (such as it is) that their guests will in the future honor their commitments of military support being pledged by dancing in the present is grounded in the association of those pledges with the Ultimate Sacred Postulates expressed in the liturgical order of which the dancing is a part. The pledge, this is to say, is sanctified.

That the sanctification of commissives – oaths, pledges, and the like – is closely related to the sanctification of reports and testimony is at least strongly suggested by the derivation of the Old English and Old Norse terms for oath or pledge, *waer* and *var* respectively, from the Indo-European stem, *wero-*, true, from which the Latin *verus*, true, and its descendants are also derived (American Heritage Dictionary, 3rd ed. 1992). Oath and truth combine, of course, in the familiar courtroom formula "I swear to tell the truth, the whole truth, and nothing but the truth, so help me God," and it seems clear that the Dakota (see p. 299 above) regarded the smoking of the calumet to constitute, in certain situations at least, an oath to tell the truth. Such oaths transform reports or accounts into testimony, and common lies into perjury.

Although the facilitation of falsehood is a fundamental vice of language, it is not the only one, and it may not even be its most consequential one. The certification of the truthfulness of questionable information and the reliability of otherwise unsubstantiated oaths does not exhaust sanctity's offices. A range of other types of expressions (often but not always) sanctified were briefly noted above. It may be helpful to list them and others here. (1) myths (which may be highly sanctified, if not ultimately sacred), (2) cosmological axioms (which may be implicit in myth or ritual), (3) rules ordaining ritual performances and constituting taboos, (4) socially transforming factive acts and utterances (e.g. rites of passsage), (5) privileged exegeses (particularly but not exclusively in literate societies with recognized priesthoods, e.g. papal dicta *ex cathedra*, the Talmud), (6) prophecies, auguries, divinations and oracles, (7) acts and utterances mobilizing occult efficacy to achieve physical effects, (8) social directives (including commandments, rules, homilies, proverbs and perhaps other forms), (9) taxonomies and other forms which, although not cast in the imperative mood, may define rank, and may organize thought and thus may direct action, (10) expressions establishing

authorities, (11) the directives of sanctified authorities, (12) te
(13) commissives, (14) ritually transmitted self-referential inf
(which may also be indexically signaled).

This list does not constitute a claim that, for instance, all myᴛʜᴇ
either sacred or sanctified, or that all taxonomies or all prophecies or all
attempts to mobilize occult efficacy are sanctified, nor is it necessarily
exhaustive, although it may approach comprehensiveness. Be this as it
may, it is clear that although ritual may be the locus of the sacred and, as
such, the font of sanctity, sanctity escapes from ritual and may flow to all
of the expressions through which a society is regulated.

This is a matter of great importance, given another evolutionary trend
that must have been associated with the emergence of language: decrease
in specificity of genetic patterning of behavior, a matter broached at the
end of chapter 5 but one which requires further discussion here. The
reduction of genetic determination of patterns of behavior and the
elaboration of conventional, or cultural, stipulation of patterns for
behavior has conferred an unparalleled adaptability upon human kind,
permitting it, as we have noted, to enter and, eventually, to become
dominant in the great range of environments the world offers. But
intrinsic to increasing flexibility for the species as a whole is a concomitant problem for the separate societies into which the species is divided:
their members are not genetically constrained to abide by the conventions governing them, and can easily (and perhaps inevitably do) imagine
alternatives, some of which may seem preferable to those prevailing.
*Sanctity in the absence of genetic specification of behavior stabilizes the
conventions of particular societies by certifying directives, authorities who
may issue directives, and all of the mythic discourse that connects the
present to the beginning, establishing as correct particular meanings from
among the great range of meanings available to the genetically unbounded
human imagination.*

To put this a little differently, as we noted briefly at the end of chapter
5, the second problem intrinsic to language is that of alternative. With an
unlimited range of cultural orders within the genetic possibilities of any
normal human individual, the adaptive capacities of the species are
enhanced, and its adaptive processes accelerated. But possibilities for
disorder are also magnified. If the particular cultural orders of the many
societies into which humanity is organized are built upon words – and
they are – then there is not only the possibility of false words, but of
many words; not only of lie but of babel; of the possibility of being
overwhelmed by alternatives. Lie and alternative are *the* two funda-

mental problems – perhaps two fundamental problems vexing the use of language. We have already noted that Martin Buber (1952) took them to be humanity's original and distinctive contribution to evil.

I argued in chapter 5 that the conception of orders alternative to those prevailing is an inevitable concomitant of the process of predication, an aspect of syntax which, along with the symbolic relation of sign to signified, is a *sine qua non* of language. If it is possible to say "Christ is God and Jove is not," it is possible to imagine and to say the converse. The conception of alternative may be the first step toward the disruption of the existent, if not toward the realization of the alternative. All social orders protect themselves, and must protect themselves, against the disordering power of the linguistically liberated imagination, and tolerance of alternatives is therefore limited in even the most liberal societies. Thus, if there are to be any words at all, it may be necessary to establish *The Word*. Words are transformed into *The Word – The Sacred Word –* by being drawn into ritual and subordinated to the canon's invariance.

Let us put this argument in explicitly adaptive terms. The very versatility that has conferred upon the species the ability to expand into all of the niches and habitats that the world presents, a versatility that rests upon the specification of patterns of behavior through language rather than through genetic processes and limited non-symbolic learning, has intrinsic to it the problem of disorder. The ability to modify or replace conventions rapidly and inventively is central to human adaptiveness, but if alternatives to the conventions in accordance with which they live can be imagined (indeed may inevitably be imagined) by the members of any society, how can they be led to abide by those presently prevailing, particularly if some of the alternatives seem more attractive? One may suggest that sanctity provides a "functional replacement" for genetic determination of patterns of behavior, a determination which becomes decreasingly specific as language emerges. The capacity for variation or alternative that is given to the species by language is disciplined by sanctity, itself a product of language. *Flexibility is neither versatility nor a simple transformation or function of versatility. It is a product of versatility and orderliness.* The innumerable possibilities inherent in words and their combinations are constrained, reduced and ordered by unquestionable Word enunciated in ritual's apparently invariant canon. A versatility that otherwise might spawn chaos is ordered into adaptive flexibility through the process of sanctification. Like lie and alternative, sanctity, a precipitate of language, but language subordinated to the invariance of canon, ameliorates the evils of alternative as well as those of lie, making it possible for humanity to enjoy alternative's undoubted blessings, adaptive and otherwise.

In light of the argument, developed earlier in this chapter, that sanctity is a product of ritual, we may recall earlier discussions of the establishment of convention. I suggested in chapter 4 that some conventions are simply products of usage. Linguistic practices in non-literate societies may provide examples of statistical norms constituting conventions. In the cases of other sorts of conventions, however, particularly conventions concerning rights and obligations, usage is full of vagary and violation. As such, usage itself is not capable of establishing all conventions. *Societies must establish at least some conventions in a manner which protects them from the erosion with which ordinary usage – daily practice – continuously threatens them.* Ritual does so, and as such it may be without equivalents. In chapter 5 I reinforced this argument by proposing ways in which liturgy "naturalizes" conventions, and by suggesting that in naturalizing them it protects them. We now may add that ritual also sanctifies whatever it encodes.

Rules promulgated by decree may also be insulated from usage, but they do not, in their promulgation, entail acceptance, and, in the absence of acceptance, there is no morally sanctioned obligation. Decrees may or may not be sanctified, but the conditions which make it possible for some men to promulgate decrees by which other men must abide have developed only relatively recently – nowhere earlier than 10,000 or 12,000 years ago – if, as is generally agreed, plant or animal domestication is a virtual prerequisite to social stratification. Ritual, intrinsic to which are acceptance and sanctification, can, in contrast, establish conventions in the absence of discrete authorities. The ritual form – the performance of more or less invariant sequences of formal acts and utterances not encoded by the performers – is more ancient than humanity itself, and may have been the primordial means by which conventions were established among humans.

In sum, as the concept of the sacred would have been inconceivable in the absence of language, so might it have been impossible for language to have developed without a concept of the sacred to resist its ever-increasing capacity to subvert, through lie and alternative, the social systems relying upon it. The implication of this argument is that the idea of the sacred is precisely as old as language and that, contingent upon each other, they emerged together in a process of mutual causation formally similar to, and in likelihood concurrent with, that which is said to have organized the interdependent evolution of human intelligence and human technology. Indeed, if human intelligence is in part a product of language, then intelligence, technology, language and the concept of sanctity emerged together in what systems theorists would call a "mutually causal deviation amplifying process" (see Maruyama 1955).

This phylogenetic proposition does not rest only upon a teleological assertion of the indispensable place of sanctity in the communication of societies relying upon symbols. In the previous chapter I suggested that the emergence of the concept of the sacred may have been inevitable as well as indispensable, a product of the conjunction of symbol and ritual, developing as the speechless rituals of our pre-verbal forebears began to absorb *some* words selected from burgeoning language, thereby subordinating them to the invariant order of canon and transforming them into *The Word*. The Word, thus established, could stand against the uncertainties and treacheries made increasingly possible by ever more words combinable by increasingly complex syntactic rules into innumerable alternative possibilities, not all of which could simultaneously serve to organize or orient social life.

3. Major variations in sanctification

There are, of course, important differences among societies in the types of expressions emphasized in their sanctified discourse. The matter is so large and complex that I can do no more here than point in the general direction of some major lines of variation.

To expand slightly on a point already noted in passing, in so-called "egalitarian" or "acephalous" societies, highly specific rules, commands, and other conventions are, in the main, directly sanctified in ritual because the development of discrete human authorities has not gone very far. In societies in which such authorities have emerged there is an increasing emphasis upon their direct sanctification; therefore, whatever specific directives they promulgate are derivatively sanctified. The sanctification of human authorities – shamans, priests, chiefs, kings, presidents, parliaments – who can issue ranges of laws, rules, and commands makes for greater adaptive flexibility than is possessed when it is only possible to sanctify laws, rules and commands directly, but these advantages may entail certain costs, for example the material cost of supporting such authorities and the possibility that they may be unwise, oppressive or incompetent. We shall return to these matters in the final chapters.

There are, obviously, also differences in the substance of the expressions sanctified and, as in the case of types of expressions, some of these differences may be accounted for in evolutionary terms. It has been widely remarked, especially by missionaries and their apologists, that the religions of contemporary state-organized societies are especially concerned with the ethical behavior of individuals, whereas the religions of tribal societies are not. It is plausible to suggest that in small-scale societies, organized on the basis of kinship, proper social conduct is in some degree assured by the heavy dependence of every individual upon limited numbers of well-known kinsmen or co-residents. Conventions of reciprocity organize these relations of interdependence, reciprocity entails its own rewards and punishments for proper and improper conduct, and the conduct of everyone is the knowledge of all. In such societies, ethical behavior may not require strong sanctification because proper conduct may be adequately insured by the logic and practice of social relations themselves. This contrasts with large-scale societies in which the division of labor is elaborate, social stratification is well developed, the relationships of all individuals are both highly specialized and widely diffused over a range of others, and many or most of these relationships are impersonal or anonymous. Proper conduct is no longer insured by the logic of reciprocity in such circumstances, and those guilty of improper conduct may often go undetected. Moreover, in stratified societies where production is for gain rather than for use, the possible rewards of unethical behavior are multiplied. It is in such societies that ethical imperatives seem to receive the explicit certification of sanctity, perhaps because they require it. In tribal societies, this is to say, ethics are an aspect of social relations, while in states they are an aspect of religion. Where there is obligation in the tribal society there is charity in states.

There are also likely to be changes in the virtues celebrated. In tribal societies generosity and bravery are likely to be admired. Renown, prestige, honor and the influence following from them are the immediate rewards of valor and openhandedness. In states, meekness, loyalty, and dutifulness (N. Brown 1972) are among the most blessed of virtues and their rewards are eschatological. To make an evolutionary statement, religions are likely to increase their concern with ethics and to postpone rewards and punishments into the next world as social relations become increasingly diffuse, specialized, impersonal and stratified, as in societies organized as states. In tribal societies, in contrast, in which discrete authorities are either absent or only slightly developed, and in which such authorities as do exist are deficient in coercive power, sanctity is likely to be associated less with what missionaries take to be individual morality than it is focused upon the organization of public action. The Maring ritual cycle, for example, and the Gadjari cycle of the Australians, coordinate the activities of large numbers of individuals whose actions cannot be commanded by others.

4. Sanctity, community, and communication

I do not wish to leave the impression that the sanctification of authorities, of directives, of testimony and of pledges exhausts the significance of the sacred in secular affairs. Indeed, emphasis upon *sanctification* might derogate the *sacred* by making it appear analytically (its identification with ultimate concerns or *as* ultimate concern, that which all else serves, notwithstanding) to be no more than an instrument of legitimation and mystification in the hands of authorities, nothing more than a mechanism in the service of whatever powers might be prevailing. I shall discuss the degradation of sanctity by power as a historical process in the final chapter, but our concerns here are even more fundamental.

In speaking of the sacred and the sanctified we are speaking of properties of certain discourses. The sacred and the sanctified are thus, aspects of communication. I wish to emphasize here the significance not only of the sanctified but of the ultimately sacred in human communication. It is of interest that the terms "communicate" and "community" are obviously cognates. "Communicate" is derived from the Latin *communicare* "to make common" (American Heritage New College Dictionary 1992). A human community is an association of persons standing upon common ground. Those who hold Ultimate Sacred Postulates in common constitute communities as fundamental in nature as those defined by descent from common ancestors, for they accept common foundations for their testimony, their pledges, their institutions and much of their general understanding of the world.

There have been times when such a role for Ultimate Sacred Postulates in the definition of communities was commonly assumed. Edward Peters has remarked, in his introduction to a volume of documents concerning Christian heresy, that "throughout the Middle Ages and early modern history, theological uniformity was synonymous with social cohesion in societies that regarded themselves as bound together at their most fundamental levels by a religion" (1980: 3). Such an assumption was probably as firmly held by Muslims and Jews as it was by Christians, among whom it was doctrinal (Ullman 1975: *passim*), and vestiges remain. British monarchs, for instance, still take an oath to defend the faith upon which once stood the polity over which they reign.

It is probably safe to propose that communication is at least facilitated by the acceptance of common Ultimate Sacred Postulates, for, in their acceptance, common grounds for trust and understanding are established. Such considerations may seem irrelevant to much of the communication in modern secular societies with their elaborate divisions of labor and high technologies. In any event, modern societies, being generally "pluralistic" are not bound together by universal acceptance of common Ultimate Sacred Postulates, although their institutions are likely to be sanctified by the Ultimate Sacred Postulates of the several religious communities whose members participate in them. Yet we know, from the prejudice and religious strife still widespread in such societies, that communication, and thus relations among those not sharing common sacred and sanctifying ground, and often burdened by historical as well as theological reasons for hostility, are likely to be distrustful, fearful and even openly antagonistic.

Common acceptance of Ultimate Sacred Postulates certainly does not guarantee trustworthiness. It would be difficult or impossible to demonstrate that acceptance even enhances it, since members of communities defined by common Ultimate Sacred Postulates violate each others' trust more than they do that of others simply because they are likely to deal with each other more than they do with others. Furthermore, in dealings with outsiders, less may be taken on trust. "Cash on the barrelhead" is not always appropriate, but it seems a fine substitute for trust when it is, especially in dealing with strangers. Certainly, it has its cost, notably that of estranging – keeping at a distance and unrelated – those dealing with one another. Their communication, then, is likely to remain specialized and impersonal, and they, consequently, are likely to remain largely unknown to each other.

The suggestion made here is not that acceptance of the same Ultimate Sacred Postulates guarantees behavior conforming to commonly held and understood moral standards, but that, in conformity to the argument concerning the entailments of acceptance advanced in chapter 4, common grounds for morality and (with sanctified elaborations) of morality are accepted and, having been accepted, constitute common grounds for judging actions as moral or immoral. While, as we noted in chapter 4, such common acceptance does not guarantee moral action, it is plausible to argue that it increases its likelihood.

Enmity between separate communities that once did, but no longer do, accept the same Ultimate Sacred Postulates, or that even have come to distinguish themselves on less fundamental grounds (e.g., on matters of ritual practice or points of exegesis) is likely to be especially bitter. Apostates and heretics have been reviled *more*, and treated worse, than infidels in the course of Christian history, possibly because their errors are taken to be willful, and to constitute betrayal as well as sacrilege.[4]

Earlier I suggested that Ultimate Sacred Postulates are low in social specificity in the sense that they usually do not specify the particular institutions in terms of which the societies in which they prevail should conduct their affairs. Their acceptance does, however, specify or demarcate communities of those whose institutions, interactions and discourse stand on common ground.

5. The sacred, the sanctified, and comparative invariance

The derivation of sanctity from the invariance of liturgy leads us to expect a correlation between the sanctity and invariance of expressions. This correlation was, in fact, first announced in chapter 8 where it was proposed that Ultimate Sacred Postulates seem to be the most invariant elements in more or less invariant liturgical orders. If this generalization holds, it has both substantive and methodological implications, proposing as it does both the process through which expressions become sanctified or sacred, and a method for identifying Ultimate Sacred Postulates in bodies of religious discourse. Also of importance are instances not conforming to the expectation that could possibly be taken to contradict or at least question one of my fundamental proposals, namely that sanctity is a product of ritual's form rather than of its substance. Questions concerning the comparative invariance of various components of bodies of religious discourse must therefore be faced.

The notion of comparative or differential invariance[5] may seem clearer on first sight than it does on second thought. We may recall that the definition of ritual offered early in this work proposes that it is only "more or less" invariant. This apparently loose language was meant to recognize several of ritual's aspects.

First, there is the matter to which chapter 3 was devoted, the relationship of variance to invariance in the transmission of ritual's two streams of messages, the self-referential and the canonical. Variations carrying self-referential information, often indexically, are not only acceptable but necessary in all ritual, and all rituals specify them. The relationship of these proper variations to the properly invariant sequence of acts and utterances comprising the canon within which these variations occur is systematic. Ritual's unique significance arises out of the relationship of variations in representations indicating the current states of participants on the one hand to, on the other, the constancy of the order in which they are participating and which they are thereby realizing. The characterization of ritual as "more or less" invariant recognizes, first, that it is in ritual's nature for its canonical component to be highly invariant in comparison to its self-referential component which, representing as it does mundane conditions and changes in them, is *necessarily* variant. Earlier in this chapter I argued that comparatively variant self-referential messages are sanctified, which is to say certified, through their association with the highly invariant canonical stream.

Secondly, the expression "highly invariant," no less than the expression "more or less invariant," including as it does a qualification, recognizes the imperfection of actual practice. Societies vary in the amount of imprecision, error, and noise they will tolerate in their rituals. No performance of a canon could ever be a perfect reiteration in every detail of previous performances, of course, but there is probably always a threshold of disorderliness beyond which a performance is regarded as invalid, inefficacious or not even an instance of the ritual it purports to be. Among the Navajo, for instance, tolerance of imperfection is slight. Reichard (1944: 12) tells us "that a single mistake not only renders the prayer void, but may bring upon the one praying the wrath, instead of the blessing, of the beings implored." Among the Maring, in contrast, tolerance for imperfection seems to be greater. An important constituent rite in the ritual uprooting of *Yu Min Rumbim* commencing the *kaiko* requires a man to pierce a red pandanus fruit while bounding (barefoot, of course) atop oven stones heated to cooking temperature. When I first witnessed this rite a few days after arriving among the Tsembaga in 1962 an ax was used by the sub-clan whose rite I was attending to strike the fruit. Some months later I innocently mentioned this to two ritually knowledgeable men who had not been present. They expressed surprise and, possibly, traces of disdain and amusement about the use of an ax, agreeing that, normally, the way of the ancestors, a way followed and considered correct, directed the celebrant to pierce the fruit with a dagger fashioned from bone taken from a cassowary's leg. Their statement conformed to the association of cassowaries and the color red with high ground, and the spiritual inhabitants thereof; and warfare, and pandanus fruit with low ground, spirits of the low ground and peace, and also to the uprooting of *rumbim* as a step in the process of mending a world torn apart by the last round of warfare. As such their position seems to have been "orthodox," or "orthopraxic." Nevertheless, they would not, when asked, declare that the use of the ax invalidated the ritual, although they were clear in saying that they themselves wouldn't do it that way.

Of greater significance than tolerance of imperfection or variation, the expression "more or less" was meant to indicate that a higher degree of punctiliousness (care, decorum, or reverence) is likely to be required in the performance of some elements of canon than of others. Some expressions may have to be enunciated more precisely than others, or a higher degree of solemnity may be required in the performance of some portions of the liturgy than of others, stricter limitations may be placed upon where or when or by whom they may be performed, or the act of performance may be subject to special stylistic constraints – particular postures must be assumed, or gestures executed, or objects manipulated, or particular modes of expression such as chanting required. Some elements, finally, may be indispensable and therefore invariably present while others are not. Illustrations abound.

In Maring sacrifices, the invocation of spirits preceding the slaughter of pigs requires a stylized form of shouting called *rauwa* (the same word denotes spirits). Although these invocations are not specified to the degree that Christian creeds are, they are highly formulaic,[6] whereas the addresses to those spirits following the invocations, although stylized, are substantively situation-specific. Among the Sioux, the canon of filling the sacred pipe and smoking it, an indispensable component of all major rituals and one representing the Ultimate Sacred Postulate is exceptionally elaborate and solemn, and the words and acts comprising it are rigorously ordered and highly formalized (see below and also Walker 1980: 82, 87, 112). In Catholic liturgy it would seem that through the "solemn dialogue prefixed to the Eucharistic prayer ... the Church obviously wishes to set off this prayer above all others, declaring at once its importance and dignity." This practice, it should be noted, "is not peculiar to the Roman Rite: it is common to every Rite in the Church" (John Miller 1959: 275). The acts following, particularly the Consecration, are especially stylized (see Fortescue and O'Connell 1962). In Jewish practice the reading of the Torah requires great care. Not a word of Torah may be changed, nor one letter added or omitted, and the corresponding pages of all Torahs must have the same words inscribed upon them. The Torah is divided into regular portions which are preceded by an elaborate sequence of benedictions and prayers including an abbreviated version of the *Shema*. They are followed by designated selections from the prophets, which are accompanied by their own sets of benedictions. The reading of prophets is not subject to restrictions as rigorous as those surrounding the reading of Torah. Torah must be read from a scroll whereas the prophets may be read from a printed book, but in comparison to the reading of the prophets, sermons, a part of modern practice, are highly variant and almost casual.[7] Furthermore, boys can be called upon to read from the prophets but not from the Torah (Idelsohn 1932: 137ff.).

Punctiliousness in the expression of Ultimate Sacred Postulates or even highly sanctified sentences is, we see, not limited to what is said. There is also the matter of who may utter such words and who may hear them uttered. In all, or in almost all, rituals some or all of the performers must meet explicit qualifications to take the parts that they do or, indeed, any part at all. Such qualifications may be based upon age, sex, physical condition, descent, initiation (including baptisms, ordinations, coronations, etc.), state of purity, state of knowledge, or upon complexes of distinctions made within several of these categories.

The consideration of constraints or limitations on the persons who may, as it were, approach the ultimately sacred or highly sanctified, along with consideration of constraints on the places (often separated from those daily frequented, often protected from quotidian behavior and often possessing special characteristics, either natural or produced by human arts of construction or consecration) at which such approaches can be made are reminiscent of the association, made explicit by Durkheim (1961, orig. English trans. 1915), of the sacred with that which is "set apart and forbidden." Be this as it may, given the centrality of the ultimately sacred and highly sanctified in human life, the social consequences of differential access to them is enormous. I have argued elsewhere (1971a: 131ff.), as have others, that differential participation in ritual entails differential access not only to the sacred and sanctified *per se* but to the construction, maintenance, and modification of meaning and value generally. As such the establishment of exclusionary qualifications for ritual participation not only provides a fundamental ground for social inequality within human societies, but may have been crucial in its primordial development, legitimation and maintenance. The nature of these qualifications, whether and how they are achieved or ascribed, and their inclusionary and exclusionary effects constitute, as well as reflect, great and fundamental differences among societies and are, thus, not only matters of great significance but also of such complexity that they cannot be broached in this work. Here I wish only to note that such qualifications, which typically become more restrictive as the relationship to the ultimately sacred becomes closer, are aspects of punctiliousness as the term is used here.

The dimensions or aspects of invariance of expression are not exhausted by specification of what is said, by whom it is said and where (and when) it is said. There is also the matter of how it is said. As Maurice

Bloch (1973) has noted, chant or song add the additional constraints of rhythm and pitch to specifications of ultimately sacred or highly sanctified words, and thus add additional dimensions to the invariance of their expression. Moreover, formalization of expression is not limited to oral aspects of performance. Postures, gestures and movements associated with their expression, as we have observed earlier, may be highly stylized, as in the consecration of the Eucharist. Stylization of behavior may achieve its highest degree when the participant is not merely a performer of the ritual but, because of claims of divinity, an ultimately sacred, or at least highly sanctified sign in the discourse of the liturgical order.

In Southeast Asia, for example, kings "were not Defenders of the Faith, Vicars of God, or Mandatories of Heaven; they were the thing itself – incarnations of the Holy, as such. The rajas, maharajas, rajadir-ajas, devarajas, and so on were many hierophonies: sacred objects that, like stupas or mandalas, displayed the divine direct" (Geertz 1980: 124). More specifically, a Balinese king, according to Geertz (1980: 126), "no mere ecclesiarch, was the numinous center of the world," and his ritual demeanor or behavior could, in fact, approach what must be a logical limit of formalization.

In struggling to characterize the king's role in this regard the phrase that immediately comes to mind is T. S. Eliot's "still point in a turning world"; for, insofar as he was an actor in court ceremonies, his job was to project an enormous calm at the center of an enormous activity by becoming palpably immobile. Sitting for long hours at a stretch in a strictly formal poste [The *padmasana*, or lotus position] his face blank, eyes blanker, stirring when he had to with a slow formality of balletic grace, and speaking when he had to in a murmur of reticent phrases ... the king *was* the Great Imperturbable, the divine silence at the center of things: The Void-Self ... inactive ... devoid of form.

(Geertz 1980: 130)

The king was thus presented, says Geertz (1980: 131), quoting Worsley (1957), "as an abstract and anonymous man who behaves in a way wholly predictable within the logic of the image in which [he has] been formed." He, says Geertz, along with holy water, hymns, lotus seats, and daggers, becomes a ritual object, a sacred sign in a system of signs in which, sitting as he did "at the point above which the hierarchy was incorporeal, he marked the threshold of the sheer ideal" (Geertz 1980: 131).

Apparently similar constraints upon the activity of high chiefs devel-oped in Hawaii and, perhaps, in other parts of Polynesia, based upon conceptions that may not have been altogether dissimilar from those prevailing in Bali. According to Valeri (1985: 147) who cites a number of sources,

the ali'is are ... thought to be free of desire, precisely like the gods. This is why they are characterized by immobility and inactivity, not only on the mythical level ... but on the real level as well: "the highest point of etiquette among illustrious Hawaiians was, *not to move*." Laziness for a high-ranking ali'i is a duty, not a vice; it is a manifestation of his absolute plenitude, of the absence of any lack, and moreover, of perfect self-control. The prescription of immobility helps explain why divine ali'i do not walk but are carried; moreover, this custom reveals that ali'i belong to a realm above (heaven) as opposed to the below, represented by ground.

We have, in passing, touched upon another index of invariance. If an element is, as we noted in the case of the Sioux canon of the pipe, an indispensable component of all of a liturgical order's major rituals, or even of some of them, that element is, in an important sense, less invariant than those confined to a single ritual. In addition to the Sioux example we may recall that Witherspoon (1977) tells us the expression *sa'ah naaghaii bik'eh hozho* is included in "nearly every song and prayer in the elaborate [Navajo] ceremonial system." We may also consider the ubiquity of the *Shema* in Jewish liturgy and the *Kalimat al Shahada* ("I testify that there is no god but God and I testify that Muhammad is his prophet") in the liturgy of Islam. Spiro (1970: 193) also observes that the Buddhist confession of faith, the *Buddham saranam dacchami* ("I take refuge in the Buddha, I take refuge in the *Dharma*, I take refuge in the *Sangha*. For the second time I take refuge ... For the third time I take refuge ... ") is "the one indispensable ritual of nibbanic [nirvana-seeking] Buddhism."

Related to the ubiquity of an expression throughout a liturgical order is its comparative frequency. The *Shema* and the *Kalimat al Shahada* are uttered several times each day by the pious, and their expression also brackets the lives of the faithful. The *Kalimat* is "repeated in the ears of the newborn babe and by the lips of the dying" (Calverly 1958: 56) and "the first Hebrew words which a Jewish child learns are the confession of faith contained in [the *Shema*] ... and every believing Jew hopes that as he approaches his end ... he will be sufficiently conscious to repeat this same confession" (Finkelstein 1971: 478). Life is thus pervaded, encompassed, and ordered by the frequent repetition of these invariant expressions.

Because the differential ubiquity of elements is implicit in the very notion of liturgical orders there is really no need for further exemplification. It is well to emphasize, however, that without such elements a corpus of rituals would not constitute a liturgical order but would, rather, remain an unordered heap of unrelated rites. The assertion that some but not all elements of liturgical orders are ubiquitous is, thus, virtually tautologous for it is by, and in respect to, such elements that distinct rituals are joined together into unified orders. It is further obvious, but also worth reiterating and emphasizing, that in the examples adduced here the ubiquitous elements are judged to be (on grounds besides their ubiquity) Ultimate Sacred Postulates, and further worth recalling that to express them is to accept them.

There is another and very different sense, also adumbrated in the last chapter, in which we may speak of differential invariance, namely differential perdurance. Some elements of liturgical orders are apparently more ancient, more enduring, and more changeless than others. We might expect Ultimate Sacred Postulates to be among a liturgical order's most venerable elements. It is obviously difficult or even impossible to know how enduring the Ultimate Sacred Postulates of non-literate societies may be, but evidence from literate societies does suggest that Ultimate Sacred Postulates may persist unchanged for very long periods while other elements enter liturgical orders, remain for a while and then disappear. For example, the Buddhist *Buddham saranam dacchami* is founded in the *Khuddaka-Patha*, part of the Pali canon which may date to the third century BC (MacDonnel 1915: 81). This would make it at least as ancient as Buddhist scriptures themselves (Spiro 1970: 193), probably even older. According to a Gaonic tradition the concise expression of the Ultimate Sacred Postulate of the Jews, the *Shema*, together, perhaps, with its first benediction, several of its associated prayers, and perhaps also the ten commandments, formed the nucleus of the liturgy of the first temple, which was consecrated during the reign of Solomon in the tenth century BC (Idelsohn 1932: 14). If this tradition is correct the *Shema* is at least 3,000 years old and it might well be older, for if it formed part of the liturgy of the first temple it might have been included in the worship of at least some of the sanctuaries maintained by tribes and even less inclusive groups before the temple was built. After the destruction of the second temple and with the increased importance of synagogue worship in the diaspora, Jewish ritual practices prevailing in different regions came to vary in ways persisting until today.[8] Nevertheless the *Shema* continues to hold a central place in the rituals of the Ashkenazic Jews of northern Europe, the Sephardic Jews of the Mediterranean, the Karaites of the Crimea, who have been separated from the rest of Judaism for 1,000 years (Idelsohn 1932: 310) and the Beni-Israel of India who have been separated yet longer (Stritzower 1971: 14). Even the Falasha of Ethiopia, whose origins are obscure, have a place for an abbreviated version of the *Shema* in their liturgy although its importance is not clear from the available account (Leslau 1951: 124).

Other elements of Jewish liturgy share an antiquity almost as great. The set of benedictions called the *Amida* was fixed and made part of the daily liturgy following the destruction of the second temple (Idelsohn 1932: 26), and the practice of reading from the scriptures seems to have been well-established by the third century BC but references to its earlier practice are well-known (Idelsohn 1932: 138).

The Roman Mass is also very ancient, having attained "a certain definitive form" by the time of Gregory the Great at the end of the sixth century, a form which has, in the main, persisted until the present (John Miller 1959: 273ff.). Some elements of the Mass antedate Gregory by centuries, of course, among the oldest being those associated with the canon of the Eucharist. It is church doctrine that the first Eucharist was celebrated by Christ himself at the *Seder* which was the Last Supper, and the canon of the Eucharist described in the *Apostolic Traditions* of the third century contains the elements still remaining crucial to the central portion of the mass (John Miller 1959: 182, 251ff.). The canon of the Eucharist, as we have already observed, expresses the Ultimate Sacred Postulates of Catholicism.

In the centuries since the Canon of the Eucharist emerged in a form which would be familiar to Catholics living today other rituals and elements of ritual, for instance such sacramentals as homage, fealty and dubbing to knighthood, and the laying-on of hands by monarchs to cure the King's Evil have emerged, persisted for a while, then fallen into desuetude (see Marc Bloch 1961 I: 145ff., II: 312ff.).

The histories of Judaism and Christianity, then, provide some evidence that Ultimate Sacred Postulates tend to persist longer than do most or at least many other elements of ritual. It is unclear how general such a relationship is, however.

For one thing, the perdurance of the Ultimate Sacred Postulates of Judaism and Christianity may be, in at least some degree, a product of writing itself. The antiquity of such postulates in literate traditions may not be a reliable guide to what goes on in societies without writing.

Secondly, there is the matter of prophets. Prophets usually claim to revitalize old Ultimate Sacred Postulates rather than to announce new ones, or are associated with new postulates only retrospectively by their followers (see, for example, Wallace's classic discussion of the Seneca prophet Handsome Lake 1972: esp. pp. 239ff., 315ff. and 330ff.), but in some instances prophets do enunciate new Ultimate Sacred Postulates. Such claims can, perhaps, be made for the Buddha, for Mohammed, and for some of the leaders of Melanesian millenarian movements.

Thirdly, although the Ultimate Sacred Postulates of Christianity and Judaism are of greater antiquity than most of the other elements of Christian and Jewish liturgy respectively, both canons include even older elements. Northern European Christian usage, for instance, is full of northern European pre-Christian usage. To this day the most highly sanctified day of the Christian liturgical calendar goes, in English speaking countries, by the name of the northern goddess Eostre. Similarly, Catholicism in general has preserved many elements of Jewish ritual. As Idelsohn (1932: 301) observed, "Nobody, in reading the pre-Christian forms of prayer in the Jewish liturgy and the prayers of the early Church, can fail to notice the similarity of atmosphere in each ... Even when one perceives ... variety in the latter form, the genus is unmistakable." The institution of reading the scriptures was taken over from the Synagogue, the response of "Amen" and the exclamation "Hallelujah" at prayer's end, the recitation of psalms, the confession and the recitation of the Decalogue, dropped from the synagogue liturgy everywhere by the thirteenth century AD (Idelsohn 1932: 91) were simply and directly continuations of Jewish usage. The heart of the *Sanctus*, retained in the Mass until this day, is a literal translation of the *Kedusha*, which remains an element of Jewish liturgy (see Idelsohn 1932: 301–308). The Canon of the Eucharist as a whole is generally derived from the Passover ritual from which, according to church doctrine, it is directly descended.

In turn, many elements of Jewish liturgy, including some remaining in contemporary practice, are known to antedate Judaism itself. Among them are not only such general features as burnt offerings, but also such specifics as divine names and epithets. *El* is an instance,[9] and the epithet (or part epithet) *Sabaoth* is also of interest. "According to repeated testimony it was part of a legend on the Ark" (cf. I Samuel 4: 4, II Samuel 6: 2; Freedman 1976: 98) in combination with the divine name Yahweh. In the expression *Adonay Sabaoth*[10] "The God of Hosts," it persists, among other places, in the *Kedusha*, a prayer of sanctification of considerable importance in Jewish liturgy. We have already noted that the *Sanctus*, an important element in the Catholic Canon of the Eucharist, translates the *Kedusha* into Latin, although retaining the name "Sabaoth" in Hebrew. deVaux (1961 II : 304) suggests that this name is pre-Israelitic in origin. If he is correct we have here an instance of a liturgical element, an important name for the divinity, persisting through three major religious traditions, Canaanite, Jewish and Christian.

We have already noted that the name "Easter" remains a direct legacy of a northern pantheon to Christ's Church, which in other places calls the same holiday by names derived from *Pesach*, the Hebrew for Passover, a Jewish festival from the liturgy of which the Mass is said to have sprung. It seems, moreover, that *Eostre* was not originally conceived by the English, nor was she even of Germanic conception, for her name "is identical with [i.e., a cognate of] Latin, Sanskrit and Lithuanian names for the goddess of the dawn" (Welsford 1921: 102).

If we permit ourselves to proceed to yet less specific or more general similarities and identities even longer continuities are to be found. The goddess Eostre, or Eostur also provided the name by which the pre-Christian English called the month approximating April (Eosturmonath), according to Bede, who tells us that sacrifices were made to her then (Chadwick 1910: 138). Because the year started on December 25 (taken to be the winter solstice), Eosturmonath may have commenced a little earlier than does April – around March 25, which approximates the date of the vernal equinox, and which was sometimes formally observed as such, at least in the early church (Jones 1943).[11] The fourteenth day of the Hebrew month of Nissan, the date of Passover, also falls close to the vernal equinox. Spring festivals are not only widespread, but must also be very ancient. It is plausible to suggest that those having currency are merely the latest in a line of descent that, although transformed again and again, has remained unbroken for many millennia, perhaps even tens of millennia.

In light of such historical counter-evidence the expectation that Ultimate Sacred Postulates will be among the oldest of any liturgical order's elements does not seem to be met. It may be well, therefore, to qualify it, proposing only that Ultimate Sacred Postulates tend to be more abiding, less transitory, more resistant to modification and change than other elements of canon. Perdurance is, after all, only one aspect of invariance, and deficiencies of antiquity could be compensated for by extraordinary punctiliousness of performance, because character as well as age may render persons or objects venerable. It also may be recalled that the eternal may be conceived to stand changeless and outside of time's flow. Prophets can, therefore, invest postulates, for the first time revealed by them, with the truth of eternity not only by asserting that they are recovering them from a forgotten historical past, but also by bringing them back from ecstatic experiences in "times out of time."

Little is lost by accepting such a qualification, and both prudence and the complexity of the matter urge it. It does not seem to me, however, that the countervailing cases adduced here invalidate the thesis that differences in the apparent invariance of expressions underlie differences in their sanctity. Moreover, we should not leave the matter at that because important aspects of sanctification and its problems may be illuminated by further discussion of apparent age or priority. We may approach them by returning to the continuities exemplified by the relationship of Easter to Eostre and Passover.

First we may recall an argument presented in chapter 2 concerning the near contradiction between human invention and sacred status that leads us to expect such continuities. Liturgical orders are seldom if ever made new out of whole cloth. Few *if any* liturgical orders are lacking in elements surviving from older ones. In some instances the surviving elements may be elements of Ultimate Sacred Postulates of the old order and, although not *by themselves* constituting the Ultimate Sacred Postulates of the new, they may contribute to, be absorbed into, or become parts of the new. The *Kedusha*, a short prayer beginning "Holy, Holy, Holy is the Lord of Hosts, the whole earth is full of His Glory" seems to have been "used as a form of sanctification during the second temple," according to Idelsohn (1932: 98), and could possible be regarded as part of an extended expression of the Ultimate Sacred Postulate of Judaism. We have noted that it survives in Catholicism as the heart of the *Sanctus*, which can be taken to be part of an extended expression of an Ultimate Sacred Postulate that also includes the doctrines of Christ's divinity, the immaculate conception, the resurrection, and the triune nature of the Godhead.

The assimilation of old Ultimate Sacred Postulates, or parts of them, into what *eventually* come to be recognized as new liturgical orders, preserves the sanctification of orthodoxy for what, at the outset, might otherwise seem heterodox, heretical, or no more than the work of man, neither divine in origin nor worthy of ultimate sacred status. New orders may continue to claim the sanctity of the old at the same time that they are distinguishing themselves from them.

It is clear that the significance of doxological or doctrinal continuity, as exemplified by the translation of the *Kedusha* into the *Sanctus*, is not only theological. The persistence of old Ultimate Sacred Postulates, or parts of them, into new orders may mask the profundity of religious transformations from the participants. The presence of familiar old Ultimate Sacred Postulates, or some of their elements, may suggest to those involved that the sacred postulates distinctive of the new order do not displace or invalidate the old but simply add to or elaborate them. It may be suggested that it is much easier and more agreeable to augment than to reject, and it makes it possible for religious transformations to be understood by those going through them to be *intensifications of acceptance*, not denials or abandonments of what had been accepted in favor of something new. We may note here that it was deliberate Catholic policy, enunciated by Pope Gregory the Great[12] to permit or even to encourage the continuation of certain pre-Christian practices during the missionization of the English, quite explicitly to ease the conversion experience. Holy days coinciding with the pagan liturgical calendar were emphasized, fanes (temples) were reconsecrated to Christian worship, and Christian feasting at times when the people were accustomed to offer sacrifices to their old gods was ordained. The missionaries even tolerated the compromise of King Redwald of East Anglia who early in the seventh century "set up two altars in one temple, one *ad Sacrificium Christi* and the other *ad Victimus daemoniorum*" (Bede 1955 II: 15; Chaney 1970: 161). Christ was, it would seem, initially accepted by the people of East Anglia as a new member of the northern pantheon, his divinity sanctified by his association with the old gods in the old places at the old times, like Yule and the feast of Eostre.

Eventually new orders become sufficiently venerable in their own rights to separate themselves more sharply from the ancestral orders from which they have sprung. Thus, although Catholic liturgy has retained Jewish elements to this day, by the year 200 AD congregations reckoning the date of Easter in a way which made it possible for it to coincide with Passover were being anathematized as "those who would celebrate Easter with the Jews." Subsequently Jewish sabbatarian practice was also gradually supplanted among Christians by the observance of the Lord's Day on Sunday. Given the covenantal significance of the Sabbath for Jews and the importance of both Passover and Easter these liturgical discontinuities were definitive (see chapter 6 above). It was not until 640 AD, almost a half century after his grandfather, Aethelbert's conversion, that Eorcenbert of Kent became the first English king to decree the overthrow of the idols still standing within his domain (Bede 1955: Book III, ch. 8).

It should not be imagined that attempts were ever made to extirpate all practices and understandings sanctified by pre-Christian usage from English religious, social and political life. There were, in fact, clear attempts to preserve some of them. It is noteworthy that in seven of the eight surviving genealogies of Anglo-Saxon royal houses descent was traced from Woden, and continued to be traced from Woden long after conversion (Chaney 1970: 29; Lappenberg 1894 I: 352ff.). Sanctified kingship was one of the axioms or foundations of early Germanic societies (Chaney 1970, Wallace-Hadrill 1971), not something easily or casually subject to experiment. The reluctance of the English to give up the doctrine of the divine descent of kings as they adopted the sanctification of kings in Christian ritual may possibly be accounted for by the limitations that the genealogies emanating from northern divinities placed upon the persons eligible to ascend the throne; Christian rituals, in contrast, in and of themselves do not similarly limit eligibility. As we have already noted, only members of royal lineages could rightfully become kings in pre-Christian English society. Such a "Woden-sprung" king could, however, be deposed and replaced by another member of the royal lineage should he through misadventure or incompetence "lose his luck" (see Chaney 1970, especially chapter 1, and Wallace-Hadrill 1971). It is here that Christian ritual had something to offer to Germanic kings. By 633, in Visigothic Spain, the crowning of the king made him a *minister Dei* and, although he was supposed to be just, pious and a father to his people, his subjects were, for their sins, to suffer his cruelty or ineptitude if he was not (Wallace-Hadrill 1971: 53ff.). But even then the English did not abandon the notion of the divine origin of kings.[13]

The liturgical, theological and, possibly, social and political circumstances prevailing antecedent to such events as the overthrow of the Kentish idols or a change in the reckoning of Easter are ambiguous, uncertain and often unstable. Bede tells us, for instance, that in the first three decades of the century kings of Kent, East Anglia, Essex and Northumbria quit Christian practice and resumed worship of northern gods for varying lengths of time (Bede 1955: Book II ch. 5, Book III ch. 1). In earlier chapters we noted, however, that vagueness is reduced by digital representation and that binary signals (being "yes/no" or "either/or" signals) are *in their very nature* free of ambiguity. I argued that ritual occurrences are in their nature binary and as such they are especially well-suited to distinguish succeeding from preceding states of affairs unambiguously. They thus impose upon the processes of nature, society, and thought discontinuities sharper than those intrinsic to the processes themselves. I suggest that this formulation holds good not only for the occurrence of established rituals but also for their replacement. The changes signaled by the replacement of one liturgical order by another are, of course, more profound than those signaled by the occurrence of established rituals. In distinguishing before from after they do not merely separate phases in recurrent cycles (as do, for example, solstitial and equinoctial rituals) or periods in such irreversible processes as lives (as do rites of passage). They distinguish epochs in the histories of people and are so construed (if earlier times are not entirely lost to memory).

The relationship of discontinuity to continuity, manifested in the relationship of liturgical orders to those from which they have separated themselves and to others coordinate with themselves emerging from the same antecedent orders, is formally similar to that prevailing in genetic processes. Minor liturgical changes may occur with considerable frequency, and contemporaneous variations in practice often emerge and are established. If Ultimate Sacred Postulates remain unchanged such variations may indicate nothing more than the adaptation of a fundamentally constant body of doctrine to regional or ethnic particularities, as illustrated by the various rites of the Roman Catholic Church.[14]

Somewhat more profound differences in ritual practice and in the interpretations of generally common Ultimate Sacred Postulates distinguish the sects or denominations of Protestantism from each other, and yet more marked ones set apart Protestantism as a whole from Roman Catholicism. Differences in Ultimate Sacred Postulates distinguish Christianity in general from Judaism in general.

Species are distinguished by the criterion of genetic discontinuity, that is to say, by ruptures in genetic communication. Liturgical orders, and the communities in which they are enacted are separated from each other by ritual distinctions which also effect attenuations or even ruptures in communication. The Protestant denominations, it is said, are not "in communication" with the Vatican, and if Ultimate Sacred Postulates form the grounds of the communication that constitute communities, then Christianity and Judaism are separated more profoundly.

It should be kept in mind, however, that despite the uncounted genetic hiations that have produced all the species, genera, orders, phyla the world has ever seen, all living organisms have descended in unbroken lines from the first simple creatures to have emerged from organic compounds in the warm seas of the archaezoic. Similarly, it is plausible to think that, despite the birth of gods and their banishment, liturgical continuity has remained unbroken from the moment when first our ancestors spoke words in ritual.

Consideration of continuity and discontinuity returns us to the matter of the differential perdurance of liturgical elements as a dimension or aspect of comparative or differential invariance.

There is a sense, tautological but nevertheless significant, in which Ultimate Sacred Postulates are always among the original elements of any liturgical order simply because liturgical orders are recognized as distinct from their antecedents by virtue of the distinctiveness of their Ultimate Sacred Postulates. When such postulates are abandoned, replaced, or even substantially modified, augmented or elaborated one liturgical order has replaced another even if many ritual elements persist. The invocation, or even the awareness, of that distinctiveness may be long postponed, as in the separation of Christianity from Judaism, and such distinctions may be retrospectively imposed by peoples on their own pasts, if they preserve any memories of antecedent orders at all.

If antecedent orders are remembered: an account based upon histories of literate societies should not allow us to forget that, as discussed in chapter 6, some components of canon change so infrequently or slowly that they are likely to seem forever changeless to those performing them. The appearance of changelessness is easier to maintain in non-literate than literate societies, for in them social memory is unlikely to penetrate much further into the past than a few generations. Anything surviving from yet earlier times is likely to be regarded as something which has forever been. Given a short social memory Ultimate Sacred Postulates, and perhaps other elements of canon as well, may become "eternal verities" or even become associated with creation itself. Ultimate Sacred Postulates, in sum, may become apparently invariant because their variation is so slow as to elude detection or so infrequent as to be lost to memory.

They become *apparently* invariant: we may remind ourselves that we are concerned with the comparative invariance of various elements of ritual, proposing a correlation between invariance and sanctity. I have argued that sanctity is a quality of discourse. *When we speak of sanctity we speak of signs and significance.* If we are concerned with the *significance* of invariance it is *apparent* invariance that finally counts. The *actual* changelessness or antiquity of an element is semiotically important only insofar as it affects the perception or understanding of that element as ancient, changeless or eternal. Appearances here are "truer" than facts.

We can recall here a problem, noted at the end of chapter 6, that literacy creates, or at least exacerbates, problems for apparent changelessness. The penetration of social memory into antiquity and the preservation of memory of the present into the distant future are virtually entailed by writing. History in some form is an almost inevitable product of literacy; it can hardly avoid exposing changes in what, in the absence of writing, would have been taken to be never-changing. Writing makes it possible to submit myth to history's judgment. The apparent thus may be polluted by the actual, and ideal structures dissolved by known events. "May be" should, of course, be emphasized. The presence of writing is one thing, widespread literacy another (Goody 1977), the reading of history or of chronicles yet another. What are unavoidable facts for historians may be unknown to common folk.

In sum, the correlation of sanctity with *apparent* invariance does not seem to me to be damaged by facts to the contrary. The unquestionableness that constitutes the essence of the sacred is a product, twice over, of liturgy's apparent invariance, a product of the acceptance intrinsic to the performance of invariant orders encoded by other than the performers, and a product of the certainty intrinsic to that which is represented as without alternative. In a later chapter we will discuss a third ground of the sacred. Here we will only reiterate that the Ultimate Sacred Postulates in which the sacred resides ground the social world as the conservation laws do the physical. Chapter 11 will be devoted to the sanctification of the *Logoi* that order social worlds.

11

Truth and order

The essence of the sacred, it was argued in chapter 9, is unquestionableness and unquestionableness is an entailment of both canonical invariance and its performance. In an earlier chapter, I argued that canonical invariance also provides the ground for the idea of eternity, and perhaps of immortality as well: the unquestionable truths of the ultimately sacred are apparently eternal. They are further extraordinary because, although they are in words, the truth to which they lay claim is not the contingent truth that other expressions may but do not necessarily possess. They claim the truth of that which is, the absolute "truth of things": not mere temporal veracity but eternal verity. There is an inversion here of what we are inclined to regard as the usual relationship of expressions to that which they signify. Statements, reports and descriptions are judged true, correct or adequate by the degree to which they correspond to the states of affairs or facts that they signify which exist independently of themselves. In contrast, if the ritual form makes unquestionable whatever it represents then ultimate sacred postulates, by being "truly said" in liturgy bring into being metaphysical facts or states of affairs corresponding to themselves. This act of creation by word, fundamentally performative in nature, is immediately mystified as constative expression. The result is that the correspondence theory of truth remains intact but is, as it were, "stood on its head."

It is this inversion which gives to the truths of sanctity their extraordinary character. Expressions truly said in ritual become the criteria against which may be assessed the contingent "truth" – propriety, morality, legitimacy, or correctness – that may be but is not necessarily a quality of practices, facts or states of affairs. States of affairs, facts, practices, conditions or understandings at odds with ritual's true expressions are *ipso facto* false or wrong, no matter how palpable or substantial they may be, and we have seen that in some traditions terms including among their meanings "lie" are used to designate them.

We may recall here that sanctity was defined at the beginning of the last chapter as a quality of religious discourse rather than of the objects of that discourse. If, however, in the inversion of the correspondence between expressions and states of affairs, expressions come to be the criteria against which palpable states of affairs are assessed, and if states of affairs, facts or practices can thereby be judged false, then it is implied, to say the least, that truth is not only a property of the religious discourse within which those expressions have a place, but of the divine or metaphysical objects those expressions denote. As we have already noted, the distinction between religious discourse and the objects of that discourse is blurred or mystified in the inversion of the correspondence relationship, and in many religious traditions truth is a quality explicitly attributed to divine objects.

What of the nature or scope of these divine objects? It is clear from discussions in the last chapter of sanctification, of the relationships of the truths of sanctity to deutero-truths, and especially from the discussion of truth and divinity in which the Nahuatl concept of Nelli was considered, that divine beings are not all that are or can be established in ritual as possessing the "truth of things." Nelli was not only a property of the first and highest deity – he who inhabited "the thirteenth heaven, of the beginning of which nothing was ever known" – but a quality with which he endowed the universe, providing it with a founding order.

The truth of divine orders as well as divine beings is established in ritual. It may even be that divine beings cannot be established in solitude because liturgical orders may need to include more than representations of the divine if their invariant features and acts of performance are to be developed sufficiently to constitute "true expression." Whether or not this is the case, we have seen that Ultimate Sacred Postulates are parts of more general canons and these canonical or liturgical orders are established concurrently with them.

We may recall here that it was suggested in chapter 8 that liturgical orders do not represent "the political order" or "the social order" or "the economic order." They represent – or re-present – themselves. This characterization was not meant to suggest futility or emptiness, for the "true expression" of a liturgical order establishes the actuality of the order represented and, possessing the truth of things, that order becomes sovereign for those accepting it. Whatever it encodes become directives, commands or, as we say, "orders." A True Order is thus imposed upon the world by the performance of the liturgical order that is its representation. Cosmic orders are made in correspondence to the complex representations of liturgical orders in their entireties.

The dimensions of liturgical orders were discussed at length in chapters 6, 7 and 8 and in the context of sanctification in chapter 10. It would be well to recall that such orders are not entirely metaphysical in content. In addition to Ultimate Sacred Postulates and cosmological axioms they include rules for social action and individual behavior and, of course, acts undertaken in accordance with some of those rules. They may also include representations of natural phenomena, both environmental and physiological. Expressions differing in rhetorical, semiotic and logical type, and ranging in their temporal values from ephemeral to eternal are found among their utterances. They are not, however, entirely discursive in their effects. Strong emotions may be generated in those who realize them, a matter that has been touched upon in past chapters but will be developed more fully in a later one. In sum, liturgical orders are meta-orders, orders of orders binding together the natural, the cultural and the social, the individual and the group, the discursive and the non-discursive into coherent wholes. Sanctified by the Ultimate Sacred Postulates at their apices, they are pervaded by the specific virtues into which unquestionableness may be transformed in its sanctifying descent from the ultimate: propriety, correctness, legitimacy, morality, reliability, truthfulness. That which is realized in the true expression of liturgical performance is the true order of the cosmos: enduring, correct, moral, legitimate, natural. As we have noted, such divinely ordained cosmic orders provide criteria in terms of which actions, events, words, ideas and even conventions may be judged and found proper, good, true, "in order" or erroneous, evil, false, "out of order." I will use the term "Logos" to refer to such world-encompassing orders.

1. Logos

Because "word" is probably the gloss most frequently given in English for Logos, and because its use in the New Testament to refer to an incarnated God is so familiar, it is necessary to make clear that I am not following this narrow and late usage when I use "Logos" to denote the cosmic orders that may be established in liturgy. I am, rather, invoking a range of meanings emphasized in earlier times, particularly as they were brought together by Heraclitus, his reporters, and his interpreters.

The history of the word is well known from texts. In Homer, according to Debrunner (1967: 72ff.), the basic meanings of the associated verb *lego* seems to be "to gather," "to count," "to enumerate," "to enter on a list," "to enlist," "to narrate," or "to say." Debrunner infers from Homeric usage that, because "the enumeration usually aims at completeness," there is also a sense of "not concealing or forgetting anything" (p. 72) and thus of wholeness or comprehensiveness. He proposes that the notion of continuous ordering is also implicit because "to gather is to pick out things ... [in some sense] alike. It implies on the one side 'succession', 'repetition', and on the other judgment, logical separation" (p. 72).

The meanings of the noun Logos parallel those of the verb. There are first, those of "collection" and the allied meanings "gathering," "assemblage," and "list." It also denotes in Homer "calculation," "account," and "reckoning" (as of numbers) (p. 72), and "narrative" and "speech" in a general sense were to be found among its early meanings. Soon after Homer's time, however, "Logos" as utterance comes to be reserved for "rationally established and constructed 'speech'," in contrast to both *epos* which "came to be almost completely limited to the sense of verse, and [from] *mythos*, to be used only for (invented or not very well established) 'history'" (p. 74).

Other early meanings seem to have been derived from these fundamental denotations. "From expressions like 'take account of' there arises the sense of 'consideration', 'review', 'evaluation', 'value', "and from such meanings it was an easy step to the meanings 'reflection' [and] 'ground'" in the sense of logical ground: "on what ground, lit. by what calculation" (p. 74). Much later it becomes "a technical term in mathematics: proposition, relation, element, in the Euclidean sense" (Kleinknecht 1967: 78). By Heraclitus' time, at the end of the sixth century BC, "With the interrelation of mathematics and philosophy, logos, as the rational relation of things to one another ... acquires the more general sense of 'order' or 'measure'" (Kleinknecht, 1967: 78).

Orders imply unifications of some sort; and the notion of binding together, the "togetherness" of all "things that are,"[1] is fundamental in Heraclitus' conception of the Logos (Heidegger 1959: 127f.), or what is understood of it from the fragments that have come down to us. In fact the term "togetherness" is hardly adequate to indicate the integration realized in Logos. Heidegger characterizes it, particularly in his reading of Heraclitus' Fragment 114 (but see also Fragment 2 [G. Kirk 1954: 57]), as the "original unifying unity of what tends apart."[2] Kirk agrees. In his summary of fragments 1, 114, 2, and 50 he states "the chief content of the Logos is that all things are one" (1954: 32). Heidegger observes that permanence and endurance are also fundamental to the philosopher ironically remembered best for the dictum "everything flows," and Kleinknecht concurs: "It is the transcendent and lasting order in which flux occurs" (1967: 81).

Logos in Heraclitus signifies, in Heidegger's words, "neither meaning nor word nor doctrine, and surely not 'meaning of a doctrine'; it means: the original collecting collectedness which is in itself permanently dominant" (1959: 128). It is an ordering principle subordinating and binding all that exists into a coherent and enduring whole. Its antithesis, *sarma*, is "that which is merely tossed down ... muddle over against togetherness" (Heidegger 1959: 133), randomness or chaos.

By Heraclitus' time Logos is taken to be accessible to humans. According to Kleinknecht,

It is presupposed as self-evident [in ancient Greece] ... that there is in things, in the world and in its course, a primary logos, an intelligible and recognizable law which then makes possible knowledge and understanding in the human logos ... [according to Heraclitus, because] the same logos constitutes the being of both the cosmos and man, it is the connecting principle which forms the bridge and possibility of understanding, [first,] between man and the world and also between men'.
                                                                              (1967: 81)

It follows, as G. Kirk puts it in his synopsis of the burdens of fragments 41, 32 and 108, that

Only one activity can be described as genuinely wise, that is the understanding of the way in which everything in the world is part of an ordered whole: everything is guided along a determinate path so as to produce a complex and essentially unified result ... only one entity can have this wisdom to the full, and so be properly called "wise": this is the divine entity (both "force and "substance" in modern terms) which itself accomplishes the ordering of the whole – fire according to fragment 64,[3] the Logos according to the more analytical approach of fragments of Group 1 ... Human wisdom which is the same in kind as the divine ... is quite separate from other forms of cleverness. It is of greater importance ... because only by possessing it can a man adequately assimilate himself to the ordered whole of which he is a part; and yet it remains within reach of all.
                                                                              (1954: 385)

These accounts make clear that the "Logos is not taken to be something which is merely grasped theoretically. It claims a man. It determines his true life and conduct. The Logos is thus the norm" (Kleinknecht 1967: 81). In later Hellenistic thought these themes are elaborated, and it becomes increasingly explicit that "the particular logos of man ... is part of the general logos ... which achieves awareness in man, so that through it God and man, or the sage or philosopher as the true man who alone has orthos logos, and who thus lives as a follower of it, are combined into a great cosmos" (Kleinknecht 1967: 85).

It is also clear that Logos possesses an irreducible social component. It not only constitutes the bridge between man and the world, absorbing both those who follow it and God into "a great cosmos," but it also must thereby bind those who follow it to each other. In his synopsis of the first group of fragments, Kirk (1954: 32) writes "The Logos according to which all things come to be is 'common' in two senses: it is universal, and it is equally apprehensible by all." Moreover, insofar as the Logos constitutes norms, as Kleinknecht proposes, it must be social, for the concept of norm has an irreducible social import. Later "the Logos as the basic fact in all life in society [becomes] ... the decisive point in the politics of Socrates and Plato" (Kleinknecht 1967: 83).

It follows from the comprehensiveness of the Logos that in its wholeness it is endowed with certain qualities, one of which is harmony. This harmony is not a product of mere compromise, however, nor does it necessarily reduce tensions (Heidegger 1959: 134). It is a harmony among things that may be in conflict, or that pull in opposite directions. Heraclitus illustrates its nature in Fragment 51 (G. Kirk 1954: 203) by pointing to the bow and the lyre. In both there must be forces working in opposite directions if they are to perform as bows and lyres. This harmony, being a harmony that contains flux, conflict and tension as well as easy agreement, is hidden; nevertheless, it is in its true nature ultimately accessible to those who will heed it, that is, hear it and follow its order.

Although not easily accessible, Logos also possesses *alethia* which, etymologically, has the meaning of "non-concealment" (Bultmann 1967: 238). It is, however, generally glossed as "truth," clearly signifying not the "truth of words" but "the truth of things." It is that which may "disclose itself as it really is ... the full or real state of affairs to be maintained against different statements." Its opposites are *pseudos*, "deception," and *doxa*, which according to Bultmann, may be understood as "appearance" or "mere opinion." As the "truth of things," *alethia* is closely related to, or synonymous with, *physis*, the meaning of which Kirk, after considerable discussion, gives as "the real constitution of a thing, or of things severally" (1954: 230). Heidegger prefers to give the sense of "being" to *physis* (1959: 125), and it is sometimes translated as "nature" or "nature's vitality and generative power."

Although Logos orders the universe, or is the order in and of the universe, it is likely to be ignored and it can be violated by humans simply because they cannot easily comprehend it. As Heidegger puts it,

> Unconcealment occurs only when it is achieved by work: the work of the word in poetry, the work of stone in temple and statue, the work of the word in thought, the work of the polis as the historical place in which all this is grounded and preserved. (... work is to be taken here in the Greek sense of *ergon*, the creation that discloses the truth of something that is present.)   *(1959: 191)*

We may be reminded here that the etymology of liturgy is *laos ergon*, "work of the people" (see the American Heritage and Oxford English Dictionaries), and we may add ritual to the works through which Logos may be known. For one thing, liturgical performances "unconceal" (to use the term selected by Heidegger's translator) or "reveal" (to put it in better English at some possible cost in meaning) that which may otherwise remain vague in the immateriality of abstraction or imprecise in the vagaries and violations of usage or stand vulnerable to confusion among the alternatives of unbounded interpretation. The canons of liturgical orders may make unambiguously manifest the irreducibly true, correct and legitimate, that which is of the Logos and not merely of interpretation, which is necessarily *doxa*, opinion. But liturgy's significance with respect to Logos does not lie only its capacity to specify it clearly and unambiguously, as we saw in chapter 4. We shall return to this matter shortly. First, there is something more to say about the Greek concept itself.

The concept of Logos was elaborated in the centuries following Heraclitus when it also seems to have become more important in social life generally. In Hellenistic times Logos became ever more explicitly "a term for the ordered and the teleologically orientated nature of the world ... [even] the principle which creates the world, i.e., which orders and constitutes it ... The world is a grand unfolding of the Logos ..." (Kleinknecht 1967: 81–82). In the mysteries it becomes that which is revealed, and its grasp induces pious awe in initiates (Kleinknecht 1967: 81). For the neo-platonists Logos becomes closely related to *eidos* and *morphe*, both of which carry the meaning "form" or "shape," the importance of which in accounts of creation generally was discussed in chapter 5.

Heraclitus took the Logos to be a "divine entity," although what he meant by "divine" or by "entity" is not altogether clear. In later pre-Christian thought, however, it becomes identified with divine beings. "By assimilation to popular religion ... logos is equated with Zeus" (Kleinknecht 1967: 81), while in Hermeticism "almost all aspects of the logos concept ... [were] comprehended in the figure of the god Hermes and others" (Kleinknecht 1967: 87).

The comprehensiveness and pervasiveness of Logos as conceived by the ancient Greeks were both overarching and profound. As Kleinknecht put it, "Thought, word, matter, nature, being and norm [and thus morality and society] are all brought together in a complex interrelation in the Logos" (1967: 83). But even this summation seems inadequate. Logos brings together the temporal and timeless, the divine and the mortal, the sacred and the sanctified, discursive reason and non-discursive emotion, assimilating them all into its wholeness and unity.

The correspondence between Logos and the orders represented in liturgy is apparent. In both, the social, moral, conceptual and material elements of which worlds are made are bound together into coherent wholes. Profound harmony is intrinsic to the unifications of both Logos and liturgy, although that harmony may be hidden beneath apparent oppositions, conflicts and discord. The "truth of things" is claimed by both, and both are conceived to be enduring.

Logos and liturgy were apparently closely related in late classical and Hellenistic times, but there is no clear evidence that an association between them was explicitly recognized in Heraclitus' day, and they may have had little or nothing explicit to do with each other during that period. The Greek conception of Logos may well have been a product of philosophical speculation and not of ritual practice. It is at any rate impossible to claim that Logos could not be conceived independently of liturgy. But conception is one thing and establishment another. To establish an order is more than to conceive it and more than to agree with it theoretically. It is to accept it as binding. It is not about the conception of Logos, but of the difficulties of its establishment that Heraclitus despairs in fragments 1 and 2:

Of the Logos which is as I describe it men always prove to be uncomprehending, both before they have heard it and when once they have heard it. For although all things happen according to this Logos, they [men] are like people of no experience even when they experience such words and deeds as I explain, when I distinguish each thing according to its constitution and declare how it is, but the rest of men fail to notice what they do after they wake up just as they forget what they all do when asleep.   *(G. Kirk 1954: 33)*

Therefore it is necessary to follow the common [universal, apprehensible to all, shared] but although the Logos is common the many live as though they had a private understanding.   *(Kirk 1954: 57)*

As Heraclitus was painfully aware, Logos is likely to elude or remain beyond reason's unaided reach. Standing between Logos and its human comprehension is *doxa*, or *idia phronesis*, terms generally taken to mean "private understanding or opinion," or "the quality of being opinionated" (see Heidegger and Kleinknecht in passages already cited). *Doxa* also denotes (mere) appearance (which can give rise to varying opinion) and *idia phronesis* carries the further meaning of practical calculation, the rationality of private advantage. In the terms of an earlier chapter, *doxa* and *idia phronesis* are deutero-truths of individuals.

The limitless diversity of private opinion and the innumerable goals of private advantage are, in their very nature, antithetical to the unification essential to Logos:

> To be joined with all things into the "great cosmos" one must, therefore, elude or reject the instructions of opinion and advantage and follow those of the logos that stands as a universal beyond all opinion and that, itself, proposes unity.[4] It is of interest that the term Heraclitus used in Fragment 1 for human incomprehension of the Logos was *axynetoi*, which is the negation of *syniemi*, "bring together."   *(Heidegger 1959: 129)*

Logos may be conceived outside of liturgy, but its establishment is entailed by liturgy and, if Logos has an irreducible social component, liturgy may even be indispensable to its establishment. Liturgical orders are "common" in the sense of Fragment 2, and to perform them is *ipso facto* to "follow the common," for to perform a liturgical order is necessarily to conform to it. It is to follow an order which stands beyond individual opinion and to override the councils of private advantage. Furthermore, the orders of liturgy are not only "grasped theoretically." They may not be grasped theoretically at all. In Kleinknecht's terms they "claim" those who follow them because, in terms of this essay, their performance entails acceptance, and acceptance in turn entails obligation. As we observed in chapter 4, such language only barely suggests the intimacy of the relationship of the performer to the order he performs. In performing a liturgical order the performers participate in it. Their breaths give voice to that order, their bodies give it substance, they substantiate that which might otherwise remain no more than speculation or conception, an incorporeal, abstract form. In becoming part of it for the time being the participants are joined with that which it represents, and with each other, into a single "great cosmos." We shall deal with the deep experiential aspects of liturgical participation in the next chapter.

To summarize, the liturgical order of a society establishes its Logos. Following ancient Greek usage I take the term "Logos" to refer to an all-encompassing rational order uniting nature, society, individual humans and divinity into "a great cosmos," to use Kleinknecht's term, which is eternal, true, moral, and in some sense harmonious. Logoi[5] are conceived to be naturally and divinely constituted but, because they are incomplete without human participation, and because human action may be understood to be requisite to their maintenance, they are, and may be recognized to be, human constructions as well. Although humans should follow them, it is within their power to ignore the Logos, or even to violate it.

2. Logoi

The use of the term "Logos" to refer generally to the cosmic orders represented by liturgical orders as wholes suggests that a family resemblance may be discerned among them. It must be emphasized that a family resemblance is not an identity. All, I think, bind together disparate elements, all transcend individual opinion, all claim, at least tacitly, to be moral and natural and to possess the truth of things, but the elements bound together and the specific principles of their unification are always in some degree unique. There are also profound differences among orders in the degree to which the ultimate is thought to be knowable and how it may be known. Variations in the sequential, simultaneous and hierarchical dimensions of liturgical orders, moreover, produce variations in the architecture of Logoi.

It is not necessary to this formulation that concepts resembling the Greek Logos be named or otherwise made explicit by the societies they order, but such explicit concepts are not rare. They are to be found in a range of societies widely dispersed in time and space and differing from each other in social type. It is of interest that the word denoting a number of them may also denote both "truth" and "order," as we have already seen in the case of Nelli. We shall examine a few more of these concepts briefly, beginning with Ma'at, which stood at the center of ancient Egyptian thought.

Ma'at has been "variously translated as 'truth', 'justice', 'righteousness', 'order,' and so on," but, Wilson (1951: 48) tells us, "no English word is always applicable." He concurs in this view with Budge (1895: cxix), who states that "there is no word which will exactly describe the Egyptian conception of Ma'at both from a physical and from a moral point of view, but the fundamental idea of the word is "straight," and from the Egyptian texts it is clear the Ma'at meant right, true, truth, upright, righteous, just, steadfast, unalterable, etc." Ma'at was the cosmic force of harmony, order, stability, and security, coming down from the first creation as the organizing quality of created phenomena and affirmed the accession of each God-king of Egypt ... Thus there was something of the unchanging, eternal and cosmic about Ma'at. If we render it "order" it was the order of created things, physical and spiritual, established at the beginning and valid for all time. If we render it "justice" it was not simply justice in terms of legal administration; it was the just and proper relationship of cosmic phenomena, including the relationship of the rulers and the ruled. If we render it "truth" we must remember that, to the ancient, things were true not because they were susceptible of ... verification but because they were ... in their true and proper places in the order created and maintained by the gods ...

(Wilson 1951: 45)

In addresses to the pharaoh it was said "Authoritative utterance (*Hu*) is in thy mouth. Understanding (*Sia*) is in thy heart. Thy speech is the shrine of truth (Ma'at)" (Frankfort 1948: 51), and he lived "under the obligation to maintain Ma'at throughout his kingdom. He labored under the enormous responsibility, as it was said of Amenhotep III, "to make the country flourish as in primeval times by means of the designs of Ma'at" (Frankfort 1948: 51).

Pharaoh was a god as well as a king, thus it is clear that gods as well as mortals were subject to Ma'at, and that Ma'at provided a place of juncture for the human and the divine, especially in the relationship among Ma'at, the pharaoh and other deities.

... it is by means of the concept of Ma'at that the essential affinity of god and king is expressed when Hatshepsut writes: "I have made bright Ma'at which he (Re) loves. I know that he lives by it. It is my bread; I eat of its brightness; I am likeness from his limbs, one with him.   *(Frankfort 1948: 157–158)*

The king maintained Ma'at by liturgical performance as well as by secular governance, and this passage may well allude to such performances.

Ma'at was personified as a woman in inscriptions and in ritual representations and has, therefore, been taken by many authorities to have been a goddess (Baikie 1914, Budge 1895, Wiedemann 1914, Wilson 1951). The deification of Ma'at is reminiscent of the identification of Logos with Zeus and Hermes, and both the Egyptian and Greek instances may exemplify a general tendency to apotheosize cosmic principles, especially in popular religious thought. Be this as it may, as seems appropriate for a goddess of truth, order and exactitude, Ma'at was said to be the "daughter of the Sun God Re whose regular circuit is the most striking manifestation of established cosmic order" (Frankfort 1948: 51). It may well be that, in accordance with Wensinck's (1923) suggestion, Ma'at was conceived by observation of the precisely regular movements of the celestial body said to have sired her. But if Ma'at was conceived in astronomy she was established in liturgy. "In a ritual performed every day the king (or his substitute, the high priest) offered to the god [Re] a small image of Ma'at seated upon a basket or basket-like vessel, a feather on her head and the sign of life in her hands" (Gardiner 1912: 480). This account suggests that Ma'at is not a quality possessed by gods themselves but something that must be given them, something that, according to Hatshepsut as cited by Frankfort, they must both "live by," or conform to, and "live on," that is, be nourished by.

There are other accounts of the origins of Ma'at. Ptah was sometimes called the "Lord of Truth" and also "He who created Ma'at" (Frankfort 1948: 389). He was not primarily a solar but a chthonic figure, in the Memphite theology being equated with the "eight weird creatures fit to inhabit the primeval slime" who served as a "conceptualization of primal chaos, and who brought forth the sun from the primordial ocean" (Frankfort 1948: 151, 154, see also above). In presiding over the formation of an ordered universe out of formless substance Ptah may be regarded as the creator of the goddess Ma'at as he is the creator, direct or indirect, of all the world's things and beings. There is not necessarily then, a contradiction between Re's paternity and Ptah's creativity.[6]

It is nevertheless the case that Ma'at, as goddess, seems rather odd.[7] Something given daily by one god to another for nurturance and guidance does not seem much like what we would ordinarily mean by the term "goddess," and other accounts suggest that Ma'at was not primarily understood to be a divine offspring of Ptah's creative labors but rather a super-divine principle informing them.

Flinders Petrie (1911: 145) tells us that "Ptah, 'the Great Artificer,' the Demiurge, shapes the sun-and-moon-eggs on his potter's wheel; he is the god of Law and Order who created all things by Ma'at, truth or exactness." If Ptah, who stands at the point of transition between unformed matter and ordered universe creates by – in accordance with – Ma'at, then Ma'at is truly primordial. In terms of our discussion in chapter 5 it may be construed as form, one of the two primitive, irreducible and unprecedented elements or properties that in creation couples with substance to make cosmos – substantial form, informed substance. In the terms of this chapter it is Logos, the true order in accordance with which all created things are bound into a cosmos.

Although Ma'at as truth, order, exactitude, harmony was primordial, events and things could be at variance with it. "That which was not

consonant with the established order could be denied as being false"
(Wilson 1951: 48). Wilson also informs us that the terms denoting the
antithesis of Ma'at were "words we translate as 'lying', 'falsehood' and
'deceit'" to which Lichtheim (1971: 145) adds that one such term, *isfet*,
generally means 'wrong', "but sometimes conveys the enlarged sense of
... 'chaos'."

Because wrong, lie, chaos, deceit are possible Ma'at, like the Logos of
Heraclitus, must be completed and maintained by gods and humans. We
have already noted that responsibility for the maintenance of Ma'at to
the god Re each day in ritual, and it was he who, through his governance,
was supposed to make the country flourish "by means of the designs of
Ma'at." But he could fail. During the disorders of the intermediate
period the prophet Ipu-wer addresses the pharaoh whom he holds
responsible for the uproar of the times:

Hu, Sia, and Ma'at are with thee. [Nevertheless] confusion is what thou dost put
throughout the land together with the noise of tumult. Behold one uses violence
against another. [Yet] people conform to what thou hast commanded (Frankfort
1948: 48). If three men go along a road, they are found to be two men: it is the
greater number that kills the lesser. Does then the herdsman [the pharaoh, who
should be "herdsman" to his people] love death? ... This really means that thou
hast acted (?) to bring such a situation into being, and thou hast spoken lies.

(Wilson 1951: 115)

It is one thing for the ordinary mortal to violate Ma'at, another for
pharaoh, who is himself divine, whose "speech is the shrine of Ma'at"
and from whose mouth *Hu* – authoritative utterance – flows. We shall
take up this special form of falsehood in the last chapter.

As Ma'at pervaded ancient Egyptian thought, so did the notion of Asha
inform Zoroastrianism which in one form or another was dominant in
Iran from the time of the Achaemenian kings in the sixth century BC[8]
until the triumph of Islam, 1,200 years later. It continues to be professed
by the Parsees, who survive in a few scattered communities in Iran but
are to be found in largest numbers around Bombay, where over 115,000
of them were living in the mid-1960s (Duchesne-Guillemin 1966: 1). Like
Ma'at, Asha is not easy to translate. It is usually rendered as "truth," but
with the proviso that it encompasses more than is usually meant by its
English gloss. Other renderings include "the order of things," "true
order," "the Right (including the idea of truth) as a cosmic force," "the
norm for decent behavior," "the guide for all actions" (Duchesne-
Guillemin 1966: 26ff.), "order," "symmetry," "discipline," "harmony"

(Masani 1968: 79), "righteousness," "order," "the mean," and "the Path" (Orlin 1976: 259). Windfuhr (1976: 269ff.), like the others, seems to prefer a conflation of truth and order. It is "a spiritual law in accordance with which the Universe has been fashioned and governed" (Masani 1968: 79). Windfuhr notes that Asha "existed as the prime principle even before the creation of the world" (1976: 277n).

Asha is one of the six or seven[9] "Holy Immortals" and is sometimes called "Asha Vahishta," which Masani renders "best Order" or "the Highest Righteousness," and which Duchesne-Guillemin gives as "Excellent Truth" (1966: 137). Asha, with the other Immortals[10], was sometimes personified as a member of the entourage of Ahura Mazdah, the godhead (Duchesne-Guillemin 1966: 25), but was also taken, like the others, to be an "Attribute of the Supreme Being" (Masani 1968: 42). These Attributes or Beings were ranked in the Gathas, the canon of hymns attributed to Zoroaster himself, but the ranking is not altogether clear to contemporary scholars. Living Parsees seem to give primacy to Vohu Manah (Masani 1965: 44) as Ahura Mazda's first creation, but an ethical primacy to Asha: "To uphold Asha at all times and in all circumstances is a duty enjoined on a true Zoroastrian. In fact, all religious teachings begin with this alpha and omega of the creed. It is the Eternal Verity, the One reality, which is the mainspring of all creation" (Masani 1968: 79). Lommel (1930: 14; cited by Windfuhr) also ranked Asha highest. Windfuhr, in general agreement, comments: "Asha existed as the prime principle even before the creation of the world; but creation is an act of mind ... Asha is realized through creation. For the creation of this time-bound world, and for its salvation, mind is the prime mover, and with it Vohu Manah [Good Mind]" (1976: 277n, his emphasis). Asha in this formulation stands in a relationship to the creative agency of Vohu Manah similar to the relationship of Ma'at to Ptah. As such it seems an instance of primordial form substantiated in creation, as discussed in chapter 5. In terms of this chapter, it is an instance of Logos. Concerning this identification A. V. Carnoy wrote long ago "there is ... a curious resemblance between the conception of Asha (= Arta) 'law of the universe', 'moral law, which manifests itself in fire', and Heraclitus' first principle, which is a fire, a law of order (logos), a moral law (man's perfection is in his conformity to the law of the universe), and a manifestation of the godhead, opposed to darkness" (1921: 867).

Asha has other claims to primacy in Zoroastrian thought. First, it is of central significance in the teachings attributed to Zoroaster himself as expressed in the Gathas. Secondly, the notion of Asha antedates Zoroastrianism. "Of all the Bounteous Immortals [i.e. 'Holy Immortals'] who surround and partake of the nature of Azura Mazdah [the godhead], Asha alone is of demonstrably Indo-Iranian origin" (Zaehner 1961: 35). Boyce (1979) also places the origin of the concept in Indo-Iranian times.

Although Asha is the order in accordance with which the world was made and is maintained, it is possible for it to be violated. That which does not conform to Asha is Druj, which is generally translated "lie," but whose meanings encompass much more. They also include "deceit," "wickedness," "evil" (Masani 1968: 45), "fault," "sin," "non-observance of the law," (as the equivalent of the Vedic tantra (Duchesne-Guillemin 1966: 27). Orlin (1976: 259) notes that Druj as "'lie' encompasses the concepts of 'unrighteousness', 'disorder', 'deceit,' and 'the non-Path'." The lie in this larger sense, which seems to have much in common with Egyptian notions of lie, was for Zoroaster the very principle of evil – "not only the opponent and denial of Asha as abstract truth ... [but] aggression against, or subversion of, good government and a peaceful ... order" (Zaehner 1961: 34). "In Darius' inscriptions the Lie is equated with 'rebellion', with those who subvert good government" (Orlin 1976: 261). Asha must be maintained by humans. All humans should be *ashevan*, "followers of the truth," but are free to be *dregvant*, "followers of the lie." As in Egypt, so in Iran: the heaviest responsibility for maintaining Asha devolves upon the king "who holds his kingdom in trust from Ahura-Mazda ... source and guardian of Truth and Order ... his was the ubiquitous problem of all princes: to administer according to principles of Authority which are seen as eternally valid in a world characterized by inconstancy and disruption" (Orlin 1976: 260). Good thought, good word, good deed, the triad forming the ethical ground of Zoroastrianism (Masani 1968: 76) contributes to Asha, but worship is itself part of Asha and is recognized to be important to its maintenance. Five brief acts of devotion are required daily of contemporary Zoroastrians. These rituals include reading the Avesta,[11] for which purpose the work is divided into daily portions arranged according to the dates upon which they are to be recited (Carnoy 1921: 865). Longer liturgies are periodic and frequent. The "central liturgical text," to use Zaehner's characterization of it, is the Yasna, an elaborate ritual requiring the recital of seventy-two chapters of the Gathas (Masani 1968: 119; Zaehner 1961: 91f.). This ritual can be construed as an extended expression of the Zoroastrian Ultimate Sacred Postulate. All rituals take place in the presence of "sacred fires," which are representations of the Godhead and of its attribute Asha; moreover, relationships among fires, of which there were three grades, seem to have represented the "true order" of political relations. The highest fires, the Bahram or Varahram fires, were both the kings of fires and the fires of kings. In Sassanian times they were set on pedestals resembling thrones and were represented on coins with crowns above them (Boyce 1979: 60, *passim*; Duchesne-Guillemin 1966: 65, *passim*; Masani 1968: 115, *passim*; Zaehner 1961: 92, *passim*).

It is generally agreed that Iranian Asha and the Vedic Rta are virtually identical conceptually. Glosses provided for Rta are reminiscent of those for Asha and Ma'at: "law of the universe," "unity of nature," cosmic law or order," "universal and eternal law," "order," "right," "truth" (Radhakrishnan and Moore 1957: *passim*). Rta prevails in the existent portion of the universe, the Sat, which is the dwelling-place of Gods and Men. There is also a "non-existent" portion of the universe, the Asat, "a region of horror inhabited by demons" (N. Brown 1972: 260), in which Anrta, lie and chaos, the antithesis of Rta, prevails. Sat is continually threatened by Asat, Rta by Anrta. The preservation of Rta is a charge of the gods, and it is the charge of men to strengthen them for this task through ritual and sacrifice (Brown 1972: 261). Both humans and gods have duties to fulfill according to Rta, and within a structurally differentiated society different persons have different obligations. Being true, that is, conforming to Rta, is fulfilling the obligations of one's segment of society or even one's specific occupation (Brown 1972: 262, *passim*). In Vedic India Rta is manifested in the social order, as Asha was in the social order of ancient Iran.

The Vedas are of great antiquity. There is evidence "to indicate with some certainty" that the Rg Veda, somewhat in the arrangement that has come down to the present day, was current fifteen centuries before Christ (Radhakrishnan and Moore 1957: 3f.), and some of its constituent hymns may be much older. The great antiquity attributed to the Iranian notion of Asha derives largely from its identity with Rta, an identity which is not only conceptual but etymological: they are cognates (Boyce 1979: 7; Masani 1968: 79; Zaehner 1961: 35). On the grounds of their close conceptual and philological relationship both Boyce and Zaehner take the Asha/Rta concept to be of Indo-Iranian age. Boyce takes the period to have ended when the proto-Indo-Iranians drifted apart to become identifiable as Indians and Iranians "perhaps early in the third millennium" (1979: 2).

We have noted strong resemblances among certain ancient notions, the Logos of pre-classical Greece, Ma'at of dynastic Egypt, Asha of pre-

Islamic Iran, Rta of Vedic India and earlier, Nelli of ancient Mexico. All are terms for cosmic order; four of them are themselves understood as truth as well as order; the fifth, Logos, claims truth as one of its inseparable attributes. Harmony, unity and eternity are also aspects of them all. In Greece, Iran, Egypt and possibly Mexico the concept seems to have been at one time or another apotheosized, but in all of these societies it is also, and primarily, a principle to which even divinities are subject, a principle standing in opposition to chaos and falsehood. In three of the instances, the notions of chaos, disorder, lie, falsehood, wrong, are covered by single terms. Logos, Ma'at, Asha, Rta, and possibly Nelli, all require for their completion and preservation the participation, or "following," of humans who are free to follow *druj, anrta, isfet, doxa, idia phronesis*. Liturgical performance was explicitly of importance in the expression and maintenance of what we are generally calling Logoi in at least three of the instances. The relationship of Logos to liturgy in the Greece of Heraclitus' time is unknown and his conception may have been entirely independent of ritual, but the association of liturgy and Logos in Hellenistic times is clear. The relationship of Nelli to Toltec liturgy, however, is not.

If the attribution of an Indo-Iranian date to Asha/Rta is correct, it may be that it antedates the emergence of the state and the development of literacy in Iran and India. It is nevertheless the case that the instances I have adduced are all of archaic civilizations, societies organized as states and possessed of literacy. Moreover, with the exception of Nelli, they flourished in more or less contiguous regions through concurrent or contiguous epochs. But similar notions may be found in regions remote from the Eastern Mediterranean and Ancient Near East among peoples who possessed neither writing nor the trappings of state.

We may return to the Sioux concept of Wakan-Tanka (also given as Wakan Tanka and Wakantanka).

Wakan-Tanka has traditionally "been glossed as 'great Spirit' or 'Great Mystery' (*wakan* 'sacred' and *tanka* 'great', 'large', 'big')" (Powers 1975: 45). "Sacred" is hardly an informative gloss in itself, but Powers analyzes "*wakan* further, noting that in relatively late usage it was applied to horses (*sundawakan*, 'sacred dog'), guns ('sacred iron', and whiskey ('sacred water'). These instances suggest that the term carries an implication of the radically exotic, or that which comes from outside the known world, for guns, whiskey and horses were recognized not to be indigenous. More certainly, these contexts suggest efficacy of an extraordinary, marvelous, or even (in the cases of guns and whiskey at least) occult and incomprehensible sort. The rendering of Wakan-Tanka as "Great Mystery" is supported by such an interpretation. Frances Reed, a native speaker with Western philosophical training, confirms it in observing that "unknowable" in the sense of being unamenable to analysis or disassembly is an aspect of *wakan* (personal communication). Etymology provides other meanings. The root *kan*, according to Powers (1975: 47), provides "the connotations of ancient, old and enduring," and Reed (personal communication) provides related glosses: "unchangeable," "given," "that which is." We may recall Black Elk's address, cited in an earlier chapter: "Our Grandfather Wakan-Tanka ... you are first. You have always been. O Wakan-Tanka you are the truth." Out of the conflation of the primordial, enduring and unchanging on the one hand with "that which is," the given, and the true on the other, eternal verity is born.

Wakan-Tanka is not only true and eternal but all-encompassing. "Although singular in form, Wakantanka is collective in meaning. Wakantanka is not personified but aspects of it are" (Powers 1975: 45). There are sixteen such aspects, arranged into four hierarchically ordered classes, each including four members. The *Wakan akanta*, "the superior *wakan*" include the Sun, the Sky, the Earth and Rock. Humans and Buffaloes are included in the third class with, among other things, the Four Winds (Powers 1975: 54). As Black Elk proclaims, "Our Grandfather Wakan-Tanka, You are everything."

Wakan-Tanka is not only all-encompassing but a unity. As Walker was told by his informant Sword in the early years of this century, "Wakan-Tanka is like sixteen different persons, but each person is *kan*. Therefore they are all only the same as one" (Walker 1917: 153). Concerning human participation in this Oneness, Black Elk prays during the construction of the sweat lodge:

We have come from You, we are part of You, and we know that our bodies will return to You ... by fixing this center in the earth, I remember You to whom my body return, but above all I think of Wakan-Tanka with whom all our spirits become as one. *(J. Brown 1971: 34)*

Ultimately there is no reality other than Wakan-Tanka. *(1971: 42)*

The comprehensiveness and unity of Wakan-Tanka and its quintessential truth and perdurance virtually entail the conception of a world-encompassing order. Sacred cosmic order is represented among the Sioux by the circle. As Tyon told Walker,

The Oglala believe the circle to be sacred because ... [Wakan-Tanka] caused everything in nature to be round except stone. Stone is the implement of destruction. The sun and the sky, the earth and the moon, are round ...Everything that breathes is round like the body of a man. Everything that grows from the ground is round like the stem of a plant ... The day, the night, and the moon go in a circle above the sky. Therefore the circle is a symbol ... of all time.

(*Walker 1917: 000*)

The largest and most encompassing representations of the circle constructed by the Sioux were encampments, metaphorically called "sacred hoops." This camp plan was given to the Sioux by the divine White Buffalo Calf Woman when she brought home the calumet (Powers 1975: 81). Having a common origin the camp circle and the pipe possess comparable degrees of sanctity. Other circular representations closely identified with Wakan-Tanka include the calumet's bowl and the seven circles, representing the seven major rituals, carved upon it (J. Brown 1971: 7). The ground plan of the sweat lodge, which is round, with the "sacred hill" to which it is connected by a short path, is a precise icon of the calumet, and so is the Sun Dance Lodge with the sacred tipi, to which it is connected by a path defined by sixteen tobacco offerings. The ground plan for the sacred ball game, the sacred tipi and sites prepared for the vision quest are also circular (Powers 1975: 185ff.).

Intrinsic to these circular representations are their centers, in which fires are made in pipes and sweat lodges, where the sacred pole is erected in the Sun Dance Lodge, at which is dug the pit in which the seeker stands on the vision quest ground, whence the ball is thrown in the sacred ball game, and where in the encampment stands the "lengthened tipi" in which councils and dances take place. The center pole of the sun lodge is associated with the sun, the most *wakan* of Wakan-Tanka's sixteen aspects, and so is fire. The sun and fire are associated, among other things, with knowledge, and knowledge is illumination. The movement from darkness to light is a movement from ignorance to knowledge. Lighting the pipe and lighting the fire in the sweat lodge provide knowledge at the same time that steam and smoke carry prayers to Wakan-Tanka, and inanimate things are given breath (Powers 1975: 181–184). It may also be that he who stands in the vision pit at first resembles in his ignorance tobacco placed in the pipe's bowl before it is ignited. Similarly the ball thrown in the sacred ball game "represents Wakantanka ... [it] is symbolic of knowledge and people's attempt to catch it represents the struggle of people submerged in ignorance to free themselves" (Powers 1975: 103).

The centered circle is a ubiquitous sacred symbol among the Sioux. Of the encampment Powers says "the camp circle was representative of unity and social solidarity. Everything inside the ... circle ... was irrefutably Oglala ... outside were the enemies, the inconsistencies of everyday life, the evil spirits, and later the white man" (1975: 41). Inside were safety and order, outside danger and disorder. The centered circle, encompassing, unifying, natural, representing Wakan-Tanka, represents orderliness in the sense of balance, a "finding and holding of the center through appropriate behavior" (Reed, personal communication). The world is often thrown out of balance, however. The grasp upon its center is loosened, proper form submerged in disorder, *wakan* weakened. According to Brown (1971: 4), the degree to which a being or thing is *wakan* "is in proportion to its nearness to its [proper] prototype; or better, it is in proportion to the ability of the object or act to reflect most directly the principle or principles which are in Wakan-Tanka ... who is One." When the world is disordered "It is only through sacred ritual that harmony can be achieved, the universe restored to its proper balance" (Powers 1975: 181). The achievement of this harmony is sometimes said to be "making roundness" (Reed, personal communication), and congregations almost always assemble in the form of circles. "When the sacred rites are performed properly, the common universe, one acknowledged to be controlled by the white man's technology, is transformed into a sacred universe, one controlled by the power of Wakantanka" (Powers 1975: 201f.).

In summary, we see in Wakan-Tanka a conception bearing a strong resemblance to Ma'at, Rta, Asha and Logos. Wakan-Tanka, like them, is a true, moral, eternal, harmonious, encompassing, unitary order. It is natural, but it may be violated by inappropriate behavior. It must be maintained through appropriate acts, especially the performance of rituals. In participating in rituals people become part of Wakan-Tanka, completing it as they "follow its logos." As they give energy and breath to Wakan-Tanka by smoking the calumet, so do they gain knowledge of the order which is Wakan-Tanka by participating in rituals.

As in the cases of Ma'at, Asha and Logos, there seems to have been a tendency to apotheosize Wakan-Tanka. Although it seems generally agreed that Wakan-Tanka was not a sentient being but an encompassing order of beings, it was addressed as if a person. In recent times, in dialogue with white men Wakan-Tanka came to be a gloss for God, or even for the Christian God. Indeed, a missionary says of the religious condition of the Sioux in 1866: "The Christians are universally distinguished from the pagans, as being worshipers of Wakan-Tanka, or, as we speak, the Great Spirit." The pagans worshipped Taku-Wakan, "that which is *wakan*," *wakan* things in their multitude (Pond 1989[1866]: 217f.).

The conception of Wakan-Tanka, emerging as it did in a tribal society in the New World, can owe nothing to the archaic civilizations of the Old World, nor to their conceptions. It grew independent of them, but perhaps not independently of the conceptions of other New World peoples. It may be that the general idea toward which the terms Ma'at, Asha, Rta, Logos and Wakan-Tanka point had wide currency in aboriginal North America in the variant forms denoted by a number of culturally specific terms. As Powers notes, the term *wakan* "has been regarded as analogous to *orenda* of the Iroquois, the Shoshone *pokunt*, Algonquin *manitou*, and Kwakiutl *nauala*, Tlingit *yek* and Haida *sgana*" (1975: 46–7.). We may also recall here the Navajo *hozho*, which seems somewhat different.

The term *hozho* is difficult to translate, perhaps because, as Kluckhohn (1949: 369) suggested, English is poor "in terms that simultaneously have moral and aesthetic meaning." The stem *zho* seems to carry an indefinite number of positive meanings, including good, favorable, beauty, perfection, harmony, goodness, normality, success, well-being, blessedness order and ideal" (Witherspoon 1977: 23f.). The "closest English gloss" of the prefix *ho*, according to Witherspoon, might be "'environment' in its total sense." As a verbal prefix *ho* denotes "(1) the general as opposed to the specific; (2) the whole as opposed to the part; (3) the abstract as opposed to the concrete; (4) the indefinite as opposed to the definite; and (5) the infinite as opposed to the finite" (1977: 24). *Hozho* thus seems to be a general and pervasive ordering principle, infinite in its dominion, the true manifestation of which is never in distinct things or beings in their separation, but in the wholeness or unity that emerges out of proper relations among the things and beings that together compose the world. In such relations Hozho, comprehending at once "the intellectual concept of order, the emotional state of happiness, the moral notion of good, the biological condition of health and well-being, and the aesthetic dimensions of balance, harmony and beauty" (Witherspoon 1977: 154) is realized or substantiated.

For Reichard, (1950: 45), Hozho (*xojon* in her orthography) denotes "'perfection so far as it is attainable by man,' the end toward which not only man but also supernaturals and time and motion, institutions and behavior, strive. Perhaps it is the utmost achievement in order" (1950: 45).

The opposite of Hozho is *hochzo* "the evil, the disorderly and the ugly" (Witherspoon 1977: 34). Reichard (1950: 125) states that "The nearest Navajo approach to the concept of sin is 'being out of order, lacking

control' ... goodness is ... closely tied up with order and compulsion
..." In an earlier work she asserts that the main difference between good
and evil, "is the presence or absence of control, for control is ritual,
decreed long since, but taught and learned" (1944: 5). It is of interest that
the stem for "know," "possess knowledge," "summarize," "be able to
analyze," "be acquainted with" is related phonetically and grammatically
as well as semantically to that for "holy," "blessed," "sanctified" (Witherspoon, citing Reichard, 1977: 187).

The very existence of the term *hochzo* makes it clear that Hozho can be
disrupted or violated, that order can be dissolved by disorder. "The
primary purpose of Navajo ritual is to maintain or restore *hozho*" (Witherspoon 1977: 34). It is surely significant in this regard that in the
performance of Navajo rituals extraordinary stress is laid upon punctiliousness. Great care is lavished upon the details of preparation previous
to ritual performance, to the collection and arrangement of objects and
to the disposal of the substances and objects used after the ritual is
concluded (Reichard 1950: 341ff.). As far as the performance itself is
concerned, the accurate production of prayer and song is requisite "in
spite of stringent restrictions and a strain on the memory" because the
reference of the prayer is to "'the tip of the speech,' the existence of the
word from the very beginning of conceivable time" (Reichard 1950: 267).

Hozho not only may be restored and maintained by ritual, but,
following an implication of Witherspoon's analysis, may itself be a
product of ritual. In an earlier chapter it was suggested that the expression
Sa'ah naaghaii bik'eh hozho may be construed to be the ultimate sacred
postulate of the Navajo. *Naaghaii*, the third person singular continuative-
imperfective mode of the verb "to go" denotes repetition, restoration and
continuous recurrence. *Sa'ah* refers to aging and to the successful completion of the life cycle in its entirety. The constituent phrase *sa'ah naaghaii*
thus denotes the continuous repetition, restoration or recurrence of a
living completeness. The meaning of *bik'eh* is "according to," "in conformity with." "What follows *bik'eh* is ... the product of or exists in
conjunction with *sa'ah naaghaii*. The by-product of *Sa'ah Naaghaii* is
hozho" (Witherspoon 1977: 23). Punctilious recurrence makes ritual the
most orderly of all events, their performance infuses their order with life.
They substantiate Hozho as no other behavior can at the same time that
Hozho predicates the performers and their performances with its order.

Hozho, like Wakan-Tanka, bears a strong family resemblance to
Asha, Rta, Maat, and Logos. Like them, it is an encompassing, harmonious and unifying world order, at once natural and moral, which humans

may violate but for which they have responsibilities of maintenance and restoration. These responsibilities are fulfilled through the performance of rituals, which not only, as it were, rejuvenate Hozho but define its terms. On the other hand, like each of the other forms of Logos that we have discussed, Hozho has qualities peculiarly its own. In none of the other Logoi is the aesthetic as important as it is in Hozho and its emphasis on happiness and health seems stronger than in the others. Truth, on the other hand, is not explicitly associated with Hozho (Witherspoon, personal communication) as it is with all of the others, nor does there ever seem to have been any tendency to transform Hozho itself into a deity. *Hozho* is never addressed, as is Wakan-Tanka. The expression "*Sa'ah naaghaii bik'eh hozho*" is, however, taken to be generative. Changing Woman, the "Supreme Mother of the Navajos," "the most blessed ... revered and ... benevolent of all the Holy People," and "the personification of regeneration, rejuvenation, renewal and dynamic beauty" is said to be the daughter of the two primordial phrases, existing eternally, that constitute the full expression, "the static male *Sa'ah Naaghaii* and the active female *Bik'eh Hozho*" (Witherspoon 1977: 201–202).

Other instances of concepts bearing a family resemblance to Logos, Ma'at, Asha, Rta, Wakan-Tanka and Hozho could easily be adduced, but the ubiquity of such concepts in tribal societies as well as in states, in the Old World as well as the New, may have already been demonstrated sufficiently. I shall, therefore, be brief in noting that Stanner (1956) has referred to "The Dreaming," the concept central to the metaphysics of virtually all of the hunting and gathering peoples of Australia as "a kind of logos of aboriginal man" (1956: 159). This Australian Logos is expressed in a mythos that tells of the institution of things – species, landscapes, customs – in the Dreamtime, a primordial epoch standing at the beginning of existence which still continues (Stanner 1956: 164; see also Meggitt n.d.: *passim*). As in the Logos of Heraclitus, unity is an aspect of the Dreamtime but, again as in the Logos, it is a unity of opposites and antitheses (Stanner 1956: 160, n.d.: 10). The cosmic order which the Dreamtime constitutes is quintessentially natural. Of the religions of the Murinbata, the aboriginal people among whom he worked for many years, Stanner says its "principle ... was to make fleshly, determinate and social life correlative with the spiritual cycle. But life in human, worldly society was at all times a function of that cycle, and subservient to it" (1956: 165). Human life, this is to say, was supposed to "follow the Logos," an aim most fully realized in ritual. "Murinbata rites were, at the most fundamental level, attempts to make social life correlative with the plan and rhythm of the Cosmos. The appropriate occasions for rites, it is true, were 'socially defined,' but the definitions were in terms of an inexorable cosmic cycle to which the social systems were made correlative" (1956: 139). Indeed, in ritual the social system becomes one with the cosmic for the time being for, when men, upon entering a ritual, take up the roles of Dreamtime beings, they are entering the Dreamtime itself (Gould 1969: 109). Participation in rituals was not merely devotional but necessary to the continuity of the dreaming itself, and thus to the maintenance of the world and what is in it (Stanner 1956: 168), such as species of plants and animals, to the generation of which many rituals are devoted among all Australian aborigines. I will only note, finally, that the cosmic order realized in ritual was understood to be absolutely true.

The Murinbata had not yet discovered that men could dispute the truth or falsity of the great events from which men themselves had issued. There was authority, divine, but the consequence of things happening to, or done by, beings greater than ordinary men. What issued was *murin daitpir*, "true words." Truth, once exhibited, remained a datum.

(Stanner 1956: 169)

Among the Walbiri, Meggitt tells us,

There are explicit social rules, which, by and large, everybody obeys; and the people freely characterize each other's behavior insofar as it conforms to them or deviates from them. The totality of the rules exposes the law, *djugaruru*, a term that may be translated as "the line," or "the straight and true way." Its basic connotation is of an established morally right order of behavior (whether of planets or of people) from which there should be no divergence ... the law is itself a basic value, for this is thought to distinguish Walbiri from all other people, who are consequently inferior. As the law originated the Dreamtime, it is beyond critical questioning and conscious change. The totemic philosophy asserts that man, society and nature are components of one system, whose source is the Dreamtime; all are, therefore, amenable to the law which is coeval with the system.

(1965a: 252–253)

Truth, unity, perdurance, order seem to be as intrinsic to the conceptions of Australian Dreamings as they are to the Logoi of North America and the Ancient Old World.

I will only mention, finally, the Maring word *nomane*. *Nomane* has a personal aspect, or rather is an element of the total personality of the individual: an entranced shaman sends his *nomane* to the house of the Smoke Woman during a seance, and a person's *nomane* survives death. The term may also refer to an individual's thought, idea, opinion or intellect carrying with it an implication of correctness, propriety or wisdom. Stupid, selfish or scheming thought is not *nomane*. The term also has a more general significance. People will speak of "our *nomane*," the *nomane* of the Maring people, designating thereby Maring tradition or culture. It includes marriage conventions, garden practices, magic – particularly that associated with warfare – conformity to rules of reciprocity, generally speaking the proper way to do things. It is both represented and exercised in the performance of the rituals comprising the warfare-*kaiko* cycle. I am not certain, but I think that individual thought may be regarded as *nomane* if it conforms to, or follows, *nomane* in the inclusive sense. It is plausible to regard *nomane* as a Melanesian variant of Logos.

The orders established in the liturgies of a range of societies resemble the order that Heraclitus called "Logos." It may nevertheless seem that despite their resemblance the association I have proposed misrepresents or distorts Heraclitus' conception. For him and those who followed him the Logos was not conventional. At least it is not clear that its validity depended upon its acceptance and it may have been thought to prevail whether or not it was comprehended. It was not a conventional order nor even an order naturally constituted but itself an order constituting both nature and convention. As such, it was an absolute that the wise would try to comprehend – by discovering changelessness beneath the world's superficial flux, by attending to harmonies vibrant in the world's tensions or even hidden beneath its disorders – in order to follow it, which is to say to live in accordance with it.

The orders represented in liturgy, in contrast, are not naturally constituted but conventionally constructed. They cannot be discovered empirically in nature but must be established performatively in society. It may seem, therefore, that what is constituted by a liturgical order is not a Logos but a pseudo-Logos.

The opposition between the naturally constituted and performatively constructed is, of course, mystified by a sleight-of-ritual (to which reference has been made more than once) in which the products of performatives immediately become the denotata of constatives. This transformation operates in the relationship between any liturgical order as a whole and its corresponding Logos, as it does with metaphysical objects generally. Although liturgical orders are social constructions the order they represent is no more understood to be invention than is that of a philosophically conceived Logos. This alone might be sufficient to dismiss the objection, but the objection, because it is founded upon an opposition that seems fundamental to the condition of the species, the opposition between the discovered and the constructed, requires further discussion.

First, if the Logos is conceived to be all-encompassing and all-integrating, as seems apparent in such statements as "it is wise to agree that all things are one," it is not simply an object, not even a divine object which, distinct from humans, should be grasped by them, or a principle to which they should comply. It is, rather, an order of which humans are parts. But, to the extent that by choice, error or ignorance, humans in the grip of *doxa* or *idia phronesis* can act against the Logos to produce *sarma* the Logos may remain incomplete or even be broken, not merely uncomprehended but unrealized or violated. Because humans can do other than follow the Logos, its completion and the preservation of its unity require them to act to bind themselves to it or to participate in it. In Heraclitus' terms, the wise agree to it. This agreement is not wise simply because it would be foolhardy to disagree, as it would be to deny the observable effects of a naturally constituted law (like that of gravity), but because wisdom recognizes the world's fragility as well as humanity's dependence upon the integrity of that fragile world. Agreement is, of course, close in meaning to acceptance, and if acceptance is a prerequisite of the completion of an all-encompassing Logos, the Logos possesses moral force as well as the force of natural law. As the Logos may be conceived to constitute nature, so may it constitute morality – and, thus, human society. Even as classically conceived, then, the Logos could not be fully known through discovery in nature for, although morality is often mystified as natural, it must be constructed, that is, conceived and established. I have argued that such construction occurs, or is at least completed, in liturgy (although, possibly, not only in liturgy) and thus morality becomes known as it becomes established. Liturgies stand in an epistemic as well as a constitutive relationship to the moral aspects of the orders that they reveal as they represent.

Logos must be constructed, and humanity's responsibility for constructing it ever again in ritual is explicit among some peoples, as we have already seen. But neither the Logos of classical conception nor the Logoi established by the innumerable liturgical orders the world has known are or could be "mere constructions" emerging from undisciplined wish or untrammeled fancy. If harmony is an aspect of an all-encompassing Logos the Logos cannot be arbitrary, for harmony must suppose an accommodation of convention to naturally constituted phenomena – laws, processes and things – which convention cannot supervene nor human action alter. These phenomena, then, may set limits upon convention and their establishment, limits which the processes of establishment themselves then make proper. Liturgical orders, as we have seen, may include among their understandings those of natural phenomena, particularly growth, decay, seasonality and organic characteristics of the species. The importance of the natural may become attenuated in the liturgies of world religions, however, for their universal claims cannot help but divorce them in some degree from the particulars of environments, often at some cost. World religions do not transcend nature, and their regional variants sometimes recognize the particulars of local geography. Their liturgies at least realize, however, the part–whole relationship of the performer to the order that he performs. This part–whole relationship may constitute not only the experiential grounding of ecological and cosmological thought, but of ecological and social commitment as well. Logoi and liturgical orders stand at the intersection of natural law and conventional understanding, an intersection at which difficulties fundamental to the species are most clearly manifest. Like all other species, humans live in a universe governed by laws they cannot alter nor even fully comprehend. Like all other sentient species they act in that world in accordance with their understandings of it. Unlike all other species whose understandings are limited by lack of language, they must construct those understandings for themselves, although they are only loosely constrained by their nature from constructing self-destructive or even world-destroying follies. These understandings may be flawed not only by the incompleteness and the imperfections of discovery, and by the willful and self-serving errors of *idia phronesis*, but also by anthropocentrism, the *idia phronesis* of groups or societies that sets them, or even the species as a whole, against the rest of the world upon which they depend. We shall return to the falsification of Logos in the final chapter.

12

The numinous, the Holy, and the divine

The Holy, it was stipulated in the first chapter, has two[1] fundamental constituents: the sacred, its discursive, logical component, those of its aspects that can be expressed in language; and the numinous, its non-discursive, non-logical, affective component; its ineffable constituent, that of its aspects which cannot be expressed in words but is, rather, experienced inarticulately.

This chapter will be primarily concerned with the numinous and, later, the divine, but because we have, so far in this book, been largely concerned with the sacred, the foregrounding of the numinous constitutes something of a transition. We have, of course, already had brief encounters with the numinous, particularly in its most common manifestation, *communitas*. Nevertheless, it may be well to take stock briefly before proceeding, the better to locate present discussions in those preceding them.

Chapter 9 argued that the locus of the sacred, in bodies of religious discourse, lies in certain expressions, labeled Ultimate Sacred Postulates, enunciated in ritual and sometimes elsewhere as well. These expressions are peculiar in that they are typically[2] absolutely unfalsifiable and objectively unverifiable, but are nonetheless taken to be unquestionable. It was further argued that this quality of unquestionableness is the essence of the sacred. Indeed, the sacred was defined as the quality of unquestionableness imputed by congregations to postulates in their nature objectively unverifiable and absolutely unfalsifiable. Sanctity is, thus, a quality of discourse and not of the objects or beings that constitute the significata of such discourse. It is not Christ that is sacred. He may be divine, but that is another matter. It is the discourse, ritual and scriptural, asserting his divinity that is sacred.

Ultimate Sacred Postulates are themselves, generally low in, or even devoid of, material significata, and they are, similarly, low in, or even devoid of, explicit social import.[3] For example, "The Lord Our God, The Lord is One," the ultimate sacred postulate of Judaism, contains not a single material term, nor does it provide explicit social guidelines of any sort. Yet, as substantively tenuous or even empty as they might seem, the *Shema*, and other Ultimate Sacred Postulates serve as fonts from which sanctity flows to other expressions – prescriptions for rituals and taboos, ethical commandments, oaths certifying testimony, vows and covenants, declarations establishing authorities (whose directives are derivatively sanctified). Such contingent expressions do include material and social terms and are directly involved in the regulation of social and material affairs.

In the course of its flow from Ultimate Sacred Postulates, generalized unquestionableness is transformed into such closely related but more specific qualities as truthfulness, propriety, correctness, morality and legitimacy. Sanctity thus escapes from the confines of religion, in the strict sense, to diffuse itself through much of society's general discourse, to bind together those orders we have called Logoi and, at a more primordial level, to ameliorate the vices, lie and alternative, intrinsic to language's virtues. Sanctity, it is reasonable to believe, is as old as language, which is to say as old as the human way of life, and has been crucial to that way of life. Indeed it may not be excessive to suggest, or even to claim, that the relationship of Ultimate Sacred Postulates to the human social world is analogous to the relationship of the conservation laws to the physical world. Both are foundational.

Chapter 9 argued that the unquestionableness definitive of ultimate sacred postulates is a function of their expression in ritual, more specifically, a product of liturgical invariance. It had previously been argued (in chapter 4) that to perform an invariant order encoded by other than the performer constitutes an acceptance by the performer of that order. Although such acceptance does not necessarily signify belief in the contents of that order, nor guarantee actions conforming to it, it does establish an *obligation* to abide by it, and an agreement to have one's actions judged by it. In chapter 9 I further proposed that such acceptance is tantamount to agreement not to question that order or the Ultimate Sacred Postulate it expresses. Such agreements not to question constitute one ground of unquestionableness.

A second ground of unquestionableness, also a product of canonical invariance, has been revealed to us by information theory. Information, in a technical sense, is that which reduces uncertainty. It is theoretically mensurable, the minimal unit being a "bit," roughly the answer to a yes/ no or an either/or question when the alternatives are equally probable. To the extent that a canon is invariant its performance cannot reduce uncertainty between or among alternatives because no alternatives are represented. So, to the extent that a canon is invariant it is devoid of information. To say, however, that a canon is informationless is not to say that it is meaningless; the meaning of informationlessness being certainty. Ritual, more particularly canonical invariance, is a way of "truly saying" the referents of Ultimate Sacred Postulates into metaphysical being by standing the correspondence theory of truth on its head. The certainty with which ritual imbues Ultimate Sacred Postulates is the second ground of the sacred's unquestionableness.

It is worth taking a moment to recognize, or even to marvel at, canonical invariance. We see, ironically enough, that the very aspect of ritual that leads the narrowly pragmatic, the hyperrational, the untempered positivist, to dismiss it as "mere ritual" makes formal public acceptance possible, and provides the wherewithal for fabricating the sacred. As such it may be indispensable to the establishment of Logoi There is no way of knowing; but if, as suggested in the first chapter, the sacred is as old as language, canonical invariance, the ground of the sacred, may be even more ancient, for invariance is as characteristic of animal as human ritual, and it is at least plausible to suggest that the sacred came into being as expressions from burgeoning language were drawn into, and subordinated to, a ritual form prevalent among our pre-verbal forebears.

Yet, as important as canonical invariance may be, language and the human way of life must, one feels, stand on more than tricks in information theory and the theory of speech acts. We further know from our own experience that the meaningfulness of ritual is not exhausted by its discursive or rational content, and that its most distinctive meanings are not entirely discursive, or discursive at all. We may also recall that in chapter 11 a modern commentator on the Heraclitian conception of the Logos was cited as stating that whereas that order is itself rational, grasp of it is not merely "theoretical" or rational. "It claims a man," says Kleinknecht (1967), which is to imply that its grasp is, in some degree, non-rational. The non-rational numinous constitutes the third ground of unquestionableness.

Whereas the numinous is not confined to ritual, ritual is its most usual locus in the form of *communitas*, as described in chapter 7. After an introduction to William James' and Rudolph Otto's formulations (with an allusion to Durkheim and further discussion of *communitas*) we will take up some common features of consciousness that constitute the ground for the numinous. We will proceed to that state of unification that James and others called "grace."

1. Religious experience, and the numinous in William James, Rudolph Otto, and Emile Durkheim

The term "religious experience" was put into general currency by W. James 1961, a work based upon the Gifford Lectures delivered at the University of Edinburgh in 1901–1902. The "varieties" of which James speaks are not as varied as they could have been, for he was mainly concerned with Christianity, and, within Christianity, mainly with experience of conversion and illumination. He did make reference to Eastern mysticism, but aside from the case of one lapsed Jew who had a vision of the Virgin Mary in an empty church he confines his attention to the experiences of Christians, mostly Protestants, in their solitude. The implications of James' discussions are, however, more general than the materials from which they are constructed.

James recognized two aspects of religion corresponding closely to the two aspects of the Holy we have distinguished. On the one hand there is what he called "institutionalized religion," on the other "personal religion." The former includes rather more than his designation may seem to denote, for he includes within it theology as well as ecclesiastical organization. It consists of discourse and institutions founded upon discourse, and as such is that portion of the Holy in this book labeled "sacred." James' interest in institutionalized religion was slight. He was mainly concerned with personal religion because, in his view, religion originates in and always remains essentially within the experience of individuals (J. Moore 1938: 6). The extent to which he identified religion with private, psychic processes is clearly indicated by his definition: "Religion ... shall mean for us the feelings, acts, and experiences of *individual men in their solitude*, so far as they apprehend themselves to stand in relation to whatever they may consider to be divine" (James 1961: 426; emphasis mine).[4]

James' emphasis on the individual was not merely the choice of a psychologist wishing to remain within his own domain. He took personal religion to be both logically and historically prior to institutionalized religion. It is historically prior because churches are based upon the personal religions of their founders (Moore 1938: 4), so "personal religion should still seem the primordial thing, even to those who continue to esteem it incomplete" (James 1961: 42). In this view he received some support from Anthony F. C. Wallace (1956) a half century later, who argued that all religions have originated in revitalization movements, themselves led by prophets guided by their own private illuminations then taken up by their followers. This entails historical as well as logical priority.[5]

Personal religion is logically and phenomenologically prior to institutionalized religion because it is based upon *experience*, a term which has a special meaning for James. Experience is one of two aspects of consciousness, the other being "thought." "Experience" refers to an immediate grasp of things. It includes sensations, emotions, and vague "feelings of relations." It covers the general area labeled "primary process" by Freudians (Fenichel 1945: 47f.), and it produces a continuous form of comprehension that James called "acquaintance-knowledge" (1890 I: 221). "Thought," on the other hand, has an instrumental function intermediate between experience and behavior (J. Moore 1938: 14). It is outside experience, but reflects on experience to produce the form of understanding that James called "knowledge about" (1890 I: 221). Although "acquaintance knowledge" is fundamental, it is inarticulate. Experience, in James' sense, is non-discursive, a continuous "stream of consciousness" that cannot be communicated in words. "Knowledge about" is a product of thought, which is logical, linguistic and, to use a term not current in James' day, digital in nature, operating upon experience which is not logical, is not verbal and is analogic or continuous in nature. "Through feelings [experience] we become acquainted with things but only by our thoughts do we know about them" (1890: I: 222).

Personal religion is, then, logically prior to institutionalized religion because the latter is constructed in discourse, whereas the former is grounded in experience. Religious experience is a form of experience, and all experience is prior to all thought. If there were no religious experience there could be no religious discourse, but religious experience, as we have already seen, does not, in James' thought, itself constitute religious discourse. Experience, being radically inarticulate, cannot report upon itself, and we interpret our feelings through discursive thought. This interpretive function is the office of religious discourse. "Conceptions and constructions are thus a necessary part of our religion" (W. James 1961: 339).

That he took religious experience to be prior to religious thought led

James to derive the "conceptions and constructions" of religion from it: "Religious experience ... spontaneously and inevitably engenders myths, superstitions, dogmas, creeds and metaphysical theologies, and criticisms of one set of these by the adherents of another" (W. James 1961: 339). This passage is dubious. It suggests that James denied much influence to the role of discursive thought, social process and material conditions in the formation of "myths, superstitions, dogmas, creeds and metaphysical theories," and that he demanded of the sensations, emotions and "feelings of relations" of religious experience an exercise of more formative skill than they probably possess. The relationship of the primary processes of religious experience and the "secondary processes" (Fenichel 1945: 49) of religious discourse are more reciprocal than James would have it, a matter to which we shall return. For now, we are forced to recognize a fallacy in James' conception of "religious experience." In his own terms it includes more than the inarticulate form of consciousness he called "experience." The term "religious" is, after all, a product of the discursive form of consciousness he called "thought." James' "religious experience," then, includes more than experiences, for it is distinguished from other aspects of experience by a product of thought, namely the term "religious." This possible fallacy should not lead us, however, to dismiss his general characterization of religious experience itself.

James explicitly states that there is no specifically religious emotion: the term "religious experience" is simply "a collective name for the many sentiments which religious objects may arouse" (1961: 40). It is to be distinguished from other experience substantively, that is, by its concern with religious objects. These are whatever one takes to be such – gods, for instance – and to this category he affixed the term "divine."[6] Despite these disclaimers James did, however, attribute qualities of a rather specific nature to both religious experience and divine objects. "There must be something serious, solemn and tender about any attitude which we denominate religious" (pp. 47f.) and, in complement, he takes the term "divine" to be properly applied only to such "a primal reality as the individual feels compelled to respond to solemnly and gravely" (p. 48). His Protestant predilections seem apparent here.

Terms like "solemn," "serious," "grave" and "tender" are gentle, or even staid, but few of the accounts of religious experience James himself provides are either gentle or staid. They are, rather, charged with "enthusiasm" (pp. 50, *passim*) and he also uses such terms as "rapture" and "wonder" (p. 225). Those moved by religious experience do not merely submit to the divine. They "abound in agreement" and embrace it

(p. 52). And they do not merely accept the order sanctified by the divine. They participate in it zealously, ardently and even joyously. Saints "run out to embrace the divine decrees," (p. 52) and, as James put it, the "main office of religion" is to "raise conduct . . . from that of doing one's duty to sainthood."

Religious enthusiasm, according to James, is founded upon, or grows out of, a deeper element in religious experience that he calls "grace." In the state of grace the worshippers abandon responsibility for themselves to the divine (pp. 233, *passim*). Following this surrender conduct previously not possible, or possible only with great pain and at the cost of difficult renunciation, becomes easy and joyous. Effort of will is replaced by an enthusiasm that not only overcomes the drives that moral exertion must otherwise tame, but actually enlists the energetic support of those drives. We shall return to grace in a later section. For now we will only reiterate that James' "religious experience" entails significant alteration in the state of consciousness. Whereas in quotidian contexts thought dominates experience, in certain extraordinary contexts among which ritual is most common, most frequent, most social and most reliable, experience becomes increasingly compelling, subordinating or, in extreme cases, displacing, thought. This proposes that religious experience, or, as Rudolph Otto would have it, the numinous, may manifest itself in a range of intensities, running from the feelings of quietude, solemnity or reverence that many people experience in low-key Western church services, to profound ecstatic or mystical experience.

Rudolph Otto's account of the numinous differs from but is compatible with that of James' religious experience. As developed in *Das Heilige* (1917, translated as *The Idea of the Holy*, 1923, second edition 1950) it is more formal, more elaborate, and less bound to Christianity. The "numinous," as he calls that which is experienced in religious experience (1950: 7), is, he says, the non-discursive, non-rational, and ineffable portion of "The Holy" which, in its entirety, embraces not only religion, but is applied by transference to another sphere – that of ethics (1950: 6). The Holy also possesses a moral and rational aspect according to Otto; the numinous is "the Holy minus its moral factor or moment and . . . its rational aspect altogether" (1950: 6). The moral-rational aspect of Otto's Holy corresponds in a general way to James' institutionalized religion and to what I have called the sacred and the sanctified. It is the Holy's discursive content, and is formulated in what Freudians call "secondary process thought" – roughly what James meant by "thought," in contrast to "experience."

The numinous, according to Otto, has both subjective and objective aspects. The subjective, he insisted, is not conceptual but is manifested primordially in what he called "creature-feeling." "It is the emotion of a creature, submerged and overwhelmed by its own nothingness in contrast to that which is supreme above all creatures" (1950: 10). Following Schliermacher, he took a feeling of absolute dependence to be a part of creature feeling. The feeling of being absolutely dependent upon an overwhelming numinous force or entity implies that that which is experienced as numinous is a presence external to the self (1950: 11). The objective aspect of the numinous is, thus, an implication of its subjective aspect. The "objective" is constituted by the sensed characteristics of that which overwhelms the creature and upon which it feels absolutely dependent. The objective aspect of Otto's numinous is thus related to its subjective aspect as James claims institutionalized religion is related to his personal religion. The subjective generates, as it were, the objective. That this approaches the tautological did not seem to trouble Otto, so powerfully did he experience the subjective.

Otto, a theologian, like James, a psychologist and philosopher, was concerned exclusively with the individual, in whom, after all, experience must be located. His discussion of the numinous takes no more account of the social contexts of their occurrence than does that of James, but it nevertheless bears a strong resemblance in certain respects to Emile Durkheim's formulation of the grounds of religious conceptions in *Les formes élémentaires de la vie réligieuse* (1912, English trans., *Elementary Forms of the Religious Life*, 1915). Like Otto, Durkheim asserts that the divine is experienced by worshippers as something which both dominates and sustains them, something superior to them and more powerful than they are, and upon which they are dependent (1961: 236–255, and *passim*). Like Otto, he recognizes that the divine has a moral force and a rational aspect, but is neither rationally comprehended nor even fully comprehensible. It is, rather, grasped in immediate experience. Unlike Otto, Durkheim takes the events in which the divine is comprehended to be the "effervescent" assemblages of ritual. For Durkheim, whose formulation was based upon Australian aboriginal ethnography, *the fundamental context of numinous experience is social rather than individual*, and, furthermore, the social characteristics of rituals themselves constitute the characteristics of the divine object. God, for Durkheim, is society mystified and apotheosized. Needless to say, in holding this view he is in the company of neither Otto nor James. We will return to Durkheim shortly.

The numinous object is a *mysterium tremendum* in Otto's famous formulation (1950: ch. 4). It is *mysterium* because it is beyond creature comprehension. It is uncommensurable with us; as Otto puts it, it is "wholly other" (1950: 25ff.). It is *tremendum* because, first, it is awful in both senses of the word: inspiring awe on the one hand, dread on the other. It is *tremendum*, second, because it has *majestas*, absolutely over-powering and perhaps all-absorbing (1950: 20ff.). It is *tremendum*, third, because of its "energy" or, as Otto's translator called it, its "urgency." "It everywhere clothes itself in ... vitality, passion, emotional temper, will, force, movement, excitement, activity, impetus" (1950: 23). It is experienced as alive in some sense. It is not merely an abstraction but a being or, if it is not a being, it is something that possesses being, or is actively "be-ing" itself.

The *mysterium* of the numinous is not only *tremendum* but *fascinans* (1950: ch. 4). At the same time that it inspires awe and dread it is "uniquely attractive" and "allures with a potent charm."

The "mystery" is ... not merely something to be wondered at but something that entrances ... and beside that in it which bewilders ... [is] something that captivates and transports ... with a strange ravishment, rising often enough to a pitch of dizzy intoxication; it is the Dionysic element in the Numen.   *(1950: 31)*

The experience of the numinous is not always Dionysic, however. The qualities of love, mercy, pity and comfort are elements of its mysterious fascination, according to Otto (1950: 31), but such "natural" qualities do not exhaust it. For Otto, experiences of bliss, beatitude and felicity are "something more," something non-rational, indescribable, and even "inexpressibly tranquil" (1950: 36). This aspect or form of religious experience can be recognized in many of the cases James describes, in accounts of Eastern mystical practices, and particularly among American Indians seeking visions in solitude.

Durkheim emphasizes the ecstatic or Dionysic in his account of the effects of ritual assemblage among Australian aborigines:

The very fact of the [social] concentration acts as an exceptionally powerful stimulant. When they are once come together, a sort of electricity is formed by their collecting which quickly transports them to an extraordinary degree of exultation. Every sentiment expressed finds a place without resistance in all the minds, which are very open to outside impressions; each re-echoes the others, and is re-echoed ... And since a collective sentiment cannot express itself collectively except on the condition of observing a certain order permitting co-operation and movements in unison ... gestures and cries tend to become rhythmic and regular; hence songs and dances. But in taking a more regular form, they lose nothing of their natural violence; a regulated tumult remains a tumult ... This effervescence often reaches such a point that it causes unheard-of actions ... They are so far removed from the ordinary conditions of life ... that they must set themselves outside of and above their ordinary morals ... If we add to all this that the ceremonies generally take place at night in a darkness pierced here and there by the light of fires we can easily imagine what effects such scenes ought to produce on the minds of those who participate.   *(1961: 246–248)*

Durkheim provides us with an account of strong numinous experience arising out of what Victor Turner a half-century later (1969) called *communitas*, which as we saw in chapter 7 is likely to be generated in communitarian ritual. Communitarian rituals are undoubtedly the most common form of cultural event in which numinous experience arises. It may well be that William James and other spiritually sensitive individuals are able to conjure up numinous experiences of the divine in their solitudes. It is clear that some Native Americans found the numinous in solitary and arduous vision quests, and that some trained and disciplined individuals can achieve numinous states in meditation. For most people in most societies, however, the way to numinous experience is through participation in communitarian ritual, for in communitarian ritual the need for extraordinary spiritual sensitivity, or the special preparations and exertions requisite to successful vision quest or meditation are regulated by the compelling characteristics of ritual itself, its tempos, its repetitiveness, its unison, its strangeness, that drive many, or even most participants from mundane consciousness into numinous experience. As westerners know perhaps all too well, not all communitarian rituals generate, or are meant to generate, the alterations of consciousness and society we call *communitas*, but it is in communitarian rituals that *communitas*, often excited, sometimes ecstatic, sometimes achieving the extreme states called "trance," is most frequently experienced.

  One of the fundamental properties of *communitas* is the blurring of distinction between self and other that, in chapter 7, and again in Durkheim's account in the present chapter, seem to extend the self-unification characteristic of numinous experience implicit in James' enthusiasm beyond the self to the congregation or even to the world as a whole. Such non-discursive consciousness of oneness with the world is intrinsic to the *communitas* of communitarian ritual whereas it does not spring naturally from the solitary cultivation of the numinous through meditation, contemplation, or the vision quest. *Communitas* can be said to constitute a non-discursive confirmation of the discursive and rational assertion of Heraclitian Fragment 50 (G. Kirk 1954: 65): "Listening not to me but to the Logos it is wise to agree that all things are one."

The revelation of the hidden oneness of all things and of one's participation in such a great oneness may be the core meaning of *communitas*. It is a meaning of what we have called "the highest order," arising as it does not out of distinction nor similarity but out of the unification of participation.

2. Order, disorder, and transcendence

That the order manifested in liturgical orders is an order heightened over that generally prevailing was discussed in chapter 7 especially, but is entailed by the definition of ritual offered at the beginning of this work, and has constituted one of its foundations. The comprehension of heightened order realized in the unison of performance is, at the least, a perception of an altered reality, but it may also encourage alterations in the perception of that and other realities. We shall return to the profound cognitive and affective consequences of participation in the heightened order of ritual shortly. First it must be recognized that unison is not all that is found in ritual, and order may be transgressed as well as heightened during rituals. In chapter 7 we saw, for instance, that in planting *rumbim* food taboos fundamental to Maring thought as well as social practice are violated. In the passage cited earlier Durkheim alludes to the violation of incest prohibition in Australian rituals. The liturgical calendars of Europe include time for carnivals, periods during which mundane order was renounced and "kings of misrule" presided over an exalted disorder. In Africa and elsewhere, "rituals of rebellion" (Gluckman 1954, Norbeck 1963), in which rulers are reviled, have been elaborated. At the heart of some rituals not order, but hilarity, confusion, aggression, and chaos, expressed in clowning, transvestism, attacks upon initiates, self-mortification, sexual license, blasphemy, and otherwise indecorous actions seem to reign. Such behavior may challenge, tacitly or explicitly, the very canons that ordain it, and Abrahams (1973) suggests that the "vitality" of ritual springs from the confrontations of order and disorder for which it provides an arena. This is to say, the liturgical orders may include not only canons of order but their antitheses as well. As Abrahams puts it "there is a simultaneous proclamation of the order of the world as seen by the group and its (almost) absolute denial" (1973: 15).

Threat to order carries the excitement of danger, and if one is both a subject of that order and a participant in the assault upon it there are, further, the complex excitements of transgression: shame, guilt, fear, abandonment, liberation and exultation. Yet more profoundly, if the order mocked, inverted, violated or renounced is taken to organize reality, then reality itself has been transformed. Ordinary canons of reality are no longer valid and consciousness is in some sense altered.

The orders of liturgy do generally manage to contain, and even to sublimate, the emotions that they themselves generate, and they may be vitalized or invigorated by confrontations with their anti-orders. But these confrontations may be more than invigorating. They may be limiting and corrective as well. Denials of order in ritual are seldom if ever absolute, and while they may be denials of this world's order, liturgical orders are usually concerned with more than the order of the world of here and now. They also proclaim an order that transcends time, an ultimate or absolute order of which the temporal order is merely a contingent part. It is the temporal, and not the ultimate, aspects of order that are most open to challenge, and that are most likely to be challenged by what appears to be anti-order. And it is the temporal and contingent nature of conventions that is exposed by ridiculing and violating them. In being exposed for what they are, they are prevented from themselves becoming ultimate. The king who is ordained by God is told – and so is everyone else – that he is no more than a man when, in the name of the self-same God, he is mocked. Liturgy's challenges to the temporal are in the service of the ultimate, for they keep the conventions of time and place in their places by demonstrating that they are not ultimately sacred, but only sanctified by the ultimately sacred. They are also thereby in the service of evolution, for they make it easier to discard temporally bound conventions when times and places change. But we are primarily concerned for the moment with religious experience, and not with evolution and adaptation, subjects to be considered in the final chapters. Here I shall only suggest, hesitantly, that violations of temporal orders, in pointing to ultimate orders abiding beyond any of their worldly manifestations, point a way toward what is taken to be transcendent of time and place, and a sense of transcendence, itself numinous, may be an element in the experience of the ritualized transgression of prevailing orders.

3. Grace

Order, disorder, and their transcendance in a meta-order of some sort may mirror formally the neurological union of opposites broached in chapter 7. Such unifications may be of a general class that includes the union of the discursive and non-discursive and the sacred and the numinous.

The sense of the unification of opposites, of harmony with the universe, of oneness with the congregation and with God brings us to the holy and to what William James and others have called "grace."

If the term "numinous" designates emotions and feelings, "acquaintance knowledge" and "direct experience" associated with religious practice, then the numinous does not exhaust religious experience because, despite James, experience in religion is not as we have already noted in passing, composed entirely of non-discursive elements. James' own account of grace speaks of a more general interpretation.

In the state of grace, according to James, the rationally guided will no longer must battle against non-rational animal drives to achieve moral ends. Will is replaced by an enthusiasm that does not simply suppress those drives but brings their energies into the service of the divine. In the state of grace individuals can reach new heights of conduct because their internal conflicts have been ameliorated. Grace, for James, is a psychic reunion in which war among parts of the self is replaced by a harmonious and enthusiastic concert of the whole self working in peace as one. This unification, by James' own account, encompasses more than the disparate sensations, emotions and feelings of relation that comprise "experience" in his strict usage. The "divine decrees" enthusiastically embraced in the state of grace include "decrees of divinity," that is, the significata of Ultimate Sacred Postulates, which are expressions in language. The postulates may not represent divinity in all its glory, but at least point toward it, give it names – God, Allah, Ahura Mazda, Ptah, Wakan-Tanka – and thus provide objects which experience can invest with numinousness. But such objects are not conceptualized in inarticulate experience. They are conceptualized in thought, and the experience of them by worshippers is not prior, but subsequent to their objectification in thought. This is certainly true as well of the enthusiastic embrace of "divine decrees properly-so-called," that is, commandments of an ethically rational nature taken to be decreed by God.

Gregory Bateson also calls the union of the discursive and the non-discursive "grace."

> I shall argue that the problem of grace is fundamentally a problem of integration, and that what is to be integrated is the diverse parts of the mind – especially those multiple levels of which one extreme is called consciousness and the other the unconscious. For the attainment of grace, the reasons of the heart must be integrated with the reasons of the reason.   *(1972e: 129)*

Bateson cites conversations with Aldous Huxley as his brief for this usage.

Aldous Huxley used to say that the central problem for humanity is the quest for *grace*. This word he used in what he thought was the sense in which it is used in the New Testament. He explained the word, however, in his own terms. He argued – like Walt Whitman – that the communication and behavior of animals has a naiveté, a simplicity, which man has lost. Man's behavior is corrupted by deceit – even self-deceit – by purpose, and by self-consciousness. As Aldous saw the matter, man has lost the "grace" which animals still have.

In terms of this contrast, Aldous argued that God resembles the animals rather than man: He is . . . unable to deceive and incapable of internal confusions.

In the total scale of beings, therefore, man is as if displaced sideways and lacks the grace which the animals have and which God has.   *(1972e: 128)*

Whether or not we care to join Huxley in beatifying the beasts, his concern with deceitfulness lies close to the problems with which this work is concerned, and he does point to a problem that may be peculiar to humankind: the alienation of parts of the psyche from each other as a consequence of the elaboration of discursive reason concomitant with the emergence of language. Whatever we may care to think about the animals, for humans, according to James, Huxley and Bateson, grace can only be achieved by reuniting elements of the psyche that language sets at odds.

In the state of grace, and in religious experience generally, non-discursive feelings, emotions, and presentiments grasp, envelop, or pervade objects of discursive thought. The numinous and the sacred unite to form the all-embracing Holy. The term "holy," sharing as it does its etymology with "whole," is appropriate for the designation of that which encompasses and integrates both the discursive and non-discursive aspects of human experience. Both words are derived from the Old English *hale*.

Alienated and warring parts of the self are not all that are reunited in the holiness of religious experience. The coordination of persons in ritual is often much tighter than in mundane activities, sometimes reaching levels that seem more typical of the internal dynamics of organisms than of social groups. To perform a liturgical order is to effect a union with others, and the ritual acts that make the reasons of the heart one with the reasons of reason may also join radically separate individuals to their fellows in unions that may seem to approach in intimacy those of the cells or organs of single organisms.

4. Grace and art

Bateson who, as we have seen, conceived of grace in a manner resembling James, took art to be "part of man's quest for grace." Art and religion seem ancient or even primordial companions, and it seems abundantly clear that representations appearing in ritual may evoke emotion and may affect cognition through their aesthetic qualities. Ritual places themselves may be works of art, and they have, since time immemorial, been embellished by works of art. I have already mentioned the paintings in Paleolithic caves, and among the most plausible attempts to explain art's origins are those taking it to emerge from, or with, religion. In chapter 5 it was suggested that the significance of works of art in ritual could lie either in the objects produced and then contemplated or manipulated, or in the act of making them, or both. It is plausible to think that the making of the paintings in palimpsest that survived from the Paleolithic in the dark reaches of caves was at least as significant as their subsequent contemplation, and that in making them artists were participating in acts of creation, or perhaps of begetting, in the earth's womb.

Whether or not the roots of art are set in the soil of religion, or whether its roots and those of religion are together set in a yet deeper stratum of the human condition, many students have remarked not only upon their association in practice but upon similarities in their evocative qualities and effects. Otto recognized an association between art and religion. In *The Philosophy of Religion Based on Kant and Fries* (1909, English trans. 1931), he suggested that religious experience may flow out of aesthetic experience. "In our experience of the sublime and the beautiful we dimly see the eternal and true world of Spirit and Freedom" (1931: 93). He also claimed that the ways in which we experience art and religion are similar. It is through what Fries had called *Anhung* or *Ahndung*, "a kind of perceptual feeling whereby the richest experiences are brought under some form of understanding which yet is recognized as totally inadequate to convey the richness of the experience itself. It is not a conception, but a 'presentiment' of a wealth of reality obscurely revealed in the experience" (J. Moore 1938: 81f.).

Susanne K. Langer's account of aesthetic experience (1953), although it does not explicitly attempt to relate it to religious experience, illuminates the way in which art may contribute to the psychic unification James, Huxley and Bateson call "grace." For Langer, art is "significant form," and its significance is "that of a symbol, a highly articulated sensuous object, which by virtue of its structure can express the forms of vital experience which language is peculiarly unfit to convey" (1953: 32). She means by "vital experience" to refer to the "dynamism of subjective experience" (31) which she identifies with feeling and emotion. Her vital experience is, thus, akin to James' experience. Like James' "experience," Langer's "vital experience" is inarticulate but art provides something like what he calls "knowledge about" it. In fact, Langer uses those very words. Artists, she says, do not convey to us through their art what James would call "acquaintance knowledge" of their own vital experience, but their "knowledge about" vital experience. This "knowledge about" is not quite the same as James', however. For him "knowledge about" is discursive. But aesthetic comprehension – both the comprehension of artists and those who contemplate art – although at a remove from experience, remains non-discursive. "If I could tell you what it meant," Isadora Duncan is reported to have said, "there would be no point in dancing it."

The difference between James' "knowledge about" and Langer's is illuminated by her use of the term "symbol" in the passage just cited. Following Peirce (see chapter 2) we have understood the term to denote signs related only by convention or law to that which they signify. In this usage words are the fundamental symbols. Symbols in this sense are the ground of language and discursive reason. For Langer, however, the relationship of what she calls "symbols" to their significata is not merely arbitrary or conventional. Her symbols are themselves "sensuous objects" whose very form is significant. Her symbol signifies by virtue of the relationship of its structure to that which it signifies. The iconic or metaphoric relationship, in which the structure of the sign resembles the structure of the signification is the most obvious but not the only possibility. Furthermore, to follow Skorupski's distinction discussed in note 3, chapter 8, Langer's symbol does not simply *denote* that which it signifies. It *represents* it. As Skorupski (1976) puts it, "It makes it present to the senses," which is to say that the significatum is grasped not merely rationally but sensuously.

Given its intermediate location among the "multiple levels of which one extreme is called consciousness and the other the unconscious," it is plausible to suppose that religious art in all its forms has a special and important (although perhaps not indispensable) part to play in the "attainment of grace," the union of the "reasons of the heart" with "the reasons of reason." Art and aesthetic experience, by the account offered here, stand midway between thought and experience. The significance of a work of art is grasped sensuously, for works of art have discursive import. They often represent objects available to our ordinary senses, as in painting and statuary, or objects of reason and thought, as in poetry, and even when a work of art does not depict, describe or represent any physical object or object of thought, as in music, it has a context. A pattern organizes the stained glass of the church window, the music played, the dance danced, at a wedding or a funeral. Since art may have discursive import as well as sensuous significance, it may focus the emotions that it is clearly able to stimulate sensuously upon *designated* objects in the physical world or in the realm of discourse.

These emotions, as well as being powerful, sometimes seem rather specific: sadness, joy, solemnity, certainty. Much subtler and more complex but nameless and even unnamable feelings may also be evoked. The particular feelings experienced may, of course, be as much a function of the ritual context as of the aesthetic qualities of the object itself. That they are at a funeral may suggest to those present that what they feel while listening to the dirge is grief, but what each of them feels may well be different. No matter. For a work of art to be successful it need not stimulate the same emotional response in all who experience it. Indeed, if emotion is in its nature not fully describable, how can anyone know if another feels as he or she does? It is likely that everyone responds emotionally to a particular object or event rather differently, for each person brings a uniquely conditioned emotional and rational constitution to it. What is important is that the work elicit a response of *some* sort. But the discursive significance of the work itself, and its place in the liturgical order may then impose tacitly or explicitly a common designation upon the varied responses of those experiencing it: seriousness, solemnity, reverence, submission, Such designations, unlike the complex, changeable and varied emotional states of the members of congregations, have clear social significance. They do not denote emotions, but what Radcliffe-Brown (1964: 40 ff.) called, rather unfortunately, "sentiments," which stand at one remove from emotions. They are emotion-laden but nevertheless socially approved attitudes concerning material, social or metaphysical objects. If art and ritual, and art *in* ritual, are successful they construct "sentiments" out of the inchoate stuff of vital experience on the one hand and objects of discursive reason on the other. They point toward grace, or holiness, that is, the reunion of the "multiple levels [of the mind] of which one extreme is called consciousness and the other the unconscious" by guiding experience to particular objects of thought.

I have been speaking of the part that both art itself and art in ritual may play in the union of the "reasons of the heart" with the "reasons of reason." The two are not equivalent. In contemplating a work of art in solitude an individual may achieve for a moment an intimation of grace.

The experience will always be in some sense unique and may even be idiosyncratic in the extreme. If, however, the work of art stands in a public place it guides the emotions of those who contemplate it to the same object and, although the sensibilities they bring to it and the emotions with which they respond to it will differ, the integrations they attain will have at least something in common. If the work of art is not an object always on display, but a performance only periodically or occasionally occurring, temporal dimensions are now added to that which is common to the experiences of the many. First, there is simultaneity. Performers focus the attention of those witnessing them on the same object at the same time. There is at least the rudiment of coordination among witnesses as well as performers in such events. Secondly, whereas paintings, statues and buildings are atemporal, temporal qualities inhere in all performances. We discussed those of ritual at length in chapter 6. The inclusion of these qualities significantly enlarges the scope of that which is shared.

Finally, if the performance is a ritual, one in which a congregation participates, commonality is further enlarged by a magnitude, for it comes to encompass all that is implicit in common participation. The members of the congregation may each experience the Ultimate Sacred Postulates not only through their ears and eyes, but coming out of their own bodies in song, or forcing entry into their bodies through the beat of drums animating their limbs in dance. The self-unification of participation in ritual is more comprehensive than that of aesthetic contemplation, for it embraces the somatic as well as mental processes, and thus may bring the acts and sensations of the body into the mind's computations.

5. Ritual learning

The alterations of consciousness of which ritual is capable are not, then, mere Dionysic ends in themselves but are, rather, in the service of the organization or reorganization of sets of understandings that include discursive as well as non-discursive elements and processes. They are in the service of the integration of those multiple levels of mind of which one extreme is called consciousness and the other the unconscious, an integration which may be, for the novice or learner in a rite of passage, a novel synthesis, a new and deeper understanding of the world.

This account suggests that the way understanding is reorganized in ritual differs markedly from ordinary learning. Anthony F. C. Wallace (1966: 259ff.) suggested several decades ago that ritual learning does not depend upon practice and reinforcement, nor upon the "law of effect (as in conditioning and instrumental learning)" nor upon the "law of repetition (as in imprinting)" but on "what might be called the law of dissociation," which is "the principle that ... cognitive and affective elements can be restructured more rapidly and more extensively the more of the perceptual cues from the environment associated with ... previous learning of other matters are excluded from conscious awareness, and the more ... new cues immediately relevant to the elements to be organized are presented" (pp. 239f.). "Cognitive and affective restructuring," or learning, in ritual typically has five stages, according to Wallace. The first, which he calls "pre-learning," precedes the ritual (typically a rite of passage). The novice may have some knowledge of the ritual itself, but more generally, he has learned the rights and obligations of the status into which the ritual is to move him, and has also learned to value them, be they those associated with manhood, wedlock or salvation. In the second phase, that of "separation," canons of ordinary reality are disrupted and the state of consciousness altered by means which have already been discussed at sufficient length. Van Gennep would have recognized the third phase, which Wallace labels "suggestion," as liminal. The dissociated novice, in his altered state, under the influence of suggestions from others, or even from himself, "recombine[s] ... cognitive material relevant to resynthesis" unimpeded by everyday notions of reality and uninhibited by mundane habits of mind (p. 241). Resyntheses may be of various depths and durations. They may be relatively transient as, for instance, in the case of temporary mood changes that serve to focus attention in rituals preceding particular activities, like hunting, or they may be irreversible changes in belief and value, as in the case of important rites of passage, or in rituals of conversion, such as voluntary adult baptism.

The two last phases of "ritual learning" may be subsequent to the ritual in which learning originally took place. Wallace calls the fourth phase "execution." In it the ritual subject is called upon "to act in accordance with the new cognitive structure." This *may* occur during the ritual itself but, if the new status is a permanent one, such action may continue throughout the subject's life (p. 241). The fifth phase is "maintenance." The lessons originally learned are, like all learning, likely to fade, and may have to be reinforced from time to time. Further rituals are a common, but not the only, mode of renewal (pp. 241f.).

In light of the importance that psychiatric theory generally puts on learning taking place in the early years of life, it is of interest that rites of passage typically reduce the novice to a state of pseudo-infancy, or even to a pseudo-embryonic condition. The stages in which ritual learning is most concentrated, the second and third, are ones in which a variety of techniques are used to strip the subject of his everyday knowledge and to divest him of his previous identity. Between ritual death and ritual rebirth the novice may be held naked, nameless, silent. It may be suggested that whatever novices learn in this reduced or regressed condition they learn with a depth and a grasp approaching that with which they learned fundamentals in their earliest years. This grasp is strengthened, this depth made yet more profound, by becoming the focus of the ritually induced neurophysiological processes discussed above. That which is learned in ritual may thus override, displace or radically transform understandings, habits, and even elements of personality and character laid down in early childhood.[7]

A suggestion of Erik Erikson's is of interest in the present context. He has proposed that the pre-verbal infant's experience of its mother resembles that which Rudolph Otto attributes to the worshiper's experience of God: she is mysterious, tremendous, overpowering, loving, and frightening. It is learning to trust her upon whom he depends utterly that makes subsequent language-learning and, for that matter, continuing socialization possible. This trust is learned in what Erikson calls "daily rituals of nurturance and greeting" (1966), stereotyped interactions between mother and child taking place dependably at regular intervals, or at times specified by the child's needs. Through the course of ontogeny the numinous emotions initially associated with mother are displaced to other objects.[8]

It may be suggested, in the light of both Erikson's account and the pseudo-infancy prevailing in some rituals, that ritual recaptures a state having its ontogenetic origin in the relationship of pre-verbal infants to their mothers. If this is the case the ground of the numinous precedes the development of any awareness of the sacred or the sanctified for, being discursive, that awareness can come only with language. There are also phylogenetic implications. If ontogeny has a phylogeny and if the mother-child relationship among humans is but a variant of the primate or even mammalian pattern, it may be that the basis of the numinous is archaic, antedating humanity, and it may further be that religion came into being when the emerging, discursive, conventional sacred rooted itself in the primordial, non-discursive, mammalian emotional processes that in their later form (when they, in turn, are bound by the sacred) we call "numinous."

6. Meaning and meaningfulness again

The understandings given by religious experience are said by those who have experienced them to be of an order of meaningfulness exceeding all others. The nature of this meaningfulness is mysterious, but we can at least approach it.

The surpassing meaningfulness of religious experience is usually associated with Ultimate Sacred Postulates. It emanates from them, or they point to it, or it is hidden in their depths. In Chapter 9 I argued that although they themselves are devoid of material terms and are empirically and logically unverifiable, they are represented by the invariance of their expression in ritual to be absolutely true. They, in turn, sanctify other sentences which do include material terms and which are engaged in the operation of society. They certify the truthfulness of testimony and invest conventions, otherwise arbitrary, with correctness, propriety, morality, and legitimacy. Ultimate Sacred Postulates, through the process of sanctification, thus stand against the dissolving power of lie and alternative, the two vices intrinsic to language, and thus make it possible to construct social systems based upon conventions specified in language. Ultimate Sacred Postulates, themselves in language, constitute the ground upon which the use of language stands.

Although Ultimate Sacred Postulates are discursive in form, and although they are the ground of all discourse, when we examine them we find our discursive, rational selves in trouble. We are faced with terms that are without material significata, and relations among them may be paradoxical. What does it mean to say that "The Lord Our God, the Lord is One"? Or that the Lord is Three, or that "All Things are One," or that "Wakan-Tanka encompasses all things"? In Ultimate Sacred Postulates, taken to be without alternative and therefore certain, discursive meaning may be rarefied to a point close to discursive meaninglessness. Ultimate Sacred Postulates stand at the limits of discursive meaning and rationality. They may be taken to be First Words, or Words of the First Being, but at any rate they are mysteries, and their paradoxical or otherwise irreducibly cryptic character declares that discursive reason cannot by itself comprehend them; that the only way to reach beyond them in anything like language is to lapse into song or nonsense syllables. We may remember here the mystical Jewish characterization of the ultimate as the "meaninglessness that encompasses all meaning" (Scholem 1969).

Although Ultimate Sacred Postulates are devoid, or almost devoid, of discursive meaning they are not devoid of all meaning, for all meaning, as this chapter has discussed, is not discursive. There are few who would argue either that a Bach suite is devoid of meaning or that its meaning is discursive. But it does not advance us to say, simply, that the meaning of Ultimate Sacred Postulates, as they are expressed or represented in ritual, is "non-discursive." It is plausible to propose that each of the "multiple levels of the mind" of which "one extreme is called consciousness and the other the unconscious" has a meaningfulness of its own, each of which is more or less discursive than the others. The number of such levels may be indeterminate, but for our purposes we recognized three "types" or "levels" of meaning in chapter 3, and these three types have, in fact, been tacitly as well as explicitly distinguished in the course of this work. Let us review them here.

There is first, the notion of meaning in its ordinary everyday semantic sense. The meaning of the word "dog" is *dog*, *dog* being distinct from *cat*, signified by the term "cat." Meaning in this low-order sense is closely related to what information theorists mean by "information," for it is based upon distinction. As we have seen, information in a technical sense is that which reduces uncertainty, the minimal unit being the "bit," which can be understood as a binary distinction, or as that which eliminates the uncertainty between the two alternatives in a binary choice. Taxonomies are the typical but, of course, not the only forms within which lower-level meaning is organized. The use of language, which distinguishes our species from all others, has removed all limits from the proliferation of low-order meaning. Chapter 3, which was concerned with the self-referential messages carried by stipulated variations in liturgical performance, dealt with this form of meaning.

There are higher orders of meaning. When we become concerned not merely with the references or significata of discursive messages, but with the *meaningfulness* of messages that may include many such meanings, we are concerned with more than, or other than, distinction. Low-order, or first-order, meaning, is founded upon distinction, but what may be called "second-order meaning" is of another sort. The sense of meaning to which questions like "What does it all mean?" point when they are asked by one confronted by a complex mass of information is not that of distinction. In answering such questions we do not attempt to multiply distinctions but, on the contrary, to decrease them by discovering similarities among phenomena that may be disparate, namely that which we seek to understand on the one hand, and that with which we are familiar on the other. These similarities among obviously distinctive phenomena become more significant than the distinctions themselves.

The paradigmatic vehicle of second-order meaning is the icon, among which metaphors are prominent. Metaphor seems to enrich the world's meaningfulness, for the significance of every term that participates in a metaphor is magnified into something more than itself, that is, an icon of other things as well. Metaphor is the stuff of which dreams and primary processes are made, and art and poetry rely heavily upon its various forms for, in their connotative resonance, metaphors are affectively more powerful than straightforward didactic statements. They can, furthermore, represent significata which didactic forms can only denote. In chapter 5, and again in chapter 8, we saw that affectively powerful metaphors are intrinsic to liturgical orders and to the Logoi they construct. As *rumbim* is to *pubit*, so is the spiritual to the mundane, the immortal to the mortal, culture to nature, man to woman, hot to cold, strength to fertility, male genitalia to female genitalia. We also saw that similarities revealed by metaphor are not only discovered but constructed. At the same time that the proximal, or familiar, term illuminates the distal, or unfamiliar, term to which it is metaphorically likened, the distal term predicates the proximal.

There is yet a higher form of meaning. Whereas low, or first order, meaning is based upon distinction, and second order meaning is based upon similarity, highest order meaning, "meaning of the third order," is grounded in unity, in the radical identification of self with other. Those who have known such meaning refer to it by such obscure phrases as "The Experience of Being," or "Being Itself" or "Pure Being." Meaning becomes a state of being. It is no longer referential, but a state or condition of subjects no longer distinct from that which is meaningful for them. Highest order, or third order meaning, signifies only itself, but it itself seems encompassing. All distinctions seem to disappear including, most importantly, the distinction between that which is meaningful, and those for whom it is meaningful. There may be an immediate, undeniable sense of union with others, or even with the cosmos as a whole, as that which is meaningful and they for whom it is meaningful become one.

There are mystics who are able to lose themselves in such unifications through contemplation, but such meaning is more usually attained in varying degrees of profundity for durations of varied length, through participation, by becoming part of that which is meaningful. The relationship of performer to performance in ritual provides a context within which such unification is facilitated.

In sum, distinction is the ground of low-order meaning, and taxonomy the paradigmatic form of its ordering. Similarity underlying distinction is the essence of second order meaning, and metaphor is its fundamental vehicle. At the heart of highest order meaning is the union of that which is meaningful and they for whom it is meaningful, and its way, the most common way to reach it, lies through participation in ritual. We observe here yet another aspect of liturgical invariance's profound significance, for it is this invariance that defines the order of which performers become parts.

The three forms of meaningfulness stipulate three different relationships of significata to those for whom they are meaningful. The semantic distinctions constituting first-order meaning are properties of messages or texts, and as such they are distinct from those who make them or attend to them. First order meaning is discursive, digital, and seems highly "objective." Second order meaning is based upon structural similarities of relations among disparate things – A:B: :C:D. Some of the elements joined together by a metaphor may be aspects of the persons using it and, as we have seen among the Maring, they may wittingly or unwittingly predicate themselves through it. Persons and significata are, as it were, drawn closer together by metaphor than they are by "more objective" first-order meanings. In highest-order meaning, as we have seen, the distance between significata and the persons for whom they are significant is annihilated as the latter become parts of the former. There is a continuum, in this hierarchy of meaningfulness, from the clear objectivity of distinctions of first-order meaning to the absolute subjectivity of third-order meaning.

This hierarchy of meaningfulness may be correlated with the hierarchy of understandings, discussed in chapter 8, that liturgy organizes. Understandings located in different levels of these hierarchies may differ in the nature of their meaningfulness. The representations of contemporary conditions are informational in a strict sense, for their significance is founded upon their variability. Iconicity in liturgical representations indicates that the meaningfulness of the cosmological axioms constituting or synthesizing their significata is of the second order. It is that of metaphor, of the deep and hidden similarity of things apparently unlike. It follows that metaphoric meaningfulness derivatively pervades the rule-ordained procedures for realizing those axioms. It may further be suggested that Ultimate Sacred Postulates evoke highest-order meaning. In ritual the performers "participate in that to which they point," to paraphrase Tillich, that is, in that which is represented by Ultimate Sacred Postulates. Highest-order meaning pervades or grasps ritual generally, but Ultimate Sacred Postulates form the focal point of the identity which defines it.

To distinguish three levels of meaning is not to propose that they are unrelated. It may be suggested that association with, or subsumption by, higher-order meanings invests those of lower order with significance and value. It may make "mere information" deeply- or highly- meaningful. Conversely, first-order meanings provide the distinctions upon which the meanings of higher order operate. Similarities among distinctive phenomena cannot be illuminated through metaphor until distinctions among those phenomena have been drawn, nor would it be possible to dissolve all distinctions into a transcendent unity if there were no distinctions to dissolve.

7. Belief

The compelling nature of highest-order meaning, although the label has not been in general currency, has often been remarked upon. James declares "It is as if there were in the human consciousness *a sense of reality, a feeling of objective presence, a perception* of what we may call 'something there' more deep and more general than any of the particular 'senses' by which current psychology supposes existent realities to be originally revealed" (1961: 62; emphasis his, see also 318ff.).Otto went so far as to argue that such feelings of presence demonstrate actual presence: "We possess in direct experience the best grounds of truth. For we experience nothing more certainly than the content and riches of our own mind, its power of acting and creating and all its great capacities" (1907: 295, cited by J. Moore 1938: 105).

The logical shortcomings of this assertion are too obvious to dwell upon. That Otto could discount them, however, is itself testimony to the convincing – even absolutely convincing – power of religious experience.

In an earlier chapter formal acceptance through liturgical performance was distinguished from belief. Acceptance, it was said, is an outward act, visible to those who accept as well as to others. Liturgical acceptance is performative. As it realizes a conventional order by conforming to it, *it establishes an obligation* to abide by whatever conventions – understandings, prescriptions, proscriptions – that order represents. The force of acceptance is, thus, moral, for breach of obligation is *the* fundamental unethical act or, more precisely, it is the one element present in all unethical acts, the element that, in fact, transforms acts otherwise devoid of moral value into wrongs – homicide into murder, sexual union into incest, seizure of objects into robbery. Liturgical orders are public, and participation in them constitutes a public acceptance of a public order, regardless of the private state of belief. Acceptance is, thus, a fundamental social act, and forms the basis of public social orders.

But acceptance is not belief, nor does it even imply belief. Whereas acceptance is an outward act, belief is an inward state, knowable subjectively, if at all. The nature of the state of conviction may preclude any possibility of indubitable indexical representation, [9] and we thus may have to take its presence in others "on faith." But this is not to deny either its reality or its force. Earlier we spoke of two grounds for the unquestionableness of the sacred; first, the agreement not to question implicit in the formal acceptance entailed by the performance of invariant liturgical orders; second, the certainty intrinsic to the invariance of the order itself. Now we find a third ground of unquestionableness: belief or conviction.

Numinous conviction and formal acceptance are complementary rather than alternative. In chapter 4 it was stated that because belief is both volatile and hidden it cannot serve, as can formal, visible acceptance, as the foundation of public social orders. It now may be added that, conversely, in the absence of belief, formal acceptance alone provides unreliable grounds for such orders in the long run. Formal acceptance, it is true, establishes obligation and it may by itself be sufficient to support, for protracted durations, the conventions to which it has bound men and women by obligation. But a liturgical order that is not supported by the *conviction* of at least some of the members of the congregations realizing it is in danger of gradually falling into desuetude, of sooner or later becoming a dead letter or, as contemporary usage would have it, "mere ritual." Whereas belief, being volatile, hidden and unpredictable, is not *in itself* sufficiently reliable to serve as the foundation of convention, it is, *in the long run*, indispensable to the perpetuation of the liturgical orders in which conventions are accepted. If liturgical orders are to remain vital they must receive the numinous support of at least some of those who participate in them at least from time to time.[10]

8. The notion of the divine

The union in ritual of the numinous, a product of emotion, with the sacred, a product of language, suggests possible grounds for the notion of the divine going somewhat beyond Maurice Bloch's ingenious but perhaps too simple suggestion. Because the notion of the divine is a human universal we must search for its ground in a universal experience or condition.

I would suggest that notions of the divine typically have at least five features. First, although divine objects may be incarnated, the quality of the divine itself is not material in any ordinary sense. Secondly, the divine exists, or, rather, "has being." It is not deemed to be, simply, a law, like the laws of thermodynamics, or an abstraction, like truth, but a being, like Zeus. Thirdly, it is powerful, or efficacious. It has the ability to cause effects. Fourth, it is something like alive. It possesses something like vitality. To use Rudolph Otto's term, it is "urgent." Fifth, it is rationally incomprehensible. The first two of these qualities could be provided by fundamental linguistic processes as they are expressed in ritual's utterances, the last two by ritual's numinous qualities, the third by both.

First, the conception of non-material entities is made possible by the symbolic relationship between sign and signified. This was explicitly recognized in chapter 1 and is implicit in most, if not all, theories of signs. Whereas concept is intrinsic to the symbolic relationship, material reference is not intrinsic to concept. If the sign is not bound to the signified there is nothing to hold the signified to materiality at all, and it can easily escape into the abstract, imaginary, or otherwise purely conceptual.

The *existence* of the conceptual may be made conceivable by the fundamental linguistic process of predication. To say that "X is a quality of Y" is to endow Y with the attribute X. The copula "is" in this sentence has, simply, a logical function, which is to invest Y with X, but this logical function has an existential implication and this implication may be unavoidable. To say that "X is a quality of Y" might be to say, or *seem* to say, that both X and Y in some sense exist, or are "real." Yet the existence entailed by predication may be no more than a conceptual existence, the mode of existence of laws and abstractions. But gods are not conceived as abstractions, nor are laws *per se* divinities, although they may be thought divine. Divine laws and principles, like Asha, Maat, Logos, and Nelli, may become divinities, but only by being transformed into Beings. Asha becomes a personage in the entourage of the Zoroastrian godhead, Ma'at a goddess, Nelli the god-goddess of duality, Logos becomes one with Zeus or Hermes or Christ. Gods are not concepts but Beings. The problem is, then, to transform the conceptual – that which is understood to exist merely as concept, law, or abstraction – into that which is deemed a Being.

The conception of the non-material as efficacious, i.e., as capable of causing effects, may contribute to such a transformation, for humans generally realize that effects are not directly caused by concepts alone (any more than, let us say, houses are built by plans alone). The efficacy of the non-material may imply the being of the non-material. The notion of the efficacy of divine beings, in turn, might well be founded upon the performativeness and meta-performativeness of language as expressed in ritual. The very invariance of ritual proposes, as Bloch has suggested, an agent to whom the efficacy of performativeness intrinsic to ritual's language can be attributed. But divine beings are not merely the products of induction from mystified performativeness, for we know that people are often convinced of their existence in the absence of effects from which they could induce, however correctly or incorrectly, such beliefs.

We must consider not only the capacities of the propositions and performatives that language may present to the worshipers but also the worshiper's experience of those utterances and acts, and the relationship between their qualities and his or her experience. A mediating or connecting term may be noted. At least in languages in which it is an independent lexical element, and perhaps in all languages, the verb "to be" may give rise to the notion of being independent of instances of being. It is of interest in this respect that the most sacred name of God in Hebrew, the tetragrammaton, is said to be a form of the verb "to be" (Brandon 1967: 655). Tillich (1957, etc.) refers to God as "The Ground-of-All-Being" and "Being-Itself." The word for trance in Java is "being" (Geertz 1965: 32).

The general predication (with Being) of that which is represented in an Ultimate Sacred Postulate may become conflated in ritual with the numinous state of "being" of the performer. Numinous experiences, even those that are much less profound than those achieved in mystical states, are widely described as ones in which the divine being is experienced as present. In James' words cited in the last section, there is "a sense of reality, a feeling of objective presence, a perception of 'something there'"; and that 'something' is, in Otto's worda, "urgent – vital, willful, forceful, passionate, excited, overwhelming." With loss of the sense of distinction between themselves and that which is meaningful, the worshipers may sense that they are participating in, or becoming one with, or at least in the close presence of, the divine being. This suggests that the divine object – that which is denoted or represented by an Ultimate Sacred Postulate – is predicated as present and urgent in ritual by the numinous experience of worshipers who take their experiences to be reactions to, or experiences of, divinity. That divinities are reflexive creations of their worshippers is, as noted in an earlier chapter, implicit in the etymology of the English word God. It is, according to both the American Heritage and the Oxford English Dictionaries, derived from an

Indo-European root meaning "That which is invoked or that to which sacrifice is made." And so, the "urgency" that the worshipers feel emanating from the god in whose presence they sense they stand is that which they have projected into it, reflected back upon them. God's Being is the sum, or rather the amalgamation of, its creatures' states of being.

The "Being" with which the numinous state of its creatures predicates the divine is ineffable because rationally incomprehensible. First, the One such numinous experiences seems to animate is of an order of being different from that of the worshiper: an order of being of which the worshiper is only a part. As parts, the worshipers may sense the whole, or even attempt to describe it, but the nature of its animation cannot be fully grasped by them rationally. Secondly, their sense of it, being numinous, is, in its nature, non-discursive although the divine itself includes discursive or conceptual elements, themselves of enormous cognitive and rational attractiveness. They do not merely account for the otherwise inexplicable but, as argued throughout this book, they sanctify, and thus establish, the world's orders. In the non-discursive comprehension of that which includes discursive elements, the non-discursive may seem to encompass, and in some ineffable sense surpass, the discursive.

Ritual is, thus, the furnace within which the image of God is forged out of the gifts of language and the powers of human emotion. This argument suggests that the idea of the divine, like that of the sacred, is as old as humankind.

9. Illusion and truth

The account of the numinous, of the state of grace, of highest-order meaning and of the divine offered in this chapter presents them as non-rational in whole or part. These conceptions are grounded, this is to say, in mental operations that do not conform either to formal logic or to the looser rationality of everyday. Nor do they or the sacred, as it was elucidated in chapter 9 seem bound by any rules of empirical reference. Indeed, such rules are contravened in the case of the sacred: if the terms of a sentence have empirical significata, the sentence is not worthy of ultimately sacred status. The account so far offered, then, is of elaborate fabrication.

Although they may recognize that religion may have made a contribution to the earlier development of humankind, critics of religion have taken it to be illusory because imagined, and deceitful because illusory. As such, they regard it and the non-rational modes of thought animating it to be something from which humankind should free itself. For much the same reasons that Durkheim took all religion to be in some sense true, Marx (1842, 1844) took it to be false (Skorupksi 1976: 32ff.). Durkheim, who rested his case largely upon Australian aboriginal material, took such conceptions to be symbolic representations of society, veils of mystification being perhaps necessary because men are likely to find the necessity of the apparently natural, and the authority of the naturalizing supernatural to be more compelling than mere rational conventions as bases for living in some degree of concord with other men and nature. Marx, in contrast, who was concerned largely with state societies, took religious conceptions not to be useful mystifications but deceptions facilitating the manipulation of the many by the few.

Freud and Marx were in considerable agreement in seeing religious conceptions not only to be illusions, but because illusory deplorable, for illusion denies to humans the illuminations which their unclouded reason could provide them, and prevents them from establishing social orders founded upon reason. But the twentieth century has taught us that the faith of the nineteenth in reason may have been too sanguine. I think we know now that conscious reason has not been an imprisoned angel that would save us if only it were freed from its bondage to the irrational. To the extent that it has been possible to free reason it has been freed, perhaps as never before, in the time of our fathers, our grandfathers, and ourselves. It has discovered evolution and relativity and the double helix, but it has also spawned monsters of such power that they threaten the existence of the species that reasoned them into being. But we do not need history to tell us that noble conceptions are not alone in being born of conscious reason. Heraclitus warned against *idia phronesis* (see chapter 11) and Bergson, recognizing that intelligence is lodged in individuals, warned against its "dissolvent power" (see chapter 10). James also expressed a distrust of rational thought when left, as it were, to its own devices because it is in the nature of thought to serve the ends of the thinker above all else. "This whole function of conceiving, of fixing, of holding fast to meanings, has no significance apart from the fact that the conceiver is a creature ... with purposes and private ends" (1890 I: 482). Elsewhere he states "My thinking is first, last and always for the sake of my doing ... " (1890 II: 333). For James rational thought is primarily an instrument serving private, self-interested, and often selfish ends. As Bergson took religion to be society's defense against the dissolvent power of human intelligence, so did James take the state of grace to provide a better ground for social conduct than rational ethical thought. In the state of grace there is a tendency for experience to pass directly and enthusiastically into conduct, bypassing the egocentrism of all rational thought, including moral thought, which can easily turn to rationalization which may become self-righteous and which is vulnerable to argument (Moore 1938: 37).

Conscious reason, then, is often narrowly self-serving. Indeed, the word "rational" in economics, the discipline that probably more than any other guides the affairs of modern societies, has come to refer to a class of activities that pits humans against their fellows and that must be, in some senses antisocial: the application of scarce means to differentially graded ends to maximize the position of the actor *vis-à-vis* others. If rationality in the economic sense is what conscious reason can come to, it may be suggested that reason alone could not provide a secure and sound basis for social life even if it could be freed from the nonrational. Fortunately, it cannot be, for the nonrational is not only the home of rage and fear, but also of art, poetry, and whatever it is that people mean by the word "love." Moreover, the understandings that eventually lead to formal theories concerning space, time, matter and energy are as likely to be grasped initially by the "left hand" of the non-rational as by the "right hand" of conscious reason (Bruner 1970).

For Bateson the problem of rational consciousness lies in its incompleteness:

consciousness is necessarily selective and partial ... the content of consciousness is, at best, a small part of truth about the self. But if this part be *selected* in any systematic manner, it is certain that the partial truths of consciousness will be, in aggregate, a distortion of the truth of some larger whole ... If, as we must believe, the total mind is an integrated network ... and if the content of consciousness is only a sampling of different parts and localities in this network; then ... the conscious view of the network as a whole is a monstrous denial of the *integration of* that whole. From the cutting of consciousness, what appears above the surface is arcs of circuits instead of either the complete circuits or the larger complete circuits of circuits.

What the unaided consciousness ... can never appreciate is the systemic nature of the mind.   *(1972e: 144–5)*

Its inability to comprehend the wholeness of the mind results, according to Bateson, in an inability to comprehend such wholeness in the world generally.

... purposive rationality unaided by such phenomena as art, religion ... and the like, is necessarily pathogenic and destructive of life; and ... its virulence springs specifically from the circumstance that life depends upon interlocking circuits of contingency, while consciousness can see only such short arcs of such circuits as human purpose may direct.   *(1972e: 146)*

Conscious reason is incomplete, and so are its unaided understandings. The common sense of conscious reason, which has its loci in individual organisms, proposes a sense of separation. Consciousness separates humans from each other, each in solitude behind his own eyes, each imprisoned by his own skin, each enclosed alone between the dates of birth and death. The common sense of separation endorses the common sense of self-sufficiency and autonomy, notions that are sanctified virtually to the point of apotheosis in Western capitalist society. But of course they are illusions. Although humans are metabolically separate from one another, and although consciousness is individual, humans are not self-sufficient and their autonomy is relative and slight. They are parts of larger systems upon which their continued existence is contingent. But the wholeness, if not indeed the very existence, of those systems, may be beyond the grasp of their ordinary consciousness. Although conscious reason is incomplete, the mode of understanding encouraged by liturgy may make up for some of its deficiencies. Participation in rituals may enlarge the awareness of those participating in them, providing them with understandings of perfectly natural aspects of the social and physical world that may elude unaided reason.

Bateson's (1972d: 448ff.) discussion of mind casts light on those aspects of nature that may be grasped by ritual's insight. He suggests that the minimum unit of an idea is a "difference which makes a difference," a *bit* in information theory. The elementary cybernetic circuits around which such units of information flow are the simplest units of mind. Mind, this is to say, is immanent in cybernetic systems. Although some such circuits are contained entire within individual consciousness, the mind of the individual is more comprehensive than his consciousness alone, as Freud long ago showed us. We also know directly from experience that our information-processing circuits include more than our brains, because in response to some messages we experience changes in our visceral states, and these changes enter into the computations that produce our total reactions to information received. Further implied here is that the information circuits that are significant to us include not only more than our brains but more than the selves our skins bound. We are dependent upon circuits that include portions of environments; some of them include many individuals, often individuals of a number of species. Whereas animals are, as a rule, quite separate from each other as far as metabolism is concerned, they are less autonomous with respect to information-processing. This is to say that matter-energy processing systems and information-processing systems are not coextensive. But the adequate functioning, indeed the very survival, of metabolically autonomous individuals as well as societies is contingent upon supra-individual information-processing circuitry immanent in social and ecological systems, and disruptions of such circuits are likely to lead to results not formally dissimilar from the effects of brain lesions or neuroses. In the absence of reliable information, total systems or their parts cease to be self-correcting. The doctrine of I–Thou which Buber (1970) proposes as an ethical dictum is in fact an adaptive imperative, and it does not denigrate Tillich's concept of the "Ground of Being" or "Being Itself" (McKelway 1964: 123ff.) to suggest that the structure of information-processing in nature accords with it. Bateson has recognized these similarities:

there is a larger Mind of which the individual mind is only a subsystem. This larger Mind is comparable to God and is perhaps what some people mean by "God" but it is still immanent in the total inter-connected social system and planetary ecology.   *(1972d: 461)*

Conscious reason may of course provide us with knowledge about the structure and function of ecological and social systems and present to us reasonable arguments for complying with their imperatives. But such knowledge and reasons are likely to be overcome by what economists call "rationality." To ask conscious reason to lead unaided the separate individuals in which it resides to favor the long-term interests of ecosystems and societies over their own immediate interests may be to ask too much of it. Sustained compliance with the imperatives of larger systems not only may require more than ordinary reason, but may have to be maintained in defiance of a consciousness that *in its nature* informs humans of their separateness. It may, indeed, require that the common sense of separation be transcended and replaced from time to time by an extraordinary sense of participation, of being joined together with entities, from which one is usually separated by the evidence of the senses and by competitive rationality, into wholes – societies and ecosystems – that are natural, but not in their nature directly perceptible.

To perform a liturgical order is to participate in it, act as part of it; and where the ritual is public, it is to join with others in this participation. Strong emotions may be engendered and consciousness altered in ritual and, as we have reiterated, not infrequently there is feeling of "loss of self" – that is, a loss of the sense of separation – and a feeling of union with the other members of the congregation and even more embracing entities, a sense of grace, and of being "claimed" by the Logos. As we have seen, it is obviously important that singing, dancing, and speaking in unison are common features of public rituals. To sing or dance in concert or in unison with others, to move as they move and speak as they speak is, literally, to act as part of a larger entity, to participate in it; and as the radical separation of the everyday self dissolves in the *communitas* of participation – as it sometimes does – the larger entity becomes palpable. Such extraordinary or even mystical experiences seem to be profoundly satisfying but, more important here, they may provide deeper and more compelling understandings of perfectly natural and extremely important aspects of the physical and social world than can be provided by reason alone. In sum, ritual in general, and religious experience in particular, do not always hide the world from conscious reason behind a veil of supernatural illusions. Rather, they may pierce the veil of illusions behind which unaided reason hides the world from comprehensive human understanding.

I emphasize "comprehensive." I do not claim that non-discursive modes of comprehension are superior to conscious reason, or even alternative to it. I have dwelled more upon the inadequacies of reason than upon the inadequacies of non-discursive comprehension because of reason's high status in contemporary thought. Understandings provided by non-discursive experience alone are at least as incomplete. The two are mutually dependent in both their secular and religious manifestations. In the absence of the numinous the sacred is cut off from human feeling, and is not only devoid of vitality but alienated from human need. In the absence of the sacred the numinous is inchoate and may even become demonic. The unguided numinous, numinousness unfocused upon Ultimate Sacred Postulates, in glorifying experience, sensation and exultation themselves, not only does not sustain *communitas*, it encourages excess, narcissism, disengagement and hedonism. But even the conjunction of numinous experience and Ultimate Sacred Postulates is no guarantee of beneficence. The numinousness of the Nuremberg rallies should never be forgotten, and in the final chapter we shall consider ways in which the sacred may be degraded, the numinous deluded, the Holy broken.

10. The foundations of humanity

Key characteristics of sacred postulates and numinous experiences are the inverse of each other. Ultimate Sacred Postulates are discursive but their significata are not material. Numinous experiences are immediately material (they are actual physical and psychic states) but they are not discursive. Ultimate sacred postulates are unfalsifiable; numinous experiences are (because directly sensed) not merely unfalsifiable but undeniable. In ritual's, union Ultimate Sacred Postulates thus seem to partake of the immediately known and undeniable quality of the numinous. That this is logically unsound should not trouble us for, although it may make problems for logicians, it does not trouble the faithful. In the Holy – the union of the sacred and the numinous – the most abstract of conceptions are bound to the most immediate and substantial of experiences. We are confronted, finally, with a remarkable spectacle:

> *The unfalsifiable supported by the undeniable yields the unquestionable,*
> *which transforms the dubious, the arbitrary, and the conventional*
> *into the correct, the necessary, and the natural.*

This structure is the foundation upon which the human way of life stands, and it is realized in ritual. At the heart of ritual – its "atom" so to speak – is the relationship of performers to their own performances of invariant sequences of acts and utterances which they did not encode. Virtually everything I have argued from the first pages of this book is implied or entailed by that form.

13

Religion in adaptation

The concerns of this book, it was announced in a near-chiasmus in its first sentence, are two: to consider the nature of religion and to explore the place of religion in nature. The second sentence declared that it is, therefore, concerned with the very nature of humanity.

The very word "human" points to the dual nature of our species. On the one hand, it is cognate with "humus," reminding us (as does the relationship of the Hebrew *adamah*, earth, to *adam*, man) of humanity's "natural nature," of what humanity has in common with all living things. Humans are no less of the earth than the earthworms that will eventually return them to the earth from which the myths of many peoples tell them they first sprang. On the other hand, "human" is as clearly and closely related to the Latin *humanitas* and *humanus*, denoting kindness, sympathy, philanthropy, politeness, refinement, civilization (C. Lewis 1891), all that presumably distinguishes humanity from the rest of life. Both *humus* and *humanitas*: humanity is a species that lives and can only live in terms of meanings it itself must fabricate in a world devoid of intrinsic meaning but subject to natural law. Humanity is not, as Geertz (1973) would have it, simply "suspended in webs of meaning." It is caught between natural laws that it never fully comprehends and meanings that it must fabricate in the absence of much to prevent it from constructing self-destructive or even world-destroying follies.

We have, so far, largely been taken up by our first concern, with the nature of religion, more specifically with the conceptions definitive of religion – the sacred, the numinous, the divine and the holy – and the linguistic, experiential and social grounds from which they are fabricated and on which they stand. I have located those grounds in ritual and ritual has been our focus – so much so that chapters 2 through 12 could

406

have been read as a treatise on the logical entailments, social consequences, and subjective effects of ritual participation. Religious conceptions and ritual as such have occupied us first not only because exploration of their internal logic is an end in itself, but because their consideration seems prerequisite to exploration of their relationships with whatever lies outside them in human society and even in nature as a whole. It has not, however, really been possible, nor have I tried, to separate radically questions concerning religion's nature from those concerning its place in nature. The universal ritual form, and universal religious conceptions – the sacred, the numinous, the holy, the divine – have been in undisputed possession of the foreground from the second to the twelfth chapters but we have frequently, even continually, touched, usually without calling special attention to the matter, upon their adaptive significance, that is, upon their relation to the social life and circumstances of humanity, and to the natural world that humanity increasingly dominates. Thus, we have been concerned with the ritual establishment and sanctification of convention, the act of acceptance entailed by ritual participation that underlies social contract, the grounding of morality and obligation, the organization of time, the establishment of Logoi, the generation of numinous emotion in support of the orders guiding social life and, at a more profound level, the amelioration of the vices of language.

At the end of the last chapter I called attention to the remarkable structure embodied in the Holy and realized in ritual: the unfalsifiable supported by the undeniable yields the unquestionable, which transforms the dubious, the arbitrary and the conventional into the correct, the necessary and the natural. Religion, this was to claim, has been the ground upon which human life has stood since humans first became human, that is, since they first spoke words and sentences. This is further to claim that the relationship of Ultimate Sacred Postulates to the conventional world parallel, as we noted in the last chapter, the relationship of such laws as those of thermodynamics to the physical world. They are its very ground. We may cite here Giambattista Vico's declaration that the gods were "the first great invention of the gentiles" (1988[1944]: 1744, para. 9, 10, *passim*), and that the rest of social life is built upon the foundations that those first great inventions laid down. Our exploration of religion in nature is thus embedded in and continuous with our account of the nature of religion.

Let us translate the phrase "the role of religion in nature" into slightly more precise and technical terms. We will be concerned with the place of religious concepts and practices in the adaptive processes of humanity. But, as we could not explore the role of religion in adaptation until we had established what we meant by "religion," neither can we do so until we establish what we mean by "adaptation." The matter was broached in section 1.2 and will be reviewed and elaborated upon in section 13.1. This will divert us from religion *per se* temporarily but will prepare us to consider religion in adaptation and, in the next chapter, maladaptation. It may help to note in advance that the underlying principle organizing our discussion now shifts from the logic of ritual and its entailments of the sacred, the numinous, the divine and the holy to the logic of adaptation, its social and material effects and its structural requisites. To put the matter a little differently, chapters 2 through 12 were essentially microcosmic, being concerned with ritual's internal workings. Chapters 13 and 14 are macrocosmic, being concerned with the relation of ritual and the concepts it generates to the social and natural world generally. Some readers may find the shift in emphasis in the next sections both abrupt and tedious, but their discussions are prerequisite to understanding what follows and I have kept it as succinct as possible.

1. Adaptation defined again

I take the term "adaptation" to designate the processes through which living systems of all sorts maintain themselves, or persist, in the face of perturbations, originating in their environments[1] or themselves, through reversible changes in their states, less reversible or irreversible transformations of their structures, or actions eliminating perturbing factors. Such processes, in very general ways similar in form as well as goal, underlie the innumerable sorts of actions undertaken by all the world's life forms in dealing with the vicissitudes they continually or intermittently face. They are universals, to be observed among pismires and empires, as much processes of life as respiration and reproduction. Some preliminary comments are in order.

First, I include within the class "living systems" both organisms and associations of organisms. The latter, among humans, may include such social groups as families, clans, tribes, states, and even societies and anthropocentric ecosystems – any association that can be shown to have inhering in it as a unit distinct processes at least occasionally initiated in response to, as response to, and in attempted correction of, perturbation. Thus, although it may be acceptable to speak of adaptive processes "inhering in" living systems, it is more accurate and therefore preferable to propose the converse: that adaptive processes define (and bound) living systems. The scope of an adaptive process distinguishes a living system (which may, of course, include others[2] and be included by yet others) from its environment.

The application of a common set of concepts to organizms and to associations of organisms, some of which are culturally governed, is likely to attract charges of organic analogizing. Such charges would, in my view, be misplaced. To say that organisms and associations of organisms are both loci of adaptive processes is to recognize that they are both subclasses of a larger class, namely living or adaptive systems, and not to propose that social systems are detailed icons of organisms (or vice versa). To recognize general similarities among systems differing in obvious respects is not to deny their differences nor the significance of those differences, but to contextualize them. We shall return to certain of these differences shortly. It may be noted in passing, however, that the organic analogy doesn't even apply very well to organisms, which are more like ecosystems than is generally thought (L. Thomas 1974).

Adaptation is a process, or category of processes, universal to life. It is to be observed in simple animals and complex societies, and its application to human affairs may provide supracultural criteria in terms of which the operations of particular societies may be assessed.

Relatively autonomous adaptive systems are what have sometimes been called "general purpose systems." The term is ugly but does convey the notion that such systems do not have special goals. They cannot be defined, as can the special-purpose systems which they include, by the production of some special product, like petroleum or pituitrin, or by some special activity, as can hearts, lungs, or fire departments. Their ultimate goal is so low in specificity as to seem a virtual non-goal. It is simply to persist. As Slobodkin and Rapoport (1974) have put it in a discussion of the difficulties of applying game theory to evolution, general purpose systems are autonomous "players of the existential game," a game that is peculiar in that the only reward for successful play is to be allowed to continue to play, a game in which the phrase "cashing in your chips" is a euphemism for losing. Individual humans and societies may, of course, mystify such goals (or non-goals) while maintaining their low specificity (e.g., "It is the goal of society to serve God."), but for them to set for themselves enduring goals as specific as those appropriate for their subsystems is likely to reduce their chances of staying in the existential game by reducing their flexibility. Central to adaptation is the maintenance of systemic flexibility, the maintenance of an ability to keep responding homeostatically to perturbations the magnitude and nature of which usually cannot be predicted, given the complexity of the universe.

I have just used the adverb "homeostatically." I do so with some reluctance because homeostasis is widely misunderstood to imply changelessness. The 1987 supplement to the Oxford Unabridged Dictionary defines it ("homoeostasis") as [1] "The maintenance of a dynamically stable state within a system by means of internal regulatory processes that tend to counteract any disturbance of the stability by external forces or influences; [2] the state of stability so maintained; [3] *spec.* in *Physiol.* the maintenance of relatively constant conditions in the body (e.g. as regards blood temperature) by physiological processes that act to counter any departure from the normal."[3]

It is clear that such terms as "homeostasis," "dynamically stable state," and the related "dynamic equilibrium" *do not* imply changelessness. Indeed, the opposite is the case. In an ever-changing world the maintenance of homeostasis requires constant change of state and less frequent and discontinuous changes in structure as well. If the maintenance of homeostasis is not synonymous with adaptive processes it is the goal of adaptive processes.

2. Adaptation as the maintenance of truth

We tend to conceive of adaptation and the maintenance of homeostasis in physical terms (e.g., the maintenance of blood temperature within ranges of viability), but in chapter 1 we recalled that Gregory Bateson put the matter into informational or communicational terms by proposing that adaptive systems operate to maintain the truth value of certain propositions about themselves in the face of perturbations threatening to falsify them. In purely organic systems such "propositions" are genetically and physiologically encoded "descriptions" of healthy structure and function (e.g. proper blood temperature range, blood sugar levels, etc.), and thus the preservation of their truth value is synonymous with the persistence of the organisms maintaining them. In human societies, as we know from chapter 1 and ensuing discussions, the matter is not so simple. Regnant propositions – those whose truth value is maintained at the possible cost of changing other parts of the system – become propositions "properly-so-called," that is, symbolically encoded statements, like "The Lord Our God the Lord is One," and the expressions such postulates sanctify (see chapters 9 and 10). The relationship of such expressions to the biological well-being and reproductive success of those who espouse them is problematic, to say the least. We will return to this and related matters, but for now two points.

First, we can only note in passing that the adaptive unit in all but human systems, the unit that responds homeostatically to perturbation is entirely, or almost entirely, constituted by genetic information (some animals add some degree of learned information). Human systems and only human systems add, for better or worse, a symbolic component. This component *always* becomes dominant, radically transforming the very nature of adaptive systems from organic to symbolic-organic, leading Leslie White to declare that the emergence of the symbol was the most radical development in the evolution of evolution itself since the appearance of life.

Secondly, it is well to make explicit that Bateson's informational definition of adaptive systems – that they maintain the truth value of certain propositions about themselves in the face of perturbations threatening to falsify them – is, in fact, his definition of cybernetic systems. This is to say that adaptive systems are quintessentially cybernetic. The cybernetic nature of adaptive processes is also indicated by the OED definition, which proposes that the existence of regulatory processes *internal* to the system is a *sine qua non* of homeostasis.

3. Self-regulation

In most general usage to say that a system is self-regulating is to say that it is cybernetic,[4] and vice versa. Be this as it may, self-regulation depends upon a limited family of mechanisms.

First, we may mention *Insulation*, in which some aspect or component of the system is held in what seems to be an invariant state by insulating it from perturbations. Examples from nature may be provided by heavy-shelled molluscs whose activities are more or less limited to opening their thick shells intermittently to filter-feed. The clearest cases among humans may include restrictions placed upon the enunciation of Ultimate Sacred Postulates in some traditions (see chapter 9 above). Most notable may well be Jewish constraints upon the utterance of God's name. During the period of the Second Temple, "The only individuals who lawfully uttered the name were the priests ... It is recorded that sages communicated the pronunciation of the name to their disciples once in seven years ... the priests themselves, after the death of Simon the Just, discontinued the pronunciation of the Tetragrammaton in the blessing ... The high priest, however, continued to pronounce the name on the day of atonement, amid the prostrations of the people. Blasphemy, the pronunciation of

God's name under other circumstances, or by other persons, was a capital offense (I. Abrahams 1909: 671f.). Such insulation has clearly been of considerable importance in the self-regulation of human societies.

Secondly, there are what Piaget (1971: 14) calls *Operations*. These are perfectly reversible processes, best exemplified by mathematical and logical formulation (1+1=2, 2−1=1). As such they are of considerable importance in thought. Although they do not apply directly to matter and energy transactions, within which inexactitude prevails and entropy is ubiquitous, they may be important in the regulation of such transactions. Elsewhere in this volume and in other essays (see Rappaport 1979a) I have described Maring ritual operations for reversing damage done to the cosmos by warfare. Of course ritual does not return the physical and social to their precise pre-war condition, but *logically* the *status quo ante* is restored.

Thirdly, there is *Time-Dependent Regulation*, exemplified by circadian rhythms in organisms and by such mechanical contrivances as traffic lights, which change from red to green at fixed intervals whether there are many or even any cars waiting. More to our point, some rituals occurring at fixed intervals form a class of regulatory mechanisms of considerable importance in social process. This matter was discussed at length in a previous chapter. We will only note here that sabbath observance assures rest at regular intervals whether needed or not, and provides a convenient framework for organizing recurrent activities.

Finally, there is *Variable-Dependent Regulation*, cybernetic regulation in the strict sense, in which deviation in the value of a variable from its ideal or reference value itself initiates a process returning the deviating value to that reference or ideal. The thermostat provides a familiar example. Having detected the deviation of room temperature from its reference value of, say, 70° F, it throws a switch activating or deactivating a heat source, thus returning room temperature to 70° F. The restored condition is quickly detected by the thermostat and the corrective program terminated by an opposite throw of the switch. That cybernetic regulation in the strict sense is important in the regulation of social systems has been argued in discussions of the Maring ritual cycle in this volume and elsewhere (see esp. Rappaport 1984).

It is, perhaps, obvious that the various regulatory modes may be embodied or, in social systems, institutionalized, in a variety of ways. Discrete regulators (e.g., chiefs, big men, kings) are important in some systems, but regulation may be the outcome of unmediated interactions among components, as in hypothetical "perfect markets" and in dynamic interactions among distinct species populations. Regulation in human societies and ecological systems dominated by humans may also reside in tradition, in ritual cycles, or in the entailments of social structure.

Self-regulation entails corrective responses, and, as already noted, corrective responses may have several effects. In some instances the stressing factor is eliminated. In others, compensatory adjustments are made within the existing structure of the system. In yet others, however, changes – genetic, constitutional, structural – in the very organization of the responding systems themselves are, and must be, made. The self-regulating processes through which living systems maintain themselves thus entail or subsume the self-organizing processes through which they transform themselves. This matter was broached in Section 1 but can be elaborated upon here.

These two classes of processes, self-regulation and self-organization, have generally been distinguished in the social sciences, forming the foci of two distinct modes of analysis, "functional" on the one hand and "evolutionary" on the other. The distinction has been overdrawn because the maintenance ("persistence," "adequate functioning," "survival") of systems in a changing world requires constant change. The connecting generalization is what Hockett and Ascher (1964) have called "Romer's Rule," after Alfred S. Romer, the zoologist who first enunciated it in a discussion of the emergence of the amphibia (1954[1933]). We may recall from chapter 1 that Romer argued that the lobe-finned fish did not come onto dry land to take advantage of its previously unexploited opportunities. Rather, relatively minor modification of their fins and other subsystems made it possible for them to migrate from one drying-up stream or pond over land to others still containing water during the intermittent droughts of the Devonian period. Such structural changes thus made it possible for them to maintain their general aquatic organization during a period of marked environmental change. In slightly different terms, self-organizing or evolutionary changes in components of systems are functions in the self-regulatory processes of the more inclusive and enduring systems of which they are parts.

Structural or evolutionary changes, such as fin to leg, may be distinguished from "functional" changes or "systemic adjustments" on such grounds as reversibility but they are not separated from them in the larger, more inclusive scheme of adaptive process. Together they form ordered series of responses to perturbations. We shall take up the characteristics of these sequences in some detail in a later section. First we shall review and elaborate what has already been said in this volume about the place of religious conceptions generally in human adaptation.

4. Religious conceptions in human adaptation

The conceptions of religion enter into both human adaptation and the adaptations of humanity. By this second near-chiasmus I mean to emphasize that the sacred and the numinous are significant both among the adaptive *properties* of the species as a whole and in the adaptive *processes* of the social units into which the species is organized.

When terms like "adaptive," "adapt" or "adaptation" are used in connection with individuals, clans, states, or populations they imply sequences of responses to perturbations, but species *as wholes* only rarely respond in unitary fashion to perturbations. When such terms as "adaptive" are used in connection with species *qua* species they do not usually refer to sequences of responses, but *to properties*, universal throughout these species, making it possible for their constituent units to adapt in the variety of ways that each of them do to the specific perturbations to which they are subjected. Much of the adaptive apparatus of any species, including ours, is not its sole possession, but in speaking of human adaptation, I mean to refer to what is not only common to humanity but unique to it. To the extent that chapters 2 through 12 have been concerned with adaptation they have been largely concerned with adaptive properties universal to and exclusive to the species. We may review, draw together and elaborate earlier discussions of this concern before proceeding.

Flexibility is central to adaptive processes, and the enormous flexibility of the human species rests, of course, largely upon a property universal to and unique to humanity, namely language. Whereas the capacity for language must have a genetic basis, there seems to be no genetic specification for any particular language nor what can be said in any language. Their possession of language not only permits but requires human groups to stipulate linguistically the rules and most of the understandings in accordance with which they live. The rules and understandings of human groups are not genetically but only conventionally specified, and can thus be modified or even changed relatively quickly and easily, even overnight. Language has thus conferred upon humanity the ability to devise a great range of organizations and practices and to process, conserve, and transmit enormous quantities of information. These gifts of language have made it possible for the species to invade and dominate virtually all of the world's regions. In Chapter 1, however, we noted vices intrinsic to the very virtues of language, problems of sufficient seriousness to undermine language's usefulness, namely lie and alternative.

These problems are fundamental. What is at stake with the lie is not only the truthfulness or reliability of particular messages, but, as stated in chapter 1, credibility, credence and trust themselves, and thus, community and communication generally. The survival of any population of animals depends upon social interactions characterized by some minimum degree of orderliness, but such orderliness depends upon reliable communication.

If the recipients of messages are not willing to accept the messages they receive as sufficiently reliable to act upon, their responses are likely to tend toward randomness, becoming decreasingly predictable, leading to yet more random responses, reducing orderliness yet further. When a system of communication accommodates falsehood how can the recipients of messages be assured that the messages they receive are sufficiently reliable to act upon (see Waddington 1961)?

It is often infeasible for receivers to verify such messages; often, indeed, there is no possible way for them to do so. How can the recipient come to rely upon such messages? This book has argued that ritual ameliorates this vice of the symbol by moving in what seem to be opposite directions. First, as argued in chapter 2 and elaborated in chapter 3, ritual seems to minimize symbol use in representations of certain consequential self-referential messages, either eschewing the symbol for the index or reinforcing symbols with indices.[5]

The signifying capacity of indexicality is, however, limited to the representation of that which is present, and we have seen that at the same time that ritual vitiates some problems of falsehood by representing indexically that which is of the here and now, it *sanctifies* its references to that which is not confined to the here and now. To sanctify is to certify. Sanctified sentences partake of, or are supported by, the unquestionableness of the Ultimate Sacred Postulates with which they are associated. To sanctify messages is to certify them.

Sanctity does not eliminate falsehood. We all know that people may lie even under oath. They may be more reluctant to do so than if no oath had been sworn, however, and it may be that sanctity decreases the prevalence of lie. It is significant in this respect that when a common lie is told under oath it becomes more than a mere lie. It is an instance of perjury, that is, a "meta-lie," a lie about telling the truth. But the problem of falsehood, as we have already observed, is not merely that of the falsehood itself, nor even of falsehood's direct effects. Much more important, it is the corrosive distrust bred by falsehood's mere possibility. On the other hand, to the extent that the recipients of messages regard those messages as trustworthy, their actions will tend to be non-random and therefore in a general way predictable. Moreover, the regularity of their responses may bring about the states of affairs they assume. To put it a little differently, the validity of some messages is a function of their sanctification. Sanctified truths, we have seen, constitute the dominant category in the class of conventional truths, those whose validity depends upon their acceptance. As far as informing behavior is concerned, conventional truths form a third class in the set that also includes the necessary truth of logic and the empirical truth of experience.

Like lies, the Ultimate Sacred Postulates from which sanctity flows are made possible by symbols, that is, by freeing signs from their significata. Thus, the quality of language out of which the problem of falsehood arose also proposed its solution through a move of astonishing – yet inevitable – simplicity and profundity. Whereas lies are made possible by the freeing of signals from material significata, Ultimate Sacred Postulates are made possible by the freeing of significata from materiality altogether, and then encompassing them in ritual's invariant order. It should be noted that if common lying is understood as the intentional transmission of information thought or known by the transmitter to be false, then Ultimate Sacred Postulates, which are in their nature unfalsifiable, cannot be vulgar, or common, lies. They can, however, be faulty in ways related to vulgar lying, a matter to be explored in the final chapter.

The emergence of sanctity in the course of human evolution may be an instance of Romer's Rule. Evolution, in light of this principle, is conservative in nature: the fundamental question to be asked of any evolutionary change is "What does it maintain unchanged?" In light of Romer's Rule, sanctity's role in human evolution has been profound. I have argued that sanctity has made it possible for associations of organisms to persist in the face of increasing threats posed to their orderly social life by the increasing ability of their members to lie.

We have seen, however, that certification of the truthfulness or reliability of questionable information through association with unquestionable postulates is only one of sanctity's offices and perhaps not even the most fundamental. All sorts of sentences may be sanctified, and sanctity thus may invest all of the sentences through which a society is ordered. This is a matter of great importance given another evolutionary trend that must have been associated with the emergence of language. I refer to decrease in the specificity of genetic determination of behavior patterns. The replacement of genetic determination of patterns of behavior by their cultural (verbal) stipulation has conferred an unparalleled adaptability upon humankind, permitting it to enter and, eventually, to become dominant in the great range of environments the world offers. But intrinsic to increasing flexibility for the species as a whole is a concomitant problem for the separate societies into which the species is divided: their members are no longer genetically constrained to abide by their conventions, and can easily (and perhaps inevitably do) imagine others, some of which may seem preferable to those prevailing.

To put this a little differently, we have noted that the second problem intrinsic to language is alternative. With an increasing range of cultural orders becoming genetically possible for any human individual, the adaptive capacities of the species are enhanced and its adaptive processes accelerated. But possibilities for disorder are also magnified. If the particular cultural orders of the many societies into which humanity is organized are built upon words – and they are – then there is not only the possibility of false words, but of too many words, not only of lie but of babel, of the possibility of being overwhelmed by alternatives. Lie and alternative are two fundamental problems – perhaps, as Buber (1952) proposed, the two fundamental problems vexing the use of language.

If falsehood is a problem intrinsic to language, so is a problem of truth, the "truth of things," the truth of "what is the case?" The conception of a desired alternative may be the first step toward its realization; it is also likely to be the first step toward the disruption of the existant. Such conceptions may be an inevitable concomitant of grammar which, along with the symbol, is a *sine qua non* of language. If it is possible to say "Christ is God and Jove is not," it is possible to imagine, to say and act upon the converse. All social orders protect themselves, and must protect themselves in some degree, against the disordering power of the linguistically liberated imagination, and tolerance of alternatives is therefore limited in even the most liberal societies. Thus, if there are to be any words at all it may be necessary to establish *The Word*, and *The Word* is made sacred, which is to say unquestionable, by canon's invariance.

To put this argument in terms of adaptation, the very versatility that has conferred upon the species the ability to expand into all of the niches and habitats that the world presents, a versatility that rests upon the specification of patterns of behavior through language rather than through genetic processes and limited non-symbolic learning, has intrinsic to it the problem of disorder. The ability to modify or replace conventions is central to human adaptiveness, but if alternatives to the conventions in accordance with which they live can be imagined (indeed may inevitably be imagined) by the members of any society, how can they be led to abide by those prevailing, particularly if some of the alternatives seem more attractive? I have suggested that sanctity is a functional replacement for genetic determination of patterns of behavior, a determination which became decreasingly specific as language emerged. The capacity for variation or alternative that is given to the species by language is ordered by sanctity, itself a product of language. *Flexibility is neither versatility nor a simple transformation or product of versatility. It is a product of versatility and orderliness.* The versatility flowing from the rich and varied thoughts, purposes, and capacities of any population if left unordered do not provide a ground for Logos but a reservoir of *doxa* and *idia phronesis*. The innumerable possibilities inherent in words and their combinations are constrained, reduced and ordered by unquestionable Word enunciated in ritual's apparently invariant canon. Sanctity orders a versatility that otherwise might spawn chaos.

Thus it is that sanctity, like lie and alternative a precipitate of language, but language subordinated to the invariance of canon, ameliorates the evils of alternative as well as those of lie, leaving humanity to enjoy alternative's undoubted blessings. In participating in a liturgical order the performer follows the Logos. In the hands of sanctity the versatility that, flowing from grammar, engenders *doxa* and *idia phronesis* is, as it were, gathered into Logos. Flexibility is thus wrought from the same materials as disorder.

As the concept of the sacred would have been inconceivable in the absence of language so might it have been impossible for language to have developed without a concept of the sacred to resist its ever-increasing capacity to subvert, through lie and alternative, the social systems relying upon it. The implication of this argument is that the idea of the sacred is precisely as old as language and that, contingent upon each other, they emerged together in a process of mutual causation formally similar to, and in all likelihood concurrent with, that which is said to have organized the interdependent evolution of human intelligence and human technology. Indeed, if human intelligence is in part a product of language, then intelligence, technology, language and the concept of sanctity emerged together in what systems theorists would call a "mutual-causal deviation amplifying process" (see Maruyama 1955). This phylogenetic proposition does not rest only upon an assertion of the indispensable place of sanctity in the discourse of societies relying upon symbols. The emergence of the concept of the sacred may have been as inevitable as it was indispensable, a product of the conjunction of symbol and ritual, developing as the speechless rituals of our pre-verbal forebears began to absorb some words selected from burgeoning language, thereby subordinating those words to the invariant order of canon, and transforming them into *The Word*. The Word, thus established, could stand against the uncertainties and treacheries made increasingly possible by ever more words, combinable by increasingly complex syntactic rules into innumerable alternative possibilities, not all of which could, simultaneously, serve to organize social life or even be true.

The sacred is not the only constituent of the Holy entering into the human mode of adaptation. There is also the numinous. In numinous experiences parts of the psyche that may ordinarily be out of touch with each other are brought together and in the ensuing "grace state," sanctified conventions, otherwise merely accepted, are enthusiastically embraced. The unifications of religious experiences may, however, bind together more than fragmented psyches and more than reunite individuals to divine decrees. They may reach outward from the individuals in which they arise to embrace others, and, even beyond, to encompass the world. We shall return to these experiences later only noting now that in them Logos may be experienced and in them, therefore, the reasons of Logos may overcome the purposes of *idia phronesis*.

I further proposed in the last chapter that religious experience provides a third ground for the unquestionableness of Ultimate Sacred Postulates. It reinforces acceptance and certainty with belief or conviction, and I argued that although belief is not *by itself* a *sufficient* ground for unquestionableness because it is volatile, hidden and unpredictable, it is *in the long run* a *necessary* ground. A liturgical order that is not supported by the conviction of at least some of those realizing it at least some of the time has become, as we say, "mere ritual," and it is likely soon to pass away. Its gods, banished from eternity, disappear into the past. If the sacred is crucial to the human mode of adaptation, so is the numinous.

5. The structure of adaptive processes

We may now turn from the place of the sacred and the numinous in the human *mode* of adaptation to their role in the specific adaptive *processes* of the societies into which humanity is organized. Even to suggest the range of social forms that have evolved in the course of human history, and the variety of ways in which the conceptions of religion have participated in them would require a volume lengthier than this one, so I must remain general. But, before discussing the place of ritual and its products in adaptive processes more needs to be said about the nature of those processes generally and, further, their structural entailments. Again, we leave religion for a little while, better able, on our return, to consider its place in adaptive processes.

We may begin where we left off at the end of section 13.1. We noted there that the view of adaptation favored in this work obliterates the distinction between functional and evolutionary responses to perturbations. Both classes – state changes and structural changes – are directed toward persistence, toward staying in the "existential game," and they are not separated in adaptive processes. They are organized into ordered sequences of responses, and these sequences as sequences have certain interesting structural properties (Bateson 1963, Frisancho 1975, Rappaport 1976a, Slobodkin and Rapoport 1974, Vayda and McKay 1975).

The responses most quickly mobilized are likely to be energetically and behaviorally expensive, but easily and quickly reversible following the cessation of stress. Should a perturbation or stress continue, however, the earlier responses are eventually relieved by slower-acting, less energetically expensive, less easily reversible changes. For instance, the response of a human moved from lowlands to very high altitudes begins immediately with panting and racing of the heart and continues, through a series of circulatory and other changes, to, after a year or so in younger individuals, irreversible changes in lung capacity and in the size of the heart's right ventricle. The ultimate change in such sequences would be genetic, although this seems not to have occurred in either the Andes or the Himalayas (Bateson 1963, Frisancho 1975). Similarly, the initial response of a town to very heavy traffic loads during peak periods may be transitory redeployment of police. But if this response is inadequate or itself causes an intolerable strain a series of less easily reversible actions may be initiated, like making certain streets one-way, the ultimate perhaps being the construction of a highway by-pass around the town, a change which is virtually irreversible. Responses earlier in the sequence are likely to be gross behavioral or physiological state changes. Changes later in the sequence are likely to be structural (constitutional in social systems, irreversible somatic change, and ultimately genetic change, in organisms and populations of organisms; formally similar sequences can possibly be observed in various psychological processes).

Earlier responses are likely to deprive the system of immediate behavioral flexibility while they continue. When a lowlander first ascends to

Lhasa at 15,000 feet he can do little more than aerate himself; the police force, while it is taking care of peak traffic, is impeded in responding to hold-ups. Living systems can ill afford to remain long in such compromised states, in states that make them increasingly vulnerable to additional perturbations, and even make it difficult for them to conduct their ordinary affairs. If they are not to be destroyed by stresses engendered by *their own* early, behaviorally expensive responses, living systems must mobilize deeper responses if particular perturbations become continuous or even very frequent. When villages become large enough, for instance, it becomes too disruptive to call out the citizenry to form bucket brigades in response to every fire, and fire departments are organized. We may note in passing that the presence of discrete agencies and institutions with special functions forms one of the main points of contrast between contemporary and tribal societies. Indeed, the proliferation of special-purpose subsystems constitutes the transition from tribal society, by definition organized mainly in accordance with segmentary principles, to modern society organized mainly in accordance with sectorial principles. It may be suggested that this transition is as much to be accounted for by the advantages of routinizing responses to perturbation as by changes in other aspects or components of culture, for instance, the technology of production.

This general account does not propose that later responses are superior to earlier ones. While the earlier responses prevail the system may well be deprived of some behavioral freedom and its thermodynamic efficiency may be impaired. But while these easily reversible responses continue the structure of the system remains unchanged. Later responses, although they may be more efficient energetically than the earlier, and although they do restore some *immediate* behavioral freedom to the system, are less easily reversible or even irreversible. This is to say that later responses may entail structural change. Both Bateson (1963) and Slobodkin and Rapoport (1974) have suggested that the *probable*[6] effect of structural change in response to *specific problems* is the *reduction* of long-term flexibility. There is likely to be trade-off, then, in adaptive response sequences, of long-term systemic flexibility for immediate efficiency or behavioral freedom. In an unpredictably changing universe it is good evolutionary strategy, they say, to give up as little flexibility as possible. Over-response is, in the long run, as dangerous to the persistence of a system as is insufficient response in the short run. (To put the matter in more familiar terms, structural change in response to particular stresses is likely to lead to increased specialization, and increased specialization to loss of flexibility and to earlier loss in the existential game, a game in which even the rules change from time to time.) Accurate calibration of response to perturbation seems generally to characterize physiological and genetic response sequences, and "evolutionary wisdom" may be intrinsic to the structure of organisms. In contrast, social systems, in which responses are in some degree the outcome of rational deliberation can make mistakes of which physiological and genetic processes are incapable. There is no way in which an organism can enlarge its heart and lungs before it pants and races its heartbeat. Towns or states, on the other hand, can build highway by-passes that they do not need. Once built they are as much part of the geography as rivers or mountains and, of course, play a significant role in changing the future development of the locality.

6. The structural requirements of adaptiveness

The account of adaptation offered here implies that *adaptiveness* – the capacity to maintain the orderliness of adaptive response sequences – has certain *structural* requirements. First, we have already noted that adaptive systems are self-regulating and that self-regulation takes several forms, prominent among which are time-dependent (or rhythmical) and variable-dependent (or cybernetic) modes. The causal structure of both is circular. In the cybernetic mode the departure of conditions from the ideal (more technically, the deviation of a variable from its reference value) itself initiates a program to reverse, and thus to nullify, the deviation. A thermostat is a simple example of a cybernetic regulator. Time-dependent regulatory devices, like traffic lights, are simpler, operating on the assumption, usually based on some sort of experience, that deviations from reference values (e.g. cars waiting to proceed) will be correlated with time and thus can, effectively, be corrected by periodic regulatory action: the light changes from red to green to red every minute or so.

But, the adaptive structure of any living system could not be a mere collection of autonomous feedback loops. They must be integrated sufficiently for the system as a whole to maintain a viable degree of coordination and coherence. General adaptations, human or otherwise, biological or social, must take the form of complex sets of interlocking regulatory operations or processes roughly or generally hierarchical in overall structure or organization with some necessarily subordinate to others (Kalmus 1967, James Miller 1965, Pattee 1973, Piaget 1971, Rappaport 1969, 1971a, Simon 1969). Adaptive systems can be regarded as structural sets of processes, and regulatory hierarchies, whether or not they are embodied in particular organs or institutions, are found in all biological and social systems.

Our discussions have approached two aspects of hierarchical organization. First, there is the simple matter of *hierarchies* of *inclusion*, the relationship of parts to the wholes in which they are included or, slightly different, the relationship of special purpose subsystems to the general purpose systems of which they are parts. This relationship is, of course, implicit in Romer's evolutionary parable. Transformations in several special purpose *subsystems* facilitating movement over dry land made it possible for the structure of the general purpose system, the proto-amphibian, to remain relatively unchanged, and thus made it possible to maintain a generally aquatic way of life during the initial stages of terrestrial adaptation. The generalization we have already derived from contemplation of those Devonian creatures is that evolution is essentially conservative, that evolutionary changes are to be accounted for by whatever it is that they maintain unchanged and, vice versa, that the *costs* of maintaining some aspects of a system unchanged are changes in other parts of the system, and such changes may be costly, radical or, in the long run, damaging.[7] We will return to such matters in the final chapter.

We are led by consideration of hierarchies of inclusion – general purpose systems made up of special purpose subsystems, in turn made up of even more specialized sub-systems and so on to the second aspect of hierarchy, that broached in chapters 8, 9 and 10, its discursive and regulatory aspect.

The connecting link between the two aspects is implicit in the relations between general-purpose systems and the special-purpose systems they include. Relations between the levels of any adaptive system do, or at least should, correspond to differences in the specificity of their goals or purposes. The goal of the proto-amphibian is to persist and reproduce. The goal of its locomotory subsystem is to contribute to that general goal in special ways. The proper goal of an adaptive system as a whole is so low in specificity as to be, virtually, a non-goal. It is merely to persist, to remain in Slobodkin and Rapoport's existential game. The goals of subsystems are, in contrast, increasingly specific. In well-ordered adaptive systems the less inclusive the subsystem the more specific its goal, purpose, or function. The function of an army, for example, is to defend the polity of which it is a subsystem. The function of its artillery is to contribute to that defense in specialized ways.

To make altogether explicit what may already be obvious: properly ordered adaptive systems are hierarchical with respect to specificity of goal or purpose. That is, their goals or purposes form continua running from highly specific in specialized subsystems to highly general at more inclusive systemic levels. In properly-ordered systems the specific goals and purposes of subsystems are subservient to the more general purposes of the more inclusive systems. To put it a little differently, the goals of specialized subsystems are instrumental, in the service of the fundamental goals of adaptive systems as wholes, which is simply to continue to play the existential game.

All of this may seem virtually self-evident but it is important to state because the specificity-generality continuum may, in human social systems, become disordered, leading to derangement of adaptive processes resulting, in turn, in serious social disruption. We shall consider instances of such maladaption in the final chapter.

The generality–specificity continuum of goals and purposes implies, if it does not, indeed, entail, temporal ordering along several lines. It is typical for low-order regulators, like factory foremen, to have to give orders more or less continuously in response to constantly changing situations on the shop floor. The resulting continuous low-order changes are likely to be as quickly modified or reversed as they are mobilized. Therefore, specialized subsystems are likely to be organized for rapid, frequent, if not, indeed, continual, detailed, reversible changes of states.

Higher-order regulators, that is, regulatory mechanisms or agencies (like legislatures) associated with more inclusive systems usually do not respond as rapidly to perturbations as do those of lower order, nor should they. Moreover, when they do respond, their regulatory output, in the form of directives, may be less continuous or more sporadic, and their directives less easily reversed than those of lower order. We may also note that there are likely to be procedures among the functions and routines of higher-order regulators for modifying or even replacing the subsystems subordinate to them. Thus, higher-order systems, and certainly adaptive systems as wholes, may retain their continuity, their identities, and even their general organizations relatively unchanged while some or all of their subsystems undergo radical transformations or even replacement. We thus note that the temporal ordering of general purpose adaptive structures may include continua of perdurance as well as of speed, frequency and reversibility, with general purpose adaptive systems as wholes sometimes persisting for what seems like, or is represented as, forever (see chapter 7), with specialized subsystems being more transitory in nature. Again, much of the discussion of temporal ordering may seem self-evident, but such ordering can become disordered with socially and materially disruptive results. We shall briefly consider such matters, and their possible amelioration by religious concepts and actions shortly.

7. Hierarchical organization of directive, value, and sanctity
The term "directive" has been introduced without comment. Directives, however, vary in mood, impact, and rhetorical force and, almost explicitly in our discussion so far, those differences do correspond roughly to differences in specificity, response speed, frequency, perdurance, and reversibility. The directives typical of low-order regulation in special purpose subsystems are the situation-specific imperatives generally called "commands" or "orders." Higher-order regulators may, in addition, promulgate the class-general directives called "rules" in some organizational contexts, "laws" in others. Yet higher-order regulators may enunciate the yet more general form of directive called "policy" or (yet higher, perhaps) "principles," or even those statements of the world's fundamental order labeled here "cosmological axioms." Enunciations of policy and principle may not be cast in the imperative mood, but nevertheless constitute directives of a very general and highly authoritative nature, to which lower-order directives are supposed to conform. They are less easily reversible than directives of lower order, in some instances because their sources are not living agents but documents, like the Torah, the Gospels, the Koran, or even the Declaration of Independence, enunciated once for all times, and as such highly resistant to the manipulation of living agents.[8]

We are led here to Ultimate Sacred Postulates which, although they are not cast in the imperative mood, constitute directives of thehighest generality (see chapters 7 and 8). They are likely to be associated with adaptive systems as wholes, and their significata – gods, ancestors, and the like – may be identified by those subordinated to them as their systems' ultimate regulators: the divine is that which all serve and that against which all is judged. Although it may seem almost tautological to so declare, in well-ordered adaptive social systems the regulatory hierarchy is thus a hierarchy of authority as well as of specificity, speed, frequency, reversibility, perdurance, and rhetorical form because those relations can become disordered, with dire results, a matter remaining to be considered in chapter 14.

We may also note here the hierarchical organization of values. As we proceed "upward" through the hierarchical structures of social systems we note a progression away from material or concrete regulatory values toward values which seem increasingly ideological. For instance, discourse concerning wheat farming is highly concrete, and the fundamental agricultural assumptions of Chinese and American wheat farmers are probably close. In both societies regulation is directed toward the availability of sufficient water, adequate soil nutrients, and a reliable supply of tractor fuel. But when economics, not merely production but rights in the product and its distribution, is discussed, phrases like "free enterprise" and "from each what he can give, to each what he needs" may begin to appear. The difference between what is connoted by these phrases is not technical, but ideological. Both are taken by those subscribing to them to be highly moral. Yet higher-order regulation is bolstered by such notions as honor, freedom, righteousness, and patriotism, and highest-order regulation may be explicitly concerned with the preservation of notions taken to be naturally or self-evidently moral, like "Life, Liberty, and the Pursuit of Happiness." These values or principles are explicitly stated to be those for the preservation of which governments and other institutions are mere instruments.

Regulatory hierarchies are *always* hierarchies of values. I have argued that in well-ordered adaptive systems, values are ordered such that they proceed from "instrumental values" at the lower levels to what may be called "ultimate" or "basic" values at the highest or next to highest levels. At the highest levels of regulation, divinity, as we have seen, is often invoked. Pharoah was the living Horus; Elizabeth is by Grace of God Queen; and even the United States is One Nation under a God in whom we trust[9] and by whom our highest principles, Life, Liberty, and the Pursuit of Happiness, are said to be given.

The association of divinity with highest-order regulation leads us to the hierarchical organization of sanctity or, rather, back to the relationship of the sacred to the sanctified discussed in the context of the hierarchical ordering of understanding the liturgical orders in chapters 8 and 9, and of the process of sanctification in chapter 10. In both of those places it was observed that continua of specificity, perdurance, concreteness, and mutability inform relations between the ultimately sacred and the merely sanctified. That these continua have adaptive significance was suggested in chapter 8. We need only reiterate here, before proceeding to the place of sanctity in adaptation that adaptive hierarchies among humans are hierarchies of sanctity as well as of the other qualities we have noted. As we saw in an earlier chapter, sanctity has its apparent source in Ultimate Sacred Postulates which are typically without material significata, but it flows from them to other sentences which do have material references: "Henry is by Grace of God King," "It is more blessed to give than to receive," "I swear in the name of God to tell the truth." In its flow from Ultimate Sacred Postulates the unquestionableness of sanctity, as we have seen, is transformed into the more specific qualities of correctness, propriety, legitimacy, morality, veracity, naturalness, and efficacy, thus transforming the dubious, the arbitrary, and the conventional into the correct, the necessary, and the natural.

We may well be reminded here that the substance of sanctified sentences is varied, and that an attempt was made in chapter 10 to list major variants. They included, among others, cosmological axioms (often embedded in and expressed through myth, scripture, or the like), ritual prescriptions, taboos, oaths, pledges, certain performatives, commandments, expressions establishing authorities, and directives issued by such authorities or their agents. Such expressions constitute the corpuses of directives out of which regulatory hierarchies in social systems are organized.

We are also reminded here that sanctity, in its descent from its source in ultimate sacred postulates, can escape from the confines of ritual to enter into the governance of society generally.

8. Sanctity, vacuity, mystery, and adaptiveness

That sanctity supports social orders is one of anthropology's most ancient truisms. That it may increase the adaptiveness of social systems is not. Flexibility is central to adaptiveness and the suggestion that the invariant, which constitutes the sacred, nurtures the flexible seems to approach paradox. Mere lability, however, constitutes chaos, not flexibility. Flexibility – ordered versatility combined with differential responsiveness – is, I have proposed, intrinsic to the hierarchical structure of adaptive systems. The ultimately sacred forms an unchanging ground upon which all else in adaptive social structures can change continuously without loss of orderliness.

The material and social emptiness typical of Ultimate Sacred Postulates is of significance in this light. We earlier observed that the substantive vacuity of Ultimate Sacred Postulates places them beyond falsification. Now it may be suggested that the self-same emptiness is of importance to the flexibility of the social systems whose discourse – in particular whose goals – they ground. Being devoid of material terms, Ultimate Sacred Postulates do not in themselves specify particular social or material goals or the proper means for fulfilling them. Specifying *nothing* they can apparently sanctify *anything*. Bound to no convention they not only can sanctify all conventions but *changes* in all conventions. Continuity can thus be maintained while allowing change to take place, for the association of particular institutions or conventions with Ultimate Sacred Postulates is a matter of interpretation. Interpretations forever remain vulnerable to *re*interpretation but the *objects* of interpretation – Ultimate Sacred Postulates themselves – are not challenged by reinterpretation. Indeed, reinterpretation may preserve and reinforce them. As long as the ultimately sacred words establishing them remain fixed and apparently eternal, ultimate goals remain *apparently* unchanged, but the conventions which they sanctify may be continually modified, transformed, or even replaced in response to the perturbations of history and environment. Even understandings of the ultimate may change while the postulates denoting the ultimate remain unchanged. In response to changing historical conditions, this is to say, the connections of the eternal unvarying truth to ever-changing history may be reinterpreted, and in light of the reinterpretation social rules and even cosmological axioms may change without many or even any of the devout becoming aware of those changes.

It may further be suggested that constant reinterpretation is both encouraged and facilitated by the typically cryptic character of Ultimate Sacred Postulates as well as by their non-material nature. What, after all, does it mean to say that God is One or Three, that Wakan-Tanka encompasses all things, that the Dreaming is primordial and continuing, or *Sa'ah naaghaii bik'eh hozho?* *If a postulate is to be taken to be unquestionable it is important that no one understand it.* It is not surprising that Ultimate Sacred Postulates are often what Catholics call "Mysteries properly so called."[10] It is ironic to note that the very features of Ultimate Sacred Postulates that lead positivists to declare them to be without sense or even nonsensical – that they are unverifiable, unfalsifiable, materially empty, lacking social specificity and sometimes incomprehensible – are those that render them adaptive, that suit them for association with a certain class of "players of the existential game," social systems at their most inclusive.

A further implication of Romer's Rule may be cited here. Although the initial effect of an innovation may be to preserve aspects of elements of the system in which it occurs unchanged, the subsequent effects of that innovation may not be so conservative, indeed, not conservative at all. The great range of novel terrestrial vertebrate forms emerged out of the genetic changes that first made it possible for the proto-amphibia to maintain an aquatic way of life in the face of drastically changed conditions. Similarly, sanctity, once emerged, provided a principle upon which the great variety of novel human social organizations could rest: it provided the ground from which the innumerable diverse human adaptations could subsequently radiate.

9. The Cybernetics of the Holy

Sanctified administrative structures, such as the governmental apparatus of a Holy Roman Emperor, are not in and of themselves complete adaptive structures but may be parts of yet more inclusive structures which, as wholes, possess cybernetic properties. Such structures as I have presented them and as they usually present themselves to those subordinate to them, appear to be "hierarchical" in the most straightforward and simple sense of the word. That is, authority and sanctity seem to flow from their apices in Ultimate Sacred Postulates and the authorities directly sanctified by them, e.g., "Charles the Most Pious Augustus, crowned by God, Great and Peace-keeping Emperor," through strata of understandings, institutions, officials, and directives into the lives of those governed by them. Ritual, however, may encompass such regulatory hierarchies in cybernetic structures in which the highest is ultimately subordinate to those whom it appears to subordinate. This ultimate cybernetic circuit has lain just below the surface of the discussion. Let us now make it explicit:

(1) Ultimate Sacred Postulates sanctify authorities, institutions, and the various forms of directives constituting regulatory hierarchies;

(2) The operations of the regulatory hierarchy affect, to say the least, prevailing material and social conditions;

(3) Material and social conditions determine in a major degree, or even define, the well-being of those subject to the sanctified regulatory hierarchy;

(4) Those subordinate to the regulatory hierarchy, the members of the community , are themselves the congregations participating in the rituals accepting, and thus establishing, the Ultimate Sacred Postulates which, in turn, sanctify the regulatory hierarchy and, often, explicitly accepting the connection of elements of such hierarchies to the Ultimate Sacred Postulates. *Thus, the validity of Ultimate Sacred Postulates and the connec-*

tion of elements of regulatory hierarchies (such as monarchs) to those postulates, is ultimately contingent upon their acceptance by those presumably subject to them. This is to say that sanctified authority is ultimately contingent, albeit this is normally mystified, upon acceptance (indirect more likely than direct) by the governed. The structure of sanctification, and thus of authority and legitimacy, is "circular," a cybernetic "closed loop."

(5) If material or social conditions are felt to be oppressive or otherwise unsatisfactory for very long the willingness or even ability of congregations to give sanctified or numinous support to the regulatory structures they take to be responsible for these conditions will be adversely affected. If there is no improvement in conditions those staffing the regulatory structures, the regulatory structures themselves, or even, in extreme cases, the Ultimate Sacred Postulates sanctifying them will, *sooner or later*, be stripped of their sanctity.

Those subordinate to them may deprive authorities or even regulatory structures of sanctity passively by no longer participating in the rituals sanctifying them, but desanctification may also be active, and desecrating acts and agents may themselves be sanctified, or at least claim sanctity. The liturgical orders of many of the African societies in which kings were divine included rituals for deposing them (these procedures often included their execution, see James Frazer 1963: 308ff.). Prophets not only may challenge the connections of incumbent authorities to the sources of sanctity but may also claim sanctified status for their own injunctions and even may proclaim new Ultimate Sacred Postulates.

(6) In sum, if authorities wish to maintain their sanctity, which is to say their legitimacy, and to maintain the sanctity of the regulatory structures over which they preside, they must be sure that those regulatory structures remain in reasonable working order and are reasonably responsive to those subject to them.

We may represent these relations, which we may label "The Cybernetics of the Holy" in an oversimplified diagram (see figure 1).

Some comments and elaborations are in order. I have asserted that the malfunction of regulatory hierarchies will *sooner or later* lead to their

Figure 1 The Cybernetics of the Holy

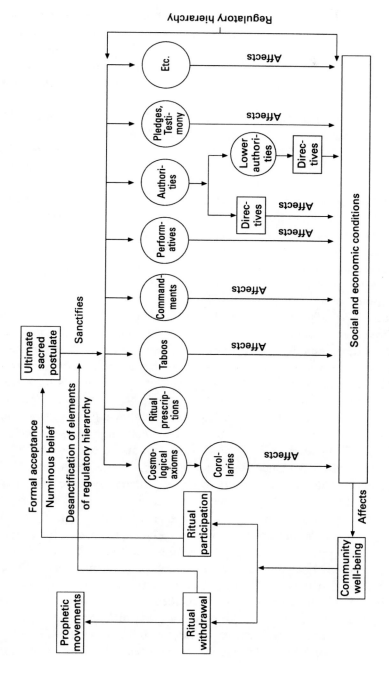

desanctification or, more likely, first to the desanctification of those who administer them. The phrase "sooner or later" is of course meant to recognize that historical conditions are always sufficiently unique to confound precise formulation, but is also meant to suggest that delay, or "time-lag" is intrinsic to, and important in, The cybernetics of the holy. For one thing, the withdrawal of sanctity from the regulatory structure or its personnel *follows* the perception that whatever misery is experienced is to be blamed on the faults or malfunctions of the hierarchy or those presiding over it. The operations of some societies may be so mystified or so complex, however, or those affected by them may be so ignorant of their workings, that their malfunctions, exploitations, or oppressions are grasped only slowly. More important: institutions and authorities at the beginning of the process of desanctification obviously still remain sanctified and are not easily or quickly divested of their sanctity. People are usually willing to put up with much hardship for the sake of God or his anointed, and it may be well that they are. Unhappy conditions are likely to be as self-limiting as they are ineluctable, and fortitude is often a better response to them than revolutionary corrective actions, which often do more harm than good. Consider the Iranian Revolution. The discussion of the temporal ordering of adaptive response sequences presented in an earlier section suggests, furthermore, that premature responses, particularly premature structural transformations, may cause difficulties in the long run as they alleviate short-run stresses. The restraint and fortitude that sanctification encourages may provide time for less profound, more easily reversible corrective responses to operate first, sanctified structural changes following only if less radical corrective measures fail. In sum, *sanctification may maintain the orderliness of adaptive response sequences.* This merits further discussion.

Responses, sanctified and desanctifying, to the malfunctioning of regulatory hierarchies may follow in an orderly sequence of increasing profundity conforming to that proposed in 13.3 as characteristic of adaptive processes generally. Gradations may be numerous, finely differentiated, subtle and diverse, and it is to be expected that the particular sequences into which they may be arranged will be changed by historical conditions. The matter is extremely complex and cannot really be developed here. It is not difficult, however, to arrange ethnographically and historically familiar instances of sanctified and desanctifying responses to oppressive regulation into an order of types differing in gravity, reversibility, and, possibly, speed of initiation and frequency as well.

In the least profound form, which may well occur earliest, support of the regulatory structure is weakened as people absent themselves from the rituals sanctifying it. A near-contemporary instance: the substantial decline in devotional practice among American Catholics, apparently in response to the encyclical *On Human Life* promulgated by Pope Pius VI, reaffirming the opposition of "The Vatican" to chemical and mechanical means of birth control. The withdrawal of an individual from participation in Catholic liturgy constitutes a self-referential message, indexically signaled, and it conforms to the logic of ritual acceptance discussed in chapter 4. It should be emphasized, in light of the discussion of reversibility in the ordering of adaptive response sequences, that absence can be as quickly reversed as undertaken. Those who absented themselves from Mass last week can return to church this Sunday.

Regulatory structures are not immediately transformed by withdrawal of support, nor do those absenting themselves necessarily seek structural transformations. They are simply demonstrating, which is to say signaling indexically, in a manner both passive and transitory, their dissatisfaction with particular operations of the regulatory structures, rather than with the structure itself. The effects of such passive demonstration can, however, be grave. The temporary withdrawal may turn into permanent defection, not a casual matter for those departing and a matter of no small consequence for the Church. It is doubtful if the persistence of Catholicism in America was ever in any danger, but decline in the numbers of its communicants was surely damaging to it as an institution. More important, the challenge to its authority in one area threatens to damage its sanctity generally. Dissatisfaction with respect to a specific low-order rule was expressed through withdrawal from participation in fundamental rituals accepting the Ultimate Sacred Postulate. We shall return to a related aspect of the matter later.

I have elsewhere (1979e: 18) suggested that a similar form of demonstration may have been an aspect of at least some of the ceremonial redistributions over which Polynesian chiefs presided. The collection of foodstuffs by chiefs and their subsequent redistribution (Sahlins 1958) could have had only slight importance, if any, in the provisioning of most Polynesian societies. Such redistributions are better construed as indices of the subordination of those who produced the foodstuffs to the highly sanctified chief who appropriated them and then redistributed them to those who produced them in the first place. But migration out of a chief's territory to the territory of another was an option in most Polynesian societies. Douglas Oliver, for instance, tells us in *Ancient Tahitian Society* (1974 II: 986) that in the Society Islands "there appear to have been no potent norms, positive or negative, against changing tribal residence." We read of a chief's complaint at having been forsaken by fickle subjects. That there was likely to be much more to such moves than could be accounted for by mere preference or fickleness is proposed on the next page of Oliver's massive work (II: 987), where he cites an account provided by Moerenhaut:

It is noteworthy that despite their despotism, and perhaps even because of their despotism, the chiefs lost no opportunity to keep on friendly terms with their subjects of whom they had such great need in their frequent wars. A native, unjustly treated by his chief, could threaten to leave him and it was rare that the latter did not seek to appease him and retain him in his service. There is something almost touching in the threats of a simple Indian to his chief, which seems to prove that the latter was more father than despotic master of his subjects. "You are angry with me," said an Indian I know, an old man now, and from whom his chief had taken the little bit of land he owned. "Ah well, I will leave the land where my fathers died ... and I shall go away with my children to die among strangers, enemies of yours." His chief, moved, went away without answering; but the next day he returned to the Indian double the amount of land he had taken with other gifts.   *(1837 II: 19n)*

Evidence is insufficient, but it may at least be suggested that in light of their detailed awareness of the natural conditions affecting production, chiefs might have been able to infer from further and otherwise unaccountable fluctuations in donations to them changes in the strength of their support. Declines could have been taken as admonitions to improve their performances and hold on to supporters, this being a matter of continuing cogency in a political milieu where smaller units were in continual danger of being absorbed by stronger neighbors (Oliver 1974 II: 986).

A more active response threatening incumbent authorities but still not necessarily terminating in their desanctification is the prophetic philippic. The Old Testament is full of instances, but prophets who would have been distressingly familiar to the Kings of Ancient Israel have certainly spoken in other societies: the fulminations of the Egyptian prophet Ipu-Wer were cited in chapter 11.

It is important that prophets are "holy men." They and their words may be sanctified by liturgical orders more or less directly, or they may present themselves as sanctified by direct encounter with whatever God is established by prevailing Ultimate Sacred Postulates. In any case, prophets claim to be closer to the sources of sanctity than those against whom they inveigh. As such they claim to be in a position to divest the objects of their fulminations of their sanctity, if they do not repent or at least reform, and such a prophet may receive the numinous support of an oppressed, angry, and rebellious populace, as events in Iran demonstrated in the late 1970s. The prophet is, as it were, "numinized" by the disaffected who become re-engaged by becoming his followers in opposition to prevailing powers.

We are led from what may be called "low-order" or "first-order" responses in which authorities are, as it were, admonished to improve their performances, to "second-order responses" in which the connection of incumbent authorities to the sources of their sanctification are challenged. In chapter 10 we noted that among Germanic people previous to their conversion to Christianity

> when the King's luck or charismatic power is maintained, the favor of the god rests with the tribe; when he has lost his "luck" and is impotent to secure the divine blessings, his people are justified, even obliged, to do the only thing possible, to replace him with another who can make the office once more effective.   *(Chaney 1970: 12)*

Germanic kingship itself was not challenged by the degradation of German kings, but kingship, or whatever other institutions prevail, can also be divested of sanctity. In "third-order responses," attempts are made to strip of their sanctity elements of existing structures or even those structures as wholes, and to sanctify others in their places. The more profound reactions frequently include the use of force, a force which is inspired and sanctified by reference to Ultimate Sacred Postulates, and which may be magnified by numinous experience. History is full of such religiously inspired movements, an obvious example being the English Peasants' Revolt of 1381, sometimes called "Wat Tyler's Rebellion," which sought, in rather inchoate fashion, to rid English society of its aristocracy (but not its monarchy), justifying itself with a slogan taken from one of John Ball's sermons, "When Adam delved and Eve span, who was then the gentleman?" (see Dobson (ed.) 1970, Tuchman 1978: 37ff.).

A more recent instance, already noted, has been the Iranian revolution led by the Ayatollah Khomeini. Less recently and less obviously, there is the American Revolution. It was not led by prophets, and it would be wrong to claim that it was religiously inspired. Nevertheless, in its founding document it explicitly divested the governance of King George III of its legitimacy, sanctifying in its placed a new autonomous government to be devoted to securing to all men the "Right of ... Life, Liberty and the Pursuit of Happiness," rights with which, it states, "they are endowed by their Creator."

Fourthly, or "highest-order" responses are those which seek to replace

Ultimate Sacred Postulates themselves. The endogenous generation of explicit attempts to repudiate old Ultimate Sacred Postulates and to consecrate new ones may not be rare in complex societies, but such attempts rarely seem to succeed in doing more than converting small numbers of individuals to what are often called "cults" remaining marginal to general historical processes. The emergence of Islam, Zoroastrianism, Buddhism, and Christianity may be among the few instances in which societies at large have adopted new Ultimate Sacred Postulates, but even these cases are equivocal, for they did not so much repudiate the Ultimate Sacred Postulates of their predecessors as add to or elaborate on them (see chapters 9 and 10).

Ultimate Sacred Postulates have been wholly discarded and replaced innumerable times in the course of history, but in most of the instances about which information is available the new ones have not been endogenously conceived. They have come from abroad and somehow been imposed upon those who have become subordinate to them. The conversion of the English to Christianity taken up briefly in chapter 10 is a case in point. It should be recalled, moreover, that conversion to Christianity in seventh-century England was encouraged by kings and had the effect of strengthening existing institutions, including kingship, rather than reforming or replacing them. Such instances do not fit the category of "fourth-order responses" as I have defined them. It may be reasonable to consider them adaptive responses of Anglo-Saxon kingdoms as wholes to perturbing forces external to themselves, but they do not constitute a phase in the "cybernetics of the holy" under consideration here. The Cybernetics of the Holy is constituted of corrective actions initiated in response to pressure from those subordinate to regulatory hierarchies for the amelioration of unsatisfactory conditions prevailing within the systems governed by those hierarchies.

It might seem that such prophetic movements as the ghost dance (Mooney 1896) that swept across the American West in the late nineteenth century, and many of the Melanesian millenarian manifestations of the twentieth (e.g., Williams 1923, Worsley 1957) would fit better into the category. Although the stresses to which these movements were responses were of foreign origin they were realized in the conditions of the here and now, among which disenfranchisement, relative deprivation, disease, expropriation of land, and social disruption were prominent, particularly in the American cases. The Ultimate Sacred Postulates of these movements, although they sometimes included introduced elements, were endogenously conceived and their representation in new rituals sanctified attempts, in some instances violent, to replace prevailing regulatory structures with others of a profoundly different nature. But such religiously inspired eruptions close no cybernetic circuit because those manning colonial administrations do not depend for the maintenance of their control upon sanctification through the liturgical performances of those over whom they stand. To the extent that their authority rests upon sanctity at all, they derive it from the societies from which they have come, not from those upon which they have been imposed. The sources of their sanctity, for instance one or another set of Christian institutions, lie beyond the reach of the indigenes whom they oppress, in the final analysis, through power. Power disrupts the Cybernetics of the Holy, a matter to which we shall return in the next chapter. Here we may note that if the conceptions of religion have a part to play in the alleviation of foreign oppression it is not so much by divesting the aliens of their sanctity as it is by sanctifying and "numinizing" efforts to overthrow them and, perhaps, to restore a native rule within which the Cybernetics of the Holy may be effective.

The corrective processes that I have called "the Cybernetics of the Holy" inhere in systems as wholes. In the last chapter we noted that the etymology of the word "holy" is shared with that of "whole." Both are derived from the Old English *hale*, from which the word "health" is also descended. In this light, the appropriateness of the term "Holy" for the larger category that includes both the discursive sacred and the non-discursive numinous becomes increasingly apparent. The sacred and the numinous, the rational and the affective, the everyday formal structure of society and its occasional ritual or festive state of *communitas*, form wholes through the mobilizations of which the ambitions of separate men and women may be subordinated to common interest while at the same time the operations of society are continually reviewed and tempered by the needs of the very same men and women. Wholeness, holiness, and adaptiveness are closely related if not, indeed, one and the same.

14

The breaking of the Holy and its salvation

To those who have lived with experiences of, or with memories of, jihads, holocausts and less lethal but nevertheless disabling forms of religious persecution the account, offered in chapter 13, of the place of religion in human adaptation, culminating in an outline of the Cybernetics of the Holy may well seem, at best, idealized and naive, apologetic and misleading. We may, however, recall here in qualification of such claims the maxim that every evolutionary advance is likely to set new problems as it ameliorates those already prevailing, and admit that the Holy and its constituents constitute no exception. We may recall, more specifically, the suggestion first offered in chapter 1 that the emergence of the concept of the sacred made the human way of life possible by ameliorating subversive possibilities intrinsic to certain aspects of language. The possibility that sanctity and other of religion's conceptions might well have problems of their own was also broached but not developed in chapter 1 and reengaged in chapter 13, particularly in discussions of the inversion, in the course of humanity's emergence from its prehuman (preverbal) forebears, of the relationship of the adaptive apparatus to the adaptive species. The species, it was suggested, became subservient to conceptions that it itself had imagined into being.

We turn now to the pathologies of religion, to the falsification of the sacred, the delusion of the numinous and the breaking of the Holy. At the end we will return to their possible revitalization in a reformulated Logos.

1. The natural and the unnatural
Let us deal first and briefly with a vice obviously intrinsic to sanctity's very virtues. If, as argued throughout this book, sanctification certifies as

438

correct and moral, or even naturalizes, the conventions of a social group, it at least tacitly implies that other conventions, those espoused by the unorthodox and the orthodox conventions of other groups, are incorrect, immoral, or even unnatural. As such they may be regarded as abominations and thus evil. Those guilty of such "unnatural acts" may therefore be regarded as other than, or less than human and, in full righteousness and justice, be treated accordingly. Sanctity may, thus, magnify what are no more than minor cultural differences into what may seem to be fundamental natural differences. It may not only envenom enmities for which it itself is not responsible but its itself is capable of defining such enmities and thus setting humans and human communities against each other.[1]

I have argued that Ultimate Sacred Postulates are typically devoid of social specificity, meaning to say that they in themselves usually[2] do not decree particular social arrangements or authority relations within the groups accepting them. But the expression of Ultimate Sacred Postulates does identify those who accept them, thereby distinguishing them from those who do not. If, as claimed in chapter 10, Ultimate Sacred Postulates provide members of communities with grounds for trust in their communication, communication between those who accept different Ultimate Sacred Postulates may well be impeded or at least limited.

We may add here that in distinguishing those who accept them from those who do not, Ultimate Sacred Postulates may set boundaries on charitable impulses and may limit the reach of human fellow-feeling. Such limitations may inhere tacitly in the acceptance and non-acceptance of Ultimate Sacred Postulates, but ritual practices, even by separate groups accepting the same postulates, can reinforce enmities. Maring *kaiko* cycles clearly distinguish "us" from enemies who conduct formally equivalent cycles based upon similar if not identical postulates, but addressed to different ancestors.

We may regard the divisive consequences of religious conception and practice to be an unfortunate, or even tragic aspect of the human condition itself. Such divisiveness may be a natural concomitant of sanctification on the one hand and of the characteristics of typical adaptive units on the other. Until relatively recently on the scale of human antiquity, that is until the emergence and spread of state organization commencing no more than 5,000 or 6,000 years ago, but not universal until recent decades, adaptive units were generally, and probably necessarily, small and were often, even usually, in competition for scarce resources with others of similar limited size.[3] One need not subscribe fully to conquest theories of the origins of the state to regard as plausible the suggestion that the amelioration of such conflict was an important factor encouraging the state's emergence.

2. Sanctity and specificity

Other problems inhering in sanctification are less obvious. I have argued that if human social systems are to remain adaptive they must remain flexible, and if they are to remain flexible the degree of sanctity accorded to the various directives composing their regulatory discourse should be inversely correlated with the material or social specificity of those directives. That is, the more specific the rule or command, the more limited the domain of an authority, the less sanctity should support it. To put it in the inverse, highly sanctified directives should be low in political, social or material specificity.

Dissonance may, however, develop between sanctity and specificity. That is, highly specific directives may become "oversanctified," come to possess greater degrees of sanctity than their narrowness, or specificity, warrants.

The results can be deeply disruptive. A case in point: the rules concerning birth control reiterated by Pope Paul VI in his encyclical *On Human Life* (1969). It seemed not only to me, a non-Catholic, but to figures important in the Church, like Hans Kung (1971), that a degree of sanctity virtually equivalent to that surrounding doctrines of faith, like the doctrine of the Immaculate Conception, was being accorded to a set of very specific low-order rules concerning non-immaculate non-conception. As a result the Roman Catholic Church suffered, as we noted in the last chapter, immediate and widespread defection, particularly in developed countries. Although most of those who discontinued devotional practices because of disagreement with the encyclical have returned to the Church, many seem to have returned, according to priests with whom I have spoken, understanding their relationship to the Church differently from before: they are less likely to acquiesce routinely to Vatican dicta on social matters of any sort, and few discuss their violations of birth control rules in the confessional booth.

In sum, what appears not only to an outside observer but to many within the Roman Catholic Church to be oversanctification of a highly specific set of rules has cost the church dearly in general authority as lay folk reject or ignore dicta of a sort that they previously would have been likely to accept. The corrosion of papal authority, moreover, has not been limited to the reactions of the laity. Theologians such as Hans Kung and Charles Curran (see Kung 1971) have not only challenged the particular encyclical in question but the infallibility of the papal authority upon which its promulgation was based.

Oversanctification of the specific impedes adaptive response to changing historical circumstances. It lurks as a continuing possibility within the process of sanctification itself and therefore may trouble societies at all levels of development. Raymond Kelly (personal communication, 1993: 153f., see also 1974) reports that the Etoro of Papua New Guinea, who, when he worked among them in the late 1960s, had only recently been contacted by the Australian administration, began to plant more gardens than they traditionally had, as a consequence of receiving steel axes. Previously, when they possessed only stone axes, they relied more heavily on sago production. Highly sanctified taboos on heterosexual intercourse during certain stages of gardens' growth had been in force since time immemorial, but with increase in reliance upon gardens the periods of sexual prohibition lengthened to an estimated 205 to 260 days per year. It is not possible to know for sure whether or not the ensuing decline in the Etoro's birth rate was a consequence of the lengthening of the periods in which heterosexual sex was prohibited, but the decline did endanger this small group's future. Kelly estimated its "half-life" at sixteen years.

Kelly's account suggests that oversanctification of the specific is likely to trouble tribal people in times of dramatically changed historical or technological circumstances (e.g. the more or less sudden introduction of steel axes) after long periods of relatively stable human-environmental relations. But oversanctification is, if anything, a more common and probably more serious problem in literate state-organized societies where ordained clergy, particularly those in possession of powerful means for enforcing their interpretations (e.g. the Inquisition) are in a position to adjudicate what is orthodox.

Orthodoxy tends to support prevailing signs and their interpretations and tends thereby to support the social or political status quo, or to return it to some specific idealized condition assumed to have been prior, primordial and certainly proper (e.g. women to be veiled, men to grow side curls and wear fringed garments).

3. Oversanctification, idolatry, and maladaptation
Oversanctification of the specific was likely to develop in pre-modern societies (and even during modern times) as a consequence of an

inflexible orthodoxy's conflation, or confusion, of specific social and ritual practices with general social and religious doctrine. But such over-sanctification is more likely to develop in highly differentiated modern societies for other reasons, for reasons intrinsic to socio-cultural evolution generally, and not only to the dynamics of sanctity itself.

Adaptive systems are, as discussed in the last chapter, general purpose systems. Their only proper goal as autonomous general purpose systems is to stay in the "Existential Game." They are, however, made up of special purpose sub-systems, agencies: departments, and firms which are defined by special goals and outputs specified by their positions within the larger systems of which they are parts, and to the persistence of which their outputs presumably contribute. But, as societies become increasingly sectorial, that is, as they become increasingly differentiated internally, their special-purpose subsystems become increasingly identified with particular individuals. These individuals, quite astutely, are likely to take the special goals and outputs of the special purpose systems in which they participate directly (the army, the automobile manufacturing industry, the media industry) to constitute their own general goals, and they frequently attempt to elevate these special goals to positions of predominance in the larger systems (societies) of which they are merely specialized parts.

Power is differentially distributed among the sectors of technologically developed societies, and the more powerful sectors – industrial firms, financial firms, business firms generally, the military – are most able to elevate their goals, or interests, to positions of predominance in the larger societies of which they are simply parts.

As the highly specific goals of special purpose subsystems are elevated to positions of predominance in the more inclusive systems of which they are merely parts they come to capture higher degrees of sanctity. Sanctity, to put the matter in vulgar vernacular terms, is "up for grabs."

An example, albeit a bit crass, is in order. If, as Calvin Coolidge declared, "The business of America is business,"[4] and if the United States is "one nation under God," a God in whom we trust (as is declared on every piece of American currency) then business and everything related to it – profit, private enterprise, consumption – become highly sanctified. Indeed, if the business of America is business, business, profit, private enterprise and consumption are tacitly declared basic, or ultimate values and as such enjoy a degree of sanctity equal to that of life, liberty and the pursuit of happiness, with which they may well be conflated.

The theologian Paul Tillich (1957: 11ff. and elsewhere) would have recognized Coolidge's dictum as an instance of what he called "idolatry," which he defined as "Absolutizing the Relative" – raising relative, contingent, and material values to the status of ultimacy. Absolutizing the relative, be it noted, cannot help but, conversely, relativize the absolute, for it identifies the absolute with the status quo and the material, in Coolidge's case, with profit, with private enterprise, with consumption. It vulgarizes, profanes, and degrades the ultimate and for that reason Tillich took it to be evil. I will add that to accord a higher degree of sanctity to propositions, interests, goals than their specificity warrants is to impede flexible response to changing circumstances by narrowing the range of conditions under which the system can stay in the existential game, or persist. Whether or not idolatry is evil, it is certainly maladaptive. Maladaptation and whatever Tillich meant by evil intersect in what he called "idolatry" and I include idolatry in the family of Falsehoods which also includes Vulgar Lies, Vedic Lies and other forms to be approached soon.

4. Adaptive truth and falsity

We have spoken of both truth and falsehood, of problems of truth and its establishment, and of types of truth. Our discussion of idolatry suggests another truth, rather different from the conventional truths earlier considered. If we can take to be "adaptively true" expressions the acceptance of which enhances chances of continuing to play the Existential Game, that is, which enhances chances of persistence, then we can take idolatrous postulates to be adaptively false. It is ironic to observe that apotheosizing the specific and material, the sine qua non of idolatry, is likely to defeat the material goal of survival. Adaptive truth is, of course, a form of pragmatic truth (James 1909).[5]

I take idolatrous postulates to be false, be it noticed, regardless of the degree of acceptance offered them. This is to say that consent and consensus are not sufficient to establish all conventional truths. The only Ultimate Sacred Postulates that can be adaptively true are those that, being devoid of material terms, do not irrevocably commit the societies accepting them to the particular institutions or conventions of any time or place. "The lie," said Martin Buber, "is from time and will be swallowed up by time; the truth, the divine truth, is from eternity and in eternity, and in devotion to the truth ... partakes of eternity" (1952: 13f.). The only way Ultimate Sacred Postulates can partake of eternity is not to avoid the particulars of time and place but to avoid being limited to the particulars of any specific time and place. It is of interest in this regard that the very qualities of non-idolatrous Ultimate Sacred Postulates that lead the rationalist to judge them illusions, delusions or nonsense are those that render them adaptively true.

5. Idolatry and writing

Oversanctification of the specific – idolatry – is a continuing problem intrinsic to what was surely one of the great advances in humanity's evolution, namely writing. A relatively recent development, writing capable of recording the fullness of what can be said developed no more than 5,000 or so years ago[6] in a few societies, but in most places was adopted much more recently.

In chapter 9 I derived the sacred from liturgical invariance, arguing that it is as old as language, which is to say that it antedates writing by tens or even hundreds of thousands of years. I further proposed that what was crucial for the establishment of the sacred was not invariance itself, but apparent invariance, the logical and semiotic entailments of what seem to be ever-unvarying-eternal-messages.

In discussing time we further noted that apparently and presumably invariant liturgies can and do change in ways unobservable to those whose temporal consciousness is confined to relatively limited durations, like the six or so generations since creation constituted by living memories in such illiterate societies as the Nuer (Evans-Pritchard 1940). It is the semiotics of invariance and not actual invariance that counts in the generation of the sacred.

The invariance of written texts is different. They are not simply, when set in stone or precisely and meticulously copied into a Torah scroll, apparently invariant. They are actually invariant, leaving much less possibility for modification or change if, indeed, any possibility at all.

Scriptural texts tend to become very specific and very concrete, not only purporting to report both history and natural history but to declare what is good, proper and true, often in rather precise, narrow and particular terms. Given their invariance (which being actual is also apparent) whole scriptures can be taken to be ultimately sacred. Indeed, in some Jewish mystical thought the Torah in its entirety is the great name of God, and God is indistinguishable from his name (Sholem 1969).

If flexibility is central to adaptiveness, loss of adaptiveness is a likely consequence of elevating whole scriptures to ultimate sacred status, and political and social conservatism is a likely outcome. Fundamentalism, the literal interpretation of highly specific texts and the granting to them of absolute authority, arises.

The fundamental problems of fundamentalism are several. First, and most often remarked, fundamentalism may resist, and thus impede, secular scholarship. This, however, is less serious than a problem that seems almost the inverse: in pitting sacred and sanctified truths against those that empirical procedures attempt to discover, fundamentalism sometimes exposes the sacred, itself the ground of conventional truth, to general invalidation, falsification, or at least high dubiety. To put the sacred in the service of, for instance, the geocentric theory of the universe in the early seventeenth century or of creationism in the late twentieth has, as its likely effect, not the defeat of modern astronomical cosmology or of evolutionary theory, but of discrediting the sacred itself as a general principle of certification, even in the domain that remains proper to it, namely sanctifying the conventions governing social life.

With respect to the sanctification of convention, writing may also tend to oversanctify the specific or, to put the matter a little more precisely, to mistake the specific expressions of moral principles characteristic of particular times or places for the general principles themselves and in doing so to trivialize or lose the general principle for the sake of maintaining the dead or stultifying letter of outmoded law. Such an argument animates the Jewish Reform movement's abandonment of the dietary laws. The Orthodox, who continue to observe these laws, relying upon the Mishnah, assembled around the year 200 CE, continue to understand the purpose of these laws to be the maintenance of the individual's and the community's holiness. Feeley-Harnick (1994: 7) writes that

their observance hallows [for the Orthodox] the individual and sets him and ... [his] group ... apart from others. In contrast, the Reform Movement resolved [in] ... 1885 that the dietary rules were the product of particular and now foreign circumstances. "Their observance in our days is apt rather to obstruct than to further modern spiritual elevation."   *(Encyclopedia Judaica 6: 44)*

There is no way to adjudicate this argument, but it is at least clear from Reformed Judaism's demographic success in the United States that by the late nineteenth century the specific rules of an ancient dietary code were no longer hallowing nor spiritually elevating to the majority of American Jews, who abandoned them without, in their view, abandoning their Judaism. For them the avoidance of pork could no longer signify holiness and even trivialized it.

6. Sanctity, power, and lies of oppression

We have noted that opportunities for idolatry may increase with the social, political, economic and technological elaboration of societies. So may other problems of sanctity and holiness. Indeed, the cybernetics of the holy may become increasingly disrupted in the course of social evolution as a concommitant of increasing scale, increasing discreteness of authorities and technological development.

In technologically simple societies authority is contingent upon its sanctification. A Polynesian chief's broad prerogatives rested ultimately upon his high degree of sanctity, and not upon his control of force. But social differentiation and technological advance, both aspects of socio-cultural evolution, place at the disposal of authorities coercive instruments at once increasingly powerful and decreasingly available to their subjects. The possession of such means of coercion reduces the dependence of the authority upon sanctity. As the authority becomes increasingly powerful it can, obviously, stand more upon power (a product, in the mathematical sense, of personnel × resources × organization; see Bierstadt 1950: 730ff.) and less upon sanctity.

This is not to say that powerful authorities necessarily, or usually dispense with sanctity. It is to say that as power accumulates the relationship between sanctity and authority is likely to be inverted. Whereas in the technologically and socially simple society the authority is contingent upon the maintenance of its sanctity, in the technologically and socially complex society sanctity may well be degraded to the status of the authority's instrument.[7]

An aspect of the sacred's degradation may be a change in the basis of the unquestionable status of Ultimate Sacred Postulates. Whereas they once rested upon the uncoerced acceptance of the faithful, often supported by numinous experiences, they later came to rest on force – heretics are burned, infidels put to the sword. When acceptance is coerced it becomes a lie: there can be no valid or binding "Yes" unless there is a viable "No." But a coerced act of acceptance is not the lie of those whose acts apparently constitute such acceptance. It is the lie of the coercer, and it fails to establish, as free acts of acceptance do, any moral obligation on the part of the coerced, regardless of the legal aspects of the matter.[8]

We have just added a member to the family of the lie, The Lie of Oppression. In lies of oppression the coercer is not only the liar but also one of the ultimate victims of his own lie, for if, as I argued in describing the Cybernetics of the Holy, both acceptance and its waning inform the regulation of society, then for an authority to coerce acceptance is for it to distort the information by which it itself is guided. Power threatens truth and threatens the cybernetics of adaptive systems, for adaptation relies upon reasonably accurate information concerning current conditions. Oppression is not only inhumane but maladaptive and, finally, self-defeating.

7. Breaking the Holy and diabolical lies

Ritual participation obviously continues and even flourishes in the established or tolerated churches of complex state-organized societies, and religious experiences continue to occur in them. If ritual participation is coerced, as it sometimes is, it does not constitute acceptance in any moral sense, but even when participation is eager it is likely to be profoundly different in adaptive significance in complex states from what it was in simpler societies. Religious experience, and acts of ritual acceptance generally, when invoked in the churches of state-organized societies are inclined not only to render to Caesar what is Caesar's but to bless him as well; and they also tend to emphasize other-worldly salvation and to become disconnected from corrective engagement with the iniquities of the here and now. Blessed are the meek. Acceptance, non-acceptance and religious experience no longer participate in the encompassing adaptive process we have called the Cybernetics of the Holy. Indeed, to the extent that the experience of ritual participation alleviates the anxieties of the faithful without correcting the causes of those anxieties it bears formal resemblance to what Freud (1907) meant by "neurosis" and to what Marx (1842, 1844) claimed were "opiates." Rituals become parts of deceits if they lead the faithful into bondage while promising salvation.

So sanctity, itself the foundation of the true and the correct, and the numinous supporting it, become false when they are subordinated to the powerful, for they falsify consciousness. But the cost is great even for those who are not deluded. For them ritual becomes empty and meaningless. Indeed, the term comes to denote empty form (Douglas 1973: 19). The act of ritual acceptance, once more profound than belief, becomes a proverbial form of hypocrisy.

But in refusing to participate hypocritically no less than in hypocritical participation, the conscious minds of men and women become divorced from those deep and hidden portions of themselves to which ritual participation introduced and bound them. The sense of grace becomes increasingly difficult to attain, for the self becomes fragmented and some of the fragments may be lost. The consciousness that remains is likely to be trapped in its own radical separation. For those not deluded or oppressed into subordination in the name of salvation there may be alienation from the deepest parts of the self.

So the sacred and the numinous may get detached from each other and from their cybernetic or corrective functions. Given the association I have made between wholeness and holiness it is not inappropriate to say that they become unholy. As holiness stands to wholeness, adaptiveness, and survival, so does unholiness stand to fragmentation, maladaption, and annihilation. It is of interest that in the Kabbalah of Isaac Luria (Scholem 1969: 110ff.) the origin of evil is not ascribed to the appearance of any particular substance or being, but to the fragmentation of a primordial unity. The disruption of the cybernetics of holiness is such a fragmentation. We may recall once again the Vedic and Zoroastrian notion of lie as violation of sacred order, but now the order itself becomes disorderly, disrupting ecosystems, oppressing men and women, leading societies into decline. Many years ago de Rougemont (1944) made a distinction between ordinary lies and what he called "diabolical lies," in recognition of the putative proclivity of "The Father of Lies" to appear as his own opposite. Diabolical lies are not simply false transmissions, but are lies that tamper with the very canons of truth. I think it not wrong to assign to this category assertions of sanctity for discourse the unquestionable status of which rests ultimately upon force, which is subject rather than superior to the authorities it sanctifies, which misleads ritual acceptance and numinous experience away from corrective effect upon the here and now, which encourages fragmentation and maladaptation while promising wholeness and heaven.

Diabolical lies are not new to this world, as Buber's (1952: 7ff.) analysis of the Twelfth Psalm informs us. The psalmist, according to Buber,

no longer suffers merely from liars but from a generation of the lie ... the lie in this generation has reached the highest level of perfection as an ingeniously controlled means of supremacy ... [removing] completely ... the basis of men's common life ... those the psalmist has in mind speak "delusion" ... they breed "delusion" in their hearers, they spin illusions for them ... Instead of completing their fellow-men's experience and insight with the help of their own, as required by men's common thinking and knowing, they introduce falsified material into his knowledge of the world and of life, and thus falsify the relations of his soul to his being ....In order that the lie may bear the stamp of truth, the liars as it were manufacture a special heart, an apparatus which functions with the greatest appearance of naturalness, from which lies well up to the "smooth lips" like spontaneous utterances of experience and insight ... all this is the work of the mighty in order to render tractable by deceits those whom they have oppressed.

(pp. 8–10)

Diabolical lies, like lies of oppression and idolatrous lies, are the products of power, and if they are not new to this world, new and increasing possibilities for diabolical lying are offered by the increasing ability of ever smaller groups of men and ever more specialized, powerful and wealthy institutions to control the flow of ever greater volumes of information more comprehensively and the disposition of increasing concentrations of energy more totally. This ability has been enhanced by advances in technology and increased social scale and differentiation, which is to say that it is correlated with what seems to have been the central factors in cultural evolution.

It thus may be that humanity's fall is one with its evolution: as its evolution has been founded upon its possession of words, so may its possession by words have sealed its fate. Of words are inevitably born not only vulgar lies and Vedic lies, which may be benign, but also lies of oppression, idolatrous lies, diabolical lies and other forms of falsehood as well that join together into the encompassing and world-dissolving "Generation of the Lie" that troubles our times even more than the time of the psalmist.

8. Inversion in the order of knowledge

We see, then, that the holy is not excluded from the generalization that new and often unprecedented problems inhere in all evolutionary advances. Over the past few centuries we have witnessed, and generally admired as heroic, the struggles of our most gifted thinkers to escape from orthodoxy's constraints. It seems clear that the success of their liberated efforts to discover the laws constituting the physical world and to demystify the social world have contributed to the growing disrepute of the sacred in particular and the holy in general. Given the ills to which holiness is prone and to which it contributes in the literate, state-organized societies which now dominate the world, we could easily regard its decline as a blessing, as a great leap forward into the liberation of the human mind. But the liberation of science and secular thought from the sacred has also had its costs. Once again, all evolutionary advances set new problems as they ameliorate older ones, and neither secularism's nor science's successes constitute exceptions.

With the Enlightenment, and more particularly with the emergence of modern science, an order of knowledge very different from Egypt's Ma'at, the Zoroastrian Asha or Maring *nomane* comes to prevail. Indeed, the new order of knowledge inverts the structure of Logoi generally.

Ultimate knowledge in all the Logoi discussed in chapter 11 is sacred knowledge, knowledge which, because numinously grasped or liturgically accepted, is unquestionable. Ultimate Sacred Postulates, taken to be eternally true, sanctify, which is to say certify, other sentences – axioms concerning the enduring structure of the Cosmos, values grounded in those structural principles, rules for realizing them. Worldly fact is, as it were, at the bottom of such hierarchies. Mundane knowledge is generally regarded as interesting and important, but is taken to be obvious, transient, low in or devoid of sanctity, and contingent or instrumental, rather than fundamental.

When, in the course of evolution, secular thought in general and scientific thought in particular, is liberated from religion this structure of knowledge is stood on its head. Ultimate knowledge becomes knowledge of fact. Facts are, to be sure, subsumed under general-izations called "theories," but theories continue to fall victim to anomalous facts. If facts are, at one and the same time, both ultimate and transient certainty disappears. Theories, moreover, are not only transient but of limited scope. Attempts to apply concepts developed in one domain to another, let us say animal ecology to human society, tend to be dismissed as "mere analogies" or even improper "reduc-tions" and what we have called "middle-order meaning," the mean-ingfulness that emerges from the recognition of similarities hidden beneath the surfaces of apparently disparate things, shrivels. Knowledge may become more precise, but it also becomes more fragmentary, and if oneness is intrinsic to the conception of Logos, Logos is threatened with dissolution.

Not only are facts sovereign but there are more of them. Facts breed facts, and as knowledge of facts burgeons the domains into which they are organized are severed into yet smaller pieces, as individuals and their knowledge become increasingly specialized. The result is the loss of the sense of the world's wholeness. *Sarma* prevails over Logos.

When facts become sovereign, what is the fate of that which had been ultimate knowledge? In the realm of fact nothing is sacred except, perhaps, the maxim "Nothing is sacred," and knowledge that had been ultimately sacred is no longer knowledge at all. It is "mere belief," belief now being reduced to the status of *doxa*. Values sanctified by the ultimately sacred are degraded to the status of tastes or preferences. They are relativized, and *idia phronesis*, in the form of economic rationality, is not only given free rein but is elevated to the status of general organizing principle and may even claim sanctity. The Business of America is

Business. *Homo economicus* becomes the moral as well as natural model of humanity.

Finally, unlike Logoi, which make moral and emotional claims on those who follow them, the new order of knowledge makes explicit that its claim on those operating in accordance with its ideals is no more than intellectual. Explorers are supposed to be disengaged from the worlds they objectively explore. Participation in scientific acts of observing and analyzing the world in accordance with scientific epistemology differs from participation in ritual acts constructing and maintaining the world in accordance with Logos. Rituals, and ultimately meaningful acts of participation in orders the performances themselves realize, become "mere rituals," empty or even hypocritical formalisms. Under such circumstances highest order meaning and the quest for it are dismissed as "mystical" or even stigmatized as "fanatical" or "weird." The world becomes a less meaningful place as the sacred certainty on which all human certainty is built, whether rock-like as Hans Kung would have it (1980: 1) or made of words as I would have it, is threatened. Ritual as an instrument for establishing the foundation of human worlds has not been devastated but it has been seriously damaged, and it is not clear that other means as effective for establishing such foundations have yet been developed or, for that matter, ever will.

9. Humanity's fundamental contradiction

The nature of humanity, it was declared in this book's second sentence and reiterated several times in later discussions, is that of a species that lives and can only live, in terms of meanings it itself must fabricate in a world devoid of intrinsic meaning but subject to physical law. We face now the maturing of the contradiction, inherent in that nature from its very beginnings, but which modern conditions or the conditions of modernity allow, or even encourage, to become acute.

The reordering of knowledge that has finally liberated humanity to explore the physical world and to discover its laws is, in its very nature not only hostile to "superstition" and "magic" but also to the sacred and sanctified conceptions on which the distinctively human components of the world are founded, and the sacred and sanctified processes through which human institutions are constructed. The epistemologies that have been spectacularly successful in illuminating the ways in which physical aspects of the world work, when shone on humanity's conventional foundations, show them to be fabrications and thus, in a world in which objectivity and fact seem to own truth, delusory.

At the same time that epistemologies of discovery may subvert the saved and sanctified understandings on which human ways of life are founded, so may understandings of the world fabricated by humans so misconstrue the world's physical nature as to lead to actions that will damage it, possibly irreparably.

It seems hardly necessary to say that the consequences of the contradiction between the epistemologies of discovery and the fabrication of meaning become increasingly pressing as a function of technical and social evolution. No skeptical epistemology threatens the foundations of the social worlds conceived and enacted into being by hunters and gatherers, tribal cultivators or even most of those living in archaic civilizations, and the destructiveness and degradation following from misunderstandings of the nature of nature are limited when technology is unpowered and social formations small.

Misconstruing the world's nature is not necessarily, or even primarily, a matter of empirical error. We are concerned here with the adaptiveness of conceptions, not with what the knowledge available at a particular historical moment takes to be empirically accurate. We are concerned with the consequences of the actions to which such understandings lead. If such actions tend to increase the actor's chances of staying in the existential game indefinitely, and if, in this age of ever-increasing human capacity to destroy the world, such actions tend to preserve the existential game itself, then the understandings upon which they are based are adaptively true even if empirically absurd. I long ago (1969, 1984 [1968]: 237ff.) argued that in a world where the processes governing its physical elements are in some degree unknown and in even larger degree unpredictable, empirical knowledge of such processes cannot replace respect for their more or less mysterious integrity, and it may be more adaptive – that is, adaptively true – to drape such processes in supernatural veils than to expose them to the misunderstandings that may be encouraged by empirically accurate but incomplete naturalistic understanding. A little knowledge is proverbially dangerous, here possibly leading to overestimates of the extent to which natural processes can be circumscribed, circumvented or bent to human purposes. The consequences of such misunderstandings may include desertification, ozone depletion, species extinctions, atmospheric warming and the social and political disruptions following upon such environmental degradation. In contradiction of the doctrine of cultural relativism it may be asserted that some of the understandings that societies construct for themselves are false because they lead those for whom they are meaningful to act in ways that are so at variance with the world's physical constitution as to make damage to it and to themselves inevitable. The lawful order of nature – through which the processes of understanding and convention must have emerged – continues to provide criteria in terms of which the appropriateness of understandings and conventions can be assessed.

10. Dissonance between law and meaning

In summary, the lawful and the meaningful are not co-extensive and they are differently known. If physical laws and the states of affairs they constitute are to be known they must be discovered and explained. In contrast, the meanings by which humanity lives must be constructed and accepted. Laws and facts and the scientific procedures for discovering them may provide some of the materials out of which meanings are made, but they do not by themselves constitute meaning, nor can they do meaning's work of organizing human action. Conversely, although constructed meanings are often represented as discovered law they do not constitute nature. Laws of the sort discovered by physics, chemistry and biology, and the states of affairs contingent upon them are the case whether or not they are known. The lawful emergence, in the course of evolution, of the ability to construct meanings more or less independent of the characteristics of the physical world did not exempt humans from physical law but did increase by magnitudes their capacities not only to conceive the social world but to misunderstand the physical world as well. Thus, as the epistemologies of discovery threaten with demystification the fabricated sacred truths on which human institutions are founded, so may meanings constructed by humans lead to actions destructive of the world's physical elements. Moreover, meanings that may have once been merely self- or locally destructive become, with increased technical power and enlarged social scale, potentially world-destroying.

Such meanings may be highly and obviously sanctified. Many years ago the historian Lynn White Jr. (1967) proposed that the postulation, in the first chapter of Genesis, of human mastery of the earth and all that inhabits it constitutes the ideological and even moral grounds of the current ecological crisis. Perhaps so, but such conceptions of mastery are not intrinsic to religion in general; respect for natural processes is at least as widespread among religious concepts, and (without too much stretching) more benign interpretations of Genesis 1: 26–31 are possible. I have no interest in defending scripture against Lynn White Jr., but what are at first sight apparently more appropriately secular conceptions seem to me more immediately destructive. I say "apparently more secular." These conceptions may also be highly, if tacitly, sanctified.

Consider the epistemology inhering in money, the dominant mode of assigning value in modern societies. Consider it especially as a means for assessing physical environments and for making decisions concerning them. Money's analytic power rests, as Simmel long ago (1950 [1900]: 414) observed, on its most peculiar and interesting ability: it annihilates quality. That is, it dissolves the distinctions between qualitatively unlike things, reducing those distinctions to mere quantitative differences by providing a common metric in terms of which all things can be assigned values directly comparable to the values of all other things. But the world on which this metric is imposed is not as simple as the metric itself. Living systems – humans, plants, ecosystems – all require a wide variety of qualitatively distinct materials to survive. Protein and vitamin C, for instance, cannot substitute for each other. You can stuff yourself with protein-rich foods but if you do not get some vitamin C your teeth will fall out. The imposition of the more–less logic of money on systems – organisms and ecosystems most obviously – that do not operate in terms of a logic of more-less or addition and subtraction, but in terms of complementarity and reciprocity among their qualitatively distinct components, is bound to be destructive. It is in the nature of such a monetized rationality to rip the top off of complex systems such as West Virginia to get at a simple substance with a substantial monetary value, coal.

There is yet more to say about misunderstandings generated by monetary epistemology and about its dangers. If money becomes the standard by which all value is assigned and compared, then it itself becomes *ipso facto* the highest of all values. This elevation of money, an economic conception and instrument is, of course, of ancient origin but in recent decades it has been formalized, elaborated, and refined in procedures called "Cost-Benefit Analyses," which have been legitimized by economics, the most influential of the disciplines attempting to analyze social processes. Indeed, so many members of the 104th Congress were persuaded by the logic of cost-benefit analysis that they almost succeeded in subjecting all health, safety, and environmental regulations to it. Given the apotheosis of money, such a development would, however, violate natural relations of contingency. Economic values, indeed all economic systems, are entirely contingent upon the prior existence of biological systems, both organisms and ecosystems. The reverse is not the case. Biological systems are not contingent upon economic systems and had been in existence for 3.5 billion years or more before anything that could plausibly be called an economic system emerged and then only in a single evolutionary line. To give precedence to economic over biological values is to subordinate the fundamental, the processes of life themselves, to values which are merely instrumental, conventional, and arbitrary (not to mention often narrow and self-serving).[9] Such subordination of the fundamental, that which is both an end in itself and indispensable to that which is contingent, both dependent upon the fundamental and, properly, subservient to it, is, as our discussions of adaptation and maladaptation make clear, maladaptive. If, for instance, ecosystemic integrity is subordinated formally to economic interest, ecosystemic degradation is more than likely. A similar subordination of biological to economic considerations is obvious in the transformation of medical practice into what is called "The Health Care Industry," an industry, like any other industry, in which successful operation is assessed on the basis of an economic "bottom line," rather than in terms of the health of the clientele.

I characterized the emergence of a monetized epistemology as an apparently secular development, a key element in an economistically defined rationality, and so it is; but when money itself becomes the ultimate standard of value, and when such an epistemology is embedded in societies whose ultimate goals and values are represented by dicta like Coolidge's famous "The business of America is business," such an epistemology becomes a theology and as such highly sanctified. We recognize it, as such, as an instance of that form of falsehood that we, following Tillich, have labeled "Idolatry" in which the relative, the contingent, and the conventional are oversanctified or even, to use Tillich's terms, "absolutized," that is, elevated to the status of "Ultimate Concern" with, consequently, the value of the fundamental, here life itself, subordinated to the status of contingency, and as such "relativized."

Although monetized epistemology, when applied to biological systems instantiates Idolatry, and perhaps the Diabolical Lie as well, it also may constitute its own distinctive form of falsehood, another member of the Lie Family. We may recall that in Gnostic understanding this world is not the handiwork of a beneficent God, but of a quasi-evil being or beings. As such it is, in its entirety, a comprehensive, world-encompassing delusion. Monetary accounts of organic, ecological, and social systems misrepresent the natures of that which they purport to describe so falsely as to distort or mislead our comprehension of the world as a whole. We can declare such comprehensive falsification of the world's nature the "Gnostic Lie." The Gnostic Lie becomes ever more dominant and dangerous as social and political, but especially economic, processes become ever more global and ever more highly powered by elaborate, expensive, and concentrated technology. Evolution has armed our powers of misunderstanding with an ever-increasing capacity, technical, economic and political, to degrade or even to destroy the world for increasingly narrow, trivial, or abstract reasons, and religion has sometimes, directly or indirectly, sanctified the agents of that degradation.

11. Postmodern science and natural religion

Human worlds, then, are worlds whose features and operations must be constructed as well as discovered by those participating in them. But a caveat should be introduced here. Although we may distinguish as classes the physically constituted from the culturally constructed, the two cannot be separated in nature, and the world is increasingly an outcome of their interaction. The continuing accommodation of discovery and construction, their never-ending need for reconciliation, the maintenance of respect for the unknown on the one hand and the mystified on the other, difficult at best, becomes ever more difficult as our capacity to destroy the world increases and the certainties of our symbolic constructions crumble.

To recognize that problems arising from our entrapment between law and meaning become ever-more acute does not mean that our condition is ever-more hopeless. Stephen Toulmin in *The Return to Cosmology* (1982) has advocated the development of what he calls a "post-modern science" which would, once again, open itself up to what was called in the seventeenth, eighteenth, and nineteenth centuries "Natural Theology," or "Natural Religion," the sorts of inquiries in which the likes of Newton took themselves to be participating.[10] Nature was God's book, a book in which God's mind could possibly be read.

According to Toulmin, a science capable of participating in such a reunion would differ in several ways from modern science as defined by Descartes and his near contemporaries.

First, it would return scientists to the systems from which the Cartesian program attempted to separate them, either elevating them or exiling them to the status of detached observers. Such a detached status is no longer tenable (if it ever was) in light of Heisenberg's recognition of indeterminacy, of the growing awareness that living systems under study have subjective as well as objective characteristics, of the realization that opinion polls affect the opinions polled, and that studies of ecological systems are interventions into those systems.

The impossibility of anything approaching a radical scientific detachment leads to a second difference. Whereas a presumably detached modern science has attempted to confine itself to the construction of theory, leaving "praxis" to engineers, plumbers, and electricians, recognition that participation in the world is unavoidable must lead postmodern science to incorporate considerations of practice into itself. The distinction between "theory" and "praxis" will be blurred.

Thirdly, if postmodern science is to be concerned with thinking and acting subjects, and not merely with inanimate objects or subjects treated as such, it must grant validity to subjectively as well as objectively derived knowledge; to Vico's *verum* as well as to Descartes' *certum*.

A fourth difference follows. Whereas modern science claims to be value-free or value-neutral, post-modern science, to the extent that it is concerned with praxis, is in its nature value-guided, for praxis implies goals. A moral dimension is thus intrinsic to postmodern science.

There is a fifth difference of a yet more general nature. As a practical matter observations demanded by modern science have required an ever more specialized division of labor. Disciplines have, therefore, necessarily multiplied and as a result knowledge is increasingly fragmented and the organization of the world as a whole has become no serious scientist's business. Postmodern science will, on the contrary according to Toulmin, revive concern with Cosmos, the world as an integrated and ordered whole, a conception banished from serious scientific consideration in the seventeenth century when the new astronomy and the subsequent Cartesian revolution made forever untenable the cosmological models based upon astronomy that had dominated thought since Babylonian times, if not earlier.

That astronomy ultimately proved an unsatisfactory ground for cosmos does not mean, however, that no good grounds for cosmological conceptions are possible, and in Toulmin's view postmodern science will be ultimately concerned (I use Tillich's expression deliberately) with the world's unity, both with the principles underlying that unity and its preservation through practice. In sum, "postmodern science" is an order of epistemology and action in which both those who seek to discover natural law and those who seek to understand the nature of meaning and its fabrication are reunited within a world which they do not merely observe, but in the creation of which they participate and which they strive to maintain.

Whereas premodern cosmology was based upon astronomy, Toulmin suggests (as have others in other words) postmodern cosmology could be grounded in ecology. Cosmologies based upon astronomy on the one hand and ecology on the other differ in fundamental respects. It may once have been plausible to believe that the stars' courses could affect us, but it has probably never been easy to believe that we could have any influence upon the stars. Indeed, their imperviousness to our manipulation was probably an important aspect of their cosmological appeal. In contrast, the reciprocity of our relations with the ecosystems in which we live is manifestly obvious, continuously experienced and consequently undeniable. Whereas the relationship of human lives to the movement of heavenly bodies was one of correspondences between radically separate systems, the relationship of humans to the plants and animals, water and soils, surrounding them is one of ceaseless and obvious transaction. Ever since plant cultivation originated, moreover, humans have become, ever more decisively, the most consequential actors in the systems which they not only seek to understand but in which they seek to live and therefore seek to maintain.

Toulmin speaks of resurrecting, modernizing, or postmodernizing the concept of Cosmos but I prefer the term and concept Logos because intrinsic to it is a recognition that the world's order is not only constituted by unmotivated tectonic, volcanic, meteorological, chemical, and genetic processes but, since the emergence of humanity, has been, in part, constructed socially and symbolically. This seems to be the case of even our most apparently naturalistic notions. The concept of the ecosystem, for instance, is not an ineluctable extrapolation from empirical procedures of discovery. It is a constructed understanding and a contested one at that (see Worster 1993: ch. 13). We may recall a caveat issued a few pages ago. Although we may distinguish as classes the physically constituted from the culturally constructed, the two classes are not always, and usually cannot be, separated in nature. The state of the world, furthermore, is increasingly an outcome of their interaction, cultural fabrication becoming increasingly determining with the growth of social scale, the elaboration of technology, and the increasing comprehensiveness of money's sovereignty.

The ecosystem concept is neither pure discovery nor pure fabrication. It may well be fair to say that it bears as much resemblance to religious conceptions as it does to the descriptive statements of modern science. Indeed, it may, as it were, mediate between them, and as such serve well as the ground for a revitalized Logos, a feature of which is integration, wholeness, or holiness. This is clearly expressed in Heraclitus' Fragment 50, which we cite yet again: "Listening not to me but to the Logos the wise agree that all things are One" (G. Kirk 1954: 65).

Although the organization of ecosystems cannot be demonstrated as such, the conception can, and has, served as a "regulative principle" (Angeles 1981: 225) providing a framework within which to formulate and investigate empirical problems rigorously. At the same time it provides a general view of the physical world in light of which people can formulate their practical and moral relationship to it. The concept of the ecosystem is not only an explanation of nature but a reflection upon nature and a guide for acting in nature. We are reminded here of the notion of adaptive truth. The concept of the ecosystem, undemonstrable, is part of humanity's means, perhaps indispensable, for maintaining a world, and itself in a world, that it itself is increasingly capable of disrupting, degrading, or even destroying through processes which it itself has initiated – ozone depletion, greenhouse warming, deforestation, desertification, nuclear waste contamination. To put it a little differently, the ecosystem concept is part of humanity's means for maintaining ecosystems: to act as if the world is constituted of ecosystems, or the one encompassing ecosystem that some call Gaia is, in some degree, performative tending to bring into being and to preserve the form of organization it assumes.

I have said that the concept of the ecosystem, which Toulmin would make central to a revitalized cosmos and I to a new Logos, bears resemblance to religious concepts, or even is at least as much religious conception as scientific hypothesis. For one thing, its truth is not demonstrable through the objective procedures of scientific epistemologies (which may, in fact, threaten it). Its validity is, therefore, like the validity of all conventions, including religious understandings, a function of acceptance.

I also prefer to think of a new Logos rather than Cosmos not only because, as noted in chapter 11, commentators agree that its comprehension is different from scientific understanding. It is not only or merely intellectual. As one of Heraclitus' modern commentators put it, it "claims" those who grasp it. Intrinsic to conceptions of Logos is commitment to realize, participate in, maintain, correct, transform, and not merely observe orders grounded in the world's ecological order. How comprehension is to be transformed into commitment is not clear. We have discussed liturgy's capacities in this regard at length, considering both formal acceptance with its attendant obligations and responsibilities and numinous conviction, but we have also noted that liturgy's capacities may have been weakened since the Enlightenment, and its weakened powers may not be sufficient to "claim" those who seem to be in some degree of control of human affairs, and who may be under the spell of monetary epistemologies. Weakened or not, ritual and related forms of action should not be ruled out of attempts to establish a new Logos grounded in the concept of the ecosystem. I myself have found, in recent work on the social impacts of outer continental shelf oil leasing and on locating a national high-level nuclear waste repository, that participation in concerted actions conforming to or supporting ecological value and theory, or directed toward the amelioration of ecological or other social disorders, is likely to resemble "witnessing" and therefore be "deeply" or "highly" meaningful to participants, and as such strongly committing. With slight increase in the formalization of some aspects of such action it might become as committing as ritual.[11]

Ecosystemic conceptions *per se* are Western and modern in origin and no Western ecologist, so far as I know, has made religious claims for them, preferring to think of them as products of scientific epistemology, nor have Western religions claimed them either. Ecosystemic conceptions are certainly not explicit in the religions of the Book but they are not, it seems to me, incompatible with those religions. Even the assertions of human domination of nature found in Genesis and elsewhere are not beyond the reach of reinterpretations that may transform exploitation into stewardship and protection, as is at least implicit in the account of Noah, in which even unclean animals are welcomed aboard. Ecosystemic conceptions which, in some non-Western societies, approach ultimate sacred status, are thus worthy of high sanctification by the religions of the West as well. High and explicit sanctification of such conceptions and the actions they encourage not only might contribute to the preservation of the world's wholeness in the face of pervasive fragmenting and dissolving forces but could contribute to the revitalization of those religions in an age of increasing skepticism and cynicism toward them.

To adapt a conception of Logos based upon ecology is not to reduce all human problems to ecological problems but to define humanity's place in the world as a whole. The moral responsibilities of humanity's unique place are nowhere more profoundly realized than in the religions of aboriginal Australians.

The world, according to Aboriginal religions generally, seems to have been given its order by "heroes" who, among the Walbiri people for example (see Meggitt 1965a: 60), entered their tribal area or emerged

from the earth at definite places, then "traveled about, creating topo-
graphical features, performing ceremonies, introducing customs and laws
and depositing spirit essences." Geography is a product of the interwoven dream tracks of many heroes, and law and custom are not fully
distinct from geography:

> All these events occurred in the long-past dreamtime, an epoch (which is also a
> category of existence) that not only preceded the historical past and present but
> also continues in parallel with them. Although the totemic beings either departed
> from Walbiri territory or vanished into the earth during the dreamtime, they still
> exist and their powers and actions directly affect contemporary society.
>
> *(Meggitt 1965a: 60)*

So the dreamtime heroes formed the world out of its primordial formlessness (see Meggitt n.d.) largely through rituals and acts of naming, and
the world's continuity is contingent upon the continued performance of
those dreamtime rituals. But "The people believe that, by performing the
appropriate rituals and songs, living men can actually "become" these
beings for a short time and so participate briefly in the dreamtime"
(Meggitt 1965a: 60).

In sum, living men, apotheosized briefly as creative beings, are themselves the dreamtime heroes and as such are responsible for the world's
creation and persistence. Given humanity's powers to construct and
destroy and its position of dominance in ecosystems that it itself can
destabilize, its responsibility, as the Walbiri, the Murinbata, and other
Australians have long realized, cannot be to itself alone but must be to
the world as a whole. If evolution, human and otherwise, is to continue,
humanity must think not only about the world, but on behalf of the
world of which it has become a very special part and to which, therefore,
it has, as Australian aborigines in some sense realize, enormous responsibilities. We may recall here one of Heraclitus' modern interpreters
(Kleinknecht 1967: 85): "The particular Logos of Man ... is part of the
general Logos ... which achieves awareness in man." The Logos, this is
to say, can reach consciousness in the human mind and, so far as we
know, only in the human mind. This proposes a view of human nature
very different from, and I believe nobler than, *Homo economicus*, that
golem of the economists into which life has been breathed not by the
persuasiveness of their theory but by its coerciveness, and from the
obsessive focus on reproduction attributed to individuals by evolutionary
biologists. Humanity in this view is not only a species among species. It is
that part of the world through which the world as a whole can think
about itself.

Notes

1 Introduction

1 For Charles Sanders Peirce, the symbol is one of a trichotomy of three classes of signs. The other two are the *Icon* and the *Index*. A sign, (or Representamen) is, for Peirce,

> something which stands to somebody for something in some respect of capacity. It addresses somebody, that is creates in the mind of that person an equivalent sign, or perhaps a more developed sign. That sign which it creates I call the *interpretant* of the first sign. The sign stands for something, its object. It stands for that object, not in all respects, but in reference to a sort of idea, which I have sometimes called the ground of the representamen. *(Buchler 1955: 99; emphasis his)*

A symbol, for Peirce, is

> a sign which refers to the Object that it denotes by virtue of a law, usually an association of general ideas, which operates to become the Symbol to be interpreted as referring to that Object. It is thus itself a general type of law, that is, a Legisign [see Buchler 1960: p. 102]. As such it acts through a Replica [see Buchler 1990: esp. p. 112]. Not only is it general in itself, but the Object to which it refers is of a general nature. That which is general has its being in instances in which it will be determined. "There must, therefore, be existent instances of what the Symbol denotes, *although we must here understand by "existent," existent in the possibly imaginary universe to which the Symbol refers.* *(Buchler 1955: 102f.; emphasis mine)*

Words, by this definition, are the quintessential symbols.

An icon for Peirce

> is a sign which refers to the Object that it denotes merely by virtue of characters of its own, and which it possesses, just the same, whether any such Object actually exists or not ... Anything whatever, be its quality, existent individual or law, is an Icon of anything in so far as it is like that thing and used as a sign of it. *(Buchler 1960: 102)*

By this definition a map is an icon of a territory, inasmuch as it bears formal resemblance to it, and what is (redundantly) called a "phallic symbol" is not a symbol but an icon.

An index, in Peirce's terminology, "is a sign which refers to the Object that it denotes by virtue of being really affected by that object" (Buchler 1960: 102). In this usage a rash indicates (is an index of) measles, a dark cloud indicates rain, a thick tongue may indicate drunkenness.

2 Bickerton (1990: 158ff.) argues that with language, and even with proto-language, a form of learning that he calls "constructional" becomes increasingly important. Constructional learning is not based directly on either the learner's or anyone else's experience or observation but on the rational

manipulation of concepts (which may, of course, have been previously derived from observation or experience). Whereas limited constructional learning probably occurs under favorable conditions among some non-human species (most notably apes and, possibly, dolphins) the complex and quasi-autonomous models of the world that Bickerton calls "Secondary representational Systems" (1990: 145, *passim*) and associates with proto-language and language provide much richer material upon which it can operate.

3 Physical anthropologists are far from agreement as to when, that is, at what stage of anatomical development, particular linguistic capacities developed.

The expansion of the cranium from the 300–600 cc range characteristic of *Australopithecenae* through the *Homo habilis* average of 659 cc (Corballis 1991: 40) to the *Homo erectus* range of 843–1067 cc (Shepartz 1993) marking or even defining the transition from *Australopithecus* to *Homo* could plausibly be associated with linguistic emergence. Because brains are metabolically very expensive it is at least reasonable to assume that early *Homo*, particularly early *erectus* or even *habilis*, were doing something new and useful with these expanding organs. It hardly seems daring to suggest that the increment could well have been associated with the early stages of linguistic development, possibly with proto-language. Wolpoff (1980: 206) also notes that structural transformations of the brain were associated, or at least coincided with, this expansion: the "evolution of language ability seems tied to the appearance of hemispheric dominance and asymmetry" and that bilateral asymmetry in size and morphology is "marked" in Chaokoutien Cranium 5 [an *erectus*]. Thus, in his view, "there is every reason to believe that *Homo erectus* was capable of human language." More recently Corballis (1991, chs 4–8, 12) has also associated the emergence of linguistic ability with brain lateralization and suggests that these capacities begin to appear with *Homo habilis*.

It is important to note, however, that other scholars have other views. Bickerton's (1990: esp. ch. 7) position is that although proto-language may have been developing from some time during the *habilis* phase of *Homo*'s evolution (probably toward the end of it, or more likely, during the *erectus* phase, pp. 136–138 *passim*), full language does not appear until some time after the appearance of *Homo sapiens*. Others (e.g. Laitman 1981, Durhin 1990) take the emergence of full language to have coincided with emergence of *Homo sapiens sapiens*, this conclusion being based on evolutionary changes in the anatomy of the upper respiratory tract that tended to improve ability to articulate.

4 It seems plausible to suppose that the proto-language, when it began to emerge, served primarily if not entirely to label concepts or "proto-concepts" (see Bickerton 1990: 91) derived *directly* from concrete non-linguistic experience. It is likely that the significata of symbols in early stages of linguistic development, although no longer imprisoned in the present, were still limited to the likes of material objects – food sources, predators, prey, enemies, landscape features, and so on – and conditions existing materially in the perceptible world – hot, cold, wet. Bickerton (1990: 181ff.) proposes, however, that "Quite early on, a handful of terms had to be developed that did not refer directly, but either referred materially or performed some

communicative function that required an abstract element for its expression." Such elements, perhaps already constituents of proto-language, would have been likely to include, as development proceeded, elements denoting negation, inquiry, relative time or aspect (before/after, completed/incomplete) relative space and direction (on/in/at, to/from, near/far, etc.), quantifiers and perhaps later, modal auxiliaries (can, must, etc.). Proto-language thus began a process whose completion marked the emergence of "full language," of the creation of "terms of its own," terms that is, to the referents of which it was not possible to point with one's finger.

Discourse *necessarily* pushes beyond the physically actual. At some point, perhaps even before full language had emerged from proto-language, and perhaps as a function of elaborating classification and even more supple and subtle uses of what Corballis (1991: 219ff., *passim*) calls "Generative Assembling Devices," it becomes possible to denote the likes of unicorns as well as bison.

If "unicorn" is without concrete referents in nature it is at least a sort of thing – animal – that does exist in the natural world, as, perhaps do anthropomorphized spirits and gods. Standing at greater distance from the physically concrete are such concepts as honor and duty.

5 I take Leslie White's definition of culture to be the most important fundamental definition ever offered:

> Culture is the name of a distinct order, or class, of phenomena, namely those things and events that are dependent upon the exercise of a mental ability peculiar to the human species, that we have termed symbolling [i.e., the invention and use of symbols]. It is an elaborate mechanism, an organization of ways and means employed by a particular animal, man, in the struggle for existence and survival.   *(1949)*

6 In Eugene Odum's terms

> An ecological dominant ... is an organism which exerts a major controlling influence on the community (1959: 251f.). As such, dominants are species that set the conditions encouraging or discouraging the presence of other species. In land communities other than those dominated by humans, plants are usually dominant. Some marine communities are dominated by plant-like animals such as corals.
> *(Odum 1959: 250–252, passim).*

7 In earlier discussions I have called it the "ordinary lie."
8 These examples are drawn from games by whose rules they are allowed or even encouraged. We are led here to the matter of play in a more general sense. In the mode of action illustrated by children playing "cowboys and Indians," or by puppies wrestling, play closely resembles deception because *in its nature* it cannot be what it apparently represents. Play is distinguished from deceit or deception or lie by tacit or explicit context markers designating the action as play. As Bateson put it, "Expanded, the statement 'this is play' looks like this: 'These actions in which we now engage do not denote what those *actions for which they stand would denote*" (1972f: 180, emphasis in original). Thus, few people would regard children playing cops and robbers or, for that matter, actors playing Romeo and Juliet, to be practicing deceit.

9 A hierarchical taxonomy of deceptions formulated by the psychologist R. W. Mitchell (1986: 21ff.) is useful here. He distinguished four levels.

Level One. The organism does or is what it does or is because it cannot do otherwise. This level, which is exemplified by palatable butterflies that avoid being eaten by looking like unpalatable ones to "experienced" blue jays (Brower 1969, cited by Mitchell 1986: 22) is genetically established. Similar morphological mimicry can be observed among plants as well as animals. If the concept of intention entails consciousness and control of actions it is obviously not implicated here.

Level Two. The organism's actions are also genetically programmed but they appear programmed to the organism's registration of acts of another organism. The influence of the receiver's actions on the sender's actions distinguishes this level from the preceding one ... the organism [is] ... programmed to "do p given that q is the case (when p and q are actions of the sender and receiver respectively") (p. 24).

This level of deception, which does not require learning or even intent (if "intent" needs to be anything more than automatic response to stimuli), is exemplified by species of predatory fireflies who, in response to the flashing of males of firefly species upon which they prey, flash the sexual aroused signal of females of that species, thus attracting males who discover, in the last moment of their lives that they are fated to be dinners, not lovers.

Level Three. The organism's actions are, as at level two, contingent upon its registration of some sort of stimulus from the potential dupes of the deceptive signals it will subsequently transmit but, unlike level two deception, these actions can be modified by learning. Thus, the level two instruction "do p if q is the case" is replaced by the more complicated and cognitively demanding instruction "do any action p given that this p has resulted in some desired consequence q in our past ... Deceptions at level three are based upon trial and error, instrumental and/or observational learning" (p. 25).

Mitchell offers a variety of instances of level three deceptions, not all of which seem to me to qualify. Some of his examples do, however, seem to be radically different from deceptions of lower type. He cites Hediger's (1955: 150f.) account of the gorilla that "lured her keeper into her cage by acting as if her arm were stuck" noted in the text above and Morris's (1986) observation of an elephant acting as if she were about to turn on a shower for another elephant, thereby forestalling a dominance interaction.

Deceptive possibilities become increasingly convoluted and ramified at higher levels. Mitchell notes that at level three "an animal can be deceived as a result of [its own] learning ... " Thus, blue jays learn to ignore palatable butterflies that resemble unpalatable ones, having experienced some sort of upset subsequent to eating the latter. This example further indicates that a deceiver can operate at one level, here level one, and the dupe at another, here at a level of learning corresponding to level three deception. A wry implication is that increased capacity for processing information increases both the number of ways to be wrong, and vulnerability to and likelihood of error.

Although intentionality is present at level three it is not clear, Mitchell observes, that the intention is to deceive. An animal may act in a particular way because it has learned, simply, that such an action will have desirable consequences. To cite the famous case of Romanes's dog (1977[1883]: 444), which simulated limping after having received extra petting following injury to his foot, Lloyd Morgan (1970[1900]: 280) argued that it may not have been attempting (as Romanes claimed) to deceive its master into believing that it was once again injured (and thus in need of attention and comforting) but had simply learned that the adoption of a certain gait is followed by petting or, to go a little further, that that particular gait constituted the message "Pet me."

At *Level Four*, however, the intention of deceit becomes patent. Mitchell characterizes deception at this level as involving

An open program ... capable of programming and reprogramming itself based upon past and present actions of the organizm being deceived. That is, the sender corrects and changes its actions both to counteract undesired acts and to encourage desired acts of the receiver. In a sense the sender becomes the programmer of its own behavior. This type of metaprogramming is typically called thinking and planning, and at this level of deception the sender actually *intends to deceive the receiver.*   (p. 24; emphasis his)

What seems to be level four deception has been reported among a number of species beside *Homo*, including arctic foxes (Ruppel 1986), and may be quite common among undomesticated as well as signing chimpanzees. Figan, whose shenanigans are described in the text above, may have been more ingenious than most other apes but he was hardly unusual in his apparently deceptive intentions. I say "apparent" because there is the possibility that Figan really did hear something out there and just happened to get back to the clearing ahead of the others. He was seen to go through his charade more than once, however, and too many instances of deceitfulness among apes have been reported by trained observers (see de Waal 1986, 1988) to doubt its occurrence.

10 Frans de Waal (1986: 225ff.) has recognized five forms of deception among higher primates. The most common and widespread, found among macaques as well as apes, is "Withholding information about one's knowledge, impulses, or intentions ..." Chimpanzees may, for instance, "keep secrets" about the location of food, and subdominant males may hide their amatory advances toward estrous females from dominants. Chimpanzees also have been observed to suppress indications that they have noticed threats toward them, thus avoiding confrontations. A closely related second class noted by de Waal is deliberate inattention to what is going on, "showing great interest in objects or events ... apparently irrelevant to ongoing social interactions" as a way to draw others with whom there have been antagonistic interactions into reconciliation. Also closely related is the "feigning of mood," a category into which bluff displays fall, as may the behavior of an elderly chimpanzee called "Yeroen." When challenged by younger males, he would begin to play in what seemed to be meant to appear to other chimpanzees (but not to trained human observers) to be high good humor. Chimpanzees also seem to be able to correct indexical mood signals that they otherwise might more or

less automatically transmit. Thus, males engaged in antagonistic bluffing displays have been observed to turn their backs on their antagonists momentarily to rearrange manually their facial expressions, which otherwise would have indicated fear.

Figan's behavior falls into the class of deceptions de Waal calls "Falsification," as does Hediger's instance of the gorilla who lured a keeper into her cage (by pretending her arm was caught in the bars) and then captured her. Six cases of "luring" have also been observed among chimpanzees (four perpetrated by the same female). In all of them, the perpetrator, shortly after an antagonistic incident she herself had initiated, signaled through facial expression, hand gestures, and so on that she sought reconciliation, but when her erstwhile antagonist approached her, the perpetrator attacked her. Also of interest is the case of Dandy, the youngest of four adult males at the Arnheim zoo who was fed in a confined space with his three senior colleagues, all of whom "picked on him" and probably deprived him of food. He solved his problem by appearing to become very good-natured and frolicsome just before feeding time, engaging the others in play, after which they ceased persecuting him.

Several comments are in order.

First, Marshall, a linguist, proposed some time ago that "The most striking differences between animal signs and language behavior is to be found ... in the rigid stereotyped nature of the former and in the fact that *they are under the control of independently specifiable external stimuli and internal ... states*" (1970: 234 emphasis mine). This contrast, if meant to distinguish between human communication and the communication system of other animals, is much too stark. For one thing, human communication is not confined to language. Blushing in humans, which *indicates* (it does not "symbolize") embarrassment to observers, is no less under the control of "specifiable external stimuli and internal [emotional] states" than is pilatory erection in chimpanzees or dogs. On the other hand, chimpanzees, and many other animals, as Mitchell, de Waal, and others have observed, have considerable control over some, or even much, of their signaling. As descriptive of the total systems of communication of entire species, Marshall's characterization may not apply fully to any, or at least many, species "higher" than fireflies.

Both Mitchell and de Waal's accounts make clear that higher forms of deception are dependent upon the ability of animals to bring at least some of the signals they continuously emit under conscious control. Some types they identify, however, as illustrated by Yeroen's strained playfulness, are deceptive only insofar as they mask the emotional states of estrus, and it is hard to see that such deception – if it is properly considered deception – deceives its targets to their harm (unless depriving them of an opportunity to inflict pain is harmful to them). It could as well be said that Yeroen, in avoiding sending a direct signal to his antagonist, is, in fact, signaling "I am not challenging you," a message which may, in fact, save everyone from harm. For one primate to act as if he has not seen another's threat display may require him to dissemble his knowledge and his emotional condition, but such actions might better be seen as exercises in rudimentary diplomacy or civility than in deception.

Our own experience tells us that the requirements of diplomacy and civility often run counter to sincerity, but insincerity and deception, although not mutually exclusive, are not one and the same. The term "sincerity" refers to the relationship of signals to the affective or attitudinal state of the transmitter, deception in its higher forms, deceitful and otherwise, to the relation between signal and intention. We will return to questions of sincerity and to the virtues of insincerity in chapters 3 and 4. For now it is sufficient to propose that insincerity may be prerequisite to social life of any complexity, and that what is meant by "socialization," the transformation of immature organisms into fully functioning members of society, is in considerable degree tutelage in "proper insincerity." To put this a little differently, sociability or civility requires members of society to distinguish between their *private* subjective, affective and cognitive states on the one hand and their *public* social expressions and actions on the other, and psychological health as well as social competence further requires that these private and public "spheres" be in some degree buffered against each other as well. Such a distinction and such buffering are as much entailed by conscious control of message transmission as are possibilities for insincerity and deception.

If an animal can exercise some degree of control over its signaling, in some degree managing its transmissions, it can exercise some degree of control over its social life. Although deception as well as insincerity may have a part to play in an organism's management of its social relations, we may again call into question some instances of what de Waal takes to be deceptive behavior in chimpanzees. Dandy's preprandial jocularity is of special interest. He, even less than Yeroen, was not misleading his three persecutors by leading them into play. His intention, de Waal proposes, was, in fact, to get them to play, and he was successful in doing precisely that. It is useful to distinguish proximate intention from deeper motive. But even if his motive for initiating play, as de Waal plausibly suggests, was not to give expression to a sudden seizure of light-heartedness but was based upon a belief that they would stop persecuting him if he engaged them in play, he was not being deceitful, otherwise deceptive, or even, necessarily, "insincere." He was, rather, displaying a high degree of what has been called "social intelligence" or "Machiavellian intelligence," an aspect, component, or form of intelligence hypothesized to be more or less distinct from "technical intelligence." Whereas the latter focuses on the understanding and manipulation of physical objects, the former emerges out of and focuses upon the understanding of social processes, and the factors (especially psychological) entering into them, and upon their manipulation (see Byrne and Whiten [eds.] 1988, esp. articles by Humphrey, Jolly, and Chance and Mead. See also Barnes 1994). All these authors have called attention to the probable importance of "social intelligence" (Humphrey), "the social use of intelligence" (Jolly) or "Machiavellian intelligence" (Byrne and Whiten), as distinct from "technical intelligence," in the evolution of intelligence generally.

We have called into question, or even disqualified, what some observers have taken to be instances of deceptive or even deceitful behavior in primates. Some instances do, however, remain – most notably Figan's ingenious distraction and, more generally, luring behavior observed among both chimpanzees and gorillas. We can easily agree that if these instances do not constitute bald-faced lies properly so-called they come very close. Furthermore, in the case of Figan, at least, whose dupes included close kin (whom chimpanzees seem to recognize as such) his behavior was truly deceitful. For reasons advanced in the main text, however, notably the limited scope of lying with pseudo-indices rather than symbols, I prefer to think of them as "proto-lies" and, in Mitchell's terms, place them by themselves in a fifth level of deception.

11 It is obvious that the disruption of their social orders is taken by most if not all societies to be evil. The association of evil itself with disorder and disruption is a somewhat deeper matter, and it may be widespread. That they are associated in Western tradition is given some etymological support by consideration of the possible derivations of the English words "symbol," "parable," and "diabolic."

It is generally accepted (American Heritage Dictionary 1992) that "symbol" is derived from the Greek *syn* "together," or "with" and *ballein* "to throw." A symbol is, thus, something which "throws things together," presumably signs with significata.

"Parable," according to the same dictionary, is derived from *paraballein*, "to set beside," which in turn is derived from *ballein* and *para*, beside. A parable is a narrative running parallel to a moral matter which it illustrates or represents.

"Diabolic," in contrast, is, according to Shipley (1945) and Partridge (1958), derived directly from the Latin *diabolus*, "devil," which in turn, is derived from the late Greek *diabolos*, Satan, which is, in turn, derived from *diaballein*, "to slander," but literally "to throw across," from, obviously, *ballein* and *dia*, "across," "through," "at right angles to" (American Heritage Dictionary 1992). "To throw across," in light of the derivations of symbol and parable which associate them with order, harmony, illumination, meaningfulness, is to disrupt, disorder, and confuse.

2 The ritual form

1 *Pace* Jack Goody, who asserted some years ago (1977: 25) that "there is a whole set of terms used in the anthropological discussion ... of religion ... above all ritual" that "are virtually useless for analytic purposes." He further asserted that attempts to define such terms are better avoided because they can only lead us into nominalistic swamps. Having respectfully noted Professor Goody's reservations concerning definitions in general and of ritual in particular, we can get on with defining it.

2 We have here, by the way, an instance of amelioration being preferable to cure, for annihilation of lie and the problems intrinsic to the conception of alternative would require the elimination of language itself. "Good enough" is better than "best" or, to be a bit more precise, the adequate is to be preferred to the perfect.

3 Kapferer writes:

I suggest a kind of definition [of ritual] which is built on the types of factors which underlie the recognition by cultural members of their action as "ritual"; which attends to the phenomenon both in its universal and ethnographically particular dimensions but in a way which does not distort the possibility of the phenomenon as it is locally or situationally displayed.   *(1983: 194)*

He then provides the following definition two sentences later:

ritual is a series of culturally recognized and specified events, the order of which is known in advance of their practice, and which are marked-off spatially and temporally from the routine of everyday life (even though such events might be vital to this routine).

Aside from his stipulation that rituals are spatially and temporally separated from everyday life, a specification which I find problematic, and aside from his addendum concerning the necessity of ritual to daily life, which I regard as unnecessary at best but, possibly, an *a priori* functional assertion of that which is properly left to discovery, his definition of 1983 is rather different from, but not in disagreement with, mine of 1974, as amended here.

4 This is not to say that ritual should be conceived as somehow analogous to grammar.

5 Myerhoff (1977: 200ff.) has suggested, at least implicitly, a distinction between what she called "nonce rituals" and what may, for sake of contrast, be called "full rituals", or "rituals properly so-called", or even, simply, "rituals." Nonce rituals are performances like "those awkward, self-conscious 'first annual' events laboring under their obvious contrivance and often touchingly transparent hopes and intentions of [their] participants." They commonly deal with the problem of their patent invention by importing, as it were, sacred elements from other rituals and juxtaposing them with the new and usually secular material that constitutes the new ritual content and purpose. They also may take established rituals as organizing metaphors. Thus a nonce ritual that Myerhoff herself observed in a senior citizen's center in Los Angeles in 1974 made use of both American graduation ceremonies and, at the same time the siyum, a traditional Jewish ritual performed when the study of a sacred text has been completed.

6 Our concerns are not psychiatric, but it is of interest that the rigid but idiosyncratic sequences of stereotyped and even bizarre behavior termed "ritual" or "ceremony" (Freud 1907) by psychiatrists which are compulsively performed in private by some psychotics and neurotics, and which must originate within their psyches, are usually experienced as "ego-alien", that is they arise out of psychic regions that are not identified by those experiencing them as part of the self (Fenichel 1945: 268ff.). The sufferer feels that the form of the behavior has been imposed upon her by some agent separate from what she takes to be herself.

Noting similarities between neurosis and religious behavior, as Freud (1907) and others have done, may be illuminating, but nothing is to be gained by identifying the two, nor am I proposing that ritual innovation is a form of obsessive-compulsive disturbance. I do no more than note that the subjective experience of conforming to an order imposed by other than the self is common to both religious and neurotic rituals, but the two can, of course, be distinguished. It may be suggested that if an invariant sequence of formal acts and utterances is performed only by the innovator it is not simply a ritual but a form of madness, and the performer is no prophet nor is he taken to be. He is taken to be, and well might be, nothing more than a compulsive neurotic or even a lunatic.

7 This usage is post-Vatican II. It was previously said that the priest celebrates the mass while the congregation assists in it (Virgil Funk, personal communication).

8 Bell (1992: 30ff.) following Geertz (1973: 113) and Singer (1959: 140ff.), discusses, in the context of the thought–action dichotomy, a third category of person possibly present at rituals, namely theorists or researchers. Their relationship to the proceedings is different from either those of participants or those of audience-like spectators. Singer noted, she tells us, that "the Hindus have rites which they can enact or exhibit, whereas the researcher has concepts which can be thought or talked about. As a consequence of this distinction the particularity of any one local ritual is contrasted with the more embracing, abstract generalizations of the researcher" (p. 30). Later she notes that "ritual as performance ... enables the integration of the theorist's abstract conceptual categories and the cultural particularity of the rite" (p. 31).

9 Dramatic characters are obviously invented by playwrights, actors and directors even when they represent historical figures.

10 This aspect of ritual is not explicitly recognized in our definition, although it may be implied by the omission of any reference to instrumentality and by its emphasis upon formality *per se.* Lack of material efficacy has been omitted for several reasons. First, it seems unwarranted to claim that all events conforming to the definition offered are efficacious in any sense. Secondly, if efficacy, non-material or otherwise, is intrinsic to ritual form this should not be asserted a priori but shown to be an entailment of that form. Thirdly, our definition is concerned with ritual's most obvious characteristics. Efficacy, its nature, and its presence or absence are not always obvious. Fourthly, it does not seem necessary or desirable to disqualify as ritual sequences formal acts and utterances otherwise conforming to our definition for which hidden material efficacy may be discovered. Apparently symbolic acts undertaken in ritual may sometimes lead through obscure causal chains to the results which they seek. We may recall here Omar Khayyam Moore's suggestion (1955) that scapulamancy really does improve the hunting fortunes of the Naskapi Indians by randomizing their hunting patterns, thereby disrupting unwitting regularities that their adversaries, the caribou, might learn. I have argued (1968) that for material reasons it really may be bad for a Maring's health for his exuvia to find its way into the hands of an enemy sorcerer.

11 "The Freudian unconscious", which Fortes nominates as a source of the occult, designates a complicated set of ambiguous, but powerful and highly affective processes. Other writers do not always use the term "occult" in Fortes' sense, but it seems fair to say that in the view of Durkheim (1961[1915], esp. chapter 7), for instance, what we are calling the "occult" arises out of the emotional responses of those participating in effervescent

rituals. Leach (1966) follows Durkheim in taking occult power to be that of society mystified in effervescent ritual. Douglas sees it emerging not only from the orders of mind and society, but also from the disorders lying beyond them and from the juxtaposition, confrontation or alternation of those orders and disorders. Such orders and disorders are manifested both in the symbolic forms that characterize ritual and in a contrasting symbolic formlessness (as for instance, the state of the initiate in a marginal phase of a rite of passage, in which he is no longer a boy nor yet a man). "In ritual form is treated as if it were quick with power to maintain itself in being, yet always liable to attack. Formlessness is also credited with powers, some dangerous, some good" (1966: 95). Abrahams (1973) has argued much more elaborately that the "vitality" of ritual may be derived from the confrontation of form and formlessness. "We can appreciate the progress," he says, "of increasing formality from observing etiquette to ... enacting a ... ritual, but what of the hilarity, the confusion, the invocation of chaos ... so widely reported in actual ritual performances?" (p. 5). These are manifested in such behavior as clowning, transvestitism, physical attacks on initiates, and the like which "arise to guarantee the maintenance of ... energies which are unfocused for the larger community" (p. 14). "Ritual," he says, "is an enactment and celebration of the potentials of a group" (p. 8). "At the heart of ritual is the experience of contradiction in the most basic terms, such as the vitality of mortality (or vice versa), or the simultaneous proclamation of the order of the world as seen by the group and its (almost) absolute denial" (p. 15).

These and other notions concerning the basis of ritual's "power" are not mutually exclusive. Indeed, they are not even in any profound way competitive, for they are seen to invoke unspecified but possibly strong emotions and cognitive responses that the analysts presume to be concomitants of ritual performance. It is not, after all, from the clash of order and disorder *per se* (as manifested, say, in the juxtaposition of an awe-inspiring object with a ludicrous one) that "vitality" springs, as flame does from flint and steel. It is, if at all, from the emotional reaction of the participant to what in some way he takes to be such a clash.

12 It seems to be an empirical fact that participation in some rituals heightens emotions, in others it has a calming effect, while in yet others it has more complex emotional consequences, and students of both animal and human behavior have generally taken ritual's emotional correlates to be significant to their understanding of it. Some, in fact, take its affective qualities to be intrinsic to their very conception of the phenomenon, and a large number of theories, for the most part functional, concerning the relationship between ritual and emotion have been proposed. Among the claims that have been made are: participation in some rituals alleviates such disabling emotions as fear and anxiety, likely to be experienced in the face of the dangerous or unpredictable (Malinowski 1922: 392 ff.); rituals of deference and demeanor protect the emotions from constant trial (Goffman 1956, Tinbergen 1964a); rituals mobilize emotional support for the social organization (Durkheim 1964, Radcliffe-Brown 1964); rituals mediate between conflicting emotions or drives (Freud 1907, Gluckman 1954, Tinbergen 1964a); the forms of some

rituals can be explained by the conflicting emotions they mediate (Freud 1907, Tinbergen 1964b); in the rituals of ontogeny that primordial emotions of the young are sublimated, that is, connected, so to speak, to socially valued ends (Campbell 1959, Erikson 1966, V. Turner 1969). For discussions of the physiological concomitants of ritual participation, see d'Aquili, Laughlin, and McManus (ed.) 1979, especially chapters by Lex and by d'Aquili and Laughlin.

13 I suggest, in disagreement with Foucault (1990: *passim*), that the term "powerful" be reserved for energy transactions, those measurable in such units as ergs, horsepower, watts, etc. When the term "power" is used in the political realm we may also measure it in material terms, such as numbers of men and resources available for forceful enterprises. Bierstadt long ago (1950) proposed that power in the social or political sense be taken to be the product, in the mathematical or metaphorically mathematical sense, of men × resources × organization).

Whereas power is the product of matter and energy, authority is to be defined in terms of information. An authority may be taken to be a locus in a communication network from which directives flow. Directives may, but need not be framed in the imperative mood. They may take the form of ontological postulates, statements of principle, or policy, they may include moral and ethical dicta, and other assertions of fact or value. The actions they may be meant to invoke may be left inexplicit or unspecified. Authorities may stand upon a number of grounds. That is to say, people may acquiesce to their directives because they are powerful, but also because they are knowledgeable, convincing, wealthy, sacred or sanctified.

14 The term "information" is used here in a broad, non-technical sense. I note this because it will be used in more technical senses later.

15 This discussion of the relationship between the canonical and self-referential is similar to Arthur Burks' (1949: 680ff.) discussion of the relationship between what Peirce called "types" and "tokens." This discussion comprises part of his argument (with which I disagree, but that is beside the present point) that "the fundamental kind of indexical sign is the indexical symbol [i.e., a linguistic expression used indexically] rather than the pure index ... "

Tokens are individual occurrences of words. If the same word occurs in two successive sentences there are two tokens. The occurrence of a token is an event and as such has a particular location in time and space. The class of all tokens of a given word (in one of its meanings, e.g. "red" as designating a color, as distinct from "red" as designating a communist) is called a "type." Types, in contrast to tokens, are without specific location in time and space. The word "red" (as symbolizing a particular color) has the same meaning whenever it occurs. This is to say that in the case of a "pure" symbol there is no difference between the meaning of the type and meanings of its tokens.

The situation is different with respect to indexical symbols. For Burks (1949: 674) an index is a sign which is "in existential relation with its object (as in the case of the act of pointing)" or "a sign which determines its object on the basis of an existential connection." Thus, the "symbol 'this' is also an index because ... it may function very much the same as the act of pointing

(p. 674). So, for instance, may such words (symbols) as "now" function as indices. It is, however, obvious that the meanings of tokens of "now" and of the type "now" do not coincide fully. Whereas the type "now" means "at the present time", precisely what the present time varies from one second to the next, so that the utterance "now" means something different at 9:01 am from what it did at 9:00 am. Burks summarizes all of this as follows:

> the common element in the meaning of a token and the meaning of its type ... [is its] symbolic meaning [an association by conventional rule] ... the complete meaning of a type (either indexical or non-indexical) is its symbolic meaning. Furthermore, the complete meaning of a token of a non-indexical symbol is also its symbolic meaning. But the symbolic meaning of a token of an indexical symbol is only part of its full meaning: we shall refer to its full meaning as its indexical meaning ...   *(pp. 681–2)*

Burks would have presented what I take to be his own thought more effectively if he had said that the full meaning of the indexical symbol includes an indexical as well as symbolic meaning. Be this as it may, in both his account and mine there is in some cases crucial distinction between the general and continuing meanings of words (or reiterated formulae like the Shema on the one hand and the meanings of their particular occurrences on the other).

Burks' analysis does not claim to be historical or evolutionary but it may, nevertheless, seem to imply that the indexical function is an addendum to a logically and therefore temporally prior symbolic function. The account I have offered would, on the contrary, take the symbolic to be an augmentation of a temporally prior indexical function. Although I disagree with Burks' assertion that the indexical symbol rather than the pure index is "the fundamental kind of indexical sign," taking it to be unduly anthropocentric, I do not take the implications of the difference to be profound for the present work. My proposal follows from a general evolutionary perspective which aims, among other things, to distinguish the rituals of humans from those of other animals in a way which conforms to general differences in human and animal communication. The capacity for indexical communication is much more widespread among animals than is the capacity for symbolic communication which is almost if not entirely non-existent among species other than hominids, and must also have been temporally prior to symbol use, even among hominids and their forebears. Burks, on the other hand, apparently assumes, as did Peirce, the existence of language and is concerned with logical relations within it. Be this as it may, Burks' discussion would support, I think, the formulation

Variant: invariant::Self-referential:Canonical::Token:Type::Index:Symbol

16 Ritual representations often have iconic aspects. But, as implied on p. 000 above there may be no pure icons and most if not all icons used in ritual rest upon the symbolic definition of at least one of the terms they join. The Worm Ourabouros, the serpent that subsists by eating its own tail, may be an icon of eternity, but before it could become so eternity had to have been conceived in words, i.e., symbolically.

17 For instance, the plants figuring in a first fruits ritual may indicate the maturation of a crop.

18 The indexicality intrinsic to performatives seems obvious but I am not aware of earlier observations to this effect.

19 It should perhaps be made clear that we are not concerned here with all of the information concerning their conditions that people transmit indexically during the course of rituals. People gossip before, after and sometimes during them, they display their wealth through wardrobe and ornament, their health through the color of their complexions and eyeballs, and their dispositions towards each other by greeting, snubbing, posture and facial expression. Rituals, being points in space and time within which people assemble, are likely to be of significance in the incidental transmission of social information, self-referential or otherwise. But such information is more or less constantly transmitted by everyone all of the time, and to cite it as a distinctive aspect of ritual would be trivial if not erroneous. We may return here to the distinction casually made earlier between events designated "rituals" and "ritual" as the formal aspect of events. We are not concerned with all of the self-referential information incidentally transmitted during all rituals by all participants, but with the messages transmitted through or by the performance of the ritual itself. What an American woman communicates during a religious service by wearing new furs or turning her shoulder upon another is not of primary concern here, nor is the noticeably enlarged spleen of the dancer in a highland New Guinea pig festival. Of concern is what it is that the woman indicates by kneeling in church, the New Guinea Highlander by dancing on the sanctified ground of a neighbor.

3 Self-referential messages

1 Widows with young children often return to their natal groups.

2 The *ringi* is prepared from a fire which is ignited underneath the fighting stones. The red spirits are called into this fire, infusing the *ringi* and the fighting stones (as well as the oven stones being heated in the fire to cook pigs sacrificed to the red spirits) with their "hotness and "hardness," i.e., their ferocity, strength, anger, and vengefulness. It is said that the red spirits themselves enter these objects and are introduced into the warriors themselves when *ringi* is applied to them with the fighting stones. Some Maring say that the red spirits themselves burn like fires in the heads of the warriors.

3 *Ringi* is said by Maring to increase their strength and ferocity and to decrease their vulnerability, but it may, in fact, increase their vulnerability, for it must distinguish principle antagonists from mere allies, with whom the enemy has no quarrel. It is a fact of Maring warfare that principle antagonists suffer many more casualties than do allies, and it may be suggested that this is because warriors take principal antagonists, rather than their allies to be preferred targets, and principal antagonists are clearly indicated by *ringi*.

4 If it is attacked while its *rumbim* remains in the ground it may defend itself. The taboo is against initiating warfare.

5 Maring men's interest in shells and plumes is so intense that it might strike a Westerner as obsessional.

6 In Maring courtship it was for the men to make themselves attractive to women, but for women to make overtures to the men.

7 My use of the term epideictic display here does not indicate, symbolize, or otherwise signify acceptance of Wynne-Edwards' theory of group selection.

8 See, for example, Piddocke 1965, Suttles 1960, Vayda, Leeds and Smith 1961, Young 1971: 220ff., for plausible suggestions.

9 We note here that although the summative and ordinal aspects of display may be distinguished, summations obviously may be put to ordinal ends.

10 It is of as much interest with regard to display as to economics that devices to aid in assessing and recording commodities given and received seem to have a wide distribution. Oliver reports that the chief beneficiary (if "beneficiary" is an appropriate term) of Soni's largesse recorded his receipts on a fern frond tally as he redistributed them. Tally sticks were in use on the northwest coast (Drucker 1965: 57), and Goodenough islanders (combining analogic and digital principles) used vine measures (Young 1971: 195).

11 Nor is any simple claim for the superiority of digital over analogic representation being advanced here. In this regard, Bateson (1972i: 412) has observed that digital signaling has not replaced analogic in human communication, although it does seem to have arisen later in the course of evolution (Sebeok 1962, 1965, Wilden 1972). Sebeok's suggestion that the digital emerged when the scanning of much larger quantities of information more exactly acquired adaptive value (1962: 439) is germane to the arguments advanced here. Both modes have, rather, been elaborated side by side, no doubt because, as Bateson suggests, they have different qualities making each of them particularly appropriate for different functions.

12 Bateson (1972d: 451ff.) characterizes the basic unit of information, the bit (bi[nary digi]t) "as a difference that makes a difference."

13 This operation is considerably less drastic than circumcision. The foreskin is slit longitudinally on the dorsal side.

14 It may also be observed that informing the parents may not be easy to distinguish from asking permission of them. Since the establishment of greater personal autonomy is an aspect of the rite, the permission of parents, even if freely given, would constitute a contradiction (like the little boy asking his mother for permission to cross the street so that he can run away from home). On the other hand, to proceed without parental permission is not merely to seek greater autonomy. It is to exercise it. As such participation in the ritual is an index of autonomy.

15 Pettitt's views are at some odds with other interpretations and accounts. Black Elk's description of Lakota (Sioux) "lamenting" (Brown 1971) does not suggest that children were coerced into searching for visions.

16 The following, from Turner's account (1967) suggests the range of factors summarized:

an important respect, *Mukanda* is a cybernetic custom-directed "mechanism" for restoring a state of dynamic equilibrium between crucial structural components of a region of Ndembu society that has been disturbed by the growing up of a large number of boys. Too many "unclean" [uncircumcised] boys are "hanging around" the women's kitchens. Not enough youths are sitting in the village forum (*Chota*) and participating in its adult affairs. It is in the general interest … to bring these boys into the adult fold and thus to correct the obstructions in the course of regular social life brought about by their presence. Given the belief that uncircumcised Ndembu males are both unclean and immature, [their] natural increase … must lead to a numerical imbalance in social influence between men and women. Uncircumcised boys belong to the women's sphere of activities and their attachment to this sphere becomes greater as time passes. *(p. 167)*

Men do not ordinarily order about or chastise uncircumcised children … after the boys have been purified and rendered "men" by *Mukanda* they must obey the elders, fulfill the norms governing each category of kinship relationship and may be punished for disobedience by any male senior to them … If there is an undue preponderance of uncircumcised boys in a village or vicinage … there may not be enough initiated boys to perform routine tasks of village maintenance, and there may be a tendency for uncircumcised boys to become increasingly less amenable to the discipline whereby structural relations are maintained. Prolonged attachment to mother, and to women's sphere, is symbolized in the fact that the foreskin is compared to the *labia majora*. When the foreskin is removed by circumcision the effeminacy of the child is removed with it. The physical operation itself is symbolic of a change of social status. Ndembu admit that it is inconvenient if there are many uncircumcised boys in a village, for circumcised men may not eat food cooked on a fire used for cooking such boys' meals nor use a platter on which they have eaten. Again, they will say that the boys in a village get sharply divided into circumcised and uncircumcised, and that the former mock the latter. *(p. 268)*

Customary beliefs about the function of *Mukanda*, then, give rise to a situation of moral and physical discomfort when there are many uncircumcised boys in a vicinage …. In such an atmosphere, the suggestion by a responsible adult that *Mukanda* should be performed is received with a certain amount of relief. *(p. 269)*

17 I am not arguing for the general superiority of ritual occurrence as a signal over other modes of signaling, nor even for that of simple binary signals in general. There are two qualities which may be desirable in a signal, but which are incompatible if not, indeed, logically opposed. On the one hand there is clarity or lack of ambiguity imparting to the receiver a certainty of what is being signaled, but inevitably, at the expense of a great deal of information. On the other hand, there is informativeness: high information content and accurate reflection of changes, imparting to the receiver detailed knowledge, but at the expense of increasing ambiguity, apparent inconsistencies, increasing need for sensitive interpretation and decreasing certainty. Most actual signals may represent compromises or trade-offs between the considerations of informativeness and certainty. Binary signaling stands, of course, close to the pole of certainty (the limiting case is the invariant signal which is altogether devoid of information, although not of meaning, a matter of great importance to which we shall return), and it may be suggested that the occurrence of ritual, to which the binary is intrinsic, is likely to be of importance where certainty rather than informativeness is crucial.

To say that certainty and informativeness are logically opposed does not mean that they may not be complementary. Ritual occurrences may signal conditions or situations and changes in them unambiguously – they are in Bateson's terms "context markers" (1972a: 289). Within the contexts established with certainty by the occurrence of a ritual there is opportunity for continuous and sensitive interpretation of more informative messages. But more than that, the occurrence of the ritual may even set the terms of such interpretation, for words, gestures and even facial expression and unconscious body movement may mean different things in different contexts. To dance at someone else's *kaiko* is very different for a Maring man from dancing at his own dance ground for pleasure. The same words uttered in court and at a cocktail party do not mean the same thing, and similar emotions are likely to be exhibited in these places in different ways. But the contexts marked by ritual are not confined to the rituals themselves; the words, expressions and gestures of an initiated man may have to be interpreted differently from those of an uninitiated youth. In sum, the certainty of ritual occurrence helps to guide sensitivity and attentiveness to appropriate interpretations of highly informative but vague and ambiguous messages.

18 The term "coherence" refers to the extent to which a change in the state of one component of a system effects changes in others. In a fully coherent system a change in any component results in immediate and proportional changes in all of the others (Hall and Fagan 1956).

4   Enactments of meaning

1 Maring dancing and *rumbim* planting are instances in which the performer transforms his own state, but not all instances of ritual transformations are self-transformations. One or more participants may change the condition of others. For an authorized person to recite a proper formula, like "I dub thee to knighthood" and perhaps to perform a proper accompanying action, like touching a kneeling man on the shoulder with a sword, is not simply to tell him to be a knight or how to be a knight. It makes him a knight and as such it indicates to him and to others that he is now a knight.

2 Foucault (1990: 92) has written that

> power must be understood in the first instance as the multiplicity of force relations immanent in the sphere in which they operate and which constitute their own organization; as the process which, through ceaseless struggles and confrontations, transforms, strengthens, or reverses them; as the support which those force relations find in one another, thus forming a chain or system, or on the contrary, the disjunctions and contradictions which isolate them from one another; and lastly, as the strategies in which they take effect, whose general design or institutional crystallization is embodied in the state apparatus, in the formulation of the law, in the various social hegemonies.

Little is to be gained by railing against others' use of words, particularly when they become as well-established as Foucault's influential definition. Foucault's conception, developed in a discussion centrally concerned with the social forces shaping sexuality is, commendably, concerned not so much with developing a theory of power as an analytic of power (1990: 82ff., *passim*). It nevertheless seems to me that such a view, despite its emphasis on analysis, can obscure fundamental differences in the nature of the efficacy of different agencies, particularly in the degree to which they are based on either physical or communicational principles. Why, for instance, does the receiver of a directive (a command, or rule, or policy statement, or declamation of principle) act in conformity to that directive? Is it that the authority (a locus in a communication network from which directives flow) is physically powerful (can bring physical force to bear upon recalcitrants), is taken to be "authoritative" (i.e., expert), is persuasive, or is sacred or sanctified? I reserve the term "power" to refer to forces or capabilities amenable to description and assessment in terms of the metrics of matter and energy, recognizing that there are other grounds upon whch authorities can stand. This is in accord with the usage of Richard Bierstadt (1950: 737).

3 This is hardly grounds for unmitigated satisfaction. The greater the information-processing capacity of a system and the greater the variety of stimuli from which it can derive information and other forms of meaning, the greater its capacity for error, disconsonance, inconsistency and confusion.

4 It is not impossible that technologically developed and literate societies, while possessing in total higher information storage and processing capacities than small technologically undeveloped non-literate societies, make lower information processing demands upon their individual members. My use of the term "information" in this passage is meant to suggest that inter-societal differences in the processing of messages is greatest with respect to low-order meaning, that is, information in the narrow sense. Technical and economic development is correlated with the elaboration of information processing. Our discussion in chapter 3 suggests, conversely, that the elaboration of information processing may damage, degrade, or reduce the communication of higher-order meanings.

5 This obviously suggests that the general nature of the adult identities toward which ontogeny strives is likely to be very different in societies in which meaningful rites of passage guide social maturation from those in which such rites are weak or absent.

6 An act or utterance is said to have illocutionary force if it achieves its effect *in* its very utterance or enactment. An effect is intrinsic to an illocutionary act or performance; the concept of illocutionary force is a secular equivalent of the doctrine of *ex opera operato*, explicitly specifying the efficacy of the sacraments of Roman Catholicism, but implicit in the thought and practice of other religious traditions. In contrast, an act or utterance is said to have perlocutionary force if it achieves its result *through* its effect upon receivers. Its effect is not intrinsic to the act or utterance itself, but is realized only if the act or utterance persuades, threatens, cajoles (or whatever) some party into taking action. (Austin 1962, esp. Lecture VIII).

7 In previous publications I used the term "factitive." Because the primary meaning of factitive is grammatical, I am reviving the obsolete first meaning of factive, "tending or having the power to make," supplemented by a more recent meaning: "to make ... a thing to be of a certain character by word or thought" (Oxford English Dictionary).

8 The identification of two classes of performative, factives and commissives, is sufficient for our purposes, but it does not conform to Austin's taxonomy. He identified five classes (1962: 150ff.).

   1 *Verdictives*, "typified by the giving of a verdict," but including also less formal judgements, e.g., assessing, grading, ranking.

2 *Exercitives*, "the exercising of powers, rights, or influence," e.g., appointing, voting, ordering.

3 *Commissives*, "typified by promising; they commit you to do something."

4 *Behabitives*, "a very miscellaneous group ... [having] to do with attitudes and *social behavior* ... apologizing, congratulating, commending, condoling, cursing and challenging" (emphasis in original)

5 *Expositives*, "make plain how our utterances fit into an argument or conversation, how we are using words or are, in general, expository ... I argue, I concede, I illustrate ... I postulate."

These categories are obviously not mutually exclusive. Austin also notes that the distinction between performatives and statements, reports, and descriptions (the class of expressions he calls "constatives (1962: 3)) is not always sharp and it is clear that illocutionary acts often possess perlocutionary force as well. Austin did not identify factives at all, but it is further clear that they cross-cut at least two of his categories, and that some (e.g., "we declare peace") have commissive entailments. All in all, it is better to regard Austin's categories, and the term "factive" as well, as designations of illocutionary *functions* rather than of distinct classes of expressions.

9 Whereas participation is, in its nature, free of ambiguity, it is obvious, but nevertheless important to note, that non-participation is not. A person's absence from a ritual may indicate non-acceptance, but it is also possible that he has a bad cold, had a previous engagement, broke his leg, or ran off with his secretary.

10 The strong form of the argument is that there is no obligation in the absence of an act of acceptance. A weaker form would hold that acts of acceptance do establish obligations, but that some obligations may exist in the absence of such acts. They may, for instance, be taken to inhere in certain relationships (e.g., a mother may be deemed to have a "natural obligation" to protect her helpless infant). Both the strong and weak forms support the account of ritual acceptance argued in this chapter.

11 Relevant definitions of convention include: A rule or practice based on general consent, or accepted and upheld by society at large (Oxford English Dictionary #10); General agreement on or acceptance of certain practices or attitudes (American Heritage Dictionary 3rd edition, #3); A practice or procedure widely observed in a group, especially to facilitate social interaction; a custom (American Heritage Dictionary 3rd edition, #4).

12 The choice of the gender-specific word "men" in this sentence is not to be taken to be sexist. It recognizes that authority extending beyond the nuclear family has, in pre-state societies, generally been vested in adult males.

13 This implies that many factives, for instance those establishing peace, are commissives as well, for the states of affairs that they establish imply obligations to behave in some ways and not in others (see Searle 1969, esp. chapter 8). Maring dancing and *rumbim* planting are instances in which the performer transforms his own state, but not all instances of ritual transformations are self-transformations. One or more participants may change the

condition of others. For an authorized person to recite a proper formula, like "I dub thee to knighthood" and perhaps to perform a proper accompanying action, like touching a kneeling man on the shoulder with a sword, is not simply to tell him to be a knight or how to be a knight. It makes him a knight and as such it indicates to him and to others that he is now a knight.

5   Word and act, form and substance

1 Augustine's doctrine of grace, however, and his connection of grace to certain rituals, especially baptism, did provide grounds for the narrower conception of sacrament that came into vogue in the twelfth and thirteenth centuries and was made doctrine in the sixteenth (Lacey 1918: 905).

2 The "big bang" theory of the origins of the universe commences creation with an undifferentiated and compacted mass of matter-energy sometimes referred to as "ylem" (from the Greek *hyle*, substance).

3 Although a terminological distinction is lacking, the Navajo distinguish conceptually words on the one hand and language as a system on the other. Language and word (*saad*) and speech (*yati*) are terminologically distinguished (Witherspoon 1977: 40ff.).

4 To say that alternative increases possibilities for disorder is not to deny alternative's role in the maintenance of order.

6   Time and liturgical order

1 The attribution of recurrence always entails the abstraction of some elements of the performance from the total, of course, simply because no performance could possibly duplicate another in all of its detail (and if it did it could carry few self-referential messages). The emphasis upon punctiliousness of performance is of especial interest in this regard. No matter how punctilious recurrence is, its recognition as such is always in some degree conventional, and societies differ in the degrees of variation they take to fall within recurrence's acceptable limits.

2 The term "succession" is applied to things other than periods, of course, notably persons and regimes. Edward VII, for instance, succeeded Victoria. This usage is in its nature ordinal but, further, it strongly implies, if it does not actually entail, the notion of periods. We speak of the Victorian and Edwardian "periods," the "Kennedy Years," the "Johnson Era."

3 The transformation of processual phases into distinct periods is not a cognitive or epistemic action exclusive to ritual. Paleontologists and geologists distinguish very long temporal units in formally similar fashion. The longest such units recognized, "eras", all but one of which (the Cenozoic) were hundreds of millions of years in length, are distinguished by the evolution of distinctive fauna during each of them and, in the cases of the succession of the Paleozoic by the Mesozoic and the Mesozoic by the Cenozoic, are thought to have been more or less radically separated from each other by massive extinctions.

4 There are in the West two celestially founded temporal orders, both of great antiquity: the astronomical and the astrological. They are, while related, different in content and very different in emphasis and in what they order. In

both orders, however, the movements of relevant celestial bodies are fixed, and predictable.

5 But both Becker (1979: 198ff.), and Geertz (1973: 393) note that one of the ten concurrent Balinese "cycles" is only one day long.

6 Lévi-Strauss' "mechanical time" is very similar to what Evans-Pritchard meant by "structural time," it being "reversible and non-cumulative. "Statistical time," in contrast, which is characteristic of historical studies, is "oriented and non-reversible" (Lévi-Strauss 1953: 530).

7 As noted in chapter 3, principal antagonists do not appeal to other local groups as such to aid them in warfare. Rather, their individual members appeal to their affines and cognates elsewhere to "help them fight." Because intergroup marriage frequencies are strongly correlated with proximity, more Kungagai-Merkai were married to Kamungagai-Tsembaga than to the more distant Kungagai and, similarly, the Kamungagai-Tsembaga had exchanged more women with the Kungagai-Merkai than with the more distant Dimbagai-Yimyagai. Therefore, considerably larger contingents from each of the two clusters supported each other than went to the aid of the other's enemies. The alignments were not altogether clear and clean, however. Some Kamungagai did come to the aid of the Dimbagai-Yimyagai and, subsequently, some Dimbagai-Yimyagai did take refuge with Kamungagai.

8 Fusion was still less than complete, however. The five clans comprising Tsembaga in 1962 were organized into three subterritorial units: (1) the eastern, consisting of the Merkai clan only (Kungagai was locally extinct, although the appellation "Kungagai-Merkai" was still current); (2) the central, consisting of a cluster of three clans, Tsembaga, Tomegai and Kwibagai, but known by the cluster name "Tsembaga-Tomegai"; (3) the western, consisting only of the Kamungagai clan. Each had planted and uprooted its own (sub-territorial) *rumbim*. For them to have joined in planting a single *rumbim* would have indicated further fusion, social and territorial as well as ritual, because it would have entailed the dissolution of boundaries between sub-territories and, possibly, corresponding cessation of inter-marriage, when cognatic replaced affinal relations as both the ground of social cohesion and as the basis of access to garden land (see Rappaport 1984: 20). Such fusion between the Kamungagai and the central cluster seemed to be in progress in 1962–1964 for the boundary between their lands was becoming indistinct, and, probably as a correlate of warfare (which had ended less than a decade earlier) and the need to maintain fighting strength, grants in garden land, permanent as well as usufructory, were freely given by members of all local clans to members of all local clans. In subsequent years, however, as a correlate and probable consequence of peace, (1) *kaiko* were discontinued by the Tsembaga (although not all other Maring groups), and (2) fission progressed between what were in 1981–1982 the eastern cluster (now the Merkai and the Kwibagai) and the western cluster (Kamungagai and Tsembaga; Tomegai had accreted to the Tsembaga clan), fissioning was indicated by a) separate conduct of certain important community rituals (especially those concerned with trapping and smoking marsupials) and b) the commencement of ceremonial exchanges between the two clusters. I take this

fissioning to have followed from relaxation of the need to assure all potential local warriors with sufficient garden land, as a consequence of enduring peace. It was striking that in 1981–1982 people gardened almost exclusively on the lands of their own sub-clan; even usufructory grants of garden land were extremely rare, grants in perpetuity, even to sub-clan brothers, were virtually nonexistent, and grants to other than clansmen that had, in the early sixties, been phrased as "in perpetuity" had, by and large, lapsed.

9 It is sufficient to note in passing that for a social unit to distinguish or separate itself from others by changes in its liturgical schedule is reminiscent of phenomena observed among nonhuman species. When closely related species again become sympatric after having been separated, the scheduling of their courtship rituals may change, becoming increasingly distinct from each other. This reduces the likelihood of inappropriate matings (Cullen 1966).

10 It also might not be amiss to propose that the Maring ritual cycle constitutes, or at least codifies, the relations of production of Maring society. By "relations of production" I mean the social relations ordering the material processes of production and the disposition of that which is produced. As such, the ritual cycle is the locus of the assumptions in accordance with which economizing behavior is organized, and morality judged, as well as of some of the specific considerations in terms of which that behavior proceeds.

To argue that ritual among the Maring is an organizing principle commensurate with capitalism, feudalism or oriental despotism, principles in accordance with which relations of production are organized in other societies, is obviously not to argue that wherever ritual appears it has such a role. Ritual is everywhere; the comprehensive regulation of production, reproduction, exchange and belligerence by ritual *per se* is probably confined to simple societies and, perhaps, to certain archaic states.

11 Eliade might have taken *rumbim* to constitute a type of *Axis Mundi*.

7 Intervals, eternity, and communitatis

1 It is hardly necessary to point out that many or even most Western religious rituals are deficient in rhythmicity.

2 Frederick C. Adams and Gregory Laughlin predict the universe will come to what may be considered its end 10^{100} years from now, give or take a few trillion years, with black holes larger than galaxies which will have evaporated, only waste products remaining: mostly photons of enormous wavelength, neutrinos, electrons and positrons. Adams, Fred and Gregory Laughlin, "A Dying Universe," *Reviews of Modern Physics*, April 1997.

8 Simultaneity and hierarchy

1 It takes up to four generations to abrogate all taboos between the descendants of principal antagonists.

2 Antagonists are not in direct communication. They are informed of each other's general intentions by neutrals.

3 That I have deliberately avoided the term "symbol" in the foregoing discussion can have escaped the notice of few readers. "Symbol" is used in many ways and as such always requires definition or discussion, if misunderstanding

is to be avoided. It is well, therefore, to reaffirm here the conception of it adopted in the first chapter where, following Peirce, symbols were taken to be signs associated by law or convention with that which they signify. As such, symbols stand in contrast to icons or indices. Given this usage, the reasons for my reluctance to follow other authors in referring to canonical signs as "ritual" symbols should be clear, for the relationships of canonical signs to their significata are not in all cases symbolic in Peirce's sense. Some authors have, in fact, emphasized other sorts of signifier–signified relations in the very act of labelling canonical signs as "symbols." Paul Tillich, for instance, long ago distinguished what he called symbols (by which he meant canonical signs most importantly) from other signs by proposing that a symbol "participates in that to which it points" (1957: 42). A vague notion of identification if not indexicality seems explicit in such participation. John Beattie suggested the iconicity of liturgical elements in arguing that the relationship between what he (in agreement with many others) called symbols and their significata is not arbitrary. They are joined by an "underlying rationale" or appropriateness: the serpent eating its own tail signifies eternity; the large-headed owl, wisdom; whiteness, purity and virtue (1964: 69ff.).

I do not deny the iconic characteristics of canonical signs, and their indexical qualities, which have already been discussed at length. I simply assert that because ritual signs stand in indexical and iconic, as well as in what Charles Sanders Peirce called "symbolic" relationships with their significata, to call them symbols at best slights their semiotic complexity and, at worst, may lead us to overlook their important iconic qualities and indexical virtues. I therefore prefer to refer to them as "canonical (or liturgical) signs" or as "ritual representations."

The term "representation" may also raise some problems. John Skorupski has noted (1976: 119ff.) that designators are of two types, those that name or denote on the one hand and those that represent on the other. Thus "Fido" names or denotes a particular dog. It does not represent him. In contrast, a serpent eating his own tail may represent eternity, but it does not name or denote it, and, similarly, whiteness does not denote or name purity, but it does represent it. Skorupski argues that because the term "symbol" has been used to refer to both denotative and representational designators confusion has resulted, and our understanding of symbolic actions has been hampered. He recommends, therefore, that the term "symbol" be reserved for representational designators only, those that simply name or denote to be called something else. This strategy, he thinks, is justified because of the importance of representations in ritual, particularly in magical ritual which is his special concern.

Thus the symbol substitutes for the thing symbolized. We are sometimes said to think in words – certainly we communicate with each other in words. *In* words *about* things ... The symbol is itself made the object of thought. It stands for, or *re-presents*, the thing symbolised. In other words, it makes it present to the senses, and is treated for the purposes of symbolic action as being what is symbolised. On this picture the logic of a symbolic action is clear: it represents or enacts an action, event or state of affairs in which the thing represented by the symbolic plays a part analogous to that which the symbol plays in the symbolic action itself.   *(1976: 123)*

Skorupski's account conforms well to both the contagious and sympathetic principles of magical efficacy and to a performative theory of occult efficacy generally. His distinction between representation and denotation is also important and useful, and he deserves our thanks for calling attention to it, providing as it does additional reasons to account for the substantial nature of liturgical signs. It nevertheless seems to me that nothing is gained and much is lost by reserving the term "symbol" for representational designators only. To call signs that represent "symbols" and signs that denote by a different name is to distinguish them too radically. On the other hand, to distinguish in a rough way between "representational symbols" and "denotative symbols" is not only to recognize their general similarities as well as their specific differences, but also encourages examination of the relationship between denotation and representation. It is worth noting in this regard that the representation of concepts which are themselves devoid of material significata is obviously contingent upon prior denotation. The Worm Ourabouros, the serpent that consumes its own tail, could not represent eternity had not eternity first been denoted, nor the large-headed bird wisdom until wisdom was named. These examples lead back to an earlier point. Although *all* denotation may be symbolic in Peirce's sense and although *some* representations are symbolic, representation is not limited to the use of symbols. The representation of wisdom by the owl is surely iconic and, as I argued in chapter 4, the representation of acceptance by ritual participation, being performative, is indexical.

Denotations, joined with icons and indices, are transformed in ritual into representations. Once such a representation is brought into being, it may be "treated as being what is signified." We come upon another reason for the use of objects or substances and the use of the body in canonical signs. When that which is represented is abstract or ineffable but the representation is substantial, the representation invests that which it signifies with reality. It is, moreover, much easier to operate upon representations if they are substantial. We may recall here Bateson's observation (1972f: 183) that "in the dim area where art, magic and religion overlap" there may be "an attempt to deny the difference between map and territory" characteristic of representative symbols and of thought founded upon them.

4 Firstness contrasts with two other conditions of consciousness for Peirce, Secondness and Thirdness. Whereas Firstness is "What the world was to Adam on the day he opened his eyes to it, before he had drawn any distinctions, or had become conscious of his own existence – that is first, present, immediate, fresh, new, original, spontaneous, free, vivid, conscious, and evanescent" (Peirce in Hoopes 1991: 189) and, we may add, absolutely inarticulate, Secondness is "dyadic, or reactive, relations between things," "the process of action and reaction when one object strikes another" (both citations Hoopes 1991: 10). "We find Secondness in occurrence because an occurrence is something whose existence consists in our knocking up against it" (Peirce in Hoopes 1991: 189). Then there is Thirdness. "Besides material force or Secondness, there is another kind of real relation that Peirce called Thirdness and we call intelligence – the representation of one object to a

second by a third, which is the essence of his semiotic" (Hoopes 1991: 10). It is "the universe of mental, i.e., cognitive, phenomena" (Hoopes 1991: 13), "the relation of one object to a second by the representation of a third, a sign" (Hoopes 1991: 116). See also Carrington (1993: ch. 3).

5 Such permanent modifications of the flesh as circumcision do not exhaust incarnation. Ritual gestures and postures may also be counted in the category, differing from those incised upon the body not merely in being both impermanent and less radically transformative but in less obvious ways. Once the scar is in the flesh the body continually, perpetually and irrevocably carries its signification. The significance of the stylized gesture or posture, in contrast, is realized in transitory acts, and its perpetuation therefore depends upon repetition. Whereas the individual is linked to the significata of the ritual scar that he bears by the fortitude of a moment or an hour in his youth, the performer of a regularly repeated gesture or posture is linked to the significatum of that gesture or posture by loyalty, a loyalty not to be denigrated if it has become simply habitual. Habit or loyalty that has become virtually autonomic has become an aspect of one's identity, and there may be other social, emotional and cognitive gratifications and rewards of participation. One may, of course, stop participating, cutting oneself away from the benefits and obligations that follow from accepting, and such an option may be less easily available to one who has been scarified. It also may be quite self-alienating.

6 See also "On cognized models", in Rappaport 1979a.

9   The idea of the sacred

1 To say that kingship is *established* in ritual is not to claim that it *originated* in ritual. The sense in which the term "establish" is to be understood here was noted in chapter 4. To establish a convention is to *stipulate* and *accept* it. It could be argued, however, that kingship in a narrow sense may always and everywhere be grounded in ritual, for kings are not simply powerful authorities. They are leaders who have been set apart from others, first by such criteria as hereditary eligibility and seniority and, subsequently, by such ritual acts as crowning. Kingship is always, or almost always, "sacred or sanctified kingship" if such phrases are taken to cover not only institutions in which the monarch is either divine himself, as in Ancient Egypt, or descended from deities, as among ancient Germanic peoples (Chaney 1970, Wallace-Hadrill 1971), or in which "kingship is descended from Heaven," as in Sumer (Frankfort 1948: 237), but also those in which the king rules by "grace of God," or is elevated to the status by sacramental acts.

2 A "mystery properly so called" is, in Catholic thought, "a truth which, though not *against* reason, so far transcends it that no created intelligence could ever discover it, and is one which, even when it is revealed, is impenetrable by any created intelligence" (Attwatter 1961: 336).

3 In an earlier formulation I defined sanctity as the quality of unquestionableness imputed by a congregation to postulates which are in their nature neither verifiable nor falsifiable. I have modified this formulation here because of difficulties with respect to non-verifiability.

4 That all liturgies do allow some choice, and hence convey some information, has been discussed in earlier chapters of this book. This disagreement with the earlier argument may seem apparent but it is not real, for the choices through which *self-referential* information is transmitted do not reduce the invariance of the *canon*.

5 Such certainty may be devoid of information but is, of course, highly meaningful in an uncertain world. One may suggest that as information increases, meaning decreases, and that burgeoning information, even more than technical development and industrialization, is responsible for the crisis of meaning that has for some centuries been afflicting the west. We shall return to the matter of meaning in a later chapter.

6 There are instances in which they may, but, for reasons discussed in the final chapter, such a degree of specification is inappropriate to their unquestionable status and, for that reason, may cause problems for the social systems in which they occur.

7 An apparent (if almost trivial) exception may be Ultimate Sacred Postulates establishing members of pantheons in which there seems to be some sort of regional specialization, or division of labor among the deities (see Weber 1963 [1922]: chs. 1, 2). Although such exceptions do not seriously embarrass the argument of this essay as a whole, or even of this chapter, several responses may be made. These include, first, the suggestion that, when they are taken as wholes, relations among members of pantheons form coherent orders, and that, therefore, it is the comprehensive postulation of the entire pantheon and its structure which comprises the Ultimate Sacred Postulate. Another, and related, response might be that western understanding of ancient or alien polytheism has often been shallow and distorted, perhaps to show monotheism off to better advantage. More profound explanations of polytheistic systems tend to soften their contrasts with monotheism; in the philosophic versions of some of them what are popularly taken to be distinct beings are understood to be aspects of single entities or orders, or mere personifications of principles rather than deities. At the same time polytheistic tendencies and elements in so-called monotheistic religions: angels, archangels, cherubim, seraphim, saints, spirits, demons are played down.

8 This point was made to me by Robert Levy, as have many others which I have not acknowledged specifically.

9 An exception might be the commands of powerful authorities. We might say that such commands are unquestionable because those who issue them have the power to enforce their wills through coercion. This is clearly a different sense of unquestionable from the one under discussion here.

10 For a succinct summary, easily intelligible to non-specialists, see White 1971. See also George Pitcher (ed.), 1964.

11 There is also a general "coherence theory of truth," in rivalry with the correspondence theory. This is not alluded to here.

12 Veracity and verity are contrasted in the American Heritage Dictionary (1992): *Veracity* implies factual accuracy and honesty, principally with respect to spoken or written expression. *Verity* applies principally to an enduring or repeatedly demonstrated truth.

13 Bateson referred to these truths as "truths the validity of which depends upon belief." For reasons that should be now apparent I have replaced the term "belief" in his formulation with the term "acceptance." Bateson did not include sacred truths in his discussion.

14 See "The Logical Categories of Learning and Communication," (Bateson 1972a). In this essay, originally written in 1964, what he earlier called deutero-learning was renamed "Learning II."

15 I must hasten to state, to avoid being at odds with the ordinary experience of readers, that I claim that ritual is the *fundamental* context in which Ultimate Sacred Postulates may be learned, but it is not the only one. The literate may read them in such books as catechisms and scriptures; and they may be presented didactically by teachers to students in their classrooms. Didactic situations are, as a rule, set in ordinary periodic time, but didactic learning and teaching also differ from the ways in which lessons are taught by the daily events of one's life: walking through the forest in April, helping one's mother plant taro, watching one's father stalk deer and imitating him, seeing a sleeping child roll into the fire, or hearing a man cough until he dies. Didactic teaching may not require any sort of extrapolation or analysis by the learner. It is deliberately and artificially focused, and its lessons are much less variant than those of ordinary experience. It is always and necessarily derivative. The lessons of science, for instance, didactically taught and learned, are derived from the ordinary experience of scientists. The sacred truths presented didactically are derived from extraordinary contexts, in particular those of ritual.

10 Sanctification

1 It was, however, reported that Edward the Confessor, said to be the first English King to have cured the disease, effected cures before he came to the throne. Interestingly, Stuart pretenders as well as Stuart kings claimed the power to heal. In fact, one of the charges made at the trial of the Duke of Monmouth was that he had "touched children for the Evil," and the last recorded instance of the rite in Great Britain occurred when Prince Charles Edward, "Bonnie Prince Charlie," performed it in 1745. Performances of the ritual by unanointed pretenders were evidently attempts to legitimize their claims by demonstration of a charismatic power associated with sanctified kingship (Axon 1914: 736ff.).

2 The social and political problems set as well as solved by the sanctification of authorities may easily be discerned in such instances. The formal as well as the substantive characteristics of these problems will be discussed in the final chapter.

3 For a brief account of Maring taboos, see Rappaport 1984.

4 This is well illustrated in the Visigothic Code of seventh century Spain:

> No person is deserving of a pardon who is proved to have renounced a good religion for a bad one. Therefore, because a cruel and astounding act of presumption should be extirpated by a still more cruel punishment, we declare, by the following edict: that whenever it has been proved that a Christian, of either sex, and especially one born of Christian parents, has practiced circumcision, or any other Jewish rite (may God avert

this!) he shall be put to an ignominious death by the zeal and cooperation of Catholics, under the most ingenious and excruciating tortures that can be afflicted, [that he may learn] how horrible and detestable that offense is, which he has so infamously perpetrated.   *Lex Visigothorum, XII, 2,16 (642–652) (Hillgarth 1969: 102).*

Although persecuted by the Visigoths, born Jews were not treated as badly (see Coulton 1924: 19ff. for a discussion of Aquinas on "Heretics-Born").

5 It would probably be more proper to speak of comparative, relative or differential variance, for invariance is an absolute term. I shall persist in my usage because, although it may be improper in a strict sense, it conveys my meaning more clearly.

6 A common invocation to Red Spirits is *Runge-Yinge, Norum-Kombri, Ana-Koka, Kanan*! (Sun-Fire, Orchid-Cassowary, Father-Grandfather, Hear!).

7 I am brought here to a problem which may at first sight seem to vex the analysis being developed in this essay, but which, I think, besets the process the analysis attempts to elucidate. If the Torah not only has a regular place in the liturgical order but an especially venerable one, one set about with special acts and prohibitions, and if there is a correlation between invariance and sanctity, is not the Torah in its entirety part of the Ultimate Sacred Postulates of Judaism? Such a view seems to be represented in the mystical conception that "the Torah is not only made up of the names of God but is as a whole the one great Name of god" (Scholem 1969: 39), or even God himself. As Gikatila expressed it, "His Torah is in Him, and that is what the Kabbalists say, namely that the Holy One, blessed be He, is in His Name, and His Name is in Him, and that His Name is His Torah" (Scholem 1969: 44). Christian and Muslim fundamentalists similarly grant ultimate sacred status to the Bible and the Koran. In fact, the defining characteristic of fundamentalists is that they take their scripture in its entirety to be absolutely and literally true. It may be that the ascription of ultimate sacred status to, or even the apotheosis of, lengthy bodies of scripture is a syndrome to which literate societies are naturally prone.

The term "syndrome" denotes disorder. As we have seen, that which gains a place in canon and is set apart from the ordinary by special prescriptions, proscriptions and high punctiliousness thereby gains a high degree of sanctity, or may even be taken to be sacred. When that which is accorded sacred status is a lengthy scripture purporting, among other things, to give an account of history, it of course comes into conflict with the characterization of Ultimate Sacred Postulates as devoid, or almost devoid, of specific social and material significata. That characterization was qualified, of course, by the term "generally" or "usually," and as a descriptive statement it does seem to conform generally to the facts. Be this as it may, the formulation may now be given normative value. Ultimate Sacred Postulates *should* be devoid of, or low in, direct social and material import. Societies are of course free to bestow high degrees of sanctity or even ultimate sacred status upon sentences with highly specific social and material content, but for them to do so is to undermine the invulnerability of the sacred to falsification and to put sanctity's truths at a disadvantage in confrontations with propositions that can claim convincing empirical support. The contemporary assault upon the concept of evolution by fundamentalist advocates of special creation is an instance of actions following from an overspecification of the sacred which threatens to disgrace sanctity itself. Problems of a somewhat different sort arise when a society grants ultimately sacred, which is to say unquestionable, status to particular social rules or institutions. These problems have, in fact, afflicted Christianity, Judaism and Islam, and we shall return to them in the final chapter. The difficulties of scripture may be ameliorated in some degree by their cryptic nature, for that which is mysterious allows for, and even demands, interpretation. There remain, then, specific questions of interpretation. Nevertheless, literacy causes problems for the sacred as it does for the eternal.

8 This is not to say that ritual practice was standard throughout ancient Israel during all periods of its history. Worship in the sanctuaries, which were the places of sacrifice previous to the construction of the temple, surely varied and worship was never fully centralized at the temple (see de Vaux 1961 II: *passim*). Important differences also distinguished Palestinian and Babylonian practice after the destruction of the second temple (Idelsohn 1932: 31, *passim*).

9 The name "El," appears either by itself or in such combinations as "El-Bethel" at the sanctuary at Bethel, and "El'Olam" at Beersheba (de Vaux 1965 II: 294), as well as in "El Shadday." "El Elyon" and the familiar plural form "Elohim," were in use among the Canaanites, according to de Vaux (1961 II: 310, *passim*) and Freedman (1976: 60, *passim*). So was "Kedosh," "the Holy One" (Freedman 1976: 71). Kabod, "Glory," according to Dahood (1980: 57), should be understood as a Hebrew name for the divinity and was also the name of an Eblaite god in the third millennium, almost 1,000 years before Moses' time.

10 The name *Yahweh*, according to Freedman (1976: 98; personal communication) and others, was originally a verb, more particularly the causative form of the verb "to be." The name Yahweh Sabaoth, inscribed on the Ark itself, and thus for the followers of Moses the most sacred of the divine names, may well have been understood as "Creator of Hosts." Later, in post-exile times, the tetragrammaton YHVH, Yahweh, became "too sacred to be pronounced" (Pope 1965: xvi) and was replaced in prayer by the term *adonay*, "Lord," or "God." If the tetragrammaton was, indeed, derived from the verb "to be," this substitution resulted in an important change in meaning.

11 Chadwick writes, "Some modern writers have taken exception to this account on the ground that it presents an impossible combination of solar and lunar reckoning. The explanation, however, may be that the solar reckoning had begun to encroach on the lunar before the adoption of Christianity. Originally the year may have begun with the interlunium nearest to the winter solstice" (1910: 138).

12 This policy was outlined in some detail in a letter sent by Gregory to Abbot Mallitus, *en route* to Canterbury in the year 601 AD. The document is of sufficient interest to cite it at length:

> when Almighty God shall have brought you to our most reverend brother the Bishop Augustine, tell him that I have long been considering with myself about the case of the

Angli; to wit, that the temples of idols in that nation should not be destroyed, but that the idols themselves that are in them should be. Let blessed water be prepared, and sprinkled in these temples, and altars constructed, and relics deposited, since, if these same temples are well built, it is needful that they should be transferred from the worship of idols to the service of the true God; that, when the people themselves see that these temples are not destroyed, they may put away error from their heart, and knowing and adoring the true God, may have recourse with the more familiarity to the places they have been accustomed to. And, since they are wont to kill many oxen in sacrifice to demons, they should have also some solemnity of this kind in a changed form, so that on the day of dedication, or on the anniversaries of the holy martyrs whose relics are deposited there, they may make for themselves tents of the branches of trees around these temples that have been changed into churches, and celebrate the solemnity with religious feasts. Nor let them any longer sacrifice animals to the devil, but slay animals to the praise of God for their own eating, and return thanks to the Giver of all for their fullness, so that, while some joys are reserved to them outwardly, they may be able the more easily to incline their minds to inward joys. For it is undoubtedly impossible to cut away everything at once from hard hearts, since one who strives to ascend to the highest place must needs rise by steps or paces, and not by leaps. Thus to the people of Israel in Egypt the Lord did indeed make Himself known; but still He reserved to them in His own worship the use of the sacrifices which they were accustomed to offer to the devil, enjoining them to immolate animals in sacrifice to Himself; to that end that, their hearts being changed, they should omit some things in the sacrifice and retain others, so that, though the animals were the same as what they had been accustomed to offer, nevertheless, as they immolated them to God and not to idols, they should be no longer the same sacrifices. This then it is necessary for Your Love to say to our aforesaid brother, that he, being now in the country, may consider well how he should arrange all things.

(Reprinted in The Conversion of Western Europe 350–370, *ed. J. N. Hillgarth, 1969: 114)*

13 The replacement of divine descent by Christian ritual as the ground of kingship's sanctity was only gradual in England. In the Saxon chronicle, *sub anno* 865 (Ingram 1823: 95), more than two centuries after the conversion of Wessex to Christianity, the name "Woden" still appears in the genealogy of its king, Aethelwulf, father of Alfred the Great. This genealogy is of interest not only as a demonstration of the persistence in English Christianity of important elements antedating the introduction of its Ultimate Sacred Postulates, but also because it indicates the manner in which at least some of such elements were assimilated into Christian doctrine. By Aethelwulf's time Woden had become sixteenth in a line of descent from "Scaef; Lamech, Methusalem, Enoh, Jahred, Malalahel, Cainion, Enos, Set, Adam the first man, and Our Father, that is Christ. Amen" (Ingram 1823: 95–6). The line of descent from Scaef through Woden to Cerdic, founder of the house of Wessex from which English monarchs to this day claim to have sprung continues to appear in a booklet prepared for tourists and available at such historical monuments as Windsor Castle, with the admonishment that "it should be regarded as legendary" (Montague-Smith 1972: 5).

Chaney, citing Magoun, observes that "this 'arcane' transition makes the West Saxon rulers collateral relatives ... of our Lord" (1971: 41f.), and he notes a Welsh parallel in the court pedigree of Hywel the Good, a tenth century ruler, who traced his descent from

"Amalech who was the son of Beli the Great and his mother Anna whom they say to be the cousin of the Virgin Mary, the Mother of our Lord Jesus Christ"; since Anna is probably Ana, or Anu, a variant of Danu, the Earth Mother, and Beli Maur may well be the god Beli of Belenus, our Lord would be the relative of the Mother of the gods.   *(1970: 42)*

Other aspects of these syncretic genealogies are of interest in the present discussion. In the West Saxon case, at least, it is clear that an old Ultimate Sacred Postulate – concerning the existence of Woden – is subordinated to, and made contingent upon, the new. As a mere descendant of Noah his existence originates in time, in contrast to "Our Father, that is Christ," who stands at the beginning of time. As a descendant of men, even of mythic men, his divinity is impugned, and as a man, albeit a legendary one, he is subordinate to the order of the Christian God. The genealogy of Aethelwulf at one and the same time both perpetuates the royal claim, perhaps still politically useful, to extraordinary descent and finally, two centuries after the conversion of Wessex, gives up the notion that extraordinary descent is from a figure who is himself divine.

14 Within a few hundred years, four fundamental liturgical types, Antiochian, Alexandrian, Gallican and Roman had appeared, and the first three each included several yet more culturally specific "Rites," that is, variant liturgical orders. The "family" of Antiochian Rites, for instance, includes an East Syrian branch, composed of the Nestorian, Chaldean and Malabar Rites, and a West Syrian group which includes Jacobite, Maronite, Armenian and Byzantine Rites. Some of these culturally specific orders eventually disappeared. The Celtic Liturgies of the Gallican group, which were celebrated in Brittany, Ireland, Scotland, Wales and parts of England for hundreds of years after these regions were converted to Christianity, were replaced by Roman usage between the ninth and twelfth centuries (John Miller 1959: 46ff.).

11 Truth and order

1 In Ralph Manheim's translation, the neologism "essent" is introduced to stand for the German "philosophical invention," *seiend* (Manheim 1959: viii). I could see no reason to introduce either of these strange terms here and have rather used the approximation suggested by Manheim himself on the first page of his translation.

2 This phrase is the meaning Heidegger gives to *xynon*, which G. Kirk (1954) glosses as "common" in the sense of both "shared" and "universal," but it does seem a reasonable gloss in some contexts.

3 For discussions of the place of fire in Heraclitus see, in addition to G. Kirk (1954), William C. Kirk, Jr., *Fire in the Cosmologocal Speculations of Heracleitus* (Minneapolis, Burgers Publishing, 1940).

4 Kirk tranaslates Fragment 50 in its entirety as: "Listening not to me [Heraclitus] but to the Logos it is wise to agree that all things are one" (G. Kirk 1954: 65). In admonishing his auditors to "listen not to [him] but to the Logos," Heraclitus is proposing that "all things are one," are not mere *doxa*, even his own, but of the Logos.

5 I am uncomfortable with the pretentious quality of the Greek plural in English, but the alternatives seem worse. The awfulness of the Anglicized "logoses" speaks for itself. A Latinized compromise, "logi" might be accept-

able, were it not for the word "logy" which, although it seems to be disappearing, continues to denote a feeling of heaviness or dullness consequent to constipation. The best course is to avoid the plural whenever possible by employing circumlocutions taking the singular.

6 Contradictions are, of course, to be expected in a mythos that developed over a period of 3,000 years, one that is notorious for local variation and from the terminus of which we are seperated by another 2,000 years.

7 Flinders Petrie (1912: 248) suggests that she was devoid of personality, a mere theological abstraction, and for this reason Akenaten did not, in the course of his short-lived religious revolution, proscribe the use of her name along with those of all other deities save Aten's. It may also be that Ma'at herself was never worshipped. There is difference of opinion on this. James Baikie claimed unequivocally that "no image of Ma'at was ever made for worship (1914: 133), while in another essay in the same volume Weidemann stated that Ma'at, who became a goddess, was "worshipped in a number of temples as a woman with the symbol for truth [a feather] upon her head. Further, the particular truth which dwelt in a particular man or deity could become incarnate in a similar figure and this type of truth might be eaten or drunk, while the king might offer it to the deity" (1914: 91). Finally, and most importantly, the relatively minor position of the goddess Ma'at in the pantheon does not seem to be sufficiently prominent to represent the sovereignty of an ordering principle to which gods as well as humans are subordinate. This may be ethnocentric, of course. At any rate, the implication is that the representations of Ma'at as a seated woman with a feather on her head were not of a goddess, but should be regarded as a mere personification of an abstraction, much like the contemporary representations of justice. Her representation as a daughter of Re, similarly, may have been a metaphor for the ineluctable statement of order intrinsic to the sun's movements. There may, of course, have been differences among various components of the population and in different places at different times in whether Ma'at was worshipped as a divinity or regarded as a principle to which even the divine was subordinate.

8 Zoroastrianism may be much older. The dates of the prophet Zoroaster himself are unclear, and there seems to be enormous disagreement among contemporary scholars on what may be likely. Zaehner (1961: 33) suggests 628–551 BC for his lifetime, and this seems to reflect majority opinion in a general and approximate way. Boyce (1979: 2), in marked contrast, says "It is impossible ... to establish fixed dates for his life; but there is evidence to suggest that he flourished when the Stone Age was giving way for the Iranians to the Bronze Age, possibly, that is, between about 1700 and 1500 BC."

9 Seven, if the Godhead, Ahura Mazda, is included; six if not. Masani speaks of seven, Windfuhr, following Lommel (1930), speaks of six.

10 The others Vohu Manah, Good Mind; Khshathra, Absolute Power or Good Rule; Armaiti, Devotion, Humility; Haurvatat, Perfection, Completeness, Health; Ameretat, Immortality (from Masani 1968 and Windfuhr 1976).

11 "Avesta" is the collective term for the Zoroastrian scriptural canon.

12 The numinous, the Holy and the divine

1 Four constituents of the Holy were noted in chapter 1: The Sacred, The Numinous, The Occult, and The Divine. Of these, the Sacred and The Numinous are fundamental, The Occult and The Divine derivative.

2 Some Ultimate Sacred Postulates may come very close to being, if not falsifiable, at least vulnerable to invalidation. Those proclaiming the divinity of living monarchs come to mind.

3 All Ultimate Sacred Postulates do have social import in that they provide a ground for distinguishing those who accept them from those who do not.

4 The edition to which citations refer is that published by Collier Books, 1961. A more recent edition, with an introduction by Jaroslav Pelikan, was published by Vintage Books in 1990.

5 James also seems to have distrusted institutionalized religion, taking it to be easily corruptible and potentially vicious:

> The baseness so commonly charged to religion's account are ... almost all of them, not chargeable at all to religion proper, but rather to religion's wicked practical partner, the spirit of corporate dominion. And the bigotries are most of them in their turn chargeable to religion's wicked intellectual partner, the spirit of dogmatic dominion, the passion for laying down the law in the form of an absolutely closed-in theoretic system. The ecclesiastical [i.e., institutional] spirit in general is the sum of these two spirits of dominion; and I beseech you never to confound the phenomena of mere tribal or corporate psychology which it presents with those manifestations of the purely interior life which are the exclusive object of our study.   (*W. James 1961: 269*)

6 James made explicit that the term "divine," in his usage, did not entail personification. "when in our definition of religion we speak of the individuals' relation to 'what he considers divine' we must interpret the term 'divine' very broadly, as denoting any object that is Godlike, whether it be a concrete deity or not" (1961: 44f.).

7 It seems clear that the sort of ritual learning Wallace describes is not appropriate for learning such mundane procedures as planting sweet potatoes, tending yams, or tracking game.

8 The bipolar nature of ritual representations emphasized by Turner (1973) and Campbell (1959: 461 ff.) is of importance in ontogeny. Such representations simultaneously signify cosmic and social conceptions on the one hand and psychic and physiological experience on the other. Through their mediation the conceptual is given the power of the experiential and the experiential the guidance of the conceptual. The experiential is "sublimated," which is to say made sublime, the conceptual is "revitalized" or made "urgent." The relationship here between conceptual form and experiential substance in representations affecting ontogeny is reminiscent of the account of creation offered in chapter 5.

9 Innumerable instances of voluntary martyrdom, it seems to me, can reasonably be accepted as indices of belief or conviction. It seems at least plausible to account for instances in which people chose to die rather than renounce Ultimate Sacred Postulates they had accepted by conviction.

10 In the course of their histories, religions – movements, denominations, cults – seem to proceed from early stages in which numinousness or enthusiasm is predominant to later stages in which heavier reliance is placed upon more

formal acceptance. Revitalizing efforts, both inside and outside organized religions in these later stages, are common and varied, as we can easily observe in contemporary society.

13 Religion in adaptation

1 This definition differs from earlier ones I have offered in that the earlier ones located the source of perturbation in the environment alone. It is also well to note that "environment" is not synonymous with "ecosystem," and here is meant to include cultural and social as well as physical and biotic elements.

2 A clan, for instance, may include sub-clans and itself be included in a phratry.

3 Systemic homeostasis may be given specific, if not always precise, meaning if it is conceived of as a set of ranges of viability on a corresponding set of variables abstracted from what, for independently established empirical or theoretical reasons, are taken to be conditions vital to the persistence of a system. This is to say that any process, physiological, behavioral, cultural, or genetic, that tends to keep the states of crucial variables (e.g., body temperature, population size, protein intake, energy flux) within ranges of viability or tends to return them to such ranges should they depart from them may be taken, other things being equal, to be adaptive.

4 The American Heritage Dictionary, 3rd edition, defines cybernetics as "the theoretical study of communication and control processes in biological, mechanical, and electronic systems, especially the comparisons of these processes in biological and artifical systems."

5 Indices reinforce symbols by establishing indexical relations between symbols. Such a relationship always exists when performative acts are performed: if a conventional act brings a conventional state of affairs into being it cannot help but indicate that state of affairs.

6 There are, of course, instances in which structural responses to specific problems have not reduced long-term flexibility. The evolution of the human hand provides an example.

7 It follows that it is possible to distinguish transformations of differing degrees of profundity. "Low-order" transformations, transformations of the[bold] internal structure of specific subsystems, may be occurring more or less continuously, but because complex living systems are, to use Simon's (1969) phrase, "loosely coupled," their effects may be confined to the subsystems in which they occur. High-order transformations, transformations in the structure of more inclusive systems, are rarer and, of course, their effects are more profound. To speak, simply, of structural transformations is not sufficient, but there are possibilities for identifying transformations of different order and to consider relations – temporal, causal, and formal – among these transformations. We shall touch upon related matters later.

Whereas the adaptive structure of all living systems must share certain fundamental features – hierarchical organization and both self-regulating and self-transforming properties (see Piaget 1971) – those of different classes surely differ in important respects. There are, for instance, differences among hierarchies in the extent to which they are organized in accordance with segmentary or sectorial principles (we may be reminded that in the former, subsystems at each level are structural-functional equivalents, in the latter they are specialized.) The increasing differentiation, in the course of evolution, of discrete special-purpose subsystems in organisms, societies, and ecosystems has been called "Progressive Segregation," and it is often accompanied in organisms and social systems, but not ecosystems, by increasing centralization of regulatory operation, or "Progressive Centralization." In organisms, we note the elaboration of central nervous systems, in societies the development of administrative structures. This contrast between the development of ecological and other systems may rest upon their contrasting bases for order maintenance. The basis of orderliness in ecosystems seems to shift, in the course of their development from "pioneer" to "mature" stages, from a reliance upon the resilience of individual organisms to a reliance upon the increasing redundance of matter and energy pathways resulting from increasing species diversity. These contrasting bases of order maintenance may, in turn, reflect differences in the degrees of coherence that different classes of systems require and can tolerate. Whereas anthropologists traditionally have been concerned with the ways in which the various components of socio-cultural systems are bound together – the jargon is "integrated" – they have generally ignored the ways in which the parts and processes of such systems are buffered from each other and each other's disruptions. I further suggest that organisms are, and in their nature must be, more coherent than social systems, and social systems more coherent than ecosystems. As a rule of thumb, the more inclusive the system, the less coherent it is and must be. The less inclusive the system, the more its internal orderliness and the effectiveness of its activities depends upon the fine coordination of its parts. An organism requires and can tolerate closer coordination of the activities of its parts than societies, and societies more (at least from time to time) than ecosystems. Coordination is probably facilitated by[bold] centralization, hence progressive centralization in organisms and societies, but not ecosystems.

  8 They are, of course, always to at least some degree open to interpretation and reinterpretation by living agents.

  9 I refer doubters to any and every piece of American currency.

10 For Catholics, a "Mystery properly so called ... is a truth which, though it is not against reason, so far transcends it that no created intelligence could even discover it and which, even when it is revealed, is in its nature impenetrable by any created intelligence." An example is the Trinitarian nature of the Divine (Attwater 1961: 336).

14 The breaking of the Holy and its salvation

  1 It seems noteworthy that the violence of religious persecution may be directly related to the cultural similarities of the antagonistic groups: the greater the similarities the crueler the persecution. Christian societies throughout the post-Roman and medieval periods dealt with their own heretics much more harshly than they did with culturally distinctive infidels.

  2 Exceptions to this generalization are constituted by instances, particularly in ancient empires and certain chiefdoms, in which the king, chief, or emperor is understood to be divine.

3 A possible lesson: even if, as this account suggests, a problem inheres "naturally " in "the human condition" it is not thereby inevitable or incorrigible. The scope of the social formations within which peace prevails now reaches the hundreds of millions.

4 A somewhat more recent statement in this same spirit was Charles Wilson's response to a question put to him during Senate confirmation hearings on his appointment to the position of Secretary of Defense during the Eisenhower administration. Asked if he thought that there might be a conflict of interest between his position as president of General Motors, a prime defense contractor, and his appointment as Secretary of Defense, he replied "What's good for General Motors is good for America."

5 To agree in the widest sense with a reality can only mean to be guided either straight up to it or its surroundings, or to be put into such working touch with it as to handle it or something better than if we disagreed. Better either intellectually or practically ... Any idea that helps us to deal, whether practically or intellectually, with either the reality or its belongings, that doesn't entangle our progress in frustration, that fits in fact, and adapts our life to the reality's whole setting will agree sufficiently to meet the require- ment. It will be true of that reality.

The true, to put it very briefly, is only the expedient in our way of thinking, just as the right is only the expedient in the way or our behaving.(James 1909: vi f.)

6 Earlier texts, such as they are, seem to be accounting records.

7 This does not mean that the authority necessarily subordinates the Church. It can go either way. It is as likely that the Pope, for instance, will subordinate the Holy Roman Emperor as vice versa. It was unclear just who was doing what to whom when, in AD 800, the Pope crowned Charlemagne "Charles the Most Pious Augustus Great and Peacekeeping Emperor." It is very likely that Charles and the Pope had quite different intents and different evaluations of the outcome. Either way, however, sanctity became conflated with, or polluted by, power.

8 It may well be that coerced acts formally identical to ritual acts of acceptance in every observable way were regarded as legally binding by such authorities as the Spanish Inquisition. My claim is that, whatever the legal consequences of such coerced acts, they did not create the moral obligations entailed by freely enacted rituals of acceptance.

9 It should be clear, but it may be well to make explicit so as to avoid misunderstanding, that I am not advocating the banishment of money or markets or production for profit, nor do I wish to discredit the discipline of economics. I am not challenging the legitimacy of any of these conceptions or practices. I am challenging the elevated, even absolute status granted to them by society at large, especially by those of influence and power in society. Like most other things, notions, and practices in this world they are fine "in their places" which are, properly, subordinate to more fundamental ecological and organic considerations. It is when they are elevated to statuses more determi- native of human action than their instrumental and contingent status war- rants that they become dangerous – or even evil. It is of interest that the Oxford English Dictionary derives the English "evil" from the proto-Ger- manic *Ubiloz*, the sense of which seems to have been "exceeding due measure," or "overstepping proper limits" (see also Partridge 1958, Parkin

1985, Macfarlane 1985, Rappaport 1993). The basic ideas seem to be transgressions of boundaries and excess.

10 It may hardly be necessary to say that what Toulmin means by "postmodern" has limited qualities in common with what literary scholars and their followers in the social sciences mean by it. Indeed, for them the phrase "postmodern science" would come close to being an oxymoron.

11 I have in mind the public testimony, formally similar to the public witnessing that forms part of the ritual in many Christian churches, usually replete with expressions of ecological and aesthetic values, offered by local residents in official public hearings on matters like Outer Continental Shelf oil leasing.

References

Abrahams, I. 1909. "Blasphemy (Jewish)," in J. Hastings (ed.), *Encyclopedia of Religion and Ethics*, vol. 2. Edinburgh: T. & T. Clark.

    1918. "Sabbath (Jewish)," in J. Hastings (ed.), *Encyclopedia of Religion and Ethics*, vol. 10. Edinburgh: T. & T. Clark.

Abrahams, Roger. 1973. Ritual for fun and profit. Paper prepared for Burg-Wartenstein Conference, no. 59: Ritual and Reconciliation, July 21–29, 1973. M. C. Bateson and M. Mead (conveners). New York: Wenner-Gren Foundation.

Adams, Fred and Gregory Laughlin. 1997. "A dying universe: The long-term fate and evolution of astrophysical objects," *Reviews of Modern Physics* 69: 337–372.

Adler, Morris. 1963. *The World of the Talmud*. 2nd ed. New York: Schocken.

American Heritage Dictionary of the English Language. 3rd ed. 1992. New York: Houghton Mifflin Co.

Angeles, Peter A. 1981. *Dictionary of Philosophy*. New York: Harper and Row

Arendt, Hannah. 1958. "What was authority?," in K. Friedrich (ed.), *Authority*. Nomo Series, vol. 1. Cambridge, MA: Harvard University Press.

Aristotle. 1941. *The Basic Works of Aristotle*. Ed. with intro. R. McKeon. New York: Random House.

Attwater, Donald (ed.). 1961. *A Catholic Dictionary*. New York: The Macmillan Company.

Augustin, St. 1991. *The Confessions*. Trans. and Intord. by H. Chadwick. Oxford: Oxford University Press. First published c. 420.

Austin, J. L. 1962. *How to do Things with Words*. Oxford: Oxford University Press.

    1970. "Performative utterances," in J. Urmson and G. Warnock (eds.), *Philosophical Papers of J. L. Austin*. 2nd ed. Oxford: Oxford University Press.

Axon, William E. A. 1914. "King's evil," in J. Hastings (ed.), *Encyclopedia of Religion and Ethics*, vol. 7. Edinburgh: T. & T. Clark.

Babcock, Barbara. 1973. "The carnivalization of the novel and the high spirituality of dressing up." Paper prepared for Burg-Wartenstein Conference, no. 59: Ritual and Reconciliation. M. C. Bateson and M. Mead (conveners). New York: Wenner-Gren Foundation.

Baikie, James. 1914. "Images and idols," in J. Hastings (ed.), *Encyclopedia of Religion and Ethics*, vol. 7. Edinburgh: T. & T. Clark.

Barnes, J. A. 1994. *A Pack of Lies: Toward a Sociology of Lying*. Cambridge: Cambridge University Press.

Bateson, Gregory. 1951. "Conventions of communication: Where validity depends upon belief," in J. Ruesch and G. Bateson, *Communication: The Social Matrix of Psychiatry*. New York: Norton.

1958 [1936]. *Naven: A Survey of the Problems Suggested by a Composite Picture of the Culture of a New Guinea Tribe drawn from Three Points of View*. 2nd ed. Stanford: Stanford University Press.

1963. "The role of somatic change in evolution," *Evolution* 17: 529–539.

1972. *Steps to an Ecology of Mind*. New York: Ballantine.

1972a. "The logical categories of learning and communication," in Bateson 1972.

1972b. "The science of mind and order," in Bateson 1972.

1972c. "Redundancy and coding," in Bateson 1972. First published in T. Sebeok (ed.), *Animal Communication: Techniques of Study and Results of Research*. Bloomington, IN: University of Indiana Press, 1968.

1972d. "Form, subsistence, and difference," in Bateson 1972. First published in *General Semantics Bulletin* no. 37 (1970).

1972e. "Style, grace, and information in primitive art," in Bateson 1972.

1972f. "A theory of play and fantasy," in Bateson 1972. First published in *A. P.A. Psychiatric Research Reports* 2, 1955.

1972g. "Conscious purpose versus nature," in Bateson 1972.

1972h. "The role of semantic change in evolution," in Bateson 1972e. First published in *Evolution* 17 (1963).

1972i. "Cybernetic explanation," in Bateson 1972.

1979. *Mind and Nature: A Necessary Unity*. New York: Dutton.

Bateson, Mary Catherine. 1973. *Notes on the Problems of Boredom and Sincerity*. Paper distributed to participants in Burg-Wartenstein Symposium, no. 59. Ritual and Reconciliation, July 21–29, 1973. M. C. Bateson and M. Mead (convenors). New York: Wenner-Gren Foundation.

1974. "Ritualization: A study in texture and texture change," in I. Zaretsky and M. Leone (eds.), *Religious Movements in Contemporary America*. Princeton: Princeton University Press.

Beattie, John. 1964. *Other Cultures*. London: Routledge and Kegan Paul.

Becker, Judith. 1979. "Time and tune in Java," in A. Becker and A. Yengoyan (eds.), *The Imagination of Reality: Essays in Southeast Asian Coherence Systems*. Norwood, NJ: Ablex.

Bede. 1955. *A History of the English Church and People*. Trans. L. Sherky-Prince. Baltimore: Penguin.

Bell, Catherine. 1992. *Ritual Theory, Ritual Practice*. Oxford: Oxford University Press.

Bergin, Thomas G. and Max H. Fisch. 1984. *The New Science of Giambattista Vico*. Unabridged. Trans. of the 3rd ed. (1744) with the addition of "Practice of the New Science." Ithaca, NY: Cornell University Press.

Bergson, Henri. 1935. *The Two Sources of Morality and Religion*. Trans.

R. Audra and C. Brereton with the assistance of W. Carter. New York: Henry Holt.

Berlin, Isaiah. 1981. *Against the Current: Essays in the History of Ideas*. Oxford: Oxford University Press.

Bettelheim, Bruno. 1962. *Symbolic Wounds*. New York: Collier Books. First published by The Free Press, 1954.

Bickerton, Derek. 1990. *Language and Species*. Chicago: University of Chicago Press.

Bierstadt, Richard. 1950. "An analysis of social power," *American Sociological Review* 15: 730–738.

Blest, A. D. 1961. "The concept of ritualization," in W. Thorpe and O. Zangwill (eds.), *Current Problems in Animal Behavior*. Cambridge: Cambridge University Press.

Bligh, William. 1937. *The Log of the Bounty*. London: Golden Cockerel Press.

Bloch, Marc. 1961. *Feudal Society*. Vols. 1 & 2. Trans. L. Manyon. Chicago: University of Chicago Press.

Bloch, Maurice. 1973. "Symbols, song, dance and features of articulation," *European Journal of Sociology* 15: 55–81.

1986. *From Blessing to Violence: History and Ideology in the Circumcision Ritual of the Merina of Madagascar*. Cambridge: Cambridge University Press.

Bochenski, Joseph M. 1965. *The Logic of Religion*. New York: New York University Press.

Bok, S. 1978. *Lying: Moral Choice in Public and Private Life*. New York: Pantheon.

Bourdieu, Pierre. 1977. *Outline of a Theory of Practice*. Trans. R. Nice. Cambridge Studies in Social Anthropology, no. 16. Cambridge: Cambridge University Press.

Bourguignon, E. 1972. "Dreams and altered states of consciousness in anthropological research," in F. Hsu (ed.), *Psychological Anthropology*. 2nd ed. Homewood, IL: The Dorsey Press.

Boyce, Mary. 1979. *Zoroastrians: Their Religious Beliefs and Practices*. London: Routledge and Kegan Paul.

Brandon, S. G. F. 1967. *The Judgement of the Dead: The Idea of Life After Death in the Major Religions*. New York: Charles Scribner's Sons.

Brenner, Charles. 1957. *An Elementary Textbook of Psychoanalysis*. New York: Doubleday.

Brower, L. P. 1969. "Ecological chemistry," *Scientific American* 220(2): 22–29.

Brown, Joseph E. 1954. *The Sacred Pipe*. Horman, OK: University of Oklahoma Press.

Brown, Joseph E. (recorder and ed.). 1971. *The Sacred Pipe: Black Elk's Account of the Seven Rites of the Oglala Sioux*. Baltimore: Penguin. First published by University of Oklahoma Press, 1953.

Brown, Norman W. 1972. "Duty as truth," *Proceedings of the American Philosophical Society* 116(3): 252–268.

Brown, Robert. 1963. *Explanation in Social Science*. Chicago: Aldine.

Bruner, Jerome. 1970. *On Knowing: Essays for the Left Hand*. New York: Athenaeum. First published by Harvard University Press, 1962.

Buber, Martin. 1952. *Good and Evil: Two Interpretations*. New York: Charles Scribner's Sons.

——— 1970. *I and Thou*. A New Translation with a Prologue, "I and You," and Notes by Walter Kaufmann. New York: Charles Scribner's Sons.

Buchbinder, Georgeda and Roy A. Rappaport. 1976. "Fertility and death among the Maring," in P. Brown and G. Buchbinder (eds.), *American Anthropological Association Special Publication* no. 8. Sex Roles in the New Guinea Highlands.

Buchler, Justus. 1955. *The Philosophical Writings of Peirce*. New York: Dover.

Budge, E. A. Wallis. 1895. *The Book of the Dead: The Papyrus of Ani*. Facsimile edition. New York: Dover Publications, 1967.

Bullough, Sebastian. 1963. *Roman Catholicism*. London: Penguin.

Bultmann, R. 1967. "The Greek and Hellenistic use of Alethia," in *Theological Dictionary of the New Testament*, vol. 1. Grand Rapids, MI: Eerdmanns.

Burks, Arthur. 1949. "Icon, index, and symbol," *Philosophic and Phenomenological Research* 9 (June): 673–689.

Burns, I. F. 1911. "Cosmogony and cosmology (Greek)," in J. Hastings (ed.), *Encyclopedia of Religion and Ethics*, vol. 4. Edinburgh: T. & T. Clark.

Byrne, Richard and Andrew Whiten (eds.). 1988. *Machiavellian Intelligence: Social Expertise and the Evolution of Intellect in Monkeys, Apes and Humans*. Oxford: Clarendon Press.

Calverley, E. E. 1958. *Islam: An Introduction*. Cairo: The American University at Cairo.

Campbell, Joseph. 1959. *The Masks of God*. Vol. 1, *Primitive Mythology*. New York: The Viking Press.

Carleton, James G. 1910. "Calendar (Christian)," in J. Hastings (ed.), *Encyclopedia of Religion and Ethics*, vol. 3. Edinburgh: T. & T. Clark.

Carnoy, A. V. 1921. "Zoroastrianism," in J. Hastings (ed.), *Encyclopedia of Religion and Ethics*, vol. 7. Edinburgh: T. & T. Clark.

Carrington, Robert S. 1993. *An Introduction to C. S. Peirce: Philosopher, Semiotician, and Ecstatic Naturalist*. Lanham, MD: Rowman and Littlefield Publishers.

Catlin, George. 1844. *Letters and Notes on the Manners, Customs, and Conditions of the North American Indians*. Republished with an introduction by M. Halpin. New York: Dover Publications, 1973.

Chadwick, H. Munro. 1910. "Calendar (Teutonic)," in J. Hastings (ed.), *Encyclopedia of Religion and Ethics*, vol. 3. Edinburgh: T. & T. Clark.

Chaney, William A. 1970. *The Cult of Kingship in Anglo-Saxon England: The Transition from Paganism to Christianity*. Manchester: Manchester University Press.

Chapple, E. D. 1970. *Culture and Biological Man*. New York: Holt, Rinehart, and Winston.

Cicero, Marcus T. 1933. *De Natura Deorum*. New York: G. P. Putnam's Sons.

Codere, H. 1950. "Fighting with property: A study of Kwakiutl potlatching and warfare, 1792–1930. *American Ethnological Society Monographs*, no. 18. New York.

Collins, Paul. 1965. "Functional analysis in the symposium 'Man, Culture, and

Animals'," in A. Leeds and A. Vayda (eds.), *Man, Culture, and Animals.* Washington, DC: American Association for the Advancement of Science.

Corballis, Michael C. 1991. *The Lopsided Ape: Evolution of the Generative Mind.* New York: Oxford University Press.

Coulton, C. G. 1924. *The Death Penalty for Heresy.* Medieval Studies, no. 18. London: Simpkin, Marshall, Hamilton, Kent and Co.

Crane, Jocelyn. 1966. "Combat display and ritualization in Fiddler Crabs," in J. Huxley (convenor), *A Discussion of the Ritualization of Behaviour in Animals and Man.* Philosophical Transactions of the Royal Society of London. Series B. Biological Sciences 251(772).

Croon, J. H. 1965. *The Encyclopedia of the Classical World.* Englewood Cliffs, NJ: Prentice Hall.

Cullen, J. M. 1966. "Reduction of ambiguity through ritualization," in J. Huxley (convenor), *A Discussion of the Ritualization of Behaviour in Animals and Man.* Philosophical Transactions of the Royal Society of London. Series B. Biological Sciences 251(772).

Cunningham, Clark. E. 1964. "Order in the Atoni house," *Bijdragen tot de Taal-Land en Volkenkunde.* Deel 120, 1e Aflevering.

Dahood, Mitchell. 1980. "Are the Ebla Tablets relevant to Biblical research," *Biblical Archaeology Review* 6(5) (Sept.-Oct.).

Daniel, E. Valentine. 1984. *Fluid Signs.* Berkeley: University of California Press.

d'Aquili, Eugene and Charles D. Laughlin. 1975. "The biophysical determinants of religious ritual behavior," *Zygon* 10: 32–57.

1979. "The neurobiology of myth and ritual," in d'Aquili *et al.* 1979.

d'Aquili, Eugene, Charles D. Laughlin, and J. McManus. 1979. *The Spectrum of Ritual.* New York: Columbia University Press.

Debrunner, A. 1967. "Lego, Logos, Pneuma, Laleo," in *Theological Dictionary of the New Testament*, vol. 4. Grand Rapids, MI: Eerdmanns.

de Rougemont, Denis. 1944. *La Part du Diable.* New York: Brentano's.

Deshpande, Madhav. 1990. "Changing Conceptions of the Veda: From Speech Act to Magical Sounds", in *Adyar Library Bulletin* Vol. 56. Adyar Library and Research Centre, Theosophical Society: Adyar, Madras, India.

de Vaux, Roland. 1961. *Ancient Israel.* Vols. 1 & 2. New York: McGraw-Hill.

de Waal, Frans. 1986. "Deception in the natural communication of chimpanzees," in R. Mitchell and N. Thompson (eds.), *Deception: Perspectives on Human and Non-human Deceit.* New York: State University of New York Press.

1988. "Chimpanzee politics," in R. Byrne and A. Whiten (eds.), *Machiavellian Intelligence.* Oxford: Clarendon Press.

Dixon, Robert M. W. 1971. "A method of semantic distinction," in D. Steinberg and L. Jacobovits (eds.), *Semiotics: An Introductory Reader in Philosophy, Linguistics, and Psychology.* Cambridge: Cambridge University Press.

Dobson, R. B. (ed.). 1970. *The Peasants' Revolt of 1381.* London: Macmillan and Co./St. Martin's Press.

Dorsey, James Owen. 1894. *A Study of Siouxian Cults.* Smithsonian Institution, Bureau of American Ethnology. Annual Report, no. 14. Washington, DC: US Government Printing Office.

Douglas, Mary. 1966. *Purity and Danger: An Analysis of The Concepts of Pollution and Taboo.* New York: Frederick A. Praeger.
   1973. *Natural Symbols: Explorations in Cosmology.* Harmondsworth: Penguin. First published by Barrie and Rocklift, 1970.
Drucker, Philip. 1965. *Indians of the Northwest Coast.* New York: McGraw-Hill. Republished by Natural History Press, 1965.
Duchesne-Guillemin, Jacques. 1966. *Symbols and Values in Zoroastrianism.* New York: Harper and Row.
Dumont, Louis. 1980. *Homo Hierarchicus: The Caste System and its Implications.* Complete revised English edition. Chicago: Chicago University Press.
Durkheim, Emile. 1961. *The Elementary Forms of the Religious Life.* Trans. J. Swain. New York: Collier Books. First published in 1912 as *Les Formes Élémentaires de la Vie Religieuse: Le Systeme Totemique en Australie.* First English edition, 1915.
Durkheim, Emile and Marcel Mauss 1963. *Primitive Classification.* Trans. and ed. with intro. R. Needham. Chicago: University of Chicago Press. First published, 1903.
Eliade, Mircea. 1957a. "Time and eternity in Indian thought," in J. Campbell (ed.), *Man and Time: Papers from the Eranos Yearbooks.* Princeton: Bollingen Foundation.
   1957b. *The Sacred and the Profane: The Nature of Religion.* Trans. W. Trask. New York: Harcourt, Brace, and World.
   1959. *Cosmos and History: The Myth of the Eternal Return.* Trans. W. Trask. New York: The Bollingen Library. First English publication as *The Myth of the Eternal Return.* (New York: Pantheon). Original French publication, 1949.
   1963. *Myth and Reality.* Trans. W. Trask. New York: Harper and Row.
Ellis, William. 1853. *Polynesian Researches During a Residence of Nearly Eight Years in the Society of the Sandwich Islands.* Vols. 1–4. London: H. G. Bohn. First published, 1829.
Erikson, Erik. 1966. "Ontogeny of ritualization in man," in J. Huxley (convenor), *A Discussion of the Ritualization of Behaviour in Animals and Man.* Philosophical Transactions of the Royal Society of London. Series B. Biological Sciences 251(772).
Etkin, William. 1964. *Social Behavior and Organization among Vertebrates.* Chicago: Chicago University Press.
Evans-Pritchard, E. E. 1937. *Witchcraft, Oracles and Magic among the Azande.* Oxford: Oxford University Press.
   1940. *The Nuer: A Description of the Modes of Livelihood and Political Institutions of a Nilotic People.* Oxford: Oxford University Press.
   1956. *Nuer Religion.* Oxford: Oxford University Press.
Feeley-Harnick, Gillian. 1994. *The Lord's Table: The Meaning of Food in Early Judaism and Christianity.* Washington: Smithsonian Institution Press.
Fenichel, Otto. 1945. *The Psychoanalytic Theory of Neurosis.* New York: W. W. Norton and Co.
Fernandez, James. 1974. "The mission of metaphor in expressive culture," *Current Anthropology* 15: 119–146.

Finkelstein, Louis. 1971. "The Jewish religion: Its beliefs and practices," in L. Finkelstein (ed.), *The Jews: Their Religion and Culture*. 4th ed.

Finnegan, Ruth. 1969. "How to do things with words: Performative utterances among the Limba of Sierra Leone," *Man* 4: 537–551.

Firth, Raymond. 1967a. *The Work of the Gods in Tikopia*. 2nd ed. London: Athlone Press.

1967b. *Tikopia Ritual and Belief*. Boston: Beacon Press.

1973. *Symbols, Public and Private*. London: Allen and Unwin.

Ford, Richard I. 1972. "An ecological perspective on the Eastern Pueblos," in A. Ortiz (ed.), *New Perspectives on the Pueblos*. Albuquerque, NM: University of New Mexico Press.

Fortes, Meyer. 1966. "Religious premises and logical technique in divinatory ritual," in J. Huxley (convenor), *A Discussion of Ritualization of Behaviour in Animals and Man*. Philosophical Transactions of the Royal Society of London. Series B. Biological Sciences 251(772).

Fortescue, Adrian and J. B. O'Connell. 1962. *The Ceremonies of the Roman Rite Described*. 12th ed., revised. Westminster, MD: The Newman Press.

Foucault, Michel. 1990. *The History of Sexuality*. Vol. 1, *An Introduction*. Trans. R. Hurley. New York: Vintage Books.

Fraisse, P. 1964. *The Psychology of Time*. London: Eyre & Spottiswoode.

Frake, C. 1964. "A structural description of Subanun 'religious behavior'," in W. H. Goodenough (ed.), *Explorations in Cultural Anthropology: Essays in Honor of George Peter Murdock*. New York: McGraw-Hill.

Frankfort, Henri. 1948. *Kingship and the Gods*. Chicago: University of Chicago Press.

Frazer, James. 1963. *The Golden Bough: A Study in Magic and Religion*. One volume abridged. New York: Macmillan and Co. First published, 1922.

Frazer, J. T. 1975. *Of Time, Passion, and Knowledge: Reflections on the Strategy of Existence*. New York: George Brazilier.

Frazer, J. T. (ed.). 1966. *The Voices of Time*. New York: George Brazilier.

Freedman, David N. 1976. "Divine names and title in early Hebrew poetry Magnalia Dei," in F. Cross, W. Lemke, and P. Miller (eds.), *The Mighty Acts of God*. New York: Doubleday.

Freud, Sigmund. 1907. "Obsessive Acts and Religious Practices," *Zeitschrift fur Religionpsychologie* 1: 4–12. Trans. in the standard edition of J. Stratchey (ed.), *The Collected Papers of Sigmund Freud*. Vol. 9. Trans. J. Riviere. London: Hogarth Press.

Frisancho, Roberto. 1975. "Functional adaptation to high altitude hypoxia," *Science* 187: 313–319.

Gardiner, Alan H. 1912. "Ethics and Morality (Egyptian)," in J. Hastings (ed.), *Encyclopedia of Religion and Ethics*, vol. 5. Edinburgh: T. & T. Clark.

Geertz, Clifford. 1965. "Religion as a cultural system," in M. Banton (ed.), *Anthropological Approaches to Religion*. ASA Monograph, no. 3. London: Tavistock.

1973. *The Interpretation of Cultures*. New York: Basic Books.

1980. *Negara: The Theatre State in Nineteenth Century Bali*. Princeton: Princeton University Press.

Giantumo, Elio (ed.). 1965. Vico, Giambattista: *On the Study of Methods of Our Time*. New York: Bobbs-Merrill/Library of Liberal Arts.

Glazebrook, M. G. 1921. "Sunday," in J. Hastings (ed.), *Encyclopedia of Religion and Ethics*, vol. 12. Edinburgh: T. & T. Clark.

Gluckman, Max. 1954. *Rituals of Rebellion in Southeast Africa*. The Frazer Lecture, 1952. Manchester: Manchester University Press.

1962. "Les rites de passage," in M. Gluckman (ed.), *The Ritual of Social Relations*. Manchester: Manchester University Press.

Gluckman, Max and Mary Gluckman. 1977. "On drama, games, and athletic contests," in S. Moore and B. Myerhoff (eds.), *Secular Ritual*. Amsterdam: Van Gorcum.

Goffman, Erving. 1956. "The nature of deference and demeanor," *American Anthropologist* 58: 473–503.

1967. *Interaction Ritual*. Garden City, NJ: Doubleday.

Goldman, Stanford. 1960. "Further consideration of the cybernetic aspects of homeostasis," in M. Yovits and S. Cameron (eds.), *Self-Organized Systems*. New York: Pergamon Press.

Goodenough, Erwin Ramsdell. 1990. *Goodenough on the Beginning of Christianity*. Ed. A. T. Kraabel. Atlanta: Scholar's Press.

Goodman, Felicitas D. 1972. *Speaking in Tongues: A Cross-cultural Study of Glossolalia*. Chicago: Chicago University Press.

Goody, Esther. 1972. "'Greeting,' 'begging,' and the presentation of respect," in J. LaFontaine (ed.), *The Interpretation of Ritual*. London: Tavistock.

Goody, Jack. 1961. "Religion and ritual: The definition problem," *British Journal of Sociology* 12: 142–164.

1977. *The Domestication of the Savage Mind*. Cambridge: Cambridge University Press.

Gossen, Gary. 1972. "Temporal and spatial equivalents in Chamula ritual," in W. Lessa and E. Vogt (eds.), *Reader in Comparative Religion*. 3rd ed. New York: Harper and Row.

Gould, Richard A. 1969. *Yiwara: Foragers of the Australian Desert*. New York: Charles Scribner's Sons.

Griaule, Marcel. 1965. *Conversations with Ogotemmeli: An Introduction to Dogon Religion*. Oxford: Oxford University Press.

Grim, Patrick. 1991. *The Incomplete Universe: Totality, Knowledge and Truth*. Cambridge, MA: A Bradford Book/MIT Press.

Grimes, Ronald. 1990. *Ritual Criticism: Case Studies in its Practice, Essays on its Theory*. Columbia, SC: University of South Carolina Press.

Gurvitch, Georges. 1964. *The Spectrum of Social Time*. Dordrecht: D. Reidel Publishing.

Hall, A. D. and R. E. Fagan. 1956. "Definition of system," *General Systems Yearbook* 1: 18–28.

Hall, Edward T. 1984. *The Dance of Life: The Other Dimension of Time*. Garden City, NY: Anchor Press/Doubleday.

Hall, Robert. 1977. "An anthropocentric perspective for eastern United States prehistory," *American Antiquity* 42: 499–518.

Hallo, W. W. and J. J. A. van Dijk. 1968. *The Exultation of Inanna*. New Haven: Yale University Press.

Harlow, H. E. 1949. "The formation of learning sets," *Psychological Review* 56: 51–65.

Harrison, Jane. 1913. *Ancient Art and Ritual*. London: Williams and Norgate.

Hawking, Stephen W. 1988. *A Brief History of Time*. New York: Bantam.

Hediger, H. 1955. *Studies in the Psychology and Behavior of Animals in Zoos and Circuses*. London: Buttersworth Scientific Publications.

Heidegger, Martin. 1959. *An Introduction to Metaphysics*. Trans. R. Manheim: New Haven: Yale University Press.

Heidel, Alexander. 1951. *The Babylonian Genesis: The Story of Creation*. 2nd ed. Chicago: University of Chicago Press.

Hempel, Carl. 1958. "The logic of functional analysis," in L. Gross (ed.), *Symposium on Sociological Theory*. Evanstan, IL: Row, Peterson.

Herdt, Gilbert (ed.). 1982. *Rituals of Manhood: Male Initiation in Papua New Guinea*. Berkeley: University of California Press.

  1984. *Ritualized Homosexuality in Melanesia*. Berkeley: University of California Press.

Hillgarth, J. A. (ed.) 1969. *The Conversion of Western Europe 350–750*. Englewood Cliffs, NJ: Prentice-Hall.

Hinde, Robert. 1966. *Animal Behavior*. New York: McGraw-Hill.

Hobbes, Thomas. 1951. *Leviathan*. Oxford: Clarendon Press. First published 1651.

Hockett, Charles F. and Robert Asher. 1964. "The human revolution," *Current Anthropology* 5: 135–168.

Hockett, Charles F. and S. Altman. 1968. "A note on design features," in T. Sebeok (ed.), *Animal Communication*. Bloomington, IN: Indiana University Press.

Homans, George C. 1941. "Anxiety and ritual: The theories of Malinowski and Radcliffe Brown," *American Anthropologist* 43: 164–172.

Hooke, S. H. 1963. *Babylonian and Assyrian Religion*. Norman, OK: University of Oklahoma Press.

Hoopes, James (ed.). 1991. *Peirce on Signs: Writings on Semiotics*. Chapel Hill, NC: University of North Carolina Press.

Huxley, Julian. 1914. "The courtship habits of the great crested grebe (*Podiceps cristatus*) with an addition to the theory of sexual selection," *Proceedings of the Zoological Society of London*.

  1966. "Introduction," in J. Huxley (convenor), A Discussion of Ritualization of Behavior in Animals and Man. *Philosophical Transactions of the Royal Society of London*. Series B. Biological Sciences 251(772).

Idelsohn, A. Z. 1932. *Jewish Liturgy and its Development*. New York: Holt, Rinehart and Winston. Republished. New York: Schocken Books, 1960.

Ingram, J. 1823. *The Saxon Chronicle with an English Translation and Notes, Critical and Explanatory*. London: Longman, Hurst, Rees, Orme, and Brown.

Jacobson, Thorkild. 1976. *The Treasures of Darkness. A History of Mesopotamian Religion*. New Haven: Yale University Press.

Jacques, Elliot. 1982. *The Form of Time*. London: Heinemann.

Jakobson, Roman. 1957. "Shifters, verbal categories, and the Russian verb," in *Selected Writings*. Vol. 2, *Word and Language*. The Hague: Mouton.

James, Charles W. (ed.). 1943. *Bedae Opera de Temporibus*. Cambridge, MA: The Medieval Society of America.

James, William. 1909. *The Meaning of Truth: A Sequel to Pragmatism*. New York: Longmans, Green, and Co. Reprinted 1914.

   1890. *The Principles of Psychology*. Vols. 1 & 2. New York: Henry Holt and Co.

   1961. *The Varieties of Religious Experience: A Study of Human Nature*. With a new introduction by Reinhold Niebuhr. New York: Collier Books. First published by Longmans, Green and Co., 1902.

   1990. *The Varieties of Religious Experience: A Study of Human Nature*. With an Introduction by Jaroslav Pelikan. New York: Vintage Books.

Jorgensen, Joseph. 1972. *The Sun Dance Religion: Power for the Powerless*. Chicago: Chicago University Press.

Kalmus, Hans (ed.). 1967. *Regulation and Control in Living Systems*. London: Wiley.

Kapferer, Bruce. 1977. "First class to Maradana: Secular drama in Sinhalese healing rites," in S. Moore and B. Myerhoff (eds.), *Secular Ritual*. Amsterdam: Van Gorcum.

   1983. *A Celebration of Demons: Exorcism and the Aesthetics of Healing in Sri Lanka*. Bloomington, IN: Indiana University Press.

Katz, Richard. 1982. *Boiling Energy: Community Healing among the Kalahari Kung*. Cambridge, MA: Harvard University Press.

Kelly, Raymond. 1974. *Etoro Social Structure*. Ann Arbor: University of Michigan Press.

   1993. *Constructing Inequality: The Fabrication of a Hierarchy of Virtue among the Etoro*. Ann Arbor: University of Michigan Press.

Kelly, Raymond and Roy A. Rappaport. 1975. "Function, generality and explanatory power: A commentary and response to Bergmann's arguments," *Michigan Discussions in Anthropology* 1: 24–44.

Kertzer, David I. 1988. *Ritual Politics and Power*. New Haven: Yale University Press.

Kirk, G. S. 1954. *Heraclitus: The Cosmic Fragments*. Cambridge: Cambridge University Press.

Kirk, William C. Jr. 1940. *Fire in the Cosmological Speculation of Heraclitus*. Minneapolis: Burgess Publishing Co.

Kittel, Gerhard. 1965. "Emet in Rabbinic Judaism," in G. Kittel (ed.), *Theological Dictionary of the New Testament*, vol. 1. Grand Rapids, MI: Eerdmans.

Kleinknecht, H. 1967. "The logos in the Greek and Hellenistic world," in G. Kittel (ed.), *Theological Dictionary of the New Testament*, vol. 4. Grand Rapids, MI: Eerdmans.

Kluckhohn, Clyde. 1949. "The philosophy of the Navaho Indians," in F. S. C. Northrup (ed.), *Ideological Differences and World Order*. New Haven: Yale University Press.

Kung, Hans. 1971. *Infallible? An Inquiry*. Garden City, NY: Doubleday.
  1980. *Does God Exist? An Answer for Today*. Trans. E. Quinn. Garden City, NY: Doubleday.
Kuntz, Paul (ed.). 1968. *The Concept of Order*. Seattle: University of Washington Press for Grinnell College.
Lacey, T. A. 1918. "Sacraments (Christian, Western)," in J. Hastings (ed.), *Encyclopedia of Religion and Ethics*, vol. 10. Edinburgh: T. & T. Clark.
La Fontaine, J. S. 1972. "Introduction," in J. La Fontaine (ed.), *The Interpretation of Ritual*. London: Tavistock.
Laitman, J. T. 1981. "The evolution of the hominid upper respiratory system and its implications for the origins of speech," in E. D. Grolier (ed.), *Glossogenetics: The Origin and Evolution of Language*. Proceedings of the International Transdisciplinary Symposium on Glossogenetics. New York: Harwood Academic Publishers. First published by UNESCO, 1981.
Lane-Poole, Stanley. 1911. "Creed (Muhammadan)," in J. Hastings (ed.), *Encyclopedia of Religion and Ethics*, vol 4. Edinburgh: T. & T. Clark.
Langer, Susanne K. 1953. *Feeling and Form: A Theory of Art*. New York: Charles Scribner's Sons.
Lappenberg, J. M. 1894. *A History of England under the Anglo-Saxon Kings*. Trans. B. Thorpe. New edition revised by E. C. Otte. Vols. 1 & 2. London: George Bell and Sons.
Laughlin, Charles D., J. McManus, and E. d'Aquili. 1990. *Brain, Symbol and Experience*. New York: Columbia University Press.
Leach, Edmund R. 1954. *Political Systems of Highland Burma: A Study of Kachin Social Structure*. Boston: Beacon Press.
  1961. *Rethinking Anthropology*. London: Athlone.
  1966. "Ritualization in man in relation to conceptual and social developments," in J. Huxley (convenor), A Discussion of the Ritualization of Behavior in Animals and Man. *Transactions of the Royal Society of London*. Series B. Biological Sciences 251(772).
  1972. "The influence of cultural context on non-verbal communication in man," in R. Hinde (ed.), *Non-Verbal Communication*. Cambridge: Cambridge University Press.
Leon-Portilla, Miguel. 1963. *Aztec Thought and Culture: A Study of The Ancient Nahuatl Mind*. Trans. J. E. Davis. Norman, OK: University of Oklahoma Press.
Leslau, Wolf. 1951. *Falasha Anthology: The Black Jews of Ethiopia*. New York: Schocken Books.
Lévi-Strauss, Claude. 1953. "Social structure," in A. Kroeber (chair), *Anthropology Today*. Chicago: Chicago University Press.
  1963. "The structural study of myth," in *Structural Anthropology*. New York: Basic Books.
  1966. *The Savage Mind*. London: Weidenfeld and Nicolson.
  1981. *The Naked Man*. New York: Harper and Row.
Levy, Robert. 1973. *Tahitians: Mind and Experience in the Society Islands*. Chicago: Chicago University Press.
  1990. *Mesocosm: Hinduism and the Organization of a Traditional Newar City in*

Nepal. With the collaboration of C. Raj Rajopadhyaya. Berkeley: University of California Press.

Lewis, C. T. 1891. *An Elementary Latin Dictionary.* Oxford: Oxford University Press.

Lewis, Gilbert. 1980. *Day of Shining Red: An Essay on Understanding Ritual.* New York: Cambridge University Press.

Lex, Barbara. 1979. "The neurobiology of ritual trance," in E. d'Aquili, C. Laughlin, and J. McManus (eds.), *The Spectrum of Ritual.* New York: Columbia University Press.

Lichtheim, Miriam. 1971. *Ancient Egyptian Literature. Volume One: The Old and Middle Kingdoms.* Berkeley: University of California Press.

LiPuma, Edward. 1990. "The terms of change: Linguistic mediation and reaffiliation among the Maring," *Journal of the Polynesian Society* 99: 93–121.

Lommel, Herman. 1930. *Die Religion Zarathustras nach dem Aresta Dargestellt.* Tubingen: J. C. B. Mohr.

Lyons, J. 1972. "Human language," in R. Hinde (ed.), *Non-Verbal Communication.* Cambridge: Cambridge University Press.

MacDonell, A. A. 1915. "Literature (Buddhist)," in J. Hastings (ed.), *Encyclopedia of Religion and Ethics*, vol. 8. Edinburgh: T. & T. Clark.

Macfarlane, Alan. 1985. "The root of all evil," in D. Parkin (ed.), *The Anthropology of Evil.* Oxford: Basil Blackwell.

MacKenzie, J. S. 1912. "Eternity," in J. Hastings (ed.), *Encyclopedia of Religion and Ethics*, vol. 5. Edinburgh: T. & T. Clark.

Malinowksi, Bronislaw. 1922. *Argonauts of the Western Pacific: An Account of Native Enterprise and Adventure in the Archipelagos of Melanesian New Guinea.* Reprinted, New York: E. D. Dutton, 1961.

   1935. *Coral Gardens and their Magic.* Reprinted, Bloomington, IN: University of Indiana Press, 1965.

Manheim, Ralph. 1959. "Translator's note," in M. Heidegger, *An Introduction to Metaphysics.* New Haven: Yale University Press.

Margoliouth, G. 1918. "Sabbath (Muhammadan)," in J. Hastings (ed.), *Encyclopedia of Religion and Ethics*, vol. 10. Edinburgh: T. & T. Clark.

Marshall, J. C. 1970. "The biology of communication in man and animals," in J. Marshall (ed.), *New Horizons in Linguistics.* Harmondsworth: Penguin.

Maruyama, Magoroh. 1955. "The second cybernetics," *American Scientist.*

Marx, Karl. 1842. "Religion and authority," in F. Bender (ed.), *Karl Marx: The Essential Writings.* New York: Harper, 1972. First published as *The Leading Article in no. 179 of the Kolnische Zeitung: Religion, Free Press, and Philosophy.* Rheinische Zeitung, 1842.

   1844. "Contribution to the critique of Hegel's philosophy of right: Introduction," in *Karl Marx and Freidrich Engels on Religion.* New York: Schocken, 1964.

Masani, Rustom. 1968. *Zoroastrianism: The Religion of the Good Life.* New York: Macmillan. First published 1938.

Mauss, Marcel. 1954. *The Gift: Forms and Functions of Exchange in Archaic Societies.* Trans. Ian Cunnison. London: Cohen and West.

McKelway, Alexander J. 1964. *The Systematic Theology of Paul Tillich: A Review and Analysis.* Richmond: John Knox Press.

McKenzie, John L. 1969. *The Roman Catholic Church*. New York: Holt, Reinhart, and Winston.

McKeon, Richard (ed.). 1941 *The Basic Works of Aristotle*. New York: Random House.

McLuhan, Marshall and Q. Fiore. 1967. *The Medium is the Massage*. New York: Random House.

Meggitt, M. J. 1965a. *The Desert People: A Study of the Walbiri Aborigines of Central Australia*. Chicago: Chicago University Press.

1965b. *The Lineage System of the Mae Enga of New Guinea*. Edinburgh: Oliver and Boyd.

n.d. *Gadjari among the Walbiri Aborigines of Central Australia, The Oceania Monographs*, no. 14. Sydney.

Miller, James. 1965. "Living systems: Basic concepts," *Behavioral Science* 10: 193–257.

Miller, John H. 1959. *Fundamentals of the Liturgy*. Notre Dame, IN: Fides Publishing Co.

Milne, L. A. 1948. *Kinematic Relativity*. Oxford: Clarendon Press.

Mitchell, Robert W. and Nicholas S. Thompson (eds.). 1986. *Deception: Perspectives on Human and Non-Human Deceit*. State University of New York Press.

Moerenhaut, Jacques-Antoine 1837 *Voyages aux Iles du Grand Ocean*. 2 vols. Paris: A. Bertrand.

Molina, Alonso de. 1571. *Vocabulario en langua Castellana y Mexicana*. Facsimile edition, *Coleccion de Incunables Americanos*, vol. 4. Madrid, 1944.

Montague-Smith, Patrick W. 1972. *The Royal Line of Succession*. London: Pitkin.

Mooney, James. 1896. *The Ghost Dance Religion and the Sioux Outbreak of 1890*. Part Two of the Fourteenth Annual Report of the Bureau of Ethnology to the Secretary of the Smithsonian Institution, 1892–93. Washington: Government Printing Office. Reprint, abridged with an introduction by A. Wallace. Phoenix Books, 1965.

Moore, John M. 1938. *Theories of Religious Experience With Special Reference to James, Otto and Bergson*. New York: Round Table Press.

Moore, Omar Khayam. 1955. "Divination: A new perspective," *American Anthropologist* 59: 64–74.

Moore, Sally Falk and Barbara Myerhoff (eds.). 1977. *Secular Ritual*. Amsterdam: Van Gorcum.

Morgan, Lloyd. 1900. *Animal Behavior*. Reprinted, New York: Johnson Reprint Corp., 1970.

Morris, Desmond. 1986. *Bodywatching: A Field Guide to the Human Species*. London: Guild.

Munn, Nancy D. 1973. *Walbiri Iconography: Graphic Representations and Cultural Symbolism in a Central Australian Society*. Ithaca and London: Cornell University Press.

Myerhoff., Barbara. 1977. "We don't wrap herring in a printed page," in S. Moore and B. Myerhoff (eds.), *Secular Ritual*. Amsterdam: Van Gorcum.

Nagel, Ernst. 1961. *The Structure of Science*. New York: Harcourt, Brace, and World.

Needham, Joseph. 1966. "Time and knowledge in China and the West," in J. T. Frazer (ed.), *The Voices of Time*. New York: George Brazilier.

Needham, Rodney. 1963. "Introduction," in E. Durkeim and M. Mauss (eds.), *Primitive Classification*. Chicago: University of Chicago Press. French edition, 1903.

1972. *Belief, Language, and Experience*. Oxford: Basil Blackwell.

Norbeck, Edward. 1963. "African rituals of conflict," *American Anthropologist* 65: 1254–1279.

O'Doherty, E. Fehean. 1973. Ritual as a second order language. Paper prepared for Burg-Wartenstein Conference, no. 59: Ritual and Reconciliation. M. C. Bateson and M. Mead (conveners). New York: Wenner-Gren Foundation.

Odum, Eugene. 1953. *Fundamentals of Ecology*. Philadelphia: Saunders.

1959. *Fundamentals of Ecology*. 2nd ed. In collaboration with H. T. Odum. Philadelphia: Saunders.

Oliver, Douglas. 1955. *A Solomon Island Society*. Cambridge, MA: Harvard University Press.

1974. *Ancient Tahitian Society*. Vols. 1–3. Honolulu: University of Hawaii Press.

Orlin, Louis L. 1976. "Athens and Persia ca. 507 B.C.: A neglected perspective," in L. Orlin (ed.), *Michigan Oriental Studies in Honor of George G. Cameron*. Ann Arbor, MI: Dept. of Near Eastern Studies, University of Michigan.

Ornstein, Robert E. 1969. *On the Experience of Time*. Baltimore: Penguin.

Ortiz, Alfonso. 1969. *The Tewa World: Space, Time, Being, and Becoming in a Pueblo Society*. Chicago: Chicago University Press.

Ortner, Sherry. "On key symbols," *American Anthropologist* 75: 1338–1346.

Otto, Rudolph. 1907. *Naturalism and Religion*. Trans. J. Thomson and M. Thomson. London: Williams and Norgate. First published as *Naturalistische und Religiose Weltansicht*. Tubingen: J. C. B. Mohr, 1904.

1923. *The Idea of the Holy*. Trans. J. Harvey. Oxford: Oxford University Press. Originally published as *Das Heilige*. Gotha: Leopold Klotz, 1917.

1931. *The Philosophy of Religion based on Kant and Fries*. Trans. E. Dicker. London: Williams and Norgate. First published as *Kantisch-Friesische Religionphilosophie und ihre Anwendung auf die Theologie*. Tubingen: J. C. B. Mohr, 1909.

1950. *The Idea of the Holy: An Inquiry into the Non-rational Factor in the Idea of the Divine and its Relation to the Rational*. 2nd ed. Trans. J. Harvey.

Palmer, L. M. 1988. *Vico, Giambattista. On the Most Ancient Wisdom of the Italians. Unearthed from the Origins of the Latin Language Including the Disputation with the Giornale de Litterati d'Italia*. Trans. with intro. and notes. Ithaca, NY: Cornell University Press.

Parkin, David (ed.). 1985. *The Anthropology of Evil*. Oxford: Basil Blackwell.

Parsons, Edmund. 1964. *Time Devoured*. London: George Allen and Unwin.

Parsons, R. G. 1918. "Sacraments (Christian, Eastern)," in J. Hastings (ed.), *Encyclopedia of Religion and Ethics*, vol. 10. Edinburgh: T. &. T. Clark.

Partridge, Eric. 1958. *Origins: A Short Etymological Dictionary of Modern English*. New York: Greenwhich House.

Pattee, Howard H. (ed.). 1973. *Hierarchy Theory: The Challenge of Complex Systems*. New York: George Brazillier.

Paul, Robert A. 1976. "The Sherpa temple as a model of the psyche," *American Ethnologist* 3: 131–146.

Peirce, Charles S. 1960. *The Collected Papers of Charles Sanders Pierce*. C. Hartshorne and P. Weiss (eds.). Cambridge, MA: Harvard University Press.

Peters, Edward (ed.). 1980. *Heresy and Authority in Medieval Europe*. Documents in Translation. Philadelphia: University of Pennsylvania Press.

Petrie, W. M. F. 1911. "Cosmogony and cosmology (Egyptian)," in J. Hastings (ed.), *Encyclopedia of Religion and Ethics*, vol. 4. Edinburgh: T. & T. Clark.

   1912. "Egyptian religion," in J. Hastings (ed.), *Encyclopedia of Religion and Ethics*, vol. 5. Edinburgh: T. & T. Clark.

Pettitt, George. 1946. *Primitive Education in North America*. University of California Publications in Archaeology and Anthropology, vol. 43. Berkeley: University of California.

Piaget, Jean. 1971. *Structuralism*. London: Routledge and Kegan Paul.

Piddocke, S. 1965. "The Potlatch system of the Southern Kwakiutl: A New Perspective," *Southwestern Journal of Anthropology* 21: 244–264.

Pitcher, George (ed.). 1964. *Truth*. Englewood Cliffs, NJ: Prentice Hall.

Pond, Gideon H. 1866. *Dakota Superstitions*. Collections of the Minnesota Historical Society, vol. 2. Reprint, 1989.

Pope, Marvin H. 1965. Introduction, Job. *The Anchor Bible*. Garden City, NY: Doubleday.

Pope Paul VI. 1969. *On Human Life*. Papal Encylical. The Vatican.

Powers, William K. 1975. *Oglala Religion*. Lincoln: University of Nebraska Press.

Quell, Gotfried. 1965. "The word emet," in G. Kittel (ed.), *Theological Dictionary of the New Testament*. Grand Rapids, MI: Eerdmans.

Radcliffe-Brown, A. R. 1964. *The Andaman Islanders*. Glencoe: The Free Press. First published, Cambridge: Cambridge University Press, 1922.

Radhakrishnan, Sarvepalli and Charles A. Moore. 1957. *A Source Book in Indian Philosophy*. Princeton, NJ: Princeton University Press.

Radin, Paul. 1923. *The Winnebago Tribe*. Washington Bureau of American Ethnology, Smithsonian Institution Thirty-seventh Annual Report. Reprinted, Lincoln, NB: University of Nebraska Press.

Rappaport, Roy A. 1969. "Sanctity and Adaptation" Paper prepared for Wenner-Gren Conference on the Moral and Aesthetic Structure of Adaptation. Reprinted in *Io* (1970), 46–47.

   1971a. "Nature, culture, and ecological anthropology" in H. Shapiro (ed.), *Man, Culture, and Society*. 2nd ed. New York: Oxford University Press.

   1971b. "The sacred in human evolution," *Annual Review of Ecology and Systematics* 2: 23–44.

   1971c. "Ritual, sanctity, and cybernetics," *American Anthropologist* 73: 59–76.

   1976a. "Adaptation and maladaptation in social systems," in I. Hill (ed.), *The Ethical Basis of Economic Freedom*. Chapel Hill, NC: American Viewpoint.

   1976b. "Liturgies and lies," *International Yearbook for the Sociology of Knowledge and Religion* 10: 75–104.

   1977. "Maladaptation in social systems," in J. Friedman and M. Rowlands (eds.), *The Evolution of Social Systems*. London: Duckworth.

   1979. *Ecology, Meaning, and Religion*. Richmond CA: North Atlantic Books.

1979a. "On cognized models," in Rappaport 1979.

1979b. "Sanctity and lies in evolution," in Rappaport 1979.

1979c. "Adaptive structure and its disorders," in Rappaport 1979.

1979d. "The obvious aspects of ritual," in Rappaport 1979.

1984. *Pigs for the Ancestors: Ritual in the Ecology of a New Guinea People*. 2nd ed. New Haven: Yale University Press. First published 1968.

1992. "Ritual, time, and eternity," *Zygon* 27: 5–30.

1993. "The anthropology of trouble" *American Anthropologist* 95(2).

1994. "Disorders of our own," in S. Forman (ed.), *Diagnosing America*. Ann Arbor: University of Michigan Press.

Read, Kenneth. 1965. *The High Valley*. New York: Charles Scribner's Sons.

Reeves, C. M. 1972. *An Introduction to the Logical Design of Digital Circuits*. New York: Cambridge University Press.

Reichard, G. 1944. *Prayer: The Compulsive Word*. American Ethnological Society Monograph, no. 7. Seattle: Washington University Press.

1950. *Navaho Religion: A Study of Symbolism*. New York: Bollingein Foundation.

Roheim, Geza. 1945. *The Eternal Ones of the Dream. A Psychoanalytic Interpretation of Australian Myth and Ritual*. New York: International Universities Press.

Romanes, G. J. 1977. *Animal Intelligence*. Washington: University Publications of America. First published, 1883.

Romer, Alfred S. 1954. *Man and the Vertebrates*. Vols. 1 & 2. London: Penguin. First published, 1933.

Ruppell, Von G. 1986. "A 'lie' as a directed message of the Arctic Fox (Alopex lagopus L.)," in R. Mitchell and N. Thompson (eds.), *Deception*. State University of New York Press.

Sahlins, Marshall. 1958. *Social Stratification in Polynesia*. American Ethnological Society Monograph. University of Washington Press.

Schechner, Richard. 1985. *Between Theatre and Anthropology*. Philadelphia: University of Pennsylvania Press.

Schneider, David. 1968. *American Kinship: A Cultural Account*. Englewood Cliffs, NJ: Prentice Hall.

Scholem, Gershom. 1969. *On the Kabbalah and Its Symbolism*. Trans. R. Manheim. New York: Schocken Books.

Searle, J. 1969. *Speech Acts*. Cambridge: Cambridge University Press.

Sebeok, T. 1962. "Coding in the evolution of signalling behavior," *Behavioral Science* 7: 430–442.

1965. "Animal communication," *Science* 147: 1006–1014.

Sebeok, T. (ed.). 1968. A*nimal Communication: Techniques of Study and Results of Research*. Bloomington, IN: Indiana University Press.

Shannon, Claude and Warren Weaver. 1949. *The Mathematical Theory of Communication*. Urbana, IL: University of Illinois Press.

Shepartz, Lynn. 1993. "Language and modern human origins," *Yearbook of Physical Anthropology* 36: 91–126.

Shipley, Joseph. 1945. *Dictionary of Word Origins*. Totowa, NJ: Littlefield, Adams and Co. Reprinted, 1979.

Silverstein, Michael. 1976. "Shifters, linguistic categories, and cultural description," in K. Basso and H. Selby (eds.), *Meaning in Anthropology*. Albuquerque, NM: University of New Mexico Press.

Simmel, Georg. 1950. *The Philosophy of Money*. First published as *Philosophie des Geldes*. Leipzig, 1900.

Simon, Herbert. 1969. *The Sciences of the Artificial*. Cambridge, MA: MIT Press.

1973. "The organization of complex systems," in H. H. Pattee (ed.), *Hierarchy Theory: The Challenge of Complex Systems*. New York: George Braziller.

Simpson, Otto von. 1964. *The Gothic Cathedral: Origins of Gothic Architecture and the Medieval Concept of Order*. 2nd ed. New York: Harper and Row.

Singer, Milton. 1959. *Traditional India: Structure and Change*. Philadelphia: American Folklore Society.

Skorupski, John. 1976. *Symbol and Theory: A Philosophical Study of Theories of Religion in Social Anthropology*. Cambridge: Cambridge University Press.

Slobodkin, L. and A. Rapoport. 1974. "An optimal strategy of evolution," *Quarterly Review of Biology* 49: 181–200.

Smith, Gerard. 1956. *The Truth That Frees*. The Aquinas Lecture 1956. Milwaukee, WI: Marquette University Press.

Smith, Jonathan Z. 1987. *To Take Place: Toward a Theory in Ritual*. Chicago: University of Chicago Press.

Soebardi. 1965. "Calendrical traditions in Indonesia," *Madjalah Ilmu-ilmu Sastra Indonesia* 3(1): 49–61.

Soloveitchik, Rabbi Joseph B. 1983. *Halakhic Man*. Philadelphia: The Jewish Publication Society of America.

Speiser, E. A. (ed. and trans.). 1964. "Genesis: Introduction, translation and notes," *The Anchor Bible*. Garden City, NY: Doubleday.

Spiro, Melford. 1970. *Buddhism and Society: A Great Tradition and its Burmese Vicissitudes*. New York: Evanston and London. Harper and Row.

Stanner, William E. H. 1956. "The Dreaming," in T. A. G. Hungerford (ed.), *Australian Signpost*. Melbourne: F. W. Chesire. Reprinted in W. Lessa and E. Vogt (eds.), *Reader in Comparative Religion*. 2nd ed. 1965.

n.d. *On Aboriginal Religion*. The Oceania Monographs, no. 11. Sydney.

Strathern, Andrew. 1987. "'Noman': Representations of identity in Mount Hagen," in L. Holy and M. Stuchlik (eds.), *The Structure of Folk Models*. ASA Monograph, no. 20. London: Academic Press.

Stritzower, Schiffra. 1971. *The Children of Israel: The Beni Israel of Bombay*. Oxford: Basil Blackwell.

Suttles, Wayne. 1960. "Affinal ties: subsistence and prestige among the coast Salish," *American Anthropologist* 62: 296–305.

Tambiah, Stanley J. 1968. "The magical power of words," *Man* 3: 175–208.

1973. "Form and meaning of magical acts: A point of view," in R. Horton and R. Finnegan (eds.), *Modes of Thought: Essays on Thinking in Western and Non-western Societies*. London: Faber & Faber.

1985. "A performative approach to ritual," in S. Tambiah, *Culture, Thought and Social Action: An Anthropological Perspective*. First published in *Proceedings of the British Academy* 65(198), 1979.

Teit, James. 1906. "The Thompson Indians of British Columbia," *Memoirs of the American Museum of Natural History* 2: 163–392.

Thomas, Lewis. 1974. *The Lives of a Cell.* New York: Viking Press.

Thomas, Owen. 1969. *Metaphor and Related Subjects.* Bloomington, NY: Random House.

Thorpe, W. H. 1968. "The comparison of vocal communication in animal and man," in R. Hinde (ed.), *Non-verbal Communication.* Cambridge: Cambridge University Press.

  1972. *Duetting and Antiphoned Song in Birds; its Extent and Significance.* Leiden: E. J. Brill.

Tillich, Paul. 1951. *Systematic Theology.* Vol. 1. Chicago: University of Chicago Press.

  1957. *The Dynamics of Faith.* New York: Harper and Row.

Tinbergen, N. 1964a "Behavior and natural selection," in J. Moore (ed.), *Ideas in Modern Biology.*

  1964b. "The evolution of signalling devices," in W. Etkin (ed.), *Social Behavior and Organization among the Vertebrates.* Chicago: University of Chicago Press.

Titiev, Mischa. 1944. *Old Oraibi: A Study of Hopi Indians in the Third Mesa.* Papers of the Peabody Museum of American Archaeology and Ethnology, vol. 22 no. 1.

Toulmin, Stephen. 1982. *The Return to Cosmology: Postmodern Science and the Theology of Nature.* Berkeley: University of California Press.

Tuchman, Barbara. 1978. *A Distant Mirror: The Calamitous 14th Century.* New York: Alfred A. Knopf.

Tumarkin, Nina. 1983. *Lenin Lives! The Lenin Cult in Soviet Russia.* Cambridge, MA: Harvard University Press.

Turner, Victor. 1964. "Symbols in Ndembu ritual," in M. Gluckman and E. Devons (ed.), *Closed Systems and Open Minds: The Limits of Naivete in Social Anthropology.* Chicago: Aldine. Reprinted in Turner 1967.

  1967. *The Forest of Symbols: Aspects of Ndembu Ritual.* Ithaca, NY: Cornell University Press.

  1969. *The Ritual Process.* Chicago: Aldine.

  1973. "Symbols in African ritual," *Science* 179: 1100–1105.

Turner, Victor and Edith Turner. 1978. *Image and Pilgrimage in Christian Culture: Anthropological Perspectives.* New York: Columbia University Press.

Ullman, Walter. 1975. *Medieval Political Thought.* Harmondsworth: Penguin.

Valeri, Valerio. 1985. *Kingship and Sacrifice: Ritual and Society in Ancient Hawaii.* Trans. P. Wissing. Chicago: University of Chicago Press.

Van Baal, J. 1966. *Dema: Description and Analysis of Marind-Anim Culture.* With the collaboration of Father J. Verschoern. The Hague: Martinus Nijhoff.

  1971. *Symbols for Communication: An Introduction to the Anthropological Study of Religion.* Assen: Van Gorcum.

Van Gennep, Arnold. 1960. *The Rites of Passage.* Trans. M. Vizedom and G. Caffee, intro. S. Kimball. Chicago: Chicago University Press. First published, 1909.

Van Lawick-Goodall, Jane. 1971. *In the Shadow of Man.* London: Collins.

Vayda, Andrew P., A. Leeds, and D. Smith. 1961. "The place of pigs in Melanesian subsistence," in V. Garfield (ed.), *Proceedings of the American Ethnological Society*. Seattle: University of Washington Press.

Vayda, Andrew P. and Bonnie McKay. 1975. "New directions in ecology and ecological anthropology," *Annual Review of Anthropology* 4: 293–306.

Vickers, Geoffrey. 1965. *Value Systems and Social Process*. New York: Basic Books.

Vico, Giambattista. 1709. *On the Study of Methods of Our Time*. Trans. Elio Gianturco. New York: Bobbs-Merrill Library of Liberal Arts, 1965.

1710. *On the Most Ancient Wisdom of the Italians. Unearthed from the Origins of the Latin Language. Including the Disputation with the Giornale de Letterati d'Italia*. Trans. with intro. and notes L. Palmer. Ithaca, NY: Cornell University Press, 1988.

1744. *The New Science of Giambattista Vico*. Unabridged Translation of the Third Edition with the addition of "Practice of the New Science." Trans. T. Bergin and M. Fisch. Ithaca, NY: Cornell University Press, 1968.

Waddington, C. H. 1961. *The Ethical Animal*. New York: Athanaeum.

Walker, J. R. 1917. *The Sun Dance and Other Ceremonies of the Teton Dakota*. Anthropological Papers of the American Museum of Natural History, no. 16 pt. 1.

1980. *Lakota Belief and Ritual*. Ed. R. DeMallie and E. Jahner. Lincoln, NE: University of Nebraska Press.

Wallace, Anthony F. C. 1956. "Revitalization movements," *American Anthropologist* 58: 264–281.

1966. *Religion: An Anthropological View*. New York: Random House.

1972. *The Death and Rebirth of the Seneca*. New York: Random House.

Wallace-Hadrill, J. M. 1971. *Early German Kingship in England and on the Continent*. Oxford: Oxford University Press.

Warner, W. L. 1937. *A Black Civilization: A Social Study of an Australian Tribe*. New York: Harper and Row.

Weber, Max. 1963. *The Sociology of Religion*. Trans. E. Fischoff with intro. by T. Parsons. Boston: Beacon Press.

Welsford, Enid. 1921. "Sun, moon, and stars (Teutonic and Balto-Slavic)," in J. Hastings (ed.), *Encyclopedia of Religion and Ethics*, vol. 12. Edinburgh: T. & T. Clark.

Wensinck, A. J. L. 1923. "The Semitic new year and the origin of Eschatology," *Acta Orientalia* 1: 158–199.

White, Alan R. 1971. *Truth*. London: Macmillan.

White, Leslie. 1949. *The Science of Culture*. New York: Farrar Strauss.

1962. *The Pueblo of Sia, New Mexico*. Smithsonian Institution, Bureau of American Ethnology Bulletin no. 184. Washington: US Government Printing Office.

White, Lynn Jr. 1967. "The historical roots of our ecological crisis," *Science* 155: 1203–1207.

Whitehead, Alfred N. 1927. *Science and the Modern World*. Cambridge: Cambridge University Press.

1927. *Symbolism*. New York: G. P. Putnam.

Whitehead, Alfred N. and B. Russell. 1910–1913. *Principia Mathematica.* Vols. 1–3. Cambridge: Cambridge University Press.

Whitrow, G. J. 1972. *The Nature of Time.* New York: Holt, Rinehart and Winston.

Wiedemann, A. 1914. "Incarnation (Egyptian)." in J. Hastings (ed.), *Encyclopedia of Religion and Ethics,* vol. 7. Edinburgh: T. & T. Clark.

Wilden, A. 1972. *System and Structure: Essays in Communication and Exchange.* London: Tavistock.

Williams, F. E. 1923. "The Vailala Maddness and the Destruction of Native Ceremonies in the Gulf Division." *Papuan Anthropology Reports* No. 4, Port Moresby.

Wilson, John A. 1951. *The Culture of Ancient Egypt.* Chicago: University of Chicago Press.

Windfuhr, Gernot L. 1976. "Vohu Manah: A Key to the Zoroastrian World-Formula," in L. Orlin (ed.), *Michigan Oriental Studies in Honor of George Cameron.* Ann Arbor, MI: University of Michigan, Dept. of Near Eastern Studies.

Witherspoon, Gary. 1977. *Language and Art in the Navaho Universe.* Ann Arbor, MI: University of Michigan Press.

Wolpoff., Milford. 1980. *Paleoanthropology.* New York: McGraw Hill.

Worsley, P. J. 1957. *The Trumpet Shall Sound: A Study of "Cargo" Cults in Melanesia.* London: MacGibbon & Kee.

Worster, Donald. 1993. *The Wealth of Nature: Environmental History and the Ecological Imagination.* New York: Oxford University Press.

Wynne-Edwards, V. C. 1962. *Animal Deception in Relation to Social Behavior.* Edinburgh: Oliver and Boyd.

Yengoyan, Aram. 1972. "Ritual and Exchange in Aboriginal Austrailia: An Adaptive Interpretation of Male Initiation Rites," in E. Wilmsen (ed.), *Social Exchange and Interaction. Anthropological Papers of the Museum of Anthropology,* University of Michigan, no. 46.

1976. "Structure, event, and ecology in aboriginal Australia," in N. Peterson (ed.), *Tribes and Boundaries in Australia.* Canberra: Australian Institute of Aboriginal Studies.

1979. "Cultural forms and a theory of constraints," in A. Becker and A. Yengoyan (eds.), *The Imagination of Reality: Essays on Southeast Asian Coherence Systems.* Norwood, NJ: ABLEX Publishing Corp.

Young, Michael. 1971. *Fighting with Food: Leadership, Values, and Social Control in a Massim Society.* Cambridge: Cambridge University Press.

Zaehner, R. C. 1961. *The Dawn and Twilight of Zoroastrianism.* London: Weidenfeld and Nicolson.

INDEX

principles in construction of time 183
Logic of Religion, The (Bochenski) 290
logical entailments of ritual form 26–7
Logoi 27
  ancient Egyptian 353–6
  Australian aboriginal 366–7
  Maring *nomane* 367–8
  Native American 360–6
  Vedic 359–60
  Zoroastrian 356–9
Logos 22, 162–3, 196, 369–70, 450
  comprehensiveness and pervasiveness of 351
  concept of a new 459–61
  concept of 350–1
  and liturgy 351–3
  qualities of 349
  range of meanings 346–8
  violation of 350, 369–70
Lommel, H. 357
Lord's Day, concept of 191, 196
loving neighbors 205

Ma'at in Egyptian thought 353–6
MacDonnel, A. A. 334
McKay, B. 420
McKelway, A. J. 403
MacKenzie, J. S. 177, 200
McKeon, R. 41, 177
McLuhan, M. 38
McManus, J. 201, 226, 226–7, 229
magic in ritual 117, 126, 149
maladaptation 441–3
Malinowski, B. 50
Mammandabari people 159–60, 166, 213–14
Margoliouth, G. 191–2
Maring people 36, 53, 57, 74
  metrics of regional system 99–100
  relationships 75, 78, 130
  settlement patterns 94, 130
  women 239–41
Maring ritual,
  addresses to ancestors 277
  adornment (personal) 80–1
  amame planting 244–8, 254
  amatory display 81
  animals 242, 249, 250, 259
  axes 78, 79, 329
  cassowaries 238, 249, 329
  charcoal (*ringi*) 75, 76–7
  coordination of ritual performances 190
  cycle and rituals 74–7, 190, 194–5
  cosmological axioms 264
  dancing and fighting 57, 78–80, 108
  death and compensation 206–7
  emotion in 259–60
  fighting stones 75, 240

  food 79, 82, 241, 250, 259
  kaiko festival 53, 77–8, 84, 190, 193
  marriage patterns 206
  misunderstanding of author's analysis 27–8
  ngimbai 201–2
  nomane 367–8
  pandanus fruit 241, 259, 329
  pouches (*mbamp yuk*) 78–9
  rumbim,
    planting 16, 75–6, 93–4, 103, 190, 193
    spatial aspect 212–13, 254
    sexual symbolism 244–7, 254
    significata 253–4, 258
  rumbin, uprooting 77, 94, 95, 98, 190
  spirits 202, 237–9, 330
  succession of recurrent processes 185, 189
  taboos 206, 207, 241, 249
  territoriality 243–4
  time and space 212–13
  variation and indexicality 74–7
  warfare 57, 75–6, 104, 112, 241, 267
  yu min rumbim 237–51, 329
  see also pigs
markers in ritual acts 112
marriage 34–5, 206
Maruyama, M. 324
Marx, K. 400, 447
Masani, R. 357, 358, 359
Mass,
  Roman Catholic 25, 29, 36, 40, 44, 52–3
  antiquity of 335, 336
  and convention 125–6
  significata of 257, 315
  and social order 270
material efficacy, lack in ritual 46–7
mating in Maring ritual 81
matter,
  creation of 155, 156
  metaphor of 149
matter and form in sacraments 154–5
matter-energy and information 109–10, 111–13
Mauss, M. 12
meaning,
  disconsonance between law and 453–6
  and energy 111–13
  in religious experience 391–5
  three levels of 70–4, 392–5
meaning and meaningfulness of religious experience 391–5
meaningful and the physical, the 108–13
meaningfulness 71–3, 100–1, 111, 113
  distinction in classification 113–14, 394
  and information 285–6
  liturgical representation 262
  and meaning 391–5

Meggitt, M. J. 130, 159, 199, 213, 260, 287, 461
Melanesian millenarian movements 336
membership in rituals 76–7, 83, 111
memory 174
Memra (utterance) 163
mending the world 262–3
messages 21, 112
  canonical 52–4, 58, 107, 118, 328
  leading to action 114
  multi-channel transmission 253
  ordinal and cardinal 82–4
  purification of 103
  reliability of 15, 415
  self-referential 52–4, 56, 58, 69, 107, 108, 118
    and invariance 328–9
    in Maring ritual 78, 82–3, 85
  simple informational 113–14
  symbolically encoded 16–17
  transmitters and receivers of 51–2, 118–19, 145
meta-factiveness of ritual 133
metafunction 126
metamessages 31, 38
metaperformativeness 124–6, 279
metaphor 140, 219, 246
  cyclical metaphor for time 183–5
  and meaning 71–2, 393, 394
  and predication 147–50
  sexual metaphor for time 186
metrics of private and public systems 99
Mexico 211, 301–4
Meyerhoff, B. 24, 26, 28
millenarian manifestations, Melanesian 436
Miller, J. 112, 191, 277, 330, 335, 422
Milne, L. A. 176
mind 402–3
  see also reason, conscious
miracle plays 136
mirrors and truth 303
Moglia, Peter 154
Mohammed, Prophet 336
Molina, A. de 302
money, epistemology of 454–6
Mooney, J. 33, 436
Moore, C. 359
Moore, J. M. 374, 375, 385, 401
Moore, S. 24, 26, 28
morality 22, 128–30
  and accuracy in performatives 122, 123–4
  intrinsic to ritual's structure 132–7
  and truth 18
movements, ritual 142–4
Mukanda rituals 92–3, 97
multivocality in ritual representation 254, 258, 268

muminai feasts 85, 88
Munn, N. D. 33
Murinbata people 366–7
Murngin people 159
music, religious 136
mysteries 154
mystery and adaptiveness 428–9
mystery plays 41
mystification of rituals 116–17
myth 31, 38, 110, 134–7
  and history 233–4
  naturalization of culture in 168
  and ritual 151–2
  sanctified 317–18, 320
  of tribal people 158–61, 213–15

Nahuatl people and pantheon 301–2
names of things, learning 160–1, 213
narrators and myth 134–5
Natural Indices 63, 65
natural processes, classes of 51–2
natural and unnatural conventions 438–40
naturalization of convention 166–8, 279
Navajo people 160–1, 163, 278, 329, 333, 364–6
Ndembu people 92, 218, 236
Needham, J. 119, 177
Needham, R. 173
Nelli, Concept of 301–3, 345
neurophysiology, consequences of ritual participation 227–30
Niasese people 180
Nietzche, F. 231
Nirvana 232
noise, psychic 103
non-material, substantiating the 141–4
Norbeck, E. 381
North American Indians *see* Americans, Native and names of groups
North Pole 60, 62
Nuer people 162, 182, 223, 444
number,
  concept of 174
  in Maring ritual cycle 77–80
numbering and the eternal 234–5
numinous,
  concept of the 1, 3, 22, 219–20, 230, 290
  and religious experience 377–81, 404

oaths and swearing 57
objectivity in meaning 74
objects, special and mundane 144–5, 147
obligation 123–4, 132, 137, 142, 264
  and liturgical acceptance 395–6
  in tribal society 325
  violations of 204

Windfuhr, G. L. 357
wine representing blood 260–1
Winnebago American Indians 92
Witherspoon, G. 160, 161, 163, 278, 333,
    364–6
Word,
    The 303–4, 322, 324
    see also Logos
words,
    naming and symbols 160–3
    ritual 141–4, 151–2
    Worsley, P. J. 332, 436

writings as sanctified expressions 319
written texts and idolatory 444–5
Wynne-Edwards, V. C. 24, 83–4

Yengoyan, A. 214, 215
Young, M. 56, 84, 88–9

Zaehner, R. C. 358, 359
Zande people 149
"Zoroastrian lies" 297
Zoroastrianism 133, 254, 356–60
    pantheon of 357–8

Cambridge Studies in Social and Cultural Anthropology

* available in paperback